HANDBOOK OF POST-TRAUMATIC THERAPY

Edited by MARY BETH WILLIAMS
and JOHN F. SOMMER, Jr.

GREENWOOD PRESS   Westport, Connecticut • London

Acknowledgment

We extend our gratitude to Virginia Reinecke and her company, The Printer's Devil, for their knowledge of desktop publishing.

Library of Congress Cataloging-in-Publication Data

Handbook of post-traumatic therapy / edited by Mary Beth Williams and
   John F. Sommer, Jr.
      p.   cm.
   Includes bibliographical references and index.
   ISBN 0–313–28143–2 (alk. paper)
    1. Post-traumatic stress disorder—Treatment.   I. Sommer, John F.
    [DNLM: 1. Stress Disorders, Post-Traumatic—therapy.   WM 170
   H2355   1994]
   RC552.P67H35   1994
   616.85′21—dc20
   DNLM/DLC
   for Library of Congress   93–14437

British Library Cataloguing in Publication Data is available.

Library of Congress Catalog Card Number: 93–14437
ISBN: 0–313–28143–2

First published in 1994

Greenwood Press, 88 Post Road West, Westport, CT 06881
An imprint of Greenwood Publishing Group, Inc.

Printed in the United States of America

The paper used in this book complies with the
Permanent Paper Standard issued by the National
Information Standards Organization (Z39.48–1984).

10 9 8 7 6 5 4 3 2 1

To George O. Kemeny, M.D.,
an Auschwitz survivor who taught me the meaning
of survival from trauma,
and
Rev. John Calvin Little,
my father whose motto, "It can be done,"
guides my life.

—Mary Beth Williams

To George B. Justus,
a friend and a Vietnam veteran whose life ended far
too early,
and
John F. Sommer, Sr., and Grace June Rumfield Sommer,
who during their lifetime instilled in me the sense of
obligation to leave the world a little better than
I found it,
and
My family—Nancy, John III, and Kaitlin—
for their patience and understanding.

—John F. Sommer, Jr.

Contents

Preface

As a specific focus of professional practice, the field of traumatology is relatively new and, according to Figley (1994), has emerged only within the past decade. However, the incidence of traumatic events in the lives of human beings in all cultures has been documented for centuries, ranging from accounts in the works of Homer to Shakespeare's plays to Ambrose Bierce's chilling stories of Civil War soldiers (Williams, 1990).

It is highly unlikely that an individual will avoid the direct experience of a traumatic event or events during his or her lifetime. However, if that person is fortunate enough to avoid direct contact with trauma, secondary exposure to the traumas of others is unavoidable. The modern technological world allows every television owner to view on a daily basis death by starvation in Somalia, death by a sniper's bullet or the trauma of organized rape in rape camps in Bosnia, and countless other examples of human pain. The secondary traumatization resulting from this constant exposure to the traumas of others may eventuate in post-traumatic symptoms.

Traumatic events, by DSM III-R definition (APA, 1987), are events "out of the range of ordinary experience." To be classified as traumatic, an event must be perceived and processed as serious enough to challenge basic assumptions of safety, predictability, justness, and fairness (Janoff-Bulman, 1992). These events, during processing, become encoded in the brain as active memory and often return in the form of intrusions (the "B" category of DSM III-R; images, dreams, reactions to triggers, flashbacks) (Horowitz, 1986). If the mind is unable or unwilling to process these intrusions, it tends to shut down and avoid them, until they become so intense that they are unavoidable and demand attention.

A traumatic stress reaction is a normal reaction to the abnormal stressor events. If that reaction continues for a period of at least one month, whether that reaction occurs immediately after the event or at some point in the future, the reaction becomes a post-traumatic stress disorder (PTSD) if the required number of symptoms is present. The primary components of the reaction are reexperiencing, avoidance/withdrawal, and physiological arousal. Associated features of generalized anxiety, depression, grief, and guilt frequently coexist with the primary symptoms.

Research studies have documented intrusive, avoidant, and physiological aftereffects of a variety of traumatic events ranging from childhood abuse to exposure to the traumas of parents, to disasters, political torture, and survival of homicides of significant others, to battering and assault, to participation in war and combat, to duty-related trauma (Kemp, Rawlings & Greene, 1991; Schlenger et al., 1988; Walker, 1984; Williams, 1990).

The specific treatment of post-traumatic stress reactions and post-traumatic stress disorder has evolved since its formalized inception as crisis intervention and treatment of veterans after the Vietnam War. The recognition that individual psychotherapy, family therapy, and group treatment of traumatic stress require a specialized treatment paradigm, as well as techniques and approaches, has led to the conceptualization of this book. It presents a compendium of specific treatment approaches for event-related traumatized populations and examines the relevance of specific methodologies for treatment of traumatized individuals (e.g., hypnotherapy, drug therapy).

The book takes an interactive approach to treatment, recognizing that traumatized individuals do not live in isolation. Family and other social support is particularly crucial in the healing process. In addition, treatment must focus on emotional, cognitive, behavioral, interpersonal, biological, spiritual, and cultural aspects of the reaction or disorder.

FORMAT OF THE BOOK

This book consists of nine parts describing generalized concerns and treatment concepts, treatment for specific populations, techniques of treatment as they apply to traumatized individuals, group treatment approaches, and needs/concerns in the PTSD field. A description of each part follows.

Part I examines the theoretical, diagnostic, and practical aspects of treatment. In Chapter 1, Wilson reviews and expands upon his 1989 interactive paradigm of traumatic stress. He presents a holistic theoretical paradigm of person-environment interactions. Chapter 2, by Litz and Weathers, describes methods to collect diagnostic information concerning PTSD: clinical interview, questionnaire/inventory, and psychophysiological techniques. The authors offer guidelines for history taking, interview sequencing, and evaluation of associated symptoms in adult survivors. Chapter 3, by Pearlman and McCann, discusses structured and unstructured approaches to taking a trauma history as part of the therapy process. It includes discussions of transference, vicarious traumatization of therapists, and the ethical concerns of history taking.

Part II examines the treatment of post-traumatic stress disorders in children and families. In Chapter 4, James offers specific guidelines for the long-term, comprehensive treatment of traumatized children from infancy through adolescence. Williams, in Chapter 5, presents the creation and implementation of a public school crisis response team and its utilization in school-based and individual student-based situations. In Chapter 6, Matsakis identifies the impacts of trauma on the family when both partners are survivors. Her chapter also provides treatment techniques for couples counseling. Chapter 7, by Sheehan, focuses on a model to help clients develop intimacy and provides treatment strategies derived from that model, including relaxation exercises and a sharing meditation. In Chapter 8 Albeck discusses the intergenerational consequences of trauma for the offspring of victims. While he focuses on adult children of Jewish Holocaust survivors, his conclusions are relevant to the children of other traumatized populations.

Part III examines treatment of survivors of violence and abuse. Chapter 9 by Salston describes treatment of survivors of homicide victims from first contact through intake and assessment to ongoing counseling and closure. The chapter also includes a compendium of specific symptom management techniques. In Chapter 10, Dutton describes domestic violence as a traumatic stressor, presents therapeutic goals, and suggests a treatment protocol or set of intervention strategies to accomplish those goals. Chapter 11 by Williams, which concludes this section, describes specific techniques for creating a safety context/environment for survivors of severe abuse both within and outside the therapeutic setting.

Part IV examines the treatment of war and combat-related trauma. Scurfield, in Chapter 12, presents sixteen traumatic stress treatment principles, which may be utilized with nonveteran populations as well. He presents a specific clinical technique of "determining percentages of responsibility" in detail in his chapter. He also discusses veteran-specific issues related to disability, women veterans, minority veterans, and prisoners of war (POWs). In Chapter 13, Daniels and Scurfield describe the integrative treatment of PTSD and chemical and nonchemical abuse problems. The chapter also describes the dynamics of the interrelationship between PTSD and chemical disorders.

Part V examines ethnic, cross-cultural, and political issues in the treatment of trauma. Parson, in Chapter 14, examines the interactive effects of ethnicity, culture, and race, discusses methods of ethnocultural assessment, and presents techniques of ethnic post-traumatotherapy. Chester, in Chapter 15, examines torture as an extreme form of trauma and lists methods of torture. She also presents sample assessment protocols and treatment strategies. Abudabbeh, in Chapter 16, discusses the treatment/mental health needs and modes of Arab Americans in general and the specific treatment of traumatized Arab Americans during and following the Gulf War.

Part VI examines disaster, both natural and of human technological origin, as a traumatic stressor and discusses debriefing, crisis response, and communitywide interventions. In Chapter 17, Foreman discusses debriefing and crisis intervention treatment strategies with three traumatic incidents: a plane crash, earthquake, and crane accident. He also includes a section on the secondary impact of disaster intervention on emergency service personnel. Young and Stein, in Chapter 18, discuss the development and utilization of the NOVA (National Organization of Victims' Assistance) Crisis Response Team Project. Suggestions for team development, selection, and functions could be utilized by other organizations that offer disaster-related debriefing services. In Chapter 19, Halpern points out that moving, although it does not officially meet the "A" criterion for a traumatic stressor, can be exceptionally traumatic for many. Intervention centers around identification and grieving of losses and development of stress management techniques. Chapter 20 by Feuer describes the creation and implementation of a peer intervention prototype for employee assistance program (EAP) committee response to workplace trauma of aircraft emergencies. Trained peer counselors learn to assess seriousness of incidents and provide support to, and intervene directly with, survivors and their families. Specific macro- and microlevel interventions are included. In Chapter 21, Gersons and Carlier describe assessment and treatment of Dutch law enforcement personnel who have chronic PTSD.

In Part VII, five specific treatment interventions or modalities are examined as they apply to survivors of trauma. In Chapter 22, Spring utilizes the symbolic, graphic language of art therapy to provide a testimonial modality for victims of sexual trauma. In Chapter 23, Vogel explains the role of creative arts therapies in the treatment of voluntary inpatient victims of trauma. She highlights the tasks and goals of art therapy, music therapy, dance/movement therapy, and psychodrama, as well as their limitations. Feldman, Johnson, and Ollayos present in Chapter 24 the rationale and methods for the use of the modality of writing for facilitating recovery in traumatized individuals. They include a variety of examples from their intensive clinical program at the West Haven (Connecticut) VA Medical Center inpatient program for Vietnam veterans. Stuhlmiller addresses the positive attributes of action-based treatment approaches, programs, and experiences in Chapter 25. She outlines principles of action-based therapy as well as stages of assessment, planning, implementation, and evaluation. In Chapter 26, Schwarz provides an in-depth understanding of the use of hypnosis in treating reactions to trauma, as well as detailed descriptions of several hypnotic techniques.

Treatment of PTSD occurs in a variety of settings and utilizes a variety of formats. Part VIII examines four types of group interventions for trauma survivors and/or their significant others and two inpatient trauma recovery programs. In Chapter 27, Brende presents a twelve-theme psychoeducational program for trauma recovery that has been utilized in inpatient and aftercare settings. The format for a two-week hospital program is described in detail. In Chapter 28, Herman explains a leader-led group therapy program for adult survivors of childhood incest, and Lawrence reviews the twelve-step model for Survivors of

Incest Anonymous, a leaderless group based on the Twelve Steps of Alcoholics Anonymous. In Chapter 29, Kaplan analyzes the responses of partners of trauma survivors and gives guidelines for the creation of a partner's group. Chapter 30, by Courtois, Cohen, and Turkus, describes the development of the Dissociative Disorders Empowerment Model specialized inpatient treatment program for adult survivors of childhood abuse. In Chapter 31 Bloom describes the creation and structuring of a generic inpatient program for the treatment of trauma. This sanctuary model is based upon concepts of the therapeutic milieu and a trauma-based approach to treatment.

Part IX, the final section of the book, presents new developments, trends, and areas of interest in the field of post-traumatic therapy. Chapter 32 by Friedman gives an overview of research findings on psychophysiological alterations associated with PTSD and current clinical findings on drug efficacy. In Chapter 33, Niles expands upon those suggestions for training and develops a training model for post-traumatic therapists, counselors, and nonprofessional trauma workers. Chapter 34, by Williams, Sommer, Stamm, and Harris, examines ethical considerations in trauma-based treatment and research. It illustrates the dangers of flawed research through Agent Orange Studies and presents suggestions for training. In Chapter 35, Danieli reviews her research findings concerning countertransference reactions faced by therapists who treat trauma survivors. She also provides some suggestions to assist both the new and veteran traumatologist as they cope with this inevitable secondary traumatization. The concluding chapter, Chapter 36 by Williams and Sommer, describes a four-phase generic treatment model that incorporates many of the principles of the previously mentioned authors. While no one treatment model can suffice for all populations, it is designed to provide a beginning point for the creation of individualized treatment programs.

_____ **Part I**

Theoretical, Diagnostic, and Practical Approaches

Part

The Need for an Integrative Theory of Post-Traumatic Stress Disorder

John P. Wilson

INTRODUCTION

The field of traumatic stress studies has grown so rapidly since the advent of post-traumatic stress disorder (PTSD) as a diagnostic category in the third edition (1980) of the *Diagnostic and Statistical Manual of the American Psychiatric Association*, that it has become a specialty discipline in the behavioral sciences (Wilson, 1989d).

This chapter reviews and expands upon an interactional paradigm of traumatic stress syndromes that developed out of the author's clinical, empirical, and forensic work with various victim populations. Based on personal and professional experiences during the last twenty years, this author has become increasingly convinced of the need for an integrative approach to understanding PTSD and its associated states, comorbid conditions, and alterations in the self-structure.

Persons affected by traumatic life events are biological organisms who possess unique personality attributes that are shaped by their families of origin and the cultures in which they grew up. At the most basic level, this implies that traumatic life events systematically impact interrelated levels of human psychological functioning. These impacts include (1) psychological changes in brain-behavior mechanisms; (2) effects on specific stages of life-course epigenetic development; (3) alterations in the intrapsychic organization of the self-structure; (4) changes to the organization of culture and society; and (5) potential alterations in the individual's capacities for attachment, bonding, intimacy, love, sexuality, and self-actualization (Wilson, 1989d). Moreover, understanding the complexity of PTSD necessitates moving beyond diagnostic descriptions in the DSM III-R or the forthcoming DSM-IV. For example, whereas the DSM III-R contains five diagnostic categories and three clusters of syptoms, there is virtually no mention as to how traumatic events affect the self-concept, identity, and intrapsychic functioning of the victim. Yet, the rich literature on the treatment of dissociative reactions such as multiple personality disorder (MPD) confirms that the personality, identity, and organization of the self can be radically changed by severe emotional and physical trauma (Putnam, 1989). By logical implication as well as clinical research, certain categories of traumatic events produce changes to the self-structure whereas others may not affect ego coherence and continuity whatsoever.

An integrative theory of post-traumatic stress syndromes should also be holistic in nature and capable of specifying both pathological and nonpathological forms of adaptive behavior and psychological functioning. In order to achieve this goal, the theory must attempt to specify the interactions among neurophysiological aspects of stress response, modalities of coping and defense, and cognitive processes of appraisal, processing, and integration of traumatic affect and visual imagery (memory), as well as cultural rituals and events associated with recovery and healing. Further, the need for a holistic, dynamic approach to understand the diversity of reactions to traumatic events requires studying the issue of resiliency and healthy coping systematically. Due to historical necessity to care for those in pain and suffering as a result of trauma, the medical and psychosocial sciences have focused on understanding PTSD as a form of psychopathology and have paid less attention to the healthy copers, those with resiliency, vitality, and the capacity to overcome adversity. How does this occur? What set of factors in the person enables resilient coping? Is it possible to learn from resilient persons what prophylaxis can be implemented to minimize the pathological effects of trauma? These and related questions hold important clues to creating effective therapeutic regimens.

ORIENTATION TO THEORIES OF TRAUMATIC STRESS

There have been many attempts over the years to develop theories of PTSD and similar conditions. The theorists who formulated their conceptualizations of PTSD were affected by the culture and historical events of the era. For example, Freud (1957) was influenced by many events in Europe, including World War I. Lifton's (1967) pioneering work on PTSD was heavily affected by his studies of Hiroshima survivors and later by the studies of war veterans (Korea, Vietnam) and mass genocide (e.g., Nazi doctors). Other researchers, such as Horowitz (1986), Laufer (1988), Green, Wilson, and Lindy (1985), and van der Kolk (1992), have combined clinical experience with empirical and laboratory-based research to create theories of an eclectic nature.

Recently Peterson, Prout, and Schwarz (1991) reviewed many of the central theories of PTSD and divided them into ten separate categories (e.g., learning theory approaches, psychobiological, object relations, psychoformative). Their review is a useful and, when supplemented by Trimble's (1981, 1985) historical analysis of the concept of traumatic neurosis, provides the reader with the ability to see similarities and differences in the various theories. However, it is noteworthy that each theory, whether stated explicitly and formally or implicitly and tacitly, makes assumptions about the following dimensions of traumatic impact on the organism: (1) changes in psychobiological state (e.g., disequilibrium, increased catecholamine production); (2) changes in learned behavior through classical conditioning or operant conditioning; (3) changes in cognitive processing, including information processing and belief and value system orientation, as well as the capacity for memory, learning, and concentration; (4) changes in self-structure and object relations; (5) changes in interpersonal relations and orientation to society (e.g., alienation); and (6) the nature of the stressors experienced within the time-space framework of a culture at a historical moment. Thus, one of the important tasks for future research will be to undertake a comparative analysis of the disparate theories using a common yardstick such as the six dimensions listed above. Such a comparative analysis will not only broaden the possibilities for hypothesis testing but enable higher-order integration of the existing scientific findings into a new, more parsimonious framework.

A POTENTIAL FRAMEWORK FOR A THEORY OF
TRAUMATIC STRESS REACTIONS

In an earlier work, *Trauma, Transformation and Healing* (1989d), this author presented a potential framework for a theory of traumatic stress reactions. Figure 1.1 illustrates the major elements of this framework in graphic form. This theory is holistic and is representative of a person-by-situation paradigm of human behavior (Aronoff & Wilson, 1985; Wilson, 1989d; Lazarus & Folkman, 1984; Dohrenwend & Shrout, 1984). Stated simply, a person-environment interactional paradigm assumes that there is a dynamic interaction between the characteristics of the person and the dimensions of the environmental situation in which a traumatic event occurs. If all of the possible interaction effects were diagramed onto Figure 1.1, the diagram would resemble a microchip with lines running to and from the various elements as well as containing feedback loops of different sorts. For the purpose of simplicity, Figure 1.1 indicates that the nature of the interaction between the person (p) and the environment (e) by which a traumatic event occurs sets up a complex process (p $\times$ e) that includes individual and/or collective responses that determine forms of stress response syndromes and post-traumatic adaptation.

THE MAJOR ELEMENTS OF CLINICAL IMPORTANCE IN
WORK WITH TRAUMA VICTIMS

Stressor Dimensions

Traumatic events are made up of stressors that are generally thought of as events or experiences that tax the coping resources of the individual (Lazarus &

Figure 1.1
Elements for a Theory of Traumatic Stress Reactions

INPUTS TO THE PROCESSING OF TRAUMA   FORMS OF STRESS RESPONSE DETERMINED BY PERSON-ENVIRONMENT INTERACTION

PERSON VARIABLES ⟶ (P x E) ⟹ ENVIRONMENTAL AND ⟶ INDIVIDUAL SUBJECTIVE ⟶ POST-TRAUMA ADAPTATION
(P)   SITUATIONAL VARIABLES (E)   RESPONSE TO TRAUMA

PERSON VARIABLES (P)

Motives

Traits

Beliefs

Values

Abilities

Cognitive Structure

Mood

Coping Style

Defensive Style

Genetic Propensities

ENVIRONMENTAL AND SITUATIONAL VARIABLES (E)

I. Dimensions of the Trauma
  a. Bereavement/Loss
  b. Imminence
  c. Duration/Severity
  d. Displacement
  e. Exposure to Death, dying, etc.
  f. Moral Conflict
  g. Role in Trauma
  h. Location
  i. Potential for re-occurrence
  j. Life-Threat
  k. Complexity of Stressor
  l. Impact on Community

II. Experience of Trauma
  a. Alone
  b. With Others
  c. Community Based (collective)

III. Structure of Trauma
  a. Single Stressor
  b. Multiple Stressor
  c. Complex vs Simple
  d. Natural vs Man-made

IV. Post-Trauma Milieu
  a. Level of Support
  b. Cultural Rituals for recovery
  c. Societal Attitudes Towards Event
  d. Opportunity Structures

INDIVIDUAL SUBJECTIVE RESPONSE TO TRAUMA

I. Emotional
  a. Affective Distress
  b. Affective Numbing
  c. Affective Balance

II. Cognition
  a. Denial/Avoidance
  b. Distortion
  c. Accurate Appraisal
  d. Dissociation
  e. Intrusion

III. Motivational
  a. Aroused
  b. Non-Aroused

IV. Neurophysiological
  a. Hyperarousal
  b. Depression-avoidant
  c. Balanced

V. Coping
  a. Instrumental
  b. Emotional
  c. Cognitive Re-structure
    1. Positive
    2. Negative
  d. Resilient

POST-TRAUMA ADAPTATION

I. Acute
  a. Pathological
    1. PTSD
    2. Other Disorders
  b. Non-Pathological

II. Chronic
  a. Pathological
    1. PTSD
    2. Other Disorders
  b. Non-Pathological
    1. Personality Alteration
    2. Character Change

III. Life-Course Development
  a. Intensification of Developmental Stages
  b. Retrogression
  c. Psychological Acceleration

Folkman, 1984). Thus, there may be different types of stressors that can have varying effects on individuals, depending on whether or not they adversely affect the persons' coping capacity or inflict physical or psychological injury. Closely related to the concept of a stressor is the notion of *vulnerability* to stress (e.g., premorbid states or personality dispositions) and the *stress threshold continuum*. The stress threshold continuum implies at least two interrelated concepts: (1) stressful events theoretically can be placed on a continuum of stressfulness, and their potential to function traumatically is objectively assessable and (2) each individual has a threshold of tolerance for different types of stressors; hence, some stressors have a higher probability value to become traumatic than do others. At present, comparatively little is known about the properties of the stress continuum-traumatic potential index or about individual differences in personality and vulnerability to qualitatively different stressor events. Some traumatic events contain stressors that occur only once (e.g., motorcycle accident) whereas others are repetitive (e.g., dysfunctional families) or nearly chronic and enduring (e.g., civil violence in politically torn countries).

A Typology of Stressor Events

In the field of traumatic stress studies it has been common, if not traditionally accepted, to define trauma by the nature of the stressors that impact on the individual. But what is a trauma? How is a traumatic event defined objectively? Is there a universal set of criteria that can be used to define traumas and applied with equal unanimity throughout the world? Alternatively, is the definition of trauma determinable only by its effects upon the individual? In addition, there may be biologically based (genetic-hormonal-neurological) differences in reactivity to trauma as well as physiological "markers" that a trauma has occurred (e.g., critical levels of neurotransmitters: cortisol, NE, or 5-HT).

Thus, a psychologically traumatic event can be construed as one in which the person has experienced an external stressor event that is injurious to the normal state (stasis) and results in a condition that reflects this injury to the pretraumatic state of being. Thus, the injury caused by a traumatic event could produce varying degrees of distress to the victim for varying lengths of time, depending on the nature of the person, the nature of the traumatic experience, and the personal and social resources available for recovery and restabilization of the psychological state.

Four Types of Traumatic Stressor Events

Terr (1991) delineated Type I and Type II stressor events. Type I stressors are unanticipated single events beyond the range of normal daily stress and are traumatic in their effects, leading to PTSD and other symptoms, such as omens, misperceptions, and misidentifications. In contrast, Type II stressors are enduring or repetitive in nature and lead to PTSD, as well as tendencies toward psychic numbing, dissociation, rage states, unremitting sadness, and denial. Terr further notes that Type I and Type II stressor events may cross over, as in the case where a Type I event (e.g., auto accident causing the death of parents) results in the children's being sent to a home with abusive relatives (Type II).

Type III stressor events are caused by compounding or additive effects of low-level, insidious stressor events, which, in time, produce effects remarkably similar to those of Type I or Type II events. Recently, Berk (1992) applied the Type III paradigm to work with institutionalized children who came from dysfunctional families. He noted eight common categories of stressors: (1) failure to provide positive role modeling; (2) failure to protect the child from continued trauma or to help him or her experience a sense of safety; (3) failure to provide structure; (4) failure to provide unconditional positive regard; (5) failure to teach the child suitable problem-solving methods; (6) failure to teach the child the norms of society; (7) chaotic, conflicted "abnormal" environments, which became the "normal" baseline of experience and arousal; and (8) overall characteristics of the environment that included high levels of inconsistency, unpredictability, role reversals, and anxiety-inducing intrafamilial or interpersonal relationships. According to Berk (1992), Type III stressor environments eventuated in the development of PTSD symptoms (e.g., irritability, exaggerated startle, sleep disturbance, detachment, psychic numbing, dissociative reactions), personality disorders or subclinical syndromes as learned behaviors, and attempts at coping with the stressors inherent in the conflict-ridden interpersonal environment.

This author proposes a fourth category of stressor event, which is defined by an alteration in a person's basic relation to the biosphere. Type IV stressor events are often anomalous and initially difficult to verify objectively by standard scientific assessment. Further, Type IV stressor events produce high levels of uncertainty and profound adaptational dilemmas as to how to cope with the stressor once it has become recognized and acknowledged by the person. An example of a Type IV stressor is a technological disaster that exposes individuals or entire communities to toxic chemicals known to be carcinogenic. In this stressor event, in many cases, the victim does not know what the dose or exposure effects may be and thus confronts a dilemma of coping and adaptation. Victims may react with chronic uncertainty, hypervigilance, and somatoform concerns as well as exhibit heightened states of depression, anxiety, and brooding. It is as if they can find no way to terminate the threat of exposure and, among other changes in functioning, now experience a serious violation of their sense of safety with the biosphere (Mother Earth). This violation is often reported in terms of attachment loss, states of disconnectedness, and increased mistrust about whether their basic human needs could be gratified without harmful risk to themselves and loved ones. Further, their chronic uncertainty extends to fears about the future in terms of their health and emotional well-being.

Person Variables

An interactive theory of traumatic stress implicitly recognizes the importance of personality variables in determining reactions to traumatic events. These personality dimensions include motives, traits, beliefs, values, abilities, cognitive structures, mood, and defensive and coping styles, as well as genetic propensities. Moreover, as discussed by Aronoff and Wilson (1985), personality traits are directly associated with cognitive styles of information processing, especially in the acquisition, processing, and goal-setting dimensions of encoding information from situations. More specifically, the acquisition of information includes the cognitive processes of selective attention, search flexibility, and search persistence. The outcome of these major components of information processing is the development of a schema for enactment that includes setting a level of aspiration and risk taking as well as problem-solving behavior.

When the personality characteristics of the individual are organized around safety-oriented needs (insecurity, anxiety, dependence, authoritarianism, approval seeking, and so on), the cognitive style of information processing under conditions of stress results in a tendency toward the reduction or constriction of information from the stimulus field, which, in turn, directly affects the processing of encoded information and the formulation of a schema for enactment. On the other hand, personality characteristics concerned with enhancing self-esteem and competency (need for achievement, dominance, internal locus of control, nurturance, and so on) tend to be associated with a cognitive style that augments and expands the search of the stimulus field under conditions of stress. As a result, there is vigilance in processing the encoded material, which can lead to effective problem solving or excessive hypervigilance, depending on how the stressor was perceived and initially appraised during the trauma.

An interactionist perspective of traumatic stress implies that personality processes affect and dynamically interact with all four categories of environmental variables to influence the specific nature of the individual's subjective response to the trauma (see Figure 1.1). An insecure person with rigid moral beliefs may, in a traumatic situation of high moral conflict, have a subjective response that includes strong affective distress, cognitive distortion as to his or her role in the event, the arousal of guilt feelings, physiological hyperarousal, and emotionally laden coping actions. As a consequence of this form of individual subjective response to the situation, pathological symptoms might be manifest immediately or after a period of latency.

Theoretically, it is possible to suggest that many different personality dimensions could be crossed with the four environmental dimensions (stressor attributes, experience of trauma, structure of trauma, and post-trauma milieu) to create a matrix of predictions regarding the five dimensions of individual subjective response and the different forms of post-trauma adaptation. Such a set of tables of predictions would, of necessity, be quite complex since there are many subdimensions that form interaction possibilities. The outcome of such an effort would yield (1) a specific set of testable hypotheses; (2) higher-order predictive explanations; and (3) the evolution of new conceptual possibilities pertaining to the explanation of traumatic stress response syndromes. It is crucial to a theory of traumatic stress that such a systematic effort be undertaken to move the field beyond models that simply assume that personality variables moderate the relationship between stressor dimensions and outcome variables.

Environmental and Situational Variables

The Dimensions of Traumatic Experiences

Traumatic events differ on many different dimensions. As Figure 1.1 indicates, it is possible to identify these dimensions as follows: (1) the degree of life threat; (2) the degree of bereavement or loss of significant others; (3) imminence or the rate of onset and offset of the stressors; (4) the duration and severity of the stressors; (5) the level of displacement and dislodging of persons from their community; (6) the exposure to death, dying, injury, destruction, and social chaos; (7) the degree of moral conflict inherent in the situation; (8) the role in the trauma (agent versus victim); (9) the location of the trauma (e.g., home versus elsewhere); (10) the complexity of the stressor (single versus multiple); and (11) the impact of the trauma in the community (e.g., a natural disaster). The more dimensions present in any particular trauma, the greater the potential for producing a pathological outcome. However, consistent with the general principle of an interactional theory, personality and situational variables (e.g., social support and economic resources) will interact with the stressor dimensions in determining post-trauma adaptation. Finally, each of these stressor dimensions can be linked to post-traumatic symptomatology independent of the personality traits of the person, which might moderate different outcome processes.

Experience of the Trauma

Traumatic events can be experienced either alone, with other persons, or in the context of a community-based experience. When the trauma is experienced alone, the individual may feel helpless, terrorized, fearful, vulnerable, and at the mercy of fate. In groups, the effect of a trauma may be different, as in the case of the Chowchilla school bus kidnapping (Terr, 1985), in that well-known social-psychological processes may operate, for example, contagion, rumors and myths, social pressure and norms of regulation, and identification with the perpetrator, as recently identified in the Stockholm syndrome (Ochberg, 1988). When a trauma affects an entire community, it can produce many secondary stressor experiences if the destruction or devastation is severe enough. Indeed, Erikson (1976) coined the term *loss of community* to describe the massive social and individual trauma incurred in the Buffalo Creek Dam disaster. The disaster not only exposed survivors to high degrees of death, dying, and destruction but also eliminated many sociocultural support systems necessary for recovery.

The Structure of Trauma

Since traumas are psychological events, they possess an inherent structure similar to that of many other social-psychological phenomena. Single-stressor events are rare and typically involve an accident that produces physical injury. Most traumatic experiences contain multiple stressors, such as combat in warfare, which may include such dimensions as life threat and exposure to death and injury. Moreover, the psychological structure of a traumatic event may be thought of as complex or relatively simple. Complexity refers to the numbr of subcomponents inherent to a trauma, the number of competing or conflicting choices to be made, and the ambiguity as to possible alternative actions in the event. A simple traumatic event is typically unidimensional and clear with respect to the nature of the event and the possible behaviors one could enact.

Post-Traumatic Milieu

An interactional theory of traumatic stress must attempt to delineate the important dimensions of the recovery environment that affect post-traumatic adaptation. Broadly conceived, the milieu that exists following an excessively stressful event can be classified on four major dimensions.

1. The level of social, economic, and personal support present has been conceived as the trauma membrane by Lindy (1988) since there is a tendency for significant others to form a protective membrane of support around the victim to insulate him or her from further stress or harm. It is assumed that the greater the level of supportive mechanisms and opportunities after a traumatic event, the more positive the stress recovery process will be, especially if there are rapid clinical intervention and nurturing support.

2. As noted by van der Hart (1983), cultures develop rituals to aid persons suffering from emotional distress. Some rituals (e.g., Memorial Day parades for war veterans) are collective expressions concerned with the event, whereas other rituals are highly specific and idiosyncratic (e.g., the sweat lodge purification ritual of Native American groups). Cultures also differ on the number, kind, and frequency of the rituals designed to heal traumatized persons (Silver & Wilson, 1988). To date, there are no systematic cross-cultural analyses of healing rituals for stress recovery as determined by the human relations area files (HRAF). However, studies of shamanistic rituals have produced important information on rituals, trance states, and their larger function in different cultures (Winkelman, 1986). Clearly, the anthropological study of various facets of traumatic stress would generate a wealth of useful information necessary for an integrative and holistic theory of traumatic stress reactions.

3. Included in a set of studies of milieus would be an analysis of the sociocultural attitudes and responses toward the victimized individual and the stressful event itself. For example, it has been widely noted that the U.S. ambivalence toward, and rejection of, Vietnam veterans contributed to their postwar problems of adjustment (e.g., Figley & Leventman, 1980). Societal and political attitudes toward traumatized persons are important aspects of the recovery environment because they determine how resources will be allocated to provide the services that are needed by the victim.

4. Beyond the resources that aid in the recovery from traumatic stress, it is

possible to speak of the opportunity structures that exist or are created. These structures facilitate an integration within the culture in terms of choosing a career, assuming personal responsibilities, and establishing a viable personal identity that has meaning and significance within the culture.

Individual Subjective Response to Trauma

Individual subjective response to trauma refers to the initial responses that occur in the wake of stressful experiences. There are five separate, but inter-related, dimensions to adaptive behavior, which can be classified as emotional, cognitive, motivational, neurophysiological, and coping resources.

Emotional

By their very nature, traumatic events upset the psychic equilibrium of the individuals affected by them. They produce powerful emotional reactions in persons because they disrupt normal homeostatic functioning on the physiological level and radically alter the optimal levels of arousal on the psychological level. Persons vary in how they subjectively experience and cope with the excessive autonomic nervous system arousal and endocrine secretions triggered by threatening and overwhelming traumatic experiences. In affective distress the person feels overwhelmed emotionally, fearful, flooded with distressing affect, and extremely anxious and may be unable to mobilize intellectual and personal resources to problem-solve effectively in the face of what has happened. Alternatively, some persons shut down emotionally when confronted with an intense and upsetting event and experience affective numbing, a state in which the capacity to feel is greatly reduced. The term *psychic numbing* was coined by Lifton (1967). Affective or psychic numbing ranges on a continuum from a stuporous, zombielike daze and psychomotor retardation to very subtle manifestations, such as impacted sensuality and difficulties in giving and receiving affection. Lifton (1988) suggested that psychic numbing involves several ego defense processes, including the mechanisms of splitting, repression, and forms of dissociation. It is also the case, at least clinically, that when affective numbing is reduced, alleviated, or suddenly "lifted" by a failure in ego defenses, the person may experience affective distress, forms of vulnerability, or a fear of loss of control.

"Affect balance" indicates that the person is able to modulate successfully both positive and negative affective states, which naturally occur in unusually stressful situations. To a large degree, affect balance is a healthy response to trauma and is associated with the cognitive ability to appraise realistically what has happened and to respond with instrumental coping that is efficacious in meeting the immediate demands of the situation.

Cognitive

The cognitive responses that occur in the immediate and long-term aftermath of a trauma refer to modalities of information processing or ways to understand the event that has occurred. In an interactional theory of traumatic stress reactions, cognitive processes are especially important because they are multidimensional and include the following: (1) perception of the events; (2) appraisal of the situation; (3) attributions of causality; and (4) a schema for enactment of a response. There are, in turn, at least five major cognitive styles of information processing that characterize how individuals encode and process the four dimensions listed above.

First, cognitive denial or avoidance refers to the tendency to deny or avoid what has happened by blocking the perception of the event; by appraising the situation as not requiring help; by forming an attribution of causality that minimizes responsibility or involvement in the larger context of the situation and leads to a schema for enactment that includes denial in fantasy; or by avoiding situations that trigger reminders of the experience or survivor guilt for a failed enactment.

Second, cognitive distortion is similar to psychic denial except that the person using distortion engages in extensive distortion in perception, appraisal, attribution, and enactment. Cognitive distortion is a mechanism that seems to ward off the intense acute anxiety and fear the individual experiences in the immediate context of the event. Distortion, like denial, is a cognitive style whose effect is to reduce, rather than augment, internal stimuli. It can be thought of as a safety mechanism that prematurely terminates a search of the stimulus field for additional information that could lead to problem-solving behavior. It incorporates a high degree of selective attention, a narrow search of the stimulus field, an intolerance of ambiguity due to affective arousal, and a low level of search persistence for information that pertains to the processes of appraisal, attribution, and enactment.

Accurate appraisal is a third cognitive process that characterizes an information-processing ability to perceive accurately what has happened in the trauma, to appraise realistically the situation in terms of the persons and events involved, to make a correct or adequate assessment about causality, and to initiate attempts to respond effectively and adaptively. The person who can accurately appraise the nature of a traumatic event is more likely to augment internal stimuli, actively scan the stimulus field, engage in a search of new or necessary information, and persist in such attempts, since the outcome of this mode of cognitive functioning is the ability to act competently in terms of personal needs and the demands of the situation.

As reviewed by Lifton (1988), much of the early thinking about reactions to trauma involved the concept of dissociation, the fourth cognitive process. As traditionally conceived, the concept of dissociation refers to an alteration in consciousness, identity, or behavior (APA, 1987). As a cognitive mechanism, dissociation is an alternative way to cope with extreme emotional distress by altering the nature of perception, appraisal, attribution, and the schema for enactment. Single episodes of dissociation in response to trauma can be thought of as severe reactions to a state of psychic overload and thus constitute a kind of hysterical reaction to overwhelming affect (cf. Braun, 1986; Freud, 1966). However, repeated episodes of dissociation as a cognitive modality of information processing probably reflect a learned approach to situations perceived to be potentially threatening. In response to the perception of threat, the individual fears being vulnerable and helpless and engages in a dissociative reaction, which could be an alteration in level of consciousness, the expression of personality, or an unconscious behavioral expression such as a fugue state. Similar to denial and distortion, dissociation is a safety-oriented cognitive mechanism in which the individual attempts to avoid situations of conflict or threat that disrupt the psychic equilibrium.

Fifth, the concept of reexperiencing some element of the traumatic event in imagery and affect is the sine qua non of post-traumatic stress disorder. Intrusion as a cognitive mechanism refers to the sudden, unbidden, and involuntary presence of visual images or distressing affect associated with the traumatic event. Intrusive images or memories may occur with or without distressing affect. When intrusion occurs without affect, it is presumed that some form of splitting, dissociation, or numbing has occurred as a defense against feelings that would overwhelm the individual. Similarly, it is possible for the individual to experience affective flooding without visual imagery or memory. In this case, there is a repression, blocking, or unconscious avoidance of the catastrophic imagery. Intrusion as an acute or prolonged response to stress refers to a state of psychic overload in which the person is immersed in the wake of the trauma. In this state, the distressing affect and imagery overwhelm the individual and absorb a great deal of psychic energy. As a consequence, the result is a state of fatigue, excessive autonomic nervous system arousal, and anxiety in preparation for the next anticipated episode of reexperiencing the trauma.

Motivation

Traumatic events can affect the motivational propensities of a person, that is, the individual differences in the strength of various motives that have emerged from psychosocial development (e.g., the need for affiliation, the power motive, the need for safety and predictability). These motives may be activated by the trauma or remain dormant. For example, the unexpected death of a loved one may arouse a motive of nurturance and lead to the active initiation of generativity, caring for others, or involvement with organizations or groups with prosocial goals and values.

Traumatic events can either give birth to new motives or transform old motives in new directions. When new motives are born from trauma, they represent a form of personality alteration, as in the case of psychosocial acceleration in ego development (Wilson, 1980). The transformation of motives seems to occur when the trauma produces a rapid change in the cognitive structure of the person in terms of the organization of the belief structure. For example, when a great deal of "de-illusionment" is produced by a stressful life event, the person may let go of belief systems that seem inoperative in light of what has happened. In this process of cognitive disequilibration, an emerging set of beliefs and values may facilitate a change in the nature, prepotency, and organization of basic needs.

Neurophysiology

Variations in neurochemical and endocrine secretion result from exposure to traumatic events. In an overly simplified way these neurophysiological processes can be classified as states of (1) hyperarousal, (2) avoidance-depression, or (3) balance. In hyperarousal, it is believed that the catecholaminergic substances of noradrenalin, serotonin, and dopamine are extremely elevated to the point that their use eventually exceeds synthesis and leads to an avoidance cycle. In this state, cholinergic substances such as cortisol and acetylcholine are elevated and result in depression, avoidance behaviors, and blocked awareness of the emotions of fear, anger, and aggression. In a balanced subsystem, exposure does not result in a pathological response to trauma. Clearly, these neurophysiological states can vary in duration, severity, and periodicity, depending on their activation by external stimuli or through associative learning. In the extreme form, chronic activation of the hyperarousal-avoidance cycle can be thought of as the neurophysiological substrate of post-traumatic stress disorder. (For a more detailed discussion of this topic, see Chapter 32.)

Coping

Lazarus and Folkman (1984) defined coping as a process and state that are a "constantly changing cognitive and behavioral effort to manage specific external and/or internal demands that are appraised as taxing or exceeding the resources of the person" (p. 41). Building on their seminal work as well as that of Kahana et al., (1988), it is possible to identify four types of coping responses to traumatic events: (1) instrumental, (2) expressive, (3) cognitive restructuring, and (4) resilient. Each of these forms of coping is thought of as an active psychological process that varies in use from one situation to another and can be employed by individuals. It is also believed that these forms of coping are associated with personality processes (traits and cognitive style) that affect the predominant use of a particular coping style. However, an interactional model of traumatic stress syndromes assumes that coping is affected by the complex interplay of situational variables and personality processes.

Instrumental coping is defined as problem-solving attempts to manage directly the demands posed by the stressors in the situation. It refers to the active initiation of either short- or long-term goal-directed behavior and contains either an implicit or explicit schema for enactment. Instrumental coping was identified by Lazarus and Folkman (1984) and many others.

Expressive coping is characterized by attempts to reduce distress and emotional arousal through a variety of cognitive and emotional strategies. At one end of the continuum are raw emotional expressions, such as anger, rage, fear, apprehensiveness, whining, and complaining. Accompanying these emotional outbursts are often cognitive mechanisms, as discussed above, of denial, distortion, dissociation, or intrusion, which attempt to reduce distress by reducing or augmenting information through safety-oriented responses to threat and vulnerability. In cognitive reducing models of information processing, there are selective attention, a low search persistence, and a narrow and limited schema for enactment.

As a consequence of this style of coping, the four major cognitive tasks of perception, appraisal, attribution of causality, and the schema for enactment are negatively affected. Generally, the negative outcome includes feelings of helplessness, hopelessness, and vulnerability and the defensive operations of denial, minimalization, repression, or psychic numbing. On the other hand, the individual may augment information from the stressor, leading to states of intrusion or dissociation induced by psychic overload, which may result in the same set of negative outcomes.

Cognitive restructuring refers to coping by reappraising and restructuring thoughts and feelings pertaining to the stressors experienced. As defined by Lazarus and Folkman (1984), cognitive reappraisal includes "cognitive maneuvers that change the meaning of a situation without changing it objectively, whether the changed construal is based on a realistic interpretation of cues or a distortion of reality" (p. 151). In positive cognitive restructuring the individual engages in cognition that augments information processing by (1) wide-scope attention to the properties and elements of the stimulus field, (2) active and persistent search for new data relevant to problem solving, and/or (3) the formulation of alternative schemas for enactment. Similarly, positive restructuring may involve complex forms of processing persistence that is strictly internal, that is, rational and intuitive modalities of rethinking ways to manage the stressor experience.

In negative restructuring or reappraisal, the person employs defensive operations such as denial or distortion to cope with the stressful event. Negative restructuring alters the processes of perception, appraisal, attributions of causality, and the schema for enactment. It also serves to reduce the level of distress and emotional arousal. Extreme forms of negative restructuring may result in grossly impaired adaptive functioning since there is a potential failure to process and assimilate information necessary for efficacious action and attempts at mastery of the situation.

Resilient coping refers to the capacity of the individual to manifest flexibility and mastery of stressful events continually without a disruption in psychic equilibrium. Resilient coping does not tax or exceed the individual's resources. The "hardy coper" (Kobasa, 1979) is characterized as having an internal locus of control, a strong sense of commitment to personal goals, and substantial capacity to meet difficult and challenging situations. In terms of cognitive processes, the resilient coper engages in accurate perception, appraisal, and attribution of the traumatic event. As a result, he or she develops an effective schema for enactment, which may be either a behavioral strategy or a form of cognitive reappraisal.

Post-Traumatic Adaptation

Individuals adapt to traumatic life events in many diverse ways. As Figure 1.1 indicates, it is possible to classify post-traumatic adaptation into both acute and chronic forms, which are either pathological or nonpathological and which occur at some stage of life-course development.

Pathological outcome possibilities are theoretically unlimited and include all the major mental and personality disorders, depending on the nature, severity, and developmental onset of a traumatic event. Clinically, however, the most common pathological outcome of traumatic experiences is the development of post-traumatic stress disorder or any other disorders that one would expect to occur in response to life threat, bereavement, loss, or the witnessing of horrible events. These include dysthymia or major depression, dissociative reactions, anxiety disorders, adjustment reactions, substance abuse as self-medication, and personality alteration.

The nonpathological responses to trauma also can be classified into several subcategories, including (1) no change in personality or behavior, (2) positive personality alteration and character change, (3) intensification of specific stages of ego development, (4) psychosocial acceleration in ego development, (5) changes in prepotency in the motive (need) hierarchy, and (6) alteration in beliefs, attitudes, and values. An interactional theory of traumatic stress assumes that there is a range of variability in the strength and degree of nonpathological outcomes. However, it is assumed here that positive changes in personality are relatively permanent and likely to be associated with resilient coping styles, greater levels of ego strength, and strong tendencies toward self-actualizing behavior (Maslow, 1970). Positive forms of character change following trauma may be construed, at least theoretically, as higher forms of psychological functioning organized in the wake of the trauma. In terms of the epigenetic development of personality and identity, three major effects are discernible: (1) the intensification or aggravation of the current stage of ego development; (2) retrogression in development, which includes not only actual regressive behavior but the reactivation of previously unresolved conflicts, distressing feelings, and prior episodes of vulnerability to stress or trauma; and (3) psychosocial acceleration, in which there is a premature emergence of cognitive capacities, qualities of awareness, modes of valuing, and philosophical outlook. Psychosocial acceleration also refers to the capacity for unusually autonomous behavior, independence from cultural norms and expectancies, a capacity for existential transcendence, and a deep sense of human spirituality that appreciates the interrelatedness of humankind and its environment.

CONCLUSION

In summary, Figure 1.1 illustrates the core elements for a theory of traumatic stress reactions. As a model, it assumes that there are dynamic person-environment interactions of great complexity that determine how individuals subjectively react to traumatic events and lead to either acute or chronic forms of adaptation, which are, in turn, either pathological or nonpathological.

The person inputs to the model include all dimensions of personality processes, such as traits, needs, cognitive style, values, and genetic propensities to stressful experiences. The environmental inputs to the processing of trauma include four major categories: (1) the dimensions of the trauma, (2) the experience of the trauma, (3) the structure of the trauma, and (4) the post-traumatic milieu. The features of the person and the environmental dimensions of the trauma codetermine the individual's subjective responses to the stressors, of which there are five categories: (1) emotional reactivity, (2) cognitive processes, (3) motivation, (4) neurophysiology, and (5) coping patterns. These five dimensions occur simultaneously within a person at different levels of awareness and ultimately determine the post-traumatic pattern of adaptation, which ranges from severe psychopathology and diminution of humanness to self-actualizing transcendence, positive character change, and altruism toward others. To study and treat victims of extreme stress is to understand the psychic struggle that begins with trauma and ends with a transformation of the spirit. An interactional approach to trauma is a template by which to approach an understanding of these human processes.

2

The Diagnosis and Assessment of Post-Traumatic Stress Disorder in Adults

Brett T. Litz and Frank W. Weathers

Since 1980, when post-traumatic stress disorder (PTSD) was officially recognized as a unique diagnostic entity in the *Diagnostic and Statistical Manual III* (DSM III; APA, 1980), great strides have been made in the assessment of this complex and debilitating disorder. In the early 1980s, when few standardized instruments were available, clinicians and researchers relied on PTSD symptom checklists with unknown reliability and validity. Now, however, in the early 1990s those interested in assessing PTSD can select from a wide range of sophisticated measures, including structured clinical interviews, questionnaires, and psychophysiological procedures (see Green, 1991; Litz et al., in press; Resnick, Kilpatrick & Lipovsky, 1991; Sutker, Uddo-Crane & Allain, 1991).

Unfortunately, because progress in this area has been so rapid and so many new instruments have appeared, many clinicians who treat trauma victims may not yet be aware of the array of assessment options currently available. The goal of the present chapter is to describe the latest developments in the assessment and diagnosis of PTSD with the hope that it will foster the widespread adoption of state-of-the-art methods and instruments by clinicians working with traumatized adults.

This chapter describes three methods of collecting diagnostic information: the clinical interview, questionnaires or inventories, and psychophysiological techniques. Whenever possible, empirical findings relevant to the various instruments in each of these categories are presented so that clinicians can make informed choices about which measures best suit their needs. However, because the assessment of PTSD involves much more than simply administering a battery of tests, much of the chapter is devoted to depicting the clinical context in which the process of evaluating trauma victims occurs. The chapter offers practical guidelines for taking comprehensive trauma histories across the life span, for sequencing clinical interviews and deciding what specific content areas should be addressed, and for evaluating comorbid problems such as depression, substance abuse, and personality disorders.

The focus of this chapter is on assessing adult trauma victims. The guidelines offered are most appropriate for working with an adult client with a readily identifiable adult-onset trauma such as combat or rape, which becomes the target of the assessment. The assessment process described in this chapter is divided into separate sections that evaluate the target trauma, pre-trauma and post-trauma functioning, and current functioning. However, many of the suggestions made regarding the assessment of trauma easily can be adapted for the adult client traumatized as a child, such as an incest survivor.

INTERVIEWING TRAUMA SURVIVORS

Although questionnaires and psychophysiological procedures are an invaluable source of diagnostic information, the foundation of the PTSD assessment is the clinical interview. At times the interview will be relatively unstructured, with broad, open-ended questions that allow the trauma victim to tell his or her story, and at other times it will be highly structured, with standardized questions that inquire about specific diagnostic criteria. Due to the breadth of information needed to develop a comprehensive clinical picture, the clinician should plan to spend several sessions on the interview in order to obtain sufficiently detailed and clinically meaningful information.

The clinician should keep several goals in mind throughout the interview. The first goal, which is fundamental to all clinical assessment but is particularly important when working with trauma victims, is to establish rapport and to create a safe and responsive interpersonal context for exploring highly sensitive material. A second goal is to evaluate the client's current functioning by inquiring about the problems the client is experiencing and by evaluating the psychological resources he or she has available for coping with those problems. Conducting a functional analysis by identifying antecedents and consequences of current problems can be invaluable in helping the clinician form hypotheses about the client's unique adjustment to trauma. The use of structured diagnostic interviews to assess current and lifetime diagnoses of comorbid psychiatric disorders also is recommended.

A third goal is to obtain a trauma-focused social history with an emphasis both on understanding the nature of the target trauma and its impact as well as on determining the extent of traumatization or victimization across the life span. In their work with combat veterans the authors often have found that the combat trauma is only one component of a learning history marked by multiple traumas and that a history of other trauma, such as early physical or sexual abuse, may have rendered a veteran particularly susceptible to the effects of combat.

Table 2.1
Overview of the PTSD Assessment

I. Presenting complaints and immediate needs

    A. Is client safe (is crisis intervention needed)?

    B. Is trauma the focus of presenting complaint?

II. Pre-trauma history (see Table 2.2)

III. Description of traumatic event (see Table 2.2)

IV. Post-trauma history (see Table 2.2)

V. PTSD diagnosis

    A. Frequency of symptoms

    B. Severity of symptoms

    C. Functional interference

VI. Assessing comorbidity

    A. Additional Axis I and Axis II diagnoses

    B. Characteristic interpersonal styles/problem areas

VII. Treatment planning

    A. Is environment safe and stable?

    B. Can client tolerate memory work?

    C. Should concurrent problem be addressed first?

    D. Is pharmacotherapy needed?

A fourth goal is to integrate the information on current functioning and historical antecedents in order to arrive at a conceptual model of the etiology and maintenance of the client's problems. Finally, the clinician offers the client clear feedback on the results of the assessment. The clinician can use the feedback session to help the client identify specific targets and issues for intervention, to discuss treatment options, and to instill accurate expectations for treatment.

The various content areas to be addressed in clinical evaluations of trauma survivors are outlined in Table 2.1, which is intended as a guide for sequencing a typical evaluation of a trauma survivor. Most of the information in Table 2.1 is collected via the clinical interview and can be corroborated by information from psychometrics, psychophysiological assessment, report of significant others, or chart review. The following sections describe clinical assessment issues regarding presenting complaints, taking the trauma-focused social history, and evaluating the target trauma.

Presenting Complaints

Trauma survivors vary greatly with respect to whether or not they attribute their presenting complaints to a specific traumatic experience. At one extreme are clients who present with unequivocal information about an experience that was overwhelming for them and that they cannot "get over," "forget about," or "get out of their head." They describe PTSD symptoms readily, with little prompting, and clearly state the reasons for seeking treatment (e.g., "I want to sleep better" or "I want to concentrate better on my work").

At the other extreme are clients who present with apparently non-trauma-related problems such as depression, relationship difficulties, sexual dysfunctions, or family discord. Careful inquiry, however, may reveal symptoms of PTSD such as recurrent nightmares or emotional numbing. In these cases, the clinician's job is to gather standard information (see Table 2.1) and to begin to form hypotheses about the possibility of a traumatic history (particularly early childhood trauma). The majority of clients, however, fall midway between these two extremes. Most clients typically report a trauma but need extensive inquiry to provide sufficient information for diagnostic decision making and treatment planning.

Taking the Pre-Trauma History

Gaining a clear understanding of a client's level of functioning prior to the target trauma is essential for developing a cogent case formulation. Taking a detailed pretrauma history serves two important functions. First, different people exposed to the same traumatic life event have widely varied reactions. Taking into account a client's learning history and personal resources prior to the trauma helps the clinician appreciate fully the unique impact of the trauma for that client. Second, the pre-trauma history serves as a baseline for making a diagnosis of PTSD. The PTSD diagnosis requires that current problems represent a decline from the level of functioning prior to the occurrence of the trauma. Table 2.2 contains the various content areas that should be explored when taking the pre-trauma history.

In every case the clinician should explore the possibility of early physical and sexual abuse. When a history of childhood trauma is reported, the clinician should form hypotheses about how periods of abuse or neglect have shaped the client's fundamental interpersonal schemas and maladaptive ways of relating to others (Horowitz, 1976; McCann & Pearlman, 1990b). The goal is to evaluate underlying beliefs the client has acquired regarding issues such as trust, self-care, and expressing needs. In therapy these underlying schemas themselves become targets of treatment (McCann & Pearlman, 1990b). For clients who deny a history of early trauma, the clinician, often in the context of an ongoing treatment relationship, should continue to be vigilant for clues suggesting such a history. Memories of early traumas often are strongly defended against and may be inaccessible to the client for extended periods of time.

Table 2.2
Specific Areas to Explore in Clinical Interviews with Trauma Survivors

I. Pre-trauma history

  A. Family history of psychopathology?

  B. Early experiences with caregivers?

  C. History of abuse (physical, sexual, emotional) or neglect?

  D. Academic and social experiences in school?

  E. Relationship history?

  F. Lessons learned/beliefs about self, men, women, trust, needs, safety?

  G. Stressful events (e.g., losses, accidents) and their impact?

  H. Substance use history?

  I. Occupational history?

  J. Physical/somatic history?

II. Traumatic experiences

  A. What was going on in your life at the time that this event occurred?

  B. What occurred directly prior to the event? How were you feeling?

  C. What happened (what were you seeing, hearing; what did you try to do)?

  D. What happened afterwards? What were the responses of those around you?

  E. Are there things that you have forgotten?

  F. What is it like to tell me?

  G. What has the event meant to you over time?

III. Post-trauma history

  A. Specific PTSD symptoms?

  B. Specific situations that are problematic?

  C. Changes in key relationships, work, leisure time, self-care?

  D. Response to further life stress?

  E. Substance use?

  F. Treatment history?

  G. Current environment and sources of support?

  H. Strengths?

Assessing the Target Trauma

The exploration of traumatic memories is a task that must be handled delicately, respecting the client's approach-avoidance conflict between wanting to reveal and wanting to conceal traumatic material (see Ruch et al., 1991). The clinician can encourage disclosure by being warm and nonjudgmental, by asking matter-of-fact questions about sensitive topics, and by remaining imperturbable as intense emotions and disturbing memories become activated and vivid for the client. However, in order to avoid activating feelings of being revictimized, clients always should be given control over what they disclose and when.

The clinician should be aware that the assessment process is much more than a means for gathering information. From the initial session on, the assessment can be therapeutic in that it involves encouraging active processing of traumatic memories. Clients often report obtaining significant relief from the several sessions required to complete an evaluation. At the very least, disclosure of traumatic memories and emotions during assessment can provide evidence contrary to a client's maladaptive assumptions about what might occur if he or she were to reveal what happened, such as the fear of "going crazy" and needing to be hospitalized or the fear of being humiliated or rejected.

One scheme that is helpful as a guide for exploring trauma memories is Foa, Steketee, and Olasov-Rothbaum's (1989) expansion of Lang's (e.g., Lang, 1985) conceptualization of how fear information is stored in memory. Foa et al. (1989) proposed that traumatic events are stored in memory in a rich multidimensional network. The trauma network (or schema; see McCann & Pearlman, 1990b) consists of information about stimuli present during the trauma (e.g., what the client saw, heard, smelled, or felt); information about cognitive, motoric, and physiological responses elicited during the trauma (e.g., what the client thought or did, how the client reacted physiologically, including "fight or flight" responses); and information that defines the meaning of the event for the person (e.g., "I am helpless, and I have no control over what happens to me"; "I can never be safe—terrifying things can happen any place, any time, and they are completely unpredictable").

Assessing traumatic experiences and understanding their impact on the trauma victim involve determining what is stored in the trauma network. While keeping the stimulus, response, and meaning dimensions in mind, the clinician should listen carefully to the client's account of the trauma, then inquire explicitly about memory elements that are absent or de-emphasized. Questions as simple as "What did you notice around you?" (stimulus elements), "What did you do while this was happening?" (response elements), and "What did you tell yourself about why this happened?" (meaning elements) can elicit abundant information regarding the client's experience of the trauma (see Table 2.2).

Clients exhibit marked individual differences in reported memory elements. Many clients focus on stimulus elements, leaving response and meaning elements out of their account of the trauma. Use of the trauma network scheme enables the clinician to ascertain which elements a client characteristically reports. This information then can be used as a guide in treatment. For example, a client who focuses exclusively on stimulus elements may be using intellectualization as a defense against accessing other aspects of the trauma such as painful emotions or intolerable cognitions. In therapy the clinician would encourage the client to explore the memory elements that are being avoided.

Obtaining sufficient information about the target trauma when a client is reluctant to discuss it or has effectively blocked traumatic memories from awareness can be an exceptionally difficult clinical task. The issue confronting the clinician is how far he or she should go when inquiring about traumatic material. Some clients are fragile and react so adversely to uncovering traumatic memories that probing for details would be inappropriate during assessment. Other clients are so emotionally numb or withdrawn that they cannot convey the severity of what happened to them, even with considerable prompting. The authors have found it helpful in their work with combat veterans to provide a clear explanation regarding the information that will be needed in order to conduct a thorough evaluation. It is made clear to clients at the outset that explicit information will be elicited from them about their traumatic experiences and the ways in which these experiences may have affected them. Also, it is emphasized that they have permission to go only as far as they feel comfortable as they begin to reveal what happened to them.

A rule of thumb is to ask for as much information as a client is willing to give, while reflecting how difficult it is to discuss what took place, then to draw on additional sources of information when available (e.g., referring clinician, chart review, significant others) to fill in any missing details. In some cases it may prove helpful to postpone assessment of the target trauma by focusing on a developmental history in order to establish rapport and ease into discussion of the target trauma.

Evaluating the Stressor Criterion

According to the DSM III-R (APA, 1987), in order to render a diagnosis of PTSD, the clinician must first establish that criterion A is met, which entails a judgment that the target trauma was an event "outside the range of normal human experience and that would be markedly distressing to almost anyone." The clinician has two major tasks in this context: obtaining a sufficient amount of information from the client and making a clinical judgment about the "stressfulness" of the event reported. In many cases the target trauma unequivocally meets criterion A (e.g., violent assault, clear life threat, severe injury) even if the client gives only sketchy information. In other cases this judgment is more difficult to render (e.g., miscarriage, death of close friend), even when clients are able to provide thorough descriptions of what happened to them. Yet, many apparently nontraumatic events can lead to significant PTSD symptomatology (see Helzer, Robins & McEvoy, 1987) and should prompt an assessment for PTSD when revealed in the context of a clinical evaluation.

It is clear from research with a variety of populations that the risk for developing PTSD is high after individuals experience so-called objective traumas such as life-threatening events (Kulka et al., 1991; Kilpatrick et al., 1989). However, there is growing consensus that subjective appraisal of threat or of the intensity of an event also is an important risk factor in the development of PTSD, independent of the degree of "objective" stress (see Davidson & Foa, 1991; Green, 1990). In recent studies, the term *low magnitude* stressor has been used to describe events that may not be considered objectively traumatic but that have been perceived as extremely stressful. Data from the DSM-IV field trials have suggested that a strict interpretation of criterion A may be inappropriate in that an alarmingly high percentage of subjects with low magnitude stressor events had significant PTSD symptomatology (Kilpatrick & Resnick, 1991). This has led several authors to suggest dropping criterion A as a requirement for the diagnosis of PTSD and move instead to a diagnosis based only on symptom reports or, at least, broaden criterion A to include subjective judgments about perceived uncontrollability and severity of experience (see Davidson & Foa, 1991).

There are several psychometrically sound questionnaires available to systematically assess the extent of exposure to "objective" traumatic stress. These scales have been designed primarily for research purposes in the area of combat-related PTSD (e.g., Friedman et al., 1986; Keane, Fairbank, Caddell, Zimmering, Taylor & Mora, 1989; Kulka et al., 1988). However, several other trauma exposure scales have been developed in the area of crime-related PTSD, including the Sexual Experiences Survey (Koss & Gidycz, 1985) and the Incident Report Interview (Kilpatrick et al., 1987). In addition, other scales have been developed to measure the effects of natural and man-made disasters (see Green, 1990).

Taking the Post-Trauma History

Next, the focus of the assessment shifts to the impact of the target trauma on the client. The specific content areas to be evaluated include the severity, frequency, and course of PTSD symptoms; changes in relationships and work and leisure activities; changes in coping strategies for handling subsequent life stressors (e.g., marital difficulties, financial strains, child rearing); substance abuse (self-medication); adequacy of social support and changes in social support network; treatment history; and personal strengths (see Table 2.2).

In making the diagnosis of PTSD it is crucial to evaluate not only the presence or absence of PTSD but also the frequency, severity, and functional impact of any PTSD symptomatology. Careful evaluation of the functional impact of trauma-related symptoms is particularly important because treatment decisions should be based on the extent to which a particular symptom (or cluster of symptoms) interferes with some important aspect of a client's normal functioning.

Evaluating Comorbid Problems

Epidemiological and clinical research suggests that in the majority of cases PTSD co-occurs with other Axis I disorders, with treatment-seeking populations evincing much higher rates of additional disorders than community samples (Bromet, Schulberg & Dunn, 1982; Frank & Anderson, 1987; Kilpatrick et al.,

1985; Sierles et al., 1983; Sierles et al., 1986). Therefore it is essential to assess routinely for other psychiatric disorders when evaluating a trauma survivor for PTSD (see Litz et al., in press; Penk et al., 1989; Resnick, Kilpatrick & Lipovsky, 1991).

High rates of comorbid depression, substance use disorders, and anxiety disorders such as panic and generalized anxiety are common (e.g., Helzer, Robins & McEvoy, 1987; Keane et al., 1988; Keane & Wolfe, 1990; Kulka et al., 1988). Other concurrent problems include coping deficits and inadequate social supports (e.g., Keane, Scott et al., 1985; Solomon & Mikulincer, 1987; Solomon, Mikulincer & Avitzur, 1988; Wirtz & Harrell, 1987), relationship or family problems (e.g., Figley & Sprenkle, 1978; Steketee & Foa, 1987), and physical health problems (e.g., Litz et al., 1992).

Three instruments are particularly helpful in evaluating comorbidity. The Structured Clinical Interview for DSM-III-R (SCID; Spitzer et al., 1990) allows the clinician to diagnose concurrent psychiatric disorders. Two standardized inventories, the Symptom Check List–90 (SCL–90, Derogatis, 1977) and the Minnesota Multiphasic Personality Inventory (MMPI; Hathaway & McKinley, 1983), are continuous measures of psychopathology that provide dimensional information on a variety of problem areas.

The SCL–90 is a ninety-item self-report inventory that measures current levels of psychopathology on nine symptom dimensions: somatization, obsessive-compulsive, interpersonal sensitivity, depression, anxiety, hostility, phobic anxiety, paranoid ideation, and psychoticism. The SCL–90 is brief and easy to administer and has been shown in preliminary studies to aid in the assessment of PTSD (Blake et al., 1990; Saunders, Mandoki & Kilpatrick, 1990).

The MMPI has proven to be useful for obtaining diagnostic and personality functioning information from traumatized patients (see Penk et al., 1988). Like the SCL–90 the MMPI is particularly helpful in that, in addition to having a variety of clinical scales, it has a scale that assesses PTSD (Keane, Malloy & Fairbank, 1984). The restandardized and modernized version of the MMPI, the MMPI–2 (Butcher et al., 1989), also has been shown to be helpful in the evaluation of PTSD and is essentially interchangeable with the original MMPI for this purpose (Litz, et al., 1991; Lyons & Keane, 1992).

For comprehensive diagnostic decision making the authors advocate the use of the multiaxial conventions of the DSM III-R, which encourages the clinician to consider a number of different dimensions in developing a comprehensive picture of a client's adjustment to trauma. Following the multiaxial scheme, the clinician would determine the presence or absence of PTSD and other Axis I disorders; determine the presence of personality disorders and indicate them on Axis II; identify serious medical or physical complications and indicate them on Axis III; rate the severity of past and current life stressors on Axis IV; and rate the client's overall level of functioning on Axis V. The clinician should consider all sources of information available (e.g., interviews, questionnaires, chart review) in completing the multiaxial ratings.

Treatment Planning

The last step of a PTSD assessment is to develop treatment recommendations based on careful consideration of all the information gathered during the assessment just described. This section briefly discusses some of the essential questions that clinicians need to consider in identifying and prioritizing targets for intervention. For a more detailed discussion of clinical decision making regarding the treatment of PTSD see Keane, Fairbank et al. (1985); Keane et al. (1992); Litz et al. (1990); Litz et al. (in press); McCann & Pearlman (1990b); and Horowitz (1976).

Is the client's environment safe and stable? Before proposing any specific intervention the clinician needs to consider whether the client's current living situation might preclude beginning any type of intensive psychotherapy. Examples of problems that might interfere with progress in therapy include unemployment, homelessness, or living with an abusive spouse. Exploring traumatic memories in therapy can be upsetting, and, if the client is already struggling to cope with stressors in his or her daily life, it might be prudent to postpone any trauma-related work.

How much uncovering work can the client handle at present? Processing trauma memories in psychotherapy is an essential ingredient of any PTSD treatment (see Fairbank & Nicholson, 1987). However, as noted above, this kind of work can be distressing. Clients often initially become more symptomatic as they begin to access long-avoided memories, even though the long-term outcome is superior to palliative approaches (see Foa et al., 1991). The uncovering of traumatic memories also requires a good deal of expertise and resources on the part of the therapist (see Litz et al., 1990). The clinician should monitor a client's progress closely and should be flexible in alternating between uncovering work and stress management or supportive psychotherapy, depending on the client's ability to tolerate his or her current level of distress.

Should concurrent problems be addressed prior to the trauma work? If a client is able to begin therapy, the clinician then needs to consider which problem to address first: the trauma itself or some concurrent problem that, if left unaddressed, could disrupt the trauma work. In working with combat veterans, the most common issue that surfaces when prioritizing targets for change is the extent to which substance abuse or dependence needs to be addressed prior to addressing PTSD issues. The authors typically recommend that clients with active substance abuse achieve a significant period of sobriety and learn relapse prevention skills before they address their trauma in treatment. For example, in a recent study Boudewyns et al. (1991) found that substance abuse or relapse was the most common reason for Vietnam combat veterans' prematurely terminating treatment.

Is pharmacotherapy indicated? For clients with comorbid affective or anxiety disorders, a psychopharmacological evaluation should always be considered, given the extensive literature supporting the efficacy of medication for these problems. Also, research has shown increasingly that pharmacological interventions help alleviate the positive symptoms of PTSD (reexperiencing and hyperreactivity), which may allow a client to tolerate therapeutic exposure to traumatic memories. A thorough discussion of pharmacotherapy issues in the treatment of PTSD can be found in Friedman (1991).

Standardized Assessment Instruments for PTSD

The assessment of trauma victims can be enhanced greatly through the use of standardized instruments and methods such as structured interviews, questionnaires, and physiological measures. The use of multiple instruments provides converging evidence that increases confidence in diagnostic decision making and treatment planning (Keane, Wolfe & Taylor, 1987). By using standardized instruments clinicians can (1) specify the current severity of a disorder for a given individual; (2) track changes in severity over time and predict course, prognosis, and response to treatment; and (3) communicate assessment results efficiently and succinctly. The following sections provide a brief introduction to psychometric theory for readers who may be unfamiliar with the principles of psychological testing, followed by an overview of instruments for assessing PTSD. Readers interested in learning more about test theory should consult Cronbach (1990) or Crocker and Algina (1986).

Introduction to Psychometric Theory

Psychological tests are evaluated with respect to two important characteristics: reliability, which refers to the consistency or replicability of test scores, and validity, which refers to the meaningfulness or accuracy of inferences, interpretations, or decisions made on the basis of those scores. Test developers often report the consistency of scores over time (test-retest reliability), over different interviewers or raters (interrater reliability), or over different items on the same test (internal consistency). Reliability for continuous measures such as questionnaires is typically reported as a correlation coefficient, which can vary between .00 and 1.00, with coefficients close to 1.00 indicating excellent reliability. Reliability for dichotomous measures such as interviews that yield present/absent diagnostic decisions often is reported as a kappa coefficient (Cohen, 1960), which also varies between .00 and 1.00 and is interpreted as the amount of agreement beyond chance.

Caution should be observed when interpreting some measures of reliability for tests measuring psychopathology. For example, a test-retest reliability coefficient based on two administrations of a PTSD questionnaire given one month apart might reflect genuine change in clinical status for some examinees in addition to measurement error. Similarly, if the PTSD questionnaire contained items that tap different aspects of the disorder, such as questions on reexperiencing, numbing/avoidance, and hyperarousal, an internal consistency coefficient might reflect differences in item content in addition to response inconsistencies.

In addition to being reliable, a good test is valid or useful for the purposes for which it is intended. Although not all measures of validity are appropriate for all tests, a test for PTSD can be said to be valid if it has items that assess the key aspects of the disorder (content validity), if it predicts something of interest such as clinical diagnosis or response to treatment (criterion-related validity), or if it correlates with other measures of PTSD but not with measures of other disorders (construct validity).

Psychological tests are often evaluated on the basis of their diagnostic utility, a type of criterion-related validity pertaining to a test's ability to predict diagnostic status (see Kraemer, 1987). Three steps are involved in determining the diagnostic utility of a test. First, a diagnostic criterion or "gold standard" must be selected. The gold standard is typically a diagnosis determined on the basis of a clinical interview but may also be a composite criterion based on several sources of evidence (see Kulka et al., 1991 for a detailed treatment of these issues in the context of the assessment of combat-related PTSD). Second, both the gold standard and the test are administered to a group of examinees. Finally, various cutoff scores on the test are investigated for their utility, or their ability to correctly predict the outcome of the gold standard. Cutoff scores divide the group of examinees in two, such that those above the cutoff are predicted to have the diagnosis and those below the cutoff are predicted not to have the diagnosis. The optimal cutoff score for differential diagnosis is the test score that leads to the greatest number of correct predictions.

Some PTSD measures have excellent diagnostic utility, but none can predict the gold standard perfectly (see Gerardi, Keane & Penk, 1989). There are two kinds of errors in prediction, false positives, which occur when an examinee scores above the cutoff on the test but does not have the diagnosis according to the gold standard, and false negatives, which occur when an examinee scores below the cutoff on the test but does have the diagnosis. Diagnostic utility often is described in terms of sensitivity and specificity, which are two measures of test performance that take into account errors in prediction. Sensitivity is the "true positive rate," or the probability that those with the diagnosis will score above the cutoff on the test. Specificity is the "true negative rate," or the probability that those without the diagnosis will score below the cutoff on the test (Kraemer, 1987). Sensitivity will be low if the test yields many false negatives, and specificity will be low if the test yields many false positives.

Structured Interviews

In clinical research on PTSD it has become standard practice to use structured interviews for diagnostic decision making because they allow investigators to specify precisely how diagnoses were made and whether the diagnoses are reliable and valid. Structured interviews also can be valuable in clinical work in that they allow the practitioner to inquire systematically about specific PTSD symptoms and comorbid syndromes. The sections that follow describe several structured interviews that might be valuable in the assessment of trauma victims.

The SCID

The SCID is the most widely used structured diagnostic interview to assess Axis I and Axis II disorders in the DSM III-R. The SCID consists of separate modules for each diagnostic category. Administering the entire SCID can be time-consuming and may be not be feasible in all clinical contexts. If the SCID needs to be shortened because of practical constraints, the authors recommend including the following modules as a minimum when assessing traumatized adults: all affective disorders, anxiety disorders, and substance use disorders, as well as the module for screening for psychotic disorders. In some clinical contexts the assessment of personality disorders also may be indicated.

The PTSD module of the SCID consists of probe questions for each of the seventeen PTSD symptoms in DSM III-R, plus questions on survivor guilt and guilt over acts of omission or commission. The wording of the probe questions is sensitive and clear. Clinicians are encouraged to ask additional questions, as needed, to determine the appropriate rating for each item. Symptoms are judged to be absent, of subclinical severity, or present and count toward a diagnosis only if they are judged to be present.

The PTSD module appears to be clinically sensitive and reliable and has been widely used in PTSD research. However, a significant limitation of the SCID is that it yields only dichotomous present/absent information about PTSD. It is not sensitive to differences in current severity of PTSD, and it is impractical as an outcome measure because, over time, it can detect only changes in diagnostic status rather than changes in symptom severity.

The Diagnostic Interview Schedule (DIS)

The DIS is a highly structured interview designed for use by nonclinicians. The DIS has much less to recommend it as a criterion measure for PTSD. The DIS does appear to have at least moderate test-retest reliability. However, the validity of the DIS has been called into question. Kulka et al. (1988) found that, although the DIS performed well when the prevalence of PTSD was relatively high, it performed poorly in a community-based sample with lower prevalence. In the community-based sample, with a composite diagnosis as the criterion, the DIS had nearly perfect specificity (.99), but very low sensitivity (.23) and kappa (.28). This suggests that, in a population with a relatively low base rate of PTSD, the DIS correctly identifies individuals without PTSD but does not do a good job of identifying individuals with PTSD.

Kulka et al. (1988) describe several possible problems with the DIS that might explain why it performed so poorly. One problem is that the wording of the probe questions may make it difficult to understand what is being asked. A second problem is that the DIS requires that the client make a causal connection between a symptom and a specific traumatic event, which, as was mentioned earlier, may be very difficult for some clients to do. Finally, because the DIS is highly structured and intended for use by nonclinicians, open-ended follow-up questions are not permitted.

PTSD Interview (PTSD-I)

Unlike the SCID and the DIS, the PTSD-I (Watson et al., 1991) yields both dichotomous and continuous scores. Watson et al. (1991) report strong test-retest reliability (.95) and internal consistency (alpha = .92), as well as excellent sensitivity (.89), specificity (.94), and kappa (.82), using the DIS as the criterion.

The PTSD-I appears to have desirable psychometric properties but is limited by its format and procedure for administration. A copy of the rating scale is given to the interviewee, probe questions for the symptoms are read aloud, and the interviewee indicates his or her rating. This format differs little from a self-report instrument, and it is not clear that the PTSD-I should even be considered a structured interview. The PTSD-I may be appropriate as a screening instrument but, if given as intended, will elicit minimal qualitative information about PTSD symptomatology.

Structured Interview for PTSD (SI-PTSD)

Like the PTSD-I, the SI-PTSD (Davidson, Smith & Kudler, 1989) appears to be a psychometrically sound interview that yields both dichotomous and continuous scores for PTSD. The SI-PTSD appears to be a useful structured clinical interview for diagnosing PTSD and measuring symptom severity. In addition to initial probe questions it provides helpful follow-up questions that encourage clients to elaborate on their descriptions of symptoms. Items on the SI-PTSD are rated by the clinician on a five-point scale, and explicit descriptions of severity are provided for each point on the scale to aid the clinician in making the appropriate rating.

Clinician-Administered PTSD Scale (CAPS)

The CAPS (Blake, Weathers et al., 1990) is a new structured interview for PTSD developed at the National Center for PTSD. The CAPS was designed for use by clinicians familiar with the effects of trauma because the authors of the CAPS felt that the task of gathering adequate qualitative and quantitative information about PTSD symptoms was best accomplished by experienced clinicians. Two versions of the CAPS are available: a current and lifetime diagnostic version (CAPS–1) and a weekly symptom-rating version (CAPS–2).

The CAPS consists of thirty items that assess DSM-III-R symptoms of PTSD, symptoms associated with PTSD (e.g., survivor guilt), and overall symptom severity, degree of improvement since an earlier measurement, impairments in social and occupational functioning, and validity of responses. Like the PTSD-I and the SI-PTSD, the CAPS yields dichotomous and continuous scores. Two unique features of the CAPS are that it has separate rating scales to determine the frequency and intensity of each symptom and it contains behaviorally anchored probe questions and scale values. Interviewers are encouraged to ask their own follow-up questions, when appropriate, and to use their clinical judgment to arrive at the best rating.

Studies on the psychometric properties of the CAPS–1 and CAPS–2 are currently under way at the National Center for PTSD, and have been presented at several national conferences. Preliminary data indicate that the CAPS has very promising reliability and validity (Blake, Weathers et al., 1990).

DIAGNOSTIC QUESTIONNAIRES

In addition to the structured interviews discussed above, several questionnaire measures of PTSD have been developed and psychometrically evaluated. These types of PTSD measures enjoy widespread usage because they are easy to administer and score, and they are useful to screen for the presence of PTSD. These questionnaires can be used either as diagnostic measures by selecting appropriate cutoff scores or as continuous measures of the severity of PTSD symptoms. For rigorous diagnostic purposes, the authors recommend a structured clinical interview and the administration of one or more of these questionnaires.

Keane PTSD Scale of the MMPI (PK Scale)

The original PK Scale (Keane et al., 1984) consists of forty-nine MMPI items that were found to differentiate between combat veterans with and without PTSD. In the original report on this scale, Keane, Malloy, and Fairbank (1984) found that a cutoff of thirty correctly classified 82 percent of the subjects.

Subsequent studies have confirmed that the PK Scale can differentiate individuals with PTSD from those without the disorder. For example, Watson, Kucala, and Manifold (1986) found that, compared with psychiatric and normal control subjects, combat veterans with PTSD had much higher PK Scale scores. They also found adequate sensitivity (.87) and specificity (.74) for distinguishing between PTSD subjects and normal controls and somewhat lower sensitivity (.73) and specificity (.53) for distinguishing between PTSD subjects and psychiatric controls. However, the group means and the optimal cutting scores on the MMPI-PTSD were much lower than in the Keane et al. (1984) report. These differences are probably due to sampling differences and different diagnostic procedures as the criterion measure.

Cannon et al. (1987) found that the sensitivity of the PK Scale was .76 and the specificity was .64 for distinguishing between groups of inpatients with and without PTSD. However, unlike Keane, Malloy, and Fairbank (1984), they found a very high rate of false positives. This difference may have been due to a much lower base rate of PTSD in the Cannon et al. study (14 percent versus 50 percent), or it may have been due to different diagnostic procedures.

With the publication of the MMPI–2 (Butcher et al., 1989) some modifications have been made in the PK Scale. The most important change is that three items that appeared twice in the original PK Scale have been deleted, resulting in a forty-six-item scale. Lyons and Keane (1992) discuss this and other changes and address the complex issue of selecting an appropriate cutoff score.

Although no reliability studies have appeared on the original PK Scale, the forty-six-item PK scale in the MMPI–2 has been shown to have strong internal consistency (.85–.87) and test-retest reliability (.86–89; Graham, 1990). The PK Scale appears to be valid in that it performs moderately well in differentiating combat veterans with and without PTSD. The PK Scale also may be useful for other traumatized populations (e.g., Koretzky & Peck, 1990; Williams, 1990), although few studies have been conducted to date.

Mississippi Scale for Combat-Related PTSD (Mississippi Scale)

The Mississippi Scale (Keane, Caddell & Taylor, 1988) is a 35-item scale designed to measure combat-related PTSD. The items were selected from an initial pool of 200 items that reflected DSM-III criteria. Additional items were included to assess substance abuse, depression, and suicidality. In the original report (Keane, Caddell & Taylor, 1988), the Mississippi Scale was found to have excellent internal consistency (.94) and test-retest reliability (.97 over a one-week interval). The Mississippi Scale also performed quite well at distinguishing veterans with and without PTSD. Using a cutoff score of 107, the sensitivity was .93, and the specificity was .89.

The Mississippi Scale appears to have excellent psychometric properties and has outperformed the PK Scale in studies where the two scales have been compared directly. In a community sample with a lower base rate of PTSD, the Mississippi Scale had greater sensitivity (.77 versus .72), specificity (.83 versus .82), and kappa (.53 versus .48). In this study Kulka et al. (1988) used cutoffs of 89 on the Mississippi Scale and 15 on the PK Scale. The MMPI-PTSD and the Mississippi Scale were compared directly in a second study by McFall, Smith, et al. (1990), who found that the Mississippi Scale had a higher correlation with the SCID PTSD module.

A version of the Mississippi Scale for assessing civilian trauma is now available from the authors, although no studies have appeared as of this writing regarding its psychometric properties. As with the PK Scale, clinicians who use the Mississippi Scale may need to adjust the cutoff score to account for working in different settings (e.g., community mental health center versus inpatient psychiatric unit) or with victims of different types of trauma.

Impact of Event Scale (IES)

The IES (Horowitz, Wilner & Alvarez, 1979) is a fifteen-item questionnaire that measures two aspects of a person's response to stressful life events, intrusion (e.g., ''I thought about it when I didn't mean to'') and avoidance (e.g., ''I stayed away from reminders of it''). The IES contains a seven-item intrusion subscale and an eight-item avoidance subscale. Horowitz et al. (1979) found that the two subscales had good internal consistency (.78 for intrusion, .82 for avoidance) and test-retest reliability (.89 for intrusion, .79 for avoidance). They also found that outpatients with stress response syndromes scored significantly higher on all but two IES items compared with new medical students and that the IES was sensitive to clinical change in the outpatients.

Horowitz et al. (1979) reported a moderate correlation (.42) between the intrusion and avoidance subscales, which indicates that these subscales are measuring related, but somewhat independent, dimensions of response to stress. Two subsequent studies (Zilberg, Weiss & Horowitz, 1982; Schwarzwald et al., 1987) used factor analysis to confirm that the IES measures the two different dimensions suggested originally by the authors.

The IES is one of the most widely used questionnaire measures of PTSD and one of the few scales to be used in traumatized populations other than combat veterans. A strength of the IES is that it explicitly distinguishes the two broad symptom clusters of PTSD, although the correspondence to DSM-III-R criteria is not exact.

The PTSD Scale of the SCL–90

Saunders, Mandoki, and Kilpatrick (1990) derived a twenty-eight-item PTSD scale from the SCL–90 (described previously), using items that best distinguished between women with crime-related PTSD and women without PTSD. They found that this scale had adequate sensitivity (.75) and specificity (.90), using DIS interview ratings as the criterion. However, the SCL–90 PTSD subscale had particularly poor positive predictive power (i.e., if the SCL–90 PTSD subscale was above the cutoff defined as PTSD, the probability that DIS diagnosis was indeed PTSD positive was .31). Because of this, the authors caution that further cross-validation is needed before widespread clinical application of this subscale.

PSYCHOPHYSIOLOGICAL METHODS

Psychophysiological assessment methods have been used primarily by researchers studying conditioned emotional responses in combat-related PTSD (e.g., Blanchard et al., 1982) and are seldom used in the clinical assessment of PTSD. This is unfortunate because physiological reactivity is a salient diagnostic feature of PTSD, and assessment of this phenomenon presents the rare opportunity to obtain diagnostic information about PTSD that is independent of a client's self-report. Evidence of physiological reactivity can be very helpful in compensation cases (see Litz et al., in press) or in cases where other assessment information is inconclusive. However, in that physiological measurement is usually costly and time-consuming, it is understandable that such methods have not been adopted widely. This section briefly describes the basic methodology and findings for those interested in applying these techniques to improve diagnostic utility.

The basic paradigm entails presenting trauma-relevant and neutral (control) stimuli while measuring multiple physiological response channels such as heart rate, blood pressure, and skin conductance. Self-reported arousal is also measured, either by Subjective Units of Distress (SUDS) or by self-report of various aspects of emotional experience such as valence and arousal (see Lang, 1985). Stimuli that have been shown to be effective in eliciting responding include slides, sounds, and narrative descriptions of the traumatic event (for a review see McFall et al., 1989).

Numerous laboratory studies assessing psychophysiological reactivity have been conducted with veterans with combat-related PTSD (Blanchard et al., 1982; Blanchard et al., 1986; Blanchard, Kolb & Prins, 1991; Malloy, Fairbank & Keane, 1983; Pallmeyer, Blanchard & Kolb, 1985). It is noteworthy that despite considerable variation in the stimuli presented, the paradigm employed, and the types of control groups used, veterans with PTSD consistently have been found to be more physiologically reactive to trauma-related cues compared with veterans without PTSD. When psychophysiological approaches are utilized in assessment, the accuracy of PTSD diagnoses can be improved considerably (see Gerardi, Keane & Penk, 1989).

In a recent study, Pitman et al. (1987) presented trauma-related stimuli that were individually tailored to the experiences of the subject rather than presenting a standard set of stimuli. Pitman et al. (1987) exposed fifteen Vietnam veterans with PTSD and eighteen Vietnam veterans without PTSD to a series of thirty-second audiotaped scripts. The scripts consisted of individualized descriptions of traumatic combat experiences recalled by each subject. They found that subjects were significantly more psychophysiologically responsive to these idiographic trauma scripts than to scripts that depicted other positive and negative events.

Pitman et al.'s (1987) findings suggest that clinicians do not need standardized stimuli to conduct an adequate psychophysiological assessment. Rather, they can create powerful stimuli simply by generating individualized scripts based on a client's traumatic experiences, regardless of the type of trauma. Also, clinicians interested in assessing psychophysiological responsivity in PTSD do not need to invest in a lot of expensive equipment to do so. Heart-rate reactivity appears to be the single best predictor of PTSD status (Blanchard et al., 1986), and this can be measured using simple and reasonably priced devices.

SUMMARY

This chapter has discussed the special issues that confront a clinician during the evaluation of a traumatized client. The assessment of PTSD requires careful attention both to the content of what is reported (e.g., the nature and extent of symptomatology) and to the process by which meaningful information about adjustment to traumatic experiences is obtained. The use of structured interviews, questionnaires, and psychophysiological techniques can help the clinician reach reliable and valid conclusions regarding the presence or absence of PTSD and concurrent problems. However, information from these instruments can inform decisions about how to proceed in treatment only when they are viewed in the context of what has been learned about the total person over the course of the assessment.

3

Integrating Structured and Unstructured Approaches to Taking a Trauma History

Laurie Anne Pearlman and I. Lisa McCann

This chapter discusses the clinical implications of combining structured and unstructured approaches to taking a trauma history, focusing primarily on survivors who present with fragmented, incomprehensible, or repressed traumatic memories. The history-taking process in these cases often involves very complex and delicate clinical issues. This chapter discusses obtaining a trauma history as an integrated part of the entire therapy process; handling complex clinical issues that emerge; addressing issues of shame, fear of disclosure, and disbelief; and attending with sensitivity to the transference issues that are inevitably evoked in this process. A discussion of clinical implications of introducing a structured questionnaire as part of this process concludes the chapter.

The approach presented here is somewhat different from the more traditional, chronological history-taking approach. A more direct, systematic approach can sometimes be overwhelming to the trauma survivor client. Many survivors have an especially great need to control the material they present in treatment, telling the more sensitive and shameful parts of their stories only as they feel safe in the therapeutic relationship. This chapter presents an approach that addresses the therapist's and client's need for historical information to be shared, as well as the client's need to control the pacing of the sharing of his or her history.

ETHICAL CONCERNS

In addition to the clinical wisdom of inviting the client to control the pacing of the history taking, this approach addresses certain ethical concerns as well. Trauma therapists must be aware of the possibility of erring on the side of opening up material that clients have no wish to explore or may not be prepared to address. Limitations can include psychological resources (self capacities and ego resources; McCann & Pearlman, 1990b), financial resources for treatment, and/or social support for the demanding process of uncovering and resolving traumatic memories. While informed consent is very difficult under the best of circumstances, clients who are unaware that they have been traumatized are in a most difficult position with respect to entering treatment without full awareness of what lies ahead. The clinician's task is complex; certainly it is not his or her desire to retraumatize clients. The therapist must continuously assess the client's readiness to manage the emerging material, provide tremendous support for the process, help the client obtain whatever external support he or she needs for this process, and allow the client to guide the treatment in terms of the therapist's attending to signs that the client is not ready to open up new material or is not able to manage the therapy psychologically or materially. In addition, it is important that the therapist not assume that she knows more about the client's history than the client knows. Good clinical and ethical practice requires following the client's lead and not leading the client according to the therapist's assumptions. With these caveats, the discussion now turns to the specifics of taking a trauma history.

THE NEED FOR A TRAUMA HISTORY

Why is a trauma history important? Most obviously, trauma-related symptoms are often distressing to clients. For many survivors, the recovery of whole memories of a trauma is essential to the resolution of intrusive imagery. As van der Kolk and van der Hart (1991) noted, at the turn of the century, Janet suggested that reexperiencing phenomena and other reenactments are indications that there is unfinished trauma business, that further aspects of the trauma need to be explored and worked through (Horowitz, 1986; van der Kolk, 1989). Helping survivors remember and ultimately speak the unspeakable is therapeutic because it assists in making sense of otherwise inexplicable emotional reactions and disruptions in interpersonal relationships. Furthermore, it helps survivors restore a sense of personal identity. One's sense of identity is based on a knowledge of one's personal history and continuity over time. When trauma is repressed and dissociative episodes occur in which there is the experience of "nonself," the sense of continuity that is essential to a cohesive identity is disrupted (Westen, 1991). Putting together the disconnected pieces of the trauma puzzle is thus essential to recovering lost or disowned parts of the self. In our view, survivors must remember as much as they feel they need to remember to develop a sense of continuity with respect to their identity and life, to account for their current ways of relating to self and others, and to experience some relief of the distress that brought them to therapy.

For these reasons, it is important to help the survivor assemble the often fragmented and confusing pieces of memories. Survivors of childhood sexual abuse often display strong needs to defend against the reality of returning memories. Helping them come to terms with reality is therefore a fundamental task in therapy. Survivors with repressed memories of childhood traumas often present with a variety of difficulties and adaptations, such as chronic depression or anxiety, suicidality, low self-esteem, sexual dysfunction, and chronic relationship difficulties (e.g., Gelinas, 1983). In these instances, the goal of taking a trauma history early in treatment is not primarily to gather historically accurate and coherent data; rather, the purpose is to begin the process of naming (and thus normalizing) traumatic events and demonstrating that the events can be discussed in therapy.

A client may present with these classic symptoms of repressed early trauma as well as seriously disrupted self capacities, ego resources, and/or cognitive schemas (McCann & Pearlman, 1990b) and yet not initially report such a history. In this case, the therapist should introduce the possibility in one of the first few sessions that people who present with these symptoms often discover something traumatic has happened to them, something they have protected themselves from remembering. When the suggestion of the possibility of childhood abuse is met with a negative response, the therapist may continue to hold the possibility open in his or her mind, remaining alert for confirmatory data such as the emergence of repressed traumatic material through reenactments, dreams, flashbacks, and so forth.

Trauma-related material in disguised forms may begin to emerge spontaneously in the client's dreams. Examples include dreams of danger and harm; dreams containing threatening, menacing, or shadowy figures; dreams related to hiding, running away, or being traumatically abandoned by loved ones; and dreams with themes of shame or humiliation. One female client repeatedly denied any memories of early abuse throughout the first year of treatment. Yet she reported a recurrent dream in which she was calling out, "Mommy, mommy, why did you abandon me?" As this was explored in the context of her personal history, the dream material grew increasingly transparent. The client began having dreams of a man with a hawk's face standing over her bed. These dreams were associated with tremendous terror. Over time, the symbolic material became less disguised, and the history-taking process moved to a different stage, wherein the client eventually discovered a history of childhood sexual abuse.

Dissociative symptoms are another cardinal sign of repressed traumatic material (Ellenson, 1985; van der Kolk & van der Hart, 1991). When clients report being in a fog, feeling spaced out, blanking out in sessions, or feeling far away and dreamy, they often are indicating that something in the session threatened to activate a repressed memory. When a subtle shift in the client's demeanor, focus, or affect is observed, the therapist might say, "I'm wondering what just happened." The client can then be guided gently to explore the associations that led to dissociation. These associations often lead directly to an earlier experience of terror and trauma.

Self and world representations (schemas about self and others) that are extremely negative and overgeneralized are often associated with severe unresolved trauma (Janoff-Bulman, 1989; McCann & Pearlman, 1990b). The TSI Belief Scale (Pearlman, Mac Ian, Johnson & Mas, 1992; Stamm, Bieber & Pearlman, 1991), which is given to all clients who come to The Traumatic Stress Institute for treatment, regardless of the presenting complaint, assesses individuals' cognitive schemas or beliefs and assumptions about themselves, other people, and the world. Individuals' responses on this instrument alert the therapist to the presence of themes related to abusive relationships as well as other traumas. This is an unobtrusive way of opening up the possibility of a history of trauma without presenting potentially distressing material to the client in the early stages of therapy.

The therapist provides feedback on the scale's results in a subsequent clinical interview. Beliefs that other people and the world are unsafe, threatening, malevolent, untrustworthy, or exploitive are explored in the context of the client's personal history. This instrument has proved to be useful for three reasons: it can activate memories related to traumatic interpersonal violations; it provides the client with a framework for understanding some of the enduring effects of trauma; and finally, it provides a basis for treatment planning, including identifying areas of disruption that must be addressed in therapy and invaluable information about transference themes that are likely to emerge in the therapy.

DEVELOPING A FRAMEWORK FOR EXPLORING THE TRAUMA MATERIAL

History taking is a joint project between the client and the therapist in which, over time, both parties must eventually be invested. Providing the client with a framework to understand the importance of exploring trauma material sets the stage for that project.

The first step in setting the frame is to educate the client about the history-taking or memory retrieval process. Clients who are beginning to recover repressed memories often find it helpful when the therapist provides a metaphor for this process, such as fitting together the pieces of a puzzle or a mosaic to make a meaningful whole.

Educating the client about the memory system and the process of recovering whole memories is also important. Whole memories consist of sensory experience (images, pictures, bodily sensations, smells, sounds, and so forth), verbal experience (e.g., what happened, when, where, or the story line), and emotions (psychobiological states) (Paivio, 1986). The therapist can explain to the client that these three parts of a whole memory often become disconnected as a result of trauma. The task of therapy is to put the verbal part, the sensory part (particularly the imagery and body memories), and the feeling state of memory together. Survivors who report memory fragments or psychobiological states that appear to make no sense are often very frustrated by these distressing and incomprehensible fragments. Every fragment is important, no matter how inconsequential it may seem at the time. With appropriate attention, over time, their historical and symbolic meanings will unfold.

There are a number of techniques that are helpful in pulling together the pieces of memories. Courtois (1988b) suggests that highly motivated survivors who want to remember and make sense of their past experiences keep a record of dreams, fantasies, flashbacks, fragments, and other pieces of information that may be part of the puzzle. Depending on the survivor's preference, these data may be recorded through writing in a memory journal, speaking into a tape recorder, or drawing pictures. For some survivors, photographs or other memorabilia from a particular period of time often stimulate the imagery system of memory. It is helpful to keep a record of these fragments as well as copies of the client's productions on file. These early pieces of information often become important clues later in the memory retrieval process.

COMMON CLINICAL DILEMMAS AND ERRORS

Pacing

Survivors may have difficulties in remembering and telling their story. The most common error in pacing the history-taking process is the premature exploration of traumatic material. Clients who reveal a great deal in initial sessions may feel overwhelmed. As a result, they may back away and end therapy prematurely. When the therapist characterizes an early session as a good session, because a lot of material was disclosed, history taking may be moving too quickly. Even when material emerges spontaneously, it is important to explore the meanings of the disclosure and assess the client's feeling of control over the process.

After a revealing disclosure, clients sometimes feel overwhelmed, ashamed, or afraid they have revealed too much. Beere (1990) described how the very process of telling the therapist what happened shames and therefore retraumatizes the client. Thus it is important to name the processes of remembering, telling, and responding emotionally to the telling as a way of monitoring and ultimately resolving these reactions. The therapist may tell the client, "You don't have to tell anything you don't feel ready to or feel safe disclosing." It is also useful to predict that these feelings of shame, terror, disgust, humiliation, and self-loathing inevitably emerge over the course of history taking. Toward the end of a session in which the client has revealed new trauma material, the therapist might say: "Sometimes after talking about difficult issues in a session, people feel uncomfortable. I wonder how you might feel later as you think back on today's session." Self-abusive clients may feel like punishing themselves after such a disclosure; this danger should be named explicitly, and alternative ways of managing these feelings should be explored.

The therapist must explore the feelings of disloyalty or fear of punishment or retaliation for telling the secret, particularly among cult abuse survivors and others who were threatened with death if they told about the abuse. The therapist should also comment upon the natural desires to repress and disavow traumatic memories as well as the struggle with the reality of traumatic events. Although the clinical resolution of these issues occurs over many months, if not years, addressing them early in the therapy process can be very reassuring. It is, in fact, an essential early step in the resolution of the traumatic material, helping to normalize the intense struggles over "speaking the unspeakable."

In most cases, it is wise to regulate the process of memory retrieval. For example, the therapist might acknowledge that, while the individual may feel a need to tell all the details, he or she may feel frightened or overwhelmed after doing so and therefore need to back off. Talking about how this process might be regulated and controlled by the client, both within the sessions and at home, conveys respect for the client's own sense of timing. The therapist may also convey that the trauma history can be revealed over a period of time, rather than all at once. This assurance gives the person permission to back away from the material in the session, particularly if he or she is struggling with intense, overwhelming emotions and appears ambivalent about proceeding. Letting a client know he or she will not be pushed to talk about something often has a paradoxical effect; by conveying that the client is in control of the process, the therapist often helps the client feel safe to disclose more.

It is also very important to check in with clients periodically about how they are experiencing the therapy process at the moment. Checking in at regular intervals as particularly painful memories are disclosed can be done by gently asking: "How are you feeling right now? Are you OK with what we are doing?" It is also very important to take five or ten minutes at the end of a session to explore the meanings and affects associated with disclosure and to allow for a sense of closure. Time to regroup and reconnect is particularly important for clients who tend to dissociate or hurt themselves after sessions. If the session has been particularly difficult or difficult trauma material has been disclosed, it is important to explore in depth what a client needs in order to soothe and calm herself or himself afterward or otherwise get the needed support.

Self Capacities

Survivors frequently exhibit impaired self capacities. Within constructivist self-development theory (McCann & Pearlman, 1990b), there are three self capacities that, taken together, contribute to the individual's ability to regulate self-esteem. The four self capacities are the ability to manage and tolerate strong affect, the ability to maintain an inner sense of connection with others, and the ability to maintain a positive sense of self. A clinical dilemma related to history taking emerges when the individual's self capacities are undeveloped or impaired by traumatic experiences. If the history-taking process evokes intolerable affect, it may result in premature termination, destructive reenactments, self-mutilation, or other behaviors aimed at warding off the overwhelming affect.

The history-taking process should be integrated into an assessment of the client's self capacities. The clinician must assess the client's capacity to tolerate affect, to experience a broad range of feelings, such as joy, sorrow, rage, terror, love, and grief. Affect tolerance does not mean that clients have no problem with affects because they do not allow themselves to feel. Many trauma survivors are desperately afraid of (or completely numb to) their feelings. An important way to assess affect tolerance is to probe gently into specific aspects of the traumatic imagery while observing the survivor's emotional responses. As Horowitz (1986), Brett and Ostroff (1985), and others have pointed out, disturbing imagery is a hallmark of the traumatic state. Likewise, imagery is the gateway to the emotions. Many survivors can give factual accounts of traumatic experiences while showing very little affect. Yet, when probing for the pictures in the mind's eye, powerful affects begin to emerge.

The therapist should watch for the following signals as this process begins. Do clients distance and become detached from the material? Do they become very distressed and report feeling out of control? Are they able to experience strong affects in the session and recover on their own? Do they resort to drug use, become self-destructive in other ways, experience somatic disturbances, or exhibit dissociative symptoms after a particularly powerful disclosure? If so, then the history taking should proceed more slowly while the therapy focuses on developing the capacity for affect tolerance (McCann & Pearlman, 1990b).

One important way to address issues related to affect tolerance is to explore the client's underlying fears about experiencing strong emotions. Often clients report fears of being overwhelmed or disintegrating, fears of not being able to stop crying, fears of going crazy, and fears of appearing weak and helpless. Normalizing these responses and conveying the strong message that the therapist will help them learn to regulate painful states are very important.

It is also important to explore the past events that engendered the meanings associated with the fears. For example, some survivors talk about "don't feel" messages from childhood; feelings may have been seen as toxic or dangerous. Survivors who equate strong affects with "going out of control" often reveal links between violence and strong emotions in their families of origin. Experiencing intense anger may be equated with, or trigger memories of, an out-of-control, rageful parent. In other cases, vulnerable feelings may be associated with a parent who is viewed with contempt because he or she was helpless and weak.

In order to tolerate strong affect, the survivor must be able to soothe and calm herself or himself. This ability may be assessed by in-depth exploration of the client's self-statements when he or she is distressed. Some individuals can be unmercifully sadistic toward the wounded self, reenacting the experience of a sadistic, harsh, or punitive abuser.

Teaching clients self-soothing statements and modeling statements for them during painful disclosures are often very helpful. Discussing how an adult comforts distressed young children, as a way both to teach self-parenting and to identify historical antecedents to the client's inability to self-soothe, is also helpful. Modeling the use of self-statements (e.g., "I'm going to be OK; I can handle this"), as well as the use of soothing imagery, often helps a client tolerate the painful process of memory work.

Second, developing the ability to connect with supportive people, internally as well as interpersonally, is also important. If the individual has particular difficulty while alone, as is often the case, developing this capacity is especially necessary. This can be accomplished over time through imagery techniques. For example, the client can be taught how to bring to mind supportive images of others when distressed by memories. These others may include the therapist, friends, family members, or even protective spiritual beings such as God or guardian angels. It is equally important to assess a client's support network and to address the development and maintenance of that network.

The third self capacity, the ability to maintain a positive sense of self, is also very important to monitor during the history-taking process. This capacity, related to feelings of shame, humiliation, and disgust, is most often impaired among survivors who feel responsible for the events or who make sense of abuse by blaming themselves. This solution allowed the child victim to protect his or her abuser and to hold on to more positive images of the abusive parent. Letting go of this defense represents a painful loss as individuals struggle with self-blame and shame.

The therapeutic approach to developing this capacity is to convey empathy for the self that is the victim of this self-loathing. The part of the self that is the recipient of self-loathing is often the split-off, disavowed representation of self as helpless, vulnerable, and yet culpable. Modeling compassion for that vulnerable self is often the first step to resolve self-loathing.

TRANSFERENCE THEMES RELATED TO TRAUMA HISTORY

Many transference themes emerge over the course of history taking. One important theme places the therapist as container of terrible affects, a theme first described by Parson (1988a). Clients test out whether the therapist can contain and tolerate intense affects and painful traumatic imagery. For example, a client might pour out graphic trauma material associated with shame and self-loathing while unconsciously looking for subtle indications of shock, dismay, or disgust. The therapist needs to address this issue directly by saying something like, "Perhaps you are wondering whether I will be able to understand and tolerate these terribly painful feelings and memories, or whether I will be repelled or overwhelmed by them, as other people in your life may have been." The process of naming the client's unconscious fears is often reassuring and models the fact that these transference issues can be acknowledged and discussed.

Themes related to boundary violations and intrusion are also very important to monitor, because childhood abuse survivors have experienced such gross boundary violations in the past. The client may feel that the therapist is "coming too close too soon," asking too many questions, or being too directive in the history-taking process. Concern about issues of boundaries and intrusion leads to a more unstructured approach to history taking, particularly during the initial sessions when the therapeutic alliance is very fragile.

Gender issues are also important to address openly. When the therapist is of the same sex as the perpetrator, there may be a theme of therapist as revictimizer, whether it is through asking questions experienced as intrusive or voyeuristic or through inviting the client to reexperience shame by not providing sufficient support for her or his disclosures. For example, there are very different meanings to a female survivor of father incest who is being asked by a male therapist and by a female therapist for details of the sexual abuse. The therapist should address these meanings directly, conveying a desire to be sensitive to them, commenting directly on any feelings of discomfort or shame.

Male therapists who work with female incest victims of male perpetrators have important countertransference themes that may impact upon this process. For example, a male therapist may go to great lengths to avoid appearing voyeuristic and intrusive by failing to probe for details about the sexual abuse. Other males are ashamed and fear becoming stimulated by a client's disclosures. Likewise, the female survivor may unconsciously attempt to sexually stimulate her therapist in order to recapitulate the incest experience as well as test out whether the therapist respects her boundaries.

The final transference theme is therapist as interrogator and judge, a theme Lindy (1988) described in relation to the Vietnam veteran. This theme is virtually universal among childhood sexual abuse survivors. The client fears that the therapist will judge him or her guilty of terrible crimes. Being sensitive to these issues is obviously very important. Clients may feel great shame, particularly if they viewed themselves as an active participant or even perpetrator of the abuse.

VICARIOUS TRAUMATIZATION AND
COUNTERTRANSFERENCE ISSUES IN HISTORY TAKING

In helping clients to open up the details of their abuse, therapists open themselves to painful and sometimes frightening aspects of humanity. Taking in clients' accounts of human cruelty and interpersonal violence has an impact on the therapist. The transformation of the therapist's inner experience that occurs through listening to clients' trauma material has been termed "vicarious traumatization" (McCann & Pearlman, 1990c). In the process of this work, therapists must be extremely sensitive both to their own responses to the particular client and the trauma themes she or he is raising (Saakvitne, 1990) and to the more general effects of the accumulation of trauma material upon themselves (Pearlman & Mac Ian, in preparation). Therapists must be aware, among other things, of the role of their own feelings in their decisions to move the client toward or away from the trauma material. Continuing therapy supervision is essential for therapists at all levels of experience; it must particularly address the effect of trauma work on the therapist and the management of these issues in trauma therapies (Pearlman & Saakvitne, manuscript in preparation).

USE OF TRAUMA HISTORY QUESTIONNAIRE

Therapists at The Traumatic Stress Institute (TSI) combine structured and unstructured approaches to taking a trauma history. A short form of an extensive trauma history questionnaire, the TSI Life Event Questionnaire (LEQ), was developed to administer to all clients regardless of the presenting problem (Mac Ian & Pearlman, 1992). The purpose of this lengthy questionnaire is to assess exposure to all the major life events commonly defined as traumatic, including combat, physical or sexual abuse in childhood or adulthood, natural or human-induced disasters, and so forth. This scale inquires about the age or ages the events occurred and, most important, the degree of subjective distress the person recalls experiencing at the time and experiences now in relation to those events.

The LEQ may be introduced at any point in the therapy. Staff clinicians use clinical judgment about the timing and ask clients to complete the questionnaire when they are deemed ready. They are told that the questions may be unsettling and may stir up uncomfortable feelings or memories. They are asked to arrive a half hour before their next scheduled therapy session to complete the form so that there is ample time to discuss their reactions in therapy.

A number of interesting issues emerge from the structured trauma history-taking process. The vast majority of clients have experienced a variety of traumatic events, some of which they have never previously reported. This finding is true even for those individuals who come for treatment for non-trauma-related issues. The reason this material never emerged previously is explored over the course of therapy. In some cases, the failure to disclose was because the individual never realized the event was traumatic or had an impact. Some people will say, "I thought these events were normal because that's just the way life is." This reaction is often defensive, a way of denying the true meanings and impact of what happened. In these cases, naming the event as potentially traumatic is often emotionally powerful, opening new avenues for exploration.

Another interesting finding relates to the distress ratings for each incident. For some clients, events that might objectively be viewed as less severe than others, such as having a miscarriage, are reported as more distressing than, for example, being physically abused by a caretaker. In some cases, clients have acknowledged that it is safer to experience emotions surrounding a more current trauma than to open up feelings repressed for many years. These preliminary findings have confirmed the view that trauma, to a large extent, is in the eye of the beholder.

Therapists must avoid imposing preconceived ideas about the meanings and impacts of these events on survivors.

The questionnaire is also useful as a basis for beginning to explore repressed memories and to address issues related to what happened among clients only beginning to discover early abuse memories. The questionnaire may be a powerful stimulus for clients who have not revealed a trauma history and who claim to have no memory of one. Often clients say that although they have no specific memories, certain questions made them uneasy and caused inexplicable feelings and imagery to begin to emerge.

For clients with only beginning memories of early abuse, the questionnaire often evokes doubt and confusion. For example, a client who had been working successfully on the recovery of traumatic childhood memories through hypnosis completed the questionnaire. She came into the next session and talked about finding it difficult to respond to certain questions because she was still not sure what was real and what was fantasy. This process has been very enlightening for both client and therapist. It provides a new opportunity for exploring the self-protective need to deny the reality of the experience.

CONCLUSIONS

A combined structured and unstructured approach to history taking provides the most information about a client's traumatic life experiences, while respecting the client's need for safety. This process must occur within the context of a safe therapeutic relationship in which meanings and affects are explored and sensitively monitored.

Important areas for therapist awareness related to history taking include the following:

- educating the client about the memory retrieval process;
- providing a framework for the recovery of traumatic material that is most respectful of the client's movement between approach and avoidance (Roth & Cohen, 1986);
- monitoring and working through the inevitable feelings of shame, disgust, humiliation, and disbelief that often accompany such disclosures;
- bolstering the self capacities so that the history-taking process is not retraumatizing; and finally,
- being alert to transference and countertransference themes that often emerge over the course of this delicate and highly sensitive process.

Asking the unaskable must occur within a therapeutic context that is respectful of the client's needs and areas of vulnerability. Clinicians must be sensitive to the meanings of such disclosures in order to facilitate healing and avoid retraumatizing those individuals who have been profoundly violated and victimized in the context of interpersonal relationships.

Part II

Treatment of Children and Families

4

Long-Term Treatment for Children with Severe Trauma History

Beverly James

A child is in the process of development, and traumatizing experiences may injure that development. Trauma may impair attachment, lead to distorted moral values, or disable learning. The child's growth can be retarded by failure to thrive or by psychosocial dwarfism. Regression, a common response to trauma, is more problematic for children because it is a return to a less mature, more helpless state, which can restimulate trauma sensations. Additionally, a child is part of a family matrix and must be treated as a member of that family. The caregivers, however, may vary considerably in their desire for the child to receive psychological services. Yet their cooperation is essential to help children cope with traumatizing experiences.

Trauma treatment for children provides direct guidance to help the child acknowledge and accept the realities of painful events. The clinical process cannot wait until the child is without fear and anxiety. Establishing safety for the child, timing interventions, and pacing disclosure are clinical decisions requiring exquisite sensitivity and skill.

Treatment for children is often complicated by a community's lack of resources or failure to commit needed assistance. Harmful caregiving practices, including multiple out-of-home placements or the use of terrorizing behavior management such as holding a child immobile while physically stimulating him or her for long periods to induce rage, can further traumatize.

This chapter offers specific guidelines for the long-term, comprehensive treatment of children who have experienced trauma. This discussion encompasses various types of trauma over age spans from infancy through adolescence.

The major issue of this chapter is how best to meet the treatment objectives

Figure 4.1
Regular Awful Stuff

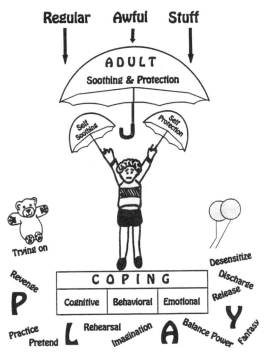

for a specific child. Discussion of specific uses of individual and group therapy is not attempted. However, as a general rule, adolescent therapy is most effective in groups, and younger children benefit from group work as an adjunct to individual therapy.

This chapter does not address immediate psychological first aid or brief therapy. Armsworth and Holaday (1993) provide a clarifying and comprehensive review of the literature regarding the effects of psychological trauma on children and adolescents.

HOW CHILDREN COPE WITH REGULAR AWFUL STUFF

Infants and toddlers learn to cope with distressing situations by using the soothing and protection typically given by caregivers. As they mature, they learn to (1) seek out soothing and protection actively from adults, (2) provide self-soothing in various ways, and (3) use their own imagination, fantasy, and physical movements (what we call play) to help them cope with distressing events. (See Figure 4.1.)

Play restores psychological homeostasis. Fear of neighborhood bullies, worries about an injured pet, and unfair treatment by parents, among other things, are often played out with children in the role of a hero who has supernatural strength and magical powers. In this mode, children give themselves exactly what they need to reduce anxieties and to resolve conflicts. Under the guise of play, they can balance power, reward themselves with fabulous riches, vanquish those who do not do their bidding, and devour their enemies. The experiences of power and invincibility enable the child to work and rework an issue until such negative feelings as fear, helplessness, and revenge are sufficiently under control to allow the child to deal with reality. Some observers may wrongly assume that a child is playing when the youngster engages in repetitive post-traumatic reenactments or aimless or frantic activity.

HOW CHILDREN RESPOND TO TRAUMA

Emotional trauma is experienced when events or situations overwhelm an individual's usual coping mechanisms. For traumatized children, soothing or play can become unavailable or insufficient to meet their needs. Children cannot borrow strength from a caregiver who is unavailable, ineffective, or perceived as the source of the trauma. Children do not engage in play if they are constricted and fearful or believe that the seriousness of their situation does not allow for play or, in cases of extreme deprivation, if they never learned or were not allowed to play.

Children often protect themselves by surrendering to what they perceive as inevitable since they cannot easily escape or fight back. This frozen, emotionally constricted response to trauma can eventually generalize, becoming a reaction to other stressful or emotional situations or to life in general. It interferes with the children's ability to grieve their losses, to obtain needed nurturing from others, and to avail themselves of the healing power of play. Everyday reminders and their own intrusive thoughts can restimulate such feelings of terror, help-lessness, and shame in children.

The child's experience of the traumatizing situation or event is strongly in-fluenced by the meaning he or she assigns to the event(s), the response of family and community, the caregiver's ability to soothe and protect the child, and the child's temperament, coping ability, and history of coping with other stressful events. Some children are resilient and survive horrendous experiences and, in some ways, may be strengthened by what has happened (Anthony & Cohler, 1987; Coles, 1967; Garmezy & Rutter, 1983). Other traumatized young people develop protective beliefs to help themselves feel safe or, in a driven manner, engage in the specific behaviors they believe necessary to ward off further traumatizing events. Among this group are those who appear symptom-free; a closer look, however, may reveal that they protect themselves with achieving academically, by reversing roles and becoming supercaregivers to others, or by engaging in secret, ritual activities.

The anxiety level of some traumatized children is so intense, long-lasting, and variable that they may appear to be attention-deficit hyperactivity disordered

(ADHD). These children, who display frantic, anxious behaviors, also have learning problems, impaired social development, and extremely strained relationships with caregivers.

Dissociation is utilized especially by youngsters with limited coping abilities. They split off conscious awareness of all or part of traumatic experiences, such as physical sensation, affect, visual memory, or all or parts of the event itself. Dissociation then can become a habitual response to stressful situations or, eventually, a disorder that interferes with everyday functioning.

GOALS OF TREATMENT

Treatment aims to enable youngsters to reestablish the use of, coping skills and to learn new ones. Through the therapy children benefit from positive caregiving, come to believe they are worthy of self-care and soothing, and accept that it is safe and acceptable to play.

Extensive, comprehensive therapy, addressing physical, cognitive, emotional, and spiritual aspects of trauma, helps to develop a relationship with children that allows them to feel safe and empowered. They can then explore, in a safe setting, events that have been traumatizing, experience that their fears and pain have been witnessed and accepted by their therapist and caregivers, who honor their survival and respect their selfhood. Children then learn to accept past realities themselves and, in turn, are then able to come to terms with their own experience and move on in their lives.

TRAUMA ASSESSMENT

Every child needs an individual, comprehensive assessment and customized treatment plan based upon a knowledge of trauma theory, child development, therapeutic parenting, attachment theory, object relations, dissociation, systems theory, and, perhaps, community resources related to the child's needs.

Evaluation/assessment must include at least the following:

Child safety. The clinician's first priority is to determine that the child is safe from harm and will not harm others. If possible, the therapist also provides guidance and support to those adults who care for the child so that the caregivers are able to provide the strict supervision that will ensure the safety of the child and his or her environment. If the needed protection cannot be provided in the home, it may be necessary to place the child in a residential setting where such supervision is available. This complex clinical decision must include considering the psychological impact of out-of-home placement against the psychological consequences for the child should he or she harm himself or herself, others, or property.

Child functioning. It is important to know the youngster's level of functioning before, during, and after the traumatic event, as well as his or her present level of functioning, quality of the attachment to caregivers, and strengths and problem areas.

Traumagenic states. Evaluation of the following traumagenic states can be useful: betrayal and loss, stigmatization, powerlessness, self-blame, destructive acting out, loss of body integrity, dissociative disorder, attachment impairment, and traumatic sexualization (Everson & James, unpublished; James, 1989).

Caregiver's functioning and abilities. Because the family is a part of the treatment plan, its strengths, resources, and limitations should be established. Assessment determines if the family is capable of being involved in the child's treatment and providing therapeutic parenting.

Resources available. Resources from many arenas may be required to provide for the needs of the child as those needs relate to traumatizing events. For example, pediatric attention, academic tutoring, physical rehabilitation, or special education placement in a school system may need to be included.

CRITICAL ASPECTS OF CHILD TRAUMA TREATMENT

Developmentally Sequenced Treatment

Trauma treatment may need to proceed sequentially at different stages in the child's development. Children's normal development can be affected by traumatic experiences if attitudes, behaviors, and self-concepts are shaped in harmful ways.

Because young persons' understanding and experience of traumatic events change as they proceed through development, they may need to reprocess those events in clinical settings several times as they gain maturity. Child victims of war, sexual abuse, or disaster may, for instance, deal initially with the reality of their losses. As they grow older, they may need to struggle with moral issues related to their own or their parents' behaviors. They may again need assistance to be able to integrate the social or political aspects of the trauma.

In this developmentally sequenced model, the psychotherapist provides treatment for current issues and identifies and teaches the family signs and symptoms that would require further professional attention. The clinician maintains a consultative relationship with the family and provides subsequent treatment as needed. Future treatment is thus perceived as evidence of maturity rather than as indicative of earlier treatment failure.

Returning to the Pain

Children rarely initiate exploration of trauma with a therapist. Clinical exploration must be sensitively approached and not attempted until the child experiences the therapeutic relationship as safe and secure—a relationship wherein overwhelming experiences and emotions can be contained. Careful timing and techniques must be used to empower the child and to help him or her deal with small, manageable pieces of the past. The objective is for the child to accept what has happened without minimizing or exaggerating the event or the consequences.

Some atrocities cannot be integrated during the initial course of therapy because of the youngster's vulnerable life position, current functioning, or both. The clinical task therefore is to help the youngster cope by acknowledging the experience in a generalized way while binding and compartmentalizing it. The clinician helps the child to establish and maintain a robust support system, to learn to ask for help, and to develop an action plan that includes skills to contend with revivifying experiences. The child is strengthened, empowered, and taught to explore the experience, little by little, when he or she is ready. The clinical decision to delay exploration of the traumatizing events must be based upon the child's clinical needs, not the needs or lack of skill of the clinician.

Involvement of Caregivers

The child's present caregiver and any anticipated/known future caregivers need to be active members of the child's treatment team. The youngster, as part of a family and community matrix, cannot be treated in isolation. It is often helpful and appropriate to have the child's extended family, teacher, day-care provider, school counselor, pediatrician, spiritual leader, school social worker, and coach be part of the treatment team.

Family or caregiver involvement allows a "witnessing" of the child's experience of trauma and affirms that the child is worthy of love and acceptance. This enables the child to anchor his or her reality and accept himself or herself. Clinical work that involves the caregivers is essential because many traumatized children experience extreme separation anxiety and have attachment disorders. Caretaker involvement not only enhances the clinical work but extends the clinical time to include the child's home care.

Hidden Trauma Reactive Behaviors

Serious issues related to trauma are frequently not identified as presenting problems and may be hidden. Hidden behaviors may include dissociation, paraphilias, obsessive play, destructive or humiliating activities, and illegal behaviors.

Direct, Open, Structured Approach

Traumatized youngsters and their caregivers generally do not trust others. Explaining the clinical process to the child (what it is and is not; how it works; why it is helpful; the roles of child, therapist, and others; goals and objectives; how we know when a course of treatment is finished) helps the child and family to feel empowered and hopeful and builds trust.

Intensity and Fun

Intense positive clinical interactions are required to penetrate the child's protective barriers. These interactions supersede the negative messages of self-blame. Fun in therapy helps the child continue with treatment and deal with difficult issues. An important treatment objective for many children is to teach them how to play and have fun.

Impact on the Therapist

Clinicians can experience secondary post-traumatic stress disorder when working intensely with damaged children. Common emotional land mines for the clinician include falling in love with the child, becoming critical of the parents, and failing to respect and strengthen the parent-child bond. Impaired clinical judgment can occur if the clinician becomes numb to the horror experienced by the child or, alternatively, becomes fascinated by that horror. The clinician's own childhood traumas can be restimulated and, if not dealt with effectively, can seriously impact effective treatment.

PHASES OF TREATMENT

Clinical work with traumatized children can generally be categorized into beginning, middle, and end phases of work. Beginning work includes learning and practicing. Middle work is directed toward exploration and acceptance of the traumatic experience. End work focuses primarily on restructuring. Between and within phases the child and therapist should pause periodically to allow for stabilization, taking time to savor and celebrate the gains that have been made. These beginning, middle, and end phases are not as neatly separated in practice as they are in theory. (See Figure 4.2.)

Beginning: Teaching and Practicing

Children need to feel strong and safe before they can explore painful areas in their lives. The therapist becomes both the child's ally and the strong, in-charge person who will keep everything manageable and safe. Therapy starts where the child feels strongest, with everyday experiences. Using movement, sound, smells, visual arts, and drama, the therapist and child have fun, get messy and wet, learn a lot, and practice what is learned.

In this phase, the clinician increases the child's comfort level by generalizing comments to other children. For example, talk is about feelings all children have, what most children think about, how their bodies respond, and descriptions of different horrible things that happen. Drama and stories provide emotional distancing and give children response options—such as "Was the bunny mad, scared, excited, or something else?"—to help them articulate everyday inner

Figure 4.2
Multidimensional Treatment for Integration of Traumatic Experiences

experiences. Talking about ridiculous and gross things like tyrannosaurus snot paves the way for later revelations of outrageous and gross things they actually experienced. The following examples of teaching and practicing areas can be utilized in the beginning phase.

Physical Mastery

Traumatized children often experience their bodies as physically vulnerable, ugly, and toxic. They may disown their bodies when trauma has included physical intrusion, such as painful medical procedures or abuse, by numbing parts of their bodies or by passively allowing others to do anything physical to them. Youngsters are often fearful of any physiological sensation that relates to emotion, such as increased heart rate, breathing changes, sweating, and tense muscles. Thus, an important treatment objective is for the child to gain body mastery and integrity.

"Wake it up! Shake it out! It's yours!" are helpful body messages. Children need to feel, in their muscles, that their bodies are powerful and belong to them and that they have some level of physical mastery.

Learning and practicing movement, exercises, dance, drama, and active play help children reestablish feelings of power and confidence in bodies and develop mastery. By moving each part of their clown bodies, bubble gum bodies, and rusty robot bodies, for example, they reclaim ownership and diminish fears, gain power over body sensations, learn to tolerate somatic sensations related to emotions, and learn to soothe, stimulate, and release emotions through body work.

It is particularly important that children who have been physically touched in hurtful ways by adults experience very positive and safe touching in the therapy setting. Touching may be by the therapist or by the caregivers with clinical guidance. Structuring short periods of time both in clinical sessions and at home when a child of any age can experience ''cuddle time'' or ''little kid time'' to be rocked, held, and stroked can benefit the child and enhance the child-adult relationship. The approach to touching must be invitational and respectful of the child's needs and fears. Prolonged tickling and other forced physical stimulation of the child's body are never appropriate.

Behavior Control

Addressing destructive and abusive behavior toward, or by, the child is the first priority of treatment. Clinical attention next focuses on behaviors that generate animosity toward the child, either by caregiver, therapist, teacher, or peers. A child who is not tolerated by those around him or her cannot have positive self-esteem.

Teaching the child to manage specific disturbing behaviors is an important priority, even if those specific behaviors seem unrelated to trauma. Never smiling, not making eye contact, or peeing in the closet can result in a failed out-of-home placement that retraumatizes the child. A clinician may be so grossed out when a child habitually picks her nose and wipes it on the therapist's desk that he or she is not able to consider countertransference issues. The efficacy of therapy is more clearly seen by caregivers and teachers when the child gains personal power over such behaviors.

There is no trick of the trade that immediately results in enabling the child to stop frightening or objectionable behaviors. Change usually occurs slowly, unevenly and is brought about by direct behavioral intervention, environmental control when needed, and psychodynamic interventions that deal with the issues and conflicts leading to the behavior.

Trauma-reactive behaviors serve children in some way. For example, children may have a rage reaction to being alone with an adult male because they consciously or unconsciously perceive this as a threat to their safety. Such behavior may appear volitional when it is not. Adults must rely on careful supervision of children to manage their behavior until they are able to do so themselves.

Empowering the child can be accomplished by eliciting the child's cooperation in behavior management. Clinical exploration helps to provide the child with some hope that behavior change is possible and will ultimately be beneficial. The child and the team of parents and teacher(s), under the leadership of the therapist, assess and clarify the specific behavior(s) over which the child is to gain power, monitor the behavior to determine triggering events and patterns, develop an action plan, implement the plan, and acknowledge and celebrate gains.

Behavior management starts at the beginning of treatment and usually continues until termination. New behavioral difficulties related to exploration of traumatizing events, changes in the child's present circumstances, and new disclosures of past events or hidden behaviors are likely to emerge during the course of treatment.

Some children are unable or unwilling to cooperate in managing their behavior. This commonly occurs when children perceive they are unsafe in their present environment or when behavior is linked to traumatizing events yet to be revealed. The clinician must carefully assess whether or not sufficient time and support have been given to help youngsters become motivated to manage their behavior. In this instance, safety and support for children at home and at school may need reassessment, and a medical evaluation of trauma-reactive behaviors may be in order to determine if medication is warranted. Behaviors that can be taught and practiced in the beginning phase of therapy are play skills, social skills, appropriate demonstrations of physical affection, assertive skills, and life skills, such as eating, personal hygiene, driving, managing money.

It is tempting to seek a quick-fix solution for frightening or disruptive behaviors. Techniques such as holding the child down and tickling/stimulating the child for long periods, forcing eye contact, yelling, taunting, controlling the child's breathing, vision, and food intake are abusive and retraumatize the child. Such methods are absolutely contrary to the goals of treatment since they are directed toward surrender, not mastery.

Cognitive Structuring

Approaching emotions in a cognitive, structured manner generally feels safe to children. Therapists need to teach them to identify and discuss complex and conflicting feelings and ideas common to all children before asking them to tell about their traumatizing experiences. This is done through therapeutic exercises, games, discussion, and example. Children are generally unable to articulate their feelings, although they may understand them. Therapists give them a language and voice for their emotions, teaching them that thoughts and feelings have names, can vary, and can appear conflictual.

Children can be helped to sort out ethical and moral issues through cognitive structuring and stories, like the following:

There was a puppy who had a best friend he liked very much, but the friend had a habit that was just unacceptable in the puppy world—he ate cow poop. This totally grossed out all the other puppies. The older dogs were more tolerant. The therapist then asks, "What are the different feelings this puppy has about his very best friend? What does he think? What does he want to do? What can he do? Is the puppy bad because he likes his best friend who has a yucky habit? Is it OK to like some parts of a person and not like other parts?"

Direct and indirect teaching helps the young person understand elements related to the traumatizing event. Education may focus on how bodies work, how hospital systems operate, the process of death and burial, how people lose control of their actions and hurt other people, how the court system works, how people live with paralysis, or how families survive forced migration. The child is helped to master learning by further elaborating through artwork, clay, sand tray depictions, psychodrama, and stories.

Therapeutic Parenting

Therapy should include teaching and practicing skills with the child's caregivers. Healing traumatized children requires therapeutic parenting, not just "good-enough" parenting. Caregivers must have the ability to provide nurturance when the child pushes away and appears rejecting; must provide guidance when the child is unresponsive or obstreperous; must set limits when they have the urge to reject the child or to do bodily harm; must protect the child who is defiant. Therapeutic parenting means caring for the child when not wanting to parent any longer. It means being more patient, consistent, and loving than ever thought possible.

Caregivers should be able to share their frustrations and concerns with the therapist. They must be able to "hang in there" when it seems they cannot tolerate one more call from the school, dangerous re-enactment, anniversary reaction, destructive act, night terror, or totally maddening nonresponsive child behavior.

Identity Cohesion

Identity issues related to trauma work with children include children's absence of core selves, loss of culture and family, and dissociative fragmentation of personality. A child who has an impaired or missing sense of a core self can be taught who he or she is by mirroring, gazing, intense looking, and identifying what is special and unique, in much the same way mothers interact with infants. The work started in this phase will be taught to caregivers and continue throughout the child's therapy.

Developmental play (Brody, 1992) helps children begin to develop a core self. The intense seeing, naming, and making special of children's attributes, such as the way they move, how they play and interact with others, how they express themselves, and how they may be experiencing situations, are helpful. Caution is warranted, however, in using this technique with sexually exploited children who may have received a similar type of attention as a prelude to abuse. Clinical work can then progress to using sensorimotor techniques (James, 1989).

Brief stories that give very specific details of idealized parenting from in utero to the child's present age totally absorb the interest of children who have unmet parenting needs. Wallas (1990) created very specific developmental stories designed to reparent adults from dysfunctional families. Her work is easily adaptable to, and beneficial for, youngsters.

Relocation, forced migration, and disasters involving lengthy separation are examples of the traumatizing situations needing the teaching and practicing of family and cultural rituals. This should include songs, games, stories, religious practices, and anything related to food. Such lessons are calming and restorative for children and for their caregivers as well.

Fragmentation of personality, which may have escalated to a dissociative disorder or multiple personality disorder, may be acknowledged in the beginning phase of treatment, but direct interventions are generally best in the middle phase. Work in this arena is most effective when a treatment foundation has been built and the child is ready to work on past traumatizing events.

Spiritual Connection

Children who have experienced frightening events and profound losses in their lives need to understand that they are more than their families, their possessions, or their bodies. They need to feel there is a core to their being that cannot be lost or taken away and that they have an inner wisdom upon which they can rely.

The spiritual nature and beliefs of a traumatized child are often damaged or may be the only place where needed strength can be found. These beliefs should therefore be addressed directly. Children can be asked to talk about times in their lives when they have felt deep joy or peace, a feeling of oneness, or sense of God. They are taught and encouraged to recapture these experiences through visualization, music, meditation, or prayer. Helping youngsters savor peaceful, strengthening experiences and teaching them how to call up these feelings as needed assist them in coping with their difficulties.

Even children who have not been exposed to religious teachings often believe that a traumatizing experience was God's way of punishing them. This belief generally emerges only through sensitive probing such as: "Some children who have cancer [use appropriate trauma] have important ideas about God and what happened to them. I wonder if you have some thoughts about God and your cancer."

Emotional Competence

Emotional competence is an area of extreme vulnerability for most children. Some appear affect-phobic, believing that if they allow themselves to acknowledge just a little of their loneliness, fear, neediness, rage, or other feelings, the floodgates will burst open, and they will be overwhelmed (annihilated), as will the therapist.

Cognitive structuring exercises about emotion are now put into action. Emotional anesthesia is reduced in steps, beginning with "feelings" of inanimate objects, then living things in general, and on to animals and children. Emotional management is taught through sound, movement, music, poetry, role play, and stories. Children learn to let themselves tolerate joy and pleasure, as well as to experience anxiety and sadness. The therapist and child actively improvise scenes such as being the single cloud in the sky that aches with loneliness, being a flower that savors the subtle warmth of being appreciated, being a terrified, lost little mouse at the shopping mall, being a puppy who gets so much loving and petting from his new masters that he thinks he will burst with happiness or just wiggle himself to pieces, or being an astronaut lost in space.

Children can be asked to focus their attention inwardly and draw where they experience sensations in their bodies. They may, for example, choose a color for anger and spread that color around the mouth, the eyes, the chest, the hands—wherever they feel anger. By using another color for fright, they are asked to color appropriate parts of their drawing, such as the chest, abdomen, or genitalia. As they pay attention to everyday feelings, they learn it is safe to feel emotions, and they begin to distinguish present emotions from past experiences.

It is important to teach children that feelings do not automatically lead to actions and that behavior can be controlled. Many youngsters fear their own aggressive desires for revenge or have experienced out-of-control violent or sexual behaviors by adults.

Middle: Exploring and Accepting the Traumatic Events

The middle phase explores traumatizing events and the child's thoughts, feelings, and behaviors related to the event(s) that transpired. The child and therapist become detectives and, in small, manageable steps, gently go over the traumatizing experiences.

Highly structured clinical sessions provide additional safety for the child. It is useful to tell the child that sessions have three parts: first we play (nondirective therapy); then we do our work (various activities related to trauma exploration and mastery); and then we play again (nurturing, joining experiences).

Trauma work has taught therapists that many of those who have survived traumatic events are unable to speak of their experiences. These memories appear to be encoded in a manner that is not readily translatable into language. Many expressions in our language support this—"unspeakable acts," "struck dumb," "mute with fear." This author's clinical approach with children and the approaches of David Read Johnson (see Chapter 24; Johnson & Miller, 1990) in treating traumatized combat veterans are similar. Initially, clients desensitize their fear of emotional expression by using everyday feelings. When the work goes directly to the trauma, the patient may be asked, for example, to "make a sound to represent how it was for you," when the person cannot put the experience into words. Expression through sound is followed by expression through physical movement, symbolic visual art, realistic visual art, symbolic language, and then, representative language.

Repetitive activities that appear related to the child's traumatizing experiences and do not reach resolution are referred to as post-traumatic play (Gil, 1991a; Terr, 1990). For example, a five-year-old client, whose history included oral rape and sodomy, spent part of every session for four months creating the identical sand tray and directed the therapist to complete the same activity. He divided the tray down the center and put all the powerful monsters and fierce animals on his side and the human and vulnerable animals on the side of the therapist. He would then annihilate the therapist's side. This might have been an attempt at mastery or, perhaps, a graphic depiction of his need for power and his vulnerability. However, the repetitiveness was also a stuckness, which had to be resolved. The therapist invited the monsters to her side for pizza and picnics and tried to negotiate a change of sides. He eventually altered the scene so that the therapist's figures were wounded, not killed, and his guys eventually joined the others for parties and Nintendo. Children who cannot control or manage certain behaviors, even those behaviors that are seemingly innocuous, can feel helpless and weird. Gil (1991a) provides a more complete discussion of interrupting post-traumatic play.

Garbage Bag Technique

Pacing the work to avoid overwhelming the child is difficult and not always possible. The "garbage bag" technique helps trauma survivors of all ages: it helps clients contain the elements of the traumatizing event and enables them to work on different elements at their own pace. It also empowers the child and helps to reinforce the reason for therapy.

The therapist works to create positive anticipation of using the garbage bag technique by directing the child's attention to other children's bags in the playroom, commenting that the youngster is just about ready for the garbage bag and that most children find it very helpful. Large paper bags on the playroom shelves are individually decorated with sparkles, wrestler/superhero pictures, feathers, and more.

A lively, vivid discussion introduces the technique while the child and therapist hold an empty bag between them. Each takes a turn placing an imaginary gross piece of garbage in the bag, noting, occasionally, how this bag would smell, look, and weigh. This is followed by a fantasy discussion of how it would be for the child to always carry the bag around in daily life, in high school, at a job interview, when getting married. The therapist tells the youngster that traumatized adults say not talking about their traumatic experiences is like carrying around a bag of garbage all their lives.

The child then is invited to participate by telling the therapist each piece of "garbage" that happened to him or her. Each yucky thing is written on a slip of paper that the therapist gives to the child to put into the bag. The child is instructed to put these things in the bag quickly, because this is not the time to have big feelings about what happened. This is also the reason the therapist does the writing instead of the child. During each subsequent session, the child gets the bag from the shelf, pulls out one piece of garbage, and does some work on that piece with the therapist. The work may involve drawing a picture, acting out what happened with puppets or using the sand tray, direct discussion, yelling out the window, "It's not my fault," or destroying a clay perpetrator. The child is told that when all the big feelings are gone or when he or she is bored with that piece of garbage, he or she can throw that piece away. The child can take a break from working on the garbage bag whenever he or she needs to, usually when present issues in the child's life need attention.

This technique literally holds and contains the trauma. Children feel relief when they walk out of the playroom and leave what represents their pain with their therapist. The garbage bag empowers children, enables them to work on issues in small manageable steps, and concretely demonstrates how much work has been done and how much is left.

Identity Cohesion: Dissociative Disorders

Children commonly use dissociation of affect, somatic awareness, or cognitive awareness to protect themselves from overwhelming emotions, thoughts, and sensations in intolerable circumstances. This process enables them to function, but its use as a protective process may, unfortunately, become so habitual and generalized in all stressful occurrences that it defeats its own purpose and dramatically inhibits functioning and development. Therapy for dissociation simultaneously proceeds along at least two tracks. The first deals directly with the dissociative behavior; the second strengthens the child and diminishes the need to dissociate.

The child's dissociative experiences and disowned parts must be revealed and directly approached in the treatment environment in order to be safely contained while the therapist helps the child toward integration. Dissociation needs to become demystified and made user-friendly to the child, the parents, and, perhaps, school personnel. This normalization can be achieved by teaching the child that dissociation is a normal process that was exaggerated in service of protecting him or her.

The first step toward integration is consistent referral to the split-off part as "that part of you that you call _____." The therapist and child identify the disowned parts of self, discuss their functions, and establish that the child has power over the splitting process. If the child is having school difficulties related to dissociation, he or she is directed not to allow other parts to take control, but only to listen and learn. This gives a clear message that the child has some control over the process. The technique generally works because these children are very suggestible.

The child is helped to examine the advantages and disadvantages of "going away" or "getting spacey" or whatever the child's or family's term is for this behavior. If he or she can be convinced there are more disadvantages than advantages, work can progress toward controlling and lessening dissociative responses. The procedure is then the same as with any other behavior the child has decided to modify, that is, monitor, determine the triggering events, formulate strategies to modify behavior, practice strategies, track progress, modify strategies if needed, and celebrate gains.

Some children may not be ready to agree that dissociation is problematic because they presently feel unsafe and fearful. The clinical focus then becomes the child's safety and what is needed to help him or her feel more protected.

Therapy also focuses on strengthening the child so that dissociation can be perceived as unnecessary. Achieving this seemingly simple objective may take considerable time and effort. Some children instantly and habitually dissociate to trigger stimuli associated with what they experienced as traumatic, such as smells or tone of voice. Giving up dissociative responses can be likened to a child giving up a baby bottle or favorite blanket. Those things, too, were useful when needed, are not easy to give up, and constitute a sign of growth when no longer needed.

Some older professional literature reports that brief therapy (Fagan & McMahon, 1984; Kluft, 1984a) can resolve dissociative and multiple personality disorders in children. Those who specialize in working with traumatized children do not see this as a common experience. Most children who dissociate have been raised in extremely dysfunctional families and have experienced ongoing abuse. These issues cannot be resolved with brief therapy.

Some children walk through the middle phase of treatment telling what occurred and feeling myriad feelings and, though the process may be difficult and painful, are not overwhelmed. Others become extremely disorganized while recalling traumatizing events.

The child's accompanying emotional and behavioral responses can be frightening or simply exhausting for caregivers and teachers. These persons must help the child learn to contain talk and play related to traumatizing experiences. For example, a child can be guided to engage in such talk only with the therapist, caregivers, and one best friend or can be asked to limit the reenactment play to his or her own home, not at school or friends' homes.

The clinical phenomenon of looking worse before getting better is most dramatic in trauma work with children because they are invited to remove the protective wrappers that have kept them from feeling pain—rationalization, projection, repression, and dissociation of all or part of what has happened. Children may be grieving past losses they were too scared or too frozen to grieve until now. A delayed response to trauma and the fact that many children will fall apart or act out in one setting and not in another can lead adults to believe the distress is not real and the behavior is volitional. This is rarely the case. Children become extremely frightened, regress, and feel small and helpless as they recount traumatic events. Allowing children to express their pain while supporting, soothing, and giving the message that they can deal with their feelings and need not do so alone requires fine clinical skills.

Acceptance by the child of all that happened related to the traumatizing event is a process of mirroring. The therapist witnesses the child's pain, glee, horror, participation, losses, shame, and more. The therapist demonstrates acceptance of what happened and respects the child's survival. The youngster, in turn, sees the therapist witness and begins to mirror acceptance of his or her own life experience. Without exaggerating, without minimizing, he or she comes to accept what is so. The therapist later helps the child's caregivers to witness the child's experience similarly, and the youngster learns physically, emotionally, and cognitively that he or she is loved. The child then accepts that he or she is worthy of self-love and self-care and grows from there.

End: Restructuring

During the final phase of treatment, traumatizing experiences are transcended, gains are consolidated, and seeds are planted for future growth. The child not only accepts the realities of the traumatic experience but learns that the event is a part of an interesting life yet to evolve.

Children who have experienced chronic or multiple trauma often have no sense of the future. Discussing, fantasizing, dreaming, planning for future possibilities such as a driver's license, learning to go places on the bus alone or getting a job need to be a part of treatment. Parents can take children on outings that relate to this future-talk, for example, taking a child to the department of motor vehicles to watch teenagers taking driver's tests. This helps children visualize some future for themselves.

Children need to spend some time talking about how old traumatizing issues might emerge in the future. Young persons who have experienced the death of a parent can benefit from talking about how they might someday wish their coach could be their dad or how they might despise a future stepfather. They need to talk about how they might feel and act in these situations.

It is important to discuss how a child's sexual exploitation by an adult is different from the sexual urges and experiences he or she will have. Abused children and their caregivers need to be disavowed of the belief that an abused child automatically becomes an abuser or marries one.

A useful metaphor for children of all ages is that of a photograph album. The therapist asks if the family has an album that shows a vacation or some other event, such as a wedding, and then asks how it would be if the children's mom, dad, or the children themselves got up every morning and stared at the album because they thought what it showed was important. The therapist then describes a ridiculous preoccupation with the album, including bringing it to church, looking at it in the bathtub, checking it out when waiting in traffic. Children readily understand that the person's functioning would be impaired unless the album was put away and brought out only as needed. The therapist then, very directly, tells children that their history makes them the fine, juicy, interesting persons that they are. While they will not forget incidents, they do not always have to remember them twenty-four hours a day. They can put their history on the shelf and take it down when needed.

At another time, the therapist may role-play a pathetic, intrusive adult, always wanting other people to look at his or her history album. The adult bothers strangers on the bus, people at the soccer game, the traffic policeman. In fact, the therapist introduces himself or herself as an album-owner instead of using his or her name, telling the child that everyone calls him or her that. This silly example helps to reinforce earlier work on self-concept, during which children learned they are more than just their history.

SUMMARY

Child trauma victims have multilevel clinical issues of Byzantine complexity that challenge therapists and stretch the therapists' cognitive, emotional, moral, and spiritual growth. The work is difficult, mental health resources are inadequate, and child clients are sometimes snatched away, without warning, for inexplicable reasons.

The primary treatment goal for most traumatized children is to help them move from a position of helplessness to one of empowerment. For children, empowerment includes being able to seek adult help when needed. Children's experiences of helplessness may be manifested in a variety of behaviors, including dangerous risk taking, extreme compliance, dissociative disorders, and more.

Children master and integrate their traumatizing experiences when they accept the realities of what happened without minimizing or exaggerating elements while examining them in small, manageable pieces. Therapists are on the cutting edge in trauma work. They are just beginning to learn about neurochemical changes, central nervous system and memory functioning, dissociation, fragmented identity, and more. The gritty survival ability of little traumatized children keeps us humble and learning.

Intervention with Child Victims of
Trauma in the School Setting

Mary Beth Williams

CASE PRESENTATION: THE TRAUMATIC EVENT

The calls in this small suburban community begin on Sunday about noon. Word is spreading with lightning speed that a fourth-grade teacher was killed in the early morning hours in a one-car accident. Members of the crisis response team of the elementary school, including the director of Pupil Personnel Services, the second school psychologist, the school social worker, and elementary school guidance counselors are notified by the team leader, the principal. Meanwhile, calls to other staff, parents of children who were in the teacher's homeroom, and students who were especially close to the teacher in her personal life are being made. At the request of the principal, the team is asked to brief the building staff early Monday morning before school begins. This briefing and time for defusing give faculty and support staff the opportunity to ask questions about what happened, express a small measure of their own grief, and then discuss and decide how to deal with the students.

Because immediate intervention is essential, crisis team members are assigned to the four classrooms and are now grouped into two teams. It is to the teams' advantage that the students have already heard about their teacher's death. They have had some time to accept the reality of the occurrence of the event.

The crisis team members and teachers discuss the accident with the students. They present the known facts, discuss normal grief reactions, and then open the floor to discussion. Everyone is alert and watches for students who are reacting in a more distressed manner than others. These students, at least for the next few days until after the funeral, will be counseled both individually and in small groups (depending on the preference of those students and the extent of their expressed grief).

The children, teachers, and even the crisis team members themselves (who were all friends of the deceased teacher) are experiencing a stress reaction. Most of these persons will put the stress behind them within a few days to a few weeks. However, at least 10 percent of those children, and possibly adults, will experience profound, long-lasting stress effects (Manson, 1989). Their cognitive symptoms may include memory loss, difficulty making decisions, difficulty with problem solving, loss of attention and concentration—factors important to successful school performance. In addition, their emotional symptoms may include anxiety, fear, grief, depression, irritability, anger, identification with the deceased teacher, and feelings of being overwhelmed or hopeless.

TRAUMATIC STRESSORS MAY LEAD TO TRAUMATIC STRESS REACTIONS

The death of a child's parent or teacher, the suicide of a classmate, sexual or physical abuse, and exposure to family violence and parental battering, as traumatic stressors, upset the equilibrium of the person involved and often result in disorganization and inability to cope. The majority of events faced by these students are what Terr (1991) referred to as Type I traumas or unanticipated single events.

The extent of the traumatic impact upon the children, however, depends on many factors, which include the perceived threat to life and limb; the time duration of the trauma; the causation of the loss (man-made or God-made, intentional or nonintentional); and the manner in which the event affects the beliefs and expectations (schemata) of the individual. Key factors are how the event fits into the child's life view (whether the child sees the cause of the trauma as lying within the self or outside the self) and the availability of social support to that child (Wolfe, Gentile & Wolfe, 1989). The course and level of seriousness of the trauma (duration, frequency of occurrence, source, type, and amount of physical impairment or violence) also impact the extent of traumatic stress that occurs. School personnel who counsel a traumatized child must determine first what beliefs the event challenges or changes in that child's mind. For example, is the event the child's first exposure to death? Does it challenge the child's conception of what is "fair" or "just"? Does the child still see the world as kind, rewarding, and benign? Or is the world no longer predictable and controllable for that child?

Traumatic events, in some ways, invalidate aspects of the child's previous view of the world. The occurrence of a sudden, traumatic event, such as the violent death of a teacher, may contribute to the genesis of later psychopathology (Terr, 1991). If the reaction to the traumatic event is long-term and chronic, denial frequently occurs after the initial outcry and alarm phase. This denial may occur even during the event itself via repression, dissociation, amnesia, or splitting into multiple personalities if the trauma is extremely severe (e.g., abuse in a ritualistic, intergenerational cult). It may remain buried for years until, perhaps, after a similar crisis occurs (e.g., the death of another close friend or authority figure), and memories, intrusive thoughts, or other images start to flood into consciousness.

The major goal for school crisis response team members in the long term is to help students and staff achieve cognitive completion and integration into a model of the world and individual assumptions that negate self-blame (Horowitz, 1976). Many of the students, in the case of the death of the teacher, recognized that they would have been unable to prevent the death by being "good" in class on Friday. Others who had misbehaved expressed the belief that they might, in some way, have been to blame because they had made the teacher upset and, therefore, perhaps not as attentive. However, the teacher was a passenger in the car and was asleep at the time of the accident. Recognition of this aspect of the accident helped students dissipate self-blame.

INTERVENTION

Establishing a School-Based Crisis Response Team

When a crisis team in a school system is established, members of that team must be willing to accept responsibility to provide needed services, even though they themselves may also be traumatized by the event. Team members must also be aware of ancillary community services and agencies, should they need to ask for outside help. A crisis response team's frontline plan of service should be defined prior to the occurrence of a crisis. Team members must be given crisis response training and be familiar with post-traumatic stress theory and intervention principles, as well as grief theory.

Members also need to know principles of group work and how to run groups as facilitators. They must be able to manage anxiety-based reactions of students and staff in a quiet, nonpunitive, direct manner and to handle intense emotional expression without "falling apart" themselves. Crisis team members must give others permission to express feelings while providing emotional support and teaching coping and problem-solving skills. They must be empathic, not sympathetic, reflective, calmative (not histrionic or excitable). They also must be willing to work extended hours, keeping a school open if the situation demands (e.g., in a hostage situation or if an event occurs during vacation).

Members must also be aware of the principles of child development and age- and stage-appropriate conceptual reasoning abilities. For example, the child's concept of death varies with age and stage of development (Staudacher, 1987).

As Hodgkinson and Stewart (1991) noted, if the team does not take steps to establish and limit its own identity and purpose, then the result will be confusion of services offered and wasted energy. The wrong person may be used for the wrong service, and services may be incorrectly conceived or badly offered. Poor service provision, or the lack thereof, can lead to resentment from students, staff, and community members and result in bad public relations and eventual questioning of the purposes or need for existence of the team. In addition, team members' individual altruistic motivations for belonging decrease. Interventions by team and individual team members in dealing with trauma are twofold. By helping students who have recently been traumatized to "debrief," team members possibly prevent or minimize the existence of long-term post-traumatic reactions. Smead (1991) noted that crisis intervention must be immediate and flexible. Mobilization of resources both within and outside the system, if the crisis is of a larger proportion, is important and necessary. Providing support, understanding, empathy, and care to a traumatized child helps that child express grief, loss, and other post-trauma emotions.

Team members may also assist children who have been traumatized in the past or over a longer period of time. Providing support and counseling to a child victim of sexual abuse who has recently revealed long-term molestation or to a child who has been exposed to serious parental violence involves more than debriefing or short-term counseling. Children traumatized over a long period of time or seriously traumatized for a shorter period of time (e.g., those children exposed to death and murder in the Stockton School massacre) need more intensive help.

According to McCann and Pearlman's (1990a) contextualistic theory of trauma, it is possible that the stressor event has impacted the beliefs and expectations of the children (their schemata). The child's beliefs about safety and trust of self and others (as well as issues of power, esteem, and intimacy toward both self and others) have often been seriously damaged and weakened by the trauma. Intervention must be designed to help the child utilize his or her capacities and resources to resolve traumatic memories as well as accompanying behavioral, cognitive, emotional, physiological, and relationship effects. Work with the traumatized child must be shaped to fit the individual profile of the child (the specific situation, belief system, environmental context, and cultural milieu). Individualization helps the child understand and cope with his or her world.

Group Meetings or Assemblies

If a school is large or if the stressor trauma impacts large numbers of students and staff, demand for crisis services is high. This demand may exceed the resources of the school, particularly if there are multiple victims who were well known (a multiple-fatality auto accident involving several teachers or an extremely beloved teacher; a mass suicide of several students) or popular (the student council president shot by a crazed, angered landowner living next to the land on which students were partying). In these instances, additional external personnel may be asked to offer assistance, for example, a crisis response team from the National Organization of Victims' Assistance (NOVA) or personnel from a local mental health agency.

Intervention preferably should occur in smaller group settings, but if this is not possible due to numbers of persons affected, the target becomes larger classroom meetings or assemblies. Students may be grouped by grade level to allow for more homogeneity (Weinberg, 1990). When large assemblies or class-room meetings are necessary, it is important to station a number of intuitive, sensitive staff at various points in the rooms to observe student reactions and approach those who are especially upset. If staff themselves are too upset to perform this function, local mental health personnel can fill in.

In a large, formal meeting, designated spokespersons must provide facts so that rumors are lessened. If the stressor event was a suicide, nothing that indicates glorification of the act or acts should be used so that possible contagion is avoided. In the case of a suicide death, there is an extremely high probability that a second suicide will occur (Lamartine, 1985). In such a situation, it is extremely important to include a suicide prevention component in the assembly (Weinberg, 1990). Students are invited to share healthy, adaptive responses they have used to cope, while avoiding self-destructive acts.

Education about the normalcy of a post-traumatic and grief reaction and the stages of healing needs to be included as part of the message of this meeting. Expression of emotion by students and staff, in measured amounts, is encouraged as everyone is permitted to release grief. Speakers may suggest ways to cope with the traumatic events that give more meaning to what has happened, if appropriate. Input from students may also be generated about what might help them cope with the event. The assembly concludes with a message of hope and a reiteration of factual information about what will happen next. This includes wakes, funerals, school schedules, and availability of personnel for small group and individual sessions, as well as repeat summary of the normalcy of post-traumatic reactions.

Those in attendance at the general meeting are given a challenging message to help restore morale and to establish a goal (e.g., plant a tree as a memorial to the teacher) to honor the deceased (Hodgkinson & Stewart, 1991). Assemblies and general meetings should last approximately one hour.

Small Group Intervention

Students whose grief reactions are inappropriate and extreme should be es-corted to waiting professionals for small group and individual sessions. In other cases, students who were especially close to the deceased or who were witness to, or are survivors of, tragedies will gravitate toward one another and to trusted adults for more intensive intervention. They often do not seek to be part of large assemblies and choose to be seen individually or in small groups. Small groups are essentially geared toward crisis intervention and are generally led by two professionals. While one professional leads the discussion or speaks, the other observes group members to note who appears to be at a greater risk of developing an acute post-traumatic stress reaction or disorder. Weinberg (1990) noted that students who are more at risk because of their level of exposure to, or involvement in, a trauma often were witnesses or observers to the deaths; were especially close friends with the victim(s); may have had a preexisting conflict with the deceased that was not resolved (National Mental Health Association, 1991); or are unable to accept the reality of the death (Raphael, Lundin & Weisaeth, 1989). At times, these students are unable to get control of their emotions and express extreme grief (e.g., in crying jags); may express extreme, self-punitive anger and self-blame; may have suicidal thoughts, insinuations, or ruminations; or may self-mutilate. As Hodgkinson and Stewart (1991) observed, leaders who meet with small groups become more identified with those students and often become recipients of less projected anger. The ideal maximum group size is fifteen.

Ideally, small groups are homogeneous in age, familiarity with the student or teacher, involvement in the traumatic event, and developmental level (Weinberg, 1990). Groups begin with an introduction of those present. The purpose of the group is stated: to allow all persons to speak to the event and its impact on them and their involvement in the event. They are cautioned to respect the boundaries of confidentiality and are encouraged to talk only for themselves. The group generally goes without a break so that everyone speaks and has an opportunity to express emotion within this supportive setting. Team leaders also discuss the normalcy of grief and traumatic reactions, correct false information about what happened during the event, and give facts about what will happen next.

Students are also asked to share what they thought about the event when they heard of it or experienced it, how they reacted, what they felt, and how they now feel. They are helped to examine current and past losses and identify proactive, empowering coping strategies they might now use (finding meaning, seeking outlets such as exercising, developing support systems, organizing a memorial, becoming a part of a funeral service). These group debriefings, according to Hodgkinson and Stewart (1991) are not aimed as "cures" for traumatic reactions. Instead, they are designed to minimize the later occurrence of disruptive post-traumatic stress reactions and therefore are, in essence, preventive. Also, through the use of these groups, members are able to recognize that a residue of loss will always be there for many of them, even though life goes on (Sandoval, 1985).

PRINCIPLES OF POST-TRAUMATIC INDIVIDUAL COUNSELING FOR CHILDREN

The utilization of basic principles and techniques for counseling of traumatized children of elementary and secondary age must be modified to fit the age and/ or developmental stage of those involved. The following principles are central to a post-traumatic counseling approach in a school setting and proceed from the perspective of psychological health.

The primary purpose of post-traumatic counseling is to help a child abreact memories. The counseling process seeks to connect all parts of the experience—

sensations, knowledge, affects, and cognitions/memories (Braun, 1989). Through this process, the memory's energy is released and "let go," and the memory becomes integrated into the child's past. Thus, the aim of post-traumatic work with a child is empowerment, acceptance, and a change in belief systems so that the child can adapt more successfully to his or her changed world.

School counselors, social workers, or psychologists must first and foremost attempt to establish a trusting relationship with the child. Traumatized children frequently find it extremely difficult to trust anyone. The professional also helps the child to trust his or her own feelings, memories, and body responses. Use of the following post-traumatic principles of counseling will help build that trust as well as work out traumatizing memories.

1. Establish a safety milieu for the child. The time spent with the school professional is a safe time in a safe location. If the school social worker learns, in the course of the meetings, that the child is still being exposed to, or is victimized by, abuse, violence, or other events, he or she must assure the child that a report will be made to the appropriate authorities. The school professional must then make that report immediately.

2. Expect testing over a long period of time. Any seriously traumatized, abused child expects to be hurt, let down, or betrayed by adults other than the abuser. The child will test repeatedly.

3. The primary response of the school professional to a traumatized child (no matter what the degree of trauma) is empathy. That caring adult must believe in the reality and individual perceptual meaning of the child's experiences.

4. The school professional needs to educate the child about the nature of grief as well as the normal stress and post-traumatic stress responses. Thus, it is imperative that he or she have a working knowledge of post-traumatic stress theory, crisis intervention theory, and debriefing techniques.

5. Only a remembered trauma can be worked through and then let go. Working through memories unblocks the energy. Additionally, working through with children frequently involves multiple repetitions to help "make sense" of an event. The school professional must have patience if the same questions are asked over and over: "Why did my teacher die?" "Why did it happen to her?" "Why did it happen to me?" "Why was I hurt by _____?" "Why isn't life fair?" The goal of memory work is to help the child construct a personal meaning of the trauma as the child learns that he or she will never totally forget what happened. However, his or her intense pain and affect, which accompanies the memories, will dissipate in time. Processing begins with the present traumatic event and may, if circumstances indicate, lead to processing of earlier incurred traumas.

6. Memory work also involves emotional release. If the school professional cannot deal with another's pain, trauma work is not for him or her. Children need to cry, and, at times, the counselor, psychologist, or social worker may cry as well. Helping a child to express anger in an appropriate manner is another part of this work. "Slime balls" to throw on walls, foam "anxiety bricks" to squeeze, "nerf bats" to hit on furniture are good tools to use with extremely angry children. The school professional

teaches children that acknowledging and expressing emotions are OK and a necessary part of the healing process.

7. Children need to identify and deal with losses that have occurred because of the trauma. In the case example, the teacher who died was a long-term substitute mother for several children. Not only did these now-adolescents lose a former teacher and friend, but they lost a very significant parent-figure who attended concerts, wrote notes, gave them presents and emotional support. Grieving losses is essential for healing.

   Children who have been molested for an extended period of time have even more traumatic losses. They have lost healthy childhood relationships, a nurturing relationship frequently with parental figures, and even childhood itself. They have also lost their innocence, control over their own bodies, privacy, and the right to eventually choose their own first sex partner.

8. As the school professional helps the child deal with losses, he or she also helps the child build self-enhancing beliefs and expectations. These beliefs build the child's self-esteem and feelings of empowerment and control. Helping a victimized child develop a "Personal Bill of Rights" might be one appropriate task in this process. It is also important to help the child identify and deal with previously held, impacted beliefs about life that have become irrational. What assumptions about self and others has the trauma violated? What dysfunctional beliefs does the child now hold? The school professional can teach the child how to identify and modify those irrational beliefs.

9. Through his or her relationship with the child as well as through the use of social skills training exercises, the school professional can help the child build appropriate peer and other-adult relationships. Specific techniques might include helping a victimized child learn to set boundaries and personal limits, be assertive, develop problem-solving skills, and develop self-control.

10. As the adult staff member builds a relationship with the child, he or she is establishing a differential diagnosis and treatment plan. Does the child have other problems, which need outside school intervention? Is family therapy needed? Is a referral to a private practitioner appropriate? Does the child express self-destructive thoughts or behaviors? Is there evidence of an eating disorder or a substance abuse problem? If so, the professional, in conjunction with other Pupil Personnel team members, frequently is a primary referral source for additional treatment and liaison with external school agencies and practitioners.

11. School professionals should be familiar with a variety of treatment methods and modes of expression. Traumatized children who have had long-term abuse or intense short-term experiences may not be able to express their pain verbally. The use of art therapy techniques, music therapy, play therapy, sand tray work, bibliotherapy, or journal writing may be extremely helpful. The use of writing therapies (particularly for upper elementary or middle and high school students) can help those students express their pain.

   Involving children in a group of similarly traumatized individuals can also be an important counseling technique. In these groups, according to Coates and Winston (1983), children can normalize and validate their feelings in a supportive, comfortable setting. The shared suffering of students helps bring them together, may lead to the development of an outside group support system, teaches tolerance for others' pain, and can have a healing impact. Group membership can provide a sense of meaning and connectedness for members.

12. The key to recovery from a traumatic event is empowerment. Empowerment of the child is the outcome goal of the school professional's relationship with that child. Empowered trauma survivors acknowledge their experiences and the accompanying effects, set appropriate self-boundaries, and have positive social skills, good self-esteem, and self-protective beliefs about safety, trust, power, esteem, and intimacy. In addition, they are able to put the trauma into a past perspective and "go on" with their lives.

CONCLUSIONS

To be sure, "time heals all wounds"—unless the wounds are buried, repressed, or dissociated and until the wounds intrude into the child's life at a later time. Also, children are, by and large, resilient. As Werner (1984) noted, children who get positive attention from others, who have a sense of meaning of life, who are bonded with caretakers or caretaker surrogates, and who demonstrate faith, hope, and humor through positive acts toward others are more likely to heal.

By helping children face their pain and their losses, school social workers, counselors, or psychologists are in unique positions of secondary prevention. Trauma may result in victims, but these school system–based professionals can help those victims become survivors.

6

Dual, Triple, and Quadruple Trauma Couples: Dynamics and Treatment Issues

Aphrodite Matsakis

What happens when one trauma survivor marries another trauma survivor or when one of the partners is a dual trauma survivor? Under these circumstances, the normal stresses of marriage are exacerbated by the presence of ghosts. The ghosts are invisible, but they have a very real impact on the psychological well-being of each member of the couple, as well as on their relationship. These "ghosts," of course, are the lingering impacts of trauma.

This chapter explores the ways in which being trauma survivors can both create conflict yet help bind a couple together, as well as other special relationship dynamics. The chapter also includes treatment suggestions.

CLINICAL BASES

The clinical basis of this chapter is individual and couple counseling with veterans with post-traumatic stress disorder (PTSD) at a Vietnam Veterans Outreach Center and a Veterans Administration Medical Center, as well as private clinical work with chemically addicted childhood abuse survivors. All were childhood abuse survivors. To date no formal research has been completed on this population. The only available clinical reports are on Vietnam veterans (Matsakis, 1989a, 1989b) and families of sexual abuse trauma survivors (Williams, 1991a).

DUAL, TRIPLE, AND QUADRUPLE TRAUMA COUPLES

In single trauma couples, one partner is a trauma survivor. In dual trauma couples, either one partner has suffered two or more major traumas or each partner has undergone a single trauma. In triple trauma couples, one partner has undergone at least two traumas and the other partner has experienced one traumatic episode. In quadruple trauma couples, each partner has experienced at least two separate traumas.

An example of a multiple trauma couple is one in which a combat veteran suffers from one set of unresolved issues regarding his war experiences and yet another set of problems from being sexually and/or physically abused as a child. At the same time, his wife or girlfriend may also have been sexually and/or physically abused as a child or in a previous relationship or witnessed the murder, rape, or suicide of a parent. Any of these events may lead to the development of symptoms of PTSD.

Couples observed in clinical practice were survivors of long-term or repeated traumas (not a onetime trauma). For example, the women were not onetime rape survivors; instead, they had been physically or sexually abused by family members for many years. Similarly, males were not just victims of a onetime mugging or a single car accident. Instead, they had been beaten to the point of bleeding by their caretakers for years or had been exposed to death and dying in war for many months.

INCIDENCE

The incidence of dual, triple, and quadruple trauma couples cannot be determined. Instead, it can only be inferred from the statistics on child abuse, domestic violence, and PTSD among soldiers.

Reliable data show that one-fifth to one-third of women surveyed report childhood sexual experiences with adult or older males. The parallel figure for males is 8–14 percent (Herman, 1981; Savina, 1987; Courtois, 1988b). In 1985 approximately 1.9 million cases of child abuse were reported (Pynoos & Nader, 1990). According to the National Center on Child Abuse and Neglect (NCCAN), approximately 4.9 children per 1,000 are physically abused annually. These are considered extremely conservative figures both by the NCCAN as well as other authorities (Matsakis, 1990).

An estimated 30 to 50 percent of wives experience physical assault in their marriages. Meanwhile at least 3.3 million children observe their mothers being beaten. All these children are prime candidates for PTSD, as are an untold number of children who observe one or more of their siblings being physically or sexually violated. The true incidence of family violence, however, is unknown. Even today, abused persons are reluctant to report abuse due to ignorance, fear of reprisals, or a host of other reasons (Savina, 1987; Pynoos & Nader, 1990). Violence in the family therefore can hardly be seen as a freakish experience that occurs to only a select few. In fact, most experts agree that the above figures grossly underestimate the true extent of the problem.

According to 1988 statistics, approximately one-third of Vietnam combat veterans have suffered from PTSD at some point since their return. Approximately 15 percent currently suffer from full-blown PTSD, and an additional 11 percent suffer from partial PTSD (Schlenger et al., 1988).

CHARACTERISTICS OF TRAUMA SURVIVORS

Impact of Trauma on Victims/Survivors and Their Relationships

While not all trauma survivors develop symptoms, many do develop full-blown or partial PTSD. PTSD is most commonly associated with war veterans; however, full-blown reactions have also been documented among battered women (Kemp, Rawlings & Greene, 1991), abused children and adults (Mowbray, 1988; Pynoos & Nader, 1990), natural catastrophe survivors (Griffin, 1987; Sudhaker & O'Brien, 1987), crime survivors (Young, 1988), sexual abuse survivors (Courtois, 1988b; Williams, 1990), and others subjected to extreme stress or life-threatening conditions (C. M. Williams, 1987).

PTSD symptoms, however, are not the only possible reactions to trauma. Other reactions include the development of chronic pain, panic disorders, psychosomatic problems, compulsions, addictions, obsessions, phobias, and memory loss and other cognitive problems. In addition, exposure to trauma can reactivate old psychological problems or stimulate latent ones, including paranoia, clinical depression, or manic-depressive illness.

Physical injuries or disfigurements and their emotional effects must also be taken into account. Mental health professionals often tend to focus on the emotional aftermath of trauma to the neglect of the physical. However, trauma often involves direct injury to the body. In general, survivors who suffer long-term medical effects or obvious disfigurements are less likely to cope effectively with their trauma than individuals who were fortunate enough to have emerged from their trauma with their bodies and appearances relatively intact (Lyons, 1991).

Relationship Problems Associated with PTSD

PTSD-afflicted trauma survivors suffer not only from emotional problems and conflicts within themselves but from a range of related interpersonal problems. The following section of the chapter identifies common PTSD-related relationship difficulties. It is not exhaustive, nor does it imply that all trauma survivors experience all of these problems all of the time. Instead, it simply outlines some of the possible, but not necessarily inevitable or universal, interpersonal effects of PTSD.

Heightened emotional vulnerability to the valuation of others. PTSD-afflicted clients often tend to overreact to the statements and behaviors of others and to interpret them as hurtful or insulting. Biochemical processes may be involved in these reactions, as well as the following reactions (van der Kolk, 1988).

Emotional numbing. Emotional numbing—the tendency to shut off emotionally, to be reluctant or unable to share on a deep emotional level, or to withdraw from others in other ways, especially intimate partners—creates numerous relationship problems, for example, hurt feelings.

Loneliness. PTSD-afflicted clients frequently suffer from loneliness and social isolation. These effects stem from low self-esteem, depression, and sense of being "deviant" due to the trauma; fears of being "triggered" into a depression or rage reaction due to comments made by others; feeling "tainted" or "cynical" and therefore different and apart from others due to loss of innocence or shattering of spiritual or religious beliefs as a result of the trauma; self-blame for their depressions, rage reactions, or wide fluctuations in mood; self-doubts created by observing their emotional shifts; confusion as to which of their problems are trauma-related and which are not; and fear of their intense anger or grief, of losing control emotionally and/or of embarrassing and/or hurting others with their intense grief or rage reactions.

Rage reactions. PTSD sufferers are subject to rage reactions during which they may verbally and/or physically abuse family members, destroy property, self-mutilate, or threaten suicide.

Depressive episodes. During the client's depressive episodes family members and friends might try to "cheer up" the client. Yet their efforts may bring about only further depression. The client feels like a failure because, even though his or her positive response is desired, the depression is too deep to permit that response.

Eventually, family members or friends also become frustrated and depressed. They, too, feel like "failures" because they have not been able to help the client substantially. On one hand, they may truly empathize with the survivor. On the other, they may also resent the client for not responding to their efforts, for being a "dead weight," or for being "overly negative."

Jealousy, resentment, and other negative emotions. Survivors typically experience jealousy and resentment toward individuals who are perceived as not having been traumatized or scarred significantly by life. Survivor guilt, although not a formal characteristic of PTSD in the *Diagnostic and Statistical Manual III-R* (APA, 1987), is nevertheless still prevalent among trauma survivors.

A war veteran or an accident survivor, for example, may experience considerable guilt over having lived while others in the trauma died or having experienced fewer or less severe injuries than these others. Similarly, an abused child or wife may experience survivor guilt over not having been able to "rescue" or minimize the physical harm of another family member toward whom the abuser was also violent.

This survivor guilt can create an underlying sense of guilt, anxiety, and low self-esteem. Punishing acts toward the self or others can follow, especially when current life stresses are high. When survivors externalize their survivor guilt, they may lash out at others, either verbally or physically, creating considerable interpersonal pain and conflict. On the other hand, when survivors internalize their guilt and punish themselves, they create a different kind of pain for themselves and their loved ones. Under such circumstances, spouses or partners, as well, can experience feelings of helplessness, guilt, and anger.

Search for a "magic rescuer." In searching for a "magic rescuer," survivors hope that they can be healed through the love and nurturance of other persons.

Despair. The belief that "nothing will help," that not even human love and comfort can do much to alleviate the suffering caused by the trauma, can create mutual alienation in families.

Difficulties handling subsequent stress. Studies have shown that trauma survivors who receive adequate social support or psychological assistance can eventually go on to function well. However, trauma survivors, especially those who have been severely or repeatedly traumatized, often do not handle stress as well as their nontraumatized peers.

Stress, whether economic or interpersonal, is often experienced by the survivor as a repeat of the original trauma. Such a reaction is not under the survivor's control. Accompanying the belief that the trauma is reoccurring are feelings of panic, numbing, and hyperalertness attendant to the original trauma. These reactions are not conducive to problem solving in relationships.

Fight, flight, and freeze reactions are also possible. These reactions make rational dialogue and verbal negotiation with others extremely difficult, particularly during stressful times when such communication is most needed.

Behavioral reenactment. When trauma survivors engage in behavioral reenactments of the trauma, they play out the role of one or more of the individuals or forces involved in their traumatic episodes. For example, a former prisoner of war can behaviorally reenact his trauma by acting as a persecutor, as a victim, or as a rescuer in various relationships.

Not all trauma survivors engage in usually unconscious behavioral reenactments. Those who do are typically those who were repeatedly or severely abused as children or who were heavily traumatized as adolescents or adults. They may include combat veterans, prisoners of war, or refugees.

Many mental health professionals view reenactments as signs of "psychopathology," "masochism," or a "self-defeating personality." However, Freud viewed them as attempts at mastery (van der Kolk, 1989). Even though the reenactments usually result in increased emotional pain for survivors and their family members and friends, Freud emphasized that they were attempts to further understand and resolve the original trauma. Reenactments involving harming others, self-destructiveness, and allowing oneself to be revictimized can wreak havoc in relationships (van der Kolk, 1989).

Substance abuse, phobias, and other secondary elaborations. If trauma leads to secondary elaborations of substance abuse, compulsive gambling, or compulsive sexual behavior, sets of associated problems become imposed on the survivor's interpersonal relationships.

Interactional Dynamics of Multi-trauma Couples

Dual, triple, and quadruple trauma couples have experienced the relationship problems of single trauma couples in exaggerated fashions. Their unique problems can include the following areas.

Projection. To the extent that partners are unaware of, ashamed of, or otherwise disown, their symptoms or traumas, they may project their feelings and fears onto each other. During anniversary times or bouts of depression or when triggered by a stimulus, individuals with untreated PTSD may blame their suffering on some action of the partner. They overreact to the partner's mistakes or foibles. If they become aware they are overreacting, they may feel immature, embarrassed, and angry at themselves. If they cannot own their own reactions, they may project their anger and self-disparagement onto the partner.

Misunderstandings and communication problems. Many misunderstandings and communication problems result from the presence of two sets of PTSD symptoms in the home. In this case each individual may not own or understand his or her trauma. Due to lack of treatment, inadequate treatment, or treatment that has not addressed the trauma, survivors are often confused and dismayed by these PTSD symptoms and the intensity of their emotions, as well as of their ''non-emotion'' or numbing.

If they are helped to understand that their reactions are normal to trauma survivors, they may then, perhaps, learn to accept, rather than deny or fight, their symptoms. Next, they need to learn how to manage symptoms and feelings so they would be minimally disruptive to their lives and relationships. However, this ideal state of affairs rarely occurs and leads to a host of interpersonal problems.

For example, in one couple, the wife, who was assaulted as a child at night while sleeping, suffers from nightmares and sleep disorders. Her combat vet husband also suffers from sleep disorders. Hence the couple may be often kept awake by each other or by himself or herself. In addition, the couple must cope not only with the vet's flashbacks, emotional numbing, depression and limited tolerance for emotional intimacy but with the wife's similar symptoms as well. In another instance, the wife experiences her PTSD symptoms during anniversary times, including her abuser's birthday, the anniversary date of the first assault, her wedding date, or when participating in activities that remind her of the original trauma, including sex. Trigger reactions are especially intense if the veteran is sexually rough or assumes sexual positions or makes sexual demands on her similar to those made by her former abuser.

Research shows that incest survivors who have yet to receive help often manifest a variety of sexual difficulties, ranging from extreme aversion to sex to a tendency to sexualize relationships or to become promiscuous (Herman, 1981; Courtois, 1988b). In some cases, the survivor flips back and forth between periods of puritanical avoidance or disdain of sex and periods of hypersexuality.

Jane, a veteran's wife, had been sexually assaulted by her brother for over eight years. At sixteen she ran away from home and supported herself through prostitution. Today she has an active sex life with her husband, yet she rarely experiences sexual pleasure, much less an orgasm. For her, sex, even marital sex, is dirty, horrible, and repulsive. Although she loves her husband, she wishes that sex was not a part of marriage.

When Jane has flashbacks during intercourse or nightmares afterward, she sometimes tells her husband, and other times she does not. If he is in a bad mood or a "PTSD mood," she usually remains silent to avoid further aggravating him. However, even when her husband is feeling well, she hesitates to speak up for fear that he will become so enraged that he will seek vengeance against her brother. Her silence also maintains her denial. When she does not explain to her husband why she is sexually disinterested or unresponsive, he easily interprets her coolness or indifference as rejection.

Identification. In multitrauma marriages, partners tend to identify with each other. The fact that they both have been hurt by life and suffer deeply binds them together. In many clinical cases neither partner usually has been willing to commit to an in-depth healing process. Yet they both insist that the partner not only needs, but deserves, help. For some survivors, their partner's healing becomes imperative. This intense desire for healing for the partner may reflect the imploring partner's own need for healing and the hope that if the spouse can achieve some inner peace, so can he or she.

Caretaker role. Adult survivors of childhood abuse often functioned as family or parental caretakers (Courtois, 1988b; Herman, 1981). Abusive parents are typically emotionally needy and immature individuals (Savina, 1987). In many cases they are also former trauma victims themselves who need comfort, care, and assurances and who often have difficulty controlling their aggression. Ironically, in many abusive homes, the abused child may be the same child to whom the abusive parent looked for emotional support and physical assistance.

When abused children grow up, they often assume a caretaking role in their relationships. Hence, to abandon a needy wife or husband might replicate the abandoning of mother or father. In this case, the weight of considering separation and divorce doubles.

Typically the female abuse survivor assumes a caretaking role in the abusive family of origin (Courtois, 1988b). However, this author has worked with many male physical and/or sexual abuse survivors who assumed physical and emotional care of alcoholic parents, siblings, and others in their families of origin. Impaired in their ability to give and receive love and/or function as adults, the men now continue this role with women.

Double anger. When trauma survivors become angry, they may experience a double anger. The first anger is at their partner; the second, toward the person(s) or institution(s) that betrayed them, let them down, abused them, or otherwise were negatively involved in their individual traumas.

Double need. Trauma survivors need more soothing and comfort than nonsurvivors. Their intense anger may stem from frustrations in meeting needs for such solace.

If a survivor turns to a mate for physical and emotional solace, the mate may or may not be able or willing to provide the needed comfort or may experience the needs of the survivor as a burden. If the mate, as a fellow trauma survivor, has similar needs for love, attention, nurturance, and reassurances, each member may compete with the other to see who will take care of the other. Alternatively, they may take turns comforting one another, or their need may turn into anger, and there may be constant conflicts over unmet needs for various forms of soothing. Special conflicts arise when one partner desires sex as a form of soothing and the other partner, due to a history of sexual abuse, associates sex with pain, guilt, or betrayal.

Ambivalent intimacy. "Come close! Go away!" is the message trauma survivors frequently give to their intimate partners. This process of desiring intimacy, yet needing to create and maintain distance has been called "ambivalent intimacy" (Palmer & Harris, 1983).

The approach-avoidance tendencies of couples with only one trauma survivor can create rejection, mistrust, insecurity, and anger in the partner. This is especially true when the survivor is unable to articulate the need for either distance or closeness. In such instances, distance may be maintained indirectly through violence, separations, substance abuse, or the generation of arguments.

In multitrauma couples, both partners struggle with ambivalent feelings toward intimacy. Under such circumstances the opportunities for hurt, disappointment, anger, and miscommunications are enormous.

Behavioral reenactments. If one partner creates chaos and misunderstandings when engaging in behavioral reenactments of the trauma, imagine the interpersonal confusion when both partners are so involved. Trust, which is almost always an issue with trauma survivors, quickly becomes eroded.

Intense loyalty and fear of abandonment. This author has observed few cases of divorce among multitrauma couples in which both partners have failed to undergo the healing process. Abuse survivors, regardless of their gender, often cherish their marriages because they were cut off from, or have exiled themselves from, their families of origin. In addition, they are accustomed to living in households where their needs are not always met. Although life with another trauma survivor may be trying at times, it may be preferable to living with an abusive parent or other family member. Another possible reason for the absence of divorce is that bonding results from both individuals' having been scarred or that one or both survivors function as a caretaker in the relationship.

Divorces have occurred, however, when one or both partners have made significant progress in dealing with their PTSD symptoms. A time comes when either one or both partners may realize that they married for the wrong reasons. On one hand, the wife may realize that she married primarily as a means of escape from a violent or abusive home. On the other hand, the husband may realize that he married out of insecurity or that he now has different needs that cannot be satisfied by his present wife. As each partner's self-esteem increases through therapy, he or she may develop interests or traits incompatible with the present partner or decide he or she deserves someone better.

TREATMENT

Assumptions

1. PTSD is real.
2. The PTSD diagnosis can coexist with other diagnoses.
3. PTSD sufferers are not "pathological" in the usual sense of the word. By definition, PTSD symptoms may develop in any individual, from the most psychologically "healthy" to the most emotionally impaired, in response to a significantly traumatic stressor.
4. The goal of treatment is to increase clients' control over their present lives. Traumas are unearthed from repression solely to increase clients' mastery and competency, not to entertain the therapist or create unnecessary pain for the clients.
5. Therapists need to be nonblaming and careful not to further victimize the victim/survivor with judgmental attitudes stemming from their lack of knowledge of PTSD, their own fears of victimization, or their inability to handle the intense affect that trauma can generate.
6. Therapists must be careful not to overpathologize clients. They must sincerely attempt to differentiate dysfunctional behaviors stemming from the trauma from other difficulties.

Traditional Couples/Family Counseling

Individual and marital problems need to be viewed not only in terms of traditional family therapy frameworks but in terms of the impact of the trauma. PTSD theory and PTSD therapy techniques must be used first, before traditional methods, in order to determine which dysfunctions in the individual and/or in the relationship are coping mechanisms related to the trauma and which serve other functions.

Traditional methods should be used cautiously for several reasons. They tend to overpathologize the emotional pain caused by the "ghosts." Additionally, they usually fail to provide adequate assistance in helping the couple to heal from their respective traumas or in teaching them how to relate positively to one another. Furthermore, traditional concepts such as codependency, enmeshment, triangulation, and symbiosis can prove destructive when used in a blaming way. Many times these tags serve primarily as a negative label for the couple without assisting them in finding the solace they seek in their marital relationship.

Traditional couple and family counseling techniques and theories can prove useful if they are employed after the trauma and its effects have been recognized and after sufficient progress has been made by both partners in understanding and healing from their own particular trauma or if they are stripped of their negative stigmatizing connotations. They are also useful if they are otherwise adapted to the special needs of trauma survivors and if they are combined with PTSD therapy and related techniques.

Method: Individual Healing

The key to working with multitrauma couples is to have each partner own and work on his or her own trauma in individual counseling. Only after each partner has progressed in this area, can couples work truly begin. However, if the couple can be seen only together, then individual therapy regarding each individual's trauma(s) should take place in the joint sessions. An adjunct or alternative to individual work on the trauma is a survivor's group.

The course of healing for each partner is similar to trauma work with any trauma survivor: uncovering the trauma, reconstructing the trauma mentally, feeling the emotions associated with the trauma, putting the trauma into an existential/spiritual framework, accepting limits imposed by the trauma, and finding positive uses for the traumatic experience. These processes are well described by Sonnenberg, Blank & Talbott (1985), Courtois (1988b), Ochberg (1988), and Matsakis (1988, 1990).

Therapist's Role

Diagnosis of PTSD. The therapist needs to assess each partner's full or partial PTSD symptoms using DSM III-R (APA, 1987) criteria. Consideration must be given to the possibility that one or both members are in long-term numbing, rather than in an intrusive phase of PTSD. Consequently, PTSD may not be apparent. Similarly, if one or both individuals are highly functioning, the PTSD symptoms may be masked behind workaholism or an intellectualized approach to life.

Dual or multiple diagnoses, including addictions. If one or both of the partners have an abuse problem with alcohol, drugs, food, or some other mood-altering substance, the substance abuse needs to be addressed directly. Couples therapy is bound to fail if one or both of the partners are practicing their addiction without being actively involved in a treatment program.

Some therapists require participation in a drug, alcohol, or eating disorders treatment program and a demonstrated willingness to practice the suggestions offered by the program, as part of the couples counseling. However, requiring an addicted partner to be totally substance-free is an impossible standard.

Psychiatric consultation. If PTSD symptoms substantially interfere with the client's functioning or ability to benefit from therapy, a psychiatric consultation is strongly suggested. Psychiatric consultation and possible medication are also recommended in the cases of manic-depressive illness, clinical depression, and any of schizophrenias or other psychiatric disorders, including the psychoses.

Education. Couples need didactic sessions on the nature of trauma, PTSD, and the social context of their particular traumas. For example, rape and incest survivors need to place their trauma in a sociopolitical framework of institutionalized sexism. Similarly, veterans need to be made aware of the centuries-long maltreatment of veterans.

In numerous wars (not just the Vietnam conflict), soldiers have been promised medical benefits and other financial compensations. In addition, to one degree or another, individuals who were willing to sacrifice their very lives for the nation or a particular cause have been implicitly promised honor and reverence by society. In reality, however, governments have all too frequently reneged on certain promises for medical care and other compensations or, alternatively, have made it very difficult for soldiers to receive their promised compensations. Thus, throughout history, soldiers have had to battle their superiors or the military bureaucracy in order to obtain promised benefits.

In addition, soldiers touted as heroes during war or during pre- or postwar patriotic frenzies were often treated as derelicts or outcasts upon their return. For example, in contrast to Vietnam veterans, World War II veterans were relatively warmly received, and many participated in homecoming parades. However, similar to many Vietnam veterans, many World War II veterans reported that their families and friends did not want to hear about their combat experiences and accepted them only when they shed—or hid—their warrior identity (Shay, 1991, 1992b).

Reframing problems in terms of PTSD. While not all of an individual's personal and relational problems stem from trauma, some do. The therapist can help clients reframe and view problems as arising from the trauma and secondary wounding experiences rather than from their own personal deficiencies.

Domestic violence: physical and sexual. If the couple is struggling with the problems of spouse abuse or child abuse or physical abuse, additional specific treatment to end the violence is necessary. Neither curbing the addiction(s) of one or both partners nor progress in individual healing will guarantee an end to domestic violence.

Violence in the family, whether physical or sexual or both, is a problem in itself. The abusing member or members need training in anger management, assertiveness, and self-care in order to cease the violence. Family members also need to fully understand, agree to, and sign a formal nonviolence contract. In this contract, violence must be clearly defined so that it includes any form of bodily assault as well as any statements or actions that indicate the intent to assault. In many areas, it is a crime not only to abuse a family member physically but also to threaten to do so. Domestic violence can range from slapping, hitting, or punching with fists, to attacks with broken glass or weapons, to murder. Other acts include burning, biting, pushing, slamming against walls, and shoving down steps.

The consequences of violence must also be clearly outlined in the contract. For example, once violence begins, even if it is with a relatively "minor" act, the victim's options need to be clarified. Following the first act of violence, the victim needs to commit to finding refuge with a friend or at a shelter or to calling the police, seeking a protection order or some other constructive action. Other techniques for preventing violence are described in the chapters on "Anger and Children" and "Spouse Abuse" in *When Anger Hurts: Quieting the Storm Within* by McKay, Rogers, and McKay (1989).

Stress management and assertiveness training. Trauma survivors tend to have difficulty managing current stress as well as being appropriately assertive (rather than passive or verbally or physically aggressive). The therapist needs to expose clients to stress management techniques and assertiveness training or, alternatively, refer them to training seminars on these issues.

Self-nurturance and self-care. Trauma survivors frequently look to others to nurture and care for them. However, they need to identify ways of nurturing and caring for themselves. As they increasingly soothe and comfort themselves, the pressure on the partner to provide the necessary comfort diminishes.

Clients can be asked to generate a list of all the compensations to which they feel entitled for having suffered the trauma and the secondary wounding experiences that followed. The compensations list should have two parts: first, those compensations to which the client is legally entitled and, second, those that are not legally mandated but that the client desires. If the client is not aware of any legal compensations, research may be necessary to generate the first list. The client then needs to consider the pros and cons of pursuing legally mandated compensations, if they exist. For example, how much time, energy, and money is the client willing to invest in pursuing his or her rights? What is the probability of success? In some cases, it may be too costly or stressful for the client to pursue such a struggle. For example, the struggle may reactivate the client's PTSD, addiction, or other problems. In other cases, the struggle may invigorate the client and help him or her externalize the anger in a constructive manner (Crnich & Crnich, 1991).

Obtaining legally mandated compensation is one form of self-nurturance and self-care. However, the outcome is largely dependent on bureaucratic or institutional response. Hence, the client is not in control of his or her reinforcers. Self-compensation, however, can be almost totally under the client's control and stands in stark contrast to the conditions of the trauma, wherein the client was out of control of his or her life.

Using the second list as a guide, the client can be encouraged to ask the following questions. What can you realistically give yourself? Are there material items, such as clothing, jewelry, or books, or experiences, such as vacations or entertainment, that are within your means and could serve as forms of self-compensation?

In the nonmaterial realm, how could you treat yourself with more loving-kindness on a daily basis? Are there ways you can respect the impact of the trauma on your personality and life-style, rather than berate yourself for having been scarred? For example, would it help to commemorate certain important anniversaries by taking some time off work, to share with others who care and are not judgmental, to have an extra therapy session, or to allow yourself extra time to write in your journal about the event? If spiritually inclined, could you give yourself extra time to meditate, pray, or engage in whatever spiritual activity you find rewarding? Are there other ways you can acknowledge, rather than deny and berate, yourself for the impact of the trauma whenever you experience the pain of the past?

Are there ways to reduce the stresses in your present life? What do you do for rest, relaxation, or fun? Is it possible for you to increase the amount of time you spend in these activities?

Couples Healing

Learning to name the feelings. Some clients need to be taught to label their feelings. This is especially true if they are childhood abuse survivors or are not psychologically insightful. They need specific instruction to learn to distinguish one feeling from another, for example, anger from grief, and to identify gradations of feelings, for example, irritation versus homicidal rage.

First, clients need to learn to distinguish feelings from thoughts and need to be given facts about feelings, for example, feelings often involve physiological reactions, that feelings are often suppressed for purposes of survival or social approval, and that feelings rarely come in pure form but, rather, in combinations of several feelings. Reviewing a list of feelings might also be helpful. Clients who are not used to dealing with their feelings may need to be instructed to stop external activity and tune into their body and emotional state in order to recognize those feelings, perhaps through meditation or some form of relaxation.

Improving communication skills. Couples may need to learn and practice basic communication skills. Many child abuse survivors were not taught how to express themselves; instead they were taught that they did not deserve to have their feelings heard or their emotional and other needs met.

Depathologizing the trauma. Clients need to depathologize their traumas and label and identify their symptoms. Depathologizing the trauma can occur only through education that teaches them that they are not alone with the symptoms common to trauma survivors and those symptoms are not signs of personal deficiency or irreparable psychological derangement. Instead, they are normal reactions to the abnormal amounts of stress involved in trauma.

Once clients can identify and accept their symptoms, they may need assistance in learning how to manage them. At this point, they may also be able to openly discuss their symptoms with the spouse.

Trigger list. The couple needs individually to compile a list of "triggers" that set off memories and uncomfortable emotions associated with a trauma.

They can then try to be sensitive to each other's "triggers." The trigger list needs to include anniversaries of events associated with the trauma.

In order to generate a trigger list, clients need first to write, tape-record, or otherwise recount a detailed description of the trauma. Clients then identify those aspects that could be serving as "triggers" in the present. As their awareness of the trauma grows, their trigger list may also grow. Clients then generate a trigger chart. They are directed to divide a piece of paper into three columns entitled, "trigger," "my reactions," and "traumatic memory."

In the first column clients list those times or instances in their present lives when they feel the adrenaline rush to fight or flight; when they suddenly become depressed, agitated, or enraged; when they "go numb," emotionally or physically or both; or when they otherwise feel "crazy" or "out of control." Sample triggers include smells, sights, sounds, people, or objects that remind the client of the trauma or events associated with the trauma. Triggers might also include current stresses, such as interpersonal difficulties at home or at work; any kind of work or emotional overload; financial or medical problems; increased crime or other neighborhood safety problems; or witnessing or being involved in a current trauma, for instance, a fire, car accident, or natural catastrophe.

In the second column, clients indicate their reactions to each trigger situation. Their reactions to each trigger may not necessarily be the same. Possible responses include any of the symptoms of PTSD; increased cravings for food, alcohol, or drugs; increased physical pain; or activation of chronic medical conditions.

In the third column, clients try to trace the trigger back to the original traumatic event, to a secondary wounding experience, or to an event somehow associated with these experiences, no matter how remote. If the client cannot remember the original event, the client should not be overly concerned. The main purpose of the chart is to help clients understand and anticipate when they might be triggered. This understanding is the first step toward change and eventual control.

Anger management. Couples need to be taught and practice basic anger management skills, for example, time-outs, relaxation techniques, and so on. Exercise programs may also be helpful as anger defusers, unless medically contraindicated.

Increasing individual mastery and competency. Couples need to be encouraged to develop individual skills, areas of competency, and interests outside the family. These outside involvements should enhance, rather than detract from, the marriage or relationship. This is especially the case if the couple is enmeshed rather than disengaged.

The interests may be educational, recreational, or social; for example, they may be courses for vocational or intellectual growth or various recreational or social activities. Trauma survivors may have difficulty identifying personal interests if coping with the trauma and subsequent problems has dominated their lives. Clients who feel that the trauma "killed" their souls, hearts, minds, or personalities need to be assisted to refind themselves, that is, to identify selves that existed prior to the trauma.

Clients can be encouraged to take time in therapy or at home, while writing in their journals, thinking, or meditating, to remember who they were prior to the trauma. Deep breathing exercises or muscle relaxation may help them to center and refresh their memories. They could consider the following questions. Before the trauma, what did you do for fun? What were your dreams and goals? What were your interests? Of the goals you had prior to the trauma, which would you like to pursue now or in the near future? Which pre-trauma interests could you realistically pursue? What would be the obstacles to pursuing these goals? Do any of these obstacles arise from your partner or what you perceive to be the demands of the relationship?

Ending the isolation. Couples should be encouraged to make friends and acquaintances outside the family. They need to develop a support system other than one another and gain a perspective on their lives that only interacting with others, especially fellow survivors, can provide.

Identifying behavioral reenactments. Couples must identify ways in which they are reenacting the trauma in their family life. As progress is made in understanding their individual traumas, the need to engage in reenactments will lessen.

Behavioral reenactments are often difficult to identify, unless the individual has reached an advanced level of understanding of his or her trauma. Ritualistic activities or nonproductive activities that occur following trigger events or dates, as well as violent or self-destructive activities, may be behavioral reenactments of the trauma.

Planning for the future. The couple should discuss and plan for anticipated life changes, such as the departure of children, career changes in career, family illnesses, and other life transitions. Such transitions are difficult for most people but are especially difficult for child abuse survivors.

Possible Outcomes

The desired outcome is a shift from victim to survivor modes of thought and behavior. A survivor is a victim who is no longer immobilized by the trauma. Survivors may still experience PTSD symptoms. However, they become able to function in a relatively consistent manner in the areas of love, work, and play.

Therapy will not end the anger, pain, or sense of loss as aftermaths of trauma. Nor will it necessarily deliver clients from all limitations imposed by traumatic experiences and their aftermaths. However, it can increase control over symptoms by increasing emotional connectedness to themselves and to others. It can also enable them to find some meaning in their pain. These goals are achieved by helping the clients remember the trauma and understand and accept their behavior and feelings during the event and afterward.

On a couples basis, therapy can help individuals own their own trauma-related pain rather than blame the partner for all or almost all their unhappiness and help them take responsibility for their own recoveries from the trauma and for other aspects of their lives rather than expecting the partner to "rescue" them or focus on "saving" them. Therapy can also increase self-esteem and teach them to request that their needs be met constructively by their mate and a variety of others.

CONCLUSIONS

In this age of shifting cultural norms, increased violence, economic instability, and decreasing family and community cohesiveness, marital counseling challenges even the most experienced and skilled practitioner. However, when the normal stresses on today's couples are exacerbated by the presence of ghosts from previous traumas, couples counseling becomes even more complex and demanding.

Before a dual, triple, or quadruple trauma couple can begin to communicate and improve the relationship, each partner needs education on the nature of trauma in general and his or her trauma in particular. In individual therapy, each partner must also begin to confront unresolved grief, anger, or guilt stemming from the trauma and learn how to cope with his or her own triggers; rage reactions; current life stresses; loneliness; depressive episodes; and despair, jealousy, resentment, and other negative emotions.

When sufficient progress is made in individual therapy, partners can then use couples counseling sessions to build on the identification they have with each other as victims/survivors of family abuse, combat, or other traumas or injustices to develop a more rewarding relationship. If the partners have acquired caretaking skills during their traumatic experiences, these skills can be used to care for each other, as well as for the self.

Counselors need to help train trauma survivors, especially family abuse survivors, to identify, express, and manage feelings, particularly in times of stress and anger, and to identify and cope with behavioral reenactments of the trauma. In order for a relationship to survive the double anger, double need, and PTSD symptoms of each partner, each partner also needs to learn to increase his or her mastery and competency in areas of personal interest and make an effort to have and enjoy relationships outside the marriage.

7

Treating Intimacy Issues of Traumatized People

Patricia L. Sheehan

> Sometimes when we touch, the honesty's too much and I have to close my eyes and hide. I want to hold you 'til I die, 'til we both break down and cry.
> I want to hold you 'til the fear in me subsides.
>
> —Dan Hill

INTRODUCTION

Intimacy is one of the most sought after and feared phenomena in life. As human beings, we want honest, open, deeply connected relationships, and yet fear causes us to avoid or destroy them when we do find them. Trauma exacerbates this fear. Clinicians who work with the traumatized are keenly aware of how difficult it is for these people to establish and maintain intimate relationships. In her clinical work with Vietnam veterans, sexual abuse survivors, and chemically dependent families, this clinician has found that it is necessary to address this fear of intimacy in order for clients to be able to sustain an intimate relationship. This chapter focuses on a model that incorporates intimacy, fears of intimacy, and trauma; supportive clinical and research findings; and treatment strategies that were derived from this model.

INTIMACY

Psychological theorists consider the ability to develop and maintain an intimate relationship to be an essential indicator of normal healthy development (Erikson, 1968; Maslow, 1954; Rogers, 1961; Shatan, 1978; Sullivan, 1953). Eastern and

Western spiritual philosophers (Callahan, 1969; Curran, 1972; Keane, 1977; Moss, 1981; Piper, 1960; Ram Doss, 1970; Theileke, 1964; Watts, 1958; Westley, 1981) view intimacy as an important path to spiritual growth and enlightenment. Intimacy is a complex concept that has been defined in various ways. From an intrapsychic perspective, intimacy is the result of an individual's achieving adequate self-knowledge and self-acceptance, which, in turn, foster the willingness to share these feelings and thoughts with another. This view of intimacy does not require reciprocity. A second view of intimacy emphasizes the interpersonal nature of the concept. Intimacy is seen as the result of interaction and can occur only between people who share something meaningful with each other. This can occur at a conscious, behavioral level or at an unconscious, inferential level (Fisher & Stricher, 1982).

In a multicultural, historical review of intimacy, Sexton and Sexton (1982) concluded that while there was lack of consensus about the precise nature of intimacy, most cultures considered intimacy to consist of freely chosen mutual self-disclosure and awareness of each other's innermost reality and private thoughts. Participants in workshops conducted by this author throughout the United States and Russia have described intimacy as involving honesty, openness, vulnerability, trust, risk, caring, acceptance, and sometimes sex. This author considers intimacy to be an honest, open, authentic sharing of thoughts and feelings between two people.

FEAR OF INTIMACY

Psychological and spiritual theorists acknowledge that fear is the major factor contributing to a person's inability to form intimate relationships (Jampolsky, 1979). Workshop participants named fears, ignorance, and pride as the causes of their problems with intimate relationships. When ignorance and pride are examined more closely, they are usually based in fear.

Fear of intimacy is an enormous concept. Feldman (1979) differentiated five different fears of intimacy. These distinctions can be used to determine the nature of a person's fear of intimacy more precisely, thereby allowing the therapist to focus treatment on more clearly defined problems. Identifying these five fears provides a better understanding of the general fear of intimacy. Identifying and understanding these five fears can also explain why the traumatized have so much difficulty with intimacy. The following section describes this clinician's view of these fears. The next section presents the rationale, clinical findings, and research that support the notion that trauma exacerbates these fears of intimacy.

THE FIVE FEARS

Fear of Merger

Fear of merger is the fear of losing identity, freedom, or control over one's life. This fear is manifested in power struggles over who controls whom and what. It may be expressed in several ways: "Don't fence me in," "Don't try to tell me what to do; you are not my mother/father," "I'm not going to be henpecked," or "I don't want to be known just as Mrs. Joe Brown." All of these statements reflect a fear that the individual is losing himself or herself in the relationship. Indeed, the most difficult task in a relationship is to stay true to oneself and also communicate and negotiate with the other person in a way that maintains the integrity and identity of both.

Fear of merger causes people to avoid communication and negotiation. They fear that if they allow the other person to deeply know them, the other person will use that information to control them. They fear that "if I give an inch, you will take a mile." Their approach to conflict resolution is: "It's my way or no way" or "You knew this was the way I am when you married me. If you don't like it, you can leave." They equate negotiation with loss and sometimes with complete annihilation.

Fear of Abandonment

Fear of abandonment is the fear of loving someone and then losing that person. It is the result of the loss of loved ones in both childhood and adulthood. Nearly everyone has experienced the pain of a broken heart; some people recover and some do not.

People manifest fear of abandonment in various ways. Some vow that no one will ever do that to them again. They avoid sexual relationships or become very promiscuous, avoiding emotional involvement. When people try to form a new lover relationship before resolving their emotional abandonment issues, they tend to form unhealthy relationships. They may get involved in an emotionally distant relationship or may form a revenge relationship in which they take revenge on the new lover for what the last one did to them. If they do let themselves get emotionally involved, they tend to be very clingy, jealous, and insecure because they are afraid the new person will abandon them as the previous one did.

Fear of Exposure

Fear of exposure is the fear of being seen. It is reflected in the thought, "If you really knew me, you wouldn't want anything to do with me." Individuals fear having their character flaws and weaknesses seen by other people. They fear being viewed as weak, stupid, undesirable, inadequate, bad, repulsive, and so on. They fear that if the other person truly sees them, they will be rejected.

Inferiority and shame are at the core of this fear. Building an intimate relationship requires mutual self-disclosure (sharing of mistakes, vulnerabilities, fears); fear of exposure inhibits or prevents this self-disclosure.

Another aspect of fear of exposure is that as individuals interact in an intimate relationship, they may also see character flaws in themselves that they have been able to deny when they are alone. They see aspects of themselves that they may not want to accept. Sometimes people choose to reject the other person rather than face themselves.

Fear of Attack

Fear of attack is the fear of being emotionally or physically hurt. Interpersonal attack can range from light verbal or nonverbal ridicule to violent physical attacks. Attack can be obvious, as in name-calling or hitting, or it can be subtle, as in teasing, put-downs, or other passive-aggressive tactics. As intimacy builds in a relationship, individuals discover each other's vulnerabilities—areas about which they feel insecure or sensitive. In a caring, compassionate relationship, there is an agreement, usually unspoken, not to use these vulnerabilities against each other. Violation of this agreement is experienced as a betrayal. The attack of an intimate partner hurts more than that of an acquaintance because the partner is counted on to be an ally and a supporter.

Fear of One's Own Destructive Impulses

Fear of one's own destructive impulses is the fear of personal anger or rage and the fear of the ability and willingness to hurt other people. Everyone has been disappointed in a love relationship. Disappointment can result in repressed or suppressed anger and resentment. As intimacy increases in a relationship, partners become more aware of these feelings and also begin to feel more vulnerable. Some people may use this anger as a protective mechanism to push the other person away, finding themselves nit-picking or exploding for no apparent reason. This is especially true in reconciling couples. Many people are afraid of their anger and may opt to avoid intimacy if it sensitizes them to these angry feelings, as it often does.

Power struggles are almost inevitable in lovers' relationships. Lovers test each other's boundaries and limitations. Most will experiment to see how far they can push the other person. Some people fear they are truly bad when they become aware of their tendencies to do this, rather than see it as a normal, but not particularly healthy, human tendency. They may avoid intimate relationships rather than face this willful, selfish side of themselves.

All human beings have some degree of all of these fears. The levels of the various fears for any person depend upon his or her past experiences, current situation, beliefs, and ability to process and recover from those experiences.

TRAUMA

The severely traumatized tend to have more problems with intimacy. Research findings support this notion. Wilson (1980) found that combat Vietnam veterans reported more severe relationship problems than Vietnam-era veterans (who served in areas other than Vietnam). In their study of 6,800 American Legionnaires, Stellman, Stellman, and Sommer (1985) found that Vietnam veterans with heavy combat exposure reported a higher divorce rate than other groups of veterans. Using the Fundamental Interpersonal Relations Orientation-Behavior instrument (FIRO-B), Shortridge (1980) found that combat veterans were less likely to express or want inclusion behavior or affection. This author found that Vietnam combat veterans scored lower on the Waring Intimacy Questionnaire than Vietnam-era veterans. The differences were even greater when the level of combat trauma was taken into account; veterans with the highest levels of exposure to combat trauma scored the lowest intimacy scores (Sheehan, 1989).

Clinical writers also invariably report severe intimacy problems with heavily traumatized Vietnam veterans (Coughlan & Parkin, 1987; Egendorf, 1982; Figley & Sprenkle, 1978; Glover, 1984; Reinberg, 1986; Shatan, 1978). Sexual abuse survivors (Bass & Davis, 1988) and adult children of alcoholics (Black, 1981) also often have serious difficulties with intimacy. Additionally, the traumatic nature of police work can cause emotional distancing and relationship problems (Sheehan, 1991).

As was stated earlier, understanding the nature of the five fears of intimacy helps one understand why Vietnam veterans and other traumatized people have had so much trouble with intimacy. The following notions explain how various traumas could intensify all five of the fears.

Fear of Merger

Fear of merger is a fear of losing freedom and control over life, or fear of losing one's identity. The Vietnam combatants lost all of these to some degree. Their choices were to enter the military, go to jail, or leave the country. Military training affects a person's sense of identity. Once they entered the military, they were told where to go and what to do. They were taught to be soldiers rather than civilians. At the average age of nineteen, they were transported into the realities of the military and Vietnam. Their rules and values were very different from those they had learned at home.

They changed; in fact, many Vietnam veterans feel as if they lost all or part of themselves in Vietnam. Their families invariably commented about how different the veterans were when they came home. The movies *Platoon* and *Apocalypse Now* depicted the severity of the Vietnam veteran's identity struggle. Both movies presented the conflict in terms of good and evil and noted that the basic battle was not fighting against an external enemy but, rather, avoiding the loss of one's own soul, the core element of identity.

As a result of Vietnam's devastating effect on them, many veterans are unwilling or unable to let anyone or anything influence them. They are afraid to trust or let anyone else have an impact on them again; they are afraid to merge. To merge, they must be willing to let another person affect their thinking and feeling, to let go of control occasionally.

Other types of trauma could also intensify fear of merger. Victims of incest, rape, and abusive parents all experience loss of control over their own bodies and lives. Their identity is assaulted. Children are not allowed to be children and frequently assume the identity of a victim or of a superhuman. Healthy merging is a temporary letting go of boundaries with another person. Abused people may have no clear distinction between merging and separating because their personal boundaries were violated and not allowed to develop normally. This violation can cause a myriad of problems and confusion with the merging experience. Sexually abused people usually have associated sex, merging, and abuse with each other, resulting in powerful, conflicting feelings.

Fear of Abandonment

Numerous experiences of Vietnam veterans were potential causes of intensified fear of abandonment. Many veterans received ''Dear John'' letters or returned home to find their loved ones involved with someone else. Of those veterans who were married before going to Vietnam, 38 percent were divorced six months after returning home (Disabled American Veterans, 1980). Friends were killed in battle. The veterans felt abandoned by their country and fellow Americans. The homecoming was a painful experience for most veterans—ranging from indifference to hostile attacks by the antiwar demonstrators.

Victims of childhood sexual and physical abuse felt abandoned by the perpetrator and the other parent who did not protect them from the abuser. All victims of violence and trauma may feel both an abandonment by God and a loss of their illusion of safety.

Fear of Exposure

Fear of exposure is the shame and guilt-based fear. Many Vietnam veterans perpetrated or witnessed what would be considered atrocities by most civilians. The intense guilt and shame they experience when they reflect on these memories cause them to believe that no one else would accept them. This fear was validated for many Vietnam veterans when they tried to talk to their families and friends who did not want to hear anything about the war, let alone its more horrific aspects.

Victims of sexual and physical abuse feel shame because they tend to believe they did something to deserve the abuse. They also see themselves as damaged and undesirable. Children in chemically dependent families are usually very ashamed of their parents and avoid having friends meet their parents or see their home life.

Fear of Attack

Fear of attack is the fear of being emotionally or physically hurt. Combat is attack. Vietnam veterans were attacked and killed by men, women, and children.

Many veterans felt that it was not safe to trust anyone. Constant hypervigilance was necessary for survival; vulnerability was associated with death. Many Vietnam veterans experienced attack from their fellow Americans when they came home. They were called "baby burners" or blamed for losing the war. Their hypervigilance and survival mind-set (that other people either were completely and consistently on their side or were the enemy) caused them serious problems with intimate relationships. When their partners were not always consistent in how they felt about something or disagreed with them, they felt betrayed or attacked.

Sexual and physical abuse are obviously attacks. Emotional attack is often the norm in chemically dependent families. Like Vietnam veterans, these victims do not tolerate feelings of vulnerability easily.

Fear of One's Own Destructive Impulses

Fear of one's own destructive impulses is the fear of one's own anger, rage, and willingness to hurt others. Many combat veterans know they can kill. They often have anger and rage from their Vietnam experiences. Knowing this causes many veterans to be afraid to express any anger for fear they will lose control and unleash a monster that will hurt or kill someone. Intimacy stirs strong feelings of love and hate. Being disappointed by a partner frequently results in anger and sometimes hate. This may be intolerable for some veterans.

Victims of abuse also have a great deal of anger and rage because of being violated. Thus, they have the same fears of being out of control and harmful to others. They also frequently associate these angry feelings with their abuser and fear they will be like the abuser if they let themselves feel angry.

Trauma intensifies fears of intimacy and, thereby, inhibits the traumatized's ability to be intimate. This important distinction implies that the link between trauma and intimacy is not a simple, direct one; fear is an important intervening intrapsychic phenomenon that affects the person's ability to be intimate.

This notion was tested in a study of the relationships among combat trauma, fear of intimacy, and intimacy (Sheehan, 1989). Using Pearson correlations and multiple regressions, combat trauma was found to be a significant predictor of fear of intimacy; it was also a significant predictor of intimacy in a simple relationship, but it was not a significant predictor of intimacy when fear of intimacy was considered in the regression. Only 12 percent of the variance of intimacy was accounted for when the effect of combat trauma and the pertinent demographic variables were regressed on intimacy, while 46 percent of the variance of intimacy was accounted for when fear of intimacy was added to regression. Indeed, when combat trauma was not included in the multiple regression, fear of intimacy and the pertinent demographic variables, by themselves, also accounted for 46 percent of the variance of intimacy. These findings support the notion that most of the effect of combat trauma, and perhaps other traumas, on intimate relationships is mediated through fear. It is important then for therapists to assess and focus more specifically on the fear component of their traumatized clients' intimacy problems, rather than simply using intimacy-building exercises.

TREATMENT

The most effective treatment strategies to help traumatized people establish or rebuild intimacy access and intervene with the fears of intimacy in an indirect or metaphorical way. Using traditional marital therapy techniques—verbal communication exercises, reframing, and so on—with couples at the Vet Center did not enable them to sustain improvement in their relationships. Relying on these traditional strategies, which had worked well with alcoholic couples, mental health clinic patients, and private practice clients, for several years, this clinician's encounters with Vet Center couples were initially very confusing and humbling.

Veterans and their partners wanted to be more intimate; both were sincerely trying and said they wanted to be emotionally closer; longing and pain filled their eyes. But one of them, usually the veteran, consistently did something to sabotage the intimate contact. He or she would be too busy, pick a fight, or leave. It became evident that the trauma-induced fears of intimacy were unconsciously causing them to be unable, rather than unwilling, to be more intimate with their partners. Therefore, treatment strategies that accessed and intervened with these fears on an unconscious level were utilized.

This author developed a treatment protocol that included several indirect approaches and metaphors that focused on healing the fears of intimacy. The treatment strategies were used in conjunction with traditional marital therapy approaches of establishing or reestablishing effective communication, correcting misunderstandings, and fostering amends and forgiveness. Soon, the couples began to make noticeable improvement. They reported less avoidant behaviors— emotional distancing, verbal attacking, and periods of separation. They also reported better communication and a greater sense of closeness and connection, which they were able to maintain from week to week. The subjective measures of success were good.

To obtain an objective measure of the effectiveness of these treatment approaches, this author used the Waring Intimacy Questionnaire (WIQ) (Waring & Reddon, 1981) to measure eight different subconcepts of intimacy before and after a series of therapy sessions in which the treatment strategies were used. The WIQ measures conflict resolution, affection, commitment, sexuality, identity, couple autonomy, compatibility, and expressiveness. It also produces a total intimacy score based on the forty most efficient items. Increases were obtained in all measures except commitment. The couples scored statistically significant increases in a paired t-test on the total intimacy score ($p = <.005$), conflict resolution ($p = <.005$), identity ($p = .02$), and expressiveness ($p = .05$) (Sheehan, 1985).

The metaphors and indirect treatment strategies are described in the following section.

Healing Metaphors

Metaphors are stories or descriptions of situations that are different from the person's situation in content but similar in theme. Theoretically, metaphors bypass resistance because they do not directly confront the issue or fear. This allows better assimilation of the information that is needed by the unconscious in order to correct the original misunderstanding caused by the trauma. For example, people who lose parents at an early age frequently have high fears of abandonment. They may consciously know that they will not always be abandoned but find themselves unconsciously defending themselves from abandonment by intimacy-avoiding tactics. Logic does not help.

Another plausible theoretical explanation for the power of metaphors is that they speak to the person's child-consciousness. This aspect of the self has been referred to as the inner child and is the focus of many healing strategies in trauma recovery, especially in literature on sexual abuse and adult children of alcoholics. It is seen as both the part of the self that is unable and/of unwilling to release the trauma-caused fear and resultant defenses as well as the source of great potential for growth if it can be given correct information.

While this clinician does not know exactly why metaphors help, clinical experience has convinced her that they do. They have been used by teachers and healers throughout the ages. Jesus told parables; Zen masters gave koans. Most of the profound human truths can be found in mythology, fables, and fairy tales.

Metaphors were used with both the veterans and their wives after interviewing them regarding their concerns and problems with their relationships. They were also initially given the Fear of Intimacy Questionnaire, which measures the five fears of intimacy (Sheehan, 1989). Metaphors were developed to address the fears that were most problematic for each person.

The beginning of the metaphor or story would pace or match the traumatic experience that triggered the fear, and the rest of the story would focus on new learning and a healing of the fear. For example, the most frequent fears of the wives were fear of merger and fear of attack.

In individual treatment, this clinician first would suggest that the wife close her eyes and focus on her breathing, then would guide her through a centering exercise and instruct her to listen to a metaphorical story. She was instructed to take from the story whatever was useful for her to lead the kind of life she wanted to lead and be the person she wanted to be.

The metaphor begins with descriptions of situations that pace or match experiences that can cause fear of attack (e.g., being hurt by the briers) and fear of merger (e.g., being caught in the briers and lost in the woods). The metaphor then creates a healing continuation of the story that involves learning new coping skills, maturity, courage, and the resultant wisdom. Theoretically, the pacing part of the metaphor attracts the attention of the wounded aspect of the personality. The healing metaphor then provides new information for better understanding and healing.

It is important to involve several of the senses when telling the stories, including sights, sounds, smells, internal feelings, tactile sensations, and tastes. This greatly enhances the images and, therefore, the power of the metaphor. It is also important to use very simple, childlike language, especially in the beginning, pacing portion of the story.

Each person's story is somewhat different, based on the person's personality, interests, and beliefs, as well as fears. Many of the veterans had high fear of abandonment. To heal this fear, the metaphor described a little boy who gets lost in a store at Christmastime. He and his mother develop a plan of action so they can find each other if they become disconnected again. This metaphor emphasized that no one is perfectly attentive to anyone else all the time and that it is important to have a plan to reconnect after they have "lost" each other. Many traumatized people, especially Vietnam veterans, feel abandoned if their partner is not always focusing on them and consistently agreeing with them. The metaphor helps to correct this destructive belief.

There are several resources available for therapists who wish to learn more about the use of metaphors in therapy. These include the writings and workshops of several of Milton Erickson's students, especially Stephen and Carol Lankton; Ron Kurtz and other practitioners of Hakomi therapy; and David Grove.

Bibliotherapy

Both partners were told to read *The Velveteen Rabbit* by Margery Williams (1969); the book is a wonderful metaphor about love, authenticity, intimacy, pain, loss, and transformation. They were also told to read *The Missing Piece Meets the Big O* by Shel Silverstein (1981); the book is a metaphor about identity formation and the unfulfilling nature of codependency.

Picture Communication Exercise

Because of recurrent misunderstandings and resultant attacks and mistrust, many couples in therapy find it very difficult to talk openly. This exercise, adapted from Naomi and Berl Chernick's (1979) work, is an excellent way to promote noncritical, safe communication, thereby reducing fear of attack and fear of exposure. It is also a good diagnostic tool to determine the strengths and weaknesses of a couple's communication patterns.

This exercise is given as a homework assignment. Both people are told to find a picture in a magazine or from any source that appeals to them. If both people are equally communicative, either one can begin to talk first. However, if the wife is more communicative, she is told to begin the exercise by talking about her picture, why she chose it, and how she feels about it. She then continues to talk about whatever comes to her mind (free-associate) for ten minutes, even if she has to talk about how difficult it is to talk for ten minutes. It is also emphasized that she is not restricted to talking about the picture; the picture is merely a springboard to begin the talking.

The husband is told to listen silently for the ten minutes and, when the wife has finished talking, to tell her what he heard her say. He is to tell her only what he heard her say, not what he thinks about it. He is not to tell her his interpretations, his view of the picture, or any of his thoughts about what she said. This eliminates criticism and conflict about who is right or wrong.

After the husband has told his wife what he heard her say, he becomes the speaker and tells her about his picture and why he chose it and then free-associates for ten minutes. She listens silently and then tells him only what she heard him say with the same restrictions of no commentary.

If the exercise is done correctly, the couple experiences being truly listened to and feeling safe when expressing themselves to the other; they can enjoy the intimacy of being in the flow of each other's thinking. If both or either of them cannot resist correcting, criticizing, or talking about their own thoughts, that becomes grist for the therapeutic mill.

Sharing Meditation

The sharing meditation is a two-person meditation that allows the couple to experience the sensations and internal feelings of love and connection with each other. Because the exercise is totally nonverbal, it is difficult to sabotage. The couple is instructed to sit facing each other, so that they can comfortably touch hands lightly. Using guided imagery, they both center by attending to their own breathing and then by imagining that they are drawing relaxing energy into themselves with every breath they take. The clinician then tells them to imagine they are drawing energy from the room as they inhale and sending it down through their arms to their partner as they exhale.

Next, this clinician suggests that the husband continue to send energy to his wife when he exhales and that she relax and becomes receptive to the energy coming from his hands to her hands, up through her arms, and into her heart. After a minute or two, the roles are reversed. The wife begins sending energy, and the husband relaxes and becomes receptive.

Both are told to center gradually and gently and bring their attention back inside themselves, neither sending nor receiving energy. They focus on the experience of being connected and, yet, very separate individuals who can be fully aware of their own experiences and also touch each other. Finally, they are guided to reorient themselves to the room and open their eyes and share their experiences with each other.

Most couples experience powerful tingly and/or warm sensations flowing between them. Many experience a merging sensation in which they lose awareness of the boundary between their hands; they seem to melt together. Most experience feelings of love, warmth, and closeness. Many couples, deeply touched by the meditation, said it reminded them of how they used to feel when they held each other. This exercise experientially reminds the couples of the loving feelings they used to have for each other before the fears became so powerful. (Audiotapes of the sharing meditation and metaphors are available from the author of this chapter).

CONCLUSION

This chapter presents a theoretical framework that incorporates intimacy, fear of intimacy, and trauma. It describes the treatment approaches, derived from this theory, that this clinician has found to be the most effective with traumatized people. If any reader wishes to share ideas and experiences with these or other treatment approaches, please contact the author.

8

Intergenerational Consequences of Trauma: Reframing Traps in Treatment Theory—A Second-Generation Perspective

Joseph H. Albeck

> . . . the generation that bears the scar without the wound, sustaining memory without direct experience. It is this generation that has the obligation, self-imposed and self-accepted . . . to describe a meaning and wrest instruction from the historical.
>
> —Cohen, 1981

INTRODUCTION

Trauma victims can be changed markedly by their experiences, sometimes in ways that impact on their children, even those born after the occurrence of the traumatic events that their parents endured. These offspring, the "second generation" from the trauma, may thus bear "the scar without the wound," since they are significantly, if only indirectly, affected.

It remains difficult to describe fully the consequences of trauma for the offspring of victims or to outline precise mechanisms by which "transmission" of victimization could occur across generations. Nevertheless, clinicians are confronted daily by adult patients who ask for help in contending with conflicts that occur in the context of histories of traumatic stress in the lives of their parents. These "second-generation" adult patients seek and deserve expert guidance about the extent, significance, and need for intervention relating to the impact on their own lives of what their parents endured.

The way professionals approach such situations is determined by their training, which is, in turn, based on what has been published to date in the literature. Unfortunately, the theories currently available in this area are somewhat limited in usefulness because of the particular concepts and terminology used by the pioneers in the field, as well as by methodological limitations of more recent studies (Solkoff, 1992). The author of this chapter, as both a member of the second generation and a professional, suggests a reframing of approach and terminology that may prove helpful to clinicians in their practical work with second-generation clients.

This chapter focuses on adult children of Jewish Holocaust survivors. The trauma suffered by Holocaust survivors is distinct from that experienced by their offspring. Unlike children of child abuse victims or children of alcoholics, no children of Holocaust survivors were directly exposed to the kind of trauma their parents experienced. This heuristic advantage for efforts to understand intergenerational consequences of trauma is maintained if child survivors, those children under age fourteen who were persecuted by the Nazis prior to the end of World War II, are defined as the direct trauma survivors they really are. Thus, child survivors whose parents survived (a minority) could be considered both survivors and, simultaneously, children of survivors. For purposes of simplicity, however, the remainder of this chapter focuses on children of Holocaust survivors who were born after the end of World War II or who were born after their parents were geographically beyond the grasp of Nazi forces. It is hoped that some of what has been learned to date about intergenerational effects of the Holocaust may prove relevant to offspring of other traumatized populations, if only as a reference point from which similarities and differences may be further explored.

TRAPS IN TREATMENT THEORY

Professional Hubris

It is important to acknowledge that current theoretical and clinical understanding of the intergenerational consequences of trauma is still in its infancy. The precise sequence of events that mediate the effects of parental trauma upon the victim's children remains poorly understood. Even the clinical language and paradigms used by professionals are still quite limited and imperfect. There is still a great deal to learn about the influences parental traumas exert on the lives of their children, during and after their formative years. Approaching this aspect of clinical work with second-generation patients as a joint venture, or as a mutual exploration into partially unknown areas, is more likely to strengthen the therapeutic relationship between patient and therapist than is a posture that exaggerates the certainty of our current knowledge of intergenerational consequences of trauma.

Overstating and Overgeneralizing Published Findings

"Shami Davidson, director of the Shlava Psychiatric Hospital in Tel Aviv, puts it succinctly: 'The trauma of the Nazi concentration camp is re-experienced in the lives of the children and even the grandchildren of camp survivors. The effects of systematic dehumanization are being transmitted from one generation to the next through severe disturbances in the parent-child relationship' '' (Epstein, 1977).

Rakoff, Sigal, and Epstein (1967) first reported that some effects of the Holocaust could be observed in children born to survivors after the end of the Nazi war against the Jews (1933–1945). These observations were based exclusively on reports from families of patients who had sought treatment at a Montreal psychiatric facility. However, years later, it remained unclear what fraction of the larger community of survivor families their cases represented. Thus, subsequent descriptions of, and theorizing about, mechanisms of the Holocaust's effects on the second generation referred to "children of survivors" as if all were clinically affected similarly. There were occasional disclaimers and caveats in published reports, including the psychoanalytic literature, but the focus on psychopathology obscured concerns about the limits of applicability of the findings. Some authors even expressed skepticism that intergenerational effects could be treated successfully (Begmann and Jucovy, 1982). Overstatement and overgeneralization marred much of the early reporting, however understandable the enthusiasm of new discovery may have been. In retrospect, it appears either that Rakoff's sample of Holocaust survivor families was extraordinarily pathological or that his descriptions and inferences were somewhat overdrawn, to make his basic and valid point: trauma can indeed affect the offspring of victims in important ways.

Vague Language and Models

The notion that trauma victims would be impaired in their parenting and thereby likely traumatize their offspring has been the basis of much clinical and research thinking about what has often been termed the "transgenerational transmission" of trauma (Frankle, 1978). However, recent and better-designed studies of children of survivors (using appropriate control groups, rigorous sampling techniques, and nonclinical populations of Holocaust survivors and their children) have not confirmed the pathological predictions of the early reports (Sigal and Weinfeld, 1989; Rose and Garske, 1987; Solkoff, 1992). These newer studies have not demonstrated the existence of the predicted psychopathology in the offspring. Children of survivors were found to be no different from matched offspring of Jews with no Holocaust histories, when large community samples were rigorously studied (Sigal and Weinfeld, 1989). There did not seem to be evidence confirming intergenerational transmission of Holocaust trauma.

Sigal (1989) attributes this paradoxical result to the fact that the early reports were based on clinical samples of a minority of those children who probably had parents with more relationship difficulties. The more recent studies were based on observations of a larger, more general population, whose parents were better adjusted. While this explanation is persuasive, other factors may be relevant. Perhaps the notion of "impaired parenting" is too vague and unidimensional. More rigorous definition and measurement of "parenting" as a concept could yield specific factors that might be involved in intergenerational effects of trauma. Researchers and clinicians alike simply do not yet know, definitively, which parental experiences, beliefs, basic assumptions, or behaviors are the critical intervening variables in the "transmission" of trauma.

Presuming a Pathological Child of Survivors Syndrome

If concentration camp survivors suffer from a "syndrome," then, perhaps, their offspring suffer from a related pathological syndrome as well. An extensive literature describing symptoms and syndromes of children of Holocaust survivors has developed over the years. This literature has recently been described by Major (1991); see Table 8.1.

Unfortunately, only a moderate degree of agreement exists among different authors about the importance of specific components of the "second generation syndrome." Some authors do not agree that eating disorders, psychosomatic disorders, or aggression should be included at all or that they describe a sub-population of children of survivors (Solkoff, 1992). Clinicians must remain cautious about presuming that such a syndrome exists, is clearly defined, or is really useful to guide clinical interactions with children of survivors. Alternative terms and concepts, as outlined later, may ultimately prove to be more helpful than the notion of a "syndrome" afflicting, or potentially afflicting, all children of Holocaust survivors.

The Tendency to Pathologize

Until very recently, psychological explanations for trauma's effects have tended to focus on intrapsychic factors at the expense of the interactive social, political, and historical aspects. This has led to a pathologizing propensity rather than the elucidation of "normal" psychological responses to "abnormal" events. Recent work by Janoff-Bulman (1989, 1992) marks a significant shift toward an approach that seeks to understand "effects" of trauma, rather than postulating psychopathology. Since the best data on Holocaust survivors' offspring suggest that psychopathological syndromes do not occur in all of their children, it may be helpful to shift the frame of reference away from a presumed psychopathology and toward a "psychology" of intergenerational effects of trauma.

A psychology would allow researchers and clinicians to seek predictable effects, without presuming that they are necessarily pathological or part of a particular syndrome, while defining and understanding effects at different points in their lives without insisting on the presence of psychopathology. A child does not have to become ill to have been affected by parental trauma, and even negative effects have different impacts, extents, and durations. Furthermore, not all effects of parental trauma are necessarily deleterious. The possibilities for growth as a result of trauma in both generations, in addition to any injuries sustained, must not be overlooked.

Table 8.1
The "Second-Generation Syndrome"

I. Symptoms Included from the Literature Concerning the Second Generation:

   Identity conflicts
   Eating disorders
   Extreme sense of responsibility
   Separation conflicts
   Difficulties in making contact
   Extreme examination anxiety
   Overachievement
   Psychosomatic disorders
   Suicidal attempts

II. Symptoms Included from the Concentration Camp Syndrome:

   Nervousness
   Holocaust-related nightmares
   Anxiety
   Concentration difficulties
   Depression

III. Symptoms Included from Post Traumatic Stress Disorder (PTSD):

   Stress reactions upon exposure to events that symbolize or resemble an aspect
      of the traumatic event
   Aggression

IV. Other Characteristics:

   Work interest in the health/social care professions
   Need felt for participation in "second generation groups."

Vagueness About What Is "Transmitted" Between Generations

The term *transgenerational transmission* suggests that the parental trauma is "transmitted" like a virus, or perhaps a radio signal, from one generation to the next. One might wonder about mechanisms: is trauma transmitted in unchanged form between the generations? Could it be subject to modification along the way? Is the child's trauma entirely different from that of the parent, or is there some overlap or relationship between the traumas of parent and child? Answers to such questions could frame the approach professionals take with second-generation clients. Yet other questions illustrate the critical roles played by language and terminology. Precisely what is it that is transmitted between the generations: a "stressor," "trauma," "victimization," a "syndrome," or a set of beliefs? Different authors use different terms. Are they really interchangeable? Most likely, they are not. Clinicians and researchers still need to develop greater consensus about terms and concepts that can help improve the accuracy of our descriptions of intergenerational consequences of trauma.

AVOIDING TRAPS: REFRAMING TERMS AND THEORY

The process of clarification might begin with the elimination of the phrase *transgenerational transmission of trauma*. For Holocaust survivors and their offspring, the singular connotation of "trauma" is misleading; no Holocaust survivor suffered only one, clearly defined traumatic event. Most suffered at least several major losses outside the norms of usual human experience or expectation. Even more misleading is the connotation that "transmitted" trauma remains unchanged during "transmission" between the generations. This subject is considered in more detail later.

INTERGENERATIONAL CONSEQUENCES OF TRAUMA

What were the traumatic stressors for Holocaust survivors? To understand the intervening steps or variables between the traumatization of parents and any effects on their offspring, one must begin with the parents' trauma histories. The term *Holocaust survivors*, broadly defined, refers to about 400,000 people who personally experienced Nazi anti-Jewish persecution between 1933 and 1945 and were still alive after Germany surrendered (Gilbert, 1987; Davidowicz, 1976). The ratio of survivors to nonsurvivors of the Nazi war against them was roughly 1:15, suggesting that even those survivors able to leave Europe before 1939 ultimately had to adapt to the knowledge of the mass murder of their Jewish friends and family. This knowledge was often traumatic to them. Such people are sometimes called "escapees." Including escapees (Jews who had the knowledge of murdered family and friends) within the definition of "Holocaust survivor" suggests that this knowledge of the mass murder of people whom they personally knew constituted a significant traumatic stressor for them. Developing an understanding of how escapees' knowledge of mass murders might constitute, or lead to, a trauma potentially capable of producing transgenerational effects could help to clarify the mechanisms by which such comparatively "mild" trauma in escapees could impact the next generation.

MODELS OF TRAUMA—EMPHASIS ON "PREDICAMENTS" RATHER THAN "STRESSORS"

Any model of trauma must include the consideration of attempted adaptive coping responses in those subjected to stress. Successful coping can result in stability or growth, while unsuccessful coping results in injury or trauma. During the attempt to adapt to a stressor, the stressed person is at a nodal point, or in a predicament. He or she is in the midst of a crisis sometimes containing opportunities for growth, as well as presenting real danger. The outcome of efforts to cope with the stressor(s) determines whether or not trauma occurs. Even when trauma does occur, it can sometimes be worked through successfully, depending on relational contexts, resiliency, and social and political factors.

As an alternative to the term *stressor*, the use of the term *predicament* helps to clarify some intergenerational effects of trauma. *Predicament* has been used in the self-help literature (Levy, 1982). It describes a phenomenon in which those who have lived with a particular problem or "predicament" subsequently develop a kind of mutual understanding that is not possible for those without that life experience. The term *predicament* seems to capture this aspect of the total experience of all trauma survivors better than does the term *stressor*, since *predicament* better connotes being on the horns of a dilemma, or being forced to make seemingly impossible choices (Styron, 1979), than does the more general term *stressor*.

Thus, it is commonplace for survivors of the Holocaust to feel that only other survivors "really" or "truly" understand them. Their "experiential" knowledge is distinct from professionals' knowledge about the Holocaust (Borkman, 1990) or the frame of reference of lay people who lack either a personal or a professional knowledge of the predicament. Escapees who have personal knowledge of the Nazis' murder of Jewish friends and relatives share a common "stressor" or "predicament," which others cannot understand in quite the same way. The actual predicament is critical to the perception of uniquely shared experience, not the coping skills involved in trying to resolve it.

The escapees' predicaments included assaults on their basic assumptions about personal physical safety, God, evil, and so on, resulting from inevitable questions raised by their direct experiences of mass murder. Basic assumptions could have been affected in varying degrees over time, thereby influencing what they consciously and unconsciously conveyed to their offspring. Janoff-Bulman (1989, 1992) described how trauma affects the assumptive worlds of victims. She noted

Figure 8.1
Predicaments Posed by Knowledge of Mass Murder in Each Generation

```
Predicament 1: For Parent
```

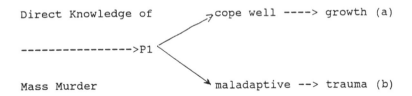

```
Predicament 2: For Child
```

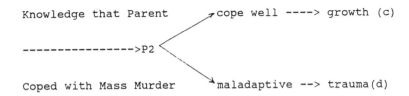

```
Predicament 3: For Child
```

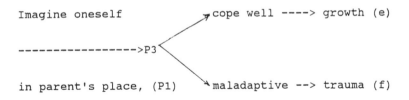

(1989) that schemas, "pre-existing theories that provide a basis for anticipating the future and guide what we notice and remember, as well as how we interpret new information" (p. 115), are modified only with great difficulty. The escapees' predicaments forced them to choose between conflicting schemas and basic assumptions about the safety of the world, the meaningfulness of the world, and the worthiness of their selves.

Escapees' predicaments were worked through individually. Their predicaments led to similar, but less intense, dilemmas for their offspring, as the children came to learn of their parents' experiences. In Figure 8.1, the parent stressed by the knowledge of murdered family members and friends is denoted by predicament 1 (P1). Predicament 2 (P2) is thus set up for the child as well, namely, dealing with a parent subject to predicament 1.

Risk of Empathic Traumatization or "Transposition"

Another predicament is created for the child simultaneously with predicament 2. Predicament 3 results from the child's efforts to imagine himself or herself in the parent's place during the parent's trauma. Kestenberg (1989) wrote that the most important aspect of the psychology of children of survivors born after the war is a tendency to think about their parents' wartime experiences as if they themselves had actually lived through them. She coined the term *transposition* to describe this phenomenon, which she asserts is a nonpathological, universal human potential.

A child who knows that his or her parents survived the Holocaust inevitably, and often repetitively, tries to imagine himself or herself in the parents' places. As Stiver (1990) has noted, children have powerful needs to feel connected to their parents, rather than to feel disconnected from them. When children of survivors cannot understand the pain of a parent, they feel barriers between themselves and others, consequently feeling alone, isolated, and guilty. The healthy yearning for connection with their parents contributes to these children's making such extraordinary efforts to imagine themselves in their parents' place. However, this imaginative experience may be so painful that they end up feeling more alienated. When children repeatedly imagine overwhelming Holocaust scenes, it may be because there has been no one to share such scenes, since parents may not be forthcoming and there are so much taboo and avoidance by others. This could lead to getting stuck for long periods, rather than finding other ways to manage the pain and discomfort with rhythms of relief.

Any traumatic experience has both overwhelming and inescapable aspects (Albeck, 1989b). Therefore, a child's empathic efforts to understand the parents' trauma could approach actual traumatization for the child as a function of his or her imaginative ability to approximate the parental experience. If the child repeatedly imagines the overwhelming scenes of Holocaust trauma without quickly escaping psychologically by changing the subject or denying its basic reality, then trauma may result, and/or the child's basic assumptions about life can be affected. However, any trauma experienced by the child will never be to the degree experienced by the parent who could not physically escape the Holocaust itself. On the other hand, unless the scenes of Holocaust trauma are imaginatively approximated and so experienced, they cannot be worked through effectively by the child. So an approach-avoidance cycle is created around the wish for connection and empathy versus the risk of experiencing the feeling of being overwhelmed.

Therapists who work with trauma victims might recognize the risk of empathic traumatization in offspring as akin to the therapist's own painful subjective experiences while trying to understand their patients' overwhelming traumas. As Havens (1979) has written, "Successful empathy can involve a transmission or sharing of bodily feelings" (p. 40). Sensitive articles have been written about vicarious traumatization (McCann and Pearlman, 1990c), burnout, and countertransference problems for therapists in these situations (Danieli, 1984, 1988a). Some children of Holocaust survivors, many of them also therapists, have struggled for years to understand the experiences of victims. This can be a painful process, as poems written by this author at age forty-one (Albeck, 1989a) may suggest. These poems, entitled ''Songs for the Last Survivor'' opened a literary window into the subjective experience of some intergenerational effects of the Holocaust, including efforts to comprehend the unimaginable predicaments survivors endured.

Toward a Psychology of Intergenerational Consequences of Trauma

Knowledge of, or fantasies about, parental predicaments ultimately forced many of the survivors' offspring to focus on the same existential questions that had long challenged their parents. The children's experience of the knowledge of mass murder could constitute a significant stressor for some children of survivors via the associated assault on basic assumptions or schemas. In the ''least case scenario'' or ''escapee'' scenario, the stressor (predicament 1) faced by Jews who escaped Europe between 1933 and 1939 is quite different from the stressor with which their children first had to deal: a stressed parent (predicament 2). When these children eventually learned or wondered about the fact of mass murder in their parents' generation, they imagined themselves in their parents' place and were additionally stressed (predicament 3).

Predicament 3, empathic traumatization or ''transposition,'' may be an important intergenerational consequence of trauma, which has not been sufficiently emphasized in the professional literature. Basic assumptions or schemas of the children may be affected by this mechanism, profoundly influencing their psychology. Facing similar predicaments may underlie the reported exhilarating sense of mutual understanding that often occurs when children of Holocaust survivors initially meet to talk about their personal backgrounds and experiences. Struggling with images of death, torture, and worse does set them apart from people whose families need not wrestle so intimately with such images. Whether a child of survivors works through such predicaments successfully is not necessarily correlated with how well or poorly the survivor-parents coped with their own trauma histories.

Predicaments of Parent and Child Are Distinct but Overlapping

The child's predicament of having to cope with knowledge of the murders of people he or she never met (predicament 3) is different from the predicament of survivor parents (predicament 1). However, it is also different in degree from predicaments of ''lay'' peers of children of survivors, who did not have to deal with murdered grandparents or lack of extended family in quite the same way.

The child of survivors is personally touched by the knowledge of mass murder. It is thus more difficult for children of survivors to psychologically escape the experience of feeling overwhelmed by clashing basic assumptions about life, safety, and worthiness of the self.

Thus, even if the parents cope successfully with personal knowledge of mass murder (predicament 1), resulting in parental growth (a), the child is still vulnerable to predicament 3. Therefore, the fact that a survivor may have coped adequately with a particular predicament does not guarantee that his or her offspring will cope successfully with their own, empathically transposed predicaments. Clearly, this model of intergenerational effects of trauma is more complex than one based on unchanged "transmission" between generations.

If the survivor parent does not cope adequately with predicament 1 and is consequently traumatized, the child faces additional, different challenges (predicament 4 and so on). Some of these challenges will be handled well, while others may be managed poorly. This model allows for the complexities of response patterns within and between the generations. It does not falsely presume that a parent who fails to cope adequately will "transmit" that failure to the children. Some children can cope, fully or partially, with failed parental efforts to resolve predicaments. This fact reinforces the desirability of speaking about the "consequences" or "effects," rather than the "transmission," of trauma between generations. It is also consistent with a general psychology of intergenerational effects of trauma, rather than a more limited syndrome of presumed psychopathology.

A GENERAL MODEL FOR PROCESSING TRAUMATIC STRESS—IMPLICATIONS FOR ASSESSMENT AND TREATMENT OF INTERGENERATIONAL EFFECTS

If some consequences of parental victimization are ultimately traumatic for their offspring, a general trauma paradigm should apply to these children as well as to the parents. The model in Figure 8.2 is loosely adapted from that of Green, Wilson, and Lindy (1985). For a more extensive description of a trauma model, see Chapter 1 by Wilson.

This general model suggests that a fact or event (1) can be stressful and, if perceived as sufficiently threatening, leads to a mental state of arousal consistent with its dangerousness (2), which then sets the emotional tone for the mental processing that subsequently occurs (3). The mental processing is influenced by the environment (5), including characteristics of the individual, such as personality, evaluative and coping styles, social class, gender, and idiosyncratic meanings attributed to the fact or event. The environment for mental processing also includes sociocultural factors (5B) such as cultural attitudes, social supports, family characteristics, and formal and informal helping organizations embedded in the then current economic and political realities. Environmental factors (5A and 5B) interact, since, for example, each individual determines the degree to

Figure 8.2
The Psychological Nature of Interfaces

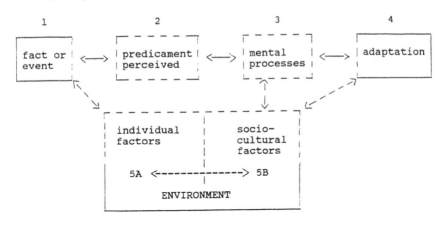

Boundaries:

_____ interpersonal

---- psychological

which he or she will accept, or deviate from, a given cultural norm. The mental processes (3) that integrate all these factors result in an adaptation (4), which can attempt to modify any part of the system. Further adaptations may be attempted, if the initial effort is unsuccessful, or catastrophic failure may result in major decompensation of mental processes, including post-traumatic stress disorder (PTSD) symptoms. The dotted lines in Figure 8.2 emphasize the psychological nature of the interfaces. The event (1) must be perceived and appreciated if it is to lead to attempts at adaptation. For example, the death of a loved one will not be fully processed until it is known or believed to be certain.

Clinical Assessment of Adult Children of Survivors

A clinician's first task is to assess the individual's presenting complaint as perceived by that patient. It is unusual for children of survivors to present for evaluation solely, or even primarily, because of concerns related to their parents' histories of trauma. A standard clinical interview yields a diagnosis and initial treatment plan that might be similar to the plan for an individual without a family history of trauma. Indeed, the fact that a patient's parents were trauma victims is often not apparent at the outset, either because the question was not asked, the patient does not think it relevant to the presenting problem, or the patient wishes to avoid the possibility of stigma associated with the "child of survivor syndrome." Furthermore, once obtaining the information that the patient is a child of Holocaust survivors, the therapist has no officially recognized diagnostic categories (DSM III-R) or standardized psychometric assessment instruments available to help in his or her work with that patient. An awareness of the previously described traps in treatment theory suggests that it cannot be presumed that the particular patient was, in fact, traumatized by the process of growing up in that particular survivor household. However, what is known about the psychology of children of Holocaust survivors can guide clinical inquiries to include several potentially important areas with the patient.

Children of survivors vary considerably in the knowledge they have about the details of their parents' lives prior to, during, and subsequent to the years of Nazi persecution (Weinfeld and Sigal, 1986). Siblings within the same family may have quite dissimilar knowledge bases. Danieli (1985) suggested that survivor families tend to cluster into four archetypes (those-who-made-it families, victim families, fighter families, and numb families) that may affect the development of the children. Eliciting the circumstances of the parents' courtship, marriage, and adaptational style in the postwar world helps to clarify precisely which issues may be salient for the particular patient or client. Children of survivors often avoid learning about the details of the parents' wartime experiences. Their degree of knowledge at the time of the clinical evaluation does not necessarily correlate with overall psychological health. Potentially traumatic information may have been shared in appropriately timed doses within the family over the years, resulting in significant growth and maturity; on the other hand, it may have been delivered prematurely or under difficult circumstances, causing unresolved confusion and psychological distancing between parent and child. Sometimes it has been gleaned inadvertently or surreptitiously from sources other than parents, exacerbating familial conflicts.

Life cycle and anniversary issues are extremely important. Kestenberg's concept of transposition may support the validity of reports in the literature (Steinberg, 1989; Almagor and Leon, 1989) that some children of survivors experience symptoms at the same age that their parents experienced Nazi traumatization. Life transitions such as graduations or marriage for children of survivors activate memories of involuntary separations in the parents. These memories may lead directly to real world distress in interactions with survivor-parents and to empathic traumatization in the children. Sensitivity to triggering of the reemergence of painful memories or actual parental flashbacks is common in children of survivors but subject to considerable individual variation. Some children of survivors go to great lengths not to upset their parents. This may seem indistinguishable from what is often conceptualized as familial enmeshment. However, it can sometimes be more successfully confronted in individual (Auerhahn and Prelinger, 1983), group (Fogelman and Savran, 1980), or family therapy (Russell, 1982; Krell, 1982) when clarified in the context of actual risk of recurrent parental pain or even recurrent PTSD symptoms (Kuch and Cox, 1992).

Clinical assessment includes evaluation of environmental factors (5A and 5B in Figure 8.2). Children of survivors differ with respect to national origin, education, social class, and even religion, since some were raised as Christians or adopted other faiths as adults. Some grew up in families that were open about their wartime experiences; others discovered for the first time in their late teens that their parents had been survivors. Some explored their family histories in religious settings; others are militantly atheistic. A careful assessment of exactly which of these factors are pertinent to the particular child of survivors is essential to any clinical undertaking.

Treatment Issues

After assessing which intergenerational issues, if any, might be most relevant to the individual child of a survivor, the clinician should remember that other, nonprofessional interventions might be helpful. For example, the general trauma model in Figure 8.2 suggests that there are important interactions between the environment (5A and 5B) and the traumatic fact or event (1). A child or grandchild of survivors who has a high school history teacher who professes that the Holocaust never occurred and was a story made up by Zionist conspirators is likely to become very upset. Conversely, public commemorations of the Holocaust by state governors or the president of the United States, particularly those in which survivors and their children participate, can have positive impacts. These ceremonies reinforce, however transiently, a belief in the potential protection and benevolence of society. Holocaust survivors and their children continue to require reassurance that this basic assumption about life applies to them. Recording survivors' videotaped testimonies about their wartime experiences can helpfully impact at the point of interface between the individual (5A) and sociocultural (5B) environment. These testimonies also help to counteract the ongoing campaigns of denial of the Holocaust that persist in the larger society.

Therapy for children of Holocaust survivors has been described at the individual (Auerhahn and Prelinger, 1983), group (Fogelman and Savran, 1980), family (Krell, 1982), and intergenerational multiple family collective group (Danieli, 1985) levels. All or none may be indicated for the particular child of survivors who presents for evaluation, depending on where along the continuum of working through the Holocaust's impact the patient is and the degree to which his or her presenting complaint is colored through the lens of Holocaust-related imagery. The perspective of a psychology of intergenerational consequences of trauma is illustrated in the following case.

Clinical Case Example

The overwhelming majority of children of Holocaust survivors who seek counseling are treated on an outpatient basis. However, the following inpatient vignette was chosen because it demonstrates that children of survivors also incur psychiatric conditions that are colored by their particular Holocaust background. The background, therefore, influences treatment prior to, during, and after acute episodes that may or may not be Holocaust-related. In this case, the complicating psychiatric diagnoses were depression, PTSD, and substance abuse.

This author received the following request for consultation "re: Holocaust survivor syndrome." It concerned a "forty-year-old, married, white female; first hospitalization for depression; is a child of Holocaust survivor; has history of sexual abuse and abuses codeine. Please evaluate and suggest possible focus for therapy."

After spending two and a half hours with this patient, this author responded to the treating psychiatrist by writing:

The patient has a 2–4 week history of symptoms consistent with diagnoses of Major Depression with panic attacks and sufficient biological signs to warrant a trial of anti-depressants if an alliance around therapy can be made strong enough to minimize her serious risk of suicide, even while waiting for medications to take effect.

The patient's particular history of being a child of a Holocaust survivor is central to the denial and intellectualization that she has used to construct a likable exterior, which has little relation to what she describes as "the black hole inside." She feels that her life is over and if she looks inside, she will melt into a puddle of craziness and never recover. What initially were ego-alien impulses to kill herself do begin to make some sense to her when put into this context, suggesting that she may gradually gain under-standing and, hence, control over these impulses as part of a longer-term psychotherapy.

Her history of childhood sexual abuse by a GI stepfather in post-war Germany and her several failed prior marriages have reinforced a personality style based on a disjunction between inner experience and external presentation. The history of sexual abuse clearly compounds the effects of family secrets, which included the patient's not learning that her mother was Jewish or a Holocaust survivor until the patient was in her late teens.

Suggestions that the patient be exposed to literature and self-help activities for children of Holocaust survivors, as well as receiving appropriate treatment for her PTSD related to her history of childhood sexual abuse, were followed. However, her lack of response to anti-depressant medication trials and her per-sistent suicidal ideation ultimately required electroconvulsive treatments, a some-what unusual choice of treatment for this age group of depressed patients. She responded favorably to the electroconvulsive therapy (ECT) and has done well since her discharge.

Subsequent to the consultation reported above, prior to the ECT treatments, this author attempted to address the patient's extreme sense of disjunction and disconnection by using his own poem as an experimental treatment tool to help her begin to speak of the unspeakable events both in her mother's and her own life. This author hoped that by being authentic about his own experience as a child of Holocaust survivors, the patient would perceive him as being empathic and able to bear witness to her own pain, rage, and sorrow. To this end, he shared several poems, including the following. The patient was then invited to share her reactions, which appear in the right-hand column. How well she was able to identify with the content of the poem and how poignantly she was able to respond are documented in the following.

My Forgone Family

My kin are gone—
grandparents, cousins, aunts,
step-relations of all descriptions,
old and young.
Children, sickly, healthy,
strong and weak—
all gone, all erased,
as if they never were.

Beautiful and handsome,
homely and shy—
they remain fixed forever
in a few cherished,
but fading photographs.

Newsreel reruns of
concentration camp scenes
pass before my eyes—
which ones should be recognized?

How do you begin to look
for family resemblances
in a pile of corpses?
Which naked ladies
with their babes in arms
might have lived
to enrich my lonely private world?

Warehouses full of children's clothes,
shoes, suitcases, and more
were preserved by the liberators
for their museums
at Auschwitz and Birkenau,
where I saw them once,
always only yesterday in my mind.

Would that cap have fit a cousin?
That tiny infant's dress,
all by itself
in the glass case—
could it have clothed
near kin of mine?

Yes! Yes!! All gone. What
color are my Father's eyes?
Did Tante Greta laugh at jokes?
Did Grandpa collect
stamps? W H Y !?!

The sepia-toned photographs
are almost as difficult to
look at as the newsreels of
Auschwitz where Mum had been
(I think).

There's a special on TV
tonight,
"Something of Evil." I can't
watch it—group doesn't want
to. Sure. Will it be forgotten
by non-Jews who just can't
relate or see?

I don't think I could survive
going through Auschwitz—
seeing the clothes—more
photos. Why can't I just
undo what was done?

I can't bear the thoughts. I
lost one baby—to lose family
torn from each other amidst
cries and tears. Surely that
was the meaning of Hell?

There are no answers
to such questions,
only anguish that
it wasn't stopped sooner,
and a strange, secret wish
that I could have rescued them,
even before I was born,
or, yet more eerily,
that if I should now
be good enough,
or smart enough, or strong enough,
I might yet somehow
save them from their fate,
undo their deaths,
and so feel myself whole again,
a part of the human family
at long, long last.

It is as if countless souls hang
from the corners of my mouth—
frowning with the sad intensity
of one who seeks revenge
when there can be none.

Is it true, therefore,
that there can be
no peace in my soul,
no smile on my face,
no humor in my heart?

If I can no longer save them,
can I force myself to look
ahead to times of joy,
not back towards pain? . . .

The smoke hurts my eyes,
though I see it not.

My tears still fall
a generation after
the ovens were stopped. . . .
I have not, today,
the charity within myself
to forgive God.

I know he can't exist,
because if he did,
I'd have to stand in line
to strike back.

I want to undo it. Undo it all.
Go back in time. Kill Hitler
before that incredible rise to
power . . . All wishes and empty
dreams. Where would you be now
Joseph? Where would I be?
Maybe we'd be neighbors, or
friends, or lovers, or cousins,
but at the very least—we'd
be. Not these tortured souls
that stand helplessly by unable
to help our Fathers and
Mothers—to cope.

I don't know if it's okay to
look for tomorrow's rainbow
at the end of today's
hurricane. Why do I make a job
of everything? Is it because I
find nothing humorous in life at
all? How can we be happy
knowing what we know? I think
sadness is inherited.

There is no God to forgive. I'm
sure of that. Would he allow
little girls to be raped? What
was he doing during WWII—
vacationing in Florida?

Can you sue God for malpractice?

Is he insured?

What compensation would ever be enough, short of the resurrection of all my lost soul-mates and playmates never known?	None. Never.
Maybe if I'd had relatives to play with while growing up, I'd have the ability to play today, to be less somber and serious, and just be comfortable, or even fun to be with, now and then.	You are fun to be with. With your laughter and smiling eyes. One would never know the pain and turmoil.

If not today,
perhaps tomorrow.

In using this somewhat unusual treatment tool, the author wishes to acknowledge the delicate balance that can exist between potentially helpful and potentially harmful therapeutic interventions. The patient's responses can be read as illustrations of both aspects of this therapeutic dilemma.

Throughout most of her comments, the patient focused on her losses and unmet needs. Indeed, in any therapeutic intervention, the patient's needs must come first. However, her final comments demonstrate how she shifted from her own needs to her perception of the needs of the therapist. By trying to reassure the therapist, she risked replicating an inappropriate childhood caretaking role. Stiver (1990, p. 8) discussed the parentification role frequently assumed by children of Holocaust survivors, alcoholics, and incest survivors: "For those who grew up in dysfunctional families, therapy may provide their first experience of not having to worry about, to take care of, and to a large extent be responsible for the important people in their lives."

Patients who come from such backgrounds might be particularly vulnerable to fall into compliant agreement with another's wishes or what they perceive to be another's wishes. Clinicians need to be vigilant about helping them to refocus on their own goals. In this case, the author is aware that sharing his own poem could have been perceived as inappropriate. However, taking this considered risk seemed warranted, since the explicitly stated goal was to help the patient move out of a dangerously lonely state into a place of connection with her treatment team. This she was eventually able to do.

The patient's initial awareness of her shared set of predicaments with other children of survivors occurred while she was hospitalized. Her efforts to imagine what life in a concentration camp might have felt like for her parent proved to be moderately stressful on one occasion and completely unmanageable and overwhelming on another. Coming to terms with her own predicaments in the context of knowledge of her parent's trauma occurred both in clinical and nonclinical situations occurred at different times across her life span. Treatment theories still offer only limited guidance about timing and dosing the complexities of working through the intergenerational consequences of Holocaust trauma.

If the therapist worked with the above patient from the perspective of a relational psychology, rather than individual psychopathology, psychotherapy might focus on clarifying the interpersonal contexts of her traumatic histories, both second-generation Holocaust trauma and first-generation sexual abuse. Specifically, by whom and when was she heard or not heard? With whom and about what were there bigger or lesser secrets? With whom and when were there real or missed relational opportunities to validate and support the impact of her experiences on her life, as well as her basic assumptions about herself? The patient's exploration of the impact of her mother's Holocaust experiences on herself first occurred while the patient was hospitalized. Her comments suggest that, for her, it was the first time these issues were felt to be addressed, validated, heard, and taken seriously. The prior, prolonged secrecy about the mother's history likely contributed to the daughter's sense of disconnection and alienation from her family's past. Secrecy about the patient's own history of sexual abuse by the stepfather certainly amplified her sense of disconnection, in turn contributing to, and being reinforced by, her failed marriages. Any psychotherapy would need to begin with external validation of her need to understand and make sense in some fashion of what in fact happened to her, as well as to her survivor mother. This patient needs to work through the assumptions shattered by her own sexual abuse history as well as whatever empathic traumatization related to her mother's Holocaust experiences. To the extent that peer support groups are available, they are likely to be most helpful. Support and education for the patient's spouse and family would also contribute to a successful working-through process.

CONCLUSION

The traps in theories about intergenerational consequences of trauma described in this chapter reflect the fact that empathy with traumatized people is painful and that there is a human tendency to avoid such pain, even among professionals. The predicament for treaters is to find an optimal professional distance from people still struggling with pain—one that allows for validation and real support, without overwhelming the treater's own legitimate need to protect his or her own basic assumptions about life, which are often significantly different from those of traumatized patients.

For traumatized people, painful emotions need to be addressed within and between the generations. It is important to remember that such painful emotions are not necessarily evidence of psychopathology. Perpetrators' actions engender painful, paradoxical emotions in victims and those close to the victims. Professionals can understand how the resulting predicaments can be handled, how their implications for basic assumptions can be processed, and how psychological functioning can be preserved to varying degrees, without invoking the notion of psychopathology. Surviving does involve pain, but pain is not the same as pathology (Lifton, 1988). This distinction is important to first- or second-generation trauma victims. Anything that unnecessarily adds to the distance between victim and treater, including a treater's silent presumption of pathology in the victim, reinforces the victim's realistic awareness of disconnection, misunderstanding, and a sense of not being accurately heard. This can contribute to the persistence of psychological isolation and disconnection, despite efforts at treatment.

The perpetrators' behavior was traumatic for the original victim. Facts cannot be undone. Only the subjective experience of human connection and understanding can help time heal the wounds inflicted on victims and their loved ones. Treaters and researchers can help in many ways but can also inadvertently do harm, even when their approaches are basically correct, but a little bit off target. The risk of harm is greatest when theoretical constructs are used to reinforce the human tendency to avoid empathic traumatization from listening to the patient's descriptions of painful predicaments (Langer, 1991). This author's hope is that future research on traumatic effects focuses more on clearly defined aspects of "parenting," on basic assumptions, on relational therapeutic psychology, and on peer and social supports to improve understanding of the fundamental mechanisms by which trauma has intergenerational consequences and the techniques by which some deleterious consequences can be minimized.

NOTE

The author gratefully acknowledges the contributions of the following persons, who have reviewed prior drafts of this chapter: Dan Bar-On, Miriam Greenspan, George Halacsz, Sylvia Hammerman, Leston Havens, Florabel Kinsler, Robert Krell, Sandra Mondykowski, Andre Novac, Irene Stiver, and Ronnie Janoff-Bulman.

Part III

Treatment of Survivors of Violence and Abuse

9

Clinical Treatment of Survivors of Homicide Victims

MaryDale Salston

REVIEW OF THE LITERATURE

Understanding the Dynamics of Surviving a Homicide

Only within the last few years has a significant amount of literature been written about survivors of homicide victims (Amick-McMullan et al., 1989). In the United States in the late 1980s, approximately 5 million people over the age of eighteen lost a family member due to criminal homicide or alcohol-related vehicular homicide (Kilpatrick, Amick & Resnick, 1990). These survivors are secondary victims. They include loved ones, close acquaintances of the victim, and witnesses to the homicide (Alexander, 1990). Yet, not much attention has been given to the survivors of these crimes except by grass-roots organizations such as Parents of Murdered Children (POMC) and Mothers Against Drunk Driving (MADD), which proclaim the message that we are all vulnerable and need to take responsibility for change. Survivors often have faced a system that revictimizes (Carrington, 1991; Getzel & Masters, 1984; Sprang, McNeil & Wright, 1989) them through media that sensationalize, friends and acquaintances who do not know how to be supportive (Rando, 1984; Range & Niss, 1990; Range & Thompson, 1987; Sprang, McNeil & Wright, 1989), clergy who do not know how to minister to their needs effectively (Greenwood Mortuary, 1988), and clinicians who do not understand the differences between grief as a result of a homicide compared with grief as a result of a nonviolent death. The survivor of a homicide victim experiences a grief that is more complex, intense, and extensive than grief following a natural loss (Amick-McMullan et al., 1989; Bard & Connolly, 1982; Kilpatrick, Amick & Resnick, 1990; Lehman, Wortman

& Williams, 1990; Sprang, McNeil & Wright, 1989; Waigandt & Phelps, 1990). National statistics indicate 23.4 percent of family survivors develop post-traumatic stress disorder (PTSD), which translates into 1.2 million individuals (Kilpatrick, Amick & Resnick, 1990). Kathy La Tour states, "Every person grieves differently at his or her own pace, for each person in the family lost the same person and at the same time, a different person" (cited in Sprang, McNeil & Wright, 1989).

PTSD is more severe and longer-lasting when the traumatic stressor is of "human design" (APA, 1980). The inherent degree of violence in homicide is a factor in the impact of the trauma upon the individual. If that individual also witnessed the homicide, impact is further intensified, and the resolution of the trauma is further complicated (Payton & Krocker-Tuskan, 1988; Pynoos & Eth, 1984; Thompson & Kennedy, 1987). The reliving of the trauma through intrusion symptoms is higher in homicide than in other types of death of loved ones or in other victimizations, such as sexual assault (Amick-McMullan et al., 1989; Pynoos & Eth, 1984; Wilson, Smith & Johnson, 1985). The avoidance symptoms are also high (Amick-McMullan, et al., 1989; Wilson, Smith & Johnson, 1985), as are physiological reliving symptoms and symptoms of physical and emotional numbing (Goleman, 1990). Traumatic reactions of children are based upon developmental stage and age (Black & Kaplan, 1988; Payton & Krocker-Tuskan, 1988; Pynoos & Eth, 1984). When a child loses a parent to homicide, the resultant intense stress threatens the development of the child (Payton & Krocker-Tuskan, 1988; Savin, 1987). "These parental deaths are not accidental or due to natural disaster. Struggles over human accountability add considerably to the child's difficulty mastering the event" (Pynoos & Eth, 1984). To add to the tragedy, when one parent kills the other parent, the child, in essence, loses them both. The child then may resort to silence, which increases the likelihood of a pathological grief response (Black & Kaplan, 1988). Often, child witnesses continue to process the trauma and grief when they are called into court. This can enhance or impede their progress (Pynoos & Eth, 1984).

Professionals Working with Survivors of Homicide

After a homicide, survivors typically first encounter law enforcement officers, emergency responders, and medical professionals. These initial contacts are usually viewed as either positive or negative, rarely as neutral, experiences.

When initial responders who choose to become involved promptly treat the survivors with respect and sensitivity, honor reasonable needs, and willingly give appropriate information, initial retraumatization generally does not occur. For example, when loved ones are informed of a murder with little compassion, when the police morgue treats the survivors coldly, when evidence is returned with blood on it, revictimization occurs.

Police, unfortunately, are often required to follow procedures at the scene of the homicide that confuse, intimidate, and frustrate the survivor and exacerbate the survivor's stress. These initial contacts become therapeutic issues in and of themselves (Sprang, McNeil & Wright, 1989). Interaction with other criminal justice professionals also may begin at this point. Most states have victim advocates or victim/witness personnel, often connected with the prosecutor's office. Although their range of offered advocacy varies, these persons provide crisis response, appropriate referrals, court accompaniment, and processing of victim compensation. Personal attorneys in a number of states provide strong victim advocacy as well.

When there is a defendant, the survivors soon begin to interact with the judge and prosecutor. Revictimization within the criminal justice system has been prevalent. Only within the last few decades have the rights of the victims, survivors, and witnesses been acknowledged through legislation, thereby curtailing retraumatization. A survey indicated 58 percent of individuals reported satisfaction in the criminal justice system; 42 percent reported dissatisfaction. Greater symptom severity was associated with the dissatisfaction experienced (Amick-McMullan et al., 1989). Thus, the entire criminal justice process becomes a clinical issue for a survivor due to its length and the potential it holds for retraumatization.

Survivors may also have the opportunity to work with mental health professionals. Child survivors may interact with professionals within the school system, for example, school administrators, teachers, social workers, and school counselors. These contacts, especially if made within a brief period following the homicide, can be beneficial if they lay a supportive foundation and address the various crises inherent in the trauma. However, it is not uncommon for professionals to provide information that can be detrimental to healing. Professionals who lack training in the area of trauma treatment or possibly experience a discomfort with the severity of the trauma experienced often unintentionally negate the feelings, thoughts, and perceptions of the survivor.

UNDERSTANDING TRAUMA

The three-stage (impact, recoil, reorganization) crisis reaction process, adopted from Morton Bard and Sangrey (1986), is therapeutically beneficial for clients. The impact stage includes the experience of shock, denial, disorientation, and confusion. Survivors also experience intense feelings of helplessness, vulnerability, and lack of control (Bard & Sangrey, 1986; Pynoos & Eth, 1984; Thompson & Kennedy, 1987). This phase can last for hours or weeks after notification of the homicide.

During the recoil stage, the survivor experiences fear, anxiety, feelings of guilt and self-blame, depression, withdrawal, anger, and rage. This stage lasts for months to years. The term *recoil* can be used to help the survivor understand the crisis process through visual imagery. Recoiling indicates movement forward and, due to various factors, a need either to "rest for awhile" or to rebound or regress. Numerous factors trigger rebounding, including reliving symptoms, complications within the system, and additional traumatization. The recoil process needs to be normalized for clients if they eventually are to move effectively into the third stage, reorganization.

The stage of reorganization, unique to each and every individual survivor of homicide, addresses these questions: "How do I incorporate this loss into my life?" "How can I make sense of something so completely senseless?" "How can I change a world reticent to change?" "After experiencing the depth of the loss of control, how do I empower myself?" This stage lasts for months to years as a process, rather than something finalized and static. Rarely does the survivor experience the trauma of homicide as completed, resolved, or healed. Every individual must experience each stage before experiencing any sense of resolution (cited in Sprang, McNeil & Wright, 1989). Effective therapy gives the survivor the tools to move out of impact, out of recoil, and into reorganization.

Some survivors find the word *healing* difficult to use, suggesting they will "get over" this tragedy as they would a bout of the flu. Therefore, it is important to reframe the image or definition of healing for the survivor. Healing, as clients have explained it, is more analogous to life after the removal of a vital organ, for example, a lung or kidney. There is a noticeable scar; there can be limitations imposed known only to them or those close to them; there is danger if something negatively affects what is remaining in their lives; there are varying levels of pain or discomfort. Healing is an ongoing process rather than the commonly expected "Get healed and move on with your life" conceptualization.

SELF-ASSESSMENT FOR THE TRAUMA COUNSELOR

Trauma counselors must continuously self-assess and evaluate their own understanding of legal, ethical, and cross-cultural issues that directly relate to providing appropriate services. Self-assessment also includes an understanding of personal responses to trauma as a means to protect and lessen retraumatization in the client and in oneself.

Legal Issues

Knowledge of specific legal issues is partially determined by the trauma counselor's own license or the license of the supervisor. Various states handle issues of threats to do harm to self or others and confidentiality of clinical notes and written records/reports in different ways. The Tarasoff ruling in California gives responsibility to the therapist to notify not only officials of a client's intention to do harm to someone but also the person toward whom that harm is directed. In one state, for example, victim compensation claim files containing psychological evaluations became public record once the claim was closed. Organizations such as the National Victim Center and the National Organization of Victim Assistance can provide information about the rights of the victim/survivor within the legal system.

Ethical Issues

Trauma counselors may work with entire families, families whose members may have different agendas or different grieving needs. Standards of confidentiality need to be established firmly at the beginning of therapy even if the homicide is a high-profile media case. Client awareness of issues of confidentiality helps give more control.

Cross-Cultural Considerations

It is essential for trauma counselors to have a general understanding of various cultures and a specific understanding of cultural beliefs regarding death and dying (Rando, 1984; Sprang, McNeil & Wright, 1989). For example, as an American Indian family prepared for the funeral services of a young female relative who had been murdered, they gathered all her belongings and her pictures to prepare them for burning. All of them had to be burned before, or at the time of, her cremation to allow her soul to be released. Nothing could remain, or it would hold her soul to the earth. It was therefore necessary for this counselor and a law clerk to work with law enforcement to release those items gathered for evidence. Fortunately, the perpetrator had confessed, and they released her property; however, that is not always the case.

The trauma counselor needs to know or determine what is culturally comfortable in the therapy process itself in order to honor and respect the cultural and/or spiritual needs of the client. Not all cultures find value in one or two hours a week of therapy in a counselor's office; they might prefer to "do" therapy at the grave site or in court hallways. For some cultures, crisis intervention may be the only therapy a counselor may be able to provide. What some counselors may label as "avoidance" or "dysfunction," in reality, may be cultural, ethnic, and spiritual beliefs or practices.

Personal Responses to Trauma

Understanding one's own personal responses to trauma helps a counselor recognize countertransference, personal reactions, or inappropriate involvement with the client. The counselor's own personal trauma history needs to be evaluated and processed. If the counselor has not finished processing the trauma, it may be appropriate to make a referral. Trauma counselors need support systems to help them debrief their own issues and the impact of those intense emotions (Talbot, Manton & Dunn, 1992).

COUNSELING THE SURVIVOR OF HOMICIDE

First Contact

The timing of the first contact with the survivor of a homicide victim depends upon the role of the trauma counselor. The counselor may work with the survivor face-to-face, on-site as a crisis respondent; may receive a call on the crisis hot line; may be working with the survivor in the emergency room of the hospital, in the police station, or in the morgue; may see the client in an agency on a walk-in basis; may receive a call from the survivor requesting an appointment. The first contact also may occur moments to years after the homicide has oc-curred. The affect and mannerisms of the survivor at that time may reflect control, denial, hysteria, shock, bereavement, rage, anxiety, confusion, helplessness, and hopelessness. Whatever the dynamics of that first contact, the survivor of homicide needs to hear the counselor say, "I am sorry [name] was murdered" (Baker & Salston, 1989).

The role of the trauma counselor, the length of time since the occurrence of the homicide, and the traumatic response of the survivor all have an impact upon the therapeutic intervention. It is very important for that first contact to be viewed as possibly the only opportunity for intervention. This viewpoint does not place responsibility on the trauma counselor to be the one to "fix everything" or provide all the necessary information. However, it encourages the counselor to show compassion or empathy without pity, to listen without judgment, to give a measure of control when everything seems out of control, and to assess whether immediate clinical intervention is necessary for the well-being of the survivor. At this time it is also important to provide written information for the survivor, if possible, regarding referrals or necessary procedures.

Intake

The clinical intake, as a foundational tool, provides the opportunity for bonding between the counselor and survivor. For this reason, it is important, if at all possible, to have the intake completed by the intended therapist. The intake process works well within the framework of "structured flexibility." The struc-ture allows the counselor to accomplish the task necessary for proper assessment. The flexibility allows the survivor to have a realistic sense of control. An effective intake model contains four parts: introduction, telling the story, assessment, and education.

Introduction

In the introduction counselors introduce themselves, explain their degree, licensure, certification, and professional experience in the field of trauma coun-seling, and, if applicable, discuss the procedural and business aspects of ongoing therapy. Clients are told that the purpose of the intake is mutual assessment (for them to assess whether they feel comfortable working with the counselor and for the counselor to assess how best to be of help to them). Many times a survivor will ask if the counselor is a survivor of a homicide. If so, it may be beneficial to self-disclose. Some loved ones of homicide victims prefer to work with a survivor. If the counselor is not a survivor but has experienced a traumatic event, he or she may want to consider disclosing this information in a generalized manner. During the introduction it is also important to address the client's questions and purpose and intent for seeking services.

Telling the Story

Once the introduction is completed, clients are encouraged to share their story of what occurred without being questioned or without being stopped because it was too horrifying to hear and without taking notes; survivors need personal contact at this time. A Rogerian style (Rogers, 1951), showing empathy, positive regard, and genuineness, is appropriate. Active listening is used only to clarify points or to help the client refocus. Clients need to be allowed to feel the feelings, to weep, to scream out in anger, to ask rhetorical questions, to laugh with a tender memory, and to be silent, unless it is clear that clients are using the silence to avoid or repress the emotions. The setting is a safe place to be who they are and to express what they think and feel.

If the counselor is working with two or more family members of the victim at the same time, each telling of the story will obviously be different. The counselor may want to "open it up" and observe who starts the story and how family members build on the story together. This interaction gives an opportunity to observe the dynamics of the family systems. As long as there is respect for each other's feelings and story-telling process, this telling can be a healthy family interaction. If criticism, correcting, or the desire of one to take control begins, then it is important for the therapist to take control and guide the relating of the story, giving everyone the opportunity to share (Harris, 1991). After the story has been told, each person is given a chance to share what he or she is feeling at the moment. The counselor also shares what he or she has heard them say, even if it is something they have indirectly said. Beginning to normalize and validate their feelings and their thoughts is essential. If homicidal or suicidal thoughts are expressed, the counselor must assess the need for possible follow-through of verbal contracts, hospitalization, and/or police action. Again, normalizing and validating thoughts and feelings, as well as clarifying the consequences, are important.

When the initial intake has been with several family members, or if the sharing of the story of the trauma has been lengthy, closure to the first session can now occur. The final portion of the intake is most effective with only one or two people in the session. If there are two people, they need to feel safe with each other and be supportive of one another.

Assessment

Assessment occurs throughout the intake process. The counselor assesses the mental and physical well-being, coping mechanisms in action, emotional stability of the client, and the patterns of thought processes used. At this point a more formalized interview process begins, using the Trauma Intake Assessment (Figure 9.1). Symptom patterns and their frequency are documented by the client's self-report. The nature or definition of each symptom is explained briefly to the client,

Figure 9.1
Trauma Intake Assessment

Symptom	3+/wk Freq.	1-2/wk Occasional	Less/1/wk Seldom	No incr. Never	Remarks
Client Name _____ Trauma _____					
Assessment Date _____ Trauma Date ____					
• Intrusive thoughts/images					
• Recurring dreams/nightmares					
• Flashbacks					
• Intense Psych. distress-sim. events					
Anxiety attacks					
Tearfulness/crying spells					
Feelings of shame/embarrassment					
Guilt feelings ("If only..")					
• Avoid thoughts/feelings of trauma					
• Avoid activities that remind					
• Can't recall specific events/trauma					
• Depression/diminished interest					
• Feel detached/estranged					
• Restricted range of affect					
• Sense of foreshortened future					
Withdrawal					
Fear					
Job difficulties					
Sexual Dysfunction					
Numbness- emotional/physical					
Helplessness/Loss of control					
Disorientation/Confusion					
• Sleep disturbances					
• Anger/rage					
• Difficulty concentrating					
• Hypervigilance					
• High startle response					
• Physiologic reactivity to reminders					
Headaches					
Muscle tension					
Nausea					
Eating disturbances					
Difficulty breathing					
Cold sweat					
Alcohol usage					
Drug usage					
Suicidal ideations					

Presently taking medication? YES ☐ NO ☐ Describe: _____

Doctor prescribing medication _____ Phone _____

* Use DSM-III-R for Assessment
*** To be used for assessment only
© 1992

** Compiled by MaryDale Salston, M.S., MFCC, CTC, 1987 (Revised 1992)
2870 4th Ave., Suite 200, San Diego, CA 92103
(619) 260-0977

in order to use common definitions. This process usually opens up the opportunity to discuss those emotional, mental, or physiological responses that the client may not even realize could be associated with the trauma of the murder. Many times the client feels more "normal" after completing the checklist. Going through the assessment, reviewing it with the counselor, and having the counselor normalize and validate the responses help the survivor to believe he or she is responding within the normal range and is not "crazy."

The assessment evaluates needs for medication, testing, and evaluation, as well as the existence of self-medication. Referrals must be made to persons trained in these areas of trauma treatment. Proper diagnosis, medication if necessary, and maintenance of that medication are essential to effective therapy. Client responses that fall outside the normal range need to be addressed through testing and diagnostic and medical evaluations. Inpatient treatment or a substance abuse treatment program may be indicated.

The frequency and severity of the survivor's symptoms are exacerbated by any combination of several major factors assessed during intake (Salston, 1992). These include the history of past trauma; the existence of a known perpetrator; the absence of a support system (Figley, 1986); mental and/or emotional instability at the time of victimization (Amick-McMullan et al., 1988); the degree of violence and fear of safety; prolonged length of time in the criminal justice system (Sprang, McNeil & Wright, 1989); and ineffective coping skills in spiritual, cognitive, behavioral, cultural, or ethnic areas.

The counselor uses an interview format to obtain the trauma history. Information concerning these factors is usually given automatically through the telling of the story and the processing of the symptom checklist. Some of the factors (e.g., whether or not the client knows the perpetrator or has a strong support system—Figley, 1983, 1986; Harris, 1991—or the time length of the process) may not have answers at the time of the intake but will be addressed over time in order to help the client understand symptom patterns, frequency, and intensity.

Education

The final aspect of the intake is education. The amount of time given to this fourth phase is dependent upon the emotional and mental well-being and specific needs of the client, the length of time since the occurrence of the homicide, and whether the client has received previous therapy in regard to this trauma or another trauma. Education about trauma and PTSD, to reiterate, normalizes and validates the client's responses. Contracts responding to suicidal or homicidal ideations need to be repeated. The counselor also explains the resources and procedures available, gives appropriate written information regarding trauma and homicide, and provides the opportunity to choose whether or not a client wants further appointments.

DEVELOPING A TREATMENT PLAN

The direction of ongoing counseling depends upon the expectations and needs expressed by the survivor, the availability of resources, and the scope of services the counselor is able to provide. Five distinct types of counseling, based upon the amount of time to be spent, are available: crisis counseling and advocacy, short-term therapy, long-term therapy, group counseling, and inpatient therapy (described in detail in Chapters 30 and 31).

Crisis Counseling and Advocacy

The counseling process of crisis resolution and victim advocacy is often chosen because of cultural, spiritual, and ethnic beliefs. In other cases a choice of crisis resolution may be indicative of the availability of a strong support system and/ or good coping skills. In other circumstances this type of counseling is not the optimum choice but is utilized because of the lack of clinical or financial resources or because the survivor is operating in various forms of denial. When the crisis breaks through denial, the survivor seeks help.

The primary goals of crisis counseling are to help facilitate the stabilization of symptoms and behaviors, to reassess symptomatology, coping skills, and suicidal and homicidal ideations, and to reassess the need for intervention from other resources. Information gained helps the survivor bring some resolution to the crisis.

In the field of trauma counseling, advocacy can be defined as any intervention with any part of the system on behalf of the client. At times a survivor needs direction, help in problem solving, or the added voice of a professional to achieve a desired goal. A counselor must make a decision as to the degree of advocacy he or she can provide based on the existing resources available. Providing information about those resources is a primary level of advocacy. At more involved levels, advocacy includes either personal interaction or communication with any, or all, of the following: police, district attorney, victim agencies, community or state aid programs, victim compensation programs, advocates of victim rights, medical personnel, schools, employers, courts, probation officers, prisons, parole boards, and others. Any degree of advocacy is therapeutically beneficial to the survivor, as long as the client learns that options are available and then requests the help. Advocacy is an important part of short-term, long-term, group, and inpatient therapy.

Short-Term Therapy

Clients frequently choose short-term therapy because of cultural and ethnic beliefs and values or the lack of financial or clinical resources. Other clients state that their feelings are too intense to deal with, and therefore they need to retreat into some aspect of denial. The counselor, in some cases, needs to encourage the client to stay in treatment long enough to learn some effective coping skills.

Foundations of short-term therapy are cognitive and behavioral models of counseling with a minimum of twelve to twenty sessions. As previously indicated, clients in the impact phase respond best to the use of a more Rogerian style. Telling the story, or parts of it, many times helps them to move out of shock and denial.

Clients who have either essentially moved through the impact phase or remained in counseling to increase their coping skills need to learn symptom management. The mutually developed treatment plan for short-term therapy is based upon the frequency and severity of the individual reliving, avoidant, and arousal symptoms. The fifteen most common types of behavioral and cognitive techniques used to manage the symptoms are addressed next.

Symptom Management Techniques

Anger management. Survivors commonly project the anger and rage onto people who are close to them, people within the system, the system itself, or the perpetrator. Examples of healthy ways to release the anger include exercise, playing sports, practicing learned self-defense, finding a safe place to scream or cry, journaling, hitting a pillow, hitting the bed with a tennis racket, hitting a punching bag, and hitting an open phone book with a rubber hose.

Breathing. When emotions are intense, persons begin to breathe in a shallow manner. The counselor can teach clients to take a "cleansing breath" when feeling anxious, out of control, angry, fearful, and/or tearful. A cleansing breath is a deep breath taken from the diaphragm, breathing in through the nose, and then blowing out slowly through the mouth. This one breath or breathing pattern releases tension.

Contracts to modify suicidal-homicidal ideations. If clients have any ideations or plans to hurt themselves or others and there is no need for medical or legal intervention, the use of a contract is essential. The contract exposes the thoughts of the survivor, commits to a plan to circumvent acting out the ideation, and makes the client accountable to talk with the counselor if the desire feels out of control. After each episode, a new contract is developed. Contracts are reviewed frequently.

Dream preparation. When clients have reoccurring, disturbing dreams, they learn to follow a cognitive procedure before going to sleep. They first need to acknowledge they may dream the dream. At this point, when the dream occurs, they need to talk through the dream, remembering to breathe and rewrite the end of a dream that replays the reality of the homicide by updating. An example of updating would be adding an ending of "And now he's with me in my thoughts" or "Now he's with God" to the present ending of "And he died there all alone." All other reoccurring dreams need to be rewritten through taking control (see nightmare control). After talking through the dream and the new ending, clients then do relaxation exercises and go to sleep.

Hyperventilation control. When breathing becomes very rapid and shallow, hyperventilation may occur. Clients are taught to open a small, lunch-sized paper bag, gather the top of the bag together around the mouth, and breathe into it from two to five minutes, depending upon the level of anxiety.

Imagery. Imagery can be used in conjunction with relaxation exercises or when clients feel out of control. One technique is to visualize a safe place. While in a state of relaxation, the counselor slowly guides clients in the development of a safe place, a place from their own reality or fantasy, in nature or made with human hands, or any combination of the above. Clients experience it with each sense. They need to see it, hear it, touch it, smell it, taste it. Clients decide where it is and what it looks like and may keep it private, unless they offer to share it with the counselor. The place belongs to clients; no one else knows where it is or how to get there. If clients want to have anyone else there, the visitor has to leave upon request. Clients need to practice relaxation and go to the safe place at least once a day, depending upon the level of anxiety. Eventually, they will be able to get to the safe place in seconds and with their eyes open.

While in the state of relaxation, after having arrived at the safe place, clients are guided to a "special room." The room is only ten steps away, counted slowly to allow the transition. Clients create this special room as they did the safe place. The client and counselor together can develop imagery in the room to help lessen symptoms. For example, if clients feel out of control, they place a control switch on the wall at the height requiring only a slight reach. While clients cannot control people or circumstances around themselves, they can take control of their responses. When they feel out of control due to anger, fear, panic, helplessness, and so on, they can decide to take control and switch it from red (out of control) to black (in control). If clients feel out of control, they can take a cleansing breath and visualize entering their special room and checking out the switch. Clients who are depressed and self-condemning can be guided to look in the mirror and see the reality of who they are. Imagery can be helpful for termination. Clients can learn to visualize a special toolbox that contains the tools (coping skills) they need to help them survive. The therapist encourages clients to "carry the toolbox" and practice these skills.

Journal writing/letter writing. Writing gives an opportunity to release intense or overwhelming emotions of depression, anger/rage, fear, confusion, sadness, and so on. Writing about feelings can break down the blocks and barriers. Journaling has no specific format, no need for complete sentences, no chronology, no rules. Letter writing allows for expression of thoughts and feelings when there is no opportunity to say them in reality. Letters are frequently never mailed. They may be to the victim, to the perpetrator, or to the system.

Nightmare control. Clients are instructed to keep a pad and pen by the bed at all times. When a nightmare occurs, the client writes it down, in detail, before getting out of bed. Then the client rewrites the ending, taking power and control, in a realistic manner.

Positive affirmations. When clients experience feelings and cognitions of depression, shame, disorientation, and confusion, they will usually begin to berate themselves. Berating compounds the responses. The counselor can guide clients to write down rational and truthful statements. Instead of "I'm stupid" or "I'm worthless," the client begins to repeat, "I am capable" or "I have value and worth."

Relaxation. Many effective forms of muscle relaxation can be practiced at home or in the office to reduce anxiety. Relaxing before going to sleep allows the body to release tension and can combine with visual imagery, for example, the safe place or special room.

Safety check for hypervigilance, high startle response, fear. Clients often obsess about the need to check locks on windows and doors and check in closets and under beds. The horror they have experienced requires that they feel safe. Counselors can give them permission to check their safety wherever and whenever they need to do so, normalizing and validating the need, encouraging them to do what they need to do to take care of themselves. Normally, the behaviors begin to diminish soon after. Reliving experiences may exacerbate the anxiety, however. If the behavior becomes phobic, systematic desensitization can be effective (Wolpe, 1969).

Self-dialogue. Self-dialogue is a cognitive restructuring process that allows the client to change maladaptive thought processes into appropriate or rational thought processes. The counselor trains the client to be aware of maladaptive self-statements while modeling appropriate self-statements (Meichenbaum, 1977). The client practices and performs these new self-statements when flashbacks occur. When a client experiences an extensive flashback, self-dialogue is less effective. Once the flashback has occurred, the client determines if the response is appropriate self-dialogue for a fear-based or helplessness-based flashback. The self-dialogue always needs to be simple and truthful. For example, when afraid, the client repeats, "This is now, not then; I am safe." If he or she experiences helplessness, an appropriate statement could be, "This is now, not then; I did everything I could do." Repetition of the self-dialogue helps diminish the intensity of the feelings.

Sleep disturbance (Baker, 1992). Survivors who have trouble going to sleep or staying asleep are told to develop a rank-ordered list of the ten things they hate most to do within their homes, with number one being the most hated chore. If they have family or roommates, they need to choose quiet chores. This list may include ironing, cleaning the grout on the bathroom tiles, polishing the silver, organizing drawers. Clients also need to develop a consistent, relaxing routine of thirty to sixty minutes before going to bed, which may include listening to soft music, reading, taking a bubble bath, or drinking decaffeinated herbal tea. If the clients are not asleep in thirty minutes, they get up and work on the number one chore for thirty minutes. After that, they go back to bed, do the relaxation exercise, and, if not asleep within twenty minutes, get up and do number two on the list. If necessary, the next night the process begins again from the top of the list. This technique is based upon negative reinforcement, not the generally used positive reinforcement of watching television, reading, or doing something pleasurable, which helps to maintain the disruptive sleep patterns. The old patterns need to be broken.

Thought stopping. Intrusive thoughts and images are usually disruptive and overwhelming and therefore need to be stopped. Various "thought-stopping" techniques recognize that the brain literally cannot be thinking of two things at the same time. In one technique, clients wear a rubber band on the wrist. When the intrusive thought or image occurs, clients either mentally or verbally say, "Stop!" while snapping the rubber band to create a physical sensation. If clients have a history of self-mutilation or have attempted suicide by cutting the wrists, they can use the hand-clapping technique by clapping hard enough to create a physical sensation. They have substituted the physical sensation, focusing on where that sensation is located, how it has "traveled," and what it feels like for the thoughts. Clients then give themselves permission either not to continue thinking about the issues or to think about them for five minutes only. Some clients will not be able to think about the issue for five minutes; for others, if the intrusive thoughts and images remain after five minutes, they will again need to snap the band or clap their hands, focus on the sensation, and give permission to think about the issue for two minutes, and another two minutes, if necessary. The whole procedure takes only ten minutes and puts clients in control. If the thoughts and images still remain, clients need to talk about them or do a relaxation exercise.

Trigger preparation. There can be both "intense psychological reactivity" and "physiologic reactivity upon exposure to events that symbolize or resemble an aspect of the traumatic event" (APA, 1987, p. 250). These events, such as similar reenactments on the news or in the movies, dates such as the anniversary date of the murder or birthdays, locations that hold significance, holidays, sensory experiences, and others, may trigger psychological, emotional, behavioral, or physiological responses that feel intense or overwhelming. Clients need to learn to identify the possible events before they occur and verbalize how they might respond to those events. Helping clients develop a plan of action to try to diminish the response or control the response can include any of the previously named coping skills. Other cognitive and behavioral techniques found to be of value include systematic desensitization (Bowen & Lambert, 1986), role-playing, and cognitive restructuring/reframing.

Long-Term Therapy

In many instances homicide trials or series of trials take four to five years, even when the perpetrator was arrested within the first month after the murder. Some cases never come to trial if a perpetrator is not identified or if the evidence is insufficient to convict. In others, plea bargaining allows for the early release of the perpetrators. A majority of families counseled by this author found themselves, ironically, going to trial after the first- or second-year anniversary of the murder. The impact of this long and emotionally and psychologically draining process is an important reason for long-term therapy.

Long-term counseling/therapy combines crisis counseling, advocacy, and all the aspects of short-term therapy. It allows clients time to process at their own rate. It does not have to be as therapist-directed; clients can also set the agenda. Long-term work gives clients time to process the grieving, address the confusion and guilt feelings, identify and effectively express the anger, and move through every anniversary date and holiday with the support of professionals.

Esoteric questions such as, "Why did this happen?"—questions that will never be answered—can be expressed and brought to some form of resolution. Over time, clients repeatedly hear that the guilt belongs to the perpetrator alone. While guilt feelings may never be extinguished, survivors may develop skills of cognitive restructuring to allow them to hear their own self-blaming messages, recognize inaccurate thoughts and feelings, and then restate the truth. In some instances, guilt has a factual basis. For example, if a client encouraged a friend to put himself or herself in a place of risk in regard to a drug or gang activity and the murder occurred at that time, the survivor may feel to blame. It is important to help that survivor accept responsibility only for encouraging the friend to participate. The victim made the choice to participate, and the perpetrator is still responsible for the murder.

Additional Clinical Styles and Techniques

Conjoint therapy (therapy with couples), family therapy, Gestalt therapy (Perls, 1973), hypnosis, and the use of symbolism are also important in trauma work. Conjoint and family therapy work well when combining pure education, structural family therapy (Minuchin, 1974), and a family systems approach (Bowen, 1978; Williams & Williams, 1987). Working with the family system helps the therapist to see the style of interaction as well as spoken and unspoken expectations. This approach also helps, for example, to identify the needs of the siblings of a murder victim, who are often expected to be supportive to their parents. It is not uncommon for family, friends, and society as a whole to minimize the impact homicide has upon the brother or sister of a homicide victim (National Organization for Victim Assistance, 1985). For this reason, it is essential to address these issues in family therapy, as well as individual therapy. The structural approach looks at issues of enmeshment and disengagement, which often affect how family members let others grieve and reorganize.

Gestalt therapy has several valuable methods to deal with feelings such as guilt, anger, and sadness (Perls, 1973). The use of ''the chair'' technique, in which the client dialogues with a visualized person seated in a chair, helps clients to express emotions and communicate important messages. Putting the victim in the chair allows the victim to ''hear'' what had been unsaid or unfinished, as well as a final ''good-bye.'' Clients can also put the ''perpetrator'' in the chair and say what they need to say without limitations. Clients can use the ''two-chair technique'' and put that part of themselves in the chair that will not let them feel and express the emotions.

Survivors or witnesses may also have blocked portions of memories that they need to clarify. Under the instruction and guidance of a trained hypnotherapist, clients may be able to break through psychic amnesia.

Personal symbolism allows a survivor to express thoughts or feelings, to honor the murder victim, or to make a statement. Symbolic acts include releasing balloons containing a message, throwing a flower onto the water, giving a gift to a needy child in the loved one's name, and lighting a candle at a victim rights rally. These acts may or may not become yearly remembrances and are healthy as long as they are not obsessively done.

The client also needs to explore, address, and process spiritual thoughts, feelings, and reactions. The issues of death, dying, pain, suffering, justice, and eternity often evoke spiritual questions. Being impacted by murder may cause the client to embrace or challenge the teachings of youth and seek clarification or more definitive answers. Feelings of anger, rage, and betrayal often need to be processed, as do spiritually oriented dreams and visions. If the counselor recognizes that he or she is not the appropriate one to address these issues, it is important to seek a pastoral counselor trained in trauma treatment to work with the client on issues of spiritual resolution.

When the survivor begins to take what has been learned in counseling and apply it to everyday life, he or she begins to experience empowerment and moves forward into reorganization, thereby often affecting changes in other individuals and systems. Closure begins when the survivor reaches this stage of healing. When therapy ends, counselor and client say good-bye and share those thoughts and feelings associated with the ending of a relationship—something the client generally did not get to do with his or her loved one.

Group Therapy

Effective therapy with survivors of trauma also takes place within a group setting. The author has found homicide groups to be most effective when co-facilitated. This allows for each counselor to process his or her own feelings, if necessary, to model mutual interaction and support, to allow for mutual debriefing between therapists, and to give different insights.

Some clients may desire to be a part of a peer support group, such as Parents of Murdered Children or Compassionate Friends. These groups are open and are not facilitated by counselors.

Decisions need to be made regarding whether the group is open or closed, has a determinate or indeterminate length of time to meet, and is structured or unstructured. These decisions are based upon the needs of the clients and available community resources. An open group allows for the ''older'' group members to model normalization and validation of thoughts and feelings to new arrivals. These older group members also model a movement forward through the stages of response to trauma. Open groups allow new members to enter when ready to do so, rather than waiting for cycle completion. An indeterminate length of time to meet allows for continual support over time. It also allows people to give themselves permission to leave the group, recognizing this when needed.

A loosely structured system allows for the therapists to guide the group through certain issues and processes, as well as for the group to set agendas. Structured aspects include everyone's telling his or her own story; therapists' teaching behavioral techniques and practices to aid in reinforcement; clients' sharing their loved one through pictures, mementos, and stories and sharing personal experiences with the legal system; exploring specific emotions and reactions; and clients' sharing ways in which they personally experienced empowerment. However, any structured part could be set aside when necessary to meet specific needs.

It is important that the client have at least some individual therapy first (Williams, 1987a) to work through the horror. Telling one's story is essential in the group; however, the group members first must need to be comfortable with possible reactions before sharing with others. Many survivors recognize that their thoughts, feelings, and reactions are not "crazy" only when they hear the same or similar responses from other survivors.

Revenge fantasies are normal for a survivor, yet that survivor often views them as horrible or disgusting. Taking time to explore revenge fantasies in group can open the door to anger, rage, sadness, and loss, as well as humor and laughter, when survivors hear the elaborate fantasies of others.

Older group members may give new survivors knowledge of what lies ahead. On a weekend retreat, the group that this author cofacilitated developed an informative and sensitive brochure for survivors, which was later distributed by local law enforcement officers. Group members also may go to court, press conferences, victim rights rallies, and other important or difficult events with each other. They bond with each other through their pain, through their growth, and through their group hugs.

CONCLUSION

Survivors of a homicide are often committed to working through the pain of their loved one's murder. They do not want to be stuck in that pain.

Through a combination of empathy, advocacy, and guidance toward the reality of empowerment, healing begins and progresses. As a trauma counselor, it is rewarding and humbling to be a part of that process.

The trauma counselor also needs to be empowered to effect change and to be willing to challenge the system to change those processes that retraumatize the survivor. Through this process, the trauma counselor is able to be a voice for those who will never be heard—the countless victims.

NOTE

This chapter is dedicated to those survivors of homicide victims with whom I have worked over the years. Through their courage I have learned and am able to share.

10

Post-Traumatic Therapy with Domestic Violence Survivors

Mary Ann Dutton

The experience of trauma resulting from domestic violence has only begun to be recognized among mental health professionals. Figley (1985) defined the conscious and unconscious actions and emotions related to dealing with stressors or the memory of stressors of a catastrophe as traumatic and post-traumatic stress reactions, respectively. This chapter describes domestic violence as a traumatic stressor, reviews the traumatic effects of domestic violence, presents a model for guiding the assessment of trauma among battered women, and discusses post-traumatic interventions with this population.

UNDERSTANDING DOMESTIC VIOLENCE

Domestic Violence as a Trauma

The DSM-IV Task Force has proposed three options for the revised diagnostic criteria to be released in 1995 (APA Task Force, 1991). The first requires that the person "has experienced, witnessed, or been confronted with an event or events that involve actual or threatened death or injury, or a threat to the physical integrity of oneself or others" (p. H:16). The second option includes the one just described but requires a second criterion: "The person's response involved intense fear, helplessness, or horror" (p. H:17). The third option, "exposure to an exceptional mental or physical stressor, either brief or prolonged" (p. H:17), is closest to the DSM III-R definition.

The first option seems most suitable for adequately taking into account domestic violence as a stressor. Requiring evidence of "fear, helplessness, or horror,'' as illustrated in the second option, may exclude those battered women whose coping style is to deny or minimize their reaction, especially while remaining in an actively abusive situation. Likewise, the third definitional option is unsuitable since, statistically speaking, domestic violence is not an "exceptional" event; it occurs all too often to be so defined. Further, option three fails to adequately define the qualitative criteria for determining a stressor as "exceptional," thus leaving it open to the judgment (and bias) of the clinician.

Typically, domestic violence is a stressor that, once established, has no clearly defined beginning and ending points. An abusive relationship can be characterized as a "state of siege" (Sue Ostoff, personal communication, 1991) in which discrete battering episodes occur as intermittent events within a cycle of violence (Walker, 1979). The most severe battering episodes may function as the extreme points on the continuum: the acute battering phase. Other less severe abusive (e.g., push, shove), as well as seemingly insignificant, behaviors (e.g., a look or tone of voice, change in pattern of behavior) may be experienced as stressors in their own right and represent the tension-building phase. The ability of these behaviors to evoke what may appear to be an uncharacteristically high level of stress can be explained theoretically by psychological principles of second-order conditioning and stimulus generalization. The "state of siege" may be briefly interrupted by the contrite, loving stage of the cycle of violence; alternatively, this phase may be characterized simply by the relative absence of abusive behavior. Thus, by contrast this period is the time when the battered woman likely perceives the most hope. In short, many of the batterer's abusive behaviors may function as traumatic stressors once the dynamic of power and control has been established within the abusive relationship.

Traumatic stressors within battering relationships can be defined by four categories: physical, sexual, and psychological abuse and abuse to property and pets (Ganley, 1981, 1989). Further, domestic violence has been described as analogous to the torture of hostages where (1) the abuser threatens to kill the battered woman and is perceived to be capable of doing so, (2) escape is not possible, (3) the battered woman is isolated from potential help sources, and (4) she perceives some degree of kindness from the abuser (Graham, Rawlings & Rimini, 1988; Scrignar, 1988).

Physical abuse refers to any behavior that involves the intentional use of force against the body of another person in such a way that there is a risk of physical injury, harm, or pain, regardless of whether the behavior actually results in such (Dutton, 1992a). Examples include slapping, pushing, hitting, punching, kicking, choking, forcefully holding or restraining, using an object to hit, twisting an arm, requiring to ingest an unwanted substance, and use of a weapon.

Sexual abuse is defined as any unwanted sexual intimacy forced on one person by another (Brownmiller, 1975) and may include oral, anal, or vaginal stimulation or penetration, forced nudity, forced exposure to sexually explicit material or activity, or any other unwanted sexually explicit activity. Compliance with unwanted sexual activity may be obtained through actual or threatened physical force or through various forms of coercion (Finkelhor & Yllo, 1983). Within an ongoing abusive relationship, sexual coercion can appear quite subtle while, in fact, exerting a powerful effect on its victim. Based on past experience with her partner, the battered woman may be able to read the specific cues to danger in her partner's behavior and understand their implicit meaning even when it is not apparent to others who are less intimately familiar with his pattern of behavior.

Psychological abuse has been operationally defined by various methods. Tolman (1989) empirically derived a two-factor model of psychological abuse: dominance-isolation and emotional-verbal abuse. Pence and Paymar (1986) described psychological abuse using the Power and Control Wheel within eight categories: isolation, emotional abuse, economic abuse, using children, using male privilege, coercion and threats, intimidation, and minimizing or denying the abuse. An extensive listing of specific examples of psychological (as well as physical and sexual) abuse is found in the Abusive Behavior Observation Checklist (ABOC) (Dutton, 1992a), which is useful either as an interview or as a self-administered assessment tool.

Abuse within intimate relationships is not an event; it is an ongoing process within which there may be identifiable episodes of relatively discrete events. The unique configuration of physical, sexual, and psychological abuse within battering relationships can vary widely. Nonetheless, this abuse clearly meets the criterion of "markedly distressing to almost anyone" (APA, 1987, p. 146); it is outside the range of what is typically considered and should be expected to be "usual human experience" (APA, 1987, p. 146).

Physical and sexual abuse is a relatively common occurrence in intimate relationships. National surveys suggest that 28 percent of marital couples report at least one violent episode during the course of their marriage (Straus, Gelles & Steinmetz, 1980), and 16 percent report an occurrence within the preceding year (Straus & Gelles, 1990). Women who are battered are also sexually abused at high rates by their abusive partners (Shields, Resick & Hanneke, 1990; Walker, 1984). Finally, women are more likely to be killed by an intimate partner than by anyone else (Browne & Williams, 1989). Thus, it must be concluded that abuse toward women by their intimate male partners is a common occurrence in our society.

Post-Traumatic Effects of Battering on Victims/Survivors

The psychological effects resulting from exposure to battering and abuse within intimate relationships can be described as post-traumatic stress reactions, including, although not limited to, those that fit within the post-traumatic stress disorder (PTSD) diagnostic category: (1) indicators of psychological distress or dysfunction, (2) shifts in cognitive schemas, and (3) relational or interpersonal difficulties (Dutton, 1992a).

Post-traumatic stress responses of psychological distress and dysfunction include (1) both intrusion and avoidance symptoms of PTSD (Dutton et al., 1990), (2) indicators of autonomic arousal, including anxiety (Rosal, Dutton-Douglas & Perrin, 1990; Trimpey, 1989), agoraphobic symptoms (Saunders et al., 1990), sleep difficulties, hypervigilance, and increased physiological reactivity, (3) affective responses to trauma, including depression and grief (Campbell, 1986), shame, rage and anger, fear, betrayal or hurt, (4) dissociation; (5) somatic complaints (Jaffee et al., 1986); (6) self-injurious behaviors, including suicidal ideation and efforts; (7) addictive use of alcohol, drugs, food, or other substances and behaviors (Stark et al., 1981); and (8) impaired functioning in various roles, including parenting, occupational, and social.

Shifts in cognitive schemas resulting from exposure to abuse include attributions, perceptions, expectations, beliefs, attitudes, and other cognitive responses that are shaped by the traumatic experience itself (Blackman, 1989; Foa, Steketee & Olasov-Rothbaum, 1989; Janoff-Bulman & Frieze, 1983; McCann, Sakheim & Abrahamson, 1988). Particularly relevant cognitions for understanding battered women's response to battering include (1) attribution of blame for the occurrence of abuse, (2) development of fear structures or loss of assumption of invulnerability/safety, (3) expectations regarding continued abuse, (4) perception of futility or diminished alternatives regarding available options for safety, (5) self-evaluation, (6) perception of some degree of tolerance of the abuse, and (7) tolerance of the cognitive inconsistency of abuse within an intimate relationship. While all of these cognitive shifts are understandable within an abusive context, distinguishing what may be a realistic appraisal of the situation (e.g., assumption of continued danger) from cognitive distortions (e.g., self-blame for abuse) is critical.

Relational or interpersonal difficulties resulting from exposure to the trauma of battering and abuse refer primarily to the battered woman's reduced ability to trust or to set boundaries and limits (e.g., having personal space, use of own time) within nonabusive relationships (e.g., with nonabusive intimate partners, friends, employers). Expecting trust within an abusive relationship is unwarranted; rebuilding trust within a formerly abusive relationship requires time and healing experience. Separately, processes of traumatic bonding (Dutton & Painter, 1981; Graham et al., 1988) that result from abuse within the relationship may eventuate in an emotional dependency and attachment to the abuser. This stronger connection with the batterer further entraps the battered woman in the abusive relationship, even when the lack of tangible resources or social support does not do so.

Assessment of Post-Traumatic Effects of Battering

Assessment of the broadly defined post-traumatic effects of exposure to battering and abuse within an intimate relationship is based on a conceptual model presented in Dutton (1992a). In addition to specific post-traumatic effects of abuse, the model identifies four additional areas of assessment: (1) the nature and extent of exposure to violence and abuse, (2) the battered woman's strategies to avoid and escape the violence and abuse and their outcomes, (3) the social, political, and economic context of the battered woman's life (e.g., an analysis of her socioeconomic status, ethnic identity, race, age, sexual preference, able-bodiedness within the dominant social structure), and (4) mediating factors, including the battered woman's tangible resources and social supports available to her, her personal strengths and inner resources, additional stressors in her life independent of the abuse, the institutional response to the violence (e.g., police response to calls, professionals' responses to prior seeking of help), her positive (e.g., "He's a good father," "He is not an alcoholic like my father," "He is kind and gentle when he isn't being abusive") and negative (e.g., "He has affairs," "He's never willing to take responsibility for the children") appraisal of her partner and relationship, and factors that may increase her vulnerability (e.g., prior childhood abuse, prior rape, dysfunctional family of origin, physical disability or illness). Further discussion of assessment in these areas can be found in Dutton (1992a, 1992b).

POST-TRAUMATIC THERAPY WITH BATTERED WOMEN

Philosophy

Overall, intervention with battered women requires attention to three primary goals: protection, problem solving or choice making, and healing the post-traumatic effects of victimization (Dutton, 1992a). The emphasis of this chapter is on the component of intervention that focuses on post-traumatic therapy: healing the psychological trauma of victimization. However, a primary focus on healing the psychological trauma of abuse can occur only after sufficient attention has been given to issues of safety and protection. Interventions to increase empowerment (e.g., decision making or choice making) may overlap both of the other two intervention components. Discussion of interventions aimed at both protection and choice making may be found elsewhere (Dutton, 1992a).

Battered women, as is the case with other abuse victims, incur injury at all levels: physical, mental, emotional, and spiritual. Healing from the psychological trauma of battering and abuse involves symptom reduction or removal, cognitive change, skill development, integration of emotions and their sequelae, and building new relationships. In order to facilitate a battered woman's process of healing, a philosophical perspective to frame the therapeutic work is necessary. Guidelines for that perspective include the following (Courtois, 1988b; Dutton, 1992b; Schechter, 1987; Wilson, 1989d):

1. All interventions should be used in a manner that empowers the formerly battered woman; interventions that cannot should be avoided.
2. Genuine nonjudgmental acceptance and validation of the formerly battered woman and her experience are required by the therapist.

Figure 10.1
Social, Political, Cultural, Economic Context

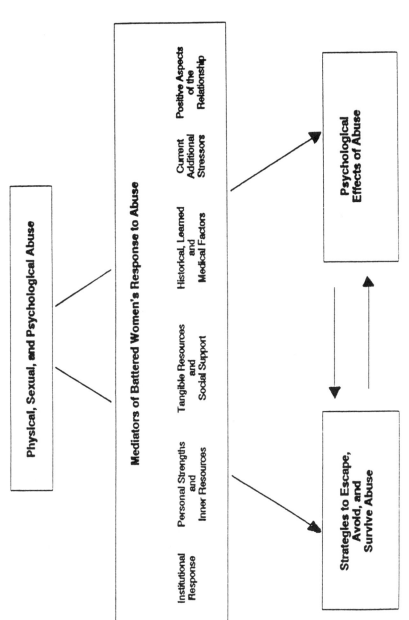

Source: Mary Ann Dutton, *Empowering and Healing the Battered Woman.* ©1992. Springer Publishing Company, Inc., New York, N.Y. 10012. Used by permission.

3. Providing immediate support and alliance to the formerly battered woman is a priority.

4. Advocating for the battered woman's safety and helping her to build options are essential.

5. The therapist's willingness to experience the battered woman's recounting and sequelae of her trauma is necessary.

6. The therapist begins with a working assumption that the indicators of distress may reflect post-traumatic stress responses, that is, that they are caused by the traumatic events even though they may be exacerbated by other factors.

7. Education about violence and abuse is therapeutic.

8. Coping strategies are viewed as indicators of strength, not pathology.

9. Substance abuse is recognized as a common method of self-medication among trauma victims.

10. The recognition that transformation or healing of the trauma may result in other positive changes for the formerly battered woman is important.

11. Prosocial action and self-disclosure are acknowledged to facilitate the stress recovery process.

12. Transformation or healing of trauma is recognized as a lifelong process.

13. Abuse and victimization are acknowledged to result in noncompensable losses.

14. The therapist assumes the right of self-determination for the battered woman.

15. The therapist recognizes that self-care is essential for the therapist as well as for the battered woman.

Therapeutic Goals

Post-traumatic therapy with battered women involves several overlapping therapeutic goals (Dutton, 1992a, 1992b). These are (1) integrating the traumatic memories imbedded within the abusive relationship; (2) processing the affect associated with trauma and abuse, for example, shame, anger or rage, fear or terror, and hurt; (3) facilitating the grief process; (4) making meaning of the abuse; and (5) establishing intimacy in relation to self and others. Intervention strategies for addressing these goals are discussed in a later section. Post-traumatic therapy deals fundamentally with the memory and emotional aftermath of abuse, not the actual physical danger of an abusive relationship. It is important to acknowledge this difference clearly since working with a battered woman to increase her safety is a distinctly different process. Post-traumatic therapy is not appropriate with battered women when safety is a primary issue.

Integrating Traumatic Memories

This goal aims toward enabling the battered woman to tolerate the memory of traumatic abusive experiences without both (1) the intrusion of overwhelming affect and physiological arousal and (2) avoidance responses characteristic of post-traumatic stress disorder (Horowitz, 1986). The battered woman's traumatic experiences typically are numerous and have occurred over a long period of time. In this respect, post-traumatic therapy with battered women is similar to therapy with incest survivors. Further, some battered women are also victims/ survivors of other forms of abuse and violence, including incest, rape, and sexual harassment. The process of working with the traumatic memories of battering therefore may trigger memories of prior traumatic events, which also require intervention. It is beyond the scope of this chapter to address fully the complex issues of post-traumatic therapy with multiple victimization. However, during the course of post-traumatic therapy with the battered woman, the therapist must be prepared to help her deal with the full array of victimization experiences that have occurred over the period of her lifetime.

Processing Affect Associated with Traumatic Memories

The goal of experiencing and understanding the emotions and affect associated directly with the trauma is integral to the process of integration described above. Battered women are often robbed of the opportunity to experience the emotional impact of their victimization fully because of the necessity of survival, which typically requires a focus on external, not internal, events. Survivors of battering may recall, on an intellectual or cognitive level, discrete abusive events but may not have an awareness of the affective experience associated with them or with the ongoing "state of siege" (Ostoff, personal communication, 1991) characteristic of the abusive relationship. Enabling the formerly battered woman to tolerate an increased awareness of her feelings and emotions related to the abuse is valuable in its own right (Korb, Gorrell & Van De Riet, 1989). Owning her experience can facilitate clearer decision making in her life choices. Furthermore, an ability to tolerate such awareness precludes the necessity of avoiding it by using psychological coping strategies or defenses that drain considerable emotional energy, which could be spent more productively.

Facilitating Grief

As a direct result of battering, women typically experience multiple losses, including loss of relationship, home, economic security, children, trust, friends, and other sources of social support, self-esteem, and freedom (Dutton, 1992a). Recognition of these losses by a formerly battered woman is essential, in part, because of the prominent role they play in her emotional life (Campbell, 1986). That is, the network of emotions experienced by the battered woman is often heavily influenced by the losses that she has experienced. Conceptualizing a component of her healing process as bereavement (Sanders, 1989) helps to recognize her emotional experiences within a familiar and normative context.

Establishing Meaning of the Abuse

This goal involves coming to terms with the shattered assumptions and other cognitive shifts that result from victimization and reestablishing a conceptual system that allows the victim to function adequately once again (Janoff-Bulman,

1985; McCann & Pearlman, 1990c). The goal is to help the battered woman make sense out of her world. In order to achieve this goal, the therapeutic tasks may involve reassigning blame for the violence and abuse away from the self to the perpetrator, increasing her perception of choice points, examining the psychological mechanisms that were (or are) required to tolerate violence and abuse and the emotional cost to her for doing so, and challenging the tolerance of violence and abuse as a viable way of life. Establishing meaning does not justify or normalize abuse; rather, the goal is to put into perspective the battered woman's experience so her life and her choices make sense to her.

Establishing Emotional Intimacy with Self and Others

The goal of establishing emotional intimacy in relationship with others does not assume that the formerly battered woman will enter or remain in a sexually intimate or romantic relationship. Regardless of her choice about this, she may need help with trusting and allowing herself to experience emotional intimacy. Helping her in this area includes (1) examining the question of whether to enter into (or remain in) a romantic relationship, (2) empowerment toward choice making, including development of her belief in the right to establish appropriate boundaries and to ask for her needs to be met and the skill to do so (e.g., saying no to a relationship that is not satisfactory, maintaining autonomy over decisions regarding one's body and use of time, asking for support), and (3) identification of sources of emotional intimacy in relationships other than sexually intimate or romantic ones, including with herself.

When a woman is interested in reestablishing a relationship with her formerly abusive partner, an additional therapeutic task needs particular emphasis: determining realistic criteria for trust and for remaining in the relationship. Repairing the trust damaged by abuse requires experience that trust is warranted.

Establishing intimacy in relation to oneself means developing a self that can provide self-nurturance and care. This requires an ongoing relationship with oneself, an opportunity to cultivate and attend to it, and recognition of its priority.

Treatment Strategies for Achieving Goals

The remainder of the chapter describes a treatment protocol or set of intervention strategies when working with battered women for accomplishing these post-traumatic therapeutic goals. No single psychotherapy approach is sufficiently comprehensive to address all of these goals adequately. An integrated combination of approaches involving components of experientially focused psychotherapies (e.g., hypnosis, Gestalt), cognitive and behavioral interventions, feminist analysis, and dynamic insight-oriented therapies (e.g., based on family systems or object relations theoretical analysis) is useful to manage the complex configuration of therapeutic issues. Whereas there are pitfalls with some of these approaches for working with battered women (or other victims of family violence) (e.g., see Bograd, 1986, for critique of family systems therapy with domestic violence), each approach can contribute something unique and not victim blaming.

Components of the treatment protocol discussed here include naming or labeling experience; recall of, and reexperiencing, specific traumatic events; expression of affect related to abuse and its sequelae; building stress management skills; feminist analysis of victimization; (re)establishing the ability to trust; and facilitating self-nurturance. All of these interventions are, of course, considered within the overall philosophical therapeutic framework, in which support and validation, empowerment, advocacy, and an understanding of the social, political, and economic context in which abuse and its sequelae occur are fully integrated.

Name or Label Experience

An initial component of post-traumatic therapy interventions is to name or label all aspects of the abuse experience that have occurred. These aspects include specific abusive behaviors, the battered woman's reactions to them, and the losses that have resulted.

Some battered women have never considered what has happened to them as abusive, and other women may have identified only portions of the abuse. Providing educational information concerning definitions of abuse is quite useful. The visual model of the Power and Control Wheel offered by Pence and Paymar (1986) and the checklist (ABOC; Dutton, 1992a) described earlier are particularly helpful in translating the abusive context into literal and concrete terms. Although the battered woman's experience obviously has been quite concrete, her recognition and labeling of it may not have been. It can be quite powerful for a battered woman to list all the examples of domestic violence and abuse to which she has been exposed (e.g., being called degrading names, slaps, punches, kicks, throwing hot coffee in face, being held forcefully to have sex, statements that imply partner will go to a prostitute if sex is not provided on command, statements that threaten to kill if she does not comply with demands). The concreteness of the task can provide a foundation for understanding, giving herself permission for, and acceptance of, her responses to her abusive situation. Extending the exercise to listing specific examples of other forms of abuse (e.g., childhood sexual abuse, date rape) experienced by the battered woman throughout her lifetime can also be similarly helpful. Without the acute awareness of the extensiveness of the battered woman's abusive experience, including all forms of abuse, both the battered woman and her clinician may fail to appreciate the reasonableness of her response to it.

Labeling specific losses that the battered woman has incurred is equally important in order to make explicit the grief process that the battered woman necessarily must experience in order to heal adequately. Assisting her to recognize these specific losses helps to provide a context for feelings of sadness, anger, longing, and emptiness. Identifying losses that are noncompensable and permanent (e.g., fifteen years of life spent in emotional isolation, unborn child

aborted due to injuries resulting from abuse, permanent loss of custody or visitation rights to her children, loss of physical mobility due to permanent injury)
is especially important in order to help her facilitate the grief process and eventually go on with her life. Other losses (e.g., temporary loss of child custody
or visitation, loss of employment, loss of economic security) also involve a
grieving process and may require problem solving, skill building, and advocacy
in order to be addressed adequately.

Helping the battered woman to label her varied and diverse internal experiences
resulting from the abuse is important, and probably essential, for healing to
occur. Affective responses or emotions (e.g., anger/rage, fear/terror, shame,
hurt, sadness) may be identified most effectively in the immediacy of her experience of them whether during a therapy session or outside it (e.g., during
experiential therapeutic work to be described later, after awakening from a
nightmare reliving an abusive episode). Attention to, and labeling, other areas
are equally important, for example, physical sensation (e.g., physiological
arousal, pain, physical numbing) and cognitive responses (e.g., attributions,
self-statements, beliefs, expectations), in order to facilitate awareness and validation of the battered woman's total experience.

In short, the process of labeling the abusive behaviors experienced by the
battered woman, the accompanying losses, and her reactions to both may facilitate what would otherwise go unrecognized or unaccepted as reality. This intervention strategy is important both as an initial step in the healing process and
as an integral component throughout it. This process of labeling can be quite
effectively accomplished in a group context, whether it be a formal therapy
group, a battered women's support group, or an informal network of friends.

Facilitate Reexperiencing of Specific Traumatic Events

A hallmark of post-traumatic therapy is facilitating reexperiencing traumatic
event(s) (Courtois, 1988b; Horowitz, 1986; Wilson, 1989). Reexperiencing the
trauma may occur spontaneously via intrusive dreams, nightmares, recollections,
or generalized stress reactions triggered by symbolic events or by means of
hypnosis, guided imagery, or other experiential therapeutic techniques intended
to retrieve it. Reexperiencing the traumatic events is most useful when it is
accompanied by a titration of the rate at which it occurs and by processing of
the experience as it is occurring, all within the context of emotional and physical
support and safety. For this reason, the spontaneous reexperiencing that occurs
outside the therapy context may not only be ineffectual but may serve repeatedly
to reexpose the battered woman to trauma, albeit symbolically. Nonetheless,
reexperiencing outside the therapy context will occur, and discussion with her
is essential concerning her response to it.

Spontaneously occurring reexperiences of trauma typically require efforts to
contain the experience and to manage the related stress so that it becomes less
overwhelming. (This discussion is elaborated upon in the section on stress management.) However, it is also possible to help the battered woman work with

her spontaneously occurring intrusive experiences by facilitating them once they occur, helping her to label feelings, encourage their expression, tolerate this experience, and recognize responses that may empower her in the here and now. This treatment strategy should be utilized only when she can safely tolerate a deliberate effort to stay with the reexperience of prior trauma. If not, the treatment protocol for spontaneously occurring reexperiences needs to focus on limiting and containing the intrusive experience.

Deliberately facilitating the reexperiencing of traumatic events that occurred within the battered woman's abusive relationship may be accomplished by simply having her recall the sequence of events associated with a particular violent episode or by using a strategy for enhancing the availability of her total experience. Such strategies may include hypnosis, imagery, drawings, journal writing, viewing photographs, reviewing police documents, or other methods that allow the prior experience to reemerge. The therapist should attempt to pace the reexperiencing process so that the battered woman can verbalize the experience as it occurs and experience its full impact. This pacing is important for labeling and adequately processing the experience as well as for maintaining contact between the battered woman and her therapist in the here and now, thus making it less likely that the experience will overwhelm her. When using deliberate efforts to facilitate reexperiencing trauma within a therapy session, it is essential to allow sufficient time for preparation of the battered woman for the experience, for completion of processing the episode, and for debriefing the experience afterward. The healing components of this strategy include increasing the ability to tolerate the memory and affect associated with the prior abusive experiences (clearly distinct from tolerating the abuse itself) and a deliberate effort toward (re)empowerment out of victimization.

This component is not typically suited to battered women's support groups or informal support networks since the experience may be quite intense and emotionally difficult, even for persons trained professionally to respond to it. In fact, this aspect of post-traumatic therapy may be the most difficult for the therapist to handle and, in some circumstances, may lead to secondary post-traumatic stress reactions (Dutton & Rubinstein, in press; McCann & Pearlman, 1990c).

Facilitate Expression of Affect

Throughout the therapy process, facilitating expression of affect or emotion is important. Expression of affect and cognitive labeling of it can go hand in hand, although either may proceed the other. The battered woman may know that she is angry but only later overtly express it. Conversely, a spontaneous expression of anger may precede her recognition that she feels angry. Clearly, expression of emotion is an integral component of the reexperiencing process; however, it extends far beyond reexperiences of past trauma. Sometimes the battered woman does not experience her emotional reaction fully when she relives the abuse; instead, the full impact may be delayed. Further, she may also experience emotional responses directed toward others besides the batterer, such as friends who failed to listen to pleas for help or the legal system or health professionals who were reluctant to acknowledge the occurrence of abuse. She may also experience joy or gratitude for having survived, for having developed a support network through her efforts to escape, or for having (re)discovered herself in the healing process.

Facilitating expression of emotion or affect may occur in many ways, such as through the use of (1) sound (e.g., crying, screaming or yelling, whimpering, groaning), (2) physical expression and movement (e.g., pounding pillows with fists, dancing, or other movement), (3) words (e.g., talking, story telling, poetry, metaphor), (4) ritual (e.g., sweat lodges, symbolic gestures), (5) music (e.g., drumbeating, composing or playing music), (6) touch (e.g., massage or other forms of bodywork), or (7) art (e.g., sculpture, drawing, painting). These activities may be geared to occur within the therapy session or between sessions, depending upon several factors. These factors might include the ability of the battered woman to tolerate strong emotion without the support of the therapist and social support available to her, access to resources needed to facilitate the activity, the amount of therapy time available, and the battered woman's own preference.

Develop Stress Management Skills

Stress management is a standard component of a treatment protocol for post-traumatic stress disorders (Courtois, 1988b; Foy et al., 1993; Peterson, Prout & Schwarz, 1991; Wilson, 1989). Not only is reducing stress important for managing intrusive recollection of traumatic material, but it is also quite useful for the myriad other stressors in her life that may be indirectly related, if at all, to the violence and abuse. Specific strategies to help a battered woman manage stress may include relaxation procedures, self-hypnosis or guided imagery, meditation, exercise, social support building, stress inoculation procedures, assertiveness training, or skill development (e.g., time management, parent training, job training).

Apply a Feminist Analysis

A hallmark of feminist therapy (Brown & Root, 1990; Dutton-Douglas & Walker, 1988; Ganley, 1989; Laidlaw et al., 1990; Rosewater & Walker, 1985) has been application of a feminist analysis to understanding social and clinical problems. A feminist analysis identifies the power imbalances inherent in the situation that are directly related to causality of the problem. These power imbalances and the oppression and exploitation that follow them are based in a hierarchical and patriarchal culture in which other bases of potential bias also exist. These other bases include race, ethnicity, social class, age, gay or lesbian identity, and able-bodiedness. A feminist analysis identifies the social, political, and economic forces that act upon the problems the battered woman faces, including the abuse itself as well as institutional and social responses to it. Such an analysis helps the battered woman to recognize that her "personal" problem of battering is indeed a "political" one as well. This recognition can readily change her focus from internal to external accountability for the abuse, providing a perspective in which the battered woman is not alone in her plight. Further, a feminist analysis can highlight empowering alternatives for the battered woman (and her advocates) in her effort to escape and heal from abuse within the complex network of both social oppression and social support in which she is imbedded.

Examination of the social, political, and economic contexts can involve an analysis of family patterns, as well. Use of the genogram (McGoldrick & Gerson, 1985) to track patterns of violence, abuse, and victimization throughout the generations can be a useful method of providing an analysis of the family as a context for understanding the battered woman's response to her victimization. A family systems perspective can bring social, cultural, and political analyses to the level of the family without relying on notions of reciprocal causality of more traditional family systems theory.

Facilitate New Experiences of Trust

Experiences of trust, which can occur first within the therapeutic relationship, are a prerequisite to emotional intimacy. Although the therapeutic relationship will not be part of the battered woman's ongoing social network, that relationship often is an integral part of her emotional support network for some time. Consistency in the therapist's support and alliance with the battered woman, honesty in communication with her, clarity regarding interpersonal boundaries, and genuine empathy and connection help build trust in the therapeutic relationship.

The therapist cannot exclusively provide the trust or emotional intimacy on which a battered woman can rely. Eventually, she needs external sources of emotional intimacy from which she can develop experiences of trust. These may occur in new relationships with friends or in new romantic relationships. An important therapy strategy is to help the battered woman select relationships that can offer intimacy and facilitate trust, monitor newly developing relationships and her feelings about them, and pay attention to violations of trust that destroy intimacy and may signal both emotional and physical danger.

Not infrequently, the formerly battered woman is interested in rebuilding trust and intimacy in a previously abusive relationship. Rebuilding trust requires a conjoint effort on the part of both the woman and her partner. This work cannot begin until the violence and abuse (including controlling behavior) have consistently stopped for a credible period of time, the perpetrator has taken responsibility for the abusive behavior, and both partners are willing and committed to work toward healing the relationship. Discussion of this therapeutic process is beyond the scope of this chapter. Refer to Bograd (1984, 1986) for further reading.

Encourage Self-Nurturance

Helping the battered woman learn to nurture herself and engage in regular self-care is essential for the healing process. Healing cannot occur with a focus on external activity alone; it requires time spent with self in a way that acknowledges personal experience and current here-and-now emotional and physical needs. Based on her prior needs for physical survival, the battered woman may be quite unaccustomed to having the luxury to spend time and energy focusing on self-awareness, much less to respond effectively to it. Issues of guilt, shame, and critical thinking may need to be dealt with for the client for whom self-care has been uncommon. The therapist can model self-nurturance by setting appropriate boundaries regarding appointment times and times available for returning phone calls, taking vacation time, and generally attending to personal and emotional needs.

THERAPIST ISSUES

Providing post-traumatic therapy to battered women, as well as other trauma victims, exacts a toll on the therapist (Briere, 1989; Dutton, 1992a; Dutton & Rubinstein, in press; McCann & Pearlman, 1990c). Recognition of that inevitability and normalizing the therapist's response (McCann & Pearlman, 1990c) are essential if the therapist is adequately to address the concerns that arise. Although a competent therapist may buffer herself or himself against the secondary trauma of being exposed to the aftermath of the battered woman's abusive experiences, it is probably impossible for any healthy human being to avoid experiencing these effects. Therapist issues include vicarious traumatization (McCann & Pearlman, 1990c), burnout, actual physical danger, or simply the emotional toll of working with intense emotional issues.

An effective therapist response includes self-care and self-nurturance (Briere, 1989; Dutton, 1992a; Dutton & Rubinstein, in press; McCann & Pearlman, 1990c). Specific strategies include the therapist's own use of personal therapy, networking and consultation, maintaining a diverse professional life, including a caseload of clients other than abuse victims, and a diverse social network, and social activism that addresses the problem on a larger scale (Briere, 1989; Dutton, 1992a). Working within a collegial supportive team is an important component of self-care and provides a check-and-balance process for monitoring the therapist's reactions.

It is especially important within a training setting to prepare novice therapists for the inevitable personal impact of working with victims. Further, training programs need to provide students with the resources necessary to respond effectively to the personal impact of working with trauma. These resources include a perspective that helps students to understand the inevitability and normalcy of the response. Students often hold the misperception that competent professionals remain personally unaffected by their work and thus remain reluctant to acknowledge the personal impact of their work to themselves and their supervisors. A supervisor's modeling recognition of these effects in herself or himself and responsible handling of them may be the most effective teaching tool. Further, providing ample opportunity for novice therapists to obtain support from their colleagues is essential. Finally, of utmost importance is helping students recognize how their own issues with power and control, including personal victimization and perpetrator histories, can dramatically influence the quality of their professional work. Supporting trainees in seeking personal therapy is nearly always recommended, if not essential.

CONCLUSION

Once the threat of ongoing abuse has ceased sufficiently to allow the battered woman the necessary emotional and physical safety, post-traumatic therapy may be helpful to heal the psychological wounds of the physical, sexual, and psychological abuse she has suffered. In some cases, however, healing the wound of prior domestic violence (and other forms of abuse) may be required in order for a battered woman to make choices and engage in decision making (e.g., to leave an abusive relationship) that advocates for her own safety and well-being. Nevertheless, even in these instances, safety remains the first priority.

A thorough assessment of all aspects of the battered woman's life and her environmental circumstances is required to understand the unique configuration of issues that she presents in post-traumatic therapy. As with most clinical interventions, the therapeutic process should be molded to the battered woman's individual needs.

Not all clinicians are suited to work with victims of trauma, especially with post-traumatic reactions, which can be quite emotionally intense. Post-traumatic therapy requires the clinician to involve her or his own emotional self, along with the intellectual and analytic self, actively. Recognizing the limitations of one's interest and emotional capacity for work in this area is essential. Nonetheless, virtually all clinicians need sufficient skill to assess and refer the battered woman adequately to appropriate resources when one is not prepared to provide them directly. The failure to recognize post-traumatic reactions in battered women (and other trauma victims) or mislabeling them as indicators of psychopathology or personality disorders is both unnecessary and an unacceptable standard of practice.

11

Establishing Safety in Survivors of Severe Sexual Abuse

Mary Beth Williams

Therapists in clinical practice are being forced to confront the existence of a traumatic history of multiple physical and sexual abuses in the lives of many clients. Many survivors reveal histories of parental violence and substance abuse, physical abuse, emotional abuse, sexual abuse by multiple perpetrators, and, in some cases, ritualized abusive experiences involving torture, bizarre sexual practices, and sadism. Their entire childhoods (and sometimes adulthoods, as well) involved betrayal, violence, pain, trauma, and mistrust.

Many of the one in three girls and one in five boys who have been or will be molested in some manner prior to becoming adults are abused by more than one perpetrator (Herman, Russell & Trocki, 1986). More recent studies have revealed that the clinical picture of incidence involves multiple events, longer duration, multiple perpetrators, and accompanying physical abuse (Williams, 1990; Gold, 1986; Fromuth and Burkhart, in press; Tsai, Feldman-Summers, and Edgar, 1979).

Severely abused clients demonstrate beliefs indicating a lack of basic security and safety and of trust in themselves and others. Invulnerability from harm is an illusion to them (McCann & Pearlman, 1990b; Jehu, Gazan & Klassen, 1988). Consequently, they frequently are anxious and hypervigilant; may consistently expose themselves to danger or reenactments of the abuse in hopes of gaining control or meaning.

These severely abused survivors also believe themselves to be damaged permanently from their experiences. They expect to be let down and abandoned. They devalue themselves, see themselves as dependent, and may avoid closeness at all costs in order to avoid repeated betrayal. Their traumatic early histories have generalized to present and future events and relationships (McCann & Pearlman, 1990b).

Many severely abused survivors have repressed or dissociated entire occurrences or aspects of their abusive experiences (Blume, 1990). Eventually, images, sensations, and memory fragments of the events intrude through flashbacks, thoughts, nightmares, and unexplained reactions to triggers suggestive of, or sensory stimuli associated with, past abuses. These visual, olfactory, tactile, and auditory triggers or cues may initiate what appears to be a psychoticlike break from reality in the survivor if he or she becomes "stuck" in their intrusive processing.

SEARCHING FOR A TREATMENT MODEL

In order to provide competent treatment for a severely abused client, the therapist needs to base that treatment on the psychological theory of post-traumatic stress. This paradigm includes the recovering of memories and associated emotions in measured doses through a collaborative therapist-client relationship and flexible strategies (Scurfield, 1985).

As Courtois (1991a) noted, a client who has been severely abused is very difficult to treat. The process of therapy requires the expenditure of a great deal of energy on the part of the therapist and a great deal of work on the part of the client. The assumptions underlying many traditional therapies (i.e., that the client comes to therapy with a basic level of safety and trust; that rapport will be easily established between client and therapist) do not generally exist. In fact, to the contrary, the process frequently is exceedingly painful and inherently unsafe to the client as it retraumatizes him or her through the exhumation of buried, dissociated memories.

The treatment of symptoms through post-traumatic therapy was first proposed by Ochberg (1988) and is described in detail by Dolan (1991). Post-traumatic therapy aims to release the emotional energy, factual information, sensations, and behavioral components of abusive memories in measured doses of reliving (Braun, 1988). Reliving every single abusive experience is not necessary. Remembering, reliving, and reexperiencing enough of the trauma to enable the client to recognize the impact of the abuse, diffuse its emotional cathexis, and diminish self-blame are all that is required.

Before traumatic early histories can be re-created, relived, or abreacted, the client and therapist together must create a safe environment both within and without the therapeutic setting. Not until basic safety is established can a client even begin to develop self capacities to moderate self-loathing, tolerate the strong affect accompanying memory retrieval, be alone without being lonely, and soothe, calm, and empower the self (McCann & Pearlman, 1990b). The work of therapy, including memory retrieval and integration, will proceed more smoothly and more quickly once safety has been established.

THE SETTING

Safety in the Therapeutic Setting

The post-traumatic therapist believes that the survivor's approach-avoidance reaction is a normal response to abnormal abusive events. This belief sets the tone of therapy. The initial responsibility for developing a collaborative relationship between client and therapist lies with that professional who uses techniques, implements strategies, and sets rules to create a safe environment in all areas of the client's life.

The therapist must be acutely aware of the scanning process used by clients as they enter the office. What triggers them? What objects appear to get their attention or are threatening to them? Clients need permission to set the boundaries, within reasonable limits, for what makes them feel safe in the setting. Do they want shades up or down? What pictures need to be removed from the wall? Is the door to be locked, unlocked, open, or shut? How can negative associations with these objects or events be desensitized? Rearranging furniture prior to a session can be traumatic and threatening in some instances (Lindy et al., 1987). Likewise, the level of tidiness in the office setting can affect clients' ability to relax. It is not uncommon for survivors to require orderly surroundings to compensate for the sense of internal disorder that they may feel. Also, the office setting needs to be made abreaction-proof, with no sharp objects available for self-mutilation (Steele and Colrain, 1991). The office setting needs to be as soundproof and secluded as possible, minimizing the outside noises and/or waiting room conversations.

Client and therapist together establish safety-oriented rituals. Rituals provide clients with consistency and predictability. Do clients meet the therapist in the parking lot if they are the first appointment, or do they meet in the office or waiting room? Do clients request/want a handshake, a nonsexual hug (only after other safety boundaries are established and with permission of clients), or a wave?

Rules concerning confidentiality and acceptability of rituals need to be established within the first few sessions. The therapist must decide how to handle paperwork. Does he or she keep process notes, process recordings, or only mental notes or take notes during a session? At what point in therapy is the client requested to complete an intake form or complete psychological instruments? In many instances, clients do not want to be "a number" or part of a research protocol. It is important to respect that request. Also, presenting clients with a complex, detailed intake form before rapport has been established can be frightening and may even cause premature termination of treatment. It may be best to wait until a later session (e.g., after the third or fourth session) to ask a client to fill out an intake form or instrument. It is more important, initially, to help the client feel relaxed and welcome. Having a pleasant physical setting decorated in warm colors and furnished with a variety of furniture, pillows, stuffed animals, and calming works of art can be conducive to relaxation and help encourage feelings of safety.

Business practices are an integral part of the therapy process and can influence a client's ability to feel safe. Procedures should be clearly identified and consistently observed. Failure to do so may cause unintentional reenactment of the inconsistent or chaotic atmosphere found in the survivor's childhood. During the first or second sessions, fee schedules and appointment length and frequency must be agreed upon. Is payment expected "up front" with responsibility for insurance reimbursement left to the client? Or does the therapist submit the bills to insurance and take only the copayment fee at the time of rendering service? In any case, is payment ever postponed? If so, what arrangements are agreed upon for a repayment schedule? How long is a typical session? What happens if a session "goes over" the allotted time, and when is that extension of the therapeutic hour allowed or planned?

It is also important to establish rules to ensure the safety of the therapist in the setting. Physical violence toward the therapist, whether intentional or unintentional, would result in immediate termination. No type of contact or advances that might be interpreted as sexual are ever to be allowed between client and therapist.

Establishing the Therapist as Safe within the Setting

Severely traumatized clients expect to be hurt, abused, or abandoned by therapists, just as they were mistreated by many others in their lives. They fear that the therapist will somehow reenact abuse (McCann & Pearlman, 1990b). Many survivors have experienced inappropriate therapy as well, which may have involved disbelief by the therapist or boundary violations, including sexual advances or inadvertent abuse. It is the responsibility of the therapist to demonstrate repeatedly to clients that he or she is a safe and trustworthy person. As McCann and Pearlman (1990b) noted, clients also may unconsciously attempt to violate boundaries as a means to test the therapist's allegiance to preserving safety.

The therapist must, first and foremost, model safety. As she or he believes in the client's telling process, as Steele (1991) noted, the therapist is aware that "telling" has subjective components of guilt, shame, externally caused injunctions, and programmed cues to self-destruction. As Herman (1988) noted, "The willingness of the victim to disclose her abuse history is entirely dependent on the clinician's willingness to hear, respect, and validate the patient's experiences" (p. 191).

Explaining to survivors that the therapist does not expect trust and is aware that he or she is not safe to them is important. There is no reason a therapist should be viewed as trustworthy. In many instances, every "trustworthy" individual in the client's life has abused that client. The therapist must earn trust, a process that may take months or years. Herman (1988) noted that establishing trust "in the context of a therapeutic alliance is the central task of treatment"

(p. 191). Self-disclosure, therefore, is never forced. The client's personal sense of pacing and timing is to be respected. The therapist models open communication as he or she reveals some information about himself or herself. The therapist can also model flexibility by choosing to use multiple techniques or strategies. The therapist must accept that the client's perceptions of events are his or hers alone. The trustworthy therapist allows the client to talk about horrible events without shunning the client, avoiding the client's gaze, or exhibiting shock and vicarious traumatization in his or her reactions (Courtois, 1991a). Internally, the therapist may be repulsed; however, motivation to help in an atmosphere of belief modifies the external reactions to that internal state of shock or, at times, even disbelief. Hodgkinson and Stewart (1991) noted that the time-limited session is the container to hold pain released by the client.

The therapeutic style must also be safe. An empathic, reflective, genuine use of self combined with nonjudgmental acceptance works best. Otherwise, the client may view the therapist as interrogator or judge (Lindy et al., 1987). The therapist recognizes that belief systems of survivors are frequently polar opposites of black and white, concrete rather than metaphoric, and based on sensory data rather than intuition (Calof, 1991). Thus, the responsive, intuitive therapist is concrete in style if necessary, in a more explicit and directive manner, while being emotionally responsive. The therapist is not a tabula rasa, or blank face. She or he models coping and an intuitive reliance on his or her own inner adviser. Casual dress, flexible seating arrangements, and body movement mirroring can help to reduce client tension and distrust. Humor and self-disclosure, within limits, also can diffuse tension and fear.

The competent, secure therapist models a strong sense of self, values, and self-liking. The therapist never knowingly inflicts pain on a client, even when pain or punishment is requested. In this process, the client is a capable, competent partner in the process of therapy. This view is in strong contrast to the general view of treatment of many sexual abuse survivors who have been diagnosed as borderline personality disorder (BPD). The BPD diagnosis portrays the client as unstable, dependent, and infantile. Briere (1989) noted that sexual abuse survivors labeled as BPD are "often considered to be relatively unresponsive to therapy" (p. 38). Briere's 1984 study affirmed, as Courtois (1988a) noted, that borderline symptoms are actually manifestations of post-traumatic stress reactions and disorders.

Presenting the framework of post-traumatic stress disorder (PTSD) theory and post-traumatic therapy within the first sessions and repeating that framework as needed are essential. This repetition helps to normalize the responses, reactions, emotional outbursts, thoughts, and emotional numbness of clients. It also provides an understandable frame for the treatment process in clients who have used their many strengths to adapt to abnormal, traumatic situations.

The therapist must be aware of possible gender issues. Is a male survivor comfortable with a female therapist? Is a female survivor safe if the therapist is a male? How does either gender of therapist approach working with a same-sex client who is homosexual?

Rules for touch and boundaries need to be established, maintained, and openly discussed throughout therapy. A client, after a period of time, may suddenly request a hug from a therapist. When is a nonsexual hug appropriate? Some therapists believe that touch should never occur. Others recognize the importance that a warm, caring nonsexual touch or hug can have in a relationship. The appropriate use of touch can extend to the client an atmosphere of hope in finding safe human contact. Touch should occur only upon request or invitation of the client within the clearly developed boundaries of good touch, bad touch, and safe touch. Helping a client to say ''stop'' in nontherapy situations, when touch is uncomfortable and confusing, is an important therapeutic lesson. The therapist should never use touch that involves control, pain, or possible sexual connotations. Touch should be used with caution to communicate caring, safety, and trust so that similar touch can later be transferred to nontherapy relationships.

The therapist must be trustworthy and follow through on promises or interventions; for example, if the therapist tells a client he or she will bring a particular book for the client to read, then the therapist must bring the book.

In work with severely traumatized clients, it is important for the therapist to commit for the ''long haul'' (i.e., long-term therapy) within the limitations of the agency or private practice setting. Post-traumatic therapy with severely abused clients is generally not short-term. Treatment is not terminated by the therapist until the individual is free from debilitating flashbacks, can put memories of abuse in the past, and remember what he or she determines is necessary to remember. Assuring the client that the therapist will be there ''as long as this process takes,'' within personal and agency limits, can reinforce beliefs of safety and build trust.

As Courtois (1991a) noted, some of these clients are ''for life.'' However, oftentimes, mitigating circumstances can affect continuation of treatment. What happens if it becomes evident that a client has multiple personality disorder and that therapist feels incompetent to treat multiplicity? What if that therapist does not want to learn what is necessary to continue with the treatment, even after a therapeutic relationship of three years? What if a client loses insurance coverage through conversion to a managed care program that limits visits to six per year? What happens if the client's insurance is used up by October, and the client has no money to pay the full fee? Is therapy put ''on hold'' until insurance coverage is reinstated in January? What happens if the client loses his or her job and can no longer afford treatment? If a therapist must take an extended leave of absence? These and other similar questions need to be addressed prior to encountering the situations. Private practice and agency policies need to be established. Waiting until the situation arises can retraumatize a fragile client.

Backup arrangements need to be arranged well in advance if the therapist is going to be away at a conference, speaking engagement, or vacation. It is quite possible that clients will be very angry when the therapist returns. They feel abandoned and rejected again. However, it is important to identify the transference issues within their angry outbursts or as demonstrated by the sudden crises they have had. As van der Kolk noted (1989), a client who is angry is healthier than one who idealizes the therapist and is overly dependent on him or her. The therapist must be able to "take" such anger, as long as the anger never involves physical violence, and its basis is discussed openly in the concurrent or later session.

Many clients try to make a therapist their best friend or primary source of social support. Boundaries about accepting invitations to a client's home (e.g., to celebrate an Alcoholics Anonymous (AA) anniversary) need to be set. These boundaries must work within both the therapist's and client's frameworks. There may be times when accepting an invitation can be extremely therapeutic. However, socializing with clients is not the ideal way to build a trusting rapport. In fact, it can undermine the relationship because the client may then view the therapist more as a friend and loved one than a helping professional.

Being a Safe Therapist Outside the Setting

A therapist needs to establish herself or himself as a safe and accessible person/object outside the office setting. One aspect of this process is setting procedures and limits for receiving phone calls from clients (when, how long, how late at night, charges for extended conversations). It is also important to have appropriate referral sources for medication consults, sources who are familiar with trauma and dissociation. Informing clients of particular colleagues who can be called upon as backup if a client encounters a crisis while the therapist is on vacation or, perhaps, ill is also important. Procedures for arranging extra sessions, should they be needed, must be established. The primary goal of this aspect of treatment is to demonstrate to clients that the therapist can be trusted to "be there" within defined limits.

Another component of being a "safe" therapist involves knowing one's own limits and boundaries. The therapist who does not take care of himself or herself first limits professional effectiveness. If the therapist is working with a client who may be dangerous, or even cult-involved, then the therapist must be cautious and not give out personal information. Therapists need to recognize when they need breaks, vacations, support from colleagues, or additional training. As Steele and Colrain (1991) noted, taking care of oneself and doing things for oneself increase the therapist's own sense of safety.

SAFETY OF THE CLIENT

Developing Client Safety for the Self

Establishing ground rules for client safety means setting limits about the use of self-destructive behaviors. Contracts to prevent self-mutilation and suicide threats or gestures may be necessary to regulate self-destructive acts. Contracts between client and therapist help the client to feel safe from self-destructive thoughts, impulses, or actions and to have alternatives should he or she become out of control. Other contracts between client and therapist or therapist, client, and the client's family can determine when hospitalization needs to be considered and where it should occur. Dissociative disorder units or appropriate day treatment programs for clients who have insurance coverage are excellent options. Hospitalization may also be necessary as a short-term, safety, or sanctuary measure during particularly dangerous times (e.g., anniversaries, ritualistic holidays).

The appropriate use of medication and appropriate type of medication to use must be discussed with a medical doctor, preferably a psychiatrist who is familiar with PTSD and dissociative disorders. It is the responsibility of the therapist to provide the name of a physician for a meds consultation. Clients may be using a variety of psychotropic medications or relying on medications for sleep and symptom modulation. Consultations frequently result in a change in, or cessation of, the use of medications. It is also important to assess substance use/abuse and arrange for detoxification prior to beginning the work of therapy if the client appears to be, or admits to being, addicted.

Clients can be encouraged to develop self-safety messages when distressed. They can write these messages on pieces of notepaper with safety symbols (e.g., a unicorn, rainbow, balloon, or whatever other object signifies safety and power) and place them in settings where their safety might be compromised. Dolan (1991) suggested, for example, that messages be put in a medicine cabinet or in a knife drawer if the client tends to self-mutilate when depressed or out of control. These handwritten messages contain reassurance, self-affirmations, or safety instructions. They are put in the potentially dangerous settings when the client's safety is not compromised. Referring to them in unsafe times can provide protection and offer suggestions for obtaining help (e.g., a message may read, "If you open this, call your therapist immediately").

Torem (1990) developed a series of healing self-affirmations for survivors to write in journals at least four times a day. These affirmations could also be included in safety messages. The objective of the frequent repetition of writing is to internalize the messages in the place of older, self-destructive messages.

Clients can be encouraged to use their dissociative abilities adaptively during extremely stressful times. One male client who had been abused by his stepfather, as had his sister, used his ability to go to a "white space" during the funeral service for the sister while his stepfather, a minister, delivered the eulogy.

There are times when a client may feel safer if another person participates in, or at least observes, the therapy session. One client brings her supportive husband with her to function as cotherapist when she is aware of the need to deal with an emerging memory of extremely sadistic abuse. Another client brings her sister as validation that the client's memories of her terrible home life are real. If a client is likely to dissociate during the drive to or from therapy, it may be necessary to help that client arrange other transportation or find a driver, thereby preventing any potential accident.

As therapy progresses, clients can be assisted to link present negative, re-victimizing behaviors to their past histories. They can learn to identify the behaviors that are, in actuality, compulsions to repeat familiar aspects of the abuse. Social skills training, including decision making, behavior rehearsal, assertiveness training, problem solving, and conflict resolution, can help the client feel and experience empowerment. The therapist also models appropriate self-protective behaviors and interactions. Clients can be encouraged to develop physical strength through activities such as weight lifting and bodybuilding, karate, or other self-defense programs such as "Model Mugging" (1990). In addition, clients can learn to identify and avoid behaviors that would be unsafe to others (and ultimately unsafe to the self). They should not be encouraged to seek revenge or make threats toward their abusers. Rather, they can use unmailed letters, audiotapes, and empty chair techniques to vent their rage.

Establishing Safe Settings outside Therapy

Clients need to establish their own visualized and actual "safe places" outside the therapy setting. A visualized safe place may be where they "went" during the abuse. This place may be inside themselves or outside themselves on a beach, within a cross on a hill, or in the middle of an open field. Visually oriented clients may find pictures to symbolize this place or may even draw it. Auditorially oriented clients may find a tape or record reminiscent of that place. A tape of Pachelbel's Canon in D Major, superimposed with the sounds of the sea, for example, has helped some clients visualize an extremely safe place. Once clients learn the visualization process, they then can learn to go to that place to relax and feel unequivocally safe. They can practice the visualizations, recognizing that their "spot of safety" may change over the course of therapy (Steele and Colrain, 1991).

Clients also need to determine the safest time of the day to deal with memories, to complete given assignments, to express emotions, or to take risks. They also need to have actual safe physical places to do the work of therapy outside the therapy session. They need to feel safe in their homes, apartments, and/or workplaces and establish self-nurturing rituals to build that safety (Dolan, 1991). If a ritualistically abused client believes that her home is not safe and is under attack, arranging a "house blessing" or conducting a religious or spiritually oriented ceremony may help provide safety. Self-identified and procured safety objects including stones, crystals, kachinas, or stuffed animals can be placed strategically throughout the living quarters to increase the feeling of safety.

Encouraging clients to identify triggers within their homes and workplaces is another part of this process. Clients also must know that their personal property is safe from intrusion from other family members. If clients are journaling, they must be sure that the journal is safe from unwanted, unsolicited reading. If necessary, they can buy a lockbox in which to put the journal and can wear the key. Designing a safe, trigger-free place in which to work is important, whether that place is a specific chair, corner of a room, or room itself. It is used during the previously identified safe time of day. Clients also can be helped to develop boundaries as to what they need or want to share with others both at home and on the job.

Helping Others to Be Safe for Survivors

According to Dolan (1991), the therapist also must evaluate realistically the presence or absence of safety in the survivor's current family system. The therapist seeks to determine if abuse is still occurring when the survivor has contact with the perpetrator or if the present environment is safe from battering, rape, or other forms of revictimization. If the situation is found to be high in lethality, then it is important to protect the survivor and the survivor's small children. The survivor also needs to be taught to evaluate and identify indicators of danger in the family rather than resort to dissociation to escape possible danger. Dolan (1991) also suggested that survivors establish an object as a safety signal for themselves and other family members. The object is to be left in a specified location, unless a family member feels at risk and then moves it. If the object is moved, then any family member is to contact the therapist immediately.

If possible, family members of severely abused clients can be included in sessions, on at least an intermittent basis. These conjoint sessions may include survivors and partners, survivors and children, or survivors and parents. Family members may also request the therapist to hold individual sessions with partners, children, and/or parents.

A survivor's post-traumatic stress reaction or disorder affects the family and family relationships and frequently results in secondary victimization of those others (Figley, 1988). Burge (1983) noted that family members need to be encouraged to express their beliefs and feelings (especially fears) openly about the survivor. During this interchange, the therapist can point out irrational beliefs and act as a calmative influence.

Goals of these sessions include the following:

1. Educate family members about PTSD and the normalcy of the client's post-traumatic stress reactions to help them reframe their view of the survivor. Too often, they see the survivor as "nuts, crazy, weird" until they learn about traumatic stress. McCubbin and Patterson (1983) noted that an educated, informed family is better able to provide social support, including emotional support (care and love), esteem support (stressing the value of the survivor in the family), and network support.

2. Help family members identify personal triggers, that is, what they do or do not do that triggers survivor dissociation, flashbacks, or self-destructive reactions. The identification of triggers is particularly important in areas of intimacy and sexual expression.

3. Allow partners and others to talk about their own transference and countertransference reactions both alone and with the survivor present.

4. Teach family members to express and deal with their own frustrated needs and cope with their own and the survivor's pain.

5. Help family members to take concrete action to solve specific problems.
6. Ask family members to discuss and assess social system safety. A more detailed discussion of this area of safety is available in Williams (1991a).

THE PROCESS OF THERAPY

While it is the responsibility of the therapist to build the therapeutic alliance through collaboration and cooperation with the client, the ultimate responsibility for healing rests with the client (Steele and Colrain, 1991). The therapist, through the process of therapy, attempts to empower the client without creating dependence and without using any confusional techniques or deliberate distortions (Kluft, 1991b). Healing means talking about what happened. If injunctions against talking as telling were programmed into the client, then the therapist needs to help the client tell by using other media or techniques (art, music, movement). The focus of telling or talking is one of mastery and uses active verbs.

The therapy process establishes a safe structure for processing trauma and doing the work that processing entails. This involves both pacing and timing. Clients must be made aware that therapy involves hard work. The process frequently includes homework assignments such as reading, journaling, creative collage making, and cognitive thought recording or stopping. Clients are requested to cooperate and participate in these assignments, if possible. However, if a client is too distraught to complete the work or chooses not to do an assignment, it is important that the therapist approach the refusal or inability without being judgmental. Discussing any difficulties with the process and looking for alternative client-chosen strategies to help deal with intrusions or avoidances empower the client and may resolve transferences if the client views homework giving as an authoritative imposition. Above all else, the therapist must remain flexible in his or her choice of techniques and strategies.

The actual "work" of therapy occurs in what Cole and Barney (1987) termed the therapeutic window, a period of moderate distress when the client is not totally blocked by denial or repression nor immobilized by the impact of intrusive memories, flashbacks, thoughts, or self-destructive behaviors. The post-traumatic therapist needs to be very sensitive to whether or not that window is open or shut. By choice, the therapist consciously may avoid, or allow the client to avoid, trauma-related material during those sessions in which the client states a need to "tread lightly" and focus more on the present.

Building Safety in Memory Retrieval

One major aspect of trauma resolution is memory retrieval and processing. Many severely traumatized clients are plagued with, and frightened by, intrusive images, thoughts, and emotions that they may or may not associate with their abuses. These memories and memory fragments must be remembered intellectually, emotionally, physiologically, and behaviorally before they can be integrated and diffused of their overwhelming energy. This abreactive process can be extremely frightening and therefore is often consciously and unconsciously avoided by survivors.

Normalizing the process of memory work by educating clients about post-traumatic stress disorder, its symptoms, and the cycles of intrusion and avoidance lessens that fear. When clients recognize that the more shocking, horrible memories generally do not resurface until the clients have processed and remembered less frightening memories, they can then view those memories as part of a growth process. In other words, memories are to be honored and encouraged, except when the client is severely stressed in current, daily aspects of life. Memories then can be avoided consciously while the client works on other needed topics.

It is not necessary for clients to recall every memory of every abuse that occurred as they "come out of the trauma closet." What is necessary is that survivors remember "just enough" to validate to themselves that they were victimized and were not to blame. Through this process, clients recognize how the trauma of sexual abuse has had an impact on their life in a variety of conscious and unconscious reenactments.

During memory work, the client frequently enters into an altered, dissociated state and actually experiences a flashback. This naturally occurring process involves a return to the mental state that occurred during the abuse. Dolan (1991) noted that this state can be identified by the therapist trained to notice lapses in verbal response time, flattening of affects, body stillness and lessening of movement, numbing of affective responses, memory lapses, or regressive behaviors in clients.

Chutis (1987) noted that flashbacks are memories of past traumas experienced as if they were happening in the present. Holding the hand of a client during the flashback, if asked or if that procedure has been established, allowing the associated emotions to be expressed in measured doses, and encouraging grieving over incurred losses are parts of this process. Also, the client can be reminded during the flashback that the event actually occurred in the past and that, through breathing and grounding techniques, the client can gain control over the memory.

Asking clients what would help them "come back" from a memory abreaction or flashback, so that the experience can be thoroughly processed prior to ending a session, empowers clients. Many varied methods for grounding or reentry exist. One frightened child alter of a client with multiple personalities stated that she needed a drink of the therapist's "magic coke" to return. Other clients return to the present when the ritual "Ready, set, go to . . . [name]" or "Are you with me, Honey Bear?" is used.

It is extremely important to allow enough time in the therapy session to process the flashback or abreaction in a linear and cognitive framework after it has ended or been interrupted by the therapist in the event the client found it too intense (Steele and Colrain, 1991). Clients must be grounded back into the present before they leave the session. Also, they need help to make sense of the memories and place them within their life context. Learning what lessons the memory teaches, what power it held over the body, thoughts, emotions, or behaviors helps clients regain control while reframing or decatastrophizing the memory.

Dolan (1991) described a four-step process to make sense of flashbacks (p. 107):

1. Identify when the client felt the same way before and in what situation.
2. Identify the triggers that led to the flashback and how the present situation and the past event are similar or show the client their similarity.
3. Identify how the current situation is different from the past and how the client is different.
4. Identify what the client could do in the here and now to feel better. Steele and Colrain (1991) noted that successful management of flashbacks prevents retraumatization through modulation of the intensity of the experience.

Part of the sense-making process of memory retrieval is helping the client identify auditory sounds (e.g., the sound of a hammer hitting a back, sexual sounds), visual images of abuse or objects into which the client dissociated, tastes (e.g., of semen), olfactory smells (e.g., of the abuser's sweat), and tactile, emotional, or behavioral associations to abuse that unconsciously restimulate the memory and lead to intrusive aspects of the trauma cycle.

These triggers are often evident within the therapy session. For example, a client may indicate a fear of a particular color or picture on the office wall. Wearing that color or putting up the picture for limited periods of time can help to desensitize the triggers or build new associations.

Flashbacks often occur during times of sexual intimacy when triggers are particularly intense. It is important for clients to learn how to ground themselves through focusing on, or using, their safety object or safe place. Clients can be empowered, should a flashback occur, to tell their partner what is occurring and stop trying to have sex until they are grounded back in the here and now. If traumatized persons are stuck in a regressed state or at a regressed age, they can ask the partner to provide comfort (Dolan, 1991).

If it seems appropriate or can help increase feelings of safety, the therapist may provide clients with transitional safety objects to use within the therapy situation, during memory retrieval, or between therapy sessions if flashbacks become intense or safety needs to be reestablished. A client-chosen rock from a therapist's collection, tapes recorded and read by the therapist of clients' favorite poems or fairy tales, musical tapes, a glowworm whose head lights up when the body is squeezed as a "grounding" device are examples of these objects. Clients may also bring their own stuffed animals, toys, medicine bundles, or dolls to therapy as "safe objects." If these objects need an additional "safety infusion," the therapist may choose to hold them during the session, when requested by the client, to invest them with personal energy.

If a client appears to be ready and willing to work on memory retrieval, those memories can be encouraged with the use of props such as childhood pictures, a body map that identifies areas of pain or illness, drawings (e.g., of the setting where the abuse took place), collages, and the selective use of acknowledged triggers. Clients may need help to link memories and memory fragments with bodily sensations and somatic representations as well. Specific pains, aches, illnesses, and bodily reactions, if allowed to "speak" through a body map drawing, artwork, or trance, can lead to memory retrieval. Memory of the types of abuse and body positions of the survivor during the abuse frequently lead to reduction or elimination of pain.

Other techniques that may help memory recall include developing an awareness wheel of a memory (Miller et al., 1989) or developing a situation in which the client watches the memory on a videocassette recorder in the mind. An awareness wheel includes sensory aspects of the trauma (what was seen, heard, tasted, touched, smelled) without evaluation; what the body did during the abuse; what the individual thought or believed during the abuse (meanings, self-talk, fantasies, images, reality-based understandings, and attached beliefs and assumptions); what was felt or hidden from feeling, what was denied or avoided in the emotional realm; what the client wanted during and after the experience for self (shoulds, intentions, motivations) and for others (revenge, relationships, forgiveness); and what was done and is being done (then, now, and in the future as a commitment).

Clients also may be encouraged to develop a new ending to a particularly troublesome memory. One client whose hand was numb remembered that her mother had locked her in a dark closet and shut the door on the hand. The pain was too intense to remember the event until the client allowed her adult self to rescue the child victim by kicking down the door and causing it to fall on the abusive mother.

Clients are encouraged to write or draw recovered memories on the life line they have been constructing. Many of these survivors have extended periods of time with no memories, partial memories, or selective memories. They have not connected the abuses of the past with present repetitive behaviors, cognitions, or body reactions. As they construct a past and a life/time line, they begin to see their life histories and life patterns.

Clients with unsafe and threatening memories can be taught to use visual imagery to counteract the emotional overload both during and after memory work. One client found an ancient, gnarled tree in a nearby field. She took a picture of that tree and carries it with her. When she is particularly stressed, she looks at the picture and reminds herself how the tree has survived in spite of disease, fire, and injury. Dolan (1991) noted that clients can also create present-oriented symbols of safety or preconceived safe settings to keep in their mind's eye. These symbols can be a person, place, or thing that reminds them of healing. During periods of intrusive symptoms, these symbols can provide comfort or serve to reorient clients to the present. Clients can also learn to permit themselves to turn off memories.

Memories can be made more manageable and understandable when they are recorded in journals at specific times in a predetermined safe setting (either during or outside therapy). They also can be drawn or symbolically represented through multimedia creations. A therapist trained in hypnosis can help a client use the natural dissociative process of trance for quicker memory retrieval (Dolan, 1991). Therapeutic stories can also stimulate memory recall (Davis, 1991). Learning to reframe memories, view memories from different angles, or identify the lessons memories have taught about self, family, and childhood also help make memories more manageable.

The process of memory retrieval can be explained using the Gestalt cycle of experience model (Kepner, 1990). The client, in a somewhat stable state of equilibrium or disequilibrium, has a memory fragment or intrusion that frequently begins with a trigger to one of the senses from within or from the environment. Triggers may be consciously unremarkable yet lead to feelings of being out of control. Clients are more open to the impact of triggers when vulnerable, as Dolan (1991) noted. This is particularly true if the client has contact with a perpetrator, undergoes intrusive medical procedures, encounters betrayal or loss, is faced with abandonment or death of a loved one, or is involved in intimacy or sexuality.

If clients are aware of that trigger, their energy gets mobilized. If they are not aware or want to avoid the trigger, they desensitize and dissociate, diminishing their awareness and suppressing their energy. Yet, the memory keeps returning, causing anxiety, tension, and pain. In therapy, clients are encouraged to take action and move toward awareness by making contact with the memory in all its various aspects of sensory information, cognitive knowledge, affect, body reaction, associated beliefs, and actions. Once contact is made, restructuring can occur, and closure of the memory can begin. The closure process empowers clients as their perceptions, ideas, and feelings of the memory are modified, integrated, and grow rather than stagnate and remain frustrated (Kepner, 1990).

Developing Beliefs About Safety

Beliefs held by survivors of sexual abuse are developed frequently as attempts to understand why abuse occurred and what role the survivor played in that occurrence. This process of cognitive appraisal may include aspects of learned helplessness. Foa, Steketee, and Olasov-Rothbaum (1989) noted that the traumatic event was extremely significant in that it "violated formerly held basic concepts of safety . . . stimuli and responses that previously signaled safety have now become associated with danger . . . [so that] the individual lives in chronic fear" (p. 166).

As Jehu, Gazan, and Klassen (1988) noted, these beliefs are often sources of mood disturbances and distorted feelings that lead to inappropriate actions. The beliefs are often self-blaming, have negative impact on interpersonal functioning, or contain externally induced introjects from the abusers. They reflect the survivor's understanding of the meaning of abuse and were developed as state-dependent phenomena.

A variety of associated triggers also become part of the fear structure of beliefs and reactivate them in "bursts of arousal (e.g., startle), reexperiencing (e.g., flashbacks) alternating with avoidance attempts" (Foa, Steketee & Olasov-Rothbaum, 1989, p. 167). To eradicate or reduce fear, these memories must be accessed, and the accompanying beliefs challenged through provision of corrective information and desensitization. However, these beliefs can be accessed fully only through reaccessing the same state in which they originally formed by means of trance, dissociation, hypnosis, abreaction, or flashback. During this state they can be modified, linked with new information to form new imprints, or challenged (Steele and Colrain, 1991). This process frequently takes multiple instances of remembering and repeated exposures to segments of the traumatic material until all components have been included.

Client and therapist together work to identify both the positive and negative self-beliefs, along with the client's beliefs about others regarding issues of safety, trust, power, esteem, and intimacy (McCann & Pearlman, 1990b). These beliefs, which Fine (1990) observed might have developed in an abusive "wartime" environment, form the assumptive world of the client and govern how he or she judges and perceives reality. Epstein (1991) found that four fundamental beliefs are likely to be challenged through traumatization:

1. The world is benign, rewarding, and pleasurable.

2. The world is meaningful, controllable, just, safe, and predictable.

3. The self is lovable, competent, and is not to blame.

4. People are trustworthy and worthy of relating to.

The use of belief inventories (Williams, 1990; McCann & Pearlman, 1990b; Jehu, Gazan & Klassen, 1988) at various points in therapy can help to identify belief structures and beliefs that need to change. Through the use of these inventories, clients who have multiple personalities can learn that different alters hold conflicting beliefs that are often incongruent with the beliefs of the host or internal self-helper.

Clients often need assistance to identify, monitor, and explore the meanings and implications of their beliefs. Clients may be shown how to examine the evidence upon which the beliefs are based. They may be asked to imagine what they would have been like as persons had they not been abused and how they could work toward becoming that self.

Clients also must identify those belief systems that originated with, and were introjected from, their families of origin and/or abusers (Calof, 1991). "I should" statements frequently reflect perpetrator-originated beliefs. Beliefs of survivors are frequently polarized into black/white, either/or, and never/always statements, without shades of gray. Helping a client to "see gray" or substitute positive beliefs and affirmations for negative ones is also part of the safety-making process.

Before a survivor can develop effective coping skills for future stressors, he or she must resolve the meaning of the original trauma and its emotional impacts. The ideal coping process, according to Roth and Newman (1991), involves reexperiencing affect in measured doses until symptoms are reduced and trauma is integrated. This coping process therefore is a change process affecting both emotions and beliefs.

CONCLUSIONS

Working with severely abused adolescents and adults is a challenging, demanding process. These clients do not have basic safety and trust, in many cases, when they arrive at the therapist's door. Treatment must therefore initially focus on safety and trust-building strategies, considerations, and techniques. This chapter summarizes a variety of potential areas for focus and inclusion. Clients need to develop safety measures to protect themselves and feel at least somewhat safe in some part of their environment before they can tackle the demanding process of memory retrieval integration and belief change. Empowered clients are better able to do the intense work necessary to free themselves from the horrors of their past.

Part IV

Treatment of Survivors of War

12

War-Related Trauma: An Integrative Experiential, Cognitive, and Spiritual Approach

Raymond Monsour Scurfield

> I'll never forget my first air assault into a hot LZ [Landing Zone]. . . . We were in the chopper, coming in to land, and we started yelling, pumping ourselves up, bouncing up and down. . . . Man, I was SO ALIVE—I've never felt so high . . . and you know, there will ALWAYS be wars, because WAR IS THE ULTIMATE THRILL!
>
> —Vietnam veteran, Los Angeles, CA
> May 1988

> When I got back from Nam, I went and got a vasectomy within a month. . . . There was NO way I was EVER going to father a son who would have to go through THAT hell that I went through.
>
> —Vietnam veteran, Tacoma, WA
> March 1991

Historically, U.S. "healthy" war veterans were faced with the general assumption that they would return home with readjustment problems that would be relatively mild and short-lived. Any lack of response by the veteran or a prolongation of symptoms beyond a few months typically has been considered as evidence of an underlying psychiatric condition rather than due to the war experience. Traditionally, there has been a rather remarkable collusion of sanitization and silence about the true impact of war on its participants and the full extent of the horror of war (Scurfield, 1992).

Connected to this collusion of sanitization and silence has been a powerful societal myth that *heroes do not or should not have any problems*. Thus, it has been difficult for veterans to admit to themselves or to others that they might be suffering from war zone experiences per se. The typical "comprehensive" psychiatric assessment of veterans presenting to the Department of Veterans Affairs (VA) with a mental health problem until the 1980s consisted of one to two lines of inquiry regarding the veteran's military history. In addition, the military view on acute psychiatric casualties was (1) a breakdown under severe stress was temporary and would pass relatively quickly with simple interventions, and the soldier would then return to duty; (2) psychiatric malfunctioning reflects individual weakness or premorbid conditions; or (3) poor leadership and weak unit cohesion were at fault (Scurfield and Tice, 1992). None of these perspectives allowed for the possibility that war itself might be traumatic and explain longer-term malfunctioning.

Not until fifteen years after almost all U.S. troops had been withdrawn from Vietnam did the United States conduct its first sophisticated and comprehensive national psychiatric epidemiologic study of the veteran. The National Vietnam Veterans Readjustment Study (NVVRS) set out to determine shorter- and longer-term sequelae of the war experience and other pre- and postwar factors. Fully 15.2 percent of all Vietnam war zone veterans were found with post-traumatic stress disorder (PTSD), and another 11.1 percent with "partial" PTSD. There was over a 30 percent prevalence rate of PTSD among veterans exposed to heavy combat stressors and among those wounded. Although premilitary and postmilitary factors also appeared important, the extent and severity of exposure to war trauma appeared to be the most closely associated with PTSD (Kulka et al., 1990).

A second and completely separate study with a different sampling strategy was conducted on 2,042 male veteran twin pairs. An almost identical PTSD prevalence rate to that of the NVVRS was reported (16.8 percent for the twin who had served in Vietnam, versus 5 percent for the cotwin who did not serve in Vietnam). In addition, there was a ninefold increase in PTSD among twins who experienced high levels of combat in comparison with cotwins who did not serve in the war zone (Goldberg et al., 1991). This study controlled for premorbid factors to a degree not possible with other retrospective studies.

The U.S. Department of Veterans Affairs has recognized that the development of war zone–related PTSD has a primary relationship to the war stressors experienced and that a specialized, rather than a general, mental health treatment regimen and strategy are necessary for severe cases. Thus, over twenty specialized inpatient PTSD units, over forty outpatient PTSD clinical teams, several dual disorder (substance abuse and PTSD) programs, and 202 Veterans Centers have been established. Congressional initiatives and "fenced" appropriations have dictated that the Department of Veterans Affairs establish or augment existing PTSD programs, and the VA has established a National Center for PTSD to provide leadership and coordinate various PTSD treatment, educational, and research activities. A number of VA professional mental health staff have attained national recognition in the field of PTSD, and the VA has extended some PTSD services beyond veterans to national disaster survivors (Armstrong, O'Callahan, and Marmar, 1991; Sorenson, 1990a, 1990b).

THE NATURE OF TRAUMA AND INADEQUACIES IN THE DSM III PTSD CRITERIA

The *Diagnostic and Statistical Manual of Mental Disorders III-R* of the American Psychiatric Association (1987) reflects new understanding and expertise, but there are continuing inadequacies with regard to PTSD. No knowledgeable clinician argues with the three major categories of symptoms listed: recurrent and intrusive thoughts, detachment and psychic numbing, and arousal (startle reaction). Unfortunately, significant core PTSD symptoms and processes are ignored. Those suffering from traumatic stress invariably experience a fundamental impact on the self. This "damaged self" (Carmen and Rieker, 1989) can be manifested by various degrees of self-denigration, very low self-esteem, self-recrimination, and a confused, conflicted, and/or shattered sense of identity (Carmen and Rieker, 1989).

PTSD victims are preoccupied with a loss of control over their feelings, behaviors, and sanity. Second, their preoccupation with blame may be directed outwardly and/or inwardly (Scurfield, 1988, 1993b). Inward-directed blame typically involves survivor guilt and shame over having survived when someone else did not and/or over behaviors of survival, rage, and depression. Outward-directed blame typically involves rage at those exempted from having to experience the trauma and toward those directly or symbolically viewed by the survivor as having "caused" or contributed to the trauma (Krupnick and Horowitz, 1981; Scurfield, 1985, 1993b).

Third, victims may experience an "existential malaise," with the survivor's becoming very confused or in conflict over what is meaningful or right in life, where the survivor fits in, and where this will all lead. A closely related phenomenon is the "broken connection" between the survivor and society; the survivor may well feel alienated, stigmatized, and discounted by society and its institutions; this is particularly likely to occur among survivors of repeated, massive trauma such as concentration camps in Nazi Germany and combat veterans (Lifton, 1979).

Fourth, to survive trauma, particularly repeated and protracted trauma, victims may feel literally disconnected within the self, between and among their cognitions, affect, physical sensations, and behaviors. This is due, in part, to the trauma-associated and profound emotional/physiological responses of rage, grief, and terror that are intrinsic to a trauma experience. These responses are potentially so overwhelming that the survivors must somehow detach from them in order not to be overwhelmed (Hammond, Scurfield, and Risse, 1992; Scurfield, 1993b). The detachment can become so profound that they may lose the ability to feel or respond with appropriate affect and accompanying physical sensations in subsequent situations (for a descriptive account of how survivors must alter affective responses in order to survive physical abuse, see Carmen and Rieker, 1989).

These symptoms are central to an appropriate and full conceptualization of PTSD. Treatment principles should be based on this expanded conceptualization.

Several factors about the trauma of war must be kept in mind when considering treatment objectives with all war veterans, regardless of number of units, personnel, and equipment involved. The core of the war experience is embedded within the context of small, military operational units. The incredible intensity of relationships that occur within a fire-team, squad, platoon, gun or armored vehicle crew, and so on is extraordinary and necessary to survival in the hostile and unpredictable milieu of the war zone.

Still, the war trauma is intertwined both with peers in this small group and with military authorities. Peer group psychotherapy with fellow and sister veterans offers an immediate and profound arena in which such issues as loss of a buddy, "shameful" behavior, "mistakes," and peer acceptance or rejection that occurred in the war zone can be directly confronted. The critical nature of possible acceptance, understanding, or rejection by peers in a treatment group is due to the fact that along with concerns about one's own safety and that of peers, perhaps the dominant dynamic and concern among military personnel in the war zone involve a preoccupation with how their attitudes and behaviors are received and accepted or rejected by the peer group (in the small operational military unit); for example, the fear of letting others down is a primary concern (Shalit, 1988). The obvious advantages offered by peer group treatment with fellow and sister veterans have led many clinicians to consider peer group treatment the modality of choice (although individual therapy may be essential, also, to help prepare a veteran for a positive therapeutic experience in a peer group) (Egendorf, 1975; Parson, 1984; Scurfield, 1985, 1993b; Smith, 1980, 1985).

There are inextricable and profound linkages between war issues and the veteran's orientation toward society and a "higher power" or God. Both of these linkages arise because military personnel are directly sanctioned by society (through the military) to be agents of killing and maiming, as well as, possibly, other traumas such as incarceration and physical abuse of prisoners. However, each individual veteran and each small operational military unit operationalize this sanction on a very personal, day-to-day basis in the war zone. Each individual and small military unit must learn to determine how this sanction to kill and maim is reconciled, if at all, with personal, ethical, moral, and, possibly, religious beliefs; Judeo-Christian mores tend to teach that no one should kill other human beings.

The task to kill becomes even more complex and difficult when religious or spiritual beliefs are invoked (or are perceived) to sanction this task. For example, chaplains in the war zone have been viewed by a number of veterans as invoking God's sanction for the U.S. military to kill and maim the enemy. Our cause is "right and good," and the enemy's by this definition must be "wrong and bad." (For additional discussion of the spiritual and religious dynamics in war, see Horowitz and Solomon, 1978; Jacob, 1987; Lifton, 1978; Mahedy, 1986).

A number of war veterans come to the decision that "to kill in cases of clear-cut self-defense" is tolerable. This line of thinking has at least two problems. First, many situations arise in a war zone in which the decision to kill or maim may clearly not be in self-defense, and many U.S. war veterans are severely troubled when women and/or children are killed (even when in self-defense). Second, veterans must come to personal terms with the issue of whether it is "right" for them and for the U.S. military to even be in this war in the first place. If there is some question about the "rightness" of the war, then the entire issue of all behavior in the war zone is brought into question.

In addition, the internal pressures that accumulate on individuals in a war zone, of course, are extremely powerful and vivid. Couple these pressures with repeatedly threatening and crisis situations, an accumulation of traumatic experiences and losses, and inevitably a number of veterans explode into acts of which they are not proud or may be ashamed. When errors in human judgment or in execution of duties occur, resulting deaths and injuries typically invoke severe reactions of guilt and shame and/or profound denial of any adverse emotional reactions.

The war veteran returns home never deconditioned or debriefed in a manner designed to counter what was instilled in military training (Eisenhart, 1975) and through repetitive war zone experience. Once again, the veteran must reconcile war zone behaviors and attitudes that clearly are not acceptable "back in the world." Or, perhaps even worse, a removal from the horrors of the war zone may precipitate a judgmental perspective toward behaviors there committed, raising ethical and moral issues perhaps at least partially masked over previously by the necessity to maintain a survival mode.

The tendency for society and its institutions to minimize or downplay the horrors of war (Scurfield, 1992) may help the veteran initially maintain a minimization or denial of what happened. However, such societal reactions also may be experienced as rejection of the veteran's experience and sacrifice of self and buddies as well as accomplishments. Conversely, a hero's welcome may provoke considerable guilt, shame, or rage if the veteran does not feel he or she has been heroic. All of the aforementioned are likely to promote or exacerbate personal issues of shame, guilt, rage, and alienation or disaffiliation from belief in society's institutions and institutionalized religion or spiritual beliefs.

War brings together in the war zone veteran a profound intertwining of extremely powerful and vivid sensations, emotions, cognitions, and images. Possessing the ultimate power of life and death over others and witnessing or carrying out this ultimate power will simultaneously or alternatively provoke bewildering, terrifying, horrifying, rageful, grief-filled, exhilarating, humbling, uplifting, stimulating, deadening, shocking, pleasurable, or intoxicating sensations, images, and cognitions. How the veteran adjusts to, processes, or detaches from, any or all of these powerful states while in the war zone may establish a pattern that continues to a large degree postwar. This is particularly likely to be the case with the veteran who returns to, or lives in, a work or community environment that is threatening, violent, nonsupportive, or unpredictable. Therefore, the impact of altering these affective responses to war trauma is one of the central areas of treatment concern.

It is important to note that war veterans typically not only are exposed to a series of traumatic events but also may experience a range of several different types of trauma (Scurfield, 1993b), of which each may have a somewhat different impact on the veteran's postwar recovery. Aspects include:

1. bereavement or loss;

2. violation of physical self-boundary (e.g., physical injury; constant threat of physical injury; and sexual or physical abuse that may not result in physical injury per se);

3. exposure to death or dying;

4. agent or perpetrator of trauma;

5. self-inflicted trauma (to include substance abuse);

6. bystander, observer, or witness of trauma; and

7. direct or indirect responsibility for the occurrence, nonprevention, continuance or cover-up of trauma that is perpetrated by others.

Abreacting and processing war trauma help veterans consider unresolved issues and the extent to which several or all of these types of trauma were experienced; working on specific issues may or may not help to resolve issues related to other categories of trauma that were experienced. Each of these factors must be attended to within the various phases of the treatment process and within the treatment principles that are discussed later.

This section has presented the stressful or problematic aspects of the war zone experience. Many powerful positive aspects also occur, including the bonding that occurs between war zone personnel; in some cases it is the most powerful bonding that is ever experienced as people learn how to survive and, perhaps, even develop and grow in the midst of a very demanding "testing ground." Maturity, self-satisfaction, teamwork, accomplishment, pride, excitement, and adventure certainly are as much a part of the war zone experience as anything else already described.

However, these positive factors are often masked over by veterans who have significant, unresolved traumatic issues from their war zone experiences. Enhancing an appropriate awareness and appreciation of positive aspects of the war zone and postwar experience is a major clinical strategy that will be discussed later.

PROBLEMATIC RELATIONSHIP BETWEEN DISABILITY COMPENSATION AND PTSD TREATMENT

There is a remarkable strength and complexity concerning the "secondary gain" dynamic among war veterans and service-connected disability compensation, for example, monetary reimbursement for a medical or psychiatric condition deemed "caused" or "exacerbated" by military service. On the one hand, the VA benefits system is an outgrowth of a noble and worthy notion—that veterans have given far above and beyond that expected or demanded of non-veterans and should be justly compensated.

On the other hand, in this author's opinion, the administrative defining, adjudicating, and carrying out of financial compensation and benefits policies for "psychiatric disabilities" in particular is fraught with a fundamental paradox. By and large, the veteran is compensated *only* as long as he or she *remains "disabled."* This sets up a situation where the veteran is *rewarded monetarily to stay sick and suffers a financial penalty to get better.*

Also, many veterans feel that the federal government and society have reneged or, at the very least, have not justly or fairly compensated veterans for their service and sacrifice for their country. Indeed, many who have been terribly wounded physically or psychiatrically, may feel that no form or amount of compensation would ever suffice. After all, what is the price of the loss of one's limbs, youth, or innocence, or loss of faith in one's country, or in a god? Consequently, many veterans view disability compensation as "just getting some of what we are due."

A further complication is that the very institution that has been established to decide on financial compensation matters *also* is the designated health care provider for veterans. At the heart of the conflict is the fact that *there is no way* that the veteran can or should *fully trust* a VA mental health provider (in the way that any client must be able to trust his or her counselor or therapist) *to the extent that the veteran perceives the VA provider to be involved in influencing or determining financial compensation matters.* The degree to which the veteran is concerned that something that he or she shares with the VA provider may negatively (or positively!) impact on possible financial compensation *will fundamentally* effect the extent to which the veteran will choose to be open and honest in the clinical relationship.

SIXTEEN TRAUMATIC STRESS TREATMENT PRINCIPLES

1. Separating Treatment and Compensation

There must be a clear distinction between being a therapist and influencing a veteran's disability rating for a service-connected condition (such as PTSD). Otherwise, it will be impossible to engage in a therapeutic trust relationship necessary for effective trauma recovery. This same conflict occurs if therapists possess a legal authority over their client, such as being able to remove a child from the home.

To minimize the negative therapeutic impact of the secondary gain dynamic intrinsic to clinical work with veterans who have any concern about VA compensation, it is imperative that the clinician undertake several actions. The clinician must recognize that there is an inherent conflictual issue between clinician and veteran when the role of the clinician in compensation matters is unclear. The reality of this dual role within the VA must be discussed frankly with the veteran very early in the treatment process. The VA Regional Office must have access to any VA medical records when evaluating a claim, and clinically documented "improvement" may indeed be taken as evidence by a Regional Office to deny a claim or reduce existing compensation rating. The clinician must seriously weigh the trade-offs in active and direct involvement in any aspect of compensation proceedings. For example, American Lake VAMC Post-Traumatic Stress Treatment (PTST) Program staff write information about a specific veteran that is routinely recorded for clinical purposes only, for example, progress notes in a medical record and a clinical discharge summary. "Special" write-ups for the purposes of supporting or clarifying a veteran client's claim with a Regional Office are not provided; a copy of the (routinely) written clinical discharge summary completed at the conclusion of a veteran's episode of treatment with the program is the only written data that will be provided.

Finally, and perhaps most importantly, the veteran must be challenged openly by the clinician: "Are you really willing to take the chance that your disability compensation claim may be reduced or denied if you improve or get better?" "Is at least 51 percent of your motivation for being here to get better?" "Do you understand that there are absolutely no guarantees about what impact your treatment might have on your compensation, and are you willing to engage openly and honestly in treatment nevertheless?"

2. Stopping Retraumatizing Behaviors

The second treatment principle is to prevent or stop retraumatizing behaviors. If the veteran is continuing, or starting to engage in, behaviors such as substance abuse, excessive thrill seeking, self-destruction, or domestic violence, then the veteran must maintain a survival mode of functioning. By definition, such behavior is characterized by constant vigilance, profound detachment, denial, avoidance, isolation, and minimization. Being in such a survival mode is very counterproductive to the "opening-up" process and establishment of a therapeutic trust relationship necessary to be able to alleviate or resolve war zone trauma issues.

3. Establishing a Therapeutic Trust Relationship

The third principle of traumatic stress treatment is the establishment of a therapeutic trust relationship. (It is important to note that the first two principles directly impact on the degree to which a therapeutic trust relationship is possible.) Many experienced clinicians argue that the establishment of a therapeutic trust relationship may be the central therapeutic task and indeed may be the core of the treatment (Haley, 1974; Carmen and Rieker, 1989). The centrality of this principle is due to the fact that trauma, by definition, is imposed by the environment. This environmentally induced violation of the individual brings into question several issues about how safe it is ever to trust the environment again and, by extension, an authority figure such as a clinician. Clients' concerns over trusting their own abilities to assess or deal with powerful internal urges and emotions or with environmental threats also come into play. Finally, aspects about the clinician (gender, race, survivor or not of the same type of trauma), the survivor's previous experience with clinicians, and the clinician's style of therapy and organizational affiliation may have profound impacts on the client's willingness and ability to engage in a trusting relationship (for some more descriptive accounts of the clinical relationship dynamics with trauma survivors, see Danieli, 1984; Egendorf, 1985; Haley, 1984; Howard, 1976; Lifton, 1978; Summit, 1989). When the clinician is a federal government employee, particularly with the Department of Veterans Affairs, "institutional transference" is particularly powerful. Veterans' issues about having been betrayed by the government, about receiving less than satisfactory services since the war, and about the military tend to be triggered by encounters with the federal government and VA health or mental health providers (Scurfield, 1985).

The issue of trust between veteran and clinician and between veteran and treatment program should be addressed in specific terms very early in the treatment process, for example, by specification of very clear boundaries concerning acceptable and unacceptable behaviors (Carmen and Rieker, 1989). For war veterans, ground rules about violence and threats of violence, confidentiality (particularly regarding written medical chart entries about war trauma and accessibility to VA medical records by a VA Regional Office or other governmental agency), and confidentiality in individual therapy sessions versus group therapy sessions are particularly important to specify and maintain.

It also seems crucial to make a clear statement early in treatment that validates the veteran's history and experiences that have led to a realistic tendency not to trust governmental authorities. Prototypical first contact comments include:

When you first walk in here, you have many valid reasons from your past experiences not to trust me, this program, or this agency. I expect that I have to earn your trust; and, considering what you have experienced both in the war and afterward, that is only natural. I ask only in return that you at least give me a chance. Please be aware if you are reacting to me because I remind you of some other authority in your life or because of something about me that Ray Scurfield has said or done, here and now.

The other level of trust is between and among you veterans here in this program. The very process of your allowing yourself and others to get close in this program will require you to start by lowering some of those very walls that you've built up in-country and over the years. Your willingness to "let others in to some degree" will bring back some of the strong negatives and positives that happened with buddies in the war zone.

The third level of trust is with yourselves. Many of you don't trust your own abilities (to control strong emotions, genuinely care or allow others to care for you), and so how can you trust others if you can't trust yourselves? So please be aware and let others know when you are reacting to them because you have trouble letting others in versus whether it is because of something they have said or done.

4. Education Regarding Traumatic Stress and Recovery

The fourth principle concerns the provision of clear and accurate verbal and written information (because of the difficulty that many trauma survivors and veterans have with memory and concentration). Prototypical comments to veterans early in treatment about PTSD may include:

Your symptoms will always get worse temporarily before they get better once you start in traumatic stress treatment or when you enter a more intensive or new phase of trauma work. This is only natural in that you are being asked to pay attention to some of the very memories that you have been desperately trying to avoid or suppress all these years. Also, you are fearful and preoccupied that you may lose control if you really let yourself get back into some of the traumatic memories, fearing that you might go back in so deeply that you will never come back out, or you will be overwhelmed by a powerful emotion, such as starting to cry and never being able to stop. It is almost impossible to totally forget about war trauma memories, because trauma literally is unforgettable. Thus, the only way you can really forget is to develop psychogenic amnesia or numb yourself out in a most extreme way, such as on chemicals. Even those affects are usually only temporary. What you can aim for is to significantly reduce the frequency or severity of a number of your symptoms and to eventually learn how to more peacefully coexist with those traumatic memories.

5. Symptom Management

The fifth treatment principle is that trauma survivors must be given practical, concrete behavioral and cognitive strategies to promote self-control over powerful emotions and physical arousal. Typically, these must include anger or anxiety management techniques and strategies (Sonkin and Durphy, 1982) and sleep disturbance, stress reduction, and relaxation techniques (Miller and DePilato, 1983; Scrignar, 1988), and some attention must be paid to symptom management practices prior to entering into intensive uncovering or exposure therapy of trauma experiences. This attention will promote veteran abilities to enhance self-control and self-confidence in tolerating and confronting troubling war experiences. To engage in provocative treatment techniques such as flooding and exposure therapies or abreactive therapies (or through research protocols) without providing clients with additional symptom management tools seems ill-advised, at best, and perhaps unethical and irresponsible. To trigger traumatic memories and accompanying sensations in a treatment session may well result in increased intrusive, recurring symptoms outside the sessions.

6. Autobiographical and Whole-Life Perspective

The sixth treatment principle is to provide the veteran with a whole-life perspective to include and not either unduly exaggerate or minimize the role of the identified trauma as well as other factors in their lives. For war veterans, applicable factors need to include prewar, war, and postwar life. This perspective is essential since most war veterans with unresolved war trauma either significantly over- or underemphasize the role that the trauma of war has played in their lives. For example, as this author explains to veteran clients: "No one ever went to war as a blank tablet; we all went as somebody. Who was that somebody?" (Veterans will be quick to point out differences between their pre- and postwar selves; however, it is equally important to clarify in what ways one was the same or similar pre- and postwar.)

Another important aspect of a whole-life perspective is that most veterans (and nonveterans as well) may have experienced trauma in their lives before and/or after the identified trauma of war. The legacy of each of these traumas and their relationship to each other is important. For a number of veterans, significant trauma experience occurred on active duty outside the war zone, in basic training or in advance training (e.g., where peers may have been injured or killed in training exercises). A number of veterans who returned from the war zone to spend additional active-duty time prior to discharge may have experienced significant trauma while adjusting to life outside the war zone. The military environment may have reinforced the denial and avoidance of war-related issues until veterans got close to discharge or were discharged; typically, it was about this time or soon after that latent reexperiencing and/or arousal symptoms might emerge. Another reason for symptom exacerbation at this time is that most military personnel will not go to a military mental health resource while on active duty for fear that it will have a negative impact on their career or type of discharge (Scurfield and Tice, 1992; Scurfield, 1992). (For a detailed discussion of the range of stressors and trauma that might face active-duty military, see Scurfield and Blank, 1985.)

Finally, the postwar lives of a number of military veterans suffering from moderate-to-severe PTSD have been characterized by dysfunction and maladaptive coping patterns (Scurfield, 1985). Consequently, there appears to be an increase in the likelihood of yet additional exposure to (civilian) trauma. Paying attention only or predominantly to premilitary and war zone issues usually will not be sufficient to significantly alter chronic and hence entrenched postwar maladaptive patterns.

7. Therapeutic Reexperiencing of Aspects of Trauma

The seventh principle describes the variety of clinical strategies that facilitate a "direct therapeutic exposure to an aspect of the original trauma" (Fairbank and Nicholson, 1987). The concept is rather simple: if detachment, avoidance, numbing, denial, minimization, and isolation were sufficient to heal from trauma, there would be little or no need for clinicians to treat survivors. All trauma survivors engage in various detachment mechanisms in order to survive the trauma at the time it is happening and to further avoid painful intrusive and recurrent reexperiencing of the original trauma for years or decades afterward. Thus trauma survivors, by definition, are experts in detachment. In more severe instances, detachment strategies have become so entrenched and powerful that what were once functional mechanisms subsequently become problematic to current life functioning. Yet, for many survivors, the painful, vivid reexperiencing phenomena have not been eliminated.

The clinical strategy therefore is to engage the survivor in ways that will promote recall and at least a partial reliving of problematic aspects of the original trauma; the underlying assumption is that such contact is necessary to eventual recovery. The objective is to "detoxify" issues embedded in the traumatic experience and attached memories and sensations to the point that a more peaceful coexistence is possible. It is important to note that detachment or covering-over mechanisms must be facilitated as well, particularly if the survivor is in a predominantly intrusive (versus a detachment) phase of traumatic stress symptomology.

A range of clinical techniques and strategies attempts to ameliorate or detoxify psychological fallout of trauma. Behavioral, exposure-based techniques (flooding, implosive) have been reported to have some treatment efficacy in reducing intrusive symptomatology (Abueg and Fairbank, 1991; Cooper and Clum, 1989; Keane et al., 1989; Boudewyns et al., 1990). However, they may increase the potential risk of substance abuse relapses and may be less effective when cognitive deficits are present (Litz et al., 1990; Abueg and Fairbank, 1991). Such techniques frequently are quite painful to the client and address only a very defined set of PTSD symptoms. They seem most appropriate, perhaps, when utilized as an adjunct within a more comprehensive treatment regimen, such as specialized inpatient PTSD units. A relatively "new" technique, eye movement desensitization (EMD), which incorporates some elements of systematic desensitization, has been reported to "defuse" negative feelings attached to traumatic memories following very time-limited application of EMD (Shapiro, 1989a, 1989b). A number of seasoned PTSD clinicians have reported to the author through personal communication the treatment efficacy of EMD when it is utilized as an adjunct to a more comprehensive therapeutic endeavor. EMD has been helpful to diminish adverse reaction to particularly vivid and painful intrusive war trauma symptoms when utilized as an adjunct to process-oriented war trauma treatment groups in the PTST Program at the American Lake VA Medical Center.

The most widely utilized and anecdotally described approaches to facilitate a "direct therapeutic exposure to an aspect of the original trauma" with war-related traumatic stress have been veteran peer treatment groups. Exposure has been at the simplest level, "simply talking about," and listening to other veterans talk about, war trauma. Good clinical judgment and skill in utilizing a variety of psychotherapeutic techniques helps war veterans to remember, discuss, emote about, and reflect on the range of problematic cognitions, emotions, and behaviors that occurred at the time of, and that are associated with recall of, the war trauma (Shatan, 1973, 1974; Egendorf, 1975; Lifton, 1978; Scurfield et al., 1984; Scurfield, 1985; Smith, 1980, 1985; Walker, 1983; Walker and Nash, 1981).

The most critical aspect in facilitating a therapeutic reexperiencing appears to be through promoting a "dosing" or modulating of emotional and cognitive reliving of aspects of the original trauma, coupled with withdrawal or detachment. In this way, the memories, accompanying effect, and psychological responses are not overwhelming and hence retraumatizing (Hammond, Scurfield, and Risse, 1993; Horowitz, 1976). Probably most critical is clinician and survivor sensitivity to the profound paradox that characterizes trauma experiences. On one hand, trauma is such a powerful experience that it is unforgettable (unless one develops psychogenic amnesia). On the other hand, trauma-reliving symptoms are so painful that it is extremely difficult to allow memories to surface and remain. Hence the "push-pull" phenomenon that characterizes post-trauma functioning among survivors with unresolved trauma-related issues.

This paradoxical dynamic of being unforgettable yet too painful and intrusive to remember becomes central to the clinical strategy. The strategy is to empower the survivor with positive and successful re-experiencing through voluntary and progressively deeper, yet "digestible" or tolerable, contact with traumatic memories. Then the survivor is helped to break off such contact. Successful alternation occurs through a series of supportive, confrontive, and clarifying encounters. Clear ground rules and the therapeutic ground rules of the facilitator in veteran peer group treatment are particularly crucial to this therapeutic task (Scurfield et al., 1984).

Activity-based therapies. A number of trauma survivors seem able to achieve a satisfactory resolution or accommodation of trauma issues through a relatively discrete series of "talking only" therapy sessions. However, a sub-group seems able to progress only to a certain point when sitting in a room and engaging in predominantly verbal and cognitive interactions.

The Post-Traumatic Stress Treatment Program that the author helped to establish and directed from its inception in 1985 through 1991 pioneered an eclectic, yet integrated, series of "activity-based therapies" to complement the many "talking therapy" groups and psychoeducational classes contained in the eleven-week intensive inpatient phase of treatment. The activities took place in a carefully planned series and were embedded within a closed membership peer group that completed the targeted eleven-week inpatient program together. They included activities as diverse as a helicopter ride (Scurfield, Wong, and Zeerocah, 1992), a trip to the War Memorial, an Outward Bound activity (Hyer et al., submitted), and an optional sweat lodge ceremony conducted at a nearby American Indian reservation by a Native American spiritual leader (Scurfield, submitted). A return trip to the war zone is, perhaps, the ultimate extension of "direct therapeutic exposure to an aspect of the original trauma" and of activity-based-action therapy (short of reimmersion in actual combat) (Gerlock, 1991; Scurfield, 1989).

Journal writing and sharing. In the PTST Program, veterans must make daily entries in a personal journal about their memories and feelings, while going through the treatment program. The journal indicates what progress or unfinished business has occurred or needs to be addressed and provides a valuable record for later. On each Friday, veterans are required to verbally share some selected sections.

8. Cognitive Reframing

The eighth treatment principle is intimately connected with the previous treatment principle. To survive trauma, individuals ascribe "meaning" to the events that occur. Many survivors "reframe" the trauma experience to help them tolerate it; however, this reframing may or may not be reality-based and might contribute to problematic post-traumatic retrospection. For example, a war veteran may conclude that he or she should have died "because people I was responsible for died." Veterans also may judge themselves to be immoral or unworthy of success because of their survival behaviors or mistakes. These veterans severely downplay mitigating environmental circumstances.

Developing an understanding and a full acknowledgment of the total reality of the trauma experience, which helps survival in emergency situations, may eventually allow appropriate reframing to occur. A veteran who repeatedly awakens from a traumatic nightmare in which he or she is just about to be killed may wake up with the message (and accompanying terror reaction), "I'm going to be killed." On the other hand, the veteran can prepare a very different message to write down and place by the bed and verbalize out loud whenever he or she awakens in the future from this dream. This message might be, "I survived."

One clinical technique developed over the past twelve years by this author helps veterans arrive at a more realistic and balanced determination of "percentages of responsibility" for a particular trauma. A frequent legacy of war has been the veteran's preoccupation and painful, incessant ruminations of anguish, guilt, shame, and self-contempt over "being at fault" or "responsible" for a trauma, usually involving death or injury to other persons.

Technique to Determine "Percentages of Responsibility"

The veteran, to no avail, has heard various arguments from others that enumerate what appear to be logical reasons for his or her not assuming so much of the responsibility (and the veteran him- or herself usually has repeatedly rehashed many of these arguments). The irrational holding onto of an exaggerated sense of responsibility prevails. A smaller sub-group of veterans manifest the opposite stance—they almost totally disavow any sense of personal responsibility for behaviors in the war-zone and, instead, blame others, such as those in military command positions (see Frey-Wouters and Laufer, 1986).

The technique enables the veteran almost always to arrive at a substantially more balanced and realistic perspective of personal versus other responsibility for a specific trauma. This technique is *not* an attempt to totally absolve the veteran of *all or to minimize* legitimate personal accountability for his behaviors *and* nonbehaviors (Marin, 1981). Rather, it facilitates a more reasonable and reality-based perspective. It also clearly has applicability to adult trauma other than war.

The following case example provides a clinical reference for the application of each of the elements of this technique. (This veteran is forty-three years old and served a tour in Vietnam primarily as a truck driver delivering and unloading supplies to various military units.)

I had finished unloading a truck full of supplies to this unit; I was really tired, and was just sitting in the cab, resting. . . . I happened to glance over and saw a guy in the distance by a tree; I assumed he was on perimeter (guard) duty. I also saw a second guy who was a little ways apart from the first guy and was moving in his direction. I assumed they were both Americans. All of a sudden, I heard this loud sound, a rifle shot. One guy looked like he was laying down next to a tree; the other guy was running away. I found out that the second guy must have been a VC [Viet Cong], and he had killed the American . . . and, I had just *sat* there in my truck and had *assumed* he was an *American!* My God, I could have checked closer, or I could have yelled out, or done *something!*

Application of the steps of assigning percentages of responsibility is as follows.

Step 1 facilitates a clear explication of the event and the survivor's perception and rationale for the degree of self-responsibility assumed. The veteran is helped to verbalize the *details* of the event, preferably in the first-person tense as if the event were occurring now. Hazy or unclear descriptions *must* be clarified *or* it must be determined that a remembrance actually *is* hazy or unclear. Then, the veteran must verbalize exactly *how much* of the responsibility he has assumed, in this case for the death of the American who was shot by the VC.

Therapist: Let me clarify something right away; are you feeling *totally* responsible for this guy's death?

Veteran: Yes . . . well, almost totally.

Therapist: Let's give a percentage to it. If we can assume that there is a total of 100 percent responsibility for this guy's death, what percentage have you blamed yourself for? You don't have to be *exact*, just give an approximation.

Veteran: About 95 percent.

Therapist: Are you sure that your responsibility is about 95 percent? Is it maybe *more* than that, or *less* than that?

This therapeutic interaction is to stimulate new thinking by the veteran regarding the percentage of responsibility that he/she has assumed responsibility for. The veteran is then challenged to *convince* the clinician and the rest of the group how it was that he *deserves* to be 95 percent responsible. The clinician must direct the group *not* to rescue at this point in order to force the veteran to *fully acknowledge "publicly"* (to the group and clinician) that which he has already decided and been persecuting himself about all these years. It is critical for the veteran to let them know *how* and *what* he has been remembering and saying to himself to remain convinced of his (exaggerated) sense of responsibility.

Step 2 challenges the survivor's exclusion or minimization of the role of others who were at the immediate scene of the trauma.

Veteran: I would give the other 5 percent of the responsibility for the death to the vet himself; I guess if he had been a little more careful maybe the VC wouldn't have gotten that close to him.

Therapist: Wait a minute. Let's look closer at this guy's responsibility. Were *you responsible for sentry duty that night?*

Veteran: No, actually I think the guy killed was one of the guys pulling sentry duty.

Therapist: And so, he is only *5 percent* responsible for allowing that VC to get that close to him that night, and he was on sentry duty, and somehow you are *95 percent* responsible for his death? Does that make sense to you?

Veteran: Well, no, now that you put it that way, maybe he was 15 percent or 20 percent responsible.

Therapist: Really? Are you sure that is a fair percentage to assign to him? Should he get more or less than 15–20 percent? [Once the veteran arrives at what appears to be a more realistic percentage of responsibility that might be assigned to the most obvious other person who bears some responsibility, the veteran is further challenged to consider how responsible is he for that other person *even being there* that night.

By the way, did you have any responsibility for that veteran being in Vietnam? [and: being in that unit, being there that night, being on guard duty, that he obeyed somebody's order to stand guard, for him being in-country or for being in the Army. . . . If the veteran claims that indeed he *did* have some influence over the other person's being in the actual situation that occurred, he then is challenged to convince the group and clinician how that person himself had *absolutely no responsibility for being there*, and how the veteran had *totally "forced"* or caused the other person to be there.]

The above strategy is also systematically applied *to all other persons who were present* at the actual scene of the trauma:

- the other veterans who were on sentry duty that night
- whoever *assigned* that deceased American to be on sentry duty
- whoever was responsible for the selection of the site where the unit was located (would this event have occurred if the unit had been elsewhere?)
- any other Americans who were in the area, and do *any* of them have *any* responsibility for what happened that night?
- the Viet Cong who actually shot the American

Therapist: Let's talk for a moment about "the enemy." *Were the VC any good at what they did?* *You* tell *us* how good the VC were at infiltrating behind perimeter lines.

Veteran: Well, of course, they were good, they were *damned* good.

Therapist: And if the men in that unit all were doing their jobs to the best of their abilities that night, does that mean that the VC would never have been able to kill anyone?" Let's get real: DOES NOT THAT VC DESERVE SOME OF THE RESPONSIBILITY FOR THE DEATH OF THAT AMERICAN?!

Veteran: Well, yes: maybe about 30 or 40 percent.

Therapist: Wait a moment; isn't that *too much* to give to someone whom you hadn't given *any* responsibility to all these years? Make sure that you are now giving what *you* consider to be a fair and realistic percentage to the enemy, no more and no less.

Thus, the veteran *comes to his own conclusion* that, indeed, his perception and remembrance of the event and delegation of blame have been extremely constricted. It may now be timely to bring to the veteran's attention that *the percentages of responsibility that the veteran has assigned to various people, including his own—now total well over 100 percent*!

Therapist: By the way, you have now assigned well over 100 percent responsibility for the American who was killed. That is impossible; that total can only equal 100 percent. Do you think that you need to recalculate some or all of the percentages you have assigned? Is yours still 95 percent, which means that all of these other people split up the remaining 5 percent?

The veteran is not specifically directed to precisely recalculate the percentages at this time. Usually a volunteer from the group will write down what percentages have been assigned to whom by the veteran during the group session) to give to the veteran after the session is over).

Step 3 challenges the survivor's exclusion or minimization of the indirect responsibility of others who were not at the immediate scene of the trauma. To not expand the circle of responsibility beyond individuals actually at the trauma site promotes continuation of an exaggerated responsibility for individual acts or nonacts that occur in the war zone. This is "society victim-bashing" of our war-veterans, that is, blaming our veterans for licensing them to be agents of death and maiming. We allow them to carry their own *and everybody else's share* of the consequences of our nation's war policy.

Thus, the veteran is now asked to consider *if senior military officials* in the war zone deserve any share of responsibility for the various traumas that occur. In other words, did the military strategies facilitate the most likely positive (military) outcome, was the minimization of loss of U.S. casualties a primary concern, and did their strategies and policies contribute to "unnecessary" loss of life and destruction among the veteran and/or civilian population in the war zone? Ultimately, does not the military command structure at its higher levels in the theater of operations deserve to receive a piece of the responsibility?

Next, the veteran considers *the war itself*. The therapist may ask, "Would any of you even have been in-country that night, if the U.S. were not fighting in Vietnam?" What percentage of responsibility for the Vietnam war should be assigned to our political leaders, and to all the civilians who sat around and watched the latest Vietnam casualty reports on television and then proceeded with their lives, irrespective of what was happening in Vietnam? (This author contends that *when, a nation goes to war, every adult in that nation bears a piece of the responsibility for every single traumatic result that occurs* [Scurfield, 1993]).

Step 4 rechallenges the veteran's sense of his/her own percentage of responsibility for behaviors and consequences in the war zone.

Therapist: Now, let us return to *you* and what *you* did and did not do, and how much responsibility you had for being in the military, for being in the war zone, for being there that night, and for what you did and did not do that night. Because you *were* there that night, you *did* sit in that truck, you *did not* say anything, and an American *was* blown away. We are not here to try and help you to explain away *any* of whatever percentage of responsibility you truly believe and feel that *you* deserve for what happened that night—once you have fully considered *all* the others who deserve some responsibility, too. And so, considering all other factors, what piece of the responsibility for that American's death do you now believe is yours?" [Once the veteran has been recentered on this issue, the clinician moves to the next step.]

Step 5 challenges the veteran to consider if he/she has been "punished" enough for his/her personal share of the responsibility for what happened.

Therapist: Now, tell us how much you have suffered and punished yourself all these years over the *95 percent* or so of the responsibility that you had blamed on yourself for this American's death. In other words, take into account *all* the times you have suffered pain from remembering and agonizing over what happened, criticizing yourself, feeling guilty, etc., etc. How much?

Veteran: A lot; I mean a whole lot: Not a week goes by these twenty-three years that I haven't relived that event.

The group and veteran then discuss the degree of responsibility that the veteran has now assigned to him/herself, and how this percentage compares with the self-punishment suffered (which has been based on a much higher assumption of responsibility). The veteran must make a clear statement to all the group members, and decides if he or she has engaged in (self-punishment) ''enough,'' ''not enough,'' or ''more than enough'' in comparison to his/her *newly assigned* percentage of responsibility. It is often helpful for the veteran to repeat this statement to *several* individual veterans in the group.

The above procedures are also utilized to address responsibility issues of veterans who seem to significantly deny that they had *any* responsibility whatsoever for particular experiences that occurred.

Step 6 explicates a non-self-destructive plan to provide additional ''payback'' for one's share of the responsibility. If the veteran concludes that he or she still has not suffered enough for this, his conclusion can, of course, be confronted by both the clinician and group. However, if the veteran can live with this reframed, less rigid percentage of responsibility, the therapist and group may now facilitate the implementation of a non-self-destructive plan. This plan provides additional payback through its positive, life-sustaining, proactive stance, rather than through self-destructive, reactive stance. The significant reframing process will require considerable readjusting of cognitions, feelings, and memories. *Step 7 is a homework assignment*, which permits the veteran some time to reflect and reframe; to refine and recalculate the set of percentages of responsibility that add up to 100 percent and truly take into account the full circle of persons and circumstances; and to develop an initial longer-range plan to provide additional payback, if any, that the survivor feels and believes he or she still must provide. The veteran provides at least a brief account to the group and therapist of the results of this homework assignment to allow for group sanction or lack of sanction. Establishing specific steps to undertake the positive, life-promoting payback plan is important, as are follow-up activities to ensure that movement has occurred.

9. Psychiatric Medications

The ninth treatment principle examines the role of psychiatric medications. This author espouses neither the essentially biologic definition of PTSD and, hence, dominantly biologic treatment regimen nor rigid requirements that veterans be free of all psychiatric and narcotic pain medications. Instead, the author strongly encourages an integrative biopsychosocial spiritual model that views biological treatment as an important adjunct to healing through psychosocial-spiritual processes (Hammond, Scurfield, and Risse, 1993). Some entrenched, traumatic stress-related symptoms (e.g., sleep disturbance, hyperactivity) are remarkably durable and appear to be relatively immune to "talking-only" therapy approaches (Scurfield et al., 1990). However, prescribing benzodiazapines as an anxiolytic for war trauma survivors who also have a substance abuse history is a concern; these drugs may exacerbate some PTSD symptoms (Risse et al., 1990). (For a more detailed discussion of pharmacological aspects of PTSD treatment, see Friedman, Chapter 32; van der Kolk, 1986, 1988.)

10. Traumatic Stress, Chemical Disorders, and Nonchemical Habituating Behaviors

The tenth treatment principle examines the very strong association (up to 92 percent) between PTSD of help-seeking war veterans and chemical (substance abuse) disorders and nonchemical problematic habituating behaviors (Abueg and Fairbank, 1991; Daniels and Scurfield, this volume; van der Kolk, 1989; Boudewyns, 1991). See Chapter 13 for a discussion of this treatment principle.

11. Facilitation of Positive Leisure/Relationship Activities and Mind-Body Connectedness

The eleventh treatment principle examines the enhancement of leisure and relationship activities and mind-body connectedness. Traumatic stress appears to be closely associated with a difficulty, if not an inability, for survivors to enjoy life. This seeming inability rests upon the preoccupation with intrusive symptomatology, the belief that one will "never get better," preoccupation with loss of control over powerful emotions, and a conviction of little control to prevent further traumatization unless one maintains a very vigilant and isolated life. Evidence that merely to target and reduce severe pathological symptoms necessarily result in an increased ability and success in promoting pleasure in one's life appears not to exist.

This lack of ability to enjoy can be so entrenched that war veterans seem to approach almost any "social" activity as if they were "embarking on a military tactical operation." These veterans must gear themselves to a tunnel vision and survival attitude in order to tolerate even an hour or three at a restaurant, market, shopping center, school activity involving one's child, and other activities in public places. To envision the possibility of enjoying oneself at such an activity is usually not even a consideration.

It is therefore very important that clinicians devote significant clinical attention to preparing war veterans to discover (or rediscover) how to attain some enjoyment in various life activities. To actualize this treatment objective, a clinician must go beyond merely encouraging engagement in leisure activities. Briefings before and after social outings must occur. Helping the veterans to visualize (concretely) the range of actions, situations, and reactions that may occur while laying out spe-

cific behavioral and attitudinal tactics to help prevent negative results and to promote more likely positive outcomes is part of this process. Clinical assistance to
optimize the ability to enjoy life (better) should be a priority treatment objective.

The veteran also must be helped to reduce hyperactive physiological system
responses. For example, if the veteran is in a marked state of constant vigilance
when eating at a restaurant, relaxing, let alone enjoying the experience, is remote.
Enhancing a positive flow between mind and body through regular practice of
various stress reduction exercises, biofeedback, meditation, and disciplined physical activities to increase mind-body interconnectedness, such as t'ai chi ch'uan,
seems to be a necessary complement to typical biopsychosocial interventions.
Utilization of these activities may also help to mitigate undue reliance on medications to achieve the same effects.

12. Significant Others

The twelfth treatment principle recognizes the fact that the impact of a trauma
inevitably goes well beyond those survivors who have been directly exposed.
The "ripple effect" (or more aptly, the tidal wave impact) of trauma has both
immediate and far-reaching consequences, which affect all subsystems: partner
and parent-child and sibling, extended family, friendship, affiliation, and vocational networks.

When the survivor is in a primarily detached phase, the survivor and significant
others generally collude to minimize, if not deny, the severity of the trauma experience and its possible impact. The overt and implicit short-term message by all
parties is "to just forget about it; it's over; let's move on with our lives." This collective denial and minimization were most recently exemplified by the aftermath
of the Gulf War (Scurfield, 1991a, 1991b, 1992; Scurfield and Tice, 1992).

On the other hand, the returning war survivor may experience intrusive traumatic stress symptomatology that causes difficulties to arise out of the reunion
challenge. Gulf War veterans and their families indicated that reported problems
appeared to relate equally to war zone (traumatic stress) and "readjustment"
(U.S. Department of Veterans Affairs, 1991; Scurfield, 1991a, 1991b).

Long-term impact of war on the veteran's significant others always exists.
Whether that impact is problematic depends largely upon the degree to which
the veteran has been able to achieve a satisfactory degree of resolution and
integration of the war zone experiences into his or her postwar life.

Longer-term complications of unsuccessful postwar adaptations on the family
system have been described (Mason, 1990; Matsakis, 1988; Scarano, 1982;
Williams, 1987a). Significant others need to be listened to, understood in their
own right and not "just" as the veteran's significant other, and included in
planning and sequencing individual, family, and group treatment (Brown, 1984;
Haley, 1985; Harkness, 1992; Herndon and Law, 1986; Matsakis, 1988; Williams, 1987a; Williams and Williams, 1985). Discussions of the impact of war
trauma on the extended family are practically nonexistent in the literature (Be-

cerra, 1982; Pina, 1985). A traumatized veteran's preoccupation with loss of emotional and behavioral control, low self-esteem, detachment, avoidant behaviors, isolation to suppress painful, intrusive reliving symptomatology, and explosive acting-out behaviors may become ingrained into the family system to the point that the family environment becomes akin to a war zone milieu. Everyone therefore must function in a state of constant vigilance or survival mode, and the entire family assumes a veteran, "vet family," or "vetling" identity. Provision of therapy for family members is essential to prevent relapse and contribute to family healing.

13. Spirituality and Religion

I cried out to God to help me, and he didn't answer. . . . He left me alone, with all this friggin' weight on my shoulders.

—S. Smith (1991)

The thirteenth treatment principle examines spiritual and/or religious aspects of the survivor's life. Trauma survivors may encounter confusion, anguish, and searching as they examine spiritual beliefs. The reaffirmation or discovery of what is missing in this "broken connection" (Lifton, 1978) is an essential aspect of recovery for many. Such searching seems particularly critical among war veterans whose trauma experiences included being a sanctioned agent to perpetration of trauma as well as witness to carnage. Veterans question very basic beliefs about the nature of human beings, morality, life and death, higher-power direction and purpose in life's experiences, reincarnation and/or an afterlife, and what life is all about while dealing with guilt and related issues of "moral pain" (Marin, 1981; Capps, 1982; Jacob, 1987; Lifton, 1973, 1978, 1979; Mahedy, 1986; H. J. Schwartz, 1984). Actions resulting in death/injury to women and children and atrocitylike behaviors ("abusive violence": Frey-Wouters and Laufer, 1986) also seem to have a special conflictual impact on religious and spiritual beliefs.

The clinician must be aware of his or her own comfort and skill levels in facilitating a veteran to deal with spiritual or religious issues related to the war experience. Active consultation or collaborative therapeutic endeavors with a VA chaplain or a community-based religious or spiritual resource may be essential.

Religious and spiritual belief systems can offer vital avenues for recovery. For example, confession and penance in the act of reconciliation can be a powerful therapeutic process within pastoral counseling and/or nonreligious clinical interventions. Profound, positive spiritual or religious outcomes of the trauma experience may include a transforming expansion of worldview and of one's relationship with a higher power. For example, a near-death experience may profoundly enhance the survivor's belief in a higher power.

14. Enhancement of Positive Aspects of Trauma and Post-Trauma Experiences

The fourteenth treatment principle recognizes that recovery from trauma includes not only a reduction or elimination of pathological or painful, negative aspects but also the enhancement of positive aspects. Such positive aspects may or may not contain religious or spiritual implications. For example, it may be a sign of health not to forget trauma; indeed, that one has persisted in life in spite of the trauma experience reflects the inner strength and courage of the survivor (Bettelheim, 1979; Frankl, 1959; Scurfield, 1985). Very few studies have investigated the positive aspects of trauma survival and post-trauma functioning (Egendorf, 1982, 1985; Card, 1983; Hendin and Haas, 1984; Lifton, 1979; Lyons, 1991; Sorenson, 1988).

The clinician must actively facilitate the survivor's attention to, and appreciation of, the positive aspects of the trauma and post-trauma experience. If not, the clinician colludes with the veteran's denial and reinforces the preoccupation with negative aspects. The survivor usually is not able to accept these positive perspectives in earlier phases of treatment; however, bringing denial to the survivor's attention early on opens up the survivor's range of challenges to be faced in the recovery process (Surfield, 1993a). Enhancement of positives is interrelated with treatment principles of a whole-life perspective, therapeutic reexperiencing, cognitive reframing, positive leisure/relationship activities, and for some, religious and/or spiritual searching.

15. Community Education and Advocacy

The legacy of trauma may include prejudicial attitudes and beliefs that can be described as "victim-bashing." Typically, the human-induced trauma survivor is blamed by others (and/or by himself or herself) for having been in the trauma to begin with and/or for continuing to have problems about the trauma afterward. The sources of such prejudice include personality theories that minimize the role of environmental factors and/or the likelihood that significant personality development occurs throughout the life cycle, and societal/political attempts to sanitize the horrors of war (Surfield, 1992a).

The fifteenth principle states that it is essential for those knowledgeable of the true and full impact of trauma to carry facts about trauma and trauma recovery to all levels and strata in our society; otherwise, clinicians do little to prevent, and indeed may abet, the secondary trauma of revictimization in and from society. An expanded role beyond treatment to advocacy (Lifton, 1978) is appropriate and necessary, including both "case services and social reform" activities in an integrated model of clinical practice (Scurfield, 1980).

16. Management of Countertransference Dynamics and Issues

The sixteenth treatment principle examines the inevitable impacts of help-seeking survivors upon clinicians. The primary reaction of the clinician is not to the survivor per se but to the trauma experienced by the survivor (Danieli, 1984). Thus, clinicians have to deal with their own issues and reactions to such profound matters as death, traumatic injury, violence, cruelty, shock, terror, grief, rage, and loss. Clinical contact triggers personal issues about war in general, the specific war, political process and the U.S. war policy, society's sanctioning of veterans to be agents of killing, what society (and the clinician) accepts as longer-term responsibilities to veterans and their impacted families, and the active or passive role of the clinician's war effort (Frick and Bogart, 1982; Newberry, 1985; Shapiro, 1984; Wakefield and Hyland, 1988; Wilson and Lindy, 1994). Countertransference issues tend to be influenced by a clinician's own personal history with war zone experiences, other trauma personally experienced, gender, and the agency setting in which he or she works.

The agency setting is a very important source of additional countertransference to the extent that the agency is facilitative of or obstructive to the provision of adequate clinical services. For example, an agency that seems almost solely concerned with "productivity" might be perceived by the employee as having a "body-count mentality." Employees of the Department of Veterans Affairs may take a passive-aggressive stance concerning agency policies, such as clinical recording requirements, and/or have difficulty actually accepting a "government employee" identity.

The definition of countertransference must include conscious and positive effects that are stimulated through clinical contact with war veterans. They include feelings of self-worth and accomplishment, positive stimulation and commitment, and a reaffirmation of the courage and strength of war survivors.

Clinicians must have routine strategies to manage countertransference dynamics. Anyone who denies this need may well be too detached from reality to be of much help to war veterans. Countertransference is an integral element of clinical work; it is expectable and normal that issues will arise that require specific attention. Good supervision, especially in a small group, addresses PTSD-related countertransference dynamics. Staff support groups are also important, though rare. Providing cofacilitators for group therapy, rotating a variety of job functions among various staff, conducting debriefing sessions at the end of each day to review (and ventilate about) clinical happenings of note are essential if staff truly are to take care of themselves (Scurfield and Tice, 1992).

TREATMENT IMPLICATIONS FOR SPECIAL
POPULATIONS IMPACTED BY WAR-RELATED TRAUMA

A number of special populations are directly effected by war trauma and exhibit distinctive traumatic aspects. Prejudice, insensitivity, and discounting are likely to occur if the client, peers, and/or clinician are not comfortable or familiar with someone who has not had the same or a similar traumatic experience or life background; if the special population person is the only member in a treatment group or is a member of a special population rarely treated in this setting; or if the content and style of sharing and interacting are actually markedly different between special population member and clients or staff.

Ethnocultural Minority Veterans

A number of active-duty personnel from an ethnocultural minority background find themselves in extraordinarily difficult situations of fighting for a country that has its own racist and classist discriminatory practices, of possibly fighting with other military who perpetuate discriminatory behaviors toward each other and/or toward the people against whom the United States is fighting. Invariably, a significant number of American military personnel includes persons whose own ethnocultural heritage may be derived in part from the enemy's country of origin. This can lead to significant intrapsychic and interpersonal conflicts, such as existed among a number of Asian American (and other minority) military personnel in Southeast Asia (Matsuoka et al., 1991) and among some American military personnel of Arab or Jewis ethnicity who served in the Persian Gulf War (Scurfield and Tice, 1992). Furthermore, prevalence rates of readjustment problems and PTSD are elevated among war veterans who are African Americans (Egendorf et al., 1981; Laufer, Gallops, and Frey-Wouters, 1984; Kulka et al., 1990) or Hispanics (Kulka et al., 1990; Barse, 1984; Becerra, 1982; Hamada et al., 1988; Holm, 1984; Matsuoka et al., 1991; Parson, 1984, 1985a, 1985b; Penk and Allen, 1991; Pina, 1985; Terry, 1984).

Critical treatment implications exist. First, it may be necessary to build a "theme" of ethnocultural factors into the treatment regimen rather than expecting that such issues will be raised. Second, clinicians and/or other veterans must be open to discussions of ethnocultural issues and factors. Adjusting admission scheduling to ensure "cluster" admissions of several members of an ethnic group at one time is necessary to promote ethnocultural sensitivity (Scurfield, submitted). Third, a number of clinical techniques may be in direct conflict with an ethnocultural veteran's values or style of interacting, such as making eye contact or expecting the veteran to express certain feelings or issues (Marsella, Chemtob, and Hamada, 1990). Issues that nonminority veterans may have with minorities are also important to discuss, as are the issues of minority veterans themselves. Finally, agency leadership must assertively recruit qualified staff of ethnocultural minority backgrounds, perhaps through "peer counselor" positions.

Physically Disabled Veterans

Physically disabled veterans, of course, may suffer longer post-war psychiatric sequelae than able-bodied veterans. Their treatment typically includes emphases on recovery from physical injuries and an avoidance of attention to emotional issues (Scurfield and Tice, 1992; Tice et al., 1988). Most physically disabled veterans suffer increased physical pain as they lower detachment mechanisms and permit appropriate abreaction or emotional processing (Scurfield and Tice, 1992). Further, it is helpful to consider the entire post-injury experience (on-the-battle-field treatment; various evacuation, triage, and stabilization phases) as ''an additional tour of war duty'' to be processed much like the processing of previous trauma that occurred in the war zone (Scurfield and Tice, 1992; Scurfield, 1992c).

Women Veterans

Women veterans experience both a general range of war and postwar trauma and gender-specific reactions. Many women veterans were exposed to discrimination, threats, and/or assault due to their gender before, during, and following war zone duty. Typical in-country, gender-specific stressors include very hostile and prejudicial attitudes and behaviors by a number of male military personnel.

Following the war zone experience, women veterans faced gender-specific discriminatory attitudes and behaviors; for example, they were viewed ''either as lesbians or whores'' to have served in the military. Until relatively recently, many programs in the VA refused to admit a woman veteran. (For more detailed accounts of issues and dynamics regarding women veterans, see Dewayne, 1984; Kulka et al., 1990; Norman, 1988; Ott, 1985; Paul, 1985; Sandecki, 1987; Schnair, 1986; Thompson et al., 1982; U.S. Government General Accounting Office, 1982; Van Devanter, 1983; Walker, 1985.)

Ex-Prisoners of War

Prisoner of War (POW) internment is characterized by a pervasively oppressive, dehumanizing, threatening, cruel, and physically harsh incarceration.

Former POWs seem to be especially vulnerable to losses (of health, spouse, job) as they get older. A particularly difficult loss is that of ''their physician'' or therapist. Thus, it is important for health care providers who work with former POWs and their families to evaluate commitment to provide a longer-term relationship honestly. Issues of shame or guilt over having been captured or not having escaped and rage and frustration over seemingly endless battles with various bureaucracies over proper recognition and benefits are important sources of powerful transference dynamics, of which the clinician must be aware (Oboler, 1987). (For other writings on ex-POWs, see Beebe, 1975; U.S. Department of Veteran Affairs, 1980; Hunter, 1978; Stenger, 1985; Ursano, 1981, 1985; Ursano, Boydstun, and Wheatley, 1981).

CONCLUSIONS

Each U.S. military venture introduces a new wave of persons who are directly or indirectly deeply impacted by the trauma of war. The subsequent collusion to minimize or deny shorter- and longer-term human costs of such wars must be vigorously and repeatedly challenged. In this author's personal opinion, the most effective way to reduce the prevalence and incidence of war-related traumatic stress is *to prevent U.S. involvement in ''unneccessary'' wars*. The price of freedom is high enough without unnecessarily adding to the rolls of our nation's veterans, their families and so many others who continue to be impacted both directly and indirectly by the horrors of war.

The range, depth, and longevity of resources necessary to address these war-related human costs adequately must be strongly advocated for and protected for the full range of persons directly and indirectly impacted by war. Knowledgeable war-related traumatic stress services must be available to all those affected, from grunts to graves registration veterans; from frontline corpsmen to medical personnel in receiving hospitals in the United States; from killed in action (KIA), MIA, and POW families to families of currently hospitalized veterans; from donut dollies to civilian stewardesses who transported U.S. troops.

NOTE

The author wishes to honor and thank the late Steven Risse, M.D., former Chief of Psychiatry, and Frank Taylor, Director, American Lake VA Medical Center, as well as the committed and skilled staff of the American Lake VAMC Post-Traumatic Stress Treatment Program, who together have made significant healing possible for many of the over 600 veterans who have been admitted to the PTSTP: Steve Tice, Anne Gregory, Russ Anderson, Diana Armstrong, Jim Burke, Jim Cariaso, Bob Coalson, Doc DeWeese, Beryl Hammonds, Jim Hardesty, John Hofstetter, Bill Hook, Carrie Johnston, Jim Kelly, Carl Kincer, Bob Lusk, Ria McEntee, Dale Miller, Alyce Neal, Tom Olsen, Art Owens, Wendy Pava and Duchess, Amy Morris, Robbie Robinson, Jerry Snead, Rico Swain, Dave Robertson, Elke (Feleafine) Zeerocah; and lest we forget: Lori Daniels, Frank Flock, Fred Gren, Jim Kelly, Shawn Kenderdine, Terry McGuire, Dale Smith, Casey Wegner, David Pauley, Duane Dailey, Nelson Korbes, Arlene Edwards, Bill Vandenbush, Allen Whitters, and Teri Wingate.

13

War-Related Post-Traumatic Stress Disorder: Chemical Addictions and Nonchemical Habituating Behaviors

Lori R. Daniels and
Raymond Monsour Scurfield

A recent landmark national study of Vietnam veterans (Kulka et al., 1990) revealed a remarkable co-occurrence between substance abuse and post-traumatic stress disorder (PTSD). Seventy-five percent of Vietnam veterans surveyed who met diagnostic criteria for PTSD also met the criteria for a lifetime diagnosis of alcohol abuse or dependence, and 15 percent met the criteria for a lifetime diagnosis of drug abuse. Another recent study indicated that of the Vietnam combat veterans requesting treatment at an inpatient PTSD program, 91.12 percent were found to have a lifetime diagnosis of substance abuse or dependence. This study also found that substance usage by patients was the primary reason for not completing PTSD treatment (Boudewyns, 1991). There appears to be a significant comorbidity of substance abuse with a range of anxiety (Kushner et al., 1990) and other psychiatric disorders (Regier et al., 1990). One could speculate that even these statistics may be conservative, given the prevalence of denial in the chemical-abusing population. In contrast to the growing clinical evidence as to the substantial comorbidity of PTSD and substance abuse, the literature is somewhat sparse (Abueg and Fairbank, 1991; Abueg et al., 1989; Baker, 1984; Boscarino, 1979; Boudewyns, 1991; Brinson & Treanor 1988; Cruden, 1985; Gordon, 1984; Helzer, 1984; Keane et al., 1988; Lacoursiere, Godfrey & Ruby, 1980; McCormack, 1988; Niles, 1989; Penk, 1986; Roy, 1983; Stanton, 1980). Traditionally, treatment of the disorders has been sequential. More recently, with the resurgence of dual disorder treatment protocols, mental health care providers are becoming increasingly aware of the interplay of psychiatric disorders and substance abuse. As a consequence, treatment provision is widening its scope to include both problem areas.

This chapter describes the relationship among chemical disorders, habituating behaviors, and PTSD; the dynamics of PTSD; survival modes to cope with protracted and repeated trauma; habituating behaviors as a coping mechanism for trauma (to include both chemical addiction and other habituating modes); "milieu management" and direct clinical treatment implications; and several impediments to successful integration of treatment for PTSD, chemical abuse, and nonchemical habituating behaviors.

THE USE OF CHEMICAL ADDICTION AND NONCHEMICAL HABITUATING BEHAVIORS AS A TRAUMA AND POST-TRAUMA COPING MODE

The authors propose that chemical addiction and nonchemical habituating behaviors are some of the most commonly utilized mechanisms to detach from, deny and minimize, and avoid or survive both protracted and repeated traumas while they are occurring and also the painful reexperiencing of trauma. Chemical addiction (i.e., overusage of drugs and/or alcohol) functions as a self-medication to suppress or avoid painful reexperiencing symptoms. For many Vietnam veterans, usage of alcohol and drugs while in the war zone was an effective acute strategy to detach from the repetitive horrors of guerrilla warfare and exposure to massive death and dying. With some individuals, this pattern of substance abuse evolved into chemical addiction in-country and continued, following their return to the United States. For other veterans, chemical usage began after returning to the United States as a form of "self-medication" to induce sleep without accompanying nightmares or other sleep disturbances. Such usage also helped to distract from, mask over, and avoid anxiety, painful memories, guilt, remorse, rage, alienation, and depression during waking hours. Wounded and physically disabled veterans also developed an addiction to narcotic medication prescribed for pain relief. Some continued to seek narcotics or "pain cocktails" or have them prescribed rather than choose alternative nonnarcotic pain management (Tice et al., 1988). Finally, a number of Vietnam veterans with PTSD did not develop chemical usage until a substantial period of time had passed since returning to the United States. Such veterans found themselves plagued with a "delayed onset" of intrusive, recurrent memories and attached feelings and arousal symptoms that they seemed to be unable to get rid of without chemical usage.

Both "street" drugs and prescribed medications have been, and are still, utilized and/or abused by a number of veterans in attempts to suppress or avoid PTSD symptoms. Unfortunately, the abuse of prescribed medications has been facilitated by unknowledgeable clinicians who recommended excessive or prolonged usage of psychotropic medications for symptom relief without directly treating underlying trauma issues.

The relationship between PTSD and substance usage may also take on different dynamics. Clinicians at the Northwest Post-Traumatic Stress Treatment Program and Substance Use/Post-Traumatic Stress Treatment Program (American Lake VAMC, Tacoma, Washington) have observed that chemical usage, in a small number of veterans, may also increase the risk of experiencing PTSD-like symptoms or that chemical usage may not be at all related to the survivor's PTSD. Therefore, the authors recommend that mental health providers thoroughly assess symptoms for both disorders to discern the dynamic interactions, if any, between the two problem areas.

Nonchemical habituating behaviors (including excessive and prolonged engagement in behaviors involving adrenaline provocation, sex, relationships, physical overexertion, eating disorders, gambling, religious obsession, spending/shopping, money, workaholism, exercise, and television) also suppress traumatic stress symptoms. Some nonchemical habituations may develop into disorders according to DSM III-R criteria, such as pathological gambling and eating disorders. The term *habituating behaviors*, as used by the authors, includes problematic, nonchemical, repetitive behaviors that may or may not meet full inclusionary criteria for a disorder according to DSM III-R.

Nonchemical habituating behaviors exert both physical and mental energies to the point that avoidance or denial of painful reexperiencing symptoms of the original trauma occurs. The development of nonchemical habituating behaviors has an etiology similar to that of chemical addiction. Behaviors such as immersing oneself in carrying out one's duties (e.g., adrenaline or thrill addiction, workaholism, and "tunnel vision") began in the war zone as a method to avoid or mask over painful traumatic realities and then continued postwar. Or, the behaviors began postwar as a defense against painful, unresolved war-associated memories and feelings, sleep disturbances, and issues such as guilt. These nonchemical habituating behaviors helped the veteran to numb out, escape, and detach from painful recollections of the war.

The inclusionary criteria for a problematic habituating behavior used in this chapter modify listed symptoms used in the DSM III-R (1987) for compulsive gambling, eating disorders, and alcohol dependence diagnoses. Many, although not necessarily all, of the following criteria must be met to define a habituating behavior as problematic:

- The individual thinks about and/or engages in the behavior frequently.
- Other people have expressed concern about the individual's identified behavior in the past and/or currently.
- The person becomes irritable, anxious, and/or preoccupied if unable to partake frequently in the behavior.
- The person may need to increase the amount of time or frequency of the behavior to achieve the desired effect.
- The individual sacrifices occupational and social obligations for the behavior.
- The person rationalizes and/or continues the behavior in spite of negative consequences that have occurred that are directly or indirectly attributed to the behavior.

- The person has attempted to stop the behavior or reduce the frequency before.
- The individual has persisted in the identified behavior longer and/or more frequently than had been originally intended.

In addition to the above criteria, the authors suggest these additional criteria to identify problematic habituating behaviors:

- The behavior "stands in the way" of personal goals the individual wishes to achieve for himself or herself.
- The person may not feel "good" about himself or herself while partaking in the behavior and/or soon afterward.
- The individual and/or others recognize that the behavior is engaged in primarily as a way to avoid interacting with others or to "protect" self or others against powerful feelings/behaviors that may otherwise be triggered.
- The individual is unable to limit the behavior and, therefore, is experiencing resultant distress in other parts of his or her life.

For those veterans unable or unwilling to readjust to "normal" postwar living, excessive thrill-seeking/risk-taking/adrenaline-rush (thrill addiction) behaviors can be another form of addiction/habituating behavior. Many veterans have admitted to repeatedly participating in highly dangerous/life-threatening activities (i.e., being involved in illegal activities, having life-styles that include excessive violence and/or consistent crisis). Excessive thrill-seeking behaviors provide an escape from the "boredom" of everyday life and feelings of disconnectedness from society. This constant survival mode is maintained as a defense against reexperiencing symptoms of the war (e.g., if one is on survival mode, one remains more detached from underlying feelings and, therefore, maintains one's energies on here-and-now demands). In addition, immersion in and preoccupation with Vietnam and other war-related books, movies, and paraphernalia are another form of thrill-seeking and escapist behavior. Some veterans have chosen to immerse themselves in the war and its accompanying memories, associations, and feelings. These individuals exhibit the "compulsive repetition" component of PTSD—they become fixated on identifying with, and reliving, earlier and incompletely processed traumatic experiences. Such immersion in the memories/attitudes of the prior trauma of war provides an escape from having to make an adjustment to the realities of postwar life. It can also be viewed as a manifestation of an arrested identity and personality development.

This view recognizes the critical importance of the specific developmental life stages in which the Vietnam veteran was at the time of Vietnam, as well as the negative impact of events on subsequent development into later life stages (Wilson, 1978). An immersion in war triggers can appear to contradict the avoidance component of a PTSD diagnosis (as listed in the DSM III-R); however, the authors recognize that the survival mode is a method of avoidance of unresolved traumas and painful feelings attached to the memories. Finally, some trauma survivors have been reasonably able to sublimate their adrenaline rushes and survival mode behaviors with occupations that accept and/or heighten these dynamics, for example, police work, fire protection, emergency medical care, and provision of acute or crisis intervention services.

A partly biological basis to continued preoccupation with the trauma may exist as well. This continuation of ''re-creating the original trauma'' may neutralize state-dependent hyperarousal through various habituating behaviors (i.e., compulsive reexposure to situations reminiscent of the original trauma). Van der Kolk (1989) described the role that endogenous opiates may play in hyperarousal state-dependent learning at the time of the trauma, in subsequent reliving experiences, and in social attachment. There appear to be several interactive dynamics between habituating behaviors and a possible biological component of PTSD. Disinhibition resulting from a chemical addiction may facilitate the occurrence of reliving experiences and thereby result in acting-out episodes, such as explosions of rage toward authority figures. (On the other hand, habitual usage of marijuana has been reported by a number of veterans to reinforce relaxation, isolation, and avoidant mechanisms.) Survivors also may become physiologically addicted in relationships to others, including compulsive reexposure to victimization of self and others (Erschak, 1984).

Habituating behaviors also play a dual role when they coexist with PTSD. Chemical addictions are both a form of self-medication against painful, intrusive, and recurrent symptoms and (physiologically and psychologically) self-inflicted retraumatization experienced by the survivor (Bean-Bayog, 1988a). For example, alcohol addiction can mask over painful memories and result in self-denigration, dysfunctional, and/or violent patterns in relationships and physical damage to the liver and nervous system. Nonchemical habituating behaviors may lead to self-induced retraumatization as perpetrator and/or recipient, that is, excessive risk taking resulting in injury, death, or violence toward others. Van der Kolk (1989) mentioned that a possible addiction to the trauma causes survivors to recreate the traumatic event in various forms throughout their lives. Being aware of these different dynamics of addiction/habituating behaviors as related to traumatic events challenges treatment providers to plan appropriate, integrated treatment for the various aspects of the disorders that could benefit the patient.

IMPEDIMENTS TO FULL INTEGRATION OF A DUAL DISORDER PROGRAM

There are several critical impediments to a successful integration of treatment of PTSD and chemical and nonchemical abuse problems within a program that is primarily a PTSD program or primarily a substance abuse program:

1. The profound denial by the survivor and many treatment providers that either or both disorders exist.
2. Denial and lack of awareness by many clinicians and trauma survivors of the full

range of addictions and/or habituating behaviors (including, but not limited to, chemical) that coexist with PTSD and of the way that such symptoms mutually reinforce the coexisting disorder.

3. Budgetary cutbacks and lack of data to support the efficacy of longer versus shorter substance abuse treatment. Many substance abuse programs have been reduced in length to the point where minimal time is available to deal with core chemical dependency issues, much less any other comorbid issues.

4. Avoidance/inability within traditional substance abuse programs to deal with PTSD issues due to lack of training and sensitization toward PTSD dynamics and their relationship to chemical dependency. Substance-abusing populations clearly are exposed to numerous traumatic experiences as part of an addictive life-style, both as perpetrator and as victim. The introduction of PTSD concepts and dynamics into a hospital-based substance abuse treatment program was recently implemented (in the Substance Abuse Program at American Lake VAMC). A unique, shared staff position was created among the Inpatient Post-Traumatic Stress (PTS) Treatment program, Inpatient Substance Abuse Program, and Veterans Outreach Center, allowing the introduction of a "generic" PTSD class. Introducing concepts of PTSD as a response to trauma exposure and delineating the symptom overlap between PTSD and substance abuse and the interactive dynamics of PTSD and substance abuse provide entrées into the more traditional substance abuse treatment program curriculum.

5. Some PTSD treatment providers seek to avoid the necessary enforcement of systematic substance abuse monitoring and the consistent application of therapeutic consequences for violations of substance abuse policies (e.g., a realistic monitoring system for a veteran with a high cocaine or alcohol abuse risk must include a urine collection and analysis frequency of at least one every two days).

6. Significant transference and countertransference issues that occur between staff and seriously physically disabled veterans with legitimate "chronic pain" conditions. On one hand, there can be considerable staff controversy over "the humaneness" and efficacy of prescribing or disallowing narcotic pain medications. On the other hand, there is a paucity of effective alternative chronic pain treatment regimens at many sites. In addition, intensive psychotherapeutic, abreactive treatment of PTSD and unresolved trauma oftentimes exacerbates physical pain symptoms and may increase patient behavior to seek medication for pain relief (Scurfield, 1993a). If the staff is not in complete agreement on this matter, "splitting" of staff by the patient is likely to occur.

7. The tendency of most clinicians not to consider substance abuse to be self-inflicted retraumatization. Their tendency is to consider substance abuse only as self-medication of PTSD symptoms or as a chemical addiction problem. Application of these concepts and substance abuse as a trauma within the framework of PTSD (Bean-Bayog, 1988a), though often lacking, are very relevant to working with war-related PTSD and other populations who abuse substances. Conversely, the interrelationship and overlap among PTSD, chemical abuse/dependence, and habituations are apparent. Many of the observed chemical dependency dynamics of dysfunctional family patterns, emotional avoidance, and relapse signals apply to the treatment of PTSD as well.

TREATMENT IMPLICATIONS

Very few treatment programs in the country have the resources and knowledge to address both addictions/habituating behaviors and PTSD concurrently or adequately. Realistically, such treatment continues to be primarily sequential. Some of the detachment and avoidance behaviors described earlier can be very functional to survival during and following the trauma, particularly to suppress potentially overwhelming feeling states and painful recollections. When such behaviors become "excessive" (addictive or habitual) following prolonged engagement, they evolve into problems per se, in addition to the problem of PTSD. Each set of problems (the PTSD, chemical disorders, and nonchemical habituating behaviors) then requires its own treatment; that is, substance abuse is not resolved only by directing interventions at the coexisting PTSD, and vice versa.

The most common clinical strategy has been to treat the chemical addictions or other habitual behaviors first or solely, at least to the point that they are stabilized and nonacute. In this way, it is possible for the survivor in subsequent PTSD treatment to have some degree of cognitive clarity in order to digest psychoeducational content and be able to feel and reexperience painful and unresolved aspects of traumatic experiences more fully, rather than to continue to deny and avoid. If the survivor continues to engage in numbing behaviors while attempting to receive PTSD treatment and if abreactive processes are considered vital to recovery, resolution of the PTSD will not occur.

It is imperative to explore in various programs how dual disorder programming may be enhanced beyond a "token" acknowledgment of the "other" disorder. For example, it appears some veterans participating in the Inpatient PTS Treatment Program at American Lake VAMC who have stabilized and, at least, are temporarily refraining from chemical abuse can successfully engage in primarily PTSD treatment. Later, these individuals can proceed to receive intensive treatment for the addiction(s), along with continued PTSD recovery support. Subsequently, the client must be involved in closely monitored abstinence-support from the chemical and/or nonchemical behavior he or she has been utilizing to avoid trauma reexperiencing symptoms. In addition, relapse prevention methods that address both addictive/habitual behaviors and PTSD symptoms should be integrated into the counseling regimen once the individuals' chemical abuse and/ or habituating behavior has been identified.

Completely ignoring PTSD dynamics when a trauma survivor is withdrawing from a chemical dependency is significantly dangerous. It is not unusual that such withdrawal may be accompanied by a reemergence of PTSD reexperiencing (including flashbacks) and arousal symptoms. The reemergence of symptoms related to unresolved traumas is often accompanied by painful feelings, which the client may be inclined to avoid and "numb out." This pattern may result in an increased risk of relapse back to the maladaptive habituative behavior and/ or may be associated with suicidal impulses or attempts. Withdrawal complications that seem to exacerbate PTSD symptoms also can occur with the use of certain prescribed medications such as benzodiazepines. Aprazolam withdrawal, in particular, has been reported to be associated with severe onset of symptoms of increased rage and homicidal ideation either to a degree never experienced before or for the first time (Risse et al., 1990).

THERAPEUTIC MILIEU STRATEGIES

At the American Lake VA Medical Center, comorbidity of substance abuse and PTSD ranges from 31 percent among inpatients in the Inpatient Substance Abuse Program (this program treats a wide spectrum of veterans including Vietnam and other veterans) to 70 percent among war veteran inpatients in the specialized Inpatient Post-Traumatic Stress Treatment Program (PTSTP) and 70 percent among the Tacoma Veterans Outreach Center clients. The PTSTP has instituted several strategies at the milieu level to address the comorbidity of chemical addictions and nonchemical habituating behaviors with PTSD treatment:

1. All veterans who are scheduled for admission to the eleven-week inpatient phase must pass urine drug screen and breathalyzer tests at the time of admission. A positive urine drug screen or breathalyzer test results in immediate discharge; that is, if an individual cannot pass an admission drug/alcohol screen, then it is evident that a substance abuse problem exists that requires treatment. This strategy is communicated clearly to the referral source and the client prior to the admission process.

2. One-half of the patient population is randomly selected to provide urine specimens on a Monday, and the remaining one-half is expected to provide urine specimens on a random day later that same week. (Direct involvement of all program staff, not just nursing staff, for example, in providing coverage for urine specimen collection is critical to reinforce the need to maintain sobriety.)

3. Every Monday morning, each veteran must announce to the community of veterans and staff that he or she is "clean and sober" since being admitted to the program. This announcement to the community is considered to be the veteran's continued "public" affirmation for sobriety to peers and staff. It underscores the importance of sobriety within the treatment context.

4. Three pages in the patients' handbook are devoted to the topic of substance abuse, its relationship to PTSD, and consequences of violating the substance use policy.

5. Each veteran who presents a significant addictive abuse history and a clinical indication that he or she may be at risk for relapse is required to attend client-run abstinence-supportive meetings once per week—Alcoholics Anonymous (AA), Narcotics Anonymous (NA), Cocaine Anonymous (CA), Gamblers Anonymous, Overeaters Anonymous, outpatient abstinence counseling, and so on—as adjunct to the PTSD counseling he or she is receiving. (One objective of this strategy is to promote the veteran's abilities to utilize peer-run, group-oriented resources productively.)

6. A first substance abuse infraction may result in immediate discharge or other consequences, depending on the circumstances. For such infractions, a "patient/staff ad-

visory committee" meets to review the infractions and recommend consequences to the full staff for concurrence or amendment. A second substance abuse infraction results in immediate discharge from the program regardless of "mitigating" circumstances. (It is essential to involve patients in reviewing infractions in order to promote a "we" rather than "we versus they" polarity between staff and patients in the enforcement of substance abuse policies.)

7. The relationship between PTSD and habituating behaviors is discussed in "PTSD Overview" classes within the first week of inpatient treatment, and the necessity for concurrent treatment of PTSD and substance abuse while an inpatient and in aftercare is emphasized.

8. All veterans attend a staff-facilitated Relapse Prevention Rap Group once per week. "Real world" strategies for dealing with one's own identified chemical addictions and nonchemical habituating behaviors while in the inpatient phase, while on weekend pass, and following discharge are discussed. Peers are encouraged to confront each other appropriately when denial or minimization of such problems occur and to assist each other to develop the most realistic relapse prevention strategies.

Peer group support has played a critical role in the treatment of both war-related PTSD and chemical disorders. Peer group treatment is considered the treatment of choice by many providers who treat war veterans with PTSD. The following factors, many of which are applicable to groups of chemical abusers as well, explain that preference (Scurfield, 1993a):

1. War-related trauma occurs within the context of a peer group, the small military operational unit.

2. Trauma survivors are inherently suspicious of persons who have not had their trauma experience.

3. Common PTSD symptoms of isolation, withdrawal, and denial can be confronted quite effectively in well-facilitated peer groups.

4. Sharing various trauma experiences by peer group members provides the individual with an additional source of "direct therapeutic exposure" to aspects of the trauma with which he or she must deal.

5. Exposure offers a "memory enhancement" function of suppressed trauma issues.

The emergence of peer-directed organizations, such as Alcoholics Anonymous and Narcotics Anonymous, has demonstrated the powerful role that peer groups can play in acknowledging, sharing, confronting, and developing a social network necessary for abstinence and assisting in preventing substance abuse relapse. Therefore, utilization of a peer group modality comprised of war veterans with both PTSD and chemical addictions and/or nonchemical habituating behaviors offers, possibly, the most powerful milieu in which to address the coexistence of both disorders. (For those patients who respond to the AA model of the twelve steps, these steps have been applied to working with PTSD by Brende (1985); see Chapter 27 in this book.)

DUAL DISORDER PSYCHOEDUCATIONAL GROUP FORMAT

All inpatients are required to participate in seven psychoeducational classes that focus on the relationship of PTSD symptoms and dysfunctional dynamics of chemical abuse disorders and nonchemical habituating behaviors. A description of those seven classes follows.

Session 1. Introduction to chemical disorders and nonchemical habituating behaviors. The definition of chemical addictions and habituating behaviors is discussed and the veterans verbally identify their various habituating behaviors, so they can be listed on the board. The identification of both chemical and nonchemical habitual behaviors by the group members is crucial in this first session. For example, a number of veterans who have been resistant to classes or treatment regarding chemical addictions may realize that other nonchemical habituating behaviors may also or instead be occurring in their lives. In addition, the etiology of psychological and physical dependency is outlined, and the criteria for problematic habituating behaviors are listed in order to assist veterans in assessing whether problematic behaviors exist in their lives and inhibit their achieving their goals.

It is important to acknowledge when the problematic habitual behaviors, identified by the habitual behavior inclusionary criteria, have also had positive impacts or functions. For example, the positive impact of exercising, as described earlier, may include stress reduction, physical exercise, enjoyment, and increased self-satisfaction in accomplishing something productive. If there is a positive aspect or function of a habituating behavior, obviously, the clinical objectives include helping the client to maintain or promote activities that provide positives, without excessively engaging in such behaviors at the expense of other life aspects.

Session 2. PTSD and the relationship with chemical and nonchemical habituating behaviors. The symptoms of PTSD are identified and applied to the habituating behavior list. Discussion centers on the interrelationship between PTSD symptoms and habituating behaviors—chemical and nonchemical—to assist veterans to understand their established cyclical patterns. This discussion assists clients in identifying if they are using chemical and/or nonchemical habituating behaviors in association with reexperiencing, arousal, or avoidance symptoms. What occurs on occasion is that the clients see an established and historical pattern of PTSD symptoms and begin to understand for themselves how they may have reinforced their dysfunctional life-styles by using substances and/or habituating behaviors. The veterans are also encouraged to explore the goals they were seeking to achieve via their habituating behaviors and to assess whether they achieved those goals for themselves in the short term or long term (Kriegler, 1991).

Session 3. Codependent and dysfunctional relationships. The relationship dynamics of the primary dyad of client and significant other (partner, spouse, lover, and so on) are discussed and diagrammed. The focus is on determining/delineating unhealthy relating patterns that may develop from inhibited communication patterns, numbing of feelings, social isolation, and rigid relationship boundaries. Veterans are encouraged to examine their own relating behaviors toward others and to identify the "rules" of relating that are consistent with codependency concepts: do not talk, do not trust, do not feel (Beattie, 1987).

Session 4. Functional and dysfunctional family dynamics. The shared characteristics of persons with PTSD and/or addictive symptoms are discussed. Relationship dynamics within a functional family system are contrasted with those in dysfunctional families, as well. The maladaptive roles that families may use to cope with ongoing problems in dealing with a traumatized family member are introduced. For example, a child may adopt the "hero" role (being a good student, taking on responsibility, excelling in sports, and so on) in order to distract the parents from their relationship problem(s) or from a specific behavior of one family member. The role is rigid, and the child is expected to fulfill that role without acknowledgment of his or her other traits. Many of the discussed concepts are consistent with chemical dependency concepts regarding dysfunctional family systems (Wegscheider, 1983).

Sessions 5 through 7. The last three sessions encourage veterans to look at relapse signals of their chemical usage/nonchemical behaviors as they relate to PTSD symptoms, in order to establish a usable relapse prevention plan based on their past behaviors. Veterans are encouraged during these sessions to focus on relapse dynamics and to analyze their past patterns of chemical disorders/nonchemical habituations and the relationship with their PTSD symptoms. For example, a common relapse pattern for both PTSD and habitual behaviors is an apparent decision to quit attending support groups and to begin isolating. Early recognition of, and intervention with, this pattern (Gorski, 1989) will lessen an increase in intrusive thoughts and the urges to use chemicals. It is crucial that group members identify and learn relapse dynamics specific to the three areas of chemical, nonchemical, and PTSD symptoms and have specific plans of action, with several alternative strategies, should symptoms reoccur.

Session 5. Introduction and assessment of PTSD and habituating behavior relapse warning signs. Veterans define and give examples of a "relapse" and various relapse behaviors. Group members are encouraged to access their own personal experiences to define relapse and to create the list that is placed on a board in full view of the group. To illustrate that relapse is a process, the list is created backwards; that is, full relapse behaviors are listed first; then follow a list of behaviors that occur just prior to the relapse; then comes another list of behaviors that preceded the previous list; then, behaviors that were occurring several steps prior to the full relapse are listed ("What was happening before the behaviors that preceded the behaviors that came before the behaviors just before a full relapse?"). The group ends up with four columns of various relapse behaviors that they, as a group, have created: early relapse stages, middle stages, later stages, and full relapse behaviors (see Table 13.1). The table shows them

Table 13.1
Four Stages of Relapse Behavior

1 *(early relapse stage)*	2 *(middle stage)*	3 *(later stage)*	4 *(full-blown relapse)*
Believing that my problems are over.	Begin to hang around with old drinking friends.	Someone dies, or gets hurt and I just give-up trying.	Depressed. Drunk all the time.
Not talking in my group.	Quit my group.	Begin isolating.	Poor personal hygiene.
Working hard.	Feeling tired/need a break.	Get into fights or argue with people.	Losing or no money.
Unrealistic expectations.	Things going too good.	Become disappointed.	Go to the woods to "bunker up."
Not get into conflicts.	Begin to verbally push others away.	Begin "socially drinking."	Not sleeping or nightmares.
Missing support group on occasion.	Believing I can gamble on occasion.	Increased intrusive thoughts of trauma.	Getting into fights.
Believing "I'm cured."	Taking on too much responsibility.	"It don't mean nothing!"	Suicidal/homicidal thoughts/gestures.
Try to control other people.	Get disappointed.	Cop an attitude about my treatment program.	Isolate myself.

The lists are not necessarily read across (column 1, 2, 3, 4), due to the behaviors being randomly listed by the veterans during the class. The veterans themselves put the behaviors together in their own personal sequence that is based on their past experiences.

the overlap of their behaviors with other behaviors within the same column and allows them to observe their own progression of the relapse pattern.

The lists are not necessarily read across (column 1, 2, 3, 4) as the behaviors were randomly listed by the veterans during the class. The veterans themselves put the behaviors together in their own personal sequence, based on their past experiences.

Each veteran then chooses three or four behaviors from each column that he or she recognizes from past relapse behaviors. He or she is assigned the written task of creating a healthy intervention for each behavior he or she indicated as a relapse behavior. For example, an early relapse signal recognized by a veteran may be, "Stopped talking in my aftercare group" or "Felt that I am 'cured,' " followed by a middle stage relapse signal of, "Stopped going to my group" or "Began to work long hours," followed by later stage relapse signal of, "My intrusive thoughts increase" or "I begin to isolate and start drinking again," followed by a full-blown relapse of PTSD symptoms and chemical or nonchemical habituating behaviors that resemble pretreatment intensity.

Sessions 6 and 7. Planned interventions of PTSD and relapse behaviors. The veterans verbally share their interventions with the class and receive feedback from other group members. In effect, this signifies the beginning stage of an aftercare plan with specific behavioral strategies. Feedback is crucial to avoid ''a plan mandated by the staff'' and to provide peers the opportunity to offer suggested changes to each plan that could be very helpful. It is not unusual for group members to edit their existing interventions by listening to feedback that is not even directed to them. Support for the interventions by the group is encouraged. This component of the class should be very positive and encouraging.

DUAL DISORDER TREATMENT

Offering a ''dual disorder'' component within an existing substance abuse or PTSD program appears to be a reasonable alternative when a primary dual disorder program is not available. Obviously, a thorough diagnosis and treatment plan that takes into account PTSD, substance abuse, and other primary and secondary diagnoses must be formulated prior to admission for therapeutic intervention. Patients with severe psychopathology for both disorders need complete inpatient hospitalizations for each, as well as extensive discharge treatment planning that addresses both problem areas (Marcus, 1990).

CONCLUSION

This chapter describes some of the dynamics of war-traumatized veterans with PTSD, chemical disorders, and problematic habituating behaviors. Clinicians and other service providers who treat individuals with PTSD diagnoses and/or chemical abuse are encouraged to recognize the possibility that nonchemical habituating behaviors incorporated into the trauma survivors' life-style may be maintaining dysfunction. Patients should be educated regarding the relationship of chemical/non-chemical habituations and PTSD symptoms. An ''either/or'' treatment and recovery approach contributes to an avoidance of treating either PTSD or substance abuse/nonchemical habitual behaviors. In addition, the ''either/or'' approach underemphasizes the powerful interplay between the two disorders and contributes to the likelihood of addictive/habitual behavior and/or PTSD relapse. Specific relapse prevention concepts appear to be applicable in the treatment of clients who manifest both addictive/habituating behaviors and/ or PTSD.

The authors have presented one approach to addressing the issues of PTSD, chemical addictions, and problematic habituating behaviors within the context of an inpatient program. Hopefully, continued strategies will evolve as clinicians become further aware of the dual diagnoses dynamic and learn about the complex issues of the dual-disordered patient. Fortunately, fully integrated dual disorder programs that treat PTSD and substance abuse issues and other major psychiatric diagnoses are currently burgeoning within mental health treatment agencies. In their clinical assessments, it is essential that treatment providers within the mental health arena continue to acknowledge, recognize, and assess the dual disorder dynamics with all psychiatric diagnoses, including any potentially problematic habituating behaviors that will likely impact upon a client's prognosis and planned treatment intervention.

NOTE

The views expressed herein are solely the authors' and do not necessarily reflect those of the U.S. Department of Veterans Affairs, the American Lake VA Medical Center, or the Pacific Center for PTSD.

The authors gratefully acknowledge Dale E. Smith and Gordon Personius for their reviews and assistance with this document.

Part V

Treatment of Victims of Ethnocultural and Political Problems

14

Post-Traumatic Ethnotherapy (P-TET): Processes in Assessment and Intervention in Aspects of Global Psychic Trauma

Erwin Randolph Parson

> Every person in different ways is like all persons, like some persons, and like no other person.
>
> —Kluckholm and Murray (1953)

THE "HARD-WIRING" OF ETHNOCULTURAL DYNAMICS

Ethnicity, culture, and race operate interactively in traumatic stress psychotherapy. They determine the nature of the therapeutic relationship, what therapist and client expect as treatment outcome, how they define the problem, and the specific process during the treatment enterprise. As a springboard into life, ethnicity is important throughout the various phases of the life cycle to most individuals—from infancy and childhood, to adolescence and adulthood, through 'lescence to senescence.

ɔiligent transcultural research is needed to understand better the role of culture in the assessment and treatment of post-traumatic stress conditions. Ethnocultural factors thus shape common and unique human responses to psychological traumatization. They determine both normal and pathological post-traumatic formations and organize the expression of post-traumatic stress disorder. So important is ethnicity to most people that it has "proved far more important than differences in philosophy or economic system" (Greeley, 1969, p. 5).

The ethnocultural self is naturally a biased self; it consists of "hard-wired" narcissistic elements rooted in deep psychological (conscious but mostly unconscious) and physiological processes and structures. The narcissistic nature of ethnoculturality makes it somewhat easier to understand the potential for healing and harm in cross-cultural therapy.

Similar to most people, psychologists, psychiatrists, and other professionals are subject or vulnerable to separating the world into "we" and "they"—replete with bias and a set of related prejudicial attitudes, beliefs, and values. It is thus essential that ethnicity-determined responses be sensitively and appropriately managed to prevent countertransference-based oppression and distortion of the victim/survivor. Embracing ethnic differences in the psychotherapeutic venture may also enrich the working and therapeutic alliances, expand the patient's self-awareness and ethnocultural identity, and thereby facilitate integration of trauma elements into a cohesive self-organization. Increasing the therapist's comfort, self-insight, and control and developing transculturally enlightened concepts, procedures, and techniques are the sine qua non of effective therapy with ethnocultural patients (Parson, 1985b, 1985c).

Introducing ethnicity in discussions of trauma is difficult for many reasons; among them are confusion, shame, guilt, anxiety, and other emotions. When most people hear the words "ethnicity" and "culture," the knee-jerk reaction is to believe that it refers exclusively to American ethnic minorities (or to minorities in other Western countries). It is important to note, however, that the term as used in this chapter is applied broadly to any clinical situation in which participants represent differing ethnic, cultural, or racial heritages, that is, in clinical situations in which victim/survivor and therapist represent both a dominant and nondominant culture (or "culture-defining group" and "non-culture-defining group" [Tyler, Brome, and Williams, 1991]).

This chapter is divided into seven major areas: ubiquity of catastrophic misery; interactive effects of ethnicity, culture, and race; ethnocultural ego identity; the aftermath of traumatic exposure; ethnic post-trauma assessment; post-traumatic ethnotherapy; and directions for future research. First is a discussion of the ubiquity of catastrophic misery.

UBIQUITY OF CATASTROPHIC MISERY: ON GLOBAL TRAUMATIC STRESS

Among the natural and man-made events that can potentially produce psychological distress, psychiatric disorders, and social dysfunctions are such seemingly ubiquitous calamities as pestilences, famines, earthquakes, fires, floods, and environmental and atmospheric damage (e.g., "global warming"). A recent area of ethnocultural strife and traumatic stressors was Los Angeles, California, as it became the epicenter or a flashpoint for ethnic tensions and violence in wake of the acquittal of four white police officers tried for the savage beating of black motorist Rodney King. In some countries today people of various ethnic, cultural, and racial groups are also subjected to psychic trauma through exposure to governmental sexual torture (Agger, 1989) and political persecution and repression that result in the "bruising of the soul" (Simpson, 1992). People also seem to be forced to endure the extreme stresses intrinsic to massive exoduses of refugees to the Western world (e.g., from Haiti, Indochina, Cuba, and elsewhere) and cultural and geographic uprootings. Other massive stressful events are associated with technological disasters (such as Chernobyl in the former USSR, Bhopal in India, and Three Mile Island in the United States).

The international awareness of global traumatic stress has resulted in five major events since 1980: the advent of "post-traumatic stress disorder" (PTSD); the establishment of the International Society for Traumatic Stress Studies and its scientific and professional publication, the *Journal of Traumatic Stress: The International Handbook of Traumatic Stress Syndromes*, edited by Drs. John Wilson and Beverly Raphael (1993); and the national and international literature on traumatic stress syndromes and PTSD.

INTERACTIVE EFFECTS OF ETHNICITY, ETHNIC SOCIO-IDENTITY, CULTURE, AND RACE

Ethnocultural existence begins with ethnicity. Ethnicity consists of biogenic (genotypic and phenotypic), sociofamilial, linguistic, socioeconomic, and experiential factors. It is "being with" one's ancestors rooted in historical, cognitive, and normal emotional narcissism. Ethnic socio-identity is the cognitive awareness and sense of emotional bonding with members sharing a common ancestry and related values, food preferences, beliefs, and customs. Culture refers to a collective of "multiple ethnic realities." The issue of race is not identical to culture, nor is race the same thing as ethnicity. In America, when people speak of race, they are often making reference to visible physical characteristics, such as skin color, that distinguish one racial group from another.

ETHNOCULTURAL EGO IDENTITY (ECEI)

As a psychological "bridging structure," ECEI connects the cultural divide, the natural sense of disjunction, and even fragmentation often accompanying the transition from one culture to another—from ethnic isolation to ethnocultural belonging and integration. ECEI transcends the individual's or therapist's ethnoculturocentrism in interacting with people of other cultures and in identifying with one's ethnic group, by which he or she finds a safe, integrative, adaptive beacon of cultural orientation.

The ECEI is based upon acquiring a sense of belonging and worthiness, a sense of competence and control, which ultimately contribute to increased management of the vicissitudes of ethnicism or racism when interacting with the dominant culture. Cognitive and emotional identification with one's ethnic group of origin is even more meaningful when the group values intrinsic customs, embues them with pride and respectability, and actively seeks to maintain and preserve them in the dominant culture's ecology.

Healthy identification with one's group of origin is not to be confused with ethnocentrism, which this author views as blind narcissism. This blindness tends to fixate the individual on the socio-identity of his or her own ethnic group. Stubborn ethnic fixity makes the individual unyielding to new information processing essential in adaptation to the dominant culture.

Ethnocultural ego identity requires action-oriented experiences; it, thus, involves learning, growth, and change processes. Piaget's (1970) reciprocal dynamic system of assimilation and accommodation in cognitive growth, referred to as "instruments of transformation," is of relevance as well to the concept of ECEI. Assimilation refers to a "process whereby an action is actively reproduced and comes to incorporate new objects into itself" (p. 63). Through assimilation, therefore, the ethnic-group person incorporates new data and experiences into existing ethnic self-schemas and structures. But these internalizations are at first distorted, biased, unstable, and impermanent.

Accommodation allows for "adjusted alignments" of newly acquired growth experience and structure with a multicultural ecologic reality. Adjusted alignment can be achieved only through action "applied to a diversity of objects" (expanded to mean people, situations, and experiences in general) (Piaget, 1970, p. 63). Adjusted alignments imply a set of refined internalizations that create intrapsychic structural change. This change provides self-continuity and a stable sense of self, which may reduce distortion of others, while increasing tolerance for ethnic dissimilarity and diversity.

The employing of assimilation and accommodation over time results in ethnocultural adaptation—from temporary mental representations to permanent schemas. The permanence of schemas provides for stability of ethnocultural self-other configurations, sense of inner continuity in time and space, and confidence in the future—or ethnocultural identity. However, when trauma strikes, even the ethnoculturally integrated self experiences the shattering of central organizing elements of identity, which often renders control operations over biopsychic and other potential problematic responses virtually ineffective.

THE AFTERMATH OF TRAUMATIC EXPOSURE: THE ETHNOCULTURAL TRAUMA RESPONSE

The trauma responses of all survivors appear to feature a homogeneous set of symptoms comprised of biological, psychological, and sociocultural elements. The biological components of trauma response appear to be the most consistent across cultures. It appears that psychological (personality defenses and coping, cognitive processing efficiency, and meaning) and sociocultural aspects of the trauma response may show greater variability in symptom expression and are determined by pretrauma variables, traumatic stress variables (i.e., onset, duration, and intensity), and the recovery environment (Green, Wilson, and Lindy, 1985; Parson, 1985c). Transcultural research in this area is needed to further clarify their relative weight. Three basic perspectives on the nature of the transcultural trauma response are identified; the universalistic, the particularistic, and the dualistic.

The universalistic perspective purports that a basic response to trauma supersedes developmental factors and ethnic, race, and cultural lines; that is, the pattern is the same transculturally and transnationally. The universalistic view also suggests that "inter-traumatic events" (i.e., rape, incest, combat, and so on) share similar properties and response patterns (APA, 1987). The particularistic position, on the other hand, holds that the trauma response is influenced by individual differences: personality, temperament, coping, age and developmental period, and ethnocultural factors. The dualistic perspective holds that common and unique patterns are both important and indispensable for meaningful conceptualization in assessment and therapy with ethnic trauma survivors.

Universalistic Trauma Response and Ethno-Biobehavioral Factors

The concepts of "ethno-biobehavior" and "ethnocultural trauma response" refers to the cross-cultural responses originating in biological alterations (Friedman, 1988; Kolb & Mutalipassi, 1982; van der Kolk, 1987c) and the cultural meaning individuals and communities ascribe to psychological traumatization. Contributing to the concept of ethno-biobehavior of PTSD is the universal clinical syndrome Kardiner (1941) reported as a result of his research with chronic traumatic neurosis in the 1920s. He had noted that, after catastrophic events, people experienced a state of being biopsychically revved up to the point of responding continually to environmental threat (even when no trace of the original threatening situation was present). Once the "biological gears" were set into operation, it seemed, the individual gave the impression of being forced to drink of the bitter waters of the past traumatic moment. The original traumatic stimuli seemed to continually drive the "engine of traumatic responses" without letting up.

Particularistic Trauma Response: Culture-Originating Affective-Behavioral Syndromes

In contrast to the universalistic perspective is the view that trauma responses vary from one ethnocultural group to another. Referred to by Simon and Hughes (1985) as "unfamiliar ways of being crazy," the so-called culture-bound syndromes (or "culture-originating affective-behavioral syndromes") are found in many countries. Ness (1985) described the "Old Hag" or "*Ag Rog*" syndromes in descendants of immigrants from the English West Country to Newfoundland: being awake but being unable to move and experiencing great exhaustion and fatigue. Hispanics, especially Mexicans, are known to suffer a condition called *susto*, or fright, which has been understood in the West as the equivalent of an "anxiety state" (Kiev, 1972). The Japanese psychoanalyst Yasuhiko Taketoma reintroduced the concept of *Amae*, a characterological state of passive-dependency, insecurity, and helplessness. China has its *shenjing shuairuo*, a somatopsychic manifestation involving headaches, weakness, irritability, poor appetite, and concentration difficulties.

Dualistic Trauma Response

Since trauma responses are complex, this perspective holds that such complexity requires a comprehensive-integrative view, rather than an either/or point of view. It espouses, instead, both universalistic and particularistic positions.

ETHNIC POST-TRAUMA ASSESSMENT

DSM III-R and ICD-10 as Transcultural Diagnostic Systems

Similar to most cultural institutions and products, classification systems are born of a society and culture. But contemporary psychiatric taxonomy has generally assumed universal applicability to persons of all racial, ethnic, or cultural groups. Some have advocated expanding the Diagnostic and Statistical Manual (DSM III-R) (APA, 1987) system to accommodate ethnocultural specificity. Others have argued for a particularistic position when diagnosing ethnocultural patients.

The DSM III-R is used widely as a transcultural universalistic instrument, especially in the form of the SCID-R (the Structured Clinical Interview for the DSM III-R) (Spitzer, Williams, Gibbon, and First, 1990). The DSM III system is criterion-referenced and so purports to reduce clinician-to-clinician variability. However, many believe the DSM III (APA,1980), III-R (APA, 1987), and DSM IV (to be published in the near future) do not readily lend themselves to transcultural applications.

This is not necessarily the case. True, this modern psychiatric diagnostic system lacks the transcultural specificity that would make it a truly cross-cultural psychiatric taxonomic system. However, to make the system more ethnoculturally sensitive, some modifications may be required. Weisaeth and Eitinger (1991a, 1991b) wrote, "If the 1990 draft of the proposed ICD-10 (International Classification of Diseases) is accepted, a diagnosis of post-traumatic stress disorder will be used internationally" (p. 1). Transcultural assessment for PTSD is most difficult. Because of the "inconsistency in available information" on ethnic groups, there is the need to "weave subjective impressions with objective facts" (Penk and Allen, 1991, p. 43).

Universal patterns were observed in children's post-traumatic stress symptomatology after a school bus disaster in Israel (Milgram et al., 1988); hostages in The Netherlands (van der Ploeg and Kleijn, 1989); Cambodian refugees (Kinzie and Boehnlein, 1989); Israeli combat veterans (Solomon, Bengenishty, and Mikulincer, 1991); survivors of volcanic eruptions, fires, tornadoes, floods, mudslides, dam break, and skywalk collapse (Baum, Hyman, and Michel, 1983; Green et al., 1990; Krause, 1987). American ethnic minorities—Native Americans, African Americans, Asian Americans, Pacific Islanders, and Hispanic Americans (Brende and Parson, 1985; Parson, 1985b, 1985c, 1991; Pena, 1985; Silver, 1984); and other survivor or victim groups.

Dimensions of Ethnic Post-Trauma Assessment

The nature of the survivor's ethnocultural ego identity must be determined during the assessment process. As noted earlier, ECEI consists of intrapsychic and external influences. The intrapsychic factors include personality, coping, and defensive organization, temperament, intellectual endowment, and affective expressions and cognitive controls. Interacting with these internal events and capabilities are the external variables: psychological trauma and related symptomatology, historical and/or current parental/family experiences and reinforcements, and the nature of psychocultural uprooting from one's country of origin and translocating to another—often alien—country or culture.

The concept of illness behavior is germane to ethnic post-trauma assessment. The concept "describes the . . . way individuals monitor their bodies, define and interpret their symptoms, take remedial action, and utilize sources of help as well as the more formal health care system" (Mechanic, 1986, p. 1). Illness behavior, therefore, is a necessary concept in assessing people from various racial, ethnic, and cultural backgrounds who have been adversely affected by traumatic stress.

Generally, ethno-post-trauma assessment incorporates the use of objective (e.g., psychometric instruments, the Wechsler scales) and projective (e.g., Thematic Apperception Test, Rorschach, projective drawings) instruments and procedures in the following ten dimensions of the assessment process.

1. The clinician expresses pleasure to meet the survivor and his or her family members; strives to build rapport by demonstrating ability to focus exclusively on the patient's self-presentation and the consciously verbalized (as opposed to unconscious derivatives and nonverbal communication, focused on much later) complaints; and projects warmth, safety, confidence, and a positive outlook in basic attitude and general approach.

2. The clinician determines the nature of the stressor, post-traumatic symptoms, and the differential contributions of both universal and culture-specific responses (as discussed previously).

3. The clinician facilitates a detailed unfolding of the client's age, gender, and racial heritage, with geographic movements, language, psychiatric history for all members of immediate and extended families, particularly those emotional reactions called "culture-bound syndromes," and familial psychohistory—father, mother, grandfathers, grandmothers, and so on.

4. The clinician uncovers the psychological process and chronology of leaving and arriving: what was said in deciding to leave, how the decision was made to leave, why the particular new country was selected, and who helped them survive (especially the initial days or weeks) after arriving.

5. The clinician determines the presence and nature of extended family systems (familial, social, supportive, helping networks) and degree of postmigration dispersion of original family members.

6. The clinician seeks knowledge of the survivor's feelings about living in the new country/culture and personal impression of how his or her ethnic group or family is perceived in terms of relative favorability and positive evaluation (compared with dominant and nondominant culture groups) by the new society's popular culture.

7. The clinician explores the victim/survivors' intrapsychic dynamics—internalizations of the new cultural experiences; self-perception, identity organization (that is, degree of emerging integration of the ethnocultural ego identity system); perceptions of the host culture vis-à-vis self over time; perceived chances for personal/familial improvement and achievements of goals in relation to country/culture of origin; relative degree of isolation or alienation from family, extended family, the ethnic community representing his or her own group, surrounding community, and the social ecology in general.

8. The clinician assesses the degree of shared ethnic identifications between self and survivor.

9. The clinician conducts an overall assessment of victim/survivor variables, therapist variables, anticipated process variables (based on clinical data gathered from the patient), patient expectations, and victim/survivor preferences—for therapy style, therapist characteristics, his or her ethnocultural identity and adaptation, and gender.

10. The clinician utilizes the best "culture-specific" assessment instruments available (based on research studies, whenever possible). It is important to note that instruments translated into various languages are not synonymous with "transcultural cognitive-experiential alignment." Missing from translations are the ethnic idioms and uniqueness of perceptual, cognitive, and phenomenological aspects of symptom expression.

POST-TRAUMATIC ETHNOTHERAPY: INTERSECTING CULTURAL AND TRAUMA ELEMENTS

Psychotherapy with victims/survivors requires transcultural understanding in order to address the recovery needs of specific patients. Knowledge of a patient's heritage empowers the therapeutic encounter by increasing the capacity for establishing a true cultural adaptational matrix. This bipersonal matrix becomes the dynamic-experiential basis for control, increased self-esteem, and change. Effective therapy in culturally pluralistic societies places the onus of responsibility for appropriate preparation on the therapist.

During the initial phase of the therapy, the therapist explores the survivor's fantasies and realistic perceptions about the therapist's ethnicity and/or gender, about his or her presenting complaints, about the process and course of treatment, and about termination. The patient's worldview, perceptions, interests, and values are intrinsic to the conduct of cross-cultural psychotherapy with victim/ survivors.

Understanding ethnoculturally different survivors may result in the sensitivity and specificity implied in the observation that Hispanics respond in therapy best when their problems are reformulated in medical terms (Meadow, 1982); African Americans do best in action-oriented therapies (Calia, 1966), while Asian Americans prefer structure and a therapist-managed interactive process (Atkinson, Maruyama, and Matsui, 1978). Patients' preference for a therapist based upon ethnic identification and demographics may also be a meaningful variable for some survivors.

Post-traumatic ethnotherapy is an intersectional view into the relationship of biphasic trauma responses in the context of diverse ethnocultural responses. This analysis begins with the stressor (history of trauma), then progresses to incursive/ intrusive phenomena, avoidance, hyperarousal, and other clinical manifestations of psychological trauma.

History of Traumatic Experience

To expand present cross-cultural understanding of the complex interaction of psychic structure and coping, phenomenology, *stressor properties* (i.e., type, intensity, duration, and so on), "holding characteristics" of the recovery ecology, and traumatopsychic symptoms, it is important that an integration of Woeber's (1969) "centri-cultural" method and valid cross-cultural instruments incorporate native customs, idioms, and meaning systems held by indigenous persons of a particular ethnocultural group. Until valid cross-culture studies are devised and conducted in the area of traumatic stress, it will continue to be difficult to discriminate between what Tseng and Hsu (1980) have called "minor psychological disturbances of everyday life" and the more serious pathological developments in cases of chronic post-traumatic stress.

Generally, however, use of descriptions that may be seen as stereotypic cannot be avoided totally. What is probably worse than the use of ethnic-born descriptions is the pretense of legitimacy for "normative stereotyping," that is, expecting all persons, regardless of their ethnic group of origin, to think, feel, and act like everyone else in American or other Western countries (the myth of the American "melting pot").

Involuntary Mental Incursion and Post-Traumatic Affective Stress Response Syndrome

Intrusive ideation, affect, and memory originating in the traumatic experience often lead to an affective stress response syndrome. The underlying biopsychic disturbances lower the capacity of survivors to tolerate strong emotions. The syndrome consists of affective symptoms and responses of depression, anxiety, fear, phobic reactions, terror, horror, sadness, grief states, shame, guilt, anger, and narcissistic rage reactions. Understanding the cross-cultural phenomenology of emotions is therefore critical to treatment of this aspect of the syndrome.

The avoidant set of mental symptoms involves "persistent avoidance of stimuli . . . or a numbing of general responsiveness that was not present before the trauma. . . . Diminished responsiveness to the external world, referred to as 'psychic numbing' or 'emotional anesthesia' " (APA, 1987, p. 248). Physiologically based arousal symptoms include difficulty falling or staying asleep, hypervigilance, exaggerated startle response, difficulty in concentrating or in completing tasks, and an unpredictable explosion or an inability to express angry feeling (APA, 1987). Clinical observation and scientific findings have shown that health-subverting effects of PTSD reverberate in the body's psychophysiological, neuroendocrine, hypothalamopituitary adrenocortical axis, and muscular systems. "Because of these physiological responses to memories, it is not difficult to understand why so [many survivors] complain of physical problems associated with parts of the autonomic nervous system: the heart, stomach, urinary tract, genitals, muscles, nerves, and blood pressure" (Brende and Parson, 1985, p. 222).

General Principles of Post-Traumatic Ethnotherapy

The goals of post-traumatic ethnotherapy combine both universal and culture-specific techniques and assumptions (Draguns, 1975, 1981; Higginbotham, 1979; Parson, 1985b, 1985c; Torrey, 1969, 1986), while espousing the integrated understanding of post-traumatic behavior and affective phenomenology. The fundamental principles of post-traumatic ethnotherapy are based upon the realization of the multiple-system impairments in post-traumatic conditions: phenomenological clouding of consciousness, cognitive-perceptual lack of control, identity disruption, "life-death" intolerance for strong affect, defective capacity for modulation of arousal and aggression, intolerance for arousal resulting in either overreactivity or underreactivity (to internal and external stimuli), the devastation of self-skills, and rupturing of social/interpersonal bonds with family, friends, community, and world. The post-traumatic affecttve intensity (and concomitant absence of controlling psychic structure) that attends therapy may be ameliorated during the early phases of the treatment through systematic preparation for therapy (Hoehn-Saric et al., 1964; Parson, 1991, in press).

The goals of post-traumatic ethnotherapy are to explore and understand the presenting complaints of PTSD and related psychological responses to the traumatic event; to alleviate post-traumatic distress; and to reintegrate "split-off" aspects of self and bring these dissociated "wandering self-fragments" home psychologically, culturally, and socially to family, work, and community. The pervasiveness of deficits inherent in PTSD disruptions requires a comprehensive model of care (Parson, 1985b, 1985c, 1990, in press).

The model features multiple forms of interventions to include individual, family (depending on degree of "culturoethnic familism"), and ecologic therapy (interaction with community/government-based service agencies to meet patients' immediate, concrete needs), stress management, and psychopharmacotherapy. Specific techniques derive from an intertheoretical approach (Parson, 1988b) that uses dynamic, cognitive, behavioral, and experiential procedures. Similar to cross-cultural therapy in general, the principles of post-traumatic ethnotherapy attend integratively to therapist variables (Marsella and Pederson, 1981; Parson, 1985b; Cheng and Lo, 1991), conceived here to be as important as client/patient variables, client variables, expectational variables, and process variables.

Personal Characteristics of the Intercultural Therapist

Relationship variables are germane to effective psychotherapy. The nature of therapist variables is seldom detailed in the literature, but they may be as important to therapy outcome as client variables. Relationships in therapy are always dynamic in nature; they are never static.

Thus, relationship issues form around ethnocultural transference, ethnocultural countertransference (Comas-Diaz and Jacobsen, 1991), and ethnocultural counterresistance. Emergence of these vital processes in therapy depends on the therapist's personality, attitude, sensitivity, capacity to process strong emotions, and willingness to "go all out" for the patient. Thus, the following factors are seen as essential qualities for therapists in post-traumatic ethnotherapy.

- The therapist demonstrates a deep, abiding respect for the survivor's capacities, limitations, values, customs, and religious preference and has the belief that the client will improve and ultimately recover.
- The therapist displays firm confidence in his or her knowledge and competence about the survivor's trauma and culture. This may be secured through specialized training (Parson, 1985b; Westermeyer, 1989).
- The therapist strives to achieve a thorough understanding of the survivor's motivation, strengths, deficits, and ethnoculturally based expectations through the ethno-post-trauma assessment process (the dual focus on PTSD and ethnicity).
- The therapist informs the ethnocultural survivor of the range and variety of available intervention options and their purposes.
- The therapist widens the assessment and therapeutic scope to include cultural/familial, personal/developmental, and trauma-originating responses.
- The therapist espouses a basic focus on coping in the here and now and highlights the survivor's strengths and abilities, while not letting deficits and pathology dominate the total therapy.
- The therapist implements a wealth of transcultural information about many ethnocultural groups.
- The therapist demonstrates transexperiential competence in terms of cognitive and experiential/affective knowledge about the survivor's specific trauma.
- The therapist demonstrates that he or she is psychologically stable, is secure in his or her identity, with personal trauma history under control, and is able to endure stress

and the affective toil demanded of the P-TET process of listening to survivors' trauma narratives and intervening in them.

• The therapist's experience features a flexible armamentarium of multiple therapies used strategically to benefit the survivor.

Post-Traumatic Phenomenology of the Victim

In therapy, "post-traumatic phenomenology" is characterized by the survivor's unique experiencing of distress energized by an admixture of emotions. This experiencing involves biopsychic processing of the post-traumatic affective stress response syndrome (mentioned earlier), consisting of guilt, shame, grief, sadness, narcissistic hurt and anguish, disappointment, anxiety, fear, terror, depression, and dissociated, "split-off" rage (Parson, 1988a, 1988b).

The admixture of these emotional reactions and the ethnic survivor's basic intolerance for strong affect and relative incapacity to regulate arousal make the development of bipersonal trust and therapeutic safety a critical prerequisite to the therapy's success. A clear understanding of the client's expectations in therapy is necessary (Higginbotham, 1977). Post-traumatic phenomenology involves the trauma-influenced self-experiencing as seen in the symptoms and expressions from the trauma.

Intercultural Intersubjectivity (ICIS): From Transcultural Perception to Intercultural Experiencing

Post-traumatic ethnotherapy is ultimately a human relational encounter that constructs a "space of safety" for the survivor of ethnocultural heritage. ICIS embraces the client's ethnic, racial, and cultural differences and recognizes that all psychotherapy is in some way cross-cultural.

A most critical procedure that must occur early in the treatment is establishing what this author calls "bipersonal synchronicity," a process of interpersonal congruence (between survivor and therapist). The concept of bipersonal synchronicity was developed to fill a void in the clinical procedures with ethnic persons in therapy. Even after achieving the cultural-clinical ideal of culture-specific knowledge about the client's group, the therapy may still remain relatively "experience-distant" and often ineffectual. Bipersonal synchronicity is conceptualized as "experience-near," closer to the victim's real feelings, beliefs, and actual distress.

Synchronicity is essential because cross-cultural relations are often experienced by most people as antagonistic to their cultural conditioning and values. Pinderhughes is correct that prejudice is "hard-wired" into even the normal psyche (Penk and Allen, 1991). Thus, nothing less than procedures aimed at "hard de-wiring" will suffice. Moreover, if people naturally tend toward "differential bonding"—that is, using affiliative-affectionate drives toward their own ethnocultural group, while employing differentiative-aggressive drives toward people of other groups (Penk and Allen, 1991)—it then follows that cross-cultural therapy will not "just happen" like magic.

It takes hard work to overcome intractable modes of cultural perception and psychophysiological imprinting. Breaking down or dissolution of rigid barriers between the principals in cross-cultural therapy must occur for meaningful interaction to become a reality. When this does not occur, stereotypes take the place of effective process and result in premature termination. When therapists try hard to keep their ethnocultural patients in therapy, they energetically "go all out" (Little, 1957) to shatter the "rigid cross-cultural wall" between self and client.

The Vicissitudes of Credible Behavior

Sue and Zane (1987) highlighted two basic processes advanced as prescriptions for underutilization of clinical services by ethnic patients: credibility and giving. Credibility refers to clients' perception that the therapist is trustworthy and effective. Giving relates to the client's experience of getting something tangible from the therapeutic encounter that works or solves an immediate problem.

Credibility and Perceived Ethnic Distance

Therapist credibility is associated with the degree of ethnic distance perceived in a specific client-therapist dyad and the degree of intrapsychic affective turbulence. The meaning of credibility is probably the same for people regardless of ethnocultural group of origin or social class. However, the techniques or specific actions utilized to achieve credibility with specific clients require divergent clinical-interpersonal pathways.

Explicit and Implicit Credibility

In the dynamics of therapy, two kinds of credibilities emerge: explicit credibility and implicit credibility. Each type of credibility features a "surface" level and a "consequential" level. Explicit credibility occurs when the client perceives client-therapist similarity that is based upon "surface-level factors" (i.e., skin color, ostensible racio-ethnic traits, and so on) and is convinced that this fact correlates with positive outcome. The client's assumption is: "You are trustworthy because you and I are alike. You will understand me fully and resolve my conflicts." The consequential or "depth" level is deemed unimportant in this case. In implicit credibility, on the other hand, the client perceives the surface-level factors as possible barriers to communication, understanding, and trust in therapy. Since the depth level is hidden from view, the client employs a "wait and see" posture. The client's assumption in this instance is: "We don't seem to have anything in common. I am doubtful you'll be able to help me with the serious problems I have. You will have to prove to me in a hurry that you can be reliable.'' The accelerated form of credibility becomes essential (discussed later). Whereas the explicit variety is easily achieved with the client, the latter takes time to consolidate and poses a real challenge to the therapist.

Trauma Victims and Credibility

Clinical observation reveals that trauma tends to increase the need for credible behavior on the part of the therapist. Therefore, survivors of the various traumatic experiences (e.g., rape, incest, physical abuse, sexual torture) are hypersensitive to the issue of credibility, regardless of race, ethnicity, or cultural differences. Adding ethnicity to the equation makes credibility even more urgent if the treatment is even to ''get off the ground'' successfully. Victims want to end the pain; they want immediate relief from what one victim called ''an inner chamber of horrors.'' If the ethnic victim/survivor in this state of mind encounters a therapist who does not understand his or her culture, the sense of vulnerability increases. If the therapist has knowledge about the culture, but the client perceives him or her to lack essential sensitivity and sophistication in working with trauma victims, the internal sense of being imperiled will escalate.

Accelerated Credibility

Victims come to therapy when they feel they have become dysfunctional in their family life, interactions with friends, relation to community, and the workplace. Victims do not feel they have the time, patience, or the essential sense of inner security and control to provide therapists with the opportunity to improve their learning curve over time. In these instances the therapist must ''hit the ground running'' and employ approaches designed to attain ''accelerated credibility.'' This writer maintains that whereas credibility may be essential for all cross-cultural therapy regardless of social class, the symbolic value of gift offering may be limited to specific ethnic groups (e.g., Asians) and to other ethnic and lower socioeconomic group survivors.

Bipersonal Synchronicity and Credible Behavior

Bipersonal synchronicity builds credibility; it impresses clients with the therapist's initiative to work hard to get to know them from within, *as they are.* This initiative makes clients feel understood, confirmed, and worthwhile. Credibility is also reinforced by the therapist's openness and willingness to ''put self on the line'' by sharing personal data relevant to the positive projected outcome of the enterprise. ''Going all out'' for the survivor builds confidence in the process, trust in the therapist, and hopefulness that change and resolution can occur.

The ''emic-etic'' axis (Berry, 1969; Draguns, 1981) is a concept used widely in the clinical and scientific literature. The emic view says that therapy and research need to be culture-specific in order to be effective and relevant to indigenous populations; the etic end of the continuum relates to the position that Western therapy and related scientific methodology are universally applicable. In therapy the process of synchronization involves the therapist's allowing the ethnocultural survivor to resonate endopsychically; it also identifies parts of the clients that the therapist can possess as his or her own. Synchronization procedures may create the "interpersonal glue" that is often missing in cross-cultural therapy.

The Cross-Cultural Perspective and Interculturality

Post-traumatic ethnotherapy is designated as "intercultural therapy" as opposed to "cross-cultural" therapy because of the intersubjective focus of P-TET. While the latter requires a "crossing over," a distally located process between two people, the former relates to a more proximally available, immediate experiential encounter that seeks to "dissolve," rather than merely recognize cultural barriers. Additionally, the notion of going across cultures suggests a purely cognitive, intellective exercise, an "encapsulated knowledge base" often without effective channels of subjective communication.

Therapy Phases and Culture-Specific Intervention

Synchronizing places client and therapist on a relatively egalitarian plane. Members of some ethnocultural groups prefer therapists who are directive, and an egalitarian relationship would not be consistent with their expectations of a professional helper. The therapist monitors the process and develops it along the lines most congruent with the client's needs and expectations. These expectations, of course, depend on the phase of psychotherapy in question.

Psychotherapy is developmentally multiphasic: it begins with an initial or orientation phase, then progresses to a phase of comfort and exploration, and then to consolidation and termination. Each phase defines the treatment challenge for that portion of the therapy and lays the foundation for succeeding phases. Thus, an ethnic survivor whose culture-based preference is for an authoritarian-styled therapist in the early phase of the therapy may, in later phases, expect and need a shift to greater power sharing in the relationship or to an egalitarian style of relating. Phasic shifts are to be expected by therapists. Therapy here thus requires a capacity for flexibility and adaptability.

Healing Idealizations

In addition to reducing bias and cultural alienation in the therapy, synchronization may in addition to credibility develop idealization, two important ingredients of effective therapy. The trauma patient is always in fear of losing control over strong affectivity, lacks self-confidence with others, may be confused and disoriented, and may manifest varying degrees of antipathy, fear, and ambivalence toward authority persons (whom they may blame for the traumatic incidents). Synchronization may be helpful here as well. In terms of the actual procedures for the bipersonal synchronizing process, Table 14.1 shows the various categories of personal qualities, traits, and experiences that guide mutual exploration in intercultural trauma therapy.

The therapist takes full responsibility for the enterprise and begins the procedure by first giving the survivor a rationale for the technique. The ethnic survivor is given the synchronizing prompt:

Though we are from different family backgrounds [racial, ethnic, or cultural], it is quite possible that we have lots more in common than meets the eye. We will do an interesting and important exercise for the success of your therapy [or counseling]. Since we are working together, it would help if you knew a lot about me as I learn a lot about you. We're engaging in what's known as "intercultural therapy" [or counseling] in which both you and I are on an equal plane. We have decided to work together to solve real problems that you got after the trauma. I will ask you lots of questions about what happened to you [the traumatic event], how you're doing now, what kinds of symptoms you've had, and things about yourself before the event and after the event. After we have completed this, we will see how many things about you are the same for me, even though we appear to be from different races or ethnic family histories. This may take a little time to do.

Ethnocultural Transference and Ethnocultural Countertransference

Once trust has been established in the treatment, transference and countertransference issues become salient clinical tools to deepen exploration. Comas-Diaz and Jacobsen (1991) highlight the dynamics of intraethnic and interethnic transference reactions. Post-trauma transference in work with ethnic survivors may involve perceiving the therapist as a rescuer who saved the patient in a natural disaster or the self-serving, uncaring authority who is responsible for the trauma. Countertransference responses are consistent with post-traumatic ethnotherapy principles. Post-trauma countertransference completes the intersubjective circular loop involving the flow of emotions and cognitions between survivor and therapist. These responses may serve as a barometer of the survivor's internal world of distress, inspiring alterations in clinical techniques and interaction in order to ameliorate these feelings and promote integration and healing.

Countertransference feelings are also a source of meaningful data about the therapist's own ethnocultural narcissism and bias. Recognition and control of these responses are possible only when the therapist becomes aware of the meaning of his or her own responses to the ethnocultural trauma survivor (Parson, 1988a).

Table 14.1
Categories of Synchronizing Factors Used in P-TET

RACIO-CULTURAL FACTORS	PERSONAL, FAMILY & SOCIAL INTERESTS	GEOGRAPHIC HISTORY	EDUCATION HISTORY	TRAUMA HISTORY
Skin Color Eye Color Hair Color Height Language Food Preferences	Mutual Experiences Hobbies, Sibling Traits Temperament, Beliefs, Values Possessions, Friendships Acculturation Experiences Communication Style Gender	Growing up, Place of Residence in Past and Today, Vacation Trips Travels Abroad	Location and Kind of Grade, High School, College Major & General Interest Occupation Social Role	Mutual Victim-Survivor Experiences, Symptoms Reaction--Type, Duration, Intensity, Recovery Experiences

DIRECTIONS FOR FUTURE RESEARCH

The world today is beset by widespread psychological trauma. A task of health and mental health professionals and organizations is to develop viable models that integrate cross-cultural information pertaining to various ethnocultural groups with the science and practice of treating human survivors of catastrophic incidents. Prevailing conceptualizations of mental disorders and clinical models of care, deriving almost exclusively from white middle-class (Euro-American) perspectives, need to be challenged and repeatedly evaluated. This narrow conceptualization of complex human dynamics not only does harm to so-called ethnic minority group patients around the world but also adversely impacts clear understanding of Western nonminority group persons as well.

The therapist's values, personality, skill, applied knowledge, and synchronicity competence are very important factors in successful intervention with victims and survivors of trauma. Therapists must recognize that each survivor is, at the same time, a participant in universal processes, a member of an ethnocultural group, and a unique individual in his or her own right.

Post-traumatic stress disorder can be found universally in the various cultures and nations of the world. As noted earlier, this presumed universality must be tempered by the realization that emic phenomenology of PTSD varies from culture to culture. More study is needed to understand the emic variation in PTSD expression and subjective illness. Scientists interested in cross-cultural PTSD are advised to avoid "the reification of a nosological category [e.g., PTSD] developed for a particular cultural population and the application of that category to members of another culture without establishing validity for that culture" (Good and Good, 1985, p. 10). This is the "category fallacy."

Though there are a number of cross-cultural studies on anxiety and anxiety disorders, depression, and schizophrenia, no cross-cultural studies on post-traumatic stress disorder have been reported to date. Meaningful cross-cultural therapy and research have always required a "decentering" from middle-class ethnocentrism to an ever-widening perspective that seeks to discover the universality of illness categories and their expression across cultures. Effort to discover emic symptomatology and disorder categories and their variations across cultural groups must begin with conducting culturally sensitive research (Rogler, 1989).

Ethnoscience or the scientific investigation into the intricacies of emic disease categories must incorporate into its system of inquiry the well-established methods of anthropological investigation or ethnography (Beiser, 1985; White, 1982). A few issues to consider in future clinical and epidemiological studies include the following:

• Epidemiologically, it is important to discover the frequency and distribution of post-traumatic stress disorder around the world.
• How does culture contribute to PTSD-related "illness behavior"?

- What are the sociocultural factors that increase risk for PTSD in a given ethnocultural group?
- What are related cross-cultural differences in cognition, perception, and attentional processes that predispose to PTSD?
- Applied in the context of post-traumatic ethnotherapy, the perennial question, "Which therapy for which individual at what time under what conditions?" could profitably address a number of pressing clinical problems in intercultural psychotherapy.
- What is the relationship between PTSD and specific culture-bound syndromes (like Koro in Quangdong, China, or the mass phenomenon of fainting and "falling" in South Africa)?

Moreover, sensitive and creative scientific investigations may yield significantly meaningful emic data that can potentially build emic-based intercultural theoretical frameworks to improve ethno-post-trauma assessment and post-traumatic ethnotherapy.

CONCLUSION

Hopefully this chapter will make a meaningful contribution to clinical therapy and to the development of outcome studies with various ethnocultural groups suffering from traumatic stress response syndromes. Assisting victims of trauma such as Cambodian, Central American, Haitian, and other refugee groups is becoming increasingly important. Ethnoculturally appropriate interventions with these and other groups from Europe coming to America offer victim/survivors an alternative to personal anguish, self-destructiveness, and impulsive acting out of pent-up intrapsychic elements from trauma. Such interventions help survivors, moreover, to overcome and integrate intrusion and fear, avoidance and numbing, anxiety and depression, isolation and alienation, hyperarousal and hypervigilance, anger and narcissistic rage, sleeplessness, and the sense of helplessness. Assisting these persons would contribute to the vitality of American and world communities, while increasing the chances for productive and contented lives.

"That Which Does Not Destroy Me": Treating Survivors of Political Torture

Barbara Chester

> They want him to live in fear, to reduce him to nothing more than wild eyes
> and a pulse that rages whenever he hears footsteps in the corridor. He knows
> that his captors are aware that the fear of torture is even better than the real
> thing in breaking down resistance.
>
> —Thornton (1988)

INTRODUCTION

Confronting the physical and emotional survival of severe trauma is a challenge
for both survivor and therapist. Severe stress reactions embody the integrity of
the mind-body interaction: the totality of the body's need to express psychic
pain and the mind's need to understand overwhelming physical hardship (and
the universal and unanswerable plea to the universe, "Why me?").

As survivors struggle with their need to integrate the unimaginable into their
daily realities, therapists, as partners in the healing process, often confront
personal limits, both as professionals and as human beings. In working with
survivors of severe trauma, the author adheres to an assumption ably stated by
author Ayn Rand and conveyed recently by a Cambodian colleague: "You can
deprive a man of reason, but you cannot make him live with what is left" (Rand,
1943).

Torture is an extreme form of trauma. It is practiced in almost half of the
world's nations, some ninety-eight countries (Amnesty International, 1988). It

is an institutionalized form of violence from which there are no escape, safety, or redress. Methods of torture are designed to break the individual and destroy his or her physical, emotional, spiritual, and social self. Thus incapacitated, he or she is released, broken, into the community, to serve as a living warning to others, a visible demonstration of the power of the regime.

After torture, a person's life becomes a process of continual conflict and vacillation between the need to remember and bear witness and the need to forget. This process is often mirrored by his or her support systems, communities, and society at large. For example, as dictatorships end, survivors of torture and other human rights abuses face their own inner needs, which conflict with the needs of the "new" society. The need to remember, name, validate, grieve, and receive compensation for unjust suffering, for example, is opposed to the societal need to forget and put an end to both the past terror of repression and the future threat of renewed military takeover, should prosecution of war crimes occur.

For those survivors released into societies in which repression continues, the choices are few, and the outlook bleak. The majority are forced, by economic, social, or political pressure or choice, to remain within their communities of terror, continually at risk for rearrest or execution. More than 14 million people have made the decision to flee persecution in their own countries and have become refugees in over 100 countries around the world. Of these, less than 1 percent are resettled in countries of third asylum, such as the United States (Shawcross, 1989).

Valiant and effective treatment programs are ongoing in countries of repression (Chester, 1990). However, this chapter is concerned primarily with the process of therapeutic intervention with victims of torture who are the "fortunate" 1 percent living their silent nightmare in exile, among strangers.

TORTURE: HISTORY, DEFINITIONS, AND PREVALENCE

It is a well-documented fact that torture, as a physical and psychological form of coercion, dates from at least as far back as recorded history (Suedfeld, 1990; Rasmussen, 1990). However, while ancient torture was an openly accepted practice and often an integral part of the administrative or criminal justice system, modern torture, like other forms of victimization, thrives on secrecy. Although sometimes used to obtain confessions in a military or quasi-military arena, torture has primarily become a tool of political repression, strategically applied to annihilate any actual or perceived dissent: "For the victims—whether imprisoned in a secret detention center in Santiago or in a special psychiatric hospital in Moscow—brutality knows no ideology because its goal is the same: to silence dissent through the destruction of healthy bodies and minds"(Stover and Nightingale, 1985, p. 8).

This situation has severe ramifications for the individual. The large majority of victims who are tortured have no information to give and nothing to confess; in short, they possess nothing of any value that allows them to stop the pain.

In addition, while the individual may be the direct recipient of actual punishment, the real target is much broader: "The victims of torture are always individuals, but never individuals alone. For every person detained, there are mothers and fathers and wives and children who wait. Torturers deprive the community of its individuals. Just as significantly, they deprive the individual of community by attacking the trust and coherence which make the fabric of any society" (Sclapobersky, 1989, p. 53).

Finally, torture has become a truly international, exportable commodity. Danish practitioners noted that when they first started working in the area, a survivor could be traced to his or her country by examining the methods of torture used. Today, torture methods are exchanged as if they were corporate trade secrets. The litany of methods is quite similar; the only cultural variations are how these methods are applied (Genefke, 1988, personal communication). Amnesty International also warns that "foreign experts are sent from one country to another, schools of torture explain and demonstrate methods, and modern torture equipment is exported from one country to another" (Amnesty International, 1975, p. 21).

Defining torture in a way that has both political and clinical meaning is extremely difficult (Chester, 1989). In addition, the United Nations at large and regional systems such as the Council of Europe and the Organization of American States have, and are developing, treaties that would criminalize the act of torture and provide for enforcement of these laws. These actions make definitions extremely important. For example, the U.S. State Department now uses rationalizations regarding cruel, degrading, and inhuman treatment or punishment to excuse not ratifying existing conventions because they are too vague.

Several treaties, declarations, and conventions against torture currently exist, most of them postdating Article 5 of the United Nations Universal Declaration of Human Rights. Several authors and practitioners (Rasmussen, 1990; Chester, 1990) utilize the Declaration of Tokyo, adopted by the World Medical Association (WMA) in 1975, as the least exclusionary document defining torture for legal purposes. According to this declaration, torture is defined as "the deliberate, systematic, or wanton infliction of physical or mental suffering by one or more persons acting alone or on the orders of any authority, to force another person to yield information, to make a confession, or for any other reason" (WMA, 1975).

Amnesty International has identified and defined several essential conceptual and practical elements of torture. These include (1) the involvement of at least two persons, the torturer and the tortured; (2) the infliction of severe pain and suffering of both a physical and a psychological nature; (3) the effort on the part of the torturer to break the will of the victim, to destroy his or her soul and humanity; and (4) the systematic and purposeful nature of the activity (Amnesty International, 1975).

It is impossible to capture the impact of torture upon the victim in the framework of legal definitions. Clients have described their experience as "stealing my soul," a "filthy intimacy," "killing my hope and belief." One young man recalls that, as a student, he often stopped in the same café to have coffee and exchange pleasantries with a waiter, approximately his same age. When this young man was arrested and accused of being part of a subversive group, one of his torturers was this very waiter, who had, in another "life," inquired after his family and his health on an almost daily basis. Such a mind-numbing perversion of reality has been described as the "un-making of the world" (Scarry, 1985).

In addition, the definition and meaning of concepts of torture, trauma, and extreme stress vary cross-culturally. In a Western sense, torture is associated with legal processes and its use in ancient times to force testimony. Southeast Asian survivors in Boston tend to view torture in terms of the Buddhist concept of karma, with which the Sanskrit/Pali derivatives of the term for torture are best associated (Mollica, 1988).

Numerous Asian and Central American clients do not fit existing explicit legal definitions as "prisoners of conscience" because the atrocities they experience occur outside the process of arrest and detention. For example, in July 1990, a medical study examined people from some fourteen villages in the Naga hills of Manipur, India, who had been tortured by security forces twenty-two months prior to the study. This team of nine physicians examined 104 victims and found that these ninety-three men and eleven women had been blindfolded; had limbs stretched for days; were beaten with rifle butts, wooden logs, iron rods; were punched in the face, chest, and ears; were kicked; were subjected to electric shock; were pricked with needles; and were starved, buried in pits, immersed in water, sexually violated, and physically humiliated. In addition to these physical tortures, most victims were subjected to severe psychological torture, including mock executions, forced observation of the torture of family members, interrogation at gunpoint, and threats of death or torture. As a result of this maltreatment, 25 percent suffered marks of visible physical trauma, and almost half exhibited obvious features of post-traumatic stress disorder (PTSD). These people had never been formally or individually arrested (Drug Action Forum, 1990).

In many cases, because they are not politically active or physically tortured, people do not view themselves as torture victims and are confused as to how to define their own experiences. For example, a woman from the Middle East was arrested or detained more than forty times in a two-year period, but only for brief occasions, never exceeding twelve hours. She was a student and refused to wear purdah or to remove her jewelry, lipstick, or nail polish. Although she was repeatedly interrogated and threatened with torture, rape, and even death, she never experienced these things in physical reality. At a certain level, however, both she and her interrogators knew that any of these acts were possible at any time. The constant stress and anxiety led to tremendous weight loss and other physical symptoms. In another instance, a man from West Africa was placed in solitary confinement for fourteen years as a suspected spy. He did not define himself as a torture victim and merely wanted an explanation of the mental health status report written for him by a staff physician at the refugee camp where he was confined after his escape.

With few exceptions, practitioners and human rights groups view torture not as an aberration, but as the logical consequence of an ailing system that is built upon the abuse of power.

In this light, torture is best viewed as a process that begins before a whip or electric prod is lifted and continues after the release from prison, or even beyond settlement in countries of asylum. This process begins with the fear and anxiety engendered by the takeover of government, suspensions of civil rights and liberties, and a political system that defines all public activity as either pro- or antigovernment in nature. For example, being poor in Chile was seen as a Marxist act under Pinochet, while wearing eyeglasses or speaking French or English was viewed as fascist or pro-American under the Khmer Rouge in Cambodia. The effects of this fear are brought home to the therapist in intake sessions during which clients hesitate or answer anxiously when asked about their levels of education or about what languages they speak.

Because of the secrecy and intimidation surrounding torture, it is difficult to estimate numbers of victims. In addition, members of the Danish Medical Team of Amnesty International noted that victims are kept in prison until physical sequelae of torture are healed. In severe cases, the victim is often executed. In addition, more modern methods of torture, such as the use of drugs or psychological techniques, are almost impossible to detect (Berger, 1980; Cathcart, Berger, and Knazan, 1979).

An Australian review noted that of 8,000 refugees arriving in Canada between 1974 and 1982, 5 percent were referred for medical and psychiatric investigation due to torture in their homeland. A center treating survivors in Paris (AVRE) estimates that 20 percent of people applying for political asylum in France have been tortured; the Refugee Health Care Center in Amsterdam estimates that about 30 percent of the 2,000 refugees arriving in the Netherlands annually have been tortured (Reid and Strong, 1987). The Center for Victims of Torture in Minneapolis reviewed reports from refugee mental health centers in Boston and Minnesota and found that 30–60 percent of refugees seeking mental health care in these areas were tortured in their homeland. In addition, an informal survey of immigration attorneys demonstrated that 10–30 percent of people seeking political asylum in Minnesota were survivors of political torture (Chester, 1987).

METHODS AND IMPACT OF TORTURE

Because the medical and psychiatric literature concerning the occurrence and effect of post-Holocaust torture is of such recent origin, research is often basic and descriptive in nature. This early literature generally focuses on documenting the types of torture that victims experience and the resultant short-term, more physical symptoms (Rasmussen and Lunde, 1980; Cathcart, et al., 1979). Even those studies that describe psychiatric or psychological sequelae often use terms that are vague ("mental symptoms") or use assessment instruments evocative of specific disorders, such as the PTSD portion of the Diagnostic Interview Schedule (Kinzie et al., 1984). In addition, due to the context of the studies, the focus and motivation of the authors are often on very immediate and practical considerations, including documentation and treatment. The Amnesty Medical Groups, for example, are concerned with investigation and documentation of torture, while groups working in countries under repression often have a more political focus and are, by necessity, concerned with emphasizing treatment within an oppressive context (Cienfuegos and Monelli, 1983).

Nonetheless, some authors do an excellent job of conveying a sense of the meaning of the experience. For example, Mollica (1988) described his patients as being "stuck" in the trauma story and "losing the world." Lira et al. (1988), emphasizing the difference between their conceptualization of the process of "cumulative trauma" and PTSD, stated, "It is necessary to realize that political repression transforms the social context, making it threatening and traumatic, with a great destructive potential which pervades the material conditions of concrete life, psychic survival and the values which constitute the meaning of life for the subjects" (p. 8). Similarly, while citing a number of symptoms of PTSD in their patients, Somnier and Genefke (1986, p. 324) depict the humiliations that force survivors to "see their dignity and identity completely destroyed," and Kordon et al. (1988, p. 103) described the conflict within a tortured person between the "image he had of himself and the image which crops up from his way of behaving in the face of a situation where certain responses are required."

The significance of timing is also emphasized in several studies. For example, while Foster & Sandler (1985) found few psychiatric symptoms reported by detainees during detention, other symptoms emerged several years afterward. A follow-up study by Boehnlein, Kinzie et al. (1983) is also interesting in this regard. In their group of twelve survivors of Cambodian concentration camps diagnosed with PTSD and treated at the Indochinese clinic, certain components of the disorder, such as sleep disturbances, showed great improvement after one year, while other symptoms, such as shame and extreme social isolation, did not. Rasmussen (1990) differentiated between various physical and emotional symptoms at time of torture and at time of examination. For example, while acute symptoms were reported by victims of *falanga* (beating on the soles of the feet) during detention, long-lasting changes in the locomotor system were discovered at the time of examination.

The issue of pre-trauma, predisposing factors was addressed by Allodi and Rojas (1985). Of all pre-trauma factors investigated in their three samples of survivors of political violence, only personality had significant correlation with the presence of psychiatric symptoms.

Psychological reactions described with regularity in the literature include lack of confidence and self-esteem, fear of intimacy, irritability or excessive expression of anger, minimization or denial, persistent shame and humiliation, sexual dysfunction, despair, and loss of previously sustaining beliefs. Some symptoms, including sleep disturbances, nightmares, and impairment of memory and concentration, are almost always mentioned in these studies (Mollica, 1988; Lee and Lu, 1989; Lira, Becker, and Castillo, 1988; Kordon, Edelman, Lagos et al., 1988; Allodi and Rojas, 1985; Somnier and Genefke, 1986). Reviewing a six-study patient series, Goldfeld et al. (1988) reported the physical examination findings and symptoms in 319 survivors of torture seeking refuge in Canada, Denmark, and Holland. The most commonly reported physical symptoms included severe headaches, impaired hearing, gastrointestinal distress, and joint pain. Physical findings included scars on the skin and bone dislocations and fractures.

Sexual abuse and rape figure prominently in the torture of women. Reports from clinics and treatment centers in Boston, Toronto, Copenhagen, and Minneapolis indicated that between one-third and two-thirds of women and girls seeking treatment for sequelae of torture reported incidents of sexual violation (Chester and Dhillon, 1991).

In general, the methods of torture can be categorized into three general groups (see Table 15.1).

ASSESSMENT

Assessment and diagnosis, including the use of psychological tests with a diversity of languages and cultures, are a complex task. In his recent report to the Refugee Technical Assistance Center at the University of Minnesota, Butcher et al. (1988) outlined both the problems and promising procedures for assessing mental health in refugee and ethnic minority clients. Whenever possible, he advised use of standard psychological tests with substantial empirical bases. In addition, procedures with straightforward face validity, provided they are translated well both culturally and linguistically, are also appropriate. All tests must be administered in appropriate language translations and with enough time to explain idioms in culturally appropriate terms. In this author's experience, a fairly long assessment period utilizing a multidisciplinary team approach is optimal. This team should minimally include a physician, psychologist, and psychiatrist. For providing comprehensive services, a social work assessment is also essential. (See Table 15.2 for a sample assessment.)

Designing and using assessment or evaluative techniques bring to light an important philosophical and practical issue in the field of torture treatment. Some practitioners, including those at the first treatment center in exile, the Rehabilitation Center for Torture Victims in Denmark, are concerned primarily with the treatment of torture status, not with related problems such as exile. The treatment is aimed at the physical and emotional results of the specific trauma experienced. The Danes, for example, repeatedly stress that the goal of the torturer is the destruction of the victim's personality and that the primary focus of treatment

Table 15.1
Methods of Torture

PHYSICAL	PSYCHOLOGICAL	PHARMACOLOGICAL
Beating	Mock executions	Use of psychotropic meds
Falanga (severe beating to soles of feet)	Threats to self or loved ones	Use of slow-acting poison
Telefono (simultaneous beating of both ears)	Noise and light	Internment in security mental hospitals
Electric torture	Use of excrement	
La barra, Helicopter (suspension from bar or hanging suspended)	Exposure to animals or insects	
Forced standing or gymnastics	Repeated release and rearrest	
Submarino, the hood (asphyxiation or suffocation in water, noxious liquid, or in a hood filled with lime)	Sensory deprivation	
Burning with cigarettes, blowtorch, or caustic substance	Sleep deprivation	
Sexual abuse		
Cajones (confined in box or restricted place).		

is to restore the personality to its former healthy state. Psychometric tests are not used, and psychiatric diagnoses are eliminated or downplayed. The client's symptoms do not dictate the treatment; instead, only the fact that the person has been tortured dictates the treatment course. In short, the emphasis is on the experience. The personality, as such, is not assessed, because it has been destroyed. What is assessed, in great detail, is the experience of torture (Somnier and Block, 1987).

One can, however, recognize that the person brings into the torture situation a personality, complete with survival skills or detriments, culture, and a lifetime of experience. Critical elements in both assessing and treating survivors of torture, in fact, include cultural assumptions about healing, beliefs about the context of pain and suffering, perspectives about the meaning of their torture and about time and process, interpretation of dreams, and expectations about life in a new country. One man from a village in the Horn of Africa, for example, viewed dreams as predictive of future events. His nightmares of torture were seen by him as portents of further torture experiences for himself or family members. An explanation of Western views—that traumatic dreams can be indicative of, and portray, past events—was both interesting and a source of relief to him.

Table 15.2
Sample Assessment

INITIAL	ONGOING	FOLLOW UP
Intake interview (includes trauma story, history of arrest, detention, flight, camp, resettlement experiences if a refugee or seeker of asylum, torture or trauma to family members)	Check trauma story for validity as new memories surface	Exit interview
Global Assessment Functioning (GAF)	GAF	GAF
Mini-Mental Status Exam Minnesota Multiphasic Personality Inventory (MMPI) Symptom Check List–90 (SCL–90) Beck Depression Inventory (BDI)	SCL–90 (quarterly) BDI (every session, if depressed)	MMPI SCL–90 BDI
Impact of Life Events Scale (Horowitz)		
Medical Examination	Compliance with medications if psychiatric interview necessary	

This type of "cultural brokering," utilizing perspectives from various cultures to address a belief or affective state, can be a rich source of therapeutic material. In addition, previous history of trauma, addiction to alcohol or other substances, physical illness, and prior positive history of mental health disorders can affect a person's response to the severe and extreme stress that torture entails.

THERAPEUTIC RESPONSES

Human beings cannot tolerate extreme helplessness, pain, and betrayal. In addition, when they confront cold and deliberate cruelty inflicted by another human being, their basic beliefs and values often shatter (Ochberg, 1988).

During and after torture, a person's life becomes a process of avoiding, at all levels, reminders of the experience. Just as torture itself narrows or eliminates choice, so does the narrowing of the world, in order to deal with it, become the main survival mechanism in the mind of the survivor. While this process was adaptive during torture, once the individual reaches safety, its continuation means that the flexibility needed for survival and growth is no longer available.

Psychotherapy is, therefore, a process of extending, widening, and elucidating options and choices. It must reverse the process of torture by restoring trust, dignity, and respect; enabling the person to "remake" his or her world at all levels; and being as strategic as the torturer. Just as the torturer uses all aspects of a person's humanness against the victim, the therapist must ally with the client to utilize every aspect of individual, spiritual, and cultural strength that is a historical and integral part of the person's psyche and community. For example, a Buddhist priest from Cambodia discussed the dilemma of working with clients whose belief in karma led them to profess that they deserved their tragic circumstances. He stated that it was necessary to look at the other side of Buddhism: lessons that teach that all living things are related and connected, lessons utilizing the strength of the community for the healing of the individual.

Bruno Bettelheim (1979), a survivor of the Nazi Holocaust, noted two issues in survivorship: surviving the trauma itself and living with an external, painful dilemma for which there is no possible solution. This second issue has led practitioners to look upon survivors as suffering from a "disorder of despair" (Ochberg, 1988) and a "disorder of hope" (van der Kolk, 1989). In a sense, intervention can be broken down into two main goals: wellness as an absence of symptoms and wellness as an "emergence," a new and integrated perspective.

THERAPEUTIC ISSUES AND STRATEGIES

It is, of course, essential to elicit the trauma story, in terms of both the events and the individual's reactions to those events. Within these stories the seeds of recovery are found. Kinzie et al. (1984) pointed out that the process of recovering memories is a risky one. Butcher (1988) stated that "if there is one point of agreement in the field, it is that the trauma story must be pursued slowly and carefully, taking the lead of the patient in terms of how far to go at any given time" (p. 35).

The trauma story must be told in an atmosphere of trust and safety. Tortured people have been involved in extremely intense and negative experiences during which they have learned to use attitudes, defense mechanisms, and behaviors in order to survive. Learning that takes place in an emotional context is very powerful and often bypasses both present context and prior knowledge (Dwortzsky, 1982).

In listening to the trauma story, the therapist becomes a participant observer and an ally (Ochberg, 1988). The therapist "normalizes" symptoms and feelings, showing them to be adaptive, though painful. It is also important to listen to, and understand, the key elements of the trauma that were most damaging to the psyche of the individual involved, the acts that "crossed the line" and "unmade the world" for that person. Emphasis can then be placed on what essential elements inside the survivor enabled him or her to survive. Two Catholic nuns tortured in Central America found strength within different dimensions. For one Sister, the experience strengthened her belief in God and the faith that God could minister to her, even in the extremity of sexual violation. The other, although experiencing a crisis in religious faith, found new power in the community of peasant people as they ministered to her, even in her extremity. The strength of one Sister was religious in nature; the strength of the other was communal and political.

While eliciting the trauma story, it is important to remember that "repetition is not mastery. . . . For torture victims, torture then continues to be the way in which the person interprets the world. The key to dealing with this damage is in giving meaning to the story . . . give voice to it. Bear witness to it" (van der Kolk, 1989).

In addition, torture victims tend to respond to environmental cues according to internal stimuli. This reliance often leads to a misinterpretation of the environment. Affective labels are attached to pain and generalized across situations. A client, for example, experiences much physical pain in circumstances under which he or she feels humiliated. Krystal (1988) emphasized that in survivors of severe trauma, emotions are often somatized and undifferentiated and therefore not usable as signals. Clients can relearn the processes necessary to identify feelings, discriminate among them, and become aware of the mind-body connection. The lack of affective response to the environment, the loss of the use of affect as a signal, and the attendant options of somatization or motoric discharge have been excellently described by both van der Kolk (1989) and Krystal (1988). These authors also beautifully elaborate the process of dissociation, described as the most dominant defense in coping with overwhelming trauma (van der Kolk, 1989).

Other important issues include countertransference, addressed ably by Danieli (1988a), Comas-Diaz and Padilla (1990), and Fischman (1991), bereavement, the need for rituals appropriate to this time and place, and the importance of making grief public. One of the most difficult issues to attend to relates to the search for meaning. In this regard, other survivor stories, either oral sharing in groups or in written form, can be extremely useful. One client, a man from Africa, was the sole survivor of his prison soccer team. As the team sat on a bench, every young man but him was shot. This tragically bizarre scenario was repeated several weeks later when he was loaded onto a jeep with ten other prisoners in the middle of the night. At each street corner, a prisoner was taken from the jeep and shot. When only he remained, the guards returned him to his cell. In surviving the guilt of these incidents and finding meaning in his life, he was inspired by the writings of Victor Frankl (Frankl, 1959). In addition, this man attended a support group of survivors from several countries.

The final goal of intervention is to integrate the experience of being "unmade" as an individual and having the world "unmade" into a new worldview with a new definition of who one is. In this light, the use of symbols and other cultural perspectives, such as the Hopi Indian conception of emergence, can be beneficial to both the client and therapist.

CONCLUSION

According to Hopi metaphysics, their world was destroyed on several occasions by cataclysm. After the survivors remained underground for a period of time, they were finally able to emerge into this, the Fourth World. Even after emergence, the People wandered for many years, migrating in all directions. The symbol for emergence is a spiral. This quintessence is a wonderful metaphor to communicate to people whose world was destroyed by trauma. The Hopi language is rich in its beautiful description of words as concepts. In addition, the language implies that, as in any growth process, all things are always in the process of becoming. *Nongakiwqat epeg* literally translates to ''from below they emerged to here at that time'' (Abbot Sekaquaptewa, 1992, personal communication).

In approaching the overwhelming issue of despair, cross-cultural symbols or metaphors can therefore help to enable the isolated and alienated individual to reconnect in a good way with the universe. However, when using metaphor to help create the possibility of a new world with the client, both partners in the therapeutic relationship must be willing to suspend previous assumptions and enter or emerge into the new world together.

Treatment of Post-Traumatic Stress Disorder in the Arab American Community

Nuha Abudabbeh

In working with a minority group it is imperative that the therapist become knowledgeable about cultural differences and try to understand the influence of the culture on the patient's ideas, thinking process, ideals, and methods of communication. The therapist who ignores the cultural differences is denying the importance of culture. In effect, he or she is being hostile to the culture, which results in the establishment of a barrier between the patient and the therapist (Katz, 1984).

While Arab Americans share many of the cultural norms prevalent in other groups, including American Indians, Afro-Americans, Asian Americans, and Hispanic Americans, certain values are specific only to Arab Americans. However, Arab Americans have sufficient variations to warrant exploration of the Arab origin of each individual. For example, an Arab American from Morocco is different from one from Palestine because they speak two distinct Arabic dialects. Other potential differences among Arab Americans include class origin, environmental setting (rural or urban), time of immigration, and level of acculturation. Despite these cultural variations, enough commonalities exist to warrant special attention from service providers (Ahmed & Adadow-Gray, 1988; Meleis, 1981; Meleis & Jonsen, 1983; Meleis & LeFever, 1984; Meleis & Sorrell, 1981).

WHO ARE ARAB AMERICANS?

Arab Americans are a heterogeneous group of 2.5 million persons tied by a common Arab ancestry. In his book, *Arab America Today*, Zogby (1990) outlines the demographic profile of Arab Americans as follows:

1. Arab Americans are mostly found in urban areas.

2. American-born Arab Americans are present in larger clusters in the northeastern United States, while immigrant Arabs are present in larger number in the western United States.

3. Arab Americans as a group are younger on the average than the U.S. population and other ethnic groups.

4. Arab Americans are less likely than other groups to have been born outside the United States, with the exception of Asian Americans.

5. American-born Arab women are twice as likely to be single than those born in the Arab countries.

6. Arab Americans in general have a higher level of education than the average American.

7. Economically, a greater percentage of Arab American households are below the poverty level than the U.S. population as a whole.

8. Unemployment among Arab Americans is low. They are more likely to be self-employed or in managerial and professional occupations. Nearly one in four Arab Americans is involved in the retail trade.

Today, Lebanese and Syrians account for nearly nine out of ten Arab Americans. In fact, Lebanon continues to be the primary nation of origin for Arab immigrants, followed by Egypt and Iraq, which have surpassed Syria (Zogby, 1990). The approximately 2 to 2.5 million Arab Americans concentrate primarily in eleven states. Rhode Island has a high percentage of Syrians. New Jersey is dominated by Lebanese and has the highest percentage of Egyptians. Pennsylvania has a high percentage of Lebanese and Syrians and a very small percentage of other Arab nations. Virginia has the largest group of Palestinians.

CULTURAL NORMS AND COMMUNICATION MODES OF ARAB AMERICANS

Variations in cultural norms and in modes of communication exist among several distinct subgroups within the Arab world. Keeping in mind limitations of making generalized statements, the following can be said to be more common shared modes of communication and cultural characteristics:

- Patrilineal family—name identification, residence, honor, property, and other rights passed through the father;
- Extended family composed of three generations related through the male heir;
- Authoritarian family structure in which elders have authority over younger family members;
- Taboo on premarital sex, particularly for women;
- Sexual segregation in the public sphere;
- Endogamy and preference for marriage within certain groups;

- Acceptability of touching between persons of the same sex;
- Preference for indirect eye contact;
- Impropriety of asking personal questions of someone met for the first time;
- Orientation toward privacy with "outsiders";
- Orientation toward modesty and reserve;
- Disdain for public reprimand;
- Flexible sense of time;
- Low regard for saving money;
- High regard for generosity;
- Preference for using "we" rather than "I."

MENTAL HEALTH NEEDS OF ARAB AMERICANS

Only four programs have developed throughout the entire United States to meet the health and psychosocial needs of Arab Americans. SIHA, which focuses more on medical needs, is in San Francisco. Two state-subsidized programs, the Chaldeon and Access, are located in the Detroit area. The Chaldeon provides counseling and other social services to the Iraqi population. Access provides a variety of services to all Arab immigrants in the area. The Naim Foundation, a Washington-based, privately funded organization with a mental health emphasis, also provides a variety of services to the Arab-speaking population.

There is little literature available describing the mental health needs and status of Arab Americans. In contrast, a growing body of literature describes traumatized Arab populations in the war zones of Lebanon and Palestine (e.g., Baker, 1989a, 1989b; Bryce & Armenian, 1986; Forhoud & Zurayk, 1990; Jamal, Shaya & Armenian, 1986; Khamis, 1990; Macksoud, 1989; Mahjoub, 1990; Punamaki, 1986, 1987; Sa'ar & Armenian, 1986; Saigh, 1986).

Historically, the Arab American community has received little attention from mental health providers. Only since the Gulf War and the events that surrounded it in late 1990 and early 1991 have Arab Americans, for the first time, become a focus of attention not only as a distinct minority in the United States but also as a traumatized population. The war that followed the Iraqi occupation of Kuwait was a traumatic event for the whole Arab American community. Also, the war itself created a sufficient number of war casualties to cause them to seek help.

The trauma experienced by the Arab American community presented itself in many different forms. In the following section, examples are drawn from the pool of referrals made to an Arabic call-in radio program on mental health issues and to the Naim Foundation.

A major role of the Naim Foundation is to help therapists develop sensitivity and competence. According to Pedersen (1988), competence is gained by developing awareness, knowledge, and skill. While the scope of this chapter is not to help the reader develop full cultural sensitivity for working with Arab clients, it describes for clinicians those initial skills needed to work with the Arab patient. It also identifies resources available to complement therapeutic work.

The reader may test his or her level of awareness of the Arab culture by answering the following questions (Pedersen, 1988):

- Is the reader able to recognize direct and indirect communication styles?
- Is the reader sensitive to nonverbal cues?
- Is the reader aware of cultural and linguistic differences among Arab subgroups?
- What are common myths and stereotypes about Arabs?
- What stereotypes do Arabs have about Americans?
- How aware is the reader of feelings about Arabs?

Three basic questions must be addressed by clinicians wanting to gain expertise in working with different cultures. What is the difference between "objective culture" and "subjective culture"? How broadly is "culture" defined? What are some culturally biased assumptions that might interfere in delivering appropriate services to Arab patients?

What is the difference between "objective culture" and "subjective culture"? The "objective" part of culture deals with visible, learned aspects of a culture. For example, an Arab man who behaves or thinks in ways that show that he respects his parents' wishes, whatever the cost may be, has learned the "objective" aspect of his culture, which includes the accepted authoritarian model. The "subjective" part of culture deals with the learned, internalized attitudes and feelings about one's culture. Subjective aspects are exemplified in the same patient's case when he feels guilty for "abandoning" his parents in his country of origin to study in the United States.

How broadly is "culture" defined? Culture can be defined either broadly or narrowly. An Arab patient's culture could be broadly defined by specifying that she or he came from Egypt or Morocco or is a Berber, Kurd, or Qopt. If one is to define a patient's culture more narrowly, it is necessary to know whether she or he came from a middle-class, aristocratic, or working-class family. Other narrow definitions would include gender, as well as political affiliation and level of education.

What are some culturally biased assumptions that might interfere in delivering appropriate services to Arab patients? Pedersen (1988) notes that Western cultural biases have little to do with geography and a great deal more to do with "social, economic, and political perceptions." He further states that just as there are many "Western" thinkers in non-Western parts of the world, there are also many "non-Western" thinkers in the Western Hemisphere. In strictly numerical terms, it is increasingly true that the "Western" viewpoint is the more "exotic." Despite that numerical reality, social scientists, including psychologists, depend on textbooks, research findings, and implicit psychological theory based almost entirely on Euro-American culture-specific assumptions. These assumptions are usually so implicit and taken for granted that they are not challenged even by fair-thinking, right-minded colleagues. The consequences of these unexamined assumptions are institutionalized racism, ageism, sexism, and other examples of cultural bias.

Pedersen (1988) identified ten Western-based cultural assumptions frequently encountered in multicultural counseling. Of these, the following five assumptions need to be considered when counseling Arab Americans.

1. "All cultures share a single measure of 'normal' behavior." Probably the most common reason for Arab students to seek help is depression; but when treating depressed Arab patients, the therapist must not think with a purely Western mind. A Western psychiatrist may diagnose the patient as dysthymic or begin a course of antidepressant therapy. Doing so, however, may cause even more fear and depression in the Arab patient because the culture identifies depression differently from the way that Americans do. If the diagnosis includes a pronouncement that depression is a mental illness from which the patient may suffer the rest of his or her life, the Western-trained psychiatrist will have to deal with yet another problem. Coming from a culture that is minimally exposed to psychological information, there is a higher likelihood of developing fear and apprehension when such definitive pronouncements are made, and the authoritarian nature of the Arab culture turns such a pronouncement by a "doctor" into absolute truth.

2. "Individuals are the basic building blocks of society." When treating an Arab suffering from trauma, it is essential to bear in mind that the family, the tribe, and the community are the basic building blocks of Arab society. Trauma may not necessarily be an individualistic trauma, as illustrated earlier by the Egyptian man whose emotional well-being was tied to the well-being of the whole Arab nation. He exhibited mood swings that reflected the status of events during the Gulf War and the mood of the rest of the Arabs.

Because the family is a culturally acceptable unit, therapists need to be encouraged to work with the entire family whenever possible. At the onset, this might seem difficult because a child, young adult, or spouse is typically targeted as the "sick" patient. In most cases, strong family ties are expressed when a family member "does what is right" by bringing another family member to an expert to cure or make well. With luck, the therapist will find that the family's belief in the expert can be used in the patient's best interests to show the family how important it is to treat the whole family.

3. "Independence is desirable; dependence is undesirable." This assumption permeates the Western model of mental health to the extent that even the most severely ill patients are expected to make it on their own. Consider the case of a young American woman who was her family's only daughter and who was diagnosed as suffering from borderline personality disorder. The parents, who were extremely wealthy, refused to help their daughter financially during a period when she was unable to hold a job. Their rationale was that she had to make it

on her own. By contrast, the Arab parent typically would go to the other extreme. Overprotectiveness is expressed by continuing to support the "children" no matter how old they are.

The extreme case of the Arab situation calls for innovation in intervention to help the parent let go of the adult child in graduated steps. It also calls for innovation in creating a model that lies between the Western independence model and the Arab overprotective model. Such a model would probably be accepted more easily by both parents and offspring.

Issues of independence versus dependence are extremely complex and important to consider when working with Arab families. This is an area where the old and new could come into conflict. Sensitivity and awareness of the Arab culture dictate a respect for the parents' values and their reluctance to let go of their children. That same respect assists the therapist to help parents allow the children to separate from them, especially when they realize that the therapist understands and respects their cultural norms and is not leading their children astray.

4. "Western concepts of 'good,' 'bad,' 'fair,' and 'humane' are considered similar across cultures." When treating Arab patients, the therapist needs to be aware that different criteria are used to make such judgments. Although it might be considered "good" to be open and willing to divulge one's private life in Western cultures, such a characteristic is considered a "bad" trait among Arabs.

5. "Counselors need to change individuals to fit the system, rather than change the system to fit the individuals." This assumption would discourage many Arabs, particularly those who are politically aware, from accepting counseling and psychology as possible avenues of help in dealing with their problems. Most Arab immigrants have suffered the consequences of institutions that have worked against them. As noted at the beginning of this chapter, many Arabs, in fact, tend to orient toward more individualistic careers. The therapist should be cognizant of these cultural phenomena, which can be complicated at times by antagonism toward American government institutions.

TRAUMA INDUCED BY THE GULF WAR

Several types of traumatized populations emerged during the Gulf War:

Non-Kuwaiti Arabs, such as Lebanese and Palestinians, who were displaced from Kuwait as a result of the Gulf War. Some refugees were intact families consisting of several children, and possibly infants, who had to flee the country with few belongings. The family was typically headed by a professional who had permanent residency status in the United States and was therefore able to enter the country. On arrival, however, the family had no shelter, no employment, no medical insurance, and only limited funds. If the family was Palestinian or Lebanese, most often it also was dealing with reawakening of the previous trauma of losing its primary place of residence.

Kuwaitis living in the United States when the occupation of Kuwait occurred.

These individuals experienced trauma related to their inability to obtain information about their families who remained in Kuwait. Anxiety and concern were further created by CNN (television) reports of violence by Iraqis. This population was additionally traumatized by what Kuwaitis interpreted as the lack of compassion by the Arab community toward their victimization. Although the Western world was "feeling" with the Kuwaitis, the majority of the Arab world was perceived as "feeling" with the Iraqis.

Iraqi Americans. Iraqi Americans were traumatized as they remained "glued" to their television sets following CNN coverage of the destruction of their country. Their inability to verify the status of family members increased their anxiety. They also were fearful of being potentially identified as Iraqis in shopping malls, for example, or of having their children so identified in school.

Palestinian Americans and Lebanese Americans. These populations relived earlier traumas, which were made worse by resurfacing in an unsafe environment. Their new environment was a homeland that "rescued" the Kuwaitis when they became victimized but did not rescue Palestinians and Lebanese when they were traumatized. These two populations felt a great deal of pain on several levels:

1. trauma resulting from civil war in Lebanon and occupation by Israelis in the West Bank and Gaza;
2. reliving the trauma by witnessing the war on television;
3. worrying about relatives in the war zone or the potential spread of war to the whole region;
4. anxiety and fear at being identified as an Arab or being victimized in the new homeland;
5. anger at not being "rescued" by Americans, when both Iraqis and Kuwaitis were in similar situations.

Arab Americans, in general. All Arab Americans expressed apprehension, anxiety, and fear of retaliation by ultranationalistic Americans. News of verbal and physical attacks against Arabs spread quickly. These fears were further intensified by media coverage of Federal Bureau of Investigation (FBI) agents harassing Arab American citizens. Feelings of victimization also were further reinforced by the knowledge that although they were not in a war zone, they could not feel safe in their new homes in the United States. News of children being hit in shopping malls and businesses being targets of arson and vandalism only further fueled the fears.

Arab Americans from those Arab countries that had decided to fight on the American/Kuwaiti side also were feeling the angst of the alliances in their daily lives. Some felt guilty about the role chosen by their governments. An Egyptian man, for example, calling in on a radio program, cried uncontrollably as he expressed bewilderment at his country's political position. Another Egyptian man, married to an Iraqi woman, sought help about how to raise his child in a home that had become irreconcilably divided.

Underlying the traumas of these specific groups was a shake-up of the concept of "What is an Arab?" Many Arab Americans were asking, "Who am I?" A whole generation of post-Nasser Arabs who had grown up with a distinct Arab identity expressed feelings of loss. An "I" that had evolved around the concept of being an Arab had been shaken to its roots. One Arab man said that he was unable to sleep after the Gulf crisis.

THE ROLE OF MENTAL HEALTH PROVIDERS RESPONDING TO THE TRAUMA

The Gulf crisis was the first time that mental health providers were faced with providing support to an Arab American population. Having learned a lesson from the psychological aftermath of the Vietnam War, American trauma experts prepared the nation to deal with the Gulf War by focusing on preventive measures. Likewise, Arab trauma experts quickly tailored preventive, as well as supportive, measures to deal with Arab Americans. For example, the Naim Foundation implemented the following services:

1. Established a hot line to receive calls, which was monitored by Arab-speaking professionals.
2. Provided agencies, such as United Nations International Children's Emergency Fund (UNICEF), International Society for Traumatic Stress Studies (ISTSS), and the Erikson Institute, with names of qualified Arab-speaking mental health professionals who could provide consultation on Arabs and trauma.
3. Organized workshops to train non-Arab professionals who needed the appropriate knowledge to work with the Arab American population.
4. Prepared a crisis intervention handbook adapted to the Arab-speaking population.
5. Organized lectures and workshops in conjunction with local Arab American organizations to educate the community about trauma.
6. Organized support groups for Arab community members.
7. Educated the community about trauma on a weekly call-in Arabic program during the Gulf War.

ISSUES THE THERAPIST SHOULD EXPLORE WITH ARAB IMMIGRANT PATIENTS

While not all Arab immigrants or Arab Americans exhibit post-traumatic stress disorder (PTSD), they face some common problems prior to their arrival in the United States that may have contributed to trauma symptoms. The following guidelines need to be explored with this population. Therapists should:

1. look for a history of imprisonment or physical abuse in the country of origin; look for possible brain damage;

2. explore losses in the family;

3. explore loss of home or other property;

4. explore economic hardships, including food intake;

5. determine educational level and occupation of parents in the home country to assess the patient's socioeconomic status;

6. ask about religious affiliation, including the sect within the religion, even if not practicing at present;

7. determine country of origin (especially if Palestinian or Lebanese) and political affiliation; and

8. determine date of arrival in the United States.

The most frequent mental health problems facing the Arab immigrant population stem from legal problems relating to residency status, intergenerational value conflicts, parenting problems, physical abuse, cultural agoraphobia, and identity confusion. Especially in the wake of the ongoing conflict in the Middle East, an increasing number of persons have presented with PTSD. The most frequently diagnosed conditions, in addition to PTSD, are depression, somatic complaints, anxiety, and panic disorder. More specific instances include the following:

1. Culture shock, because for most Arabs the values of the lost country are so significantly different;

2. Difficulties arising from adjusting to a lower status of living;

3. Difficulties arising from being in a society where they have lost social status;

4. Difficulties as a result of language barriers;

5. Changes in the family resulting from changes in the role of different family members;

6. Continued attachment to relatives at home, which can lead to anxiety and worry;

7. Lowered status as an Arab immigrant in a society perceived as not understanding or respecting Arab culture;

8. Loss of the natural support system, such as the extended family.

PTSD AMONG ARAB AMERICANS

In recent years, and particularly since the Intifada, diagnoses of post-traumatic stress disorder have been increasingly accepted. In fact, PTSD is associated with a "noble" and "patriotic" cause, such as the struggle for independence. Also it has paved the way for acceptance of other stress-related disorders, such as depression and anxiety.

The Naim Foundation and the Arab Network of America (ANA) have played major roles in popularizing mental health issues among Arabs in the United States, owing in large part to weekly call-in radio programs on Arabic mental health. The program usually begins with a discussion of either a major psychosocial problem, such as the stressful effects of acculturation in a new society, or psychiatric problems, such as PTSD, dysthymia, or schizophrenia. Listeners are allowed to ask any questions they wish, whether related to mental health or not. Since the program was established in 1989, the foundation has received significantly more requests for help from the Arab American community.

Although PTSD appears to be prevalent among those recently immigrated from war-torn areas in the Occupied Territories, Lebanon, Iraq, and Kuwait, no statistics are available on the actual number of persons suffering from PTSD. Moreover, members of ethnic groups are frequently misdiagnosed, and PTSD could be misdiagnosed as dysthymia or anxiety.

Depression and anxiety seem to be the most prevalent symptoms among traumatized Arabs. Substance abuse is not a common method used to numb their pain. There is, however, abuse of short-acting antianxiety medications, such as Valium. Most of these drugs are usually purchased without a prescription in Arab countries, and immigrant Arabs who had problems prior to their arrival in the United States usually have sufficient amounts of the drugs to control their symptoms. In most instances, these people contact the foundation to renew their prescriptions.

Symptoms of PTSD were evident in the calls received on the Naim Foundation's call-in program. Several mothers, for example, called about children's nightmares and behavior problems, which they could not connect to some other traumatic event. Exploring the matter with them confirmed that these children had immigrated from Lebanon or the Occupied Territories and were reliving early traumas.

The radio program also publicized the foundation's availability to conduct workshops and to participate in town meetings with other Arab American organizations. It is probably safe to assume that those who participated were suffering from some type of emotional problem, possibly from PTSD. A much larger number of persons participated in the town meetings than in the workshops, probably reflecting a need for concrete, didactic intervention.

Another group of Arabs came to the attention of the Naim Foundation only because they had very serious PTSD symptoms, such as depression. A Lebanese student, for example, was unable to maintain his grades and had sleep problems and recurring nightmares. He had been in Lebanon during the civil war, and his parents remained there while he pursued an academic career. He was placed on Xanax by his physician, and the student health service referred him for counseling after recognizing that he was suffering from PTSD. An Iraqi student became suicidal and began using alcohol excessively but refused to seek assistance from a mental health professional. His friends called the foundation. Staff suggested that he be brought to the offices, not to see a mental health professional but to visit ''Arabic'' style. He agreed to come and, once at the foundation, was able to discuss most of the major issues facing him.

The Naim Foundation has found the following approaches helpful when dealing with Arab American clients with PTSD:

1. being flexible and tolerant when dealing with clients; they will frequently change therapy hours and cancel sessions, events that should not necessarily be interpreted as resistance;

2. educating the Arab American community about mental health by participating in community events;

3. providing telephone counseling to out-of-town clients who are so committed to anonymity that they feel safer receiving counseling in this manner;

4. providing clients with concrete assistance on such matters as finding an attorney or even a travel agency;

5. reaching out to other institutions, such as mosques or churches;

6. being fully aware, as therapists, of the political issues related to the Arab minority;

7. providing a safe atmosphere for revealing clients' "secret" fears and traumas. Because many of these individuals arrive from backgrounds where, at times, they could not trust even their own family members, the most challenging aspect of the work is to help them establish complete trust. To build and maintain such an atmosphere, the foundation has had to be extremely diligent in building networks with the community as well as with other mental health providers.

No individual PTSD client known to the foundation has pursued ongoing treatment to date, even though the three individuals with the most severe cases of PTSD are still suffering from some symptoms. All three of them have been "adopted" by their community and feel a certain sense of security knowing that the community will never abandon them. None of them are considered abnormal; in fact, all are respected for their suffering. All three, short of committing themselves for treatment, remain attached to the foundation in one way or another. The Gulf War affected only one of them, leading to excessive drinking and suicidal ideation. The other two channeled their feelings of pain into constructive political work. The two with less severe symptoms continue to consult with the foundation when a major event occurs in their lives.

CONCLUSIONS

Arab Americans are as likely to seek treatment as any other population, when educated to the need and alerted to the symptoms of specific psychiatric problems. However, the Western definition of trauma does not translate into the Arab definition of trauma. The strong bonds that exist among Arab families seem to buffer family members from events that otherwise might be experienced as catastrophic. Knowledge of these bonds and buffers adds to understanding of what contributes to resilience.

Although some Arabs present with PTSD, it is difficult to gather an accurate history of trauma. Traumatizing events other than those that are war-induced, such as those related to family members or sexual acts, are difficult to elicit. This failure to disclose resulted not necessarily from repression or amnesia, but from a need to keep "dishonorable" information from strangers.

Arab Americans are beginning to become more familiar with issues related to mental health. This change is positive because, with education, it is obvious that this population is able to seek help. Moreover, once in treatment, this population is very respectful of the authority of the "healer" and makes good "clients." It is probably more realistic to plan for short-term treatment, and the most effective mode of treatment, in addition to pharmacological intervention, seems to be cognitive therapy. Family therapy is highly recommended whenever possible. On the other hand, treatment, at times, remains a challenge, with high value placed on privacy and certain topics remaining taboo. Still, when cultural barriers between therapist and client are minimized, working with this population is encouraging.

Part VI

Treatment of Disaster Victims

Immediate Post-Disaster Treatment of Trauma

Clay Foreman

INTRODUCTION

A traumatic incident is often sudden, violent, improbable, or unpredictable, impacting innocent victims in a random fashion. It appears to be more difficult to deal with a human-caused incident than a natural disaster (McFarlane, 1988). The lives of witnesses to a tragedy may be seriously disrupted as they experience and reexperience disturbing stereotypic reactions. Research studies addressing the human aftermath of disaster have defined the course of those reactions and the antecedents for development of symptoms (Bolin, 1985; McFarlane, 1988; Raphael, 1977). Other studies, though fewer in number, have suggested behaviors and coping strategies that promote recovery (Lindy and Grace, 1985). Social support has been found to be highly related to survivors' and combat veterans' experiencing fewer symptoms (Keane, Scott, et al., 1985; Solomon, 1987).

In this chapter, the author draws upon current research and his own professional experience relating to three traumatic incidents from northern California. Aspects of trauma, features of survivors, and subsequent provision of services are presented and discussed.

Traumatic Incidents

Certain features of traumatic events contribute to the greater likelihood of the development of post-traumatic stress disorder (PTSD) among survivors and rescue workers (Baum and Davidson, 1985; McFarlane, 1984). The personal threat of death or serious injury or witnessing death or serious injury to another can be very disturbing and is potentially a high-risk factor for the development of

PTSD (McFarlane, 1992). The experiences of terror, personal danger, and separation from coworkers have also been demonstrated to correlate highly with later emergence of PTSD symptoms (Foreman, 1990). Social and family support need to be encouraged, as they have been found to promote recovery (Solomon, 1985), while use of alcohol or other substances (Jelinek and Williams, 1987) and avoidance of discussions of the traumatic event contribute to a greater continuance of intense symptoms over extended periods.

Exposure to repeated traumatic incidents appears to promote enhanced coping skills and improved stress reduction strategies; that is, repeated exposure seems to provide the individual some inoculation. However, in the long run, greater involvement with traumatic incidents means a greater opportunity for one of the events to become personally traumatic. This "personally" traumatic event is often not a dramatic incident, such as an earthquake, and is often an incident that had previously been handled well. Sudden, violent, unexpected, or unpredictable traumatic incidents tend to break through the defense mechanisms more easily (Lindy and Titchener, 1983; Warheit, 1985). The familiarity or similarity of the scene, situation, or participants also increases the vulnerability of the witnesses and rescue workers.

INCIDENTS

The Sun Valley Mall Plane Crash

A small private plane crashed on Monday, December 23, 1985, into the Sun Valley Shopping Mall in Concord, California. Around 8:30 P.M., a small private plane with three passengers strayed off course on its approach to Buchanan Field. Below, 50,000 Christmas shoppers were milling about the mall. The man dressed as Santa Claus took a break and walked away from the long line of excited children and weary parents.

Suddenly, the airplane crashed, tearing through the sheet metal roof, spilling aviation fuel down through an open area in the second floor onto Santa's chair and display on the first floor. A few seconds later, the fuel ignited, burning shoppers and filling the mall with dense acrid smoke. Within fifteen minutes, seventy-six people suffering burns and smoke inhalation were transported to local hospitals; seven people died.

The Loma Prieta Earthquake

At 5:04 P.M. on Tuesday, October 17, 1989, the San Francisco Bay Area shook for fifteen seconds. The epicenter for this 7.1 earthquake was 7 miles east of Santa Cruz, California. Death and destruction radiated 150 miles northwest to the Marina District of San Francisco.

The Loma Prieta earthquake wreaked havoc across the Bay Area. The upper deck of a viaduct for Interstate Highway 880 alongside Cypress Street collapsed on numerous cars and their occupants. The rescue of survivors was accomplished during the first twelve hours, except for one man, Buck Helms, who was found on Friday morning, October 20, after rain caused an eighteen-inch shift of the structure. Bodies of most of the victims were removed during the five days following the earthquake.

The Crane Accident

At around 8:30 A.M. on Monday, November 19, 1989, a freestanding tower crane working on a downtown San Francisco building began to swing wildly, compromising its integrity. The operator's cabin, power plant, boom, and nineteen-ton counterweight fell sixteen stories to the corner of California and Kearney streets. The collapsed crane carried four construction workers to their deaths, killed a passing school bus driver, and injured twenty-two others.

The accident occurred adjacent to the corporate headquarters for the construction company, whose employees looked down ten and eleven floors to the carnage below. Thus many of the construction workers were directly exposed to the physical destruction of coworkers. Because the crane had crushed a small school bus and dug an eight-foot hole in the street, numerous onlookers reported their first thought to be that a number of children had been killed.

IMPACT ON SURVIVORS

Traumatic incidents offer very real threats to individuals, who, in turn, experience the stress response (Selye, 1946). The autonomic nervous system reacts to shunt blood from the internal organs to the large muscles, while a surge of adrenaline increases the heartbeat and blood pressure and quickens breathing. The endocrine system adds hormones that increase pain tolerance. This stereotypic stress response, the means by which the body prepares for danger, is often termed the "fight or flight mechanism."

The above stress response commonly causes those involved to experience some distortion of their sensory perceptions, such as tunnel vision, selective hearing, extreme pain tolerance, sluggish movement, and time either slowed or speeded up. An absolute clarity or immobility of thought may be noted. It is not unusual for survivors to report a sense of unreality, extreme detachment, and even purported extrasensory perceptions.

During the immediate terror of the plane crash at the shopping mall, most people moved rapidly away from danger. For some, the initial panic was accentuated by the loss of light and poorly identifiable exits. Others reported being swept over, and separated by, a crowd that stampeded in a wild panic. Many stopped quickly and returned to assist others, while others fled to the parking lot. One woman reported she had driven home before realizing she had forgotten her teenaged son at the mall.

One man with fifty years of experience as an engineer in chemical plants described how he was transfixed where he stood, as he watched the roof being torn apart. He resorted to prior coping strategies and analyzed the construction of the roof. This survivor did not view himself as immobilized, but rather as analytical and in control.

POST-TRAUMA INTERVENTIONS

The aim of post-trauma services is to reduce the effects of the intensely emotional and stressful incident. The goal, therefore, is to reduce stress and facilitate the resolution of post-traumatic stress reactions and, ultimately, to prevent PTSD (Lystad, 1988; Hartsough and Myers, 1985; Pichot, 1991).

Preemptive Interventions

Interventions that preempt traumatic stress reactions include safety programs, disaster planning, emergency service training, and educational programs. Training prepares individuals for the sights, sounds, activity, and confusion of emergency situations, so that the real events will be less unexpected or foreign.

Referring to an example from police training, Solomon (1987) describes the use of fear as a legitimate aid to survival during potentially lethal situations. An officer may not have expected to experience fear during an incident and may have difficulty when it occurs. Training reframes the experience of fear as an ally, sharpens the mind, and heightens the senses. Hence fear enhances survival, rather than, as feared, being a weakness or something that possibly leads to inappropriate action. Training prepares the officer, helps control a moment of fear, and allows the officer to complete the appropriate tactical response.

Primary Prevention

Solomon and Bengenishty (1986) described the Israeli model for postcombat interventions, including principles of proximity, immediacy, and expectancy. Postcombat intervention should be brief and focused on the trauma and deduction of trauma-related symptoms. Psychological interventions should occur as close to the front lines (or event) as is possible to facilitate smooth return to combat units and to lessen the stigma of having been evacuated. Immediacy of triage and treatment shortens the length of separation and feelings of dysfunction. Expectancy is the most important, overriding belief that the individual will recover and again become fully functional. These principles can apply to civilian life as experienced and trained professionals organize mental health interventions immediately following community disasters and other traumatic incidents.

Decompression

Decompression is a term adapted from scuba diving. When a diver has been underwater, increased pressure allows nitrogen bubbles to enter muscle tissues from the blood vessels. The length and depth of the dive combine to influence the degree to which nitrogen enters the muscles, and the ascent must be gradual to allow reabsorption of the nitrogen into the blood. This lethal process is reversible if the diver stops at certain intervals during the ascent and allows nitrogen to return to the blood. This is analogous to the length of time, participation, and degree of the discomfort of the actual emergency work.

At the Cypress Street structure, sessions were held next to the command post in a tent within the food service area located between the Red Cross and the Burger King food stations. Sessions also occurred along Cypress Street, where team members spoke with crews while they were on break. These brief contacts served as "decompression sessions," as well as opportunities to encourage workers to report to the tent, which was clearly marked "Debriefing Tent."

Conventional wisdom dictated that debriefing occur within twenty-four hours of demobilization from the rescue operation. While most emergency incidents are completed within eight to twelve hours, the Cypress Street operation lasted five days before most crews were demobilized. This situation was unusual, even by emergency work standards. Therefore, the duration and scope of this situation necessitated on-scene services.

Counselors soon recognized that they could provide effective interventions during operations, without distracting the workers from their tasks. Local fire departments and the air force also had crews crawling beneath sections of the structure; their own peer counselors provided informal debriefing after each shift.

The workers discussed their gruesome tasks and concerns for the victims and victims' families. They particularly needed to discuss their respect for the remains of the victims and anger when situations seemed disrespectful. They needed to discuss filth, maggots, rats, body fluids, looted bodies, and victims' last actions, as well as other sights and smells.

The air force crew described what it was like to be between the decks while others worked on top. Although they had recovered bodies from other situations, nothing had prepared them for their current task. With quiet determination they did what they could to hasten the completion of their assignment.

Defusing

At times, survivors and workers need emotional release for pent-up frustration, anger, fear, or guilt. Intervention can be provided individually or in small groups. Often workers are uncomfortable if they display vulnerability or intense emotions in front of others. Their thoughts, feelings, and reactions may be too personal or too ego-dystonic to tolerate "public" display. In fact, such a display could prove disruptive to the later cohesiveness of the working unit. In such situations, private contact with intensely distressed individuals might be useful, although often there may be resistance from the individual and coworkers.

Defusing is a supportive and active discussion that assists the focusing of frustration, resentment, fear, and anger from the immediate situation; this is not an opportunity to recount past grievances. The primary goal is to allow pent-up feelings to be expressed and discussed so that they can be placed in perspective and not continue to dominate the immediate work.

Defusing can be modulated in the group to develop support, encourage communication within the work group, and plan effective action to increase efficiency. Although this is not a time to dwell on "working through" emotional issues, the mere expression and validation can reduce or eliminate the disruptiveness of such intense feelings.

Defusing helps to diminish the reactions and the subsequent distortion of memory; that is, it helps to place events during the incident into the proper time frame and sequence. This helps reduce depersonalization and dissociative features of the individual's experience.

At the Cypress Street structure, communication was poor. The airmen worried about their safety as equipment moved and worked directly above them. Occasional violent rocking from aftershocks punctuated the constant shaking of the entire structure and further disturbed them. They wanted to feel in control of the situation in which they were working, yet they could not even redirect the other workers without interrupting their own work. Merely discussing and acknowledging their fear and frustration gave them some measure of perspective and sense of internal control.

Discussion Sessions

It is common to offer weekly meetings for survivors of disaster. These discussion sessions can be open-ended and free-form or topical and directed to a specific group. These are not group therapy sessions yet may appear as such to therapists. Some people may talk, and others simply listen. Although people voluntarily come to these sessions, it is not often easy to get them to talk about the details of their experience.

However, once survivors begin to talk, they do so compulsively; yet they often avoid the most upsetting details. These details are introduced only when the therapist is viewed as able to tolerate their disturbing nature. Any trauma is horrible; however, survivors believe they have experienced the worst thing imaginable. Therefore, they need to protect others from the full impact. Until survivors talk of these "worst things imaginable," they are doomed to face them alone.

At the Cypress Street structure, a male counselor observed the reluctant and minimal conversation of a defusing session. The group was sitting quietly, listening to the female counselor describe common reactions, thoughts, and experiences from other incidents. Some of the workers stated they did not want to "talk to a girl." What was needed was an icebreaker.

To start the conversation, a well-timed comment must be something nonthrea-tening that acknowledges common reactions. For example, the counselor may ask if anyone has had problems sleeping or eating or has been losing track of time. Mentioning other, more intrusive reactions is too emotionally loaded. Without an icebreaker, rescue workers often sit quietly and, though visibly shaken, simply nod their heads.

The male counselor introduced himself and asked, "How many of you went to work in construction to dig bodies out of concrete?" This statement, decidedly stark and to the point, put their current experiences into perspective. This situation was indeed beyond previous expectations. The counselor explained the reason for having the sessions was that this incident was beyond anyone's normal expectations. The entire group began to talk and, from then on, met with the female counselor.

Secondary Prevention

Secondary prevention includes the provision of services after the occurrence of some symptoms of distress that may, or may not, indicate a post-traumatic stress reaction. Some individuals may be in crisis or may be extremely agitated, disorganized, or withdrawn. Others may have difficulties sleeping, eating, con-centrating, or returning to usual activities. They may also experience symptoms of unbidden images, vivid reexperiencing, and other intrusive imagery.

A middle-aged couple who had been at the mall during the plane crash called this counselor because the husband was unable to travel through a freeway tunnel to attend counseling sessions. In addition, he was self-employed and not able to concentrate sufficiently to draw up bids; thus he was in danger of financial collapse. The couple had become separated during the panic of the crowd and came to an earlier session complaining about the husband's anxiety.

This couple was helped to plan a day-long fishing trip on the bay. The planning process helped to mobilize the husband's usual obsessive-compulsive style. The trip's success rewarded his sense of mastery. The wife became more comfortable with her own reactions as her husband stabilized. They began to meet their immediate needs and were then able to continue to process and work through their trauma experiences.

Crisis Intervention

Persons who are acutely distressed, disoriented, dissociated, threatening, or even suicidal will require immediate crisis intervention. At the command post of the crane accident, a young construction worker was being comforted by a supervisor. This support seemed to be going quite well, yet the supervisor was relieved to step aside for the crisis team. About eight hours earlier, the worker had observed another worker drive over the edge of the top deck and crash 100 feet below. The driver survived, yet the worker was clearly obsessing on the incident. The worker in crisis, though oriented, expressed intense unrealistic guilt and showed significant dissociation. He was helped by reframing his fragmented recall to correspond with the actual circumstances of the truck accident.

In another instance, a construction worker on top of the Cypress structure had caused concern among the other workers. A counselor was asked to assess and intervene with this worker, who seemed to believe that the end of the world was at hand. He repeatedly referred to a biblical passage he stated as "Matthew 24." The counselor expected that the passage would have been from the Book of Revelation.

The worker (W) rattled on intensely to the counselor (C):

C. "This is a horrible scene, right here on this structure." [This statement was an attempt to bring the topic into the present reality.

W. "Matthew 24 says, 'Then two men will be in the field: one will be taken and the other left.' " [His reference appeared to relate to the random deaths on the structure.]

The counselor was uncertain how to respond. There was no minister on the structure or within several blocks. The situation was less than ideal. It was the middle of the night on a shaky, half-collapsed bridge, and the counselor stood there with a half-crazed man who thought it was the end of the world. Although police were available and could have handcuffed him, this would have been poor form. Workers at disaster sites develop strong ties to one another, even without much interaction. Police at the scene would want this worker to be dealt with decisively, but gently.

C. "Armageddon, the final destruction before the second coming of Christ. Is that what you are talking about?"

W. [Referring to the sky.] "The lightning comes from the east and flashes to the west, so also will the coming of the Son of Man be."
[The counselor was concerned that the worker thought Christ was coming through the clouds.]

C. "Where is Christ?"

W. "In heaven sitting at the right hand of God the Father. See the lightning. It starts there and travels there. . . . Lightning comes from the east and travels to the west, just like it says in Matthew 24." [His voice had risen from a whisper to a shout.]

Lightning in the east was reflected on the edges of breaks in the clouds to the west. The moon had disappeared. Although intense and agitated, the worker's comments had a basis in reality. Still, the task was to bring him safely down to street level. Personal information was discussed. He was not there with coworkers; his house had been damaged, and his family was distressed and in a shelter. He was personally traumatized by the earthquake and under significant stress. Yet as the discussion continued, he became more calm and grounded.

The worker was alone in this difficult situation; this aloneness put him at risk.

Although his demeanor, statements, and beliefs seemed bizarre, he had operated the equipment well and had otherwise behaved appropriately. In spite of this disturbed ideation and traumatic stress reactions, he maintained ego strength and was able to function. He relaxed as the counselor put his experience and reactions into perspective by giving him information on the expected, or typical, course of traumatic stress reactions. Religion was important in his life, and his beliefs were consistent with the teachings of his church. He felt he had done enough. He had been working for six hours; now others could operate the equipment. He indicated that he wanted to go to help his family. He was less concerned about his home and more interested in the emotional welfare of his family. His plan seemed consistent with his pre-trauma life-style. The counselor (this author) escorted him to the crane, which returned to Cypress Street, fifty feet below.

Debriefing

Debriefing, as a formal procedure, developed out of work with emergency services and combat veterans. Various models of formal debriefing require hands-on training and usually include videotapes of disaster scenes to provide some degree of exposure to the visual and auditory experiences of the events. Such exposure has some inoculation value. It may help therapists to realize whether or not they can tolerate such images. Those who cannot are best advised not to enter the disaster field. Disaster work has a very powerful impact, which may cause secondary traumatic stress reactions in the therapists. Team members engaged in debriefing, therefore, also require debriefing and stress management.

At the Cypress Street structure, both the work and trauma were ongoing. Workers were exhausted, and formal debriefing was not possible. The time frame for debriefing depends on the physical demands of the work but generally should occur after workers have demobilized and rested.

Organizational dynamics and politics dictate the constituency at debriefing sessions. Generally, decision makers are separated from line workers. Groups being debriefed may be asked to determine the dividing line between worker and management groups. For example, in police departments, some line officers want their sergeants present while others do not wish the sergeants to join them. After the crane accident, the company constructing the high rise requested and received formal debriefing for the entire staff. Separate sessions were held for corporate executives, mid-management, and construction workers.

Construction worker sessions included line supervisors and various grades of construction workers. All were encouraged to discuss their experiences and reactions, in dynamic sessions. A one-week follow-up confirmed the apparent benefit of the sessions. Workers who had been obviously distressed during the first session had improved greatly by the second. Workers who missed the first session made a point of attending later ones after they had dialogued with their peers in the interim. On one occasion, an executive who had missed his session joined in a session with the construction workers, because he did not want to be left out.

The debriefing format used by this author includes educational components near the beginning and, again, near the end of the session. A figure representing the course of post-traumatic stress reactions was displayed to illustrate the initial educational phase. This provides a framework for the individual's internal confusion and establishes common terms and concepts. Coping skills are discussed, and communication is improved within the group. During the later teaching phase, the leader mentions that excess coffee, alcohol, drugs, survivor guilt, and not talking about one's experience can lead to PTSD, a reaction that may become a lifelong fixture.

Traumatized individuals consistently experience a sense of loss and a sense of not being in control, during and after a traumatic event. The sense of loss may be for a loved one, for possessions, for familiar features in the community, or for something too vague to be readily determined. Sometimes they experience a loss of innocence, a sense that the world will never be the same. People who demarcate their life stories with phrases such as "before the incident" or "since the incident" offer clues that may suggest PTSD.

The second core issue revolves around a sense of loss of control over one's life. A sense of having control must be reestablished. Decompression and debriefing are tools to aid the individual to regain a sense of control in his or her life. The earthquake was strongest and briefest in Santa Cruz. Twin waves traveled through a paved parking lot, rhythmically lifting cars as easily as ocean waves rock boats at a dock. Later inspection revealed that the parking lot was left flat and relatively unblemished. During formal debriefings participants were asked, "Who here believes the earth is solid?" When none answered, they were asked, "How many would have laughed at this question two weeks ago?" All laughed. Such icebreakers also pointed to a loss of the basic tenet that the earth is solid and dependable.

PROFESSIONAL CONSIDERATIONS

Just after the plane crash a group of thirty-five local community mental health workers, from a potential pool of 148 therapists, came together to volunteer to provide counseling to the survivors. Of these workers, ten actually met with groups of survivors. After two weeks, three workers were still providing services to survivors.

Such a falloff among local volunteers has been found during disaster training and following other disasters. Such work is intense and demanding, but even more so, professionals are not experienced or prepared by their education to provide services in such unstructured, noisy, and chaotic conditions.

Perhaps 20 percent of mental health professionals may desire to learn specifics about disaster psychology in formal training. Others are either not interested, believe they can study the topic on their own, or believe they are already equipped to provide whatever services are needed, without additional training. Of those who take formal training, possibly 10 percent will be able to function effectively at an actual scene; others can be of great benefit in various capacities, such as shelters, mortuaries, support groups, crisis units, and office settings.

Training needs to include participation in actual drills with emergency services. These drills prepare therapists more adequately and help determine therapists' appropriateness for different tasks. Sanner (1983) found mild traumatic reactions among those participating in mass casualty drills, which speaks to the screening effect for individuals who can operate during actual disasters. Unfortunately, most mental health disaster planning is only on paper, and therapists are seldom included in local disaster drills. Yet they, too, need to practice their procedures and refine the delivery of services within the context of the drills, in order to improve techniques and to establish the flow of debriefing. In urban areas of California, the American Red Cross has begun to provide mental health training programs that combine classroom format with role-playing involvement in local disaster drills.

After a disaster, mental health services need to be finely critiqued and dissected, so that improvements can be made in future delivery of post-trauma services. This aspect of emergency work needs to occur after all incidents. Critiques can be brutal and unpleasant but must be tolerated because of the benefit for later operations. This writer does not know of research that has documented the benefits of debriefing or other post-trauma interventions. Formal outcome studies of proper after-incident critiques are needed for training and for the legitimacy of such services.

Establishing Credibility

The ability to provide post-trauma services requires the professional to establish credibility as an expert, able to handle the matter, and personally acceptable. The difficulty for a mental health professional to establish credibility with police officers has been discussed by Benner (1982). A counselor at the Cypress Street structure introduced himself as a ''shrink who routinely works with police and with rescue workers at places like this.'' He concluded with the additional facts that he was a former U.S. Marine and Vietnam combat veteran. This introduction established him as familiar with scenes such as this, as well as with police and military operations. The police officers then introduced themselves, expressing both reluctance and interest in debriefing.

This session was joined by a psychologist who proudly mentioned his affiliation with a major university and his experience in disaster research. He then mentioned that he had worked for a long time with chronic schizophrenics. The session ended before it began. The police officers began to fidget and frown at each other immediately after hearing the psychologist introduce himself. The officers revealed less information than they had during their original debriefings. The psychologist gave information on possible reactions and encouraged to approach trauma team members at any time. Immediately following the session, the first psychologist was approached by several of the officers who had concerns about which they were able to talk.

The second psychologist meant no harm, and certainly, among the type of people he normally encountered, his credentials were impressive. Police officers also have a long experience with "chronic schizophrenics," as have most graduate students. However, they see no similarities between the highly disturbed citizens they encounter and themselves. Nor do they want to talk to someone who works with schizophrenics, especially in a situation where some officers may be experiencing unfamiliar reactions that lead to concerns for their own sanity.

Know Who Is in the Session

It may be important to do some screening prior to beginning a session, especially if the participants are strangers. As with the above example, it is important to interview and prepare other professionals, and it is advisable to screen survivors for excessive stress reactions or prior mental or emotional problems.

Following the 1985 plane crash, the initial sessions had no prescreening of participants. A chronic mentally ill woman who was a survivor of the incident and had strong reactions joined the group discussion. However, she did not fit well with the others in the group. As an elderly gentleman described how he had grabbed a young girl to smother the flames that were engulfing her, the woman yelled, "You raped her!" This gentleman was very distressed and could not understand this woman's belief that he had molested a little girl. In a follow-up session two years later, he brought up his continued distress over the response of this woman. The group would not allow the woman to be removed, and she continued to be disruptive. Survivors become very protective of each other, and therefore, the professional must tread lightly, mindful of being an outsider.

Emergency Service Personnel

When talking with others, emergency service workers are careful to avoid details they have seen or experienced, so as not to injure the listener with the horror of these personal recollections. Such concern creates distancing in their interpersonal relationships and adds to difficulty in their marriages. However, the grisly details are exactly what the worker must discuss during post-trauma interventions. Counselors who work with emergency service personnel need to be qualified by experience and training to listen to the goriest and most disturbing of graphic details.

It is vital for the counselor to establish credibility with emergency service workers before any intervention can be successful. Nonemergency workers, who have not had prior exposure to extreme situations, are much more accessible and appropriate for a general therapist to counsel. They, too, desire to protect the listener, but they are not so heavily defended and thereby are more accessible.

Beyond an individual's race, creed, color, ethnicity, or community lies a clear and tightly knit emergency service subculture. This subculture demands the same respect and appropriate approach as does any other subculture. Successful entrée occurs when the therapist is either a member of an allied profession or has gained specific and direct experience with the particular type of emergency work. If the counselors are not already compatible and comfortable with emergency service workers, little is likely to be accomplished during a post-trauma debriefing or other intervention.

Prior Trauma

Prior traumas can be vividly reexperienced during a current traumatic incident and again during recall of the more recent incident. A confusing and disorienting kaleidoscope of past and current memories, sensations, and experiences can typically mix together and may lead to a fugue state. The fugue state is an extremely rare occurrence in which the individual dissociates from the immediate surroundings and finds himself once again in the midst of a previous traumatic experience.

A survivor of the plane crash reported having only an auditory recollection of the incident. Her sporadic and disconnected record of events persisted, and a full year later, she returned to the "first anniversary" sessions with no change in her recall. Her only identified current problem was that she taught school and was unable to sing Christmas carols with the children. Her denial was so deep that she did not connect her difficulty to the Christmas carols playing at the moment of the plane crash.

Mental health staff described her as a "therapy junkie." Although she had attended numerous other traditional therapy groups, she was screened and deemed to be an appropriate member for the sessions. She was not chronically mentally ill, in spite of long-standing psychological difficulties. During the first sessions, she seemed to ask other survivors questions as to whether specific events had occurred, some of which were clearly not part of this incident.

During the "first anniversary" sessions, she related an auditory memory of a childhood trauma, which included being shot in the head. The counselor suggested that the trauma of the plane crash and the trauma of this earlier incident had become tangled in her recall. A visit to the mall with other survivors (some of whom had not yet made a return trip) facilitated some recall of her visual memory. Later, she recovered other sensory memories of the plane crash and improved her recall for both traumas. She also became better able to separate those two traumas. By the second anniversary, she was fairly free of disturbing reactions to the plane crash and resolved the earlier trauma through appropriate therapy.

Know When to Refer

During a later session with the construction crew, a burly worker with long, unkempt hair and a tattoo on his biceps reading "Born to Die" sat to the side. He was almost imperceptibly vibrating. His glazed eyes seemed to stare at something 1,000 miles away. A Vietnam veteran, he appeared unable to control the intrusive recollection of his wartime experience of twenty years earlier. When he was asked, "You were just there, weren't you?" he nodded affirmatively.

His very rare fugue state was recognizably difficult for him to retract. Fortunately, a trauma team member was a Vietnam veteran, and by using Vietnam veteran jargon, he established credibility and rapport. The construction worker was able to return completely from that fugue state. The two men, discussing the current setting, discovered various triggers for the fugue state. These environmental triggers included smells of the tent, bodies, and diesel fuel exhaust, sounds, and sights, as well as the rain and the paramilitary nature of the operation. Debriefing of these reminiscent features and the intruding reexperiencing occurred. The worker was given the telephone number of the local Vet Center and was accompanied to the phone to make the initial call.

DISCUSSION

Implicit and explicit in the case scenarios is the philosophical tenet that the behaviors of these workers were "normal reactions to an abnormal event." This cliché reassures those individuals that it is the external event that is abnormal. Furthermore those "normal" reactions may well be adaptive from an evolutionary perspective. Of course, evolution is concerned with species survival, leading to an understanding of "normal reactions" within the context of the species rather than within the individual.

A unique brain structure enabled humans to evolve and gain mastery over their environment. Early on they developed the ability to discern and recognize reoccurring environmental patterns. Next emerged a modest ability to predict cause and effect, followed by the development of speech and, eventually, writing, allowing the organism [human] to imagine a variety of outcomes without having to take immediate action, making choice possible (Becker, 1971). Although humans were not physically equipped to overpower nature or other animals, their complex human brains could efficiently analyze situations and, through the facilitation of communication, plan and implement strategies to control the environment.

Basic planning abilities would have been disrupted when an individual was overwhelmed by a traumatic event. Thus, traumatic stress reactions may have developed processes to reestablish cognitive control over environmental hazards, that is, return to a state of equilibrium. The emotional features of the event maintaining the increased anxiety drive the need to "solve the lapse in control" that initially had allowed the trauma to occur. Turner and Gorst-Unsworth (1990) discussed incomplete emotional and cognitive processing as central features interfering with resolution of the sequelae from torture. Solomon, Gerrity, and Muff (1992), Foa et al. (1991), and Davidson and Foa (1991) found cognitive therapy reduced symptoms better than did other forms of therapy. These cognitive approaches initially reduced symptoms better than did counseling, flooding, or remaining on the waiting list. After three months, however, flooding was the superior method.

Traumatized individuals can be distressed by perceptual distortions, intense emotions, extreme reactions, and loss of basic beliefs about life, the world, or people. Debriefing provides a framework and terminology for these previously unexperienced phenomena. As the individual begins to identify and label these reactions, he or she begins to regain cognitive control.

During discussion groups following the 1985 plane crash, a young, athletic police officer reported overwhelming guilt. As the plane tore into the roof directly above his head, he sprinted away from immediate danger, in essence, abandoning his family. Several minutes elapsed, he and his wife believed, before he returned to guide the family to safety. Others in the group had also been present at the same time and helped to place specific events into the proper sequence and time frame. Their reconstructions showed that he had sprinted forty feet and had returned within six seconds. His and his wife's perceptions of time had been greatly distorted and the proper sequence of events had been distorted.

Demands made on mental processes of survivors can be understood in terms of integration and assimilation. These cognitive processes were identified by Piaget (1969) as basic to cognitive development and continue into cognitive processes of adaptation to a new understanding of the world and self and integration of new perceptions into the ego. Emotions run their course toward resolution only after the cognitive equilibrium has been restored.

The ideal end result of the individual's cognitive adaptation is finding "a silver lining for the trauma cloud," that is, something positive that resulted from the trauma experience. This process may take years, if, indeed, any specific catastrophe can ever have positive aspects. For example, the loss of a child to a drunk-driving accident led to the development of the organization Mothers Against Drunk Drivers, Inc. (MADD). The founder pointed to this as a very effective therapeutic endeavor. Clearly, positive results do not resolve the horror of the trauma, yet they can provide a purposeful focus for the survivor's later productivity.

CONCLUSION

Intervention specific to the trauma and related topics relieves much of the tension evident in traditional psychotherapy sessions. The therapeutic contract focuses on the individual's return to the pre-trauma level of functioning, not on psychoanalyzing a neurosis or facilitating psychological growth. Although the proselytizing construction worker seemed bizarre, he was a normal person having normal reactions to an abnormal event. Intervention focused on the event, not on his emotions or beliefs, which were distractions. He was helped to make his own decisions and then to act upon them. This small act of empowerment enabled him to regain functioning to meet the needs of himself and his family. Whether he needed further counseling is not known, but from other instances, it is quite possible that he did not need further support.

The majority of rescue workers and survivors come to only one session and, indeed, seem to benefit well from only one psychoeducational session (Foreman 1990). The case is well made as to the benefits of debriefing for support personnel (Armstrong, O'Callahan, and Marmar, 1991) and for the debriefers themselves (Talbot, Manton, and Dunn, 1992). These groups of workers tend to avoid adequate stress reduction, thereby disserving themselves and promoting their own burnout. Debriefing should be an expected part of demobilization for all workers involved in disaster responses.

Post-trauma services can be an important adjunct to emergency service operations. Certainly, during an operation, the completion and demobilization of crews should take precedence over debriefing services. Yet, during an ongoing and lengthy incident, experienced professionals provide important consultation to the incident commander. Such consultation revolves around changes in the working conditions to reduce hunger, fatigue, stress, and subsequent traumatic stress reactions.

The professional should prepare to be asked to speak to other agencies, including the media. When presenting to the media, he or she should provide off-camera education to the reporters, repeat the question asked, and give a crisp, clear, brief answer. The brevity of the answer is important; otherwise, the broadcast will not convey what the speaker intended. Broadcast and print journalists offer the opportunity for community education and outreach and thereby can be viewed as important tools for the mental health professional.

Proper training and education in post-disaster services must be embraced and encouraged by local, state, and federal agencies, as well as professional organizations. During the immediate post-disaster phase there is opportunity for reduction and even actual prevention of significant psychological distress. Conversely, there is opportunity to cause further and additional psychological damage through poorly planned and implemented services. Therefore, it is vitally important for disaster psychology to be recognized as a special and select area for research, development, and provision of well-organized services led by experienced mental health professionals.

18

Responding to Community Crisis

Marlene A. Young and John H. Stein

INTRODUCTION

In 1975, a small group of victim service providers, academics, representatives of the criminal justice system, and others banded together to form the National Organization for Victim Assistance (NOVA). Its mission was to establish rights and services for victims of crime and crises.

To accomplish that mission, NOVA's founders promulgated three purposes: national advocacy for legislative and social change, the development of training and education programs for persons who work with victims, and provision of services to NOVA's members. These purposes served the organization well for a few years, but by 1980, when NOVA opened its national headquarters in Washington, D.C., it had become clear that a national organization in this field must also provide some direct services. Victims who could not get adequate support in their home communities were calling NOVA for help, and in some of these hundreds of cases, mere information and referral services were insufficient. Thus, in 1980, NOVA formally ratified its fourth purpose: providing advocacy and counseling services to victims who contact the NOVA staff, whenever such services are unavailable elsewhere.

As a result of this additional purpose, NOVA staff developed a training program to teach volunteers to respond to telephone crisis calls in the off-hours and to provide supportive counseling and advocacy. NOVA also developed local victim services in the District of Columbia through a combination of volunteer crisis counselors and a mental health referral system. The emphasis in these efforts was, and remains, on crisis intervention and management. However, it took on a new dimension as a result of a telephone call from Michael Turpen on August 22, 1986.

Turpen, then the attorney general of Oklahoma, had for some years used NOVA's legislative information services and was knowledgeable about its other work. Upon contacting NOVA, he explained that less than an hour earlier, someone had shot and killed a dozen or more people in the post office in Edmond, a community abutting Oklahoma City. "I don't know how to even ask the question," he continued. "All I can tell you is, we've got a whole city in crisis. Is there some way you can help?"

NOVA's response was to recruit seven volunteers, all trained crisis counselors, to fly immediately to Edmond for a group intervention of approximately forty-eight hours. Its mandate was to work with community mental health center staff and other caregivers to help them design and carry out a response plan for the overwhelming trauma in the community. To meet that charge effectively, the team followed informal guidelines hastily drawn up by NOVA's executive staff, guidelines that have evolved into protocols for the dozens of later teams that have served communities in trauma through the Crisis Response Team (CRT) Project.

THE NOVA CRISIS RESPONSE TEAM PROJECT

The following sections of the chapter describe the circumstances under which a NOVA CRT becomes involved in community crises and what a team does in the community.

Definitions

A CRT is composed of a group of trained crisis intervenors who respond within twenty-four hours to a call for assistance in the aftermath of a communitywide, trauma-inducing event. All are volunteers. NOVA's philosophy is that outsiders coming to a community in crisis should not be seen as profiting from their interventions. Moreover, the authors' experience demonstrates that a community is more receptive to outside intervention if it is perceived as truly benevolent.

Initially, people experienced in providing crisis intervention were recruited as team members, but an additional requirement now is the successful completion of NOVA's forty-hour training course. It has become increasingly clear that team members function better if they have received training based on a common model. At least two National Crisis Response Team Training Institutes are held in Washington annually, and NOVA conducts such institutes in other communities on request.

NOVA eventually expects to offer an advanced forty-hour course, incorporating the wealth of information gathered in the ongoing experiences of the CRT Project. Since 1986, the project has fielded over three dozen teams at the sites of mass murders, newly discovered serial murders, train, plane, and bus crashes, and devastating storms. The way in which members of a given team are selected is discussed in a later section.

The term *community crisis* refers to the emotional aftermath of a community-wide, trauma-inducing event. *Community* in this context often refers to a geographically defined community such as a neighborhood, town, or city. However, it also can be defined in terms of a school community, an employment community, a religious community, a professional community, and so forth. These latter groups are often more cohesive than geographic communities. To illustrate, whenever a law enforcement officer is killed in the line of duty, dozens, even hundreds, of strangers will join the funeral cortege in the uniforms and vehicles of far-distant police agencies, in testament to the pain inflicted on an entire profession.

Communities can also be established by the event itself, creating "transitory communities," such as those found in the aftermath of plane crashes, wars, hostage takings, and the like. Survivors of such events often feel more closely tied to the people with whom they survived, or to the loved ones of those who did not, than to friends from home or the workplace.

The traumatic event is usually a sudden, random, arbitrary catastrophe that causes multiple deaths or life-threatening injuries. Sometimes, however, the point of trauma is not the violent incident but its public revelation. This was the case in Cincinnati, Ohio, in August 1987, when it was revealed that Donald Harvey had killed at least fifty-four people at several hospitals in Ohio and Kentucky over a sixteen-year period. Similarly, the arrest of Jeffrey Dahmer in July 1991 in Milwaukee precipitated a community crisis when the revelation that he had killed at least fifteen young men in especially grisly ways over a ten-year period was made public.

In some circumstances, a community may plunge into crisis after the victimization of one person, rather than many. For instance, the kidnapping and murder of a retired newspaper publisher in Kankakee, Illinois, caused that community great trauma. This was, in part, because he was prominent but also because he was buried alive while the kidnappers awaited their ransom (he died of either suffocation or a heart attack). He also lived in the same neighborhood as his assailants.

So, too, was a disgruntled taxpayer's killing of the mayor of the rural town of Mt. Pleasant, Iowa, a regionwide trauma, since the victim was a revered figure in that community. Obviously, the assassinations of John Kennedy, Martin Luther King, Jr., and Robert Kennedy were each, in turn, a cause of national, and indeed international, trauma.

Beyond the number of dead and injured, other considerations that may lead to a communitywide crisis include:

• Incidents involving multiple eyewitnesses.

• Incidents wherein the direct victims have a special significance to the community

affected, as may happen with the assassination of a public figure or the killing of a child in a day-care center.
- Incidents subjecting the community to exposure to carnage or misery.
- Incidents calling for numerous rescue workers.
- Incidents attracting a great deal of attention.

Pre-Disaster Preparation

When a community crisis occurs, the response must be executed as quickly as possible. NOVA has established pre-disaster understandings with graduates of its CRT training programs. Those understandings include knowledge of the CRT's goals, the kinds of services offered, and the protocols for selecting team members and for their performance on-site. Thus, the growing network of CRT training graduates has proven effective in sizing up the extent of the trauma when disaster strikes their home communities and in quickly mobilizing either local or national CRT teams, as needed.

Other training programs, of course, also look to establish the same kind of readiness to manage the emotional dimensions of disaster. That is all for the good. Participants have indicated that NOVA's training puts especially rigorous expectations on team members. Whether or not that perception is accurate, NOVA works hard to instill a certain clarity, simplicity, and discipline in the roles of team members so they know what to expect of themselves and their teammates in what are always chaotic situations.

The Goals of a CRT

The overriding purpose of dispatching a CRT to a community is to assist the community in mobilizing its response to the crisis. All of the CRT goals derive from this ultimate purpose.

The first goal is to help local policymakers and caregivers plan their response for the initial two or three days and then to establish their long-term responses for the next year. That planning process starts with the phone calls that lead up to the team's being dispatched. It continues with what is always the first meeting, once the team is assembled on-site, with the public and private sector leaders who are the formal and informal managers of the disastrous situation. As a part of that process, NOVA helps community leaders identify all available local caregivers, such as mental health professionals, peer counselors and natural helpers within an employment group or community, family or friends, clergy members, teachers, and so forth.

The team also helps the community identify populations that are especially vulnerable to severe crisis reactions or long-term stress reactions. While some populations are obviously at risk (rescue workers, direct victims and their families, eyewitnesses), others are not always so obvious (schoolchildren, representatives of the media, and emergency shelter managers).

A third goal of that initial meeting is to plan an immediate series of disaster-related training courses on the emotional aftermath of catastrophe. Even if local caregivers have had previous experience and training in responding to disasters, they are asked (usually through the appropriate community leadership) to attend the three-hour training. In the aftermath of catastrophe, many community members momentarily forget their professional training. Moreover, caregivers who go through the same short training session together are more likely to function as a team in the days and months ahead. To underscore the importance of this training, NOVA requires all of its own team members to attend these sessions, even if they are conducting the training.

The fourth goal of the planning session is to map out a number of group "debriefing" or "defusing" sessions with members of the high-risk population. While a pair of the NOVA team members facilitates the two- to three-hour sessions, these are also designed to be a service to the local caregivers, who are expected to attend the debriefings. The authors' consistent impression is that local colleagues appreciate the team's taking the lead on these initial sessions, for several reasons.

Given the critical timing of an emergency situation, the fact that the Crisis Response Team takes on the first debriefings gives the local caregivers time to get their own thoughts in order. Since virtually none of them have done such a debriefing, and the three-hour "brush-up" training has not equipped them for what is a difficult discipline to master, they appreciate the "modeling" the CRT team gives them. Typically, the local caregivers facilitate debriefings after the team has left and usually feel they have benefited from an internship under fire. In addition, for some high-risk populations, debriefing leaders from outside the local community are almost imperative because of concern for confidentiality and privacy.

A fifth goal is to assist local leaders and caregivers, when requested, to deal with other outside influences on the community, notably the media. While some communities prefer to deal with the media through their own public information officers, most are grateful for the help of the CRT members in getting a calming message to the public through the media and in serving as a buffer on questions that the press now routinely want answered on the emotional status of direct victims and other community members.

Other intrusive forces may damage a community's efforts to cope with catastrophe. It is not unusual for the community to become a battleground of competing "disaster lawyers" and less-than-altruistic insurance adjustors. Sometimes mental health professionals converge uninvited on disaster scenes, adding to the chaos. The very disruptiveness of these intrusions underscores the importance of NOVA's being invited guests of community leaders. Given that status, the CRT can be used as a mediating force with other outsiders. The NOVA CRT screens all outside caregivers volunteering to help or, in other situations, serves as an adviser to local managers in dealing with numerous, well-meaning volunteers.

In reviewing these goals with community leaders, the CRT's team leader also gives the backgrounds of the team members. Community leaders, in most cases, respond to the team's concerns with extraordinary dispatch. It is common, for example, for officials to leave the meeting with a set of caregivers identified, a proposed training schedule, and a similar schedule of debriefings. Just as commonly, those who are asked to assist in the next few hours readily comply with the request.

Levels of Service

Not all communities that suffer a tragedy want outside help. That is determined through NOVA's initial outreach, which begins as soon as word is received of the tragedy. It usually occurs through phone calls to NOVA's network in the criminal justice and victim assistance communities in the vicinity of the disaster.

NOVA responds by outlining several levels of service. The first level is simply an offer to transmit written materials and handouts describing how to deal with the emotional aftermath of disaster. These materials usually include outlines of the CRT protocols, basic crisis reactions, long-term stress reactions, crisis intervention techniques, and group debriefing techniques, along with handouts for the public and a special outline on how children deal with trauma. Virtually all communities with which NOVA has contact in these circumstances receive basic materials by express mail or facsimile machine.

The second level of service is a more intensive telephone consultation on crisis response. Initially, service was given in an ad hoc manner. When a local caregiver would call with questions, NOVA would respond. However, it has been found to be more useful if the following procedures are followed when providing such service.

First, the person who serves as the local contact is expected to call a designated NOVA staff member twice daily for about a week; the service is more productive when both sides stay in fairly close contact. Second, the NOVA staff member (who has served on NOVA's CRTs and training teams) provides the local contact with written materials as well as an abbreviated training by telephone on some of the critical issues arising from the particular disaster. Third, the NOVA staff member agrees to be available to address any additional questions as needed on a twenty-four-hour basis. Fourth, if requested, the NOVA staff member performs a number of other services: offers help to deal long-distance with the media or other potentially disruptive elements, conducts a telephone debriefing session of local staff or volunteers, and offers a follow-up review of the disaster response with recommendations and predictions for future issues.

The third level of service is the provision of an on-scene supplement to an existing local team. Originally, no such service was offered since there were so few local teams, least of all ones with any familiarity with NOVA's training or protocols. However, NOVA has conducted some forty-five state and regional trainings throughout the United States, and some states therefore have more than adequate personnel to handle disasters in their jurisdiction.

When asked to provide a consultant on-site, NOVA will do so, at least when the lead, local caregiver has been through the training and is confident that the other local staff and volunteers are capable of following that model. One or two experienced members of NOVA's national CRT roster are selected to go to the community to provide consultations on the special attributes of the disaster. The outsiders provide disinterested intervention to help resolve local political roadblocks impeding the local team's work and help train a wider group of caregivers.

The fourth level of service is the deployment of a full CRT, with four to ten members, to work in the community for two days. The procedures followed by such a team are described more fully later.

Guidelines for Selecting Team Members

Selecting individuals for participation on a CRT is a complex task. The process takes into consideration the demographics of the community, at-risk populations, and the characteristics of the team members themselves. The primary consideration in the selection process is to make the team as isometric with the community and its most vulnerable groups as is possible. The philosophy behind this approach is simply that people tend to be more open with those who are similar in nature to themselves.

The professional makeup of a team usually includes:

- a law enforcement representative (patrol officer experience is preferred, even if the representative is now a commanding officer)
- a psychologist or psychiatrist
- victim service counselors
- a member of the clergy
- a member of a medical profession
- a child counselor
- a person experienced with media relations

One individual may wear more than one professional hat. For instance, two training graduates who have been used as team members are both clergymen and full-time victim service professionals; another is a registered nurse who is also a specialist in trauma counseling for children; and one law enforcement officer is also a paramedic. Each has proven to be an excellent liaison with fellow professionals.

When examining the demographics of a community, an effort is made to determine the racial and ethnic mix, the socioeconomic background, the educational background, the rural or urban nature, languages spoken, religious background, age groups represented, and so forth. Demographic characteristics that are unusual or dominant in the community should be reflected in the makeup of the team. Thus, when a team was sent to Inkster, Michigan, a majority-black community, special efforts were made to have African Americans on the team. A NOVA team sent to Puerto Rico had Hispanic team members, while a team sent to a southern community whose disaster most affected a fundamentalist Christian congregation included a clergy member from a fundamentalist denomination.

The idea of demographic sensitivity is applied with some imagination. For example, a team that responded to the predominantly white University of Mississippi, after a group of white sorority sisters on a walk-a-thon was struck by a truck, fairly reflected that bereaved community. One team member was a black victim counselor, chosen at NOVA's suggestion and with the host's warm approval. That team member facilitated one of the most poignant sessions, debriefing members of a black sorority who felt both a kinship with their killed and injured classmates and pain at not feeling included in grieving ceremonies occurring around the campus.

Perhaps the most difficult aspect of team selection is putting together individuals who have personality characteristics that support the team ethos. Some of those characteristics include leadership abilities, tact, diplomacy, flexibility, common sense, and stamina. Perhaps the most important attribute is the ability to focus on the team's needs to the exclusion of personal needs.

Roles of Team Members

NOVA's model for a Crisis Response Team starts with the designation of a team leader. That individual's role is to serve as the official liaison between the team and community, to make assignments on-site, to be spokesperson for the team with the media (if there is no "media person" on the team), and to debrief and care for team members. The leader must be a person who has the professional and personal attributes that make him or her seem automatically credible to the community. Thus, most often, the team leader is a psychologist or psychiatrist, since the title "Doctor" engenders respect in most sectors of society. While this approach may offend ideals of how merit should be earned and recognized, the pragmatic reality is that the team will not be around long enough to overcome a host of suspicions or to build the credibility it needs in order to do its work.

While the team leader is usually a volunteer from outside NOVA's staff, the team manager is usually a member of NOVA's headquarters staff. The manager serves as the liaison between the team and NOVA's headquarters and provides a quantity of materials and briefing papers that will help the team respond better. The manager also handles logistics and needed supplies and makes a report to headquarters at the conclusion of the response.

As indicated above, an optional goal for the CRT is to serve as a liaison with the media, if the community so requests. The designated person handles all media inquiries, sets up press conferences when necessary, and serves as public spokesperson for the team unless the team leader is designated to do so.

Other team members perform duties as assigned. These may include presenting or copresenting the three-hour training segment, facilitating debriefings, handling individual counseling sessions, providing secretarial support to the team, and running errands.

Behavioral Guidelines for Team Members at the Site

The following guidelines, although seemingly simplistic, were developed to give team members written guidance for a number of situations for which persistent questions have arisen.

All team members go to the actual disaster site if possible, although this is not always possible. When a truck crashed into a school bus near Carrolltown, Kentucky, in 1988 and killed twenty-four children and three adults, a CRT assembled in Radcliffe, some sixty miles away, where all the victims and survivors lived. However, in most cases, the team visits the actual site of the tragedy. Such a visit is required for two reasons. First, seeing the site provides team members with more credibility to community members and those involved in debriefings. While the team members have not suffered the direct impact of the disaster, they have been witness to its effects. Second, by observing the site, the team members can get special insights about what happened. When NOVA sent a team to Indianapolis after an air force plane crashed into a Ramada Inn near the airport, team members recognized that one of the high-risk populations was employees of a bank across the street from the motel. No one had mentioned that, during its descent, the plane demolished the bank's roof.

No one talks to the media without permission of the media liaison. This rule, common to any organization with a public information office, seeks to create one voice for the group. It helps to control the spread of misinformation, militates against conflicting views or advice, and generally avoids embarrassment for the team, the hosts, and the victims.

No "morgue" humor is allowed except in the privacy of team meetings. Whether morgue humor is a healthy outlet for anyone in extremely grim situations is disputed. The authors have found that team members tend to find humor in some of the bizarre circumstances that occur in the midst of chaos and tragedy and, on balance, believe that such humor is both a normal and salutary coping mechanism. However, it is always totally inappropriate for "outsiders" to seem to take lightly any catastrophe when in the presence of those who are experiencing it from the "inside" even when the "insiders" themselves find relief in a spontaneous bout of morgue humor.

Team members should not make appointments without clearing them with the team leader. This rule evolved after an incident when some team members made appointments on their own. Spontaneous responsiveness can undermine a sense of teamwork when it disrupts the scheduling of team activities. The problem typically arises when a community member is particularly affected by a training or debriefing session and seeks out a private meeting with the facilitator. NOVA's general philosophy is that such meetings may promote a bond between the community member and the team member that is inappropriate to the short-term nature of the CRT. Therefore, it is far better for team members to connect those community members to local caregivers.

The team members should treat mealtimes and other functions as opportunities for the group to be together, whenever possible. One of the best ways to reduce stress for team members at the disaster site is to provide them with the support of their peers. For this reason, NOVA encourages team leaders to organize breakfast and dinner as team events and, if possible, to schedule other team meetings or events when the schedule allows.

However much they might be provoked, team members should not make derogatory remarks about the behavior or actions of local community members. Such problems should be taken to the team leader. It is common for team members to observe behavior by community members (including caregivers) that seems inappropriate or harmful. Team members should refrain from quickly responding in a critical manner, remembering that a great many community members are in crisis and that some of their decisions may be perceived as "wrong." The tools of crisis intervention should be used in these situations: reassurance, validation, and understanding. Yet, if the problem has potential for continuing disruption, the team leader may choose to raise it privately with the local host.

Team members should not make demands on local hosts for food, transportation, copies of materials, and so forth, except in an emergency. These should be requested through the team manager. The purpose of this rule is to try to avoid imposing, in any way, on local community members. They have too much to think about regarding the catastrophe without addressing the needs of outsiders. That said, community members generally do everything possible to help the team. People are quite vulnerable in crisis and usually want to "give back" to those who are trying to help. Team members should be careful not to take undue advantage of these vulnerabilities.

Physical comfort for team members is not a priority. Team members may go without food, sleep, or exercise, may be subject to weather extremes, or may endure second-rate food or accommodations. In one community, team members conducted some debriefings in an unheated community center on a cold winter night. In another, they had to facilitate debriefings all night long. On the other hand, one community arranged accommodations at a first-class hotel, with no expense limit on incidentals and personal chauffeurs for all team members as they went about their activities. In short, a community does what it can to accommodate the team, which is expected to accept whatever is offered in good grace.

In the 1990s, it may seem strange to be discussing a "dress code," given the free-flowing, individualistic fashions of the time. NOVA teams nonetheless observe a dress code.

As a rule, the code requires team members to dress professionally and conservatively, unless team members are told of a modification. (One team that went to a small, agricultural community was encouraged to bring slacks and jeans, a suggestion endorsed by the hosts.) In addition to the general rule, team members are encouraged to wear the symbols of their professions, such as a clerical collar or law enforcement insignia.

When the Disaster Happens

As indicated before, NOVA reaches out to offer help whenever reports are received that a community has been struck by a major tragedy. The staff calls the local victim assistance program, law enforcement agency, county commissioners, state officials, or others who are in a position to make a quick decision about NOVA's offer of service.

Speed is of the essence; the aim is to send the team to the community within twenty-four hours of the event. This is based on what is perceived to be a common "time line of access." During the first day or two after the traumatic event, the community members are usually feeling shocked, vulnerable, and receptive to offers of outside assistance. Over the next five days, those close to the trauma typically vacillate between a state of emotional numbness and a state of emotional flooding. They are often exhausted and begin to resent the continuing barrage of activity surrounding their lives, many times feeling that since they survived the first two days of the crisis, they are probably over the worst part.

This change in emotional tone is accompanied by an increasing reluctance to accept outside assistance. While a few teams have indeed been welcomed five or six days after the event, by the time that the eighth or ninth day comes, there is normally an effort to put a stop to the preoccupation with the crisis.

Interestingly, NOVA's experience has been that if the community decided against a CRT during these initial stages, it may very well contact NOVA for assistance about six months after the crisis to set up a training program for a local team to deal more effectively with future crises.

With each outreach call to the community, the NOVA staff member identifies herself or himself and explains NOVA and the types of services the Crisis Response Team project can provide. Referrals to other sites that have received assistance are made so that a community can "check references" should it have any doubts about NOVA's capabilities.

The person contacted in the community (the local contact person or "LCP") is asked to explore whether community leaders would welcome NOVA's assistance. The LCP also is asked to make certain local arrangements—housing accommodations, local transportation, the compilation of press reports on the disaster, and so forth—should a team be dispatched. It is onerous to ask the LCP to do this legwork, but in most major disasters it is impossible to do these things from a distance, as was learned early on. When the first team was sent to Edmond, Oklahoma, after the post office shooting, it was not troubling to be unable get through to a recommended hotel, but it was somehow assumed that the team members could get one or two rental cars and nearby hotel rooms. That proved inaccurate, as the media had already booked them all.

While the LCP is doing the work at the local level, NOVA staff begins to put prospective team members on standby for the next three days. This often starts before NOVA has received an affirmative response from the community in order to ensure that a team can be assembled upon receiving a green light.

The aim is to get eight to fourteen people on standby, even though only four to ten people are asked to serve on the team if assistance is requested. In part, there is a certain amount of hedging against personnel problems arising with prospective team members. The major reason for the enlarged pool is to provide more choices in order to assemble the team that best mirrors important local demographics.

While placing people on standby, NOVA also begins to arrange potential travel plans for each team member. People on standby are asked to be ready to go to the nearest airport with one hour's notice.

Should the LCP find an affirmative consensus among local decision makers, the NOVA organizer then asks the LCP to provide a more detailed report on the community, including:

- demographics (ethnicity, socioeconomic group, chief employment, education level, age, and religious affiliation) for the community as a whole as well as for the most affected subcommunities
- previous history of traumatic events in the community
- political concerns, broadly speaking, ranging from misperceptions about the team on the part of some leaders, to preexisting tensions among community leaders, to conflicts among groups in the community
- insights on the personalities of major figures involved with the disaster

Finally, the LCP is asked to locate a headquarters for the team at the site. That headquarters should include at least one, and preferably three or more, telephones, as the lack of immediate communication facilities or a place to contact others interferes with the intervention effort.

Once the LCP has provided the supplementary information, NOVA executives make a final choice on team members. Each selected member is contacted and provided travel arrangements (airline tickets are prepaid for most team members), and efforts are made to get them to the airport closest to the site within an hour of each other, if possible.

The LCP is asked to prepare the following supplies for all training and debriefing meetings: flip charts, markers and tape, coffee, soft drinks, and other refreshments if possible, and ashtrays. Smoking is permitted at all of these sessions, although the smokers are segregated in one section of the room. While controversial, the policy is that a time of crisis is not the moment to mount an anti-smoking campaign.

The crisis is monitored on local and national news media from the time of the initial outreach until well after the team returns home. The NOVA staff clips articles from "national" newspapers, and the LCP is asked to save local reports.

Once the CRT arrives in the community, the strategy for responding to a crisis generally first involves team members' meeting each other at the airport, after which the team meets with the LCP or the LCP's designee. The team then visits the site of the tragedy, and, following that, team members participate in a planning meeting with the local community's leadership to get acquainted with one another and their missions. Then, the team reviews the impact of the disaster, the sequence of rescue and recovery events under way, the likely high-risk population groups, and the network of caregivers who are available to respond to the immediate and long-term emotional aftershocks of the disaster. In the typical planning meeting, the community leaders effectively pinpoint likely victim groups and caretaker groups, determine how to reach those groups quickly, and decisively map a strategy of where and when the groups will be scheduled for trainings or debriefings starting the next morning.

Should the leaders agree, the CRT's press liaison then holds a press conference to review the predictable stresses that community members may be experiencing and previews some of the concerns that the team addresses during its visit. This is the start of an education process seeking to demonstrate the predictable normality of many community members' shock or disbelief, their bouts of anger, grief, fear, self-blame, and frustration, and their anxiety about what lies ahead. Given the predictability of these patterns, NOVA is often able to prepare a press announcement in advance in case the media liaison is asked to hold one or more press conferences.

Typically, starting the next morning, members of the team conduct one or more three-hour training sessions for local caregivers who are involved in responding to the emotional aftermath of the crisis. These sessions are usually structured in four forty-five-minute segments, covering the crisis reaction and crisis intervention techniques, long-term stress reactions, group debriefing techniques, and trauma reactions in children.

Group debriefings are then held for identified high-risk groups, those who survived the life-threatening incident, loved ones of those who did not, neighbors who witnessed it, emergency personnel who responded to it, school counselors, and so on. Sometimes, team members are called on to conduct ten or more of these model sessions prior to leaving the community. In addition, NOVA urges the community leadership to organize and publicize at least one private, evening debriefing for anyone who wants to attend. One of the more experienced team members normally facilitates that session.

Debriefing sessions are never more than three hours long and many are only half that. They are designed to relieve some of the emotional pressure that community members face. The lead debriefer assists the group to identify, first, some of the reactions that people experienced in the immediate aftermath of the tragedy and, then, during the next two or three days, if that much time has elapsed since the event. The last segment asks the participants to estimate the reactions they might expect to have in the near and distant future and how they might cope with these stresses. When appropriate, facilitators also ask them to suggest ways in which they might try to create something constructive in tribute to those who had been harmed by the tragedy.

Throughout, participants are encouraged to describe their experiences, and the lead debriefer validates what appear to be normal kinds of reactions. A teammate records emotionally laden phrases used by participants on a flip chart visible to all. At the end, the facilitator reviews these flip chart entries to reaffirm the normality of these patterns of extraordinary distress. Further validation is then provided by distributing handouts on the crisis reaction and long-term stress reactions.

All debriefing sessions are held in a confidential atmosphere. While the NOVA volunteers cannot guarantee that every participant will observe the policy of confidentiality, team members do guarantee that they will not repeat anything attributable to any specific member of the group. Each evening, the team leader conducts a debriefing of the CRT members. These less formal (yet quite serious) debriefings are important to alleviate the stress that members may be facing and to maintain the cohesion of the team.

Prior to leaving the community, the NOVA CRT meets once more with representative local decision makers to discuss the long-range problems resulting from the disaster and convey recommendations for coping with those problems. Typical recommendations are to urge the establishment of a specialized, twenty-four-hour crisis line; provide suggestions for dealing with any upcoming holidays or other significant community events; set forth ideas for organizing or establishing memorials; or suggest ways to deal with schoolchildren's problems.

If the leadership wants the team to conduct a closing press conference, it is prepared to do that also. Finally, NOVA's CRT holds a closing internal debriefing session just before team members depart.

Post-Disaster Follow-Up

NOVA staff undertake several procedures after the CRT leaves the community. Often the local community members and members of the CRT have formed warm, supportive relationships. When the CRT leaves, the local community members, particularly the LCP, may feel vulnerable, alone, and at a loss without that outside support. Because of this possibility, the time spent in the community is limited to forty-eight hours. However, even with that limitation, there is a sense of sadness when the two groups separate.

To help fill that void, the NOVA team manager is responsible for communicating with the local hosts and helpers to express the team's appreciation and ideally stays in touch at regular intervals in the year following the disaster.

CONCLUSIONS

Virtually everyone who works with trauma victims recognizes that the rapid, skillful provision of crisis intervention services gives many victims the insight and tools to manage their own recoveries. These immediate services can mitigate their stresses while legitimizing a future course of supportive counseling or therapy, as needed.

Mobilizing this model of crisis service in the wake of calamity, when many have been killed, injured, or put in fear for their lives, is a formidable undertaking. NOVA's experience, however, is that a team of crisis intervenors who share a common training experience and disciplines can help a community take on that task.

The principal resource is not the team itself but the community's own caregivers. When it succeeds, the team leaves in place people who share a common plan and a sense of confidence that they can carry it out.

In working with individual victims, crisis intervenors find that critical institutions many times play a negative role in the victim's recovery. Therefore, the clumsiness, impatience, and misguided compassion victims may face from the criminal justice system, their families, their clergy members, or their employers serve only to compound their distress. However, when members of these institutions are taught some of the fundamentals of crisis reactions, as well as how to respond helpfully, the institutions often develop a more tolerant and supportive atmosphere in which to deal with the victim's problems. Some become powerful allies in the victim's slow process of healing. This, too, may be a benefit of the CRT, when the message reaches a large number of community members whose positions support the community's recovery efforts.

As this is being written, NOVA Crisis Response Teams have been welcomed in over twoscore communities in states of acute distress. Every case has been unique, and a few compelled the team to improvise in order to be of service, for example, when a team arrived at the site of a remote train crash and never found the local hosts who had invited them there.

In the authors' view, the creative ingenuity required of the typical CRT does not argue for a more flexible approach to the team members' core duties. On the contrary, it seems all the more important that different community members who have undertaken a training or debriefing by different members of a NOVA team should be able to pursue their plans together based on some common groundings and understandings.

Thus, to repeat at earlier point, NOVA aspires to conduct "graduate" training programs for experienced team members, not only to consider lessons that only those who have been to disasters are likely to develop but also to practice the basics of training and debriefing with one another.

While NOVA's "national teams" are likely to grow in number and expertise, the most dramatic growth in this field is of local crisis response (or "critical incident") teams. This growth is likely to transform the entire field of victim assistance in the United States over the next decade. Instead of seeing crisis counselors working with certain victims, crisis responders working with a different group of victims, and mental health professionals assisting yet a third such group, it seems more likely, for example, that the crisis counselor called to a crime scene at an apartment will note that many of the residents of the building are having a crisis reaction to the event. Therefore the counselor will invite a small team to come in to help them deal with those stresses. Just as the new alliance of crisis counselors with qualified therapists is increasing the depth of services, so does the existence of the local CRT promise to increase the reach of services beyond the immediate victim to others profoundly affected by what happened.

It is far too soon to say that a seamless continuum of services is ready to respond skillfully in all the known traumas in any community in the United States to the victims, the victims' loved ones, and to others significantly affected by the traumatic event. Yet that ideal is much closer to realization with the development of the Crisis Response Team model and its extraordinary usefulness in the alleviation of communitywide suffering.

19

Relocation: Treatment of a Family Crisis

Judith Halpern

INTRODUCTION

Moving day. Families watch the moving truck arrive. Labels marked "handle with care" cover containers. Moving means excitement, opportunity, new experiences, or, on the other hand, moving means images of crying kids, frazzled adults, isolation, loneliness, and loss.

Moving does not meet the "A" criterion for a traumatic stressor event. In America, everyone or his or her ancestors moved to get here. According to the Census Bureau, one in five Americans move each year, and the average American female moves eleven times in her lifetime (Cutler, 1989). Thus, moving is more of a normative than an unexpected event. This very fact, however, leads to denial and minimizing of the myriad losses and stresses of a move.

Individuals and families describing their moving experiences frequently focus on the positive aspects of moving; people who have experienced multiple moves often focus on the ease with which they have learned to accomplish this task. However, if one listens carefully to what is being said or notices hidden connections, moves take on a more disruptive aura.

One young woman reported that as a military "brat" she loved moving until the move from England to the United States when she was twelve years old. She described how her mother and siblings stood in the airport crying their eyes out when it was time to leave. Her father, however, was looking forward to the transfer and seemed unaware of the other family members' pain. Years later, when she complained that he never talked to her, he said, "But you haven't been nice to me since you were twelve." Neither was aware of the concurrence between the move she hated and the age he named.

This anecdote reflects a beginning recognition of many of the traumatic aspects of moves. First, moving is more disruptive than individuals expect, even when it is a relatively short-distance move, within a five-mile range. Place and space organize relationships and interactions. Second, moves appear to be cumulative in impact. The comment "I liked to move. The moves were wonderful experiences until we moved to [a particular place]" is fairly common to hear in clinical practice. This phenomenon appears related to issues of cumulative loss. A client may report, "I didn't have the energy to make new friends again." Third, the impact of a move is intensified during times of particular developmental sensitivity or self-awareness. Moves in the junior high school years and in the senior year of high school are especially emotionally disruptive; moving pre-schoolers is likely to produce physical illness or sudden disruptions in the developmental process, for example, night terrors or separation anxiety. Fourth, women are more troubled by relocation than men.

Relocation, whether five miles away to a new house or halfway across the world to a new job, is a crisis for each family member. Issues of distance moved, the voluntary versus forced nature of the move, opportunities available in the new location, the amount of warning the family had prior to the move, the history of the family, and the family's developmental stage have different meaning for different members of the family. To a child, no move is volitional. To a pre-schooler, much of the preparation for a move may not be integrated cognitively. Therefore, from the child's perspective, he or she is unprepared. To a teenager, no opportunity counters the fears and pain of losing friends and attempting to make new ones. To a trailing spouse, the career cost of repeatedly leaving a job may not be recognized until peers have moved into management (department chairman or administration), and the spouse is still working at the same level as he or she was twenty years earlier. In these resulting losses, disruptions and transitions accumulate to create family crises. However, conceptualizing moves as crises can lead the family members to expect a rapid resolution.

Crisis literature presents a four- to six-week framework for the process while normal adaptation to a move requires much longer. While it is generally believed that it takes two years to adapt after a move, McCollum's (1990) study found that only one-third of her subjects felt at home within their new homes at the two-year follow-up.

Conceptualizing a move as a crisis, however, helps to clarify the intervention framework. A crisis represents both a danger and an opportunity. The format for intervention focuses on helping clients restore coping techniques that were impaired when the clients' normal adaptation failed under the pressure of overwhelming stress: "The intervention process in this approach emphasizes brief, prompt, intensive helping activity in the immediate crisis situation, so as to restore functional equilibrium for individuals and groups" (Siporin, 1975, pp. 147–48).

Moving choices and adjustments are complicated by national history and personal myths, from Horace Greeley's "Go west young man" to the more personal crediting of our freedom, prosperity, and, sometimes, our very lives to our ancestors' decisions to move to this country. Early immigrants relied upon systems of support and acculturation processes to survive relocation. The emotional impact of leaving home, for example, to a nineteen-year-old with a newborn in arms, who may never see home or parents again, is rarely mentioned. National and family myths told us that moving is an opportunity, a challenge, and an adventure. When stories are told of Grandma missing the boat, no one wonders about the ambivalence of the victim about the move and the influence of those mixed feelings on events.

Hester Street (1975) is a film about Jewish immigrants on the lower East Side of New York City. When the heroine refuses to give up her wig and all it represents, the refusal is framed as a conflict between her husband's pressure on her to adapt and her wish to maintain her religious identity rather than an attempt to maintain continuity of identity and connection with her homeland. As a result of this communal denial, advice given about moving generally focuses on adaptation, to the exclusion of mourning.

As a consequence, clinicians see people who are in total denial about the meaning of the moves, even recent moves, in their lives. Instead, they expect rapid resolution of their discomfort. The clients' denial is reactive to the community's denial and avoidance. Treatment of this type of disorder requires resolution of the mourning process in order to free energy for the adaptational tasks, the social denial, and the clients' need to see themselves as flexible, creative, independent, and a good sport. The inability of clients to see what they do not expect or want to see can complicate treatment.

As an example, a twelve-year-old boy was brought to therapy because he was resisting school attendance, as well as team practice for well-loved sports. Instead, he was haunting his parents' footsteps. The family had moved forty miles to a new location the previous summer, and this boy, the youngest child and a talented athlete, had failed to make friends in the new community.

His lack of friends was seen as a major problem by the parents; the young man, though, shrugged it off. "I can make friends if I want to," he said. In brief therapy he got in touch with, and ventilated, his anger at his parents for moving him from a home and community he loved for reasons unimportant to him. Once his anger was expressed and validated, he ceased to express it defensively and proceeded to make friends, returning to his previous level of separation and individuation. To ensure this resolution, the therapist needed to recognize that the anger was flowing from the unresolved mourning process and to facilitate its expression.

It is not surprising that this young man was angry or that he was unable or unwilling to share his anger directly with his family. He may not have trusted others' abilities to tolerate his feelings. Many parents become defensive when their children express anger. Also, children rarely have the necessary skills to express angry feelings in appropriate and acceptable ways. Quick resolution of the situation occurred because the symptoms erupted within months of the move and were easily recognized as being related to it.

When very young children develop symptoms three or more months after a move (e.g., when a twenty-one-month-old develops night terrors), the symptoms may not be connected by caretaker or consultant to the disruption. Therefore simple remedial or preventive steps, such as arranging the new bedroom to be just like the old one, are not instituted. When two preschoolers cannot go to sleep in their new separate bedrooms the first night in the new home, many parents may recognize the trauma signals and even put the children together until they have adjusted to the new move. When these symptoms are separated in time from the physical move, they are not as easily connected or appropriately responded to. Time lapse in symptom formation also occurs in adults, complicating assessment and intervention.

REVIEW OF THE LITERATURE

An analysis of literature examining the impact of moving reveals a major conflict in the conclusions. Some articles and studies simply assume that moving is disruptive and proceed to analyze the reasons for the disruptions (Meyer, 1987; Seidenberg, 1973). Additional research conducted from a sociological perspective minimizes the disruptive impact of moving with statements such as, "Modern life can provide community without propinquity. Technology has lowered the barriers posed by distance" (Fisher, 1987, p. 186). Excluding from this study moves of more than fifty miles and interviewing one adult member of each household, with preference given to a male adult when available, Fisher (1987) reported that 39 percent of moves were involuntary. This study concluded that most moves were motivated by a search for better housing and that most participants were pleased by the results. Rossi's (1980) study, based on a questionnaire format, reached similar conclusions.

Two recent studies utilized a more open-ended approach. McCollum (1990) interviewed a series of women referred to her in sequence by Welcome Wagon (a national organization representing retail interests that greets new members of the community) several times over a two-year period. Wertsch (1991) interviewed eighty military children several times. Neither researcher used a random sample or a control group, so it is possible that the findings were skewed. However, subjects revealed a depth and intensity of feelings in sharp contrast to the findings of the Rossi (1980) and Fisher (1987) studies.

McCollum (1990), addressing the response of female adults to relocation, was surprised by the lack of preparation for the move by the women. The lack of welcoming response to the mover by the receiving community, the length of time that adjustment took, and the subjects' self-denigration for their difficulties were seen as reasons for difficulties adjusting to the new community.

The myth that moving is an exciting, stimulating opportunity apparently interfered with the ability of these highly educated, sophisticated women to examine basic issues such as the cost of housing, the job market, and the climate in the new community before they decided to move. For many subjects, the move was precipitated by the spouses' job opportunities or training needs. Therefore the issue of women's identity and obligations, in the biblical sense of "whither thou goest," may have clouded their judgments or perceptions. However, some of these women relocated for their own careers; these subjects also failed to examine the relevant issues adequately.

McCollum (1990) also found that in spite of the general belief in the relocation industry that it takes two years to adjust to a move, only one-third of the women in the study felt at home after two years. The questions of what "home" means and what it takes to feel "at home" are, of course, crucial to understanding the impact of relocation. Durkheim's (1973) concept of anomie, a state or condition of individuals or society characterized by a breakdown or absence of social norms or values (as in the case of uprooted people), summarizes the experience of these subjects.

McCollum (1990) suggested that relocation is actually a euphemism for dislocation and concluded that feeling at home means that the house has become an extension of self and an expression of self and that home is a parental representation, enfolding, safe, strong, and warm and a realm of mastery. Women feel shame, guilt, and anxiety about the inner turmoil they experience after they move. The pain described related to their loneliness and isolation. Two-thirds of the movers were unable to make new close friends within two years. They reported, "No one knows who I am" or "I don't know who I am." They felt invisible because they lacked complex networks involving meaningful roles and supports. Thus McCollum (1990) commented that the opposite of love is not hate; it is indifference.

Wertsch (1991) focused on the long-term impact of multiple military moves on children. Relevant questions for these children are "Where are you from?"— a question her subjects could not answer comfortably—and "How many different schools did you attend from kindergarten through high school?" The children had a sense of rootlessness and exhibited progressively increasing intense difficulties. These subjects did not necessarily fight moves as children. First, they had no choice. Second, they were propagandized to be positive and upbeat. Third, for some at least, moves were a way to avoid responsibility and commitment. They did not have to worry about the long-term consequences of social difficulties or a bad reputation; next year they would be somewhere else. They also learned to be chameleons. Adults frequently speak of the flexibility and creativity children develop in coping with moves. It may be, if Wertsch's (1991) research were replicated, that multiple family moves during childhood are predictors of difficulties with responsibility, commitment, and intimacy in adulthood.

The crucial question is, What is the impact of relocation on identity and productivity? For persons who relocate in pursuit of their career (either for a job or for training), vocational identity is, in part, transported. Social credentials for the trailing spouse or child, however, are not transferable. Seidenberg (1973) reported one woman's inability to find volunteer work in her new parish after a move of only one mile and a half. Another woman reported her children were still complaining about a move across the road, three years after the fact. The transferability, or lack thereof, of credentials, identity, and relationships is therefore a frequent concern.

Research investigating stress and coping with stress also examines the impact of moving. Moving, as change in residence, gets only 20 points on Holmes and Rahe's (1967) "Social Readjustment Scale." The Social Readjustment Scale assigns point values to various positive and negative life changes based on cross-cultural research as to how people experience the earlier impact of various changes. Cumulative scores of 150 points within one year indicate a fifty-fifty chance of illness, and a score of 300 points or more means a 90 percent chance of illness and injury. An individual might accumulate a total number of points in the year the family relocates in the 250- to 300-point range. These numbers are confirmed when participants in relocation workshops complete the scale.

Any approach to resolving the crisis precipitated by a relocation decision must incorporate information and research on dealing with stress. Popular magazines or newspapers constantly provide advice on managing stress. Briefly, those in crisis are advised to acknowledge feelings, share concerns, seek information, get help, exercise, eat properly, distract themselves, find things to laugh about, maintain perspective, keep busy, and follow expert advise. However, this advice is very hard to follow when feeling helpless and isolated or humiliated by the feelings of incompetence that a new house and new community evoke.

The problem of helping children cope with the stress is compounded by adult feelings of guilt and/or responsibility for the child's discomfort. In recent studies of children Coles & Dugan (1989) found that the skills children need to develop resiliency are the ability to tolerate frustration, so that they can continue efforts that may not be immediately gratifying; social skills that allow them to relate to, and locate, both peer and adult nonfamilial resources for education and support; the ability to recognize the limits of personal problems and responsibilities so that energy is not drained in caretaking others; and the ability to acquire, maintain, and pursue long-term goals.

CLINICAL PICTURE

The client who is reacting to the unresolved crisis evoked by relocation appears in the clinician's office in two different guises. The client may state directly, "We moved last year, and I'm still upset and [or] angry about the move." This client may be consciously sad, angry, anxious, or fearful and relate the symptoms to the issues of the relocation, consciously linking the discomfort and the household move. Such presenting symptoms may also appear in a child or in the marital relationship.

A forty-five-year-old woman named Susan sought help for mild depressive symptoms that she associated with a move from southern California to New York City. She was married and the mother of two grammar school children. Her husband's employer had terminated the company's operations in California, and he had a choice to take severance pay or transfer to New York. Susan loved California and had a perfect, professionally satisfying, well-paid part-time job there. She lived in a town where she had a network of supportive friends. However, her husband's health was fragile, and a period of unemployment might debilitate him. He promised that if they moved to New York, his increased income would permit her to become a full-time mother. They moved.

The family was unable to find affordable housing even on her husband's new salary. Susan was upset by the differences in structure of her children's new school. She had difficulty sleeping, lost her appetite, and was discouraged about her new home.

Susan knew she missed her old home. However, her focus on solving her housing problems (they were renting temporarily), on the issue of whether or not she would have to work, and on adapting to her new home was interfering with the incomplete mourning for her old home and all its meaning. The process was intensified by the loss of her own mother in early adulthood. The need to grieve for her lost home reopened wounds related to her mother's death. Susan therefore resisted the work and needed support and interpretation to tolerate the pain.

The second presentation of an unresolved moving crisis involves a client who has no idea that his or her current discomfort is related to a move. For example, a family presented for help with their young adult son's failure to get a job after finishing college. It quickly became apparent that the young man was drinking excessively and met the criteria for alcoholism, while the parental couple was in a state of constant conflict in which the wife "nagged and bitched," in his words, and the husband was "lazy and irresponsible," in her words. The family had moved to Washington, D.C., from New England when the son was a preschooler. Father had felt fortunate to "land" a government job with security and regular pay raises. The family moved. However, the mother had been born and bred in New England, and her parents, sister, aunts, and cousins, who were her major social network, still lived there. She missed them when she moved and resented her husband for taking her away from them. These feelings increased as he withdrew in response to her anger. The clinical task of helping her work through the anger and pain from the move that had happened twenty years earlier was long and slow. Gradually, this work, combined with the son's alcohol treatment, resulted in improvement for all family members.

INTERVENTION AND TREATMENT

Relocation meets the criteria for a stressful life cycle change, which may become a clinical crisis for some families. Crises can lead either to mastery and ego growth by increasing an individual's coping repertoire or to failure and the impairment of functioning. When the client is in crisis, the indicated approach includes (1) rapid intervention, (2) diagnosis of the precipitating cause of the dysfunction and of the extent of the disruption of functioning, (3) assessment of the most pressing aspect of the situation on which to focus, (4) establishing specific goals with the client for the work to be done together, and (5) implementation of change by defining and completing tasks that enable the client to learn new coping skills. The client and the clinician can then review and assess the progress, enhancing the client's self-esteem, by reinforcing the view of self as competent and effective. It is important for the clinician to recognize the disruptive effects moving has on the family and individual functioning and to offer support, education, and guidance, as well as more traditional dynamic or cognitive interventions.

The stress of a move requires both the individual and the family as a unit to work through the loss the move represents and to mobilize resources and coping strategies for reintegrating in the new community. Denial of the losses or failure to mourn the lost home and attachments can drain the energy required to adapt to a new location. The mourning process can be viewed as a series of stages: denial, anger, bargaining, depression, and acceptance. The cost of moving for most people is high. The need to connect to a community and to be known to others and affirmed by them is great. Feelings of inadequacy and insecurity occur when the systems of coping with our physical environment are disrupted by a move and feelings of competence are threatened.

The active stage of a crisis is four to six weeks in duration. This time constraint does not mean that the transitional tasks of the relocation process are resolved so quickly; instead, it means that when a crisis in functioning is precipitated by the move, the crisis stage itself lasts a few weeks. However, it appears that reestablishing homeostasis after a move takes the average person more than two years (McCollum, 1990). In practice, many cases coming to the clinician's attention involve treatment of a transitional process that has become stuck, usually in one of the stages of the mourning process.

The immobilized client is defensively fixated in a particular style of response and must be helped to be ready to give up the particular defense that has become dysfunctional. For example, the client may be in denial and therefore fail to recognize the connection between the symptoms and the losses, or a client may be in a rage that makes him or her unwilling to resolve the issue. The goal of therapy is not necessarily to resolve all the issues raised by a move but rather to be sure that those impediments to the client, whether individual, couple, or family, that inhibit working through the process independently are removed. Failure to address issues of loss and reintegration has long-term consequences.

Intervention Issues

The first issue is to help the client identify losses and disruptions caused by the move. Frequently, the mourning process has gotten stuck; getting that process back on track leads to a fairly rapid resolution of the clinical crisis that has temporarily overwhelmed the person's coping capacity. McCollum (1990) commented that subjects frequently criticized themselves for their difficulties, saying: "Why am I having such a hard time? Everyone moves." Universalizing the response and helping clients identify the multiple stresses they are experiencing are enormously helpful.

A second treatment goal is to help clients acknowledge how stressful the experience of moving was and to teach them stress management techniques. Helping clients find the energy to understand and use the techniques outlined in the popular literature on stress management becomes part of the intervention plan. Clients contract to complete tasks that include daily exercise, eating well-balanced meals, and going to see a funny movie. Tasks worked on during the therapy include development of assertiveness training skills, accepting the reality of the move, framing the move in a way that enhances the client's ability to accept it, and defining adaptational tasks that can be acted on effectively and immediately.

The following community reactions to relocation can also increase the pressures on the family: the social denial of loss; the receiving community's unavailability to new families; the belief that moving is not a big deal; the pressures on the family to be positive and "patriotic" about the move, particularly in corporate and military transfers; and intolerance of members of the receiving community for nostalgia about the former home because expression of the longing for that home is perceived as a devaluing of the current residence.

Educating clients about the impact of the disruptions of multiple moves is often necessary. This may include a review of the history of relationships through multiple moves and how the moves had been viewed. A woman who makes multiple moves may have paid a price in security and connectedness for her opportunities and experiences. She may have become tired of reaching out to people, leading to withdrawal, isolation, and depression, which interfere with competence and skill acquisition. Cumulative impacts on coping skills require carefully timed interventions, in order to help a client mobilize the resources to mourn the losses and acquire new skills for adapting to the community.

A third goal in intervention focuses on the receiving community. McCollum (1990) found that those people who adapted best to a new community had social sponsors in that environment. However, few people are fortunate enough to find sponsors.

In a similar vein, neighbors and colleagues may view new arrivals as poor emotional risks since they may be there only temporarily. They may also be reluctant to get involved with people who appear needy and have reduced competence. Though the residents may want to be needed, they may fear being overwhelmed. Movers are advised not to compare their new communities unfavorably with their past ones and to put on their happy face so people will want to have them around. Faking happiness inhibits connections with members of the new community because the resulting relationships may not feel authentic and nurturing. Small support groups of six to ten members are appropriate resources, but they are hard to find. These groups facilitate expression of feelings and support, meet frequently, and have a structure that enhances safety and openness. Treatment also must take into consideration the difference in social norms and styles in different parts of the country and around the world. Adults who have relocated across regional lines may always feel as if they are speaking a "foreign language" socially.

Helping children handle the stress of moving involves teaching many of the same techniques. In addition, however, the therapist needs to evaluate the child's ability level in the following four areas: social skills; ability to establish and pursue long-term goals; ability to tolerate frustration; and ability to establish appropriate boundaries in dealing with emotional problems. According to Coles and Dugan (1989), these skills are essential if a child is to survive a crisis. Assessing these skills, recognizing that their development may be impacted by the move itself, and providing appropriate interventions to assure that their development gets back on track, if necessary, are part of appropriate treatment.

Treatment

Treatment of the stress reaction involves identification and modification of the defenses that the person is using to ward off the pain of loss and the cultural denial that supports these defenses. These defenses are frequently dissociative in nature and require specialized knowledge of the dissociative disorders to facilitate effective intervention. Working through the mourning process related to these losses and the development or strengthening of the coping skills needed for adaptation to the new community complete the treatment.

Education about the meaning of associated losses and the function of the symptoms as attempts to protect the ego from pain is required. This education must be combined with empathy and support, as well as respect for the individual's defenses. Theoretically, disruptions in functioning in a healthy person faced with the stress of relocation should respond to short-term intervention based on crisis theory. However, it is not uncommon to find historically that these issues were addressed inadequately in previous losses. The evocation of those accumulated, unresolved issues complicates the mourning process. In these cases, treatment may require a more extended period as the defenses against the pain of loss are explored and are repeatedly worked through, as each layer of memory is worked through. The length of treatment depends upon the client's individual history and the rigidity and degree of dysfunction of the defenses.

Once those losses have been acknowledged and worked through, the client is ready to turn the emotional energy previously invested in containing pain, fear, and anger toward forming new attachments and establishing a new role in the new community. Assessment of the extent of the client's interpersonal skills, the strength of the adaptive ego, and the history of previous social integration helps to determine the form and extent of intervention needed to facilitate this part of the process. A client who has functioned successfully in multiple settings and who was immobilized by cumulative unresolved issues that erupted in mid-life will need less help with the adaptation process than a client who shows a history of gradual withdrawal and isolation that has interfered with friendships, work, school, and community involvement for many years.

To summarize, treatment is based upon a knowledge of crisis intervention, ego psychology, and the dynamics of dissociative processes used in coping with overwhelming trauma, an aspect of ego psychology. Understanding the individual's history, defenses, ego strength, and goals also helps to determine the exact design and length of the intervention.

CONCLUSIONS

Relocation is a major disruption in the development of the individual, impacting on identity, competence, relationships, career, and education. The unwillingness of a community to acknowledge this fact has led to the diminution of rituals for welcoming newcomers and a failure to develop and facilitate the development of new structures. Churches, community centers, women's centers, and schools could offer newcomers' support groups and help establish sponsoring families for new families or individuals. Both the military officer and corporate executive need to be educated to use support resources for employees and their families as means to enhance productivity and therefore improve scores on performance reviews.

When clinicians are unaware of the impact of a single move and the cumulative impact of multiple moves, the effectiveness of an intervention with appropriate treatment can be lessened. The importance of place and home to the human animal, though not easily defined, is crucial to individual functioning, as is the importance of belonging and community. Relocation can be costly and should not be undertaken cavalierly. However, when a move does occur, the resulting disruptions need to be addressed as quickly and as clearly as possible.

20

The Association of Flight Attendants Employee Assistance Program Responds to Workplace Trauma: A Dynamic Model

Barbara Feuer

INTRODUCTION

Traumatic events have always occurred in the workplace, and their consequences have affected countless workers. However, the sequelae of work-related trauma have been seriously explored only in the last ten years. Furthermore, although employee assistance programs (EAPs) are responsible for assisting employees experiencing emotional behavioral problems that affect their abilities to do their jobs adequately, the EAP field has only recently recognized the need to address this critical issue (Yandrick, 1990).

In 1981, the author made a presentation at an Association of Flight Attendants (AFA) Safety Training and met several flight attendants who had been in serious critical incidents, including crashes that had resulted in injuries and fatalities. Although these incidents had occurred many years earlier, when those involved began to discuss their experiences during an informal presentation, it was painfully obvious that most of them still had emotional wounds that had never healed; they were literally walking wounded. Because these survivors had received no professional mental health assistance in the aftermath of their traumatic encounters, many issues still remained unresolved. Tragically, they continued to be victimized by memories of their traumas. Yet, this maladaptive outcome was avoidable. If they had received the appropriate emotional support they needed, their symptoms certainly would have been minimized or prevented altogether (Farberow & Gordon, 1979; Hartsough & Myers, 1985; Mitchell, 1988).

By 1987, the need to integrate a workplace trauma intervention plan into existing EAP services could no longer be ignored. After a Pacific Southwest Airlines crash (in which all on board, including three AFA members, perished), the process of operationalizing a well-defined EAP response to workplace trauma (aircraft emergencies/critical incidents) for AFA members began (Feuer, 1987).

At the first EAP training following the crash, the EAP staff initiated an informal needs assessment by asking participants what could be done to help them more constructively to proactively prepare for critical incidents. Their answer was unanimous. They wanted a how-to resource manual to serve two primary purposes: (1) to explain what to do when a critical incident happened and then (2) to explain how to do what needed to be done. In addition, they wanted this primer to include information that would (1) help them to prepare in advance to respond most effectively and (2) include specific guidelines to help them assist members in need, both at the scene and in the aftermath of the disaster.

RATIONALE

The decision to incorporate a workplace intervention plan within the EAP's delivery of services was motivated by a number of unanswered questions. What are the effects—immediate and long-term—of extraordinarily stressful events on victim/survivors and those who help them? What kinds of interventions are most effective to empower those who have been traumatized so that they recover and emerge as healthy survivors? In a comprehensive review of disaster literature, Baum, Fleming, and Singer (1983) inferred that technological hazards are more likely to have long-term mental health consequences than are natural incidents (Solomon, 1989).

Also, the importance of early recognition and treatment of post-traumatic stress responses has been documented extensively in work with victims of rape and violent crimes, survivors of natural disasters, and incest survivors (Kivens, 1980). Early intervention after the initial traumatic event can prevent or significantly lessen the post-traumatic effect on those involved. The literature emphatically supports the author's hypothesis that crisis intervention efforts, including critical incident debriefings that occur as soon as possible after the traumatic event, minimize human suffering and later disabilities, as well as medical, treatment, and legal costs (Dunning, 1990; Barnett-Queen & Bergmann, 1988; Lawson, 1987; Mitchell, 1983). If unacknowledged, what begins as a natural human reaction to a life-threatening external event can lead to limiting, often debilitating interpersonal and intrapsychic response patterns (Burgess and Holmstrom, 1976).

Over the past few years, there has been an increasing awareness across a wide variety of occupational settings that certain events that occur at the worksite can have a significant psychological impact on workers. A variety of health hazards exist at the workplace that can result in employees' experiencing feelings and reactions typical of victimization responses (Lawson, 1987). Business and labor can no longer afford to ignore the effects of trauma in their workplace, as it rarely goes away by itself. The costs in morale, attendance, sick leave, personnel turnover, productivity, and profits are simply too great.

The impact of workplace events on members/employees and work organizations is not fully understood, and victim/survivors in many instances continue not to be taken seriously by their employers, unions, workers' compensation boards, or their EAPs. The situation is often compounded when a workplace injury neither results in dramatic physical impairment nor produces significant medical symptoms. Too often in these less serious critical incidents, the emotional impact upon those involved is minimized by health care providers, the work organization, family members, and frequently those who are directly affected (Lawson, 1987).

Directly impacted workers are not the only ones affected. Coworkers are quite clearly affected by the realization that they, too, could have been harmed. This is certainly true for flight attendants, who are a cohesive, kin-like subculture (Volpe, 1982).

There is a surprising lack of research in the area of workplace trauma intervention (Dunning, 1990). A workplace trauma response is operationalized via trauma intervention training for peer counselors. The model builds upon already existing crisis intervention skills and, taking the process several steps further, gives peer counselors resources to:

• Proactively prepare for the eventuality of a critical incident;
• Assess the level of intervention necessary when an incident occurs;
• Respond appropriately through effective intervention strategies, including formal and informal debriefings, one-on-one crisis counseling, education and information dissemination, and advocacy; and
• Follow up with victim/survivors after the situation has stabilized.

The model also addresses the critical, but often overlooked, issue of helping the helpers and secondary victimization.

PROBLEM STATEMENT

The challenge was to develop a trauma intervention prototype that would meet the needs of EAP committee members, who must respond in the aftermath of critical incidents for the AFA, which represents 33,000 flight attendants from eighteen airlines, from large carriers like United Airlines and USAir, to small regionals like Henson and Air Wisconsin. Among the eighteen, not one management group had taken the time necessary to formalize an emergency response protocol for the most directly involved employees—the flight attendants and pilots. On the other hand, the Association of Flight Attendants had responded to aircraft emergencies in instances involving its members since it began operations in 1972; the EAP has been directly involved since 1982.

Some critics believe that airlines are generally more concerned about what would happen if the flying public knew that flight attendants were traumatized after their involvement in critical incidents. It often appears their primary concern was the fear that passengers would choose to fly another airline. Ironically, based on numerous conversations with the author in the course of writing the manual, flight attendants have reported that despite any trauma they experienced as a result of involvement in a critical incident, their experiences have made them more careful, vigilant, and aware on the job, rather than less so.

Butcher and Hatcher (1988) recommended that psychological intervention programs be integrated into existing airport disaster programs. They also reported that the airline crash response personnel they interviewed, regardless of how they handled their disaster roles, all wanted more training and on-site psychological consultation. This finding underscored the need for a well-planned and organized emergency response plan after a critical incident.

Although the complete prevention of traumatic incidents at the work site is unattainable, the goal must be the prevention of maladaptive behavioral outcomes—for those directly involved and for the work organization as a whole—simply because there is no emergency response plan in place. These sequelae must be avoided, particularly within a high-risk work environment like the airline industry.

The EAP emergency response protocol was developed to maximize the goal of providing the best help possible to those directly involved after a critical incident, whether they be witnesses, the general membership, or family members. Such a complex, multidimensional undertaking demands the input of many different people at various levels of a work organization: labor, management, the employee assistance program staff, and employees themselves.

Most workplace trauma intervention efforts usually focus on the demands of the critical incident, leaving little time for consideration of anything other than the physical well-being of the involved members, their families, and the flight attendant group within the directly impacted base (Dunning, 1990). Generally, little or no consideration is given to the potential psychological injuries of those involved as part of the intervention effort. Most companies are wary of any discussion that suggests job-related duties and conditions might produce psychological injury to workers (Dunning, 1990), including those directly involved, as well as those who were part of the emergency response team. Figley (1983) described a reaction known as secondary victimization; persons close to the victim (emergency response teams) may suffer signs and symptoms similar to those of the victim.

DESIGNING A SOCIAL ACTION MODEL

The focus of this chapter is the impact of traumatic events in the workplace. Although first-aid kits and fire extinguishers are regarded as essential safety equipment, little or no support is available for mental injuries resulting from a critical incident. Yet these injuries are just as much the result of the traumatic event as are physical injuries.

It often seems that not a week goes by without mention in the evening news of a near miss, an emergency evacuation, an aircraft malfunction, or worst of all, a crash. In the event of any of these aircraft emergencies, passenger safety is the flight attendant's primary responsibility. Each time a flight attendant reports for duty, more so now than ever, he or she confronts the possibility of being involved in a critical incident (Feuer, 1988). It is not difficult to see that the burden on the cabin crew can be significant, especially if there are any injuries or loss of life. These factors strongly support the need for the implementation of crisis response plans at the workplace.

The goal of crisis intervention is the reduction of mental disability and the promotion of people's capacities for dealing with crisis (Goldston, 1977; Hoff, 1984). Bloom (1979) described a model for organizing primary prevention efforts under this crisis perspective. This approach involves:

- Identification of the stressful event (in this case, the critical incident) and the persons experiencing the stressor (the affected population);
- Research into the harmful consequences of the event, with hypotheses about how to reduce harmful outcomes; and
- Research and evaluation of interventions aimed at reducing the harmful consequences.

In describing the characteristics of acute grief, Lindemann (1944) established the basic framework for defining the symptomatology of a crisis reaction:

- Psychological and physical distress triggered by stimuli that remind the victim of the trauma;
- Feelings of derealization and depersonalization;
- Preoccupation with images of the traumatic event;
- Feelings of guilt, hostility, and anger;
- Emotional distancing;
- Depression;
- Compulsion to talk about the event; and
- Dependency on those who could motivate the victim to action (support systems).

Caplan (1964) went one step further by associating the concept of homeostasis with crisis intervention. He contended that the human organism constantly endeavors to maintain a homeostatic balance with the outside environment. When this delicate balance is threatened by either physiological or psychological forces, the human organism engages in problem-solving activities designed to restore this delicate balance. In a crisis situation, however, the individual is faced with a problem that appears to have no immediate solution, hence the idea that a crisis is an upset of a steady state.

Rappaport (1965) defined a crisis as an upset of a steady state occurring when one finds herself or himself in a hazardous situation. She thus added to the definition of crisis by noting that the normal problem-solving mechanisms of the individual are not adequate to achieve a balanced state, thereby throwing the individual into disequilibrium. She also believed that the three related factors of a hazardous event (critical incident), a threat to life goals, and inability to respond with adequate coping mechanisms usually produced a state of crisis.

The Emergency Response Manual is loosely organized within this crisis framework and includes three primary components:

- Identification of the stressful event (in this case, aircraft emergencies),
- Study of the consequences of the traumatic events, and
- Recommendations for intervention strategies whose goals are to reduce the harmful consequences of the stressful event.

The model maps out an approach to deal with issues of sociological dimensions (the life and survival of the community in question under traumatic conditions), as well as issues of a psychological dimension (the survivor's long-term mental health response to post-traumatic stress).

At the microlevel, a better understanding of these two critical areas enables EAP committees to better comprehend the mental health/emergency response implications in the aftermath of a critical incident. This understanding is achieved by bridging basic community psychology concepts that address issues on the community, interpersonal, and intrapsychic levels. Thus, the recovery (intervention) environment is dealt with on macro/community, interpersonal/family-friends-workplace and micro/intrapsychic-individual levels (Lindy & Grace, 1985).

Education and training attempts to make the flight attendant community and the aviation industry more aware of the consequences of job-related trauma on their most important assets—their employees. *The Emergency Response Manual* focuses on a response model that incorporates not only social action strategies, but interpersonal approaches as well.

Peer Support

In her ethnography of the flight attendant subculture, Volpe (1982) found a strong sense of cohesiveness that goes beyond professional identity. Because this group, as in the case of police, fire fighters, and nurses, has a strong professional identity, it is especially affected when a critical incident occurs within its ranks. Their long-range problems (which emerge after the emergency phase of the crash) can be particularly debilitating if no effort is made to deal with the impact of the critical incident on the general flight attendant population (Lawson, 1989). Survivors often experience such chronic problems as withdrawal from employment, family life, or society, psychosomatic ailments, or habitual anxiety.

A key element of the model is the debriefing process (Mitchell 1983, 1988;

Barnett-Queen & Bergmann, 1988). This approach differs from the more traditional mental health approach, which tends to view the locus of responsibility
for dysfunction as residing within the individual. Mitchell (1988) hypothesized
that the debriefing process is most effective if built upon a foundation of existing
peer support. Workers are part of an organization that existed before the incident
and will exist after the event. Under these kinds of circumstances, an emergency
response effort after a critical incident represents an extension of the already
established mechanism for internal response to troublesome incidents (Gist,
1990).

Thus, participation in the routine events of any organization or community is
the foundation upon which an effective critical incident response is built. Post-
trauma intervention work is an extension of routine consultation and education
(EAP) services; it cannot be effective as a unique intervention reserved only for
the major catastrophe (Gist & Lubin, 1989).

The trauma intervention model extends core responsibilities of the EAP to
provide help to members and their families. AFA's peer referral EAP not only
effectively identifies and refers members in need of EAP services, it goes further
than other models in its inherent ability to support recovery (Feuer, 1988).

Microlevel Outreach

Mitchell and Trickett (1980) suggested the use of network analysis to enhance
mental health outreach efforts. This technique requires skills in linking individuals with community resources. These key peer counselor responsibilities include:

- Identifying trauma specialists who are available to assist during debriefings for involved
  flight attendants as well as the general flight attendant community and family members
  and
- Finding referral sources experienced in dealing with acute trauma, as well as loss and
  grief issues.

A substantial amount of time is devoted to the topic of case management at both
basic and advanced EAP trainings for peer counselors.

An explicit message communicated by the national EAP department to all
peer counselors is that they are in the best position to determine which clinicians
will work best with members of their own peer group. They receive in-depth
training in linking individuals to appropriate treatment resources. Delegating this
responsibility is a means of empowering them to feel a sense of ownership, that
it is really their program and they are its stewards. An implicit theme woven
throughout *The Emergency Response Manual* is the idea that a truly effective
response after any traumatic event is enhanced by empowering members to help
other members.

All new EAP peer counselors receive materials, including resource information about matching clients and clinicians and about community treatment resources, as well as interview questionnaires geared toward helping the peer counselors assess the appropriateness of treatment providers.

Macrolevel Outreach

As is the case with most other communities, the flight attendant community is not prepared for critical incidents. Members are required to participate in forty hours of emergency training when they are hired, as well as twelve hours of annual recurrent safety training (four hours on security issues and eight hours of hands-on instruction) mandated by the Federal Aviation Administration. Nonetheless, postcritical incident feedback from numerous involved members underscores the lack of psychological preparation.

Farberow and Gordon (1979) noted that flight attendant victim/survivors and the general flight attendant group need specific information about what happened in the aftermath of aircraft emergencies, as well as information about available services. Unfortunately, those in charge of corporate communications at the majority of member airlines appear to operate under the assumption that less is better and often delay transmittal of critical facts. Experienced EAP team members have noted that the inability to get accurate and clear information about the status of their coworkers and passengers encourages secondary traumatization among those directly involved and the flight attendant group in general.

The AFA leadership, at its headquarters in Washington, D.C., as well as in the field, comprises flight attendants who also experience some of the same ripple effect after a critical incident. Therefore, ferreting out details of exactly what happened and the status of the involved cabin crew members, as well as disseminating this important information to the membership and the media, often in the face of little cooperation from the airlines, has always been a top priority at AFA. (See Table 20.1).

ASSESSING THE SERIOUSNESS OF THE CRITICAL INCIDENT

Assessing the seriousness of a traumatic event is an important concern in developing an effective emergency response paradigm. Involvement in a critical incident affects each member in a unique and personal way. The manual therefore is designed to give EAP committee members the information they need to understand post-traumatic stress reactions within a contextual framework that takes into consideration vital preexisting, impact, and post-impact psychosocial factors.

When considering the seriousness of the critical incident, it is also helpful to consider the following (Lawson, 1987):

Table 20.1
Assessing the Appropriate Emergency Response

ASSESSING THE APPROPRIATE RESPONSE

	SERIOUS	LESS SERIOUS	LEAST SERIOUS
CRITICAL INCIDENT	● Crash ● Hijacking ● Bomb explosion ● Severe turbulence with injuries ● Aircraft malfunction with fatalities ● Natural disaster	● CPR/fatalities ● Evacuation ● Sabotage threat ● Abnormal abort ● Rapid decompression ● Turbulence with injuries ● Natural disaster ● Bankruptcies/ mergers/strikes ● Primary/secondary violence/threats *	● Turbulence ● Aircraft malfunction ● Planned preparation ● Bankruptcies/ mergers/strikes ● Primary/secondary violence/threats
INTERVENTION	At the site/domicile Formal Debriefings/ Crisis Counseling for: ● Involved flight attendants ● Family members (optional) ● General flight attendant group Systemwide: ● Committees in crew lounges ● Debriefings(optional) ● Emergency response resource materials available	At the domicile Formal/Informal Debriefings for: ● Involved flight attendants ● General flight attendant group (optional) Systemwide: ● Committees in crew lounges (optional) ● Emergency response resource materials available ● Informal debriefings (optional)	Within 24 hours contact: ● Involved flight attendants
EMERGENCY RESPONSE TEAM	At the site/domicile: ● Local/MEC EAP Chairs ● EAP committee ● Post-trauma specialist	Systemwide: ● EAP committees ● Post-trauma specialists (optional)	At the domicile: ● EAP committees
FOLLOW-UP	EAP committee ● For 1 year	EAP committee ● As needed	EAP committee ● As needed

* Robbery, homicide/suicide, sexual/physical assault.

- Did those involved experience the critical incident as a life-threatening one?
- Do they have feelings of betrayal by the employer?
- Do they feel able to change jobs or earn a comparable living in another setting?
- What is the past and present mental and psychosocial status of those involved?

These questions are also discussed in *The Emergency Response Manual*. Providing the answers enhances the effectiveness of peer counselors to identify accurately work-related traumatization and post-traumatic stress responses among those involved in critical incidents.

SOCIAL SUPPORT AS A MEDIATOR

Informal social support systems help individuals cope with stresses associated with crises. Such systems are more likely than formal service networks to be called upon for emotional support (Solomon, 1985). A victim's ability to recover is associated with the number of available nonkin support systems. The stronger these systems and the greater their number, the more likely it is that needed resources will be available to victim/survivors (Drabek & Key, 1976; Bolin & Trainer, 1978). Nonkin networks are also of value because they constitute a social medium through which emotional support is transmitted after a disaster (Solomon, 1985; Smith, 1983). The EAP response is a survivor-based, time-limited health care delivery program that is designed to function within the trauma membrane. Survivors join together with mental health professionals and indigenous caregivers (emergency response teams) to form these new service systems. Informal social networks offer advantages that professional intervention modes do not. Among these are personal involvement of network members and the voluntary and reciprocal nature of the interaction (Caplan, 1964).

Support systems or survivor networks take on special prominence in the recovery following a traumatic event. One function of the network is to safeguard the more traumatized members from harm; another is to promote psychic healing (Lindy & Grace, 1985). Because these functions are core peer counselor responsibilities, they are implicit within the design of the trauma intervention model described in *The Emergency Response Manual*.

INTERVENTION AND RECOVERY ISSUES

In general, research on victims usually focuses on one or more of four general areas of etiology, diagnosis, treatment, or prevention of long-term consequences of trauma (Solomon, 1985). The manual concentrates on prevention and treatment (intervention) in particular. The provision of crisis intervention assistance by peers as soon as possible after a traumatic event can prevent or significantly lessen the severity of later disturbances (Farberow and Gordon, 1979).

Lindy and Grace (1985) suggest that mental health professionals can take steps to strengthen and build social support networks after a disaster by training indigenous paraprofessionals and community gatekeepers to (1) detect the psychological effects of disaster exposure and (2) refer individuals with problems to mental health professionals. This is the guiding principle of the AFA EAP strategy. Peer counselors learn to recognize signs of problem behavior among their coworkers; learn to intervene when necessary; and learn to refer to the appropriate treatment professional or self-help group (Feuer, 1987).

The EAP staff recognized that the nature of social networks within the work environment is an important influence because of the sense of cohesiveness and sameness that transcends individual members (Volpe, 1982). They therefore retained a social anthropologist to study the flight attendant subculture. This author and staff then built upon this inherent social support dimension to design a model that acknowledged the importance of peers as potential change agents. The effectiveness of this approach is that peer pressure is the leverage for getting help and is a powerful reinforcer of healthier behaviors.

Intervention by peers (when those peers work closely with mental health professionals trained in trauma intervention) is an effective means to help those directly impacted, as well as the general work population (Farberow & Gordon, 1979; Mitchell, 1988). The fact that peers can easily put themselves in the shoes of the involved flight attendants enhances the potential effectiveness of the trauma intervention efforts. Peers have already established a sense of trust, empathy, and rapport—three integral elements of the helping process.

Critical incidents require major revisions in one's assumptions about the world. They host lasting, rather than transient, implications. When they occur abruptly, they are particularly disruptive (Parkes, 1988). Under these circumstances, social support systems that effectively provide stabilizing directions for adaptation can constitute a crucial "buffer" for those so affected (Cohen & Wills, 1985). "Buffering" is one of the primary responsibilities of the emergency response team immediately after a critical incident and a key function of the local EAP committee once the situation has somewhat stabilized. Flight attendants not only work together in a confined space but lodge, eat, and socialize with other crew members during rest periods. These combined personal, professional, and social relationships put peer EAP committee members in an ideal position not only to observe possible problems among their coworkers but to intervene effectively because they already function as "health experts in the workplace" (The AL-MACAN, 1986).

SPECIFIC INTERVENTION STRATEGIES

At the Macrolevel

In addition to recognizing and responding to the emotional sequelae of work-site trauma on an individual level, it is also important to focus on environmental variables and macrolevel interventions. Soldiers leave the war zone, and attempts are made to protect sexual assault victims from their attackers, but workers return to the work site (Lawson, 1987).

Fear reactions are minimized if frightening events can be predicted and if people can anticipate a measure of personal protection (Lawson, 1987). Providing job safety and health training for flight attendants is standardized within the airline industry, but it is often insufficient in terms of time and effort. Hands-on training, both when a flight attendant is hired and, subsequently, during yearly recurrent trainings, has been replaced by videotapes and self-directed learning at many airlines. Simulation activities and experiential exercises that enhance the learning curve immeasurably have been replaced by cheaper and less effective methods.

Identifying macrolevel interventions in the area of preventive mental health is particularly crucial since workers must return to the site of the traumatic event—figuratively and usually literally. To the extent that post-traumatic stress responses continue to be ignored and the need for environmental interventions is discounted in favor of an individual stress model, personal and interpersonal distress continues to result from occupational trauma (Lawson, 1987, 1989).

The EAP emergency response model attempts to counter this phenomenon in several ways:

- A key element of the emergency response is advance planning and preparation, which includes education and information dissemination to the membership about workplace trauma and its effects.

- Additionally, in the immediate aftermath of a crisis, one-on-one crisis counseling, informal and formal debriefings, and educational efforts seek to mitigate the impact by preparing those directly involved and others less directly involved as to what lies ahead, including potential problem areas.

- Finally, any workers who develop mental health problems in the aftermath of a critical incident are aware that there is a group of trained peers who can help on an ongoing basis.

At the Microlevel

In the aftermath of a traumatic event at the workplace, victim/survivors need a variety of services: crisis counseling, legal advice, information regarding workers' compensation benefits, and sometimes ongoing psychological intervention tailored to the individual's specific stress responses (Lawson, 1987). All of these services have been incorporated into the EAP response after a critical incident.

Often, victim/survivors do not initiate discussion about personal involvement in the critical incident, particularly if there has been no physical injury. However, if health care providers and employee assistance counselors approach every injury as a potential critical incident, the exact nature of the victim's response is more likely to emerge. When it is determined that an injury has been traumatic from the patient's perspective, many employees respond with relief to the direct discussion of the psychological effects of trauma (Lawson, 1987).

Use of a psychoeducational approach (crisis counseling, debriefings) gives individuals in crisis a sense of cognitive control. This technique also helps decrease the sense of guilt and isolation experienced by individuals with stress symptoms. Cognitive controls also act as a normalizing function, an important element in the recovery process.

Helping the Helpers

When a traumatic event occurs in the workplace, numerous EAP representatives who comprise the emergency response team arrive almost immediately. Although they are closely involved in efforts to work with the victim survivors, the membership, and the family members of those involved during the post-impact phase of the incident, little or no attention is paid to their emotional and physical needs. Emergency workers rush in to rescue, treat, and, in the case of the EAP emergency response team members, help and comfort victims. Many researchers have investigated the impact of these calamities on the victims, but few have studied the effect on workers (Hartsough & Myers, 1985). This critical issue would not be overlooked in planning and developing the EAP emergency response plan.

Disaster (job-related trauma) work presents significant emotional and physical challenges to emergency workers. Exposure to distressing sights and sounds, coupled with difficult working conditions, may lead to physical illness or emotional problems. It can also lead to "burnout," with the workers unhappy and unable to perform successfully.

When workers are given appropriate support in a work situation designed to accomplish organizational goals while at the same time addressing human needs, they usually find their lives enriched by this work and are better able to maintain a sensitive and caring attitude toward the victims. This premise underscores the importance of addressing the issue of helping the helpers. Not including information on this critical area in the development of a response to workplace trauma results in an incomplete and inadequate response plan. Critical incidents, resulting from natural disaster or human-induced violence or negligence, are most frequently described by the number of lives lost or physical injuries suffered. The focus of the event is generally on physical damage, evidenced in pictures of destruction, fire, explosion, rubble, bodies, and so on. To most organizations responsible for the solution of critical incidents, the parameters of the event lie between the first person threatened with injury and the last possible victim survivor recovered and the cause of the event investigated (Dunning, 1988, 1990).

The primary components of the AFA EAP workplace trauma intervention model include crisis counseling, medical assistance, peer support and advocacy, and follow-up and referral, when necessary. Subsequent to a critical incident, resources, both fiscal and staff, are chronically stretched beyond the point anticipated by pro-active preplanning efforts (Dunning, 1990).

EAP peer counselors also work full-time as flight attendants and must deal with their own family and marital problems, as well as the emotional and psychological issues that impact members and their families. When a critical incident occurs, they are nonetheless overwhelmed, despite specific training in workplace trauma, crisis intervention, and communication skills.

CONCLUSIONS AND RECOMMENDATIONS

Problem anticipation and strategic planning are essential elements in any successful work organization. Enlightened companies are well aware of the importance of having an emergency procedures manual and appropriately involve occupational nurses and physicians in the development of the medical response aspects of the plan (White & Hatcher, 1988). Unfortunately, two important features of workplace trauma response have been largely neglected: (1) the psychological response to trauma and (2) the problems created by the occurrence of a critical incident at the workplace. A modest investment of time to incorporate a trauma response plan that addresses the emotional needs of workers and their families is one of the best investments a company can make.

EAP committee members usually have minimal training in the helping fields prior to joining the EAP. Yet frequently, they find themselves dealing with difficult and overwhelming problem situations. Unlike most mental health professionals who can choose their clients and the types of problems with which they want to work, EAP committee members do not have such an option. Thus an implicit goal of *The Emergency Response Manual* is to support peer counselors as they respond to a wide range of critical incidents at work. Support comes from this step-by-step guide, which includes information needed to:

- Proactively prepare for the eventuality of a critical incident;
- Determine the most appropriate intervention(s), based on the severity of the incident and the response of the cabin crew;
- Respond effectively through the implementation of a range of intervention strategies, including informal and formal debriefings, one-on-one crisis counseling, education and information dissemination, and advocacy;
- Follow up with victim/survivors after the situation has stabilized; and
- Recognize symptoms of burnout/helper stress and take steps to counteract their potential negative impact.

The manual also guarantees, as much as possible, a consistency in terms of the breadth and scope of the emergency response after critical incidents involving AFA members. It provides a level of quality assurance heretofore missing by giving EAP committees a blueprint for an effective emergency response protocol, including a breakdown of the kinds of critical incidents to which the EAP responds; the most appropriate and effective intervention strategies; suggestions for emergency response team composition; and, finally, a time frame for effective follow-up.

This model relies upon peers as change agents. Other helper groups are able to utilize the manual as a basis for the design of trauma intervention models that meet the needs of the populations they serve. The paradigm of the model has wide applicability for work settings that are non-hierarchical and less unsupervised (e.g., teachers, nurses, police, fire fighters, lawyers, physicians).

When there is an aircraft emergency, whether it be a sudden loss of altitude, serious turbulence, or a hijacking, it is never just the passengers who are affected. Members of the cockpit crew are left to confront their own demons while struggling to land the plane safely. But the members of the cabin crew are forced to be with 50, 100, or possibly several hundred agitated, terrified and powerless individuals, perhaps for only several moments but, just as often, for several minutes, a half hour, an hour, even several hours—with each second feeling like a lifetime.

At such a time of crisis, flight attendants have the opportunity to apply the skills they have learned as safety professionals and human relations "experts": calming hysterical passengers, comforting crying children, calling out the emergency procedures, and making sure that everyone is doing whatever possible to maximize survivability. But their role is a dichotomous one; although they are safety professionals, they are victims as well. When and if the plane lands safely, their role during the critical incident is often minimized or overlooked completely, while the captain's account of landing the plane is front-page news, along with tearful accounts from passengers.

Flight attendants are human beings who are affected by these traumatic events. Thus, it is imperative that decision makers from management and labor recognize the need for effective interventions by peer counselors. Otherwise, the costs are too great, and these decision makers may lose their most valuable asset—the human one.

21

Treatment of Work-Related Trauma in Police Officers: Post-Traumatic Stress Disorder and Post-Traumatic Decline

Berthold P. R. Gersons and
Ingrid V. E. Carlier

CASE EXAMPLE

A 45-year-old police officer was referred to the first author after many types of psychological treatment. The officer had been in the police service for twenty-two years. For eighteen years, sleep was possible only with the help of sleeping tablets. He was convinced that despite an enormous lack of cooperation and understanding from his superiors, he had managed to track down some very dangerous suspects. However, insufficiently informed colleagues sent in to arrest the suspects died in the attempt. The officer wept bitter tears that they, and not he, were the victims. His condition went steadily downhill; he suffered from panic attacks accompanied by hyperventilation, anxiety sweats, and phobic symptoms. Sleep became impossible because he was on constant alert and, to the despair of his family, was extremely irritable. Friends and acquaintances slowly but surely began to stay away.

At this stage, the officer's post-traumatic stress disorder (PTSD) was fairly limited to prominent avoidance behavior, symptoms of increased irritability, suicidal tendencies, and mistrust of others, at times so out of proportion that he completely lost sight of reality. The officer was offered six sessions to develop a working relationship before the routine treatment protocol began. Of primary importance in therapy, however, was that he had seen his father's death in a road accident as a young boy. Yet he had not come to terms with, and harbored severe guilt feelings about, the incident. With the help of a photograph of his father and an ongoing letter, he gradually worked through this trauma. He took 125 milligrams of Amitryptiline a day to improve his sleeping pattern. The officer revealed that he felt an enormous anger toward the police service, an anger that he had always managed to keep under the surface. Treatment became more and more supportive and structured. At termination, he had achieved a reasonable equilibrium, although he remained fairly tense and his later social functioning was limited. He was granted full discharge from the police service on the grounds of ill health. Although he regained some control over his life, he had to accept his feeling that much of his life was destroyed by his work experience.

INTRODUCTION

Work-related trauma is a major contributing factor to police stress (Ostrov, 1986). As part of normal day-to-day duties, expectations of the officer include encountering critical incidents of sudden death (Herman, 1989). Deaths generally occur within one of the five following categories: traffic collisions, suicides, homicides, non-traffic-related accidents, and the taking of human life by officers. The latter is, obviously, one of the most difficult situations officers may have to face (Stratton, Parker & Snibbe, 1984). Besides involvement with death, an officer is also supposed to cope with several other critical incidents, such as responding to deeply depressing social situations (for instance, abuse scenes), situations involving victims of serious (traffic or other) accidents, hostage situations, riot control situations, violent confrontations, raid or eviction situations, (failed) resuscitation of citizens, and assistance in disaster situations.

The officer is expected to deal with these incidents in a professional and, if appropriate, compassionate manner. Police officers may experience variable levels of difficulty in coping with a particular incident. After involvement in an incident, some officers may have dreams or nightmares in which they see themselves reliving the incident over and over. These symptoms are necessary to regain emotional balance, and they usually disappear after a couple of weeks.

Unfortunately, in about 10 to 35 percent of the cases the incident becomes a real trauma for the officer. Stress is internalized, or a combination of fear, confusion, and anxiety sets in after the incident. Other officers retreat into a period of isolation that affects their job performance and damages family relationships. In these cases, the aforementioned symptoms last longer than a few weeks and become more intense and extensive. Symptoms can result in a posttraumatic stress disorder (APA, 1987) or some other kind of stress disorder (Gersons, 1989; Horowitz, 1976).

Recognition of PTSD in law enforcement personnel is important; appropriate treatment may prevent long-term psychosocial impairments (such as divorce, alcoholism, violence, isolation, difficulty in holding employment, suicide). According to the DSM III-R (1987) criteria, PTSD has an acute form (symptoms within six months after the traumatic event) and a chronic form (onset after six months). Treatment outcomes in the chronic group are generally poor (Solursh, 1988). For example, in a private practice office setting, Burnstein and colleagues

(1988) reported that as chronicity increased, the dropout rate increased, ultimately reaching 81.8 percent.

The chronic form of PTSD is often characterized by a rearousal of symptoms in the face of an immediate, emotionally disturbing event, for example, exposure to another critical incident. At extremely high risk therefore are those chronic PTSD sufferers employed in services with frequent exposure to violence and its aftermath: police, firemen, other security officers, and mental health counselors (Long et al., 1989).

Persistence of PTSD in a chronic form may lead to additional complications, such as character change, beyond the symptoms associated with the original disorder (PTSD). This character change is often an indication of the process of post-traumatic decline. A person experiencing a decline syndrome increases his denial and numbing of the trauma, entering a phase of frozen overcontrol (Titchener, 1982). In this case the traumatic experience, which is almost always combined with some form of object loss, activates an intrapsychic conflict the magnitude of which brings about much devastation of the personality. The conflict demands extraordinary defensiveness similar to the altered adaptation and change in character described in the survivors of a disaster (Titchener & Kapp, 1976; Green, Grace & Gleser, 1985).

The chronic form of PTSD is diagnostically and therapeutically complex (Bleich, Garb & Kottler, 1986). Virtually no documented empirical evidence about the effects of chronicity other than a few clinical reports and some exploratory findings on combat veterans exists (Long et al., 1989). This chapter focuses on the general diagnosis and treatment of chronic PTSD and the specific process of post-traumatic decline. The chapter first describes some basic diagnostic characteristics in the assessment of chronic PTSD. Second, it offers a review of treatment studies and explains therapeutic implications. The chapter then offers some conclusions.

ASSESSMENT OF CHRONIC POST-TRAUMATIC STRESS DISORDER

In general, *chronicity* as a term refers to the persistence of a disorder (or a disease) across time (Long et al., 1989). Chronicity may be operationalized on several dimensions, for instance, length of time between onset of a disorder and current evaluation, frequency of re-occurrence of a disorder, intensity of episode, overall severity of disorder, estimated length of time a person meets criteria for classification of the disorder, and number of inpatient psychiatric hospitalizations occurring within a specified time period (Long et al., 1989). At least two chronic PTSD forms can be discerned: delayed PTSD and post-traumatic decline. The first is included in DSM III-R (APA, 1987); the second is not (yet). This chapter focuses primarily on the process of post-traumatic decline (PTD).

Post-Traumatic Decline

One chronic PTSD form can also arise from the acute and subacute syndromes of post-traumatic stress disorder. In this case, there is no delayed onset; instead there are a persistence and deepening of the PTSD symptoms as well as some disabling character changes. The resultant deep and extensive psychic impairment is sometimes highly resistant to therapeutic change (Titchener, 1982). The term *psychic impairment* acknowledges not only the existence of a painful experience and persistent symptoms but also that the experience has enduring, perhaps permanent, effects on the individual's mental functioning (Lindy & Titchener, 1983). Psychic strain weakens previously stable psychological structures leading to character change and may, if unchecked, go on to progressive post-traumatic decline (Lindy & Titchener, 1983). The latter refers to a negative spiraling encompassing deleterious changes in character structure, faulty management of tension states, and damaged object relations.

The acute phase, forerunner of decline, consists of shock effects; fear; inexpressible feelings of loss; disorganization of thinking; impairment of memory, concentration, and judgment; and interference with comfortable regulation of affect. Next follow altered attitudes in human relationships, including regressive deterioration of trust in others, alternating with unrealistic dependency and pathetic longings for help from others. This changed sense of the reliability of relationships reflects the sudden cruelty of the trauma experience, which causes a drastic change in worldview from trust to distrust and failing confidence.

When decline begins, a growing hypochondria takes over, and somatic symptoms may become the focus of the person's life. Withdrawal from gratifications at work and social life leads to isolation, distrust, and this preoccupation with the physical self (Titchener, 1982). The life of the body predominates over the life of the mind, and somatic concerns take the place of interest and pleasures. The sufferer infrequently complains of mental symptoms. If he does, he alludes to topics far removed from the essential problems of fear of reoccurrence and explosive aggression.

The reexperiencing of the traumatic event is more severe in PTD than in acute PTSD. In PTD the threshold for triggering flashbacks and nightmares is very low; the experiences recalled are detailed and particularly grim; the experiences may lead to violent behavior without conscious awareness; memories follow one another with a relentlessness that allows no respite for long periods of time; and remembering the traumatic experiences often means reliving them as their vividness and emotional intensity overwhelm the capacity for current reality testing (Rosenheck, 1985).

It seems that in the case of PTD, the ego itself undergoes profound and pathological alterations that include the use of more primitive defense mechanisms, such as splitting operations, projection, and masochistically turning-into-opposite. These defenses give rise to relatively severe "narcissistic" disturbances in the spheres of interpersonal relations and employment. In contrast to this process, in the acute form of PTSD, periods of hyperarousal and reexperiencing are evidence of an ego that has remained relatively intact and still tries to defend itself against the "bad objects" that intrude upon it from the "outside."

In individuals experiencing PTD, psychic numbing, derived from hopeless indifference, predominates. Persons feel little, if any, pleasure or pain; affective and cognitive experiencing and functioning are deadened. Isolated and unable to trust, they make less and less use of relationships in the outside world, reaching the life-style termed "psychic conservatism," also called "pan-phobic orientation to life," or the fear of living, dying, and enjoying success (Titchener & Kapp, 1976). This is a state of pervasive personality constriction in which all possible irritants and stimuli from within, as well from outside, are shut out of consciousness. The aim of life becomes enduring, rather than seeking novelty, excitement, and gratification beyond those required for existence.

The survivor, in efforts to self-medicate impending panic states, frequently turns to alcohol and/or drugs. Increased acting out and "taking the law into one's own hands" can lead to actual prosecutions. Withdrawal from meaningful personal relationships and intimacy can lead to divorce. The survivor is seen by others as cold, irritable, uncommunicative, and self-centered (Parson, 1988a). Withdrawal of ambition and investment in work leads to job failures and economic decline (Lindy & Titchener, 1983).

Parson (1988a) stated that PTD is not a real "character disorder." The intrapsychic and interpersonal problems and symptoms that an individual with PTD often presents to the clinician, particularly during the acute phase of a post-traumatic reaction, may seem more pathological than the ordinary manifestations of neurotic psychic conflict. Yet, in a true character disorder, the entire personality functions to stave off the formation of symptoms and anxiety. Post-traumatic symptoms with attendant high levels of anxiety represent a "thawing out" of heretofore "stable," enduring personality patterns. Such thawing necessarily obviates the designation of a character disorder. That is, a character disorder develops by psychic necessity to protect the individual, rather than subject him or her to the emotional trouble and inner chaos that characterize PTSD pathology.

Parson (1988a) therefore suggested the term *fluid character pathology* instead of *character disorder* for chronic PTSD forms such as PTD. This term addresses the "bi-state" of both acuteness of symptom expression and chronicity of behavior patterns and conveys the notion of malleability or crisis. Crisis often provides an opportunity for new growth-promoting insights and an acceleration of self-actualizing trends within the personality of the individual. Essentially, "fluid character pathology" combines DeFazio's (1978) three categories of trauma-induced symptoms: classical post-traumatic stress symptoms of frightening nightmares, heightened autonomic responsibility, and rage reactions; dissociated somatic symptoms; and characterological traits resembling those found in borderline conditions and narcissistic disorders.

The DSM IV PTSD Committee is presently considering the inclusion of a residual category called disorders of extreme stress not otherwise specified (DES-

NOS). The proposed criteria for DESNOS overlap with the symptoms of PTD and include seven categories: (1) alterations in regulation of affect and impulses; (2) alterations in attention or consciousness; (3) alterations in self-perception; (4) alterations in perception of the perpetrator (applies only to victims of interpersonal violence); (5) alterations in relations with others; (6) somatization; and (7) alterations in systems of meaning. DESNOS is used when the individual has developed chronic and severe symptomatology that cannot be classified either as an acute stress disorder or as PTSD. Symptoms may begin immediately or soon after the stressor or at a later developmental stage. Usually the stressor involves prolonged periods of involuntary dependency and helplessness, such as repeated episodes of interpersonal victimization (including being held hostage) or repeated episodes of torture. More rarely, the symptoms develop from a single catastrophic episode. Also, in some cases, the symptomatology develops from a stressor that does not involve interpersonal victimization, such as a natural disaster associated with loss of family and community (Spitzer, 1989). A structured interview for DESNOS (SCID-DESNOS) is currently being developed (van der Kolk et al., 1991).

TREATMENT

Treatment protocols for post-traumatic stress disorder are designed according to the assumed different pathogeneses. Few controlled studies upon which to base definite treatment conclusions have been carried out so far (McFarlane, 1989). For example, Lindy (1988) evaluated psychoanalytical short-term treatment of twenty-three Vietnam veterans with existing PTSD of longer than 15 years. The selected patients averaged 35.3 years of age and had reasonable social functioning. A set treatment protocol, utilized by the therapist, allowed interpretations of the transference, resistance, and earlier traumas. The findings were evaluated after eighteen months of treatment through the use of the SCL–90, Shock-Coping Scale, and Psychiatric Evaluation Scheme. The expected decrease in avoidance symptoms did not materialize, although there was a slight drop in the reexperiencing symptoms. Most of the patients were, nonetheless, satisfied with the treatment. Therapists and researchers alike blamed the lack of any solid results on the "chronicity" of PTSD.

Treatment Protocol

The following treatment protocol is part of the longitudinal Dutch research project called "Critical Incidents in Policework" (senior researcher at the project is the second author). The duration of the project is summer 1989 until summer 1994. The goals are prevention and treatment of PTSD in law enforcement personnel. The results will have implications for selection, training, early diagnosing, and treatment of officers with work-related trauma. The treatment protocol is based on the following assumptions:

1. PTSD is a physioneurosis; the neurophysiological system becomes disturbed, manifesting itself in heightened alertness, startle responses, and sleep and concentration difficulties. Antidepressive medication is sometimes appropriate in these cases.

2. PTSD is a consequence of stagnated coping, arising from the incomprehensibility of a traumatic experience that cannot be pinned down or given an appropriate place in the total picture of life. It is of little importance, therefore, whether or not the patient is suffering primarily from reexperiencing symptoms or whether the memories have, in fact, been "successfully" averted, leaving a legacy of numbing and detachment. When flashbacks are in the forefront, emotions such as anger and grief cannot be fully released and accepted.

3. PTSD is part and parcel of a person's total life history. Older traumas and those with which one has not yet come to terms merge with more recent ones. Psychotherapy focuses on both the past and the present.

4. Long-term intensive psychotherapy can sometimes be appropriate, irrespective of whether or not the traumatic experience played any significant role in the actual condition.

For these reasons, treatment was structured in the following manner. The patient is first asked to write a detailed and chronological account of the traumatic experience. The purpose of this exercise is to call to memory each event as precisely as possible. Recall has generally not been previously possible because of the severity of the emotions attached to the events. To achieve recall, the following procedure is used.

After a short relaxation with the eyes closed (alternating lower arm and hand muscle tightening and relaxing exercises, usually three times in succession), the patient is helped, step by step, by means of imaginary "guidance," to bring the traumatic event back to "life" as authentically as possible. Questions about, or the naming of, context points of the event, such as wind, fresh air, darkness, odors, the time of day, autumn, and so forth, enhance the level of reality. Emanating emotions are acknowledged as such by the therapist and called by name.

Recall material or "linking objects"—such as photographs, newspaper reports, and clothing—are used to bring the experience nearer to home. The most powerful and widely used method of bringing memories back in all their intensity is hypnotherapy. Between the sessions, preferably on a daily basis and during a set half hour of the day, the patient is encouraged to commit the traumatic experience to paper, giving vent to emotions and submitting them to the written word.

The chronological account is then placed in the "Malan" triangle (Malan, 1979). Of what did the trauma remind the patient? What came into his or her mind? What were his or her emotions? What are the feelings toward his or her therapist in this connection?

The treatment also includes time for the here and now. Consequences of the trauma upon the family (interactions and communications within the family) and upon the place of work (secondary victimization) are discussed. A single invitation is sent as standard practice to the spouse or partner. Amitryptiline, up to 150 milligrams per day, is prescribed for patients suffering from persistent sleeping problems and depression (see Bleich, Garb & Kottler, 1986; Falcon et al., 1985; Lerer et al., 1987; Friedman, 1988; Kinzie & Leung, 1989). Once the traumatic experience has been successfully reexperienced and the intense emotions related to it fully released, the patient is encouraged to take leave of the event by means of a "leave-taking" letter (van der Hart & Boon, 1988; Gersons, 1988).

This eclectically structured scenario includes elements of both hypnotherapy and short-term psychodynamic psychotherapy. Marmar and Freeman (1988) and Horowitz (1986) suggested that considerable energy must be spent on extracting from the patient as detailed an account as possible of the traumatic experience, bringing emotions out into the open and making avoidance impossible. Use is also made of leave-taking rituals, sometimes in combination with antidepressives. Van der Kolk (1987a) noted that medication is essential to help patients relive the emotions that overpowered them. Its sedative effects may improve patient compliance by improving depression and anxiety and make the patient more amenable to psychotherapeutic interventions (Basoglu, Marks & Sengün, 1992). The aim of treatment is to reactivate the coping process by emphasizing "turning passive into active," through regaining control of one's own life and one's own emotions and restoring trust in others. Hypnosis has a definite healing effect because it enables the trauma victims themselves to recall and relive the long-suppressed memories and images associated with the trauma, but this time under their own control. The hypnotic trance alone, according to Spiegel (1988; Spiegel & Cardena, 1990), facilitates the "abreaction," as Freud intended it, through the medium of "reexperience" (Brende, 1985). Kingsbury (1988) and Venn (1988) also share the viewpoint that the therapeutic effects of hypnosis lie in the patients' regaining control of their emotions and safety. These positive claims have yet to be confirmed or denied on the basis of controlled studies.

When treating post-traumatic decline, this protocol is changed accordingly. In treatment the patient learns to recognize the handicaps that emerge from "the frozen state." The aim of therapy is not so much to resolve the psychotrauma but, instead, to regain stability over reactions and behavior. The patient learns a new coping repertoire to regain control over life. Of utmost importance is the understanding by the therapist that the patient suffering from post-traumatic decline has lost basic trust in human beings, as well as in himself or herself. The task of the therapist is to help the person involved to restore trust in human beings as much as possible. Other basic character patterns intertwine with PTD, for instance, a paranoid trait or an affective trait. Therefore as treatment begins to develop a working relationship, the patient will test the credibility of the therapist. Treatment should not start with a rapid working through of emotions and farewell to the trauma. Instead, the therapist must recognize that the trauma or traumas have shaped the individual so that he or she has not only lost control but, even worse, lost confidence in others. The treatment first helps to restore confidence and regain some control before the patient is helped to accept the happening of so many devastating traumas. If the therapist moves too fast and does not take into consideration the PTD background, serious depression and/or suicide may result.

CONCLUSION

The picture presented by, and the treatment of, PTD differ from that of more acute PTSD. Officers suffering from PTD exhibit a mixture of deep humiliation, feelings of being burned out in the wake of multiple traumas, and connections of present traumas to previous ones. Officers' desire to return to the traumatic environment of the police force becomes more ambivalent or is sometimes non-existent. This implied withdrawal from a worthwhile occupation, in which they had gladly invested much of their lives, is couched against the background of their personal life experience.

It is difficult to draw a sharp line between PTSD and PTD. However, the assessment of the different conditions is very important so as to design treatment and facilitate a good prognosis. The elements of the protocol for treatment of PTSD can be encompassed in the treatment of PTD in an essentially different context. However, it is important to add rehabilitation in a case of PTD because, in most cases, the return to the workplace is no longer possible. More research is needed to increase knowledge of, and to improve, treatment programs for PTSD and PTD.

_____ **Part VII**

Creative Therapeutic
Approaches

22

Art Therapy as a Visual Dialogue

Dee Spring

ARTISTIC DIALOGUES IN THE TREATMENT OF PTSD

A visual dialogue is a collection of drawings created by one individual. Visual dialogues are composed of artistic symbolic language that evolves in a phenomenological manner over a period of time. The symbolic language is a projection of the threat (wedge forms) that was introjected during the original experience of sexual trauma. The dialogue also indicates the guilt (disembodied or highly stylized eyes) that was telepathically transmitted by the perpetrator to the victim at the onset of trauma. Later, the guilt becomes magnified, and victims claim it as their own. This guilt is rooted in the myth, "I must have done something to provoke it."

During the process of creating individual dramas on a tangible, visual surface (art piece), historical narrative and associated affect are captured. Form as content is used in the artistic dramas to reflect reenactments and personal metaphors as attempts to gain mastery over the traumatic experience take place. The symbolic language in graphic form and the artistic characteristics of drawings done by victims of sexual trauma have been documented by Spring (1988b).

In graphic form, the visual dialogue reveals artistic characteristics other than eyes and wedges, as well as characteristic colors (red and black). These characteristics are constructed within fragmented compositions (see examples of artwork later in this chapter), along with a discernible energy and reoccurring dissociative elements, which produce a floating effect. In addition, the dialogue corresponds to victims' progress in treatment in terms of memory retrieval and conflict resolution, which provide a tableau representative of past, present, and future. The process of creating a visual dialogue heals the invisible wounds through private, nonverbal testimony without fear of the original consequences, resolves conflict, and develops personal strengths. Victims gain identity through their artwork while moving through the six stages of restoration (Figure 22.1).

Sexual trauma is defined as a category of experience and includes incest, rape, molestation, or any combination of these forms of sexual abuse. The compositions reveal this category of experience in the form of coded messages that are deciphered through victims' nonverbal testimony. The nonverbal testimony is translated into verbal communication as victims move through the restoration stages. The decoding of the messages in the drawings incorporates primary post-trauma responses of victims as recognized throughout the voluminous literature on sexual abuse.

Decoding usually includes specific colors, symbols, and artistic characteristics (see Figures 22.2, 22.3):

1. depression (black), low self-esteem, and unworthiness
2. involvement in abusive relationships (drama drawn of situations)
3. sexual dysfunction, a reaction to the trauma (disembodied genitalia or defined areas on the body)
4. sleep disturbance because of intrusive thoughts and memories (confused lines, fragmentation)
5. severe guilt (disembodied or highly stylized eyes)
6. spontaneous, uncontrolled rage (red) or passivity cloaking the rage (faint lines)
7. feeling threatened, paranoia, phobias (wedge forms)
8. physical reactions designated by "something toward the middle" (drawings or intense color on body parts)
9. dissociation, memory impairment, and amnesia (gray, floating objects, circles)

These symptoms, which are reflected in the artwork, are further complicated by the development of learned helplessness (Seligman, 1975), an accommodation syndrome (Summit, 1983), body memories (Watkins, 1949), chronic hysterical reactions (Freud, 1896), fear of lack of control, fear of space violation, and fear of lack of a means of escape. The traumatic experience that encompasses betrayal, secrecy, isolation, severe conflict, and revictimization is revealed in victims' artistic dramas.

The use of art therapy with victims of sexual trauma provides a modality for personal testimony through silent, but revealing, artistic communication by the use of projective means. Although the properties of artistic projection are well documented, literature on the treatment of sexual trauma with art therapy is scarce and primarily aimed at children. Wohl and Kaufman (1985) and Malchiodi (1990) wrote about the artwork of abused children from violent homes. Stember (1977) and Spodick (1983) discussed cases of sexually abused children. Garrett and Ireland (1979) described group art therapy with adult rape victims, and Yates and Pawley (1987) wrote about imagery and artwork with an adult victim. Spring

Figure 22.1
Stages of Victim Restoration

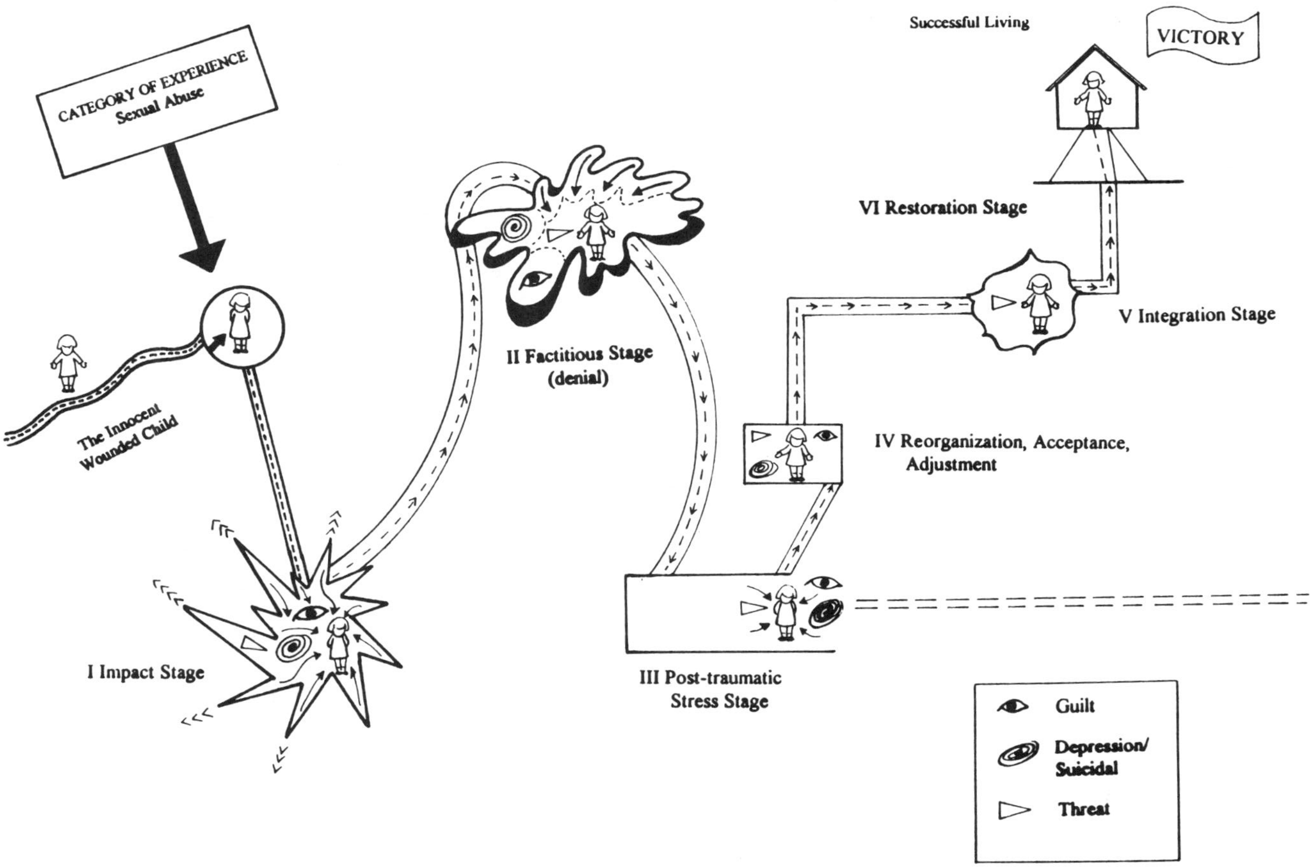

Figure 22.2
Example of Guilt

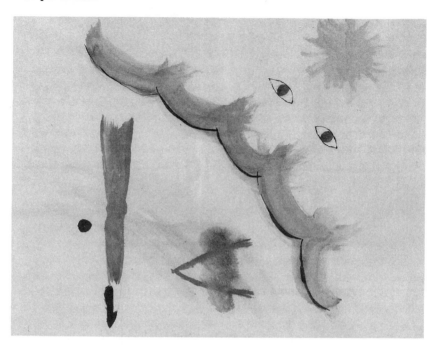

(1976–92) focused on adult victimss of sexual trauma. Spring conducted the only empirical research on art therapy and the symbolic language of sexual abuse (Spring, 1988b).

Many of the 2,500 credentialed art therapists work with individuals who suffer sexual trauma, but few have contributed to the research literature or documented the modality's usefulness in the treatment of this population. This is unfortunate since the Federal Bureau of Investigation (FBI) estimates that 1 in 3 women have been sexually abused, according to reported crimes over the past fifteen years. The FBI also stated that only 10 percent of all rapes are reported. In Lagomarisino's congressional report (1991), he states that "a woman is raped every 6 minutes." In 100 days, 24,000 rapes occur, and in one year, there are 87,600 reported. According to the FBI's formula, 876,000 actual rapes occurred in years prior to 1991. The rate of sexual abuse, not just rape, occurring in an individual's life may be closer to 80 out of 100 women and 33 percent of men. Most sexual abuse is not reported to statistics-gathering agencies. Therefore, it seems reasonable to conclude that current statistics do not accurately reflect the reality or magnitude of this menacing mental health problem. The consequences of sexual abuse result in chronic post-traumatic stress necessitating long-term psychotherapy and in lifelong effects that must be constantly monitored and self-corrected by the victim.

Figure 22.3
Example of Threat

CASE EXAMPLE: SUMMER'S EXPERIENCE

Summer was a 29-year-old divorced, Caucasian musician who lived with her 9-year-old son. During a rehearsal in a sound studio, she was raped. She was knocked unconscious when she was attacked from behind. When she regained consciousness, she sought aid from coworkers. No one had seen the rapist, and no stranger had signed the security log at the front desk. Summer's story was not believed. Instead, she was asked if she had been drinking and had imagined the attack. After much insistence and hysterics, local law enforcement was called. She was taken to a local hospital for a routine rape examination, and evidence was gathered.

Following several hours at the hospital, she was taken to the police station for several hours of interrogation by officers, all male, who asked such questions as: "Why were you rehearsing alone?" "Why were you dressed in that low-cut blouse and tight jeans?" "Who had you been flirting with prior to the alleged rape?" Summer was outraged by this line of questioning because she had made no sexual overtures to anyone.

At the conclusion of the questioning, the officers made remarks such as: "With that figure and those clothes, I'd be inclined to rape you too," "Flaunting it is asking for it," and "I'll just bet he was a stranger!" She reported that she felt emotionally destroyed and had lost all respect for law enforcement officers.

When she arrived home, a close male friend was waiting for her and was angry that she was late for their date. She related her story to him. He told her that this was the most dramatic story he had ever heard to cover up being late for a date. He discounted the lump on her head and her bruised face, abruptly left, and did not reenter her life.

At this point, Summer proceeded to try to wash away the feeling of contamination by several long, severely hot showers. She forced herself to take care of her son while attempting to explain to him what had happened. She was unable to sleep and did not report for rehearsal for several days. Out of fear, she refused to answer the phone. She lost two musical engagements and drank large quantities of alcohol to medicate her pain.

A concerned friend went to Summer's home since she had not heard from her for several days. Summer told her story. The friend suggested that Summer call a local hot line, which she did. After several attempts, she reached a crisis intervenor who told her that she needed only crisis intervention, not ongoing counseling; after a short adjustment period she would be "just fine." The crisis intervenor advised Summer to call the police department to get an update on her case. The police told Summer that due to a heavy caseload, her case had been put on hold.

Following this report, Summer's friend insisted that she contact the mental health center. Summer complied and was told that there was a three-week waiting list. She scheduled an appointment with the only professional who specialized in sexual assault. Summer felt relieved but anxious about the three-week wait.

She returned to work but continued to drink heavily when alone. She pretended that she was "just fine." The police department continued to persuade her to be patient with its heavy caseload and eventually dropped the case. Several years later, this rapist was captured and convicted after he had raped four other women in the same vicinity as the rehearsal studio.

Summer kept her appointment with the sexual assault therapist and explained that she had lost all sexual desire, could not stand to be touched, and was frightened of all men. She received a diagnosis of sexual dysfunction with anxiety attacks. The sexual assault was discounted as being of little significance. She was told that the sexual dysfunction and anxiety were causing the problems in her life. She was given potent tranquilizers for her anxiety attacks, was told the symptoms would subside, and was given an appointment time three weeks later.

After two additional sessions with this professional, Summer dropped out of therapy. She became highly promiscuous as a means to make all men pay for what had happened to her. She was nonorgasmic, had no sexual desire, and was somewhat sadistic toward the men she attracted. During this time, she had a flashback of physical and sexual abuse by an uncle as a nine-year-old child.

Four months after the rape, she admitted herself to the county medical center and was diagnosed as bipolar with situation anxiety and sexual dysfunction. She was medicated, dismissed, and referred to a prominent psychiatrist for psychoanalysis. The psychiatrist advised her that she had probably imagined the rape because of her problems with sexuality. Thus, her desire to punish men was certainly relevant, and this would be the topic area that would receive his attention. She was given more medication.

By this time, Summer had a stockpile of medication and was drinking excessively. She had become unreliable at her job, isolated, and continuously in crisis. Friends and significant others stayed away from her. She sent her son for an extended visit with his father as she felt incapable of caring for him. She saw the psychiatrist four additional times and dropped out of therapy.

Approximately eight months after the rape, her landlord found her unconscious on her kitchen floor. As the police rushed her to the medical center, she mumbled about being raped. An astute police officer who had taken a class taught by this author was alerted. He made arrangements to be called when Summer was ready for discharge and telephoned the author for a consultation. On his off-duty time, he met Summer at the hospital and brought her to the office. She willingly told her story of the rape and what she could remember about her childhood abuse. The art therapy treatment model discussed in this chapter was immediately initiated.

Summer remained in therapy for nine months, then relocated and established a highly successful modeling agency. She remarried and returned to her normal sexual pattern and social drinking habits. Three years later, upon follow-up, she was well-adjusted and had not reentered therapy. (See Figures 22.4, 22.5, 22.6, 22.7 and 22.8.)

THE USE OF VISUAL DIALOGUES IN ASSESSMENT

The first five directed, sequential drawings of a visual dialogue (as in Summer's experience) do not directly address sexual abuse. Rather, they are generic and are used for assessment, history gathering, and observation of recurrent symbolic language. These drawings give direction for memory retrieval, abreactive work, and conflict resolution. The drawings define victims' beliefs about self and others, their place in the world, family, and their social support system, if one exists. The drawing assessment also brings historical and current stressors into focus. The drawing assessment is coupled with two self-reports: (1) a screening for multiple personality disorder and (2) a screening for the post-traumatic stress level.

The post-traumatic stress disorder (PTSD) self-report is specific to victims of sexual trauma and may indicate a history of sexual abuse and the degree of conscious recall. If memories are repressed, scores may be low and show a conflict between operational patterns and the actual score. This report discriminates on seven levels: (1) no post-traumatic stress, (2) other event indicated, (3) more investigation, (4) suspicious, (5) indicated, (6) highly probable, and (7) a certainty.

Along with the five assessment drawings and the two self-reports, a written autobiography is assigned. The first color palette for interpreting victim roles

Figure 22.4
This Is Me. I Am ... (#1)

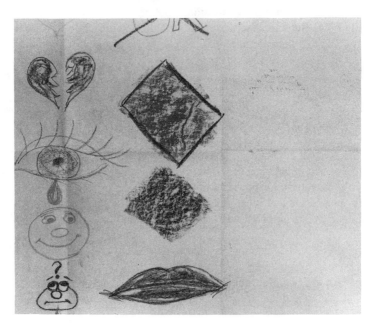

and scripts within the drawings is a component of the assessment. This color palette designates the internal adversarial system (symbolic internal civil war) and is useful in defining the major conflicts to address in treatment.

Six weeks are normally required to complete the assessment, which provides a direction for the process of psychotherapy. Life patterns, corresponding artistic and dream themes, and conflicts usually begin to surface in the first five drawings. The assessment materials indicate whether or not and on what level sexual trauma needs to be addressed. The assessment procedure may begin the retrieval of buried memories with associated affect or may stimulate the resolution of conscious memories and associated affect. The six stages of restoration (Figure 22.1) align with changes observed in the artistic drama of the visual dialogue as the unconscious is brought under conscious control. This strategic and sequential process is explained in the next section.

THE USE OF VISUAL DIALOGUES IN TREATMENT

Stage I: Impact

Many times, treatment begins with the victim's statement: "I must have made it up. It doesn't seem real." The aim of therapy is, obviously, to bring the

Figure 22.5
My Space

unconscious under conscious control through the ''cooperation of memories'' (Freud, 1896). The artwork simplistically massages the memory bank through the use of an altered state of consciousness paralleling the victim's dissociated state at the onset of trauma. The art assessment is designed to capture symbolic language rather than directly address the suspected or remembered sexual trauma. The assessment is designed to cultivate trust; acquaint the individual with the art therapy modality in terms of expression, rather than artistic talent; alleviate anxiety about exposing the creative self; and gather basic historical information in three forms: artistic, written, and verbal. The prescriptive package of directed, sequential art tasks is designed to indirectly address the traumatic past: to bring into view dissociated memories revealed through symbolic language and begin the process of deciphering the coded messages in the artwork.

Close observation of the reoccurring themes and patterns revealed in the assessment phase, which includes the three forms of communication, provides the stepping-stone for the next phase of treatment.

Stage II: Factitious

Conflict resolution is the next phase and evolves through memory retrieval and abreactions. The aim of therapy, at this point, is to interfere with the tendency ''toward gradual self-destruction and help alter the balance in the direction of live pursuits'' (Firestone, 1989, p. 155).

Figure 22.6
My Life's Road

Figure 22.7
My Family and Me

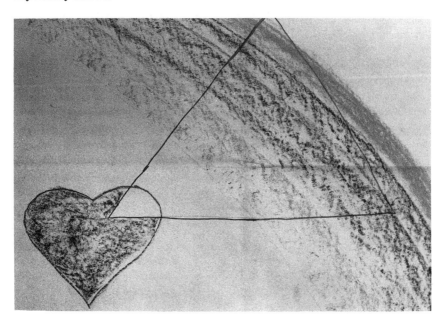

Figure 22.8
This Is Me. I Am ... (#2)

The creation of the visual dialogue begins to bring about emotional equilibrium as victims draw out conflicts on a visual surface. Victims define this as "creating a middle ground" since their belief system operates on a black and white, all-or-nothing basis. Some of the major conflicts for victims are life versus death, good versus bad, pain versus pleasure, control versus lack of control, and sabotage versus taking charge.

A series of sixteen conflict drawings is assigned as homework. These drawings make visible the ongoing internal chaotic structure and turmoil created by the original trauma. The procedure of completing the conflict drawings gives victims opportunities for creating a fantasized "middle ground" as emotional equilibrium is cultivated and projected onto the external environment. Through visual magnification and exposure of current situational problems and reenactments, the artwork exposes indecisiveness, dysfunctional relationships, guilt, rage, threat, denial, and secrecy. The drawing series is done in concert with memory retrieval and management of rage. Rage is managed by victims' completing a huge "red" painting that is continuously worked on until the individual has attained a sense of physical and emotional relief. Through this artistic process, victims increase assertiveness, objective decision making, and taking charge of life. Dependency and relationship "bondage" diminish; therefore there is a reduction in helplessness, which leads to resolution of family-of-origin issues.

Victims acquire the necessary strength and skills to advance to the next level of restoration, which is addressing the emotional cycles that are ongoing. These cycles may resemble cyclothymia or bipolar disorder. At this point, the paranoid overlay, created by victimization, begins to diminish, and internalized guilt belonging to the abuser begins to be put into proper perspective.

Stage III: Post-Traumatic Stress

Once the conflict component of the visual dialogue is completed and a symbolic peace treaty has been negotiated, the next phase of treatment begins. This phase enables victims to accept their historical narrative, thereby making sense out of their experience through their artwork. They begin to understand that their history has been the foundation for their emotionality or the lack of it (numbing); thus denial is brought under control. This phase is often marked by the eruption of body memories (somatization). Victims are prone to headaches, stomach and colon distress, vaginal pain, body aches and pains, an illusion of serious illness, and a lowered resistance to respiratory problems. Body affiliations to dissociated memories may be drawn as circles or "something towards the middle." Body memory realization leads to the next phase of restoration, which is the identification and connection of mental pictures to associated affects. The next phase of treatment involves three-dimensional artwork.

Stage IV: Reorganization and Acceptance

Object making is a powerful method of capturing what cannot be expressed in words or drawings. Object making addresses the magnitude of feelings that have been too terrifying to acknowledge or too overwhelming to manage. Holding and handling an art object provide a different dimension of personal control. This procedure activates the tactile senses as a means to teach the victim to recognize and identify feelings in order to synthesize traumatic experiences. This part of the visual dialogue includes the creation of a "monster" (representation of the abuser) and walks victims through the cycle of emotions created at the onset of trauma: hurt, anger, guilt, depression, and grieving (the loss of a childhood not realized). To address these feelings, victims are asked to create five objects: "My Hurt Locker," "Anger-Stuffing Bag," "My Guilt Trap," "My Depression Chamber," and "My Tear Collector." A final three-dimensional composite piece is constructed at the end of this phase as a means to assist victims to conceptualize how the magnitude of feelings has influenced the management of life's situations and how numbing has served as a survival tool.

Stage V: Integration

The fifth phase of the visual dialogue directly addresses the last stages of the sexual trauma which incorporates past and present sexual relationships and resolves family-of-origin issues. During this phase, family drawings are repeated in order to assess victims' current perspective relative to family, extended family, and other current intimate relationships.

Normally, in the fifth phase, the drawing compositions have begun to change, as have the colors used for those drawings. The second part of the color script palette is introduced to assess the level of internal turmoil and how the traumatic experience and family and intimate relationships have been reframed. Have the memories been put into the position of a "bad memory" without continuing to distort or interfere with daily living? The PTSD Self-Report is repeated to measure the level of post-traumatic stress, as well as which remaining areas (guilt, rage, depression, and so on) need to be the focus of therapy. Subsequently, therapy evaluates victims' restoration process and is directed toward termination.

Stage VI: Restoration

The evaluation for termination includes a complex and extended art task titled, "A Trip to a Healing Spring," which is based on the myth of the Fountain of Youth. This task incorporates all the tools acquired throughout therapy and demonstrates resolution of the traumatic effects. Following this task, victims write and illustrate "A Management Plan." This task is designed to address implementation, maintenance of goal setting, and follow-through without sabotage. During this process, victims continue to make decisions about life-style change or relationship change, as well as family-of-origin issues.

Termination usually occurs after two years of intensive psychotherapy when it is determined that there is no measure of PTSD. Four of the assessment drawings are completed and compared with the original assessment (second "This Is Me. I Am . . . " is deleted from the illustration). Both color palettes are used in this procedure. The management of lifelong effects is thoroughly discussed to assist the individual in the management of distressing moments that may be triggered by success. Accomplishments may become a threat "as they begin to approach long dreamed-of goals. These real successes interrupt a fantasy process that these individuals have relied on since childhood" (Firestone, 1989, p. 359). This represents a "change of identity that they find difficult to tolerate" (Firestone, 1989, p. 359). There must be a clear understanding that what happened to them "originated in childhood" and was "reactivated later in life" by circumstances personally designed to gain mastery over traumatic experiences (Firestone, 1989, p. 193).

The framework of the preceding treatment model includes victims' simultaneous participation in an art therapy group and individual psychotherapy. Since victims tend to isolate and see themselves as "different and weird," involvement with other victims who have experienced similar trauma is advantageous. Victims may remain in group after individual therapy has been concluded as a way to maintain support as they make the transition to independence and successful living.

CONCLUSION

Victims are often dispossessed, yet their nonverbal ability to externalize the internal chaos and personality fragmentation can be addressed via a creative method that interprets the coded messages and behavior reenactments. Art therapy parallels the dissociative process of the victim as another altered state of consciousness. The modality helps to bring the unconscious under conscious control. Victims want something "tangible to hold onto" (Spring, 1983). Art tasks that exhibit a symbolic language, composed in a phenomenological manner, provide visual records of creative trauma resolution. The victim can choose to review that artistic record at any time. The emotional charge has been lifted during psychotherapy through the creation of the artistic visual dialogues. These dialogues fill victims' desires to understand where they have been, where they are currently, and where they are going in the successful management of life.

Successful management means using the victim's creativity, regardless of its form. After all, during traumatic experiences, victims creatively learned to use dissociation to numb feelings in order to survive painful intrusions. It is advantageous for victims to have the opportunity to use their creative skills in treatment. They need to recognize that they do, indeed, have control over something in their lives. The creation of visual dialogues provides such an opportunity. The process of projection works whether or not victims talk directly or indirectly about the traumatic experience at the time an art task is completed. Artwork provides an opportunity to tell secrets without the spoken or implied threat of the consequences that were part of the original trauma. Artwork provides a referent for historical visual narrative and for future work as well. The victim can leave the projected images frozen in time and space on the art product and walk away from what they cannot communicate verbally at the moment. The process of creating art enables victims to be less obsessive-compulsive in their thinking and acting.

Art therapy provides a vehicle for victims to sufficiently translate overwhelming events, emotions, and dissociative episodes into verbal communication since they can talk about the art piece in terms of metaphorical content. Victims can draw what they do not have words for, since their art addresses the obscene, the unimaginable, and the unbelievable, as well as internal, ongoing terror and feelings of overwhelming threat, guilt, rage, and loss. The emphasis in art therapy for this population is gathering what is unspeakable, projecting it onto the art medium, and converting it into verbal testimony.

Art therapy can be used as a primary or adjunctive therapy. It combines dynamically with all other therapies and approaches to shorten time spent in therapy. Victims' creativity influences the restoration process. Art accesses the internal communication system and subsequently reflects the traumatic experiences in form and color, which results in proficient reasoning relative to reframing the sexual trauma. The art tasks externalize the internal civil war and the wish for the magical rescue. Conflict resolution and the externalization of the internal civil war and of the wish for the magical rescue lead to emotional equilibrium for victims.

Victims achieve psychological equilibrium only when they arrive at "a particular solution to the basic conflict between reliance on an internal fantasy process for gratification (and survival) and seeking satisfaction in the external world" (Firestone, 1989, p. 75). Firestone also concludes, "It is characteristic of the damaged child to attempt to reproduce the circumstances of the earlier environment, no matter how miserable they were" (p. 77). Victims may attempt to "provoke treatment similar to that received in the original family, if the child's use of distortion as a defense is insufficient" (p. 77). Therefore, the use of art and creativity in treatment brings these patterns into visual view rather than through destructive circular thinking patterns.

In summation, the use and research of art therapy for this population are recommended. The tangible products of art, as a personal testimony and internal drama, are a dramatic replication of a category of experience that is not under the control of family, psychotherapist, or abusers. Victims' creativity and artwork may be the only thing that they exclusively own.

23

Creative Arts Therapies on a Sanctuary Voluntary Inpatient Unit for Men and Women Who Have Experienced Abuse and Psychological Trauma in Childhood

Jean Vogel

INTRODUCTION

At some point in time according to Bloom (Chapter 31), "often due to a current overwhelming stressor, a retraumatization, or a developmental impasse," victims of trauma may require hospitalization because "their defenses are overwhelmed and their symptoms become so disabling." She also noted: "It is the essence of trauma that a person's sense of safety in the world is seriously compromised. In the treatment of victims of trauma, it is impossible to overemphasize the importance of the provision of a safe environment. This sense of safety must encompass physical, emotional, and social levels of care."

By creating a sanctuary for patients, a healthy, functional, emotionally and physically safe place also evolves for staff. Within this milieu, creative arts therapists dare to be creative, challenge themselves and each other, and generate meaning and value. In this setting, there seems to be a more relaxed, fluid attitude where roles become less easily defined.

SANCTUARY PHILOSOPHY IN ACTION

Creative arts therapists meet together five days a week. They may work together or separately with a group or two groups as determined by the needs of the patients. Census in and of itself is rarely a consideration. The following "checklist" is reviewed long before the group begins:

- Therapists learn what has occurred in their sixteen-hour absence from nursing, other staff, and rounds.

- To insure continuity, therapists communicate with other group therapists in order to gather information regarding their groups and specific work of group members.

- Therapists are visible to patients through informal chats and/or individual sessions as needed, when a patient requests them or when a therapist feels they would be advantageous.

- Therapists brainstorm ideas as an important warm-up and help to establish short-term and long-term group goals based on patient need. Brainstorming needs to occur regardless of whether the therapists work together or alone.

- Sometimes groups may be at an impasse (usually involving issues of safety) or exhibit fragility. A patient may be "ready" to do abreactive and empowering work, and the opportunity exists to do the work without the group. Although in-group work is usually preferred, because it decreases isolation and increases the sharing of feelings and experiences, exceptions are made. Therapists take the patient where she or he is. It is unfair to hold back individuals who are further ahead in their recovery process. "Out-of-group" work can also be useful for patients who are experiencing memory retrieval from ritualistic cult abuse as well as empowerment work focusing on reclaiming power, mind, and soul "stolen" through cult programming and other cult behaviors.

- One to several staff members may assume significant roles in the patient's life to assist in the expression of relevant feelings and thoughts. These sessions can be quite intense; often, they symbolize a major turning point in the individual's work. Frequently, the person shifts from a victim attitude of "learned helplessness" to a survivor attitude of self-empowerment around the trauma(s). This process has been termed "staff psychodrama." It involves preparation and scheduling for both patient and staff.

- On occasion, creative therapists and psychiatrists plan for a family session involving role play. Patients may go to great lengths and take risks to confront their family of origin about previously held secrets (often held for years) regarding incest, physical abuse, or emotional trauma. If family members abruptly cancel a session or simply do not appear for a planned confrontation, the individual is given an opportunity to have his or her own "family session" via role play in order to disclose the secrets, express feelings, and formulate goals. This type of work is particularly useful when an individual has, over time, been timid in the group setting.

Creative arts therapy groups occur daily at consistent times with the same leaders. However, the specific type of group depends on the needs of the patients. For example, art therapy may meet four times in one week, if patient needs require, or several sessions of psychodrama in a row may occur, regardless of what the formal schedule may indicate. Although patients know they will be attending creative therapies daily, they are also aware that these groups are not run "for their own sake." Instead, they happen on behalf of patients. Continual communication among patients, staff, and creative arts therapists leads to decision making. Where the patient group as a whole seems to be in the recovery process determines which kind of group would be most beneficial.

Therapeutic autonomy also ascertains who seems emotionally ready to attend groups and who needs more one-to-one intervention. The patient who is experiencing overwhelming intrusive flashbacks, nightmares, sleep deprivation, increased dissociative behavior, and/or self-destructive behavior requires more support and structure from nursing staff. Creative arts temporarily takes a back seat. However, exceptions to this rule occur, based on daily assessments of individual needs. Reasons for these decisions are always explained to patients. Sometimes the reverse process occurs. Patients may come to therapists and explain why attendance in group would not be beneficial to them. If fear or avoidance seems to be the major reason for the hesitancy, patients are always encouraged, but never forced or verbally manipulated, to attend.

The sanctuary model, as a growing, evolving process, has fostered the development and ongoing cultivation of a cotherapy team for creative arts therapists. Yalom (1985) urged therapists to choose a cotherapist responsibly because "it is far too important and too binding a relationship" to do blindly (p. 422). In addition to being highly skilled in their own methods—art therapy, psychodrama, movement therapy, music therapy—cotherapists need to have extensive knowledge of group dynamics, group processes, stages in the development of groups, social psychology, sociometry, family systems theory, trauma theory, and knowledge of all forms of abuse.

Courtois (1988b) stated that research on incest group therapy unanimously supports the need for cotherapy:

The intensity of the group process and emotional content places great demands on the therapists. A co-therapy model allows for mutual therapist support and shared observation and processing group interaction patterns and issues. It has the potential for lessening the intensity of transference, particularly the idealization of the therapists (p. 263).

Courtois (1988b) also argued that strong justification for a same-sex cotherapy team exists, although the appropriateness has not been documented through research. Female incest survivors may only be able to "express feelings (of anger and disappointment) in an atmosphere where they are not triangulated with a male authority figure (p. 264)." If men and women participate in the same group, according to Gil (1988), it is best to have male and female cotherapists: "This will give each client the opportunity to identify with a therapist of the same sex, and it will also allow for interactions with a role model of the opposite sex. Many adults who were abused as children have learned to fear all the members of the same sex as the person who hurt them" (p. 205).

As the sanctuary model evolved, an opposite-sex, same-age cotherapy team was also developed to meet the specific needs of an ever-growing post-traumatic stress population. Negative transference issues primarily center around female patients who exhibit hostility toward the male therapist, who represents the abusive parent or offender. Sometimes the negative transference is also directed against the female therapist, who represents the unprotecting, uninvolved parent. Another variation on this theme is the "splitting" of the cotherapy team into the "good parent" who is idealized versus the "bad parent" who is feared (Courtois, 1988b; Yalom, 1985).

The program currently utilizes a same-sex, not same-age, cotherapy team. Splitting into "good" and "bad" parents occurs with this dyad, as well; however, its frequency appears to be somewhat reduced. A younger cotherapist can become a feared or, more commonly, an idealized sibling. The older therapist, on the other hand, continues to be viewed as the "good" or "bad" parent. Interestingly, the frequency and intensity of "good" parent and "bad" parent transference seem to decrease with a same-sex team. The previously discussed opposite-sex cotherapy team, adept at working through transference issues, has experienced no apparent decline in the ability of the group members (primarily females) to confront issues and vent feelings regarding their mothers and their abusers, who may have been one and the same. However, the process to get to the point of confrontation seems to take longer than in groups with a same-sex team.

When a group becomes bogged down or completely stuck due to transference issues, the solid therapy team relationship can help to solve the impasse. The therapist to whom the transference is not directed (either negative or positive) can begin the unraveling process within the group context in order to tease out how issues and feelings mirror the patients' own life experiences. This level of support decreases the defenses of the targeted therapist, and resolution is more easily achieved.

GROUP RULES

Group rules are few but important. It is crucial that the group be a safe place in which to do the work of therapy. Aggressive verbal attacks and physical violence are not permitted. Bolting from the group is discouraged. If patients have difficulty with group content, another patient, a therapist, or some other dynamic, those patients are encouraged to stay in the group and address the issue. If unable to tolerate remaining in the group, then they are escorted to the nursing station. A nurse then talks individually to these patients. They can then return to the group, if their emotional state allows. The key is not to have individuals isolate themselves. Staff does not punish patients because of the flight response.

Patients are ethically bound, and therapists are legally bound, to confidentiality within the group. In a psychiatric unit, confidentiality extends to the system. This system, the entire team with the patient, then determines the best possible treatment goals. It is not appropriate, however, for a patient to discuss group interactions with visitors unless they are within the context of his or her own work. The above rules are repeated at fairly frequent intervals because of the high turnover of patients and the need to ensure safety for all.

CREATIVE ARTS THERAPY GROUPS

> Be assured that the most destructive forces of incest we endured are no
> match in the long run for the creative forces of our spirit.
>   —Thomas (1989, p. 38)

Crucial to the success of creative arts groups is the necessity for group members
to be believed, to be taken seriously, to get validation from the group, to be
consoled if they need consoling, to get support during dissociative states and
intrusive flashbacks, and to be encouraged to recognize that the strength to heal
from the impact of their traumas lies within themselves. Part of the function of
the therapists is to provide the environment in which to do these tasks.

Art Therapy

Art therapy within the framework of the sanctuary model aims to help patients
visualize their issues and begin the process of identifying and expressing feelings
through their artwork. Patients are often given a specific task to draw. Some
examples are:

1. Draw the problem you are working on.
2. Draw the problem that brought you to the unit.
3. Draw what you are feeling.
4. Draw yourself doing something about your problem.
5. Draw the worst thing that ever happened to you.
6. Draw your inside self and outside self.
7. Draw a safe place for your child within—then draw your adult taking your younger
   self to the safe place.
8. Draw what is on your mind.
9. Draw the problem[s] as you see it [them]. On a separate sheet of paper, draw your
   feelings as they surfaced while you drew. On a third sheet of paper draw one thing
   in your life that you would like to be different than it is now. On a fourth sheet of
   paper draw yourself making an intervention to realize the change you want.

Guided imagery instructions may also be provided as patients are asked to draw
what they see from their imagery.

The art therapist stresses that the group is not an art class and that anyone
can draw lines, shapes, and forms. Group members are encouraged to avoid
being judgmental toward their own and others' work. They are asked to tape
their drawings to a wall and gather in a semicircle. It is the responsibility of
each group member to examine all of the drawings closely in order to provide
feedback. The feedback session is guided by the art therapist and cotherapist.

In art therapy the group members, often for the first time, begin to encounter their traumas in nonverbal ways. They start the processes of looking back, remembering, and feeling. They are encouraged to express feelings and to put words to their tears, to a tight fist, or to a rapidly swinging leg. As time passes, group cohesiveness builds trust, and the therapy relationship strengthens. Members begin to feel safe enough to identify and grieve their numerous losses.

"Distorted beliefs and childhood rules and messages fostered within the abusive environment are optimally challenged in the group context" (Courtois, 1988b, p. 248). Beliefs are replaced by new information aimed at a specific belief: dysfunctional family rules are replaced with functional ones, and "old tapes" reflecting self-hate are replaced by self-nurturing messages. Replacement is an arduous process; very often the patient's volume knob is turned on "loud" and hears destructive, double-bind information. Patients are encouraged to turn the volume knob to "low" and eventually to "off," in order to hear more accurate, non-double-binding messages.

Music Therapy

Music therapy is often seen as an experiential therapy. "Within the music therapy session the individual comes to terms with and manipulates a part of his/her environment, a musical part in this case" (Parente, 1989, p. 307). According to Parente (1989), this process can be nonverbal, nonthreatening, and even pleasant; it provides the person with the opportunity to discover potentials and experience control of his or her environment (p. 307).

Part of the music therapist's responsibility is to have patients temporarily focus on feelings of satisfaction and fulfillment resulting from the influence of the music, while taking attention away from the trauma issues and symptoms. For example, specific songs can be used to "promote a healthy orientation to reality through ideas" and challenge faulty perceptions and beliefs (Parente, 1989, pp. 309–10). One such song, says Parente (1989), is "Pippen." In this song the main character, faced with many obstacles in his life, chooses to do more than just exist.

When patients spontaneously create their own music, those who otherwise feel they do not deserve the attention and support of the group can be encouraged to experiment with these new behaviors. For example, patients are encouraged to make sounds in a leadership manner and receive musical support from others, thereby interrupting their previously passive, timid music choices. These new behaviors enable patients to develop insight into their musical expression and realize that they are able to receive support from others (Nolan, 1989, p. 173).

Music therapy also requires a safe environment in which to take the risks that involve readdressing developmental tasks surrounding issues of abuse. When individuals have felt out of control of at least some aspects of their environment and undeserving of participation in that environment, music therapy is a gentle approach to reinforce the good things in their lives, increase spontaneity, challenge distorted perceptions, and lay the foundation to encourage assertive choice making.

Dance/Movement Therapy

"The flow of a group dance/movement therapy session is established as the therapist facilitates the patients' spontaneous movements and connects them to the movement of others with such methods as mirroring the action, extending it, changing it, or moving in opposition to it" (Stark, Arlwynne & McGeehan, 1989, p. 124). For example, a stretching movement of the arms and hands could be extended into a pushing movement, or a tapping foot could be exaggerated to become a stomping foot. Thoughts and feelings, as they surface, are then verbalized: "I'm stomping on my abuser" or "I want to push my father away." "The therapist must be alert and responsive to the group's ability to tolerate these expressions" (Stark, Arlwynne & McGeeham, 1989, p. 125).

Once the effect is fully developed, expressed, worked through, and moved to closure through movement, the group then verbally processes what has just occurred, again through movement. This processing helps to increase group intimacy; integrates physical, emotional, and intellectual parts of patients; and addresses developmental tasks.

As in the other creative arts therapies, the development of feelings of trust and safety is paramount. The dance/movement therapist uses his or her own body to empathize with, and mirror, patients' movements kinesthetically. The therapist thereby creates a feeling of "being with" the patients. Some interventions to increase trust and nurturance involve touch and massage. It is important for the therapist to recognize a patient's resistance and ask permission to touch in healthy ways. For some trauma victims, this may be one of the first times that they have been invited to experience safe touch—touch that involves appropriate boundaries and does not exhibit an imbalance of power.

Individuals with eating disorders and/or histories of abuse tend to cut off body sensations with numbing, depersonalization, and bingeing, to name a few defense mechanisms. Body awareness helps individuals focus on sensations and feelings within their bodies and the movement potential of body parts. The following is an example of this process.

Patients are asked to lie down in a comfortable position on their backs with arms at their sides. The therapist asks them to start with deep breathing to promote relaxation and to enter a state of inner concentration and body level attention. After a few minutes of breathing, patients are asked to scan a variety of memories or sensations; they scan their bodies from head to toe, one body part at a time, for places where there are tension and holding. Next, they scan their bodies part by part for both pleasant and unpleasant memories associated with each body part. Last, they scan their minds for memories related to their bodies from birth forward to the present. The patients may note outstanding memories, especially early traumas. Images are later brought to consciousness through verbalization or movement enactment (Stark, Arlwynne, McGeehan, 1989, pp. 131–132).

Psychodrama

"It is important to recognize Moreno's work because his ideas about the essence of healing of both individuals and communities have continuing relevance today" (Blatner & Blatner, 1988, p. 2). Psychodrama, in the context of the sanctuary model, attempts to capture this essence of healing.

Psychodrama is a group method of psychotherapy in which patients enact relevant events in their lives, rather than talk about them. Group members have the opportunity to help the protagonist explore the enactment by participating in the roles of auxiliary egos. The director/therapist is responsible for the protagonist, the auxiliaries, and the group.

A variety of therapeutic modalities, if used with care, can increase self-awareness, produce insight, and help identify, express, and integrate feelings. "The difference between psychodrama and most other methodologies, however, is that psychodrama comes closest to the natural scenarios of people in everyday life" (Yablonsky, 1981, p. 4). Since enactments replicate core experiences as closely as possible, a person experiences emotions in action.

Another important aspect of psychodrama is that it is a mirror of life, not only for the central protagonist or star having a session, but for the group present at the session. For the star, the real world slows and the time can be taken to look at critical and emotional issues by acting out key life scenes. . . . Group participants are encouraged to witness aspects of their own lives that become manifest in the session. (Yablonsky, 1981, p. 5)

Yalom (1980) argued that Sartre, as he came to terms with the meaning and meaninglessness in life, took "a leap into 'engagement,' into action, into a project" (p. 4). Yalom (1980) went on to say that "the creative path to meaning is by no means limited to the creative artist" (p. 435). Yablonsky (1981) argued that creativity and spontaneity—the ability to respond "adequately to a new situation or to enact a new response to an old situation"—are the attributes that make us human (pp. 244–47). A primary outcome of creativity is to become more humanistic in social relationships.

Patients on the unit have endured horrific abuse and trauma. The opportunity exists in a sanctuary program for the cotherapist or other staff to play the role of perpetrator, living or deceased, in order for the patient to confront his or her abuser. Thus, through psychodrama, patients can enact a "new response to an old situation." Patients must be willing to confront, but only if they are well along in their healing process, exhibit clear boundaries, and have good ego strength.

Sometimes, confronting one's abuser(s) symbolically through the experience of psychodrama is as terrifying to the patient as if it were an actual family session. The patient fears he or she will be physically attacked by the abuser for "rocking the boat" and disclosing "the secret." Often the patient was verbally threatened as a child and/or experienced physical abuse or witnessed physical abuse. The patient also may feel hopeless because the abuser in actuality will not hear the confrontation, and so the individual asks, "What good is it to confront? Why bother?" The patient also may fear that the abuser somehow will "make good" on his or her threat of "If you tell, I'll kill you [or someone close to you]!" and regardless of confidentiality, the abuser will "know" of the disclosure.

Addressing the need to feel safe in a confrontation is crucial. The thought of confronting one's abuser(s), even though only in symbolic form, seems to cause a temporary regression. The adult self seems to depart temporarily. Staff must assure the individual that no physical harm will occur, reinforce ethics of confidentiality, encourage here-and-now reality testing and replace dysfunctional family rules with functional rules.

Sometimes the patient needs to gain distance from the potential confrontation. Having the patient choose a group member to play the role of the patient's child within provides the potential opportunity for the individual to remain empowered in the adult state. This also allows the adult to comprehend how vulnerable, frozen, and terrified that child was. This process allows the adult to give the child a voice. This "voice" can disclose previously unexpressed thoughts and feelings concerning the abuse, as well as grieve accompanying losses. The adult voice can portray how the trauma or traumas impacted and currently impact the individual's life. The adult also, besides giving the child a voice, places that child in a safe place via imagery and then "takes" her or him "there." The adult can also nurture that child by saying things this child most needed to hear growing up. The adult may choose to express anger at the younger self for not having acted in certain ways. Another adult may want to reach out in loving ways but does not know how. Role reversal can be helpful in this situation. Often the "child" has responses that are unavailable to the adult who is stuck or blocked because of misplaced anger. Role reversal can help to unblock specific needs and wishes with which the adult is frequently not in touch.

Psychodrama provides not only the opportunity for emotional discharge but also the much-needed next step of integration of feelings and memories and empowerment of the self. "The therapist must constantly emphasize the fact that there is a difference between what was, what is, and what will be. The adult needs encouragement to feel empowered and capable of change" (Gil, 1988, p. 174).

In addition, the therapist can say to an individual who views confrontation as a purposeless exercise in futility because of the abuser's denial, "You are doing this for yourself—not the abuser—for yourself—to give yourself the opportunity to work through all of the unexpressed feelings, to let that child be heard and validated, to let yourself grow, to empower yourself, and to begin the process of moving on with your life and living it.'' The choice to do this work belongs to the patient.

Blending Creative Arts Therapies

Each one of these modalities may enhance another. For example, an entire drawing or part of a drawing can be concretized or ''brought alive'' psycho-dramatically. The use of psychodramatic techniques in art therapy can help a patient to express thoughts and feelings more readily. Movement therapy can be an excellent warm-up to psychodrama and it can enact art therapy drawings.

Moreno (1991) noted that creative arts therapists can ''realize an expanded approach that transcends the possibility of either discipline used separately'' (p. 331). He spoke of how ''music can enhance the depth and spontaneity of a psychodramatic enactment, just as the psychodramatic enactment can enhance the depth and spontaneity of the musical expression'' (p. 339). The expertise of therapists joining together in an interdisciplinary approach to facilitate a group has tremendous psychotherapeutic potential.

CASE EXAMPLES

The following three examples are of individuals healing from abuse and psychological trauma. In the first two examples, the core of the work was done in one session; in the third example, in two sessions. The action depicted in the three examples captures the essence of different stages of healing.

A male patient has observed and participated in other people's psychodramas. Actively involved in art therapy and other groups on the unit, he requested to focus on his father's inability to be emotionally involved with him as a boy. The session began with family sculpting as a warm-up. As roles developed, he began to talk to his ''father'' and cry over how he felt his father did not like him. The action moved into a scene where his ''father'' told him, ''You're a sissy.'' At this point, a memory surfaced that apparently had been deeply buried. He recalled his mother's attempt to drown him in a backyard pool as a small boy. He remembered choking, gasping for air, and feeling terrified and vulnerable. He had body memories and began to choke; he could not get air. The action was frozen. As his anxiety increased, the director instructed him to take slow, deep breaths. He was also reminded that he was a grown man, he was not in a pool of water, and no one was drowning him at that moment. In time, after his anxiety decreased, he asked to continue the work. The action resumed. He remembered how his father told him, ''Mommy is sick—don't upset her,'' and he began to feel the shame he felt when he went to his father for nurturing and was told, ''You're a sissy.'' He cried and, after some time, began to feel anger and was able to direct it at the ''mom'' who tried to drown him. He was totally spent by this work and sat back to get support from the group and to hear others' connections and interpretations. As a result of remembering the drowning event, he began to see how it and his parents' behavior impacted his life and how they may have contributed to his previous suicide attempt.

A second example portrays a man who was sexually abused by his mother and had never expressed his feelings about the abuse directly. He truly believed he was bad, "rotten to the core," and the cause of his mother's poor health. His father frequently told him, "You are killing your mother." His mother was dead at the time of the psychodrama. After many group and individual sessions, he began to realize that he was OK and that he neither deserved to be sexually abused nor needed to feel responsible for his mother's health. He began the process by venting pent-up rage. Kneeling on the floor, with the director/therapist by his side, he hit a cushion with a bataca (a foam bat) and put words to his blows—words that freed him from his previously locked-up secret; his toxic, internalized messages; and his distorted, self-deprecatory beliefs. He then moved into a scene at his mother's grave and began to let go of her (emotionally) while looking at his younger self with compassion.

He began to give less power to the memories that previously had him caught in a trap. He had been repeating those patterns in his family of choice where he set himself up to be both victim and persecutor, depending on the issues at hand. He understood the link and felt the losses in his marital relationship. Over time, he took that leap into action and was determined to act consistently in healthier, more nurturing ways in his marriage.

In the third example, a woman in a psychodrama session explained that she had three teenage children, one of whom had asked her to drive her to the mall to buy an item to wear to a dance. This woman, "mom," complained that she was tired from work and refused to drive her daughter. Daughter, in turn, asked her brother to drive her. He agreed, and the younger teenage brother decided he wanted to go, too. Some time went by, and mom received a telephone call informing her that her daughter and older son were in the emergency room of a local hospital due to an auto accident. She was told that her other son was trapped in the car, and rescue workers were using the jaws of life to extricate him. Psychodramatic techniques revealed that mom, while driving to work earlier that morning and listening to her radio, had heard the song "In the Living Years." She made a mental note to tell her daughter, from whom she felt estranged, how much she loved her when she got home. However, her daughter never regained consciousness and died shortly after the accident. Her two sons survived the accident, which had been caused by a drunk driver.

This woman and her family experienced psychological trauma. The mother had been depressed for several years after her daughter's death, felt emotionally dead, and entertained suicidal thoughts at the time of hospitalization. In this group, she spoke of her loss as if she were made of stone, as though the tragedy had happened yesterday. She was stuck in the grieving process and resistant to finishing unfinished business. "If I don't deal with it, then maybe she is not really dead." She was given a tape of "In the Living Years" and was asked to play it. While sitting back and listening to the words, tears began streaming down her cheeks. The words soon came: "If only I had driven her that night," Why did I not tell her how much I loved her?" "I wish I could let her know how much I care." Mom was open, and while holding her "daughter" (played by a group member), she sobbed and sobbed and expressed her love for her. However, mom was unable to "let go" of her daughter and physically held onto her. She became angry because she just needed "to be" with her "daughter." She was allowed "to be," and the action was frozen here. Sharing ensued (this two-hour session was continued into the next day).

The song "In the Living Years" was playing softly before group members entered the next day. The last scene was unfrozen, and mom was again holding her "daughter." She continued to talk to her daughter about her love for her, about the difficulties they had in their relationship, and how she did not want to let her go. After time, she asked her daughter, "Do you want to go?" and roles were reversed. Then mom, as the daughter, spoke of the limbo she felt she was in, how she wanted to be set free and wanted her mother to be a mother to her brothers—in the living years (and a wife to her husband). When roles were reversed again and mom heard these words from her "daughter," she was then able to let go. The next scene showed mom taking her "daughter" to the entrance of heaven, where her own deceased mother awaited the arrival of her granddaughter. Again, through role reversal, mom learned that her daughter was in good hands, and this gave mom peace of mind. As mom returned from heaven, her family was waiting for her. She literally ran into their arms and said, "I am back" and hugged them all. The action ended, and de-roling and sharing began.

These particular psychodramas allow the reader to connect with the sorrow, anger, and pain of the victims of trauma. In the third example, the mother was able to work through her pain, express and integrate her feelings, and choose life. She was able to shift from being a victim of her losses to a survivor of her tragedy. She took a "leap into engagement," reconnected to the outside world, and transcended her trauma. The action depicted in the three examples captures the essence of different stages of healing. The autonomy, flexibility, and support provided by the sanctuary model and the people behind that model enabled this therapist to work with a woman who had been extraordinarily emotionally stuck. Through that work, the therapist was able to "be with" her as she moved to the other side. Psychodrama is an intense level of work that necessitates rich sharing and support from group members. The psychodrama process celebrates the hard work that staff (all persons on the operating unit) and patients do to create a safe place, a sanctuary.

POSTSESSIONS

Cotherapists must process their therapy groups daily. It is also crucial that cotherapists inform the nursing staff about any significant information or suspect patient behaviors. The information is then communicated to the next shift as a means to guide one-on-one interactions. Significant information also needs to be reported to psychiatrists and social workers. Creative arts therapists also provide time for one-on-one talks with patients who are having flashbacks or feeling self-destructive as a result of group interactions. It is important for the therapists to be available or to set future times to be available. All of these interventions help to foster the patient's safety and trust while on the unit.

LIMITATIONS

Creative arts groups historically have experienced a lack of supportive and informed policies. There is often a vast chasm between the ideal and the reality of what occurs. Yalom (1985) argued that "the therapy group's effectiveness, and often its very existence, is heavily dependent upon administrative backing" (p. 460). In other words, if the medical director does not believe that psychiatric nurses, occupational therapists, creative arts therapists, social workers, or psychologists should do psychotherapy, groups are undermined and become ineffective, unsafe places for patients. Furthermore, group leaders become ineffective and feel devalued. Although not necessarily insurmountable, these feelings lead to less competent therapeutic interventions.

In addition to the "issue of professional territoriality" of which Yalom (1985) spoke, he also addressed the concern of therapist autonomy. He questioned how a therapist leads a group when "one has almost no control over the membership—a group in which there may be floridly psychotic individuals sitting side by side with better functioning, integrated members" (Yalom, 1985, p. 452). When this lack of autonomy exists for therapists, it can lead to chaotic group dynamics, decreased safety for patients in the group, and further undermining of the therapist's abilities to facilitate a group with therapeutic effectiveness.

Limitations for creative arts therapists often beset more traditional psychiatric settings. Often, creative arts groups are used as fillers to keep the patient occupied. Group boundaries are intruded upon as evidenced by frequent "pulling" of group members from a session. With the advent of the sanctuary model, many of these issues have been eliminated.

SUCCESSES

When a humanistic trauma-based approach such as the sanctuary model is utilized, energy of therapists is directed toward patients' needs. These needs include fostering a patient-therapist partnership, emotional, physical, and social safety, empathic listening, and facilitating the healing process.

Established standards of patient care existed twelve or more years ago and continue to evolve and grow today. Under the sanctuary model, support, encouragement, and respect exist for the group and for exploration and implementation of new developments in the field of trauma and creative arts. Support is fostered, as well, for the continual development and autonomy of the creative arts therapist.

CONCLUSION

The sanctuary model is based on an alternative concept not generally found in more traditional psychiatric settings. The model reflects a profound understanding, sensitivity, and determination to provide a humane, safe environment for victims of trauma.

Within the context of creative arts therapies, patients healing from trauma can work toward trauma resolution. In addition, genuine, competent group leaders and coleaders who are consistent and autonomous enable patients to develop therapeutic partnerships, feel valued, gain a healthier sense of self, encourage their creative spirit, and foster the internalization of tools for recovery.

The Use of Writing in the Treatment of Post-Traumatic Stress Disorders

Susan C. Feldman, David Read Johnson, and Marilyn Ollayos

This chapter presents the rationale and methods for the use of the modality of writing in the treatment of post-traumatic stress disorder (PTSD). It discusses three elements of writing that have relevance for the treatment of PTSD and the associated syndromes of survivor guilt, incomplete mourning, alienation from others, and demoralization. The authors then describe specific applications of written work in a comprehensive PTSD program for Vietnam veterans, including the various types of writing and stages in the process of writing.

How can writing facilitate the recovery of traumatized people? What are the unique qualities of writing in comparison to speaking, drawing, or meditating, and how can these qualities be utilized in PTSD treatment? This chapter presents three answers to these questions: (1) writing is, in its essence, the preservation of memory, and therefore is a defense against death anxiety; (2) writing is a private dialogue with the self, a private confessional in which shame can be overcome and fragmented experience can be integrated; (3) writing is a means of bearing witness to the unspeakable horror of trauma; it serves as a bridge to the world by turning private image into public language.

WRITING AS A DEFENSE AGAINST DEATH ANXIETY

The moment of trauma brings the victim to the edge of death, to nonexistence. In the aftermath of trauma, victims often succumb to a deadening or a numbing of experience (van der Kolk, 1987b). PTSD victims remain unable to gather strength against the fear that all that they care about will disappear into this hole. The existential anxiety of nothingness looms everywhere. The impulse to counter this ephemerality of life is a healthy one: to ensure that the memory of the trauma will not be forgotten; to memorialize, concretize, and preserve the memory forever; to make substantial again what is fundamentally vapor: the human spirit (Levi, 1965).

In this context, writing serves as a means to achieve this preservation of memory and self. People have always placed power in the written word. Committing oneself "on paper" rather than just in speech means that the person is serious and obligated, as if writing something down makes it more real. Recording on paper propels ambiguous and fleeting inner states into the consensual world, in a language that is not personal but collective. Inner experience is translated into communal experience. What is transient becomes embodied and permanent, ultimately in the form of the book or scripture. Ironically, the self that fears death is given life, though a living image is turned into an inert sign.

If the moment of trauma is fundamentally an act of destruction, then writing serves, symbolically, as a restitutive act of creation. To victims of trauma, the act of writing calls forth the realization, "I exist; I am not gone." Once written, the piece acquires its own autonomy: it is no longer in the victim. Writing is a birth.

For these reasons writing can be especially effective in expiating survivor guilt. The victim feels guilty that others have died and are gone, while he or she survived. Writing about these dead comrades brings them to life. The memorializing through writing gives them new substance, and their lonely wandering in the survivor's mind can come to a close.

In contrast, expiation of personal guilt for atrocities, errors, or selfish acts is not treated effectively through writing, for writing also concretizes these sins. The survivor/perpetrator is left to agonize over these acts, now heightened in intensity by the power of the public expression. Once on paper, shameful acts can become permanent accusations against the survivor. In cases of personal guilt, more transient media—such as speaking or enactments—are preferable, since the horrible event is acknowledged by the witness for a moment, and then it is gone. By surviving this moment, the victim pays his or her dues for the transgression.

WRITING AS A DIALOGUE WITH THE SELF

In order to write, one must read at the same time. As the words form in one's head, are written on the page with the hand, and are read by the eyes, one's thinking is affected. The pen gives shape to the last sentence or word as another pushes into view. The writer is both creator and audience. As creator, one gives form to personal images. As audience, one tries to understand them as others would. One's personal imagery struggles to fit in with rules of grammar, syntax, and vocabulary in this dialogue between self and other. Thus, writing implicitly calls for analysis, reflection, and transformation of thought, and this coincident self-awareness strengthens the observing ego. As different parts of the self assert themselves for a hearing within the creator, the writer as reader exerts a controlling influence, serving as referee and integrator.

Unlike thinking to oneself, the act of externalization involved with writing creates autonomous images with which one can converse. Once written, they cannot be magically altered by whim or psychic defense. For traumatized individuals, whose sense of fragmentation in identity, time, and emotion is so profound, writing provides a safe arena for integration. Review and reenactment can take place continuously and with some sense of containment. The page becomes that holding environment for pieces of feeling that otherwise would evaporate, leaving the sufferer in puzzlement.

Writing is a private affair, at least initially, and therefore provides emotional distance. Unlike the situation where one is asked to speak about one's traumas to another, the need for interpersonal defenses against shame, humiliation, and judgment by the other is minimized (Gorelick, 1989). Because the medium of writing allows for careful editing, rather than the spontaneous editing one must do while speaking with another, a sense of safety and control exists. The desire to confess to others is given practice, alone, where one can sort out feelings.

However, one is then left alone with intrapsychic defenses that are unlikely to be challenged. For this reason, writing is often not the best way for amnestic or traumatized patients to access their memories during initial stages of treatment (Johnson, 1987). Writing serves as a helpful approach with patients who have developed conscious awareness of their experiences but who have not processed or revealed them to others.

WRITING AS TESTIMONY TO OTHERS

Jean-Paul Sartre, in *What Is Literature?* (1967), asserts that the writer does not write for himself alone. Writing is a fundamental act of commitment to the world; through writing, the person is thrown into the world. In contrast, the act of the trauma separates the person from the world. Writing is thus a public act that represents the return of the victim to the world, confronting the sufferer with the reality that bad things can happen for which responsibility must be taken. Writing gives this testimonial solidity and validation, which provide a foundation for transcending shame and achieving forgiveness.

Presenting one's writing to an audience gives distance to the original shameful event. The audience is transformed into both the witness and—through identification with the writer—the victim. Victim and audience are brought closer together. Writing therefore serves to link the victim to the world. The result is the empowerment of the victim. Writing reasserts the sense of personal control over the trauma, elevating the victim into the role of teacher/expert/helper.

The public performance of poetry or prose readings can have profound effects on the course of treatment of PTSD patients precisely because the reparative work already done by putting feelings into language is enhanced by presentation to a live audience. What was initially a private horror now becomes shared.

Everyone becomes a witness through this act of performance to the traumatic or shameful event. More importantly, we hear what one person chose to do in that circumstance. This, Sartre (1967) noted, is the fundamental act of freedom occasioned by writing. At the same time that it brings the individual into the collective, writing asserts the complete freedom of the individual in the face of tragedy.

TRADITIONS OF BIBLIOTHERAPY

Bibliotherapy and poetry therapy have been utilized extensively in therapeutic settings since the 1940s. Clinicians have discovered the power of reading and writing poetry and literature to help patients express their feelings, learn about themselves through the experiences of others, and gain confidence and self-esteem by becoming authors of meaningful writings (Brand, 1980; Hynes & Hynes-Berry, 1986; Leedy, 1969; Lerner, 1978). Bibliotherapy is part of the larger field of the creative arts therapies, in which a wide range of symbolic media are used to access, work through, and then communicate internal states. The role of creativity and aesthetics in healing is becoming increasingly appreciated, and a number of authors have proposed sophisticated integrations of the creative arts and psychotherapy (Barker, 1985; McNiff, 1981; Robbins, 1989; Rothenberg, 1988).

The use of bibliotherapy and poetry therapy with traumatized populations has been increasingly reported (Berger & Giovan, 1990; Bowman, 1991; Mazza, Magaz & Scaturo, 1987; Pardeck & Pardeck, 1984; Sartore, 1990; Watson, 1980; Williams, 1991c). Several authors have used poetry in the treatment of grief reactions (Berger, 1988; Mize, 1975).

However, these reports are largely anecdotal, and few models of treatment for PTSD with writing have been developed to guide clinicians. Johnson (1987) proposes a three-stage model of treatment for the creative arts therapies, involving (1) access to the traumatic material, (2) working through, and (3) integration into society. He asserts that bibliotherapy and poetry therapy have the most applicability in the latter stage of treatment, due to their reliance on developmentally higher media of representation (words) and their power in providing a form for bearing witness.

THE NATIONAL CENTER FOR PTSD PROGRAM

In this chapter, specific ideas for utilizing writing in the treatment of PTSD are illustrated with examples from our intensive clinical program at the National Center for PTSD at the West Haven, Connecticut, Veterans Affairs Medical Center. The 27-bed unit admits Vietnam veterans in cohorts of fifteen for a four-month course of treatment. They receive intensive individual, group, family, and milieu therapy; a psychoeducational program; and many other rehabilitative treatments. The creative arts therapies, including art therapy, music therapy, poetry therapy, and drama therapy, are integral parts of the treatment. These alternate modalities of treatment collectively support an environment in which creativity and spontaneity of the patients are encouraged. The treatment program is staged in three phases. Phase One focuses on the accessing of personal histories and life events, placing the veterans' experiences into a developmental perspective. Phase Two provides intensive education about managing symptoms, confronting negative attitudes, improving family relationships, and discovering positive aspects of the self. Phase Three emphasizes reconnecting with support structures in the community, mourning past losses, and rededicating oneself to long-term therapeutic goals. The work of the program is celebrated in public presentations of a play, art show, poetry reading, and speaking engagements at local high schools. While the methods described are being used by Vietnam veterans, they can also be used with equal or even greater effectiveness by other traumatized populations.

The Writing Program

The various forms of writing therapy utilized in the program include descriptive, reflective, creative, and expository writing. Each of these forms of writing has specific applications.

Descriptive Writing

In Phase One, the veterans are asked to write their autobiographies. They are given worksheets with guiding questions to help them through four phases of their life: childhood, adolescence, military, and postmilitary. A weekly group meeting is used to help them keep on track, to share selections from their ongoing writing with others, and to give them opportunities to share what they are learning from writing their autobiography. Time is given for them to write during the group.

At times as I flew over the jungles I could see the large bomb craters, as if they were a pathway for all to see, the destruction that war creates, the once beautiful landscape, and then there were the monuments of the bare trees that agent orange had so mercifully killed and had raped the earth of all that existed for so many years only to end up destroying many of our own men in later years here at home.

—G. S.

As a young boy I remember growing up on my uncle's farm. We were very poor. My uncle had many different animals. The one I remember the best was the cow, because the day the cow had a calf my uncle made us stay in the house. It started to rain. Mom was cooking supper in the kitchen, and I had taken one of the baked potatoes and put butter on it. I remember holding the potato with a small towel because it was so hot. I stood in the doorway, the rain was coming down real heavy. It had been a hot day and

I remember how cold the rain felt as I stood near the door. When the rain stopped, I remember going out and seeing a beautiful rainbow. The calf had been born.

—K. L.

A second descriptive writing project requires veterans to write down each of their five most traumatic memories. Then, each week in the traumatic memories group, they are given thirty minutes to write about one memory, beginning with the least intense. For the next hour, each one reads it to the group, as the staff and other group members serve as witnesses to the writer's experience. At the end, there is time for comforting and a brief discussion. This writing task provides an experience of proactively accessing and sharing traumatic material, while maintaining emotional control. This process counteracts the usual mode of dealing with traumatic material: avoidance followed by flooding.

When we were about 50 meters from the woodline we received a heavy volume of fire. I struck the ground as rounds hit around me. My guys were wounded in the open, or were dead. I made believe I was dead, too. I waited. Could they see me breathe? Some guys got up and tried to run to the woodline they came from. No one made it. In my mind I wanted to run so bad. . . . Did they know I was alive? But I wanted to run. So bad. And I waited. And waited. I could feel my heart beat. What a strange feeling. People just tried to run one at a time. You could hear them get hit. Some of them screamed. And I wanted to run. But time stood still. And I played dead. And nothing was ever as still, not the night, not a statue, as I was and felt. I just wanted it to get dark. It is [as] if all my life I am in daylight, waiting for the night to come, so I can run. What is time or a heart beat? Now when I want to run I can. Because it feels so good. And finally the night did come, and I ran to safety. And the night still comes. And I run and run and run.

—F. T.

The order had come to pull back. The Lieutenant was in front of me. Blond hair with his eyes forward. A West Pointer, the son of a general, it was he who had led us into the trap. He had only been in country one month.

The short burst from the AK hit home. A bullet entered the forehead of the Lieutenant. As he fell, he uttered, "Oh, my God." The short burst almost found me. Not more than a couple of inches separated my eyes from the explosion of rock as the bullet struck. My face bled. The lieutenant was dead. Just the chance of war that I am alive and the West Pointer, the son of a general is dead. Unavoidable and without reason. Oh, my God.

—F. T.

Both of these forms of descriptive writing are used in the early stages of treatment, are supported by small groups, and focus on past experiences.

Reflective Writing

Each veteran is given a journal to record his or her daily thoughts. The journal writing is done alone, in private, and focuses on the present, helping the writer to attend to his or her own internal process (Fox, 1982; Progoff, 1981). Inner reflection and concentration are also victims of PTSD and need to be given time and space to be practiced again at the veteran's own pace. A specific time in the evening is set aside for journal writing. A journal group meets weekly to provide support, identify patients who are having difficulty, and give patients an opportunity to read selections to each other.

I'm in bed trying to sleep and I hear "Bao Chi" repeated over and over—I look to my right and I see on the floor a shadowy outline of a body which then picks itself up, looks at me, and walks across the room and goes through the wall to the outside. He is in NVA uniform without the helmet and he is bleeding from chest wounds. I can't see his face very well, it's too dark. I couldn't see most of the faces I shot at. But I do know I killed a few because of the blood trails—they never left bodies. We never found their bodies.

—J. B.

I took a walk through the fields and jungles of Viet Nam and I will tell you how I feel. I do not know what's going on, but I've been away for so long. I can't come back and still think things are alright [*sic*]. I've spent too much time in the land of chaos and confusion. Everyday [*sic*] and night ghosts continue to walk my mind. I have been living behind walls that have made me alone. I have been searching for peace which I have never known. Father, please forgive me for I have done wrong. I must have had the strength of ten men to hide my memories behind the walls I have. But look at me now. Hundred and sixty pound weakling.

—J. L.

The veterans are encouraged to reflect on the positive aspects of their lives. The purpose is to remind them of the good part of themselves that they have forgotten or of which they have been unaware since Vietnam. The following is a list of specific themes:

1. What qualities about yourself do you feel are admirable?
2. Describe a positive experience with a female (sister, wife, teacher).
3. Write about a good friend of yours.
4. Describe an experience with someone who acted as a mentor who showed you how to do something.
5. Describe a skill or hobby you do well.
6. Describe a gift someone gave you (e.g., appreciation for music) and the person who gave it to you.

These tasks are usually met with great resistance, and many veterans state that they have never had positive experiences. However, the emergence of positive qualities in the veterans' writings inspired each one to reexamine long-held assumptions about their lack of worth.

What is the meaning of happiness for me?

Is it love? Is it hope?
What is happiness?
To me it is sadness, It is my nightmares.
It is my flashbacks, It is my PTSD.
This is my happiness.

—J. L.

Creative Writing

Later in the program, as the veterans' ability to access and symbolize their internal experience has improved, especially through the use of art and drama therapies, they are encouraged to write poetry. Quite often poetry begins to emerge spontaneously in these veterans, who find that the nonlexical freedom of poetry can carry their emotional messages more effectively. The program culminates in a poetry reading (associated with an art show) in which each veteran reads his or her poem in front of an invited audience. Later, copies of these poems are printed and displayed in frames on the walls of the unit. The reception is always poignant—those attending are touched emotionally and express empathy and gratitude to the veterans—which helps to heal the anger the veterans have held so long toward a society they perceive as indifferent or cruel.

Like the dew, rising
To kiss the morning sun
I'm rising, I'm rising
To be with the ones I love
Like the light dancing
Where the river waters run
I'm dancing, I'm dancing
Soon to that painless place above.

—J. L.

Little Boy

it should have been
    a happy day
that June.
Medcaps are supposed to heal
not hurt.
we came with our medicine
    and compassion
that day.
we wanted the war to go away. . . . .

for a little while.
it had seemed so long ago
that we had heard
children's laughter.
Such a strange sound
until I realized
the laughter was
my own.
i saw you little boy,
with the bright
shining eyes
that reached into my soul
touching
the awakened child in me.
your smile was so full
of innocence
God,
how you touched me.
Why did you choose
that moment to run
between the ARVN convoy?
i watched as the truck
claimed you . . .
spreading your heart and soul
along that dusty road.
Why did i have to be
the last one
you saw
before
the light
failed?
Why?
little boy
it should have been
a happy day.

if we had not come
> to heal

would the sun still touch your smile
> or mine?

—W. B.

Funeral

Do you wrestle with dreams?

Do you contend with shadows?

Do you move in a kind of sleep?

> Time has slipped away

> Your life is stolen

> You tarried with trifles

> A victim of your own folly.

—C. G.

Most of the veterans have never written before and never considered themselves capable of creating artistic and poetic imagery. The experience of writing is a validation of continued inner growth and their ability to create. Some of the veterans have written at earlier points in their lives but, since Vietnam, have neglected this aspect of their creative selves. The writing requirement reconnects them to the neglected aesthetic sensibility of the self. When family members are introduced to the writing, hope in the healing process is inspired as they see tangible proof that the veterans' inner world is not deadened but, indeed, is capable of experiencing emotions. For most families, this is a stunning revelation, for they have only known the angry, bitter, and distancing qualities of the veteran. The writing may also be the first time the veteran has revealed his or her war experiences to them. Being able to understand what the veteran endured in war allows the family to move toward greater intimacy.

The Grunt

He is dirty and dingy, wears a helmet and a flak jacket and a faded uniform. His hands are ripped and torn from contact with barbed wire and rough, sharp branches of jungle undergrowth. His wrists are swollen from mosquito bites and his clothes are spotted with blood from the open holes in his skin left by one of the many leeches which dropped off his body after satisfying their appetites. His clothes are ripped and torn from the rough terrain and his feet are waterlogged, swollen and sore.

His pockets are full and his boots are mudcaked. His eyes never stand still; they move and squint and twitch. He is nervous, aware of every sound, for he operates in a never never world where the difference between death and one more tomorrow depends upon what he sees or does not see, what he hears or does not hear.

He is the one who dies a thousand times when the night is dark and the moon is gone and he is the one who dies once and forever when the enemy rifle belches flame. He is the one who lives as close to war as it is possible to get: May God watch over his soul.

—M. C.

Expository Writing

As part of the latter stages of treatment, in which veterans focus on communication with others in the world, they are given the opportunity to write about their opinions in three forms: the *Book of Remembrance*, the letters to the living, and the ceremony for the dead.

The unit has a *Book of Remembrance*, a large bound book in which veterans in the program are asked to place one piece of writing that will remain as a memorial to their own experience. The *Book of Remembrance* becomes a place where memories of the dead, observations about the war or treatment, and loving good-byes are placed. The purpose of this book is to bear witness to the Vietnam veteran's experience, to educate society, to become a living history so that the world will not forget this event.

The concept is derived from the literary and archival work of Holocaust survivors, whose message to the world is "Do not forget." As Holocaust survivors have found ways to educate society, now Vietnam survivors, who were initially forbidden to tell their experiences, are given a formal opportunity to record their views. The message is that survivors must bear witness, must undertake the burden of educating society.

Many veterans resist this task because their anger at society is so deep. "No one has ever cared to listen before" and "Nothing I can say has any value" are both expressions that emerge before this process begins. However, these attitudes shift as the veterans approach the end of the program. The basic human need to be remembered is kindled as they see this large and impressive book and read the selections from other veterans before them. In this process, they become aware that their unique experience is important enough to record.

Twenty years ago I was discharged from the U.S. Army; but the transformation only took place on paper. That discharge paper did nothing to deprogram my mind. Three years of being taught how to kill and actually killing, and the fear-inspired anger from being immersed in life and death situations during combat operations programmed us for a one way flight, with death being our companion and the return ticket in our minds.

Men like me have been forced to bare [*sic*] the burden of the twentieth century's mistaken war . . . alone, unaided, and struggling with an obvious combat caused mental illness . . . all the while our minds have been on active duty without pay . . . For me that has been since March 24th, 1970 . . . and it has been one hell of a heavy price to pay for "freedom."

—J. S.

Dear America,

It has been almost twenty years since the last shots were fired in Vietnam. For many veterans it seems like yesterday. Now we are faced with a similar situation in the middle east. Haven't we learned anything from our past? I think not.

I had the opportunity to go into our local high school to speak with the students, who are at the age we were when Vietnam started. I was shocked and angered at how little they have been taught about this period in America's history. We have done a great injustice to our young by trying to hide from them the horrors and mistakes of war. Now it is their turn to go out into the world and they are not prepared. We have given them nothing.

Please America, this time if the shooting starts let us remember our returning troops will need our love and support more than ever before in their lives.

—S. H., December, 1990

A second form of expository writing is the letters to the living. Here veterans are encouraged to write to people in their lives with whom they have lost contact, in order to express their desires and regrets. Some of these letters are sent, and some are only written. Many veterans have used the letter format to express feelings of love to their children—something that they cannot do in person. The following excerpt is from a letter written by a PTSD patient to his 14-year-old daughter. During the writing in his therapy session, W was able to cry, process his feelings toward his daughter, and put into words what he could never verbally express. The letter was written after a difficult weekend where he had verbally insulted her. He had never been able to let her know how much he valued and treasured her.

Dear V:

I am writing this letter to you to convey some ideas and feelings that you may not quite understand at this time but hopefully will develop insight into on your way to adulthood. . . . You have very unique personal qualities that never cease to amaze me. . . . The way you play as a carefree young lady, inquisitive of nature's simplest beauties, the launching of dandelion seeds by a mere puff of your breath. . . . I appreciate your ability to absorb and understand my times of anger, loneliness, joyfulness. . . . As you walk through the tears of life may you continue to realize that Daddy's umbrella of love, faith and understanding will always be there.

—W. W.

Another veteran wrote the following to his daughter after many months of emotional isolation. He continued to be unable to visit her, even though, with considerable encouragement, he was able to send this letter.

Dear S.,

I have really missed our talks. They are very important to me. I go through an awful lot of pain related to my Vietnam experiences and have suffered with memories of killing, of terror, of meaningless death and destruction. I am constantly reminded of the war in my nightmares and in waking thoughts—in the guilt I feel in living when so many others died. But I do not want the war to ruin my relationship with you. I am happy life is going well for you. You deserve so much—all that you want. I love you more than you will ever know. You are with me always, Dad.

—R. R.

The ceremony for the dead is conducted in Phase Three. Veterans are required to write down the names of their dead buddies as well as a farewell or a tribute to them. At a local memorial to Vietnam, they read the names out loud and then place the paper in a large urn. After all the veterans have done this, the urn is set on fire, and the ashes rise into the air in a symbolic gesture of release.

This ceremony provides a framework for completing the mourning work avoided during the trauma. The war left survivors with the task of mourning the real losses of buddies, body parts, lovers, and family members, as well as the symbolic losses of innocence, youth, and prewar values. The losses continue to block spontaneity and creativity. Veterans were not able to mourn for the following reasons:

1. Veterans have often cut themselves off from traditional religion. They were angry at the clergy for their ambiguous role in the war. Returning from Vietnam, they did not attend church or pursue the clergy's spiritual counseling.

2. They were expected by society not to discuss the war and therefore had no sanction to talk about dead buddies. PTSD was not recognized as an illness requiring therapeutic intervention.

3. Veterans often were sufficiently disconnected from fellow war veterans by virtue of individualized tours of duty. Consequently, it was very difficult to locate the families of dead buddies and share in their grief.

4. Survivor guilt was a primary symptom, and the veteran often felt guilty about the death of others. Having little counseling by which to resolve this issue, the veteran often kept the dead buddies symbolically alive by communicating with them in a pathological manner.

5. Vietnam veterans were so filled with anger that there was little room for grief.

To My Buddy and Good Friend "Joe Square"

The thoughts of you are so strong within me, that at times it seems that you are alive and with me as I wander through this empty life alone and half scared to death. Yes, the thoughts of you are sometimes warm and comforting. At other times the thoughts are about anger and hatefulness and the warm and comforting thoughts are about when we played together as kids growing up in the neighborhood, in school, riding around in your car. . . . There are times I think about things that happened to you that robbed me of your human presence and turned my anger into a hateful beast of prey, which in turn made my life a living hell. And Joe, my friend, here on these few lines, I shall try to release you from within, by giving you a proper burial that will only leave me with pleasant thoughts of you and try to carry on within a life worthy of the death that you accepted so that I can continue to live on. I salute you my loving brother in mind, body and spirit. I hope to meet you on the battle field in the sky.

—L. S.

I'm writing this letter with a sad heart.

Phil, when I landed in the Nam

you took me under your wing.

you taught me to stay alive

you taught me values.

you taught me to trust

that's why it is so hard for me to understand

why God took you that day in August 1970.

the day you died, a big part of me went with you.

I still miss you.

I know you are with God

because of the good you did on earth

so today I'm saying good bye

and I love you.

—R. G.

During the ceremony for the dead veterans often open their dialogue with God again; to give up their dead buddies, they need to release them to someone or something larger than themselves. This is a profound challenge because many trauma survivors have lost faith in a loving, protecting, or even concerned God and succumb to existential despair. Writing becomes a way to make one's plea to God, to make him accountable for what has happened: "Answer this, God, if you can! Why were you silent—and how will you help me regain faith and love in myself or in you?" When these words form, unlocking the suppressed existential rage, the trauma victim takes another step toward recovery. Ultimately what is required is a change in attitude toward one's own suffering through a fundamental reevaluation of one's being (Frankl, 1969).

Did I tell you that I met God once? Well, I did. He was working as forward air controller—flying around the blue Delta sky in a single-engine prop job. He told us to back off a couple hundred meters—that he could see gooks ahead running for a small hamlet. I couldn't see them, but I was just walking point—I wasn't God. We backed away until the Phantoms came, screaming through the sky to bring righteous destruction to those waiting below.

I was fifty meters from the still smoking hooches when I saw the face of terror. It belonged to a young mother walking toward us—in one arm she cradled a tiny, headless baby. She stared into our eyes and offered each of us the dead baby. We turned away. We could not touch the child. We could only walk away. Something inside each of us had broken.

I'm so sorry, mama, your tears still burn my memories like acid—they burned away all that I felt was good and meaningful. What is left on this earth for people like me?
Did I tell you that I met God once?
Well, I did.

—W. B.

Process of Writing

Generally, patients arrive in desperation and are unable to express themselves in any way. Whether in crisis or just getting by, they are employing strong intrapsychic and interpersonal defenses in order to keep going and not become overwhelmed with their feelings. Though they wish desperately to decrease the internal pressure, they are fearful of losing control and exploding. Any expressive demand on them raises tremendous anxiety. Therefore, the program offers them a staged approach to treatment that allows them to go one step at a time. The process of each writing component generally follows this sequence:

1. Requirement to write, usually with structured guides, and beginning in group sessions, then on their own.
2. Requirement to read their writings and share with fellow veterans and staff; this may evoke catharsis of emotion or demonstration of vulnerability.
3. Receiving feedback from the group, including verbal reassurance and physical comforting.
4. Identification of similarities and differences in experiences among group members.
5. Sharing the written work with significant others.

The overall experience, beginning with writing and culminating with giving and receiving comfort, provides veterans with a corrective experience of having exposed themselves and been accepted. This allows veterans to take the risk of opening up and sharing their writing with family members—a feat that may be less difficult than communicating spontaneously. Significant others generally voice admiration, provide positive feedback, and experience greater hope for the future.

Patients' writings develop in stages from defensive, to conventional, to conflictual, to authentic writing forms. The *defensive stage* is characterized by constriction and resistance. Veterans are fearful of revealing embarrassing or distressing feelings or thoughts and do not know how to control their expression. Writings are short, uncommunicative, incomplete, and veterans may complain that they do not have much to say or that they cannot remember.

I was in the world

I was in Nam

I came back to the world

Now I'm nowhere.

—B. K.

Resistance to writing is often substantial. Many veterans resist for the following reasons:

1. "It hurts too much to put it into words. I would rather let the pain remain inside."
2. "I don't want to remember. I want to forget."
3. "I can't concentrate: I can't remember. This proves to me how much damage Vietnam did to me."
4. "The last time I told someone, they rejected me. It was right after I returned, and I swore never to tell anyone again. No one cares."
5. "I alone can carry and preserve the memory of the dead. To give up their memory would be to betray them and render their deaths meaningless. I alone can do them justice."

In the *conventional stage,* anxiety and constriction have lessened, but patients write in generic, global ways about their experiences, following predictable themes similar to those of other veterans. Traumatic memories are described in terms that avoid the important details that make them come alive for the reader. The therapist often feels that either something important is missing or the veteran is making the whole thing up.

She gave me a gift of life.
She gave me a gift of caring.
She gave me the gift of hope.
She gave me the gift of love.
Now these gifts are gone.
And now I go on searching for what I lost.

—J. L.

Thirteen thousand miles is a long way
home, you have to keep on walking.
Half way around the world is a long
way home, you have to keep on walking.
There is help along the way, but
you have to keep on walking.
There is friendship along the way just
keep on walking.
There is love along the way, so keep
on walking.

When you see the help take it, when
you find the friendship keep it, when
you feel the love hold onto it,
For once you have the help from the friends who
love you, you will have
finally walked your way home.

—O. S.

In the *conflictual stage,* veterans begin to allow conflicting, contradictory, and fragmentary pieces of their internal world to emerge. The form of the writing suffers and appears more fragmented or confused. Affective arousal is again much greater, and one can sense that the veterans are struggling with themselves. Sometimes, at this stage, veterans will frighten themselves and revert back to the conventional stage. Hopefully, they respond with greater engagement and interest, motivated by a desire to clarify their feelings. This will lead them to the stage of authentic writing.

Incoming, Take Cover

Over and over
Day after miserable day
If death is at my heels
then touch me so this hell will be through.
Blood is all around me
my dead Buddy has gone home

Where the hell is my rocket
What's taking it so long or will I be one of the agonized to go
    home alive to tortures, nightmares, endless marriages, to be
    kept alone, the only way to survive in VA hospitals, endless
    shrinks, medication after medication
Over and over till death finally
touches a shattered
decrepit old man.

—J. LaP.

Trying to start, to end. Hoping for a rebirth.
Burying.
There's a lot of targets around.
One step back, two steps forward.
To part ways, to join.
To stay, to run,

and only yesterday, I was playing with toys.

It don't mean nothin'

I am alone. I am not alone.

Hope

Don't think. Just do it. Got to join in the dance.

I'll try for today.

Saddle up for life.

We all didn't wear flowers in our hair.

—R. T.

In the *authentic stage,* veterans find their voice, and powerful, clear, and emotionally laden writing emerges that is deeply poignant. The beautiful, awe-inspiring, creative work that emerges from traumatized individuals when they develop sufficient courage and confidence to speak out is amazing. Truly, art is born out of trauma.

Bac si

why did you move

so quickly?

i know that you

saw me

and the Death i held

in my arms.

i didn't want to shoot

but you moved

so quickly.

did you believe that you

could outrun

my bullet?

your death?

me?

me.

my bullet behind your left ear

entering your brain

ending your dreams

beginning my own.

such a small hole to cause so much

damage

in us both.

Bac si

i carried you from

the dirty canal

and lay you atop the hard paddy dike.

it was then i saw your bag

and its medicines—

so few for such a dirty war—

i touched your face

and saw the pictures

in your plastic wallet.

why, Bac si

why did you move?

I didn't want to

kill you

and end your dreams.

but you moved Bac si

too quickly

forgive me Bac si

please

—W. B.

CONCLUSION

Primo Levi, in *The Reawakening* (1965), observes, "I write what I would never dare tell anyone." Herein lies the anguish of the trauma survivors of Vietnam. Returning to a conflicted nation, they were warned never to reveal their experiences as victims and victimizers. This taboo was one of the ways their experience remained frozen in its original form, blocking an integration of past with present experience, preventing mourning, resolution, and reintegration of self, family and society.

In the PTSD program, the written word becomes one vehicle that allows expression of the previously inexpressible, in a form that can be acceptable not only to self but to others. Poetry, narrative, letter, and memorialization become aids in the journey home.

Various forms of writing are utilized in order to harmonize with the developmental tasks of the PTSD program. Primary among these tasks is integrating the experience of Vietnam into the entire life sequence, thereby widening the veteran's narrow focus on Vietnam as the only significant life experience. Sharing one's life history with empathic and interested veterans and staff becomes a healing counterpoint to the disinterest and rejection previously signaled by society and family.

Elie Wiesel, one of the great writers on the Holocaust, stated that "memory may be our only answer, our only hope to save the world from ultimate punishment, a nuclear holocaust" (Stern, 1982). Those who work with Vietnam veterans have a responsibility to encourage the bearing of witness through the written word. It is only too clear that people's memory is short, that the past repeats itself, that the textbooks used in high school do not teach children about war and its impact, that the lessons of Vietnam are even today obscured and forgotten. Those who treat Vietnam veterans have the unique opportunity to facilitate the transformation of suffering into meaning. The writing process unearths evidence of both impersonal horror and deep humanity. Out of this, we rediscover hope and faith and yet are sobered by the recognition of tragedy.

The principles and methods of treatment described in this chapter are applicable to survivors of trauma in general. The integrated treatment of PTSD requires antidotes for amnesia, fragmentation, and nothingness. Moments of terror frozen inside the victim can be thawed, expelled, and transformed into reasons to live. Writing, as an important form of human expression, has unique characteristics that can facilitate the healing process. These consist of its externalization of feeling into concrete form, emotional distancing by circumventing interpersonal demands, shifts in awareness between creator and observer, and use of consensual language to communicate to others.

But writing is of little therapeutic value if there is no audience. The patient-writer demands of the therapist-audience a heavy responsibility: to be present, to maintain integrity, and—most importantly—to listen.

I Was a Wall unto Myself

There before those panels I bowed my head and cried, my tears mingling with the mist and the occasional splattering rain drop, and looking up to cry out my first and final good bye, I could see their faces. . . . I stood frozen in time. . . . "Good bye, I love you!" I yelled . . . transfixed . . . more lonely than words could describe.

A voice called to me . . . my wife's perfume drifted across the few feet that separated us. She held out her hand. Thunder rumbled. We walked slowly, silently, her hand in mine. . . . Walked away from the Wall and on towards the Lincoln Memorial . . . on into the fog and the mist. I was not at peace. I still am not at peace. . . . But I am healing.

—M. A.

25

Action-Based Therapy for PTSD

Cynthia M. Stuhlmiller

One of the most powerful, yet generally overlooked, approaches to treatment of post-traumatic stress disorder (PTSD) involves learning through action-based experiences. This age-old approach has been widely used in a variety of therapeutic settings, yet its application and effectiveness have received little attention in the PTSD literature. This lack of interest is particularly puzzling because traumatic assault involves an integrated mind/body experience. Approaches that consider the roles of the body and of bodily action in traumatic expression and recovery are vital adjuncts to traditional therapies. In addition, the skyrocketing cost of psychiatric treatment, the enormous number of individuals needing treatment, and the paucity of programs available necessitate a look at alternative means. This chapter illustrates the power of action-based approaches in the treatment of PTSD and suggests ways to apply the principles and strategies of action-based treatment to PTSD. The origins of action-based approaches can be traced back to two main roots: the theories and philosophy of experiential education and the principles and techniques of the Outward Bound program.

ACTION-BASED PROGRAMS FOR PTSD

Although hard evidence is lacking, the success of programs employing action-based therapy provides compelling testimony of their effectiveness. Brief descriptions of the following programs illustrate how and why these approaches are particularly important for treatment of PTSD.

VisionQuest

The program developed by VisionQuest predates the field of PTSD treatment by ten years, yet its relevance derives not only from the traumatized population it serves but also from the metaphors it uses, which are currently being applied to areas of PTSD treatment. VisionQuest was founded in 1973 by corrections professionals who were disappointed by the lack of success of traditional rehabilitative services for troubled youths. This unique approach is based on the teachings and ceremonies of Native American cultures, dramatizing the traditional rites of passage that guide the transition from childhood to adulthood. Emphases are on physical fitness and learning about the self, issues, and problems; the program works as well to instill honor and commitment through building positive relationships with peers and adults.

VisionQuest offers a variety of therapeutic activities ranging from quests including hiking, horseback, or bicycle expeditions to cross-country wagon train and OceanQuest sailing challenges. In Buffalo Soldiers, an advanced program designed specifically for minority youths and based on the all-black 9th and 10th Cavalry Buffalo Soldier troops of the U.S. army in the 1800s, "recruits" retrace the steps of their forefathers. They learn to face and overcome adversity without anger, aggression, and self-destructive behavior. As a "troop," they learn about U.S. history, receive training in precision foot drills, and become involved in the antidrug war. Through outreach activities with school groups, graduates of the program become positive examples for other struggling youths.

Ending Violence Effectively

The founders of Ending Violence Effectively (EVE) also recognized the value of wilderness therapy as a tool for healing. Since 1981 they have worked with survivors of rape, incest, physical and verbal assault, sexual harassment, and other forms of trauma. In addition to traditional counseling services, they use techniques that integrate the mind and body, such as relaxation training, movement and meditation, massage, and hypnosis. A three-day wilderness program offers participants an opportunity to express strong feelings. "We have found that inclusion of this program as part of treatment has supported and hastened the healing process for survivors. Wilderness therapy is a path to learning pragmatic ways of changing one's behavior, of testing new skills, of stretching, reaching, and growing beyond one's limits" (Agosta & Loring, 1991).

Programs for Vietnam Veterans

The first documented accounts of the application of Outward Bound techniques to a PTSD population involved Vietnam veterans from the Northampton VA Medical Center's PTSD Unit in May 1983 (Rheault, 1987). As Vietnam veterans themselves, the group leaders recognized the need to help other veterans build self-esteem, learn to take responsibility for themselves, and overcome seemingly insurmountable obstacles. These veterans had the unique problem of having known courage, selflessness, dedication, interdependence, and responsibility in combat, yet they were feeling guilty about their experiences and condemned for their part in the war. The founders believed that if these veterans could recapture those qualities in a positive context, they would take a big step toward regaining their feelings of self worth and self-confidence (Rheault, 1988).

The program typically involves four days in the wilderness following some preparatory work at the hospital. Small groups (8–10 veterans) hike, camp, climb mountains and do technical rock climbing and rappelling, learn white-water rafting, practice survival skills, and work with ropes. At night, they gather around a campfire to talk about the activities and emotions they experienced during the day (Rheault, 1988).

"Success, failure, fear, courage, laughter, tears, helping, being helpful, despair, exultation, dealing with heat, cold, fatigue, blisters, thirst and sore muscles are all part of the regimen, but best of all is the sense, usually, of having done what seemed impossible and feeling real closeness and camaraderie" (Rheault, 1988 p. 7). After the course, some veterans made important breakthroughs, were more ready to engage in serious counseling, and felt the responsibility and the capability to turn their lives around (Rheault, 1988). The power and effectiveness of this course are evident in the metaphors drawn from the experience. Patients found that the wilderness setting duplicated aspects of Vietnam—"everything except the shooting, wounding, and killing."

The first Outward Bound course for female Vietnam veterans began in 1988. Participants typically spend three days on a thirty-foot ketch, a day climbing rocks and rappelling, and another day on a ropes course. Working together as a group helps build trust and allows the women to share painful memories and acknowledge each other's war experiences (Holman, 1989).

Other clinicians have integrated Oriental grounding and balancing techniques and Native American healing practices, such as thermal detoxification, into their treatment of traumatic stress syndromes (Colodzin, 1989; St. Just, 1991). Wilson (1989d) and colleagues suggested that shamanistic healing should be part of post-traumatic treatment. The ceremonial and purification rituals used to reintegrate warriors into their communities have been found particularly valuable for Vietnam veterans. These rituals involve community support, giving the warriors a meaningful place within the cultural context, honoring them for their sacrifices, and diminishing their sense of isolation and withdrawal (Silver & Wilson, 1988).

In addition, purification in the sweat lodge ritual also holds physical, symbolic, and metaphysical significance. The extreme heat, sensory deprivation, singing, and restricted mobility in the sweat lodge may contribute to the altered production of biogenic amines, endogenous opioids, and catecholamines, thereby contributing to improved mental states (Wilson, 1989d).

In 1985, a team of clinicians set out to replicate, in part, methods learned from the Sioux Indians (Wilson, 1989). Fifteen PTSD-diagnosed veterans completed a six-day wilderness expedition. Treatment included individual counseling sessions, group experiences and desensitization exercises, daily sweat lodge rituals, Native American ceremonies for release and healing, shared responsibility for the basic housekeeping duties, and family-oriented therapy.

Research with these veterans was conducted before and after the experience using a variety of measures, including the Symptom Checklist–90 (Derogatis, 1973, 1977a), Impact of Event Scale (Horowitz, Wilner & Alvarez, 1979), Vietnam Era Stress Inventory (Wilson & Krauss, 1985), Witnessing Atrocity Scale, and Participating Atrocity Scale (Laufer, Frey-Wouters & Gallops, 1985). The one- and three-month follow-up scores showed a significant reduction of symptoms for all psychopathology measures. The Impact of Event Scale and Vietnam Era Stress Inventory also showed reductions in intrusive imagery and avoidance behavior associated with war experiences (the measure of avoidance was not statistically significant until the three-month follow-up). The researchers speculated that avoidance as a coping mechanism may be more resistant to change than other behaviors (Wilson, 1989d).

RATIONALE FOR ACTION-BASED APPROACHES FOR PTSD TREATMENT

The following sections of the chapter address the positive attributes of action-based approaches to PTSD treatment. Table 25.1 suggests ways in which these approaches specifically relate to each symptom of the *Diagnostic and Statistical Manual* (APA, DSM III-R) definition of PTSD.

Action-based approaches for the treatment of PTSD address the biopsychosocial and spiritual components of the disorder. Physiologically, traumatic stress experiences alter organismic functioning. In general, bodily reactions to an extreme stress event involve fight-or-flight mechanisms, endocrine secretions, and increases in catecholamines and adrenergic substances (Wilson, 1989d, p. 26). These neurological processes are so powerful that they can encode themselves in the person's hypothalamic-limbic system and can be reactivated in other conditions of stress. The three symptom groups associated with this state-dependent experiential learning are "1) reexperience and intrusive imagery; 2) avoidance, detachment, emotional constriction, and depression; and 3) physiological hyperarousal and 'overdriven' motor activity and nervous system functioning" (Wilson, 1989d, p. 26).

Action-based techniques can stimulate the arousal and imagery that are associated with the original trauma and that may not be easily accessible through relatively passive means. Skilled, action-oriented therapists witness and guide the response by helping the participant distinguish between the traumatic experience and the representative situation, thereby allowing the exploration of alternative coping options and suitable reframes.

Over time, immersion in a traumatic event leads to reduced production of serotonin, catecholamines, norepinephrine, and endogenous opioids (Wilson,

Table 25.1
Action-Based Therapeutic Approaches to DSM III-R Symptoms of PTSD

DSM-III-R-DEFINED SYMPTOMS OF PTSR	ACTION-BASED THERAPEUTIC APPROACHES
Symptoms of Re-experience	
• Recurrent, intrusive, distressing recollections of the event	• Activities often simulate the traumatic experience in a symbolic, metaphoric, or representative way, offering the therapist an opportunity to guide the individual through the experience using action and control techniques.
• Recurring, distressing dreams of the event	
• Reliving of the event	
• Intense psychological distress at exposure to events that symbolize traumatic event	
Symptoms of Avoidance	
• Efforts to avoid thoughts or feelings associated with the trauma	• In active recapitulation of experience, more details are recalled and can be dealt with.
• Avoidance of activities and situations that arouse recollections of the trauma	• Bonding and trust are facilitated and accelerated through specifically designed exercises.
• Inability to recall important aspects of the trauma	• Many of the activities provoke fun and laughter, counteracting symptoms of ahedonia.
• Diminished interest in significant activities	
• Feelings of detachment or estrangement from others	• Experiential exercise is integrated with the past; emphasis is on the present and on transformation for the future.
• Restricted range of affect	
• Sense of foreshortened future	
Symptoms of Arousal	
• Difficulty sleeping	• Physical activity promotes fatigue and rest.
• Irritability or outbursts of anger	• Alternative experiences illustrate the ability to express and control self in other ways.
• Difficulty concentrating	
• Hypervigilance	• Activities require engagement and careful attention, thereby promoting concentration.
• Exaggerated startle response	
• Physiologic reactivity	

1989d). These reductions are associated with the avoidance, emotional constriction, and depressive symptoms of PTSD. The role of regular exercise in increasing these chemical levels and leading to a sense of well-being is well known. Strenuous or physically challenging action-oriented approaches therefore will reverse the effect at a chemical level. Also, environmental conditions, such as the heat of sweat lodges and hot springs and altitude changes during mountain hikes, can decondition the chronic hyperaroused neurophysiological state associated with PTSD. The resultant healthier state is conducive to new modalities of thinking and experiencing.

The physiological conditions of PTSD that account for the symptoms of avoidance, emotional constriction, detachment, alienation, and depression also account for the resultant social and psychological difficulties of traumatized individuals. Inability to trust, ruminative self-defeating and self-limiting thoughts, feelings of despair, hopelessness, and irritability and anger seriously impair the person's ability to form meaningful relationships with others.

Action-oriented therapy provides alternative forms of living and relating. Activities are geared for success, with a focus on abilities rather than disabilities. Through doing, participants discover that they have capabilities and some power and control over their lives. Learning from a positive encounter can become as permanently etched on the brain as learning from a traumatic experience.

Action-based therapy turns passive therapeutic analyses and interactions into active and multidimensional experiences that augment "talking" therapies. The self-reflective stance required in psychotherapy may impede self-disclosure when the patient is unable to process information in cognitive ways or is able to direct and divert attention from particular issues. Individuals reveal themselves through their actions. Action-based therapy provides an opportunity to observe how the participant actually relates to others, solves problems, and copes.

PRINCIPLES OF ACTION-BASED THERAPY

The action-based approach may not be suitable for every therapist. Therapists must have the willingness to be flexible, be able to provide leadership, demonstrate some level of enthusiasm, be uncomfortable at times, participate, think on their feet, and have interpersonal skills to build and maintain the participants' respect and confidence. They must also be comfortable with self-disclosure. If the therapist has strict codes and boundaries of practice that prohibit self-disclosure or interactions that involve physical activity, action-oriented treatment is not appropriate. These practice requirements may account, in part, for the resistance or skepticism of some practitioners who have been schooled in traditional psychotherapeutic techniques. In addition, participation in action-based activities may have therapeutic effects for the therapist. If the therapist's own issues emerge in the context of working with others in this forum, it is important to acknowledge the connection but shelve personal work for a later time.

Action-based techniques offer the therapist an opportunity to experience the participant in a different way. The focus of work is no longer on correcting individual deficits, but, instead, these techniques enable participants to reveal aspects of control, possibility, and strengths. At the same time, they give clues to where the participant is stuck or limits the interactions with self and others. The techniques can be rewarding for both participant and therapist as they share the success of accomplishment.

Anyone new to, or unfamiliar with, action-based therapy should take part in an activity led by a trainer or therapist with expertise in the approach. In doing so, therapists become aware of their own strengths, vulnerabilities, and issues, and clarify what they bring to the experiential setting that will be useful to the work. Therapists also discover whether they are suited to the work, how they would develop their role, and what applications are possible in their practice.

Some therapists may feel more comfortable in a less active role, such as a participant-observer in a training session. Defining this role and purpose to the participants at the outset of any activity (''I am here today strictly as an observer'') is essential. It may be difficult, however, to encourage participation if the therapist does not model the activity on some level.

After the therapist is fully aware of the drawbacks and possibilities of action-oriented therapy (outlined at the top of Table 25.2) and has established a willingness to attempt the work, adhering to the following principles will help to ensure success. These principles are organized within the framework of the nursing process: assessment, planning, implementation, and evaluation.

Assessment

The therapist's first step in planning any therapeutic intervention is to make a thorough assessment of self, clientele, and resources. Action-based treatment of PTSD requires consideration in the following areas.

Know One's Self

Therapists must be clear as to what they bring to the therapeutic setting that may facilitate or hamper effectiveness. For example, if they tend to be competitive, they must constantly try to avoid the tendencies that are antithetical to the process of therapy.

Know One's Clientele

It is essential that the therapist know the participants' biopsychosocial and spiritual histories as well as their traumatic experiences. It is best if clients provide stories directly, but carefully reported secondhand information may suffice. An awareness of the issues most common, prominent, and troubling to participants not only enables better planning of the action-based strategy but also allows for skilled recognition and intervention as material emerges in the context of the exercise. The therapist must also know the cognitive, social, and behavioral capabilities required for participation. Careful screening of physical capacity is required regardless of the activity.

In addition the therapist needs to know the stage of the treatment to plan interventions accordingly. Some action-based therapists insist that experiential exercises work best in the middle phase of treatment, whereas others find initial action-based techniques can ready people for treatment as well as serve as diagnostic tools. Still others use action-based exercises for confidence building and closure during the end phase of treatment.

Table 25.2
Advantages and Disadvantages of Action-Based Approaches

ADVANTAGES

for the therapist:

- Therapist experiences a different relationship with the participant—one that captures the person's resourcefulness, possibility, and control

- Informal setting of action-based therapy and shared participation in experiences can remove barriers while placing therapists in an approachable, trusted position, with participants still maintaining clear and appropriate boundaries.

- Therapist, as a colearner with the group, makes personal discoveries.

- Therapist has opportunity to work in a different and enjoyable forum.

for the participant:

- Treatment is inexpensive ($110 per day versus $300 or more for inpatient work).

- Program can accelerate therapeutic process by enhancing trust, bonding, self-disclosure.

- Program is powerful catalyst and expediter in the therapeutic process.

- Program doesn't require self-reflective stance.

- Program experience is empowering.

- Approach has recreational aspects.

- Participant has no way to fake experience.

- Participants bring who they are to the encounter.

- Program provides much-needed affirmation of self and sense of possibility: "You can do it differently" with regard to memories of trauma, feelings of personal limitations, saying goodbyes.

- Participants develop strong bonds rapidly.

- Participants experience and practice coping with stress in a controlled environment.

- Program allows physical rejuvenation and health feelings to be evoked in the context of empowerment.*

- Impatience can be examined.*

- Prescreening helps to guarantee safety.*

- The learnings needed to work effectively as a group bring a sense of personal worth and heroic involvement.*

- Participants have a clear choice about whether to participate.*

DISADVANTAGES

for the therapist:

- Therapist may feel threatened, insecure, or unable to interact with participant in less traditional setting because of the activity and level of self disclosure required.

- Exercises can stimulate powerful reminders of traumatic events in both participant and therapist. Therapist may not be prepared to deal with or possess the skills required to act in a safe responsible way in an alternative setting. Therapist must delay working on own issues.

for the participant:

- If issues are not dealt with properly in the context of the activity or in the aftermath, psychological harm or regression can result. Therapist must be willing to follow up and bring closure to the experience.

- Program may stimulate painful memories of trauma the person has been trying to avoid.

- Program may overwhelm and stress participant beyond current coping capacity.

- Improper transfer of learning may decrease effectiveness or experience.

Table 25.2   (continued)

- Activities are clearly doable and geared for
  success.*

- Activities can be metaphorically designed.

- Activities can be tailored to include any population,
  including limitations.

- Activities can include family, alumni to support and
  model.

- Program serves as a diagnostic tool.

- Accomplishments are very clear and noted:
  mileposts of success are marked throughout the
  activities.

- Success on a gradient is guaranteed, evoking
  motivation and a "thawing." Success is vital to the
  activity.*

- Problem-solving and decision-making skills are
  taught and experienced.*

- Social skills are enhanced.*

- Leadership is explored (including self-esteem and
  willingness to perform).*

- Promise and hope appear in participants' vision.

- Expression of grief and emotions such as fear and
  joy is encouraged in a safe environment.*

- Staff participation enhances experiential
  review/debriefing.*

Source: Material denoted by an asterisk is from R. Taini, Thoughts regarding the use of (ropes)
    activities with post-traumatic stress disorder Vietnam veterans. Unpublished notes (Colma, CA:
    Proaction Associates, 1991).

Know One's Resources

The therapist needs to assess the amount of available time, the settings and
exercises that are possible, the amount of money needed to set up the activity,
and the kinds of support in terms of consultation, expertise, and leadership that
are available. Support is particularly vital in a team treatment situation to ensure
lasting value of the treatment and therapeutic follow-up.

Planning

Establish Goals

The goals and objectives of action-based treatment should be based on the
assessment and be clear, reasonable, and appropriate to the treated population.
Particular issues that will likely be addressed through the activity should be
spelled out (see Table 25.1). In addition, the therapist should delineate what
will be done and why and how goals fit within overall treatment plans.

Although some therapists claim to have witnessed miracles, cures are not a reasonable expectation. Goals must be attainable by all participants. For example, an overall goal of action-based treatment is for the participant to experience success and feel empowered. Therefore, challenges must be calibrated to cover a range of abilities. A series of progressive activities that allow participants to look at powerful issues in a graduated, safe manner should be considered. Participants need to understand that they are competing only with themselves and that participation alone constitutes successful accomplishment. Thus, the exercise must be designed to ensure at least a minimal level of success while challenging participants to take safe risks and stretch "one step beyond."

Goals specific to PTSD include developing trust, gaining acceptance, taking responsibility for feelings and actions, achieving the concentration required for clear communication, learning active listening skills, and experiencing the self in a different forum. Participants are given the opportunity to explore their strengths, weaknesses, fears, problem-solving skills, and coping techniques, as well as to have fun.

Select or Design the Activity

Two schools of thought have developed around the issue of whether to tailor the activity to the population. A growing number of clinicians have explored and developed powerful metaphoric activities based on the specific issues of their clients. Gass (1991) provided an illustration of an adventure experience structured to create therapeutic change for substance abusers through metaphoric transfer. The activity, called "Path to Recovery," requires the participant to travel through a maze or web of ropes that symbolizes the obstacles of addiction and blocks the path to a substance-free life. The journey through the web and out into the world of abstinence requires asking for help, bumping into others, keeping hold of the lead rope, and helping others. To let go of the rope during the exercise is metaphorically to lose a chance to achieve abstinence.

Other clinicians do not place as much emphasis on specific metaphoric designs, suggesting that selecting a general, safe, and challenging activity allows the metaphors specific to the individual to emerge (Koller, personal communication, November 1991). The argument is that an activity holds something slightly different for each participant; therefore, attempts to design metaphors may actually limit the experience.

The activity, whether selected or designed, depends on the size and nature of the population, goals, stage of treatment, and resources. Hikes, camp-outs, wilderness expeditions, ropes and challenge courses, rock climbing, rafting trips, and sweats are most frequently and successfully used in PTSD therapy. Rafting, for example, is most often selected for the residents of the American Lake VA Medical Center's inpatient PTSD unit because everyone, even the most physically disabled, can participate.

A growing number of clinicians are attempting to simulate the environments where the trauma occurred or are returning participants to the actual site of the traumatic event. At the American Lake PTSD unit, helicopter rides re-create an air assault, enabling therapeutic interventions as the trauma is relived. Staff members have also led trips to the battlefields of Southeast Asia (see Chapter 12 by Scurfield for more detail). This practice has also been used for Holocaust survivors, who return to the ovens and crawl in and out of them to symbolize the power of survival.

On a smaller scale, a number of exercises, such as the trust walk or trust fall, and metaphorically tailored games, such as scavenger hunts found in fair play and environmental education books, are good strategies for exploring many clinically significant issues. These activities can also be used as warm-up exercises for more intensive work.

Outings, such as roller skating, picnics, shopping, and visits to local community attractions, and longer trips, such as gold-panning expeditions, beach trips, hikes, and ski trips, are therapeutic as well. Because PTSD manifests itself in problems of living, virtually any action-oriented encounter serves as a microcosm, representing the participant's unique experience with the world. The job of the therapist is to assess the participant's interpersonal style, level of self-confidence, communication skills, control over thoughts and actions, experiences of stress, and coping techniques, while gently directing and intervening on the spot.

Plan for Transfer

To enhance the transfer of the therapeutic experience into the person's daily life, a program must emphasize the connection between present and future situations. Planning can involve several techniques, as follows (Gass, 1991).

The therapist must:

1. Design conditions for transfer before activities actually begin, that is, have the participant set goals for experience, define goals, and place goals in writing to firm up the commitment.

2. Create elements in the participant's learning environment that will likely be similar to those encountered in future situations.

3. Provide participants with opportunities to practice the transfer of learning while still in the program.

4. Have the consequences of the experience be natural, not artificial.

5. Provide means for participants to internalize their own discoveries.

6. Include past successful alumni if possible.

7. Include significant others in the learning process.

8. Whenever possible, place more responsibility for the experience with the participant.

9. Develop focused processing techniques that facilitate the transfer of learning.

10. Provide follow-up exercises that aid in the application of transfer.

Plan for Safety

Action-based therapy utilizes the power of context. Creating a safe, supportive, and competent arena to explore traumatic material is particularly important (Rozynko & Dondershine, 1991). Just as an activity can be powerful and beneficial, it can also be physically and emotionally dangerous and harmful. Therapists must use extreme caution at all times. Consequently, safety issues must be carefully considered in the planning phase. The therapist should not attempt anything that provides uncertain safety. Backup and emergency plans are always needed, "just in case."

One frequently used safety method is the well-known buddy system, which partners participants together for the duration of the activity. In addition to the therapeutic effects of having people assume some responsibility for each other, the buddy system provides an extra measure of safety. The rule of thumb is never to let a participant walk off alone unless a buddy and/or the leader has been informed.

Plan the Rules

The rules of a program must be as clear as its goals. One especially important rule in action-based programs is that participants have the right to say no or pass. People need to be able to make informed choices and to be accountable for those choices as they gain empowerment. The therapist must be ready to explain all risks and possible consequences of an activity and to be supportive whether the participant chooses to take part or pass. Although giving clients the right to say no might sabotage an activity, this outcome is infrequent when activities are well planned and well explained. Coercion of participants is to be avoided as an ethical concern. Failure to recognize and accept ethical responsibility is likely to result in disaster.

Include Other Staff

Whenever possible, the therapist should involve a coleader, activity trainer, other skilled therapist, or staff member in planning. If colleagues give input from the beginning, they are more likely to support and assist in therapeutic efforts. Collaboration is especially important in the intervention and evaluation stages.

Involve the Participants

If at all possible, participants should be involved in the planning phase. Early investment helps to generate enthusiasm, foster a sense of capability and control, and provide a therapeutic opportunity to experience responsibility and follow-through. Ultimately it will help ensure the success of the program. Participants themselves may select the activity based on what they would like to explore, learn about, or rediscover.

Gather Equipment

Some activities such as wilderness expeditions require extensive camping equipment, supplies, and extra time for preparation. The preparation stage is also an ideal opportunity to engage participants.

The video camcorder has been of great value as an educative and evaluative tool to document the activity. If the therapist intends to use a camcorder, advance planning as to how it will be used and what consent form participants need to sign is necessary.

Implementation

Introductions

Once the group has convened, introductions are a first step and give the therapist the opportunity to set the tone for the activity. A number of creative techniques are available for helping participants get acquainted. If the participants know each other, they may offer something new about themselves, such as favorite places, foods, colors, cars, and so on. The object of introductions is to have participants become familiar with one another, establish a beginning level of comfort, and above all, have fun!

Explanations

The therapist needs to explain the following aspects of any activity: purpose and goals, potential risks and benefits, time limits, rules of conduct, options, emergency plan, and typical concerns. This is also the time to initiate a buddy system, make others aware of any special medical situations, and discuss confidentiality. The therapist needs to inform participants of his or her responsibilities as a leader, participant, observer, or whatever role he or she assumes.

Rules to deal with threats of harm to self and others are established, as are rules regarding confidentiality among participants. In general, participants are free to share anything about their own personal experiences during and after the activity with anyone they choose. However, they must agree not to discuss anything that would reveal the identity of other participants to nonparticipants.

Begin

The therapist uses his or her best intuition and communication skills to begin the activity. Coleaders or trainers keep frequent eye contact and respond to any signs of distress. A therapist-participant soaks up the experience, keeps an eye on the activities of others, and makes mental notes for later. It may be appropriate to point out therapeutic connections along the way, depending on the therapist's role, the activity, and how well the therapist knows the participants.

Because action-based activities often stimulate reliving of traumatic experiences, the therapist needs to be free to work with the material as it emerges. It is also helpful if the therapist has had prior experience. In these circumstances, the therapist guides in much the same way as for any other flashback.

One of the best ways to effect change is through role modeling. Fun and enthusiasm are usually contagious. Admitting fear, challenge, and doubt; laughing at oneself; and verbally rewarding oneself go a long way. PTSD clients often feel uncomfortable acknowledging and expressing emotions. They need to be reminded that, beyond following the agreed-on rules of safety, there is no right or wrong to the experience. Underscoring the positive whenever possible and being a supportive cheerleader are significant roles for the therapist.

If a participant does decide to pass or say no to a portion of the activity, he or she needs to acknowledge why. It is also helpful for the therapist, at some point, to explore the real and symbolic consequences of that choice with the participant. For example, a woman refused to participate in part of a ropes course challenge. Despite the support and encouragement of her husband and the group, she stood firm with "no." The husband felt very disappointed and wished she could have shared in the group's success. The therapist needed to explore her reasons for purposely excluding herself, the effect exclusion had on her and others, and what choices worked best for her.

Evaluation

Experiential Review

Reflection/review is a critical component of any action-based approach. The therapist needs to allot time for each participant to describe the experience and to express feelings. This period allows participants to comment on what they discovered about themselves and others; what they found particularly encouraging, helpful, challenging, frightening, or enjoyable; and what they wish they had done differently. During this time, trainers and/or therapists, as colearners, should share their experiences, personal discoveries, and observations of others. If this is a one-shot program with no follow-up, the therapist should avoid issues that cannot be reasonably dealt with during the review. Participants may be encouraged and even assigned to express themselves in journal writing. Written evaluations are also good information-gathering tools; some participants may feel uncomfortable speaking in a group. This reflective period also provides an opportunity to collect data on specific aspects and outcomes of the experience.

Watching a videotape of the activity is a good way to review participation and analyze individual experiences and interactions. Because some of the activities are extremely powerful, the therapist may have the group generate a list of how to deal with what has emerged. Some form of follow-up is also usually in order.

Saying Good-Bye

If the experience was long or intensive, participants will typically want to swap phone numbers and addresses and offer hugs, handshakes, and good tidings as they leave. Closure must be sensitively dealt with, as endings often recapitulate part of the traumatic experience. At the same time, it affords an opportunity to "do it differently."

Reviewing the Experience with Other Staff Members and Trainers

The therapist will probably want to get together with all staff involved in the activity and process the experience from a personal and a professional standpoint.

Reporting

In keeping with the commitment to pass along pertinent information to other therapists, the therapist will want to note impressions before they fade. Notes, evaluations, and videos are invaluable for later use when the therapist has obtained the consent of participants to release the information.

Summary

These principles of practice for action-based experiences provide a rationale and framework to enhance therapeutic assessment and treatment of PTSD. Action-based therapy is not designed to replace other therapeutic interventions and practices; instead, it focuses on enhancing established treatment objectives by providing a richer therapeutic environment for change.

CONCLUSION

Many clinicians in the PTSD field have come to realize that the experience of trauma is far from peripheral or unimportant; in fact, it can become the core of a person's life, negatively affecting social, psychological, physical, and creative well-being. They recognize also that all forms of activity (recreation, leisure, hobbies, group associations, cultural involvements, and entertainment) are therapeutic in promoting and maintaining emotional health. Clinicians have the responsibility to draw on these areas to help their clients realize their aspirations, overcome traumatic and difficult situations, and rediscover their potential.

Action-based therapy is beginning to win increasing recognition as an important tool in the treatment of PTSD. Its psychological implications go far beyond its use in rehabilitation. The possibilities for action-based applications are flexible and varied, affording an unlimited opportunity for self-discovery.

Our society is increasingly characterized by blind conformity and a collective groping for identity and meaning. Experts predict that the remainder of this decade will be marked by a return to rituals and adventuring as means of self-discovery. Advances in the prevention and treatment of psychological trauma are also possible. Without scientific validation of the therapeutic efficacy of action-based PTSD therapy, however, the possibilities will remain undocumented and less generally accepted.

26

Hypnotic Approaches in Treating PTSD: An Ericksonian Framework

Robert A. Schwarz

INTRODUCTION

Researchers have found links between hypnotizability and severity of symptoms in Vietnam vets with post-traumatic stress disorder (PTSD) (Stutman & Bliss, 1985); as well as higher hypnotizability profiles in Vietnam vets with PTSD than normals or other psychiatric patients (Spiegel, Hunt & Dondershine, 1988). A variety of reports describe the utilization of hypnosis in treating post-traumatic stress disorder (Brende, 1985; Brende & Benedict, 1980; Ebert, 1988; Gilligan & Kennedy, 1989; McMahon, 1986; Mutter, 1986; Silver & Kelly, 1985; Spiegel, 1981). The hypnotic procedures and techniques to treat PTSD are supportive, uncovering, abreactive, or integrative (Brende, 1985; Peterson, Prout & Schwarz, 1991). Peterson, Prout, and Schwarz (1991) present a broad description of these different facets of hypnotic treatment.

This chapter provides a more in-depth understanding of how hypnosis is useful in treating reactions to trauma, as well as in-depth descriptions of several hypnotic techniques. In addition, the problem is approached in a more holistic manner. Each of the techniques described incorporates more than one of the above-mentioned facets of hypnotic approaches to PTSD. An understanding of the relation of hypnosis and PTSD can be an invaluable component of treating survivors of trauma. Many professionals who work with survivors of sexual abuse and other trauma typically state that it would be inconceivable not to be able to think in terms of trance and hypnosis.

A STATES OF CONSCIOUSNESS MODEL OF TRANCE AND TRAUMA

Lankton (1985) described a states of consciousness (SoC) model of hypnosis that is particularly well suited to understanding hypnotic treatment of PTSD. A SoC is considered to be a unique, dynamic pattern or configuration of psychological structures, an active system of psychological subsystems, a "SoC molecule" consisting of various "atomic sub-structures." These substructures can include feeling states, patterns of attention, degree of sympathetic and parasympathetic arousal, quality of internal dialogue and mental images, memories, and so on. Colloquially speaking, a SoC is a state of mind. During everyday life people use different SoCs for adapting to varied roles and situations. Various SoCs contain discrete, as well as overlapping, sets of resources and limitations. The use or misuse of these sets determines the "utility or liability of any particular SoC." (Lankton, 1985, p. 28). For example, a father would not want to use his high-powered work SoC while he is changing his child's diaper or having a romantic dinner. In these situations the high-powered work SoC would be a liability.

Furthermore, the shifting and combining or recombining of SoCs are rule-governed. In other words, some mental states are strongly connected, while others are weakly connected or not connected at all. For instance, a victim's visual memory of the trauma may easily lead to fear or sadness, rather than feelings of security. The person certainly has SoCs that contain security, but they are usually not readily accessible from the SoC that contains the visual memory of the trauma. Changing the rules of recombination of SoCs is one of the major uses of hypnosis in treating trauma, as this chapter shows.

The idea that rules govern the recombining and shifting of experience within and between SoCs supports Shor's (1959) ideas about consciousness and trance. Shor postulated that each person has a generalized reality orientation (GRO), which is a "network of associations, memories and learning that supports, interprets and gives meaning to all experiences" (Schwarz, 1984). In other words, the GRO is the set of rules that govern how we organize our various SoCs. These rule-based shifts of SoC let each of us experience a "normal" or familiar reality. Trance occurs when the rules of GRO have either been rendered nonoperational or been significantly altered in some manner. A traumatic experience significant enough to meet Criterion A of the *Diagnostic and Statistical Manual III-R* for PTSD (APA, 1987) is quite likely to be beyond the flexibility of the GRO, thereby rendering it at least partially nonoperational. As a result, the person's consciousness becomes altered. In other words, the person goes into a trance.

Trance states occur in many situations other than formal hypnosis (e.g., daydreaming, meditation, getting lost in a book). Hypnosis is present when there are the development of a trance state and the construction of a special, temporary orientation to a small range of experience (Shor, 1959). In trauma situations, the limited range of experience is usually one of danger, lack of personal resources, and uncontrollability. Perhaps this is one of the reasons the perceived threat of significant harm increases the chance of the development of PTSD by 800 percent (Kilpatrick et al., 1989).

STATE-DEPENDENT ASPECTS OF TRAUMA

Erickson (1980a, 1980b) viewed trance as a particular psychological state that made it easier to reassociate and reorganize one's inner experience. While these facets make it useful for therapy, the knife unfortunately cuts both ways. Trauma by its very nature breaks the GRO and therefore induces a trance. The same psychological mechanisms that make it easier to reassociate and reorganize SoCs toward flexibility and resourcefulness can also produce highly limiting and rigid SoCs that become dysfunctional. During a traumatic event, persons not only are overwhelmed by the stimuli but are in a nonresourceful state and susceptible to ideas and suggestions (helpful or non-helpful) from others as well as themselves. In other words, abusers may directly or indirectly tell persons that they are no good. Accident victims may tell themselves that they are no good, because they should have been stronger.

Rossi and Cheek (1988) stated the individual's reactions to the trauma become state-dependent. In the language of this chapter, the physiological reactions, emotions, thoughts, meanings, and so on become linked together in a traumatic SoC. Even though this SoC may be partially or completely dissociated (and therefore partially or completely out of awareness), it can influence the individual in dramatic ways, not unlike a powerful post-hypnotic suggestion.

SYSTEMIC VIEW OF TRAUMA AND STATES OF CONSCIOUSNESS

The importance of taking a systemic view of understanding trauma has been discussed by a variety of authors (Green, Wilson & Lindy, 1985; Peterson, Prout & Schwarz, 1991). The role of the social support system has been particularly stressed. Lankton's model also postulates that SoCs are partially induced, maintained, and systemically reinforced by the social stimuli. Not only do family members, friends, and social networks elicit and support certain responses and SoCs from a traumatized individual, but different types of responses made by the traumatized individual elicit different responses and SoCs from the environment. For instance, a crying patient who tells people about the intrusive traumatic memories that are occurring tends to elicit different types of behaviors and SoCs from family members than a person who is yelling and angry and avoids telling anyone what is happening.

PRINCIPLES OF HYPNOTICALLY BASED THERAPY

According to Erickson (1980a, 1980b), recovery or cure takes place as a function of a reassociation and reorganization of the client's inner experiences, learnings, and associations. In other words, a presenting complaint can be viewed as a specific SoC molecule or pattern of molecules. Therapy breaks up the connections between the atoms of this state and/or adds or replaces them with other atoms, for example, feelings of confidence or safety. Therapy recombines the components of the SoCs involved in the symptom. A specific symptom state can be made up of a variety of atomic components such as negative internal dialogue, hyperactivity in the sympathetic nervous system, mental pictures with both negative content and structural properties that act as cues for danger, and internal feeling of powerlessness. Therapy involves changing some or all of these components. Just as in chemistry, altering a molecule changes its properties. The "trick" to efficient therapy is to know which components relate to the biggest change in the client's state.

The Utilization Principle

The utilization principle (Erickson, 1980a, 1980b) suggests that any behavior, emotion, or psychological mechanism that the patient brings to the therapeutic situation can and should be utilized by the therapist as part of the therapy. Whatever psychological mechanism a patient uses to produce psychiatric symptoms can also be utilized as a resource to solve the problem. One of the chief aspects of the response to trauma is dissociation, which, following the utilization approach, becomes one of the chief resources for resolving PTSD.

Mastery Orientation

Despite the myth that hypnosis means losing control, psychotherapy utilizing hypnosis usually involves the injunction to have more mastery over one's own experience. This therapy is active and involves the direct alternation of perception, sensation, and memory. Clients are asked to make mental images and then alter the images or their sensations. Clients learn that they can change something that previously was unchangeable. They actually learn to regain control of their own functioning.

Solution Orientation

Hypnosis, from an Ericksonian perspective, includes a strong solution and future orientation. The question to be answered is, What would the solution to this problem look like and sound like and feel like? Therapists have certain ideas about how one overcomes trauma. Also, clients might have certain ideas about what they will be like once they overcome the trauma. One of the problems that clients have is that they do not pay attention to their own ideas about what a solution might look like and sound like; they may not even think it is possible. This is usually called a lack of hope. One of the injunctions of hypnosis is that as a result of the experience the client will be different, will change, and will move toward a solution.

What is known about how people heal from trauma? In other words, what is known about the molecule of healing? Most persons who overcome traumatic situations and return to a well-functioning life describe recovery as the ability to:

1. regain access to resources and apply them to appropriate contexts. They regain access to good feelings, relatively positive belief systems, and good self-images. These are applied to, and maintained by, supportive relationships and satisfying life tasks.

2. maintain appropriate boundaries;

3. honor and value previously dissociated parts of the self, associating them back into devalued and dissociated parts while being in the present in ways that value and honor all parts;

4. learn to place the trauma in a larger context so that they can dissociate from the abused self and associate into a larger self; can shift attention from past to present and future; and can learn from the trauma.

Suggestions, whether using formal hypnosis or informal hypnotic communication, are geared toward these ends. Therapists should not dictate in an authoritarian manner that these are the exact goals toward which the client should be working. Nevertheless, therapists can resemble navigators of a sailboat and keep directing clients toward these or similar goals. Of course, sometimes if the desired goal requires heading right into the wind, it will be necessary to "tack" (to move at an angle to the wind away from the direct route and then later make a course correction).

Need for Resources

Trauma treatment commonly asks the client to tell the story of the trauma event in order to review the trauma to have a catharsis. The problem that can occur is the client goes back to the trauma without the necessary resources and simply becomes traumatized again. This iatrogenic problem occurs when treating trauma cases. The integration of traumatic experience via catharsis and review tends to be more complete and speedy if the review occurs with a resourceful state in the foreground. In many therapeutic modalities, the therapeutic relationship is considered to be the important resource that makes the difference. While it is true that the therapeutic relationship is an important resource in itself, the degree of resourcefulness can be significantly increased by accessing the client's own resourceful states. The inability to keep resources in the foreground of experience when remembering or working through traumatic material is perhaps the single biggest impediment to recovery from trauma.

What defines a resource or, more precisely, a resourceful state? A resourceful state is a state of consciousness that allows persons to have an effective, empowering, and adaptive choice as to how they respond. For any given situation the needed resources are decided by the client. When traumatized people are asked what resource or emotional state would have made the events or memory of the events less traumatic, they cite common themes of safety, security, strength, mastery, competence, or "knowing that I will survive." It is important to note that relaxation is generally not one of the resources this author's clients pick. Therefore hypnosis or desensitization using relaxation as the main resource does not meet these criteria.

An initial job of the therapist is to elicit these needed resources. Sometimes clients know exactly what they need. Other times, therapists need to use their own experiences, either in general terms or as empathic responses to the story of the client, to generate possibilities. These are then offered to the client in a twenty questions manner (e.g., Do you think you would have needed a feeling of power?) to negotiate the needed resources. Clients usually do not name the resource that is perhaps the most important, dissociation.

The next job of the therapist is to find or build these resourceful states even if the resourceful state comes entirely from another context. For instance, the resource of safety may come from a memory of being with one's dog or competence from experiences of winning a race. Once built, these states must be associated or anchored to specific cues so that they can easily be activated and maintained.

Under "normal" circumstances, these resourceful states would not be available during a trauma and would fade into the deep background. Trauma overwhelms the system. By using trance, associational cues (anchors), and focusing of attention, therapists assist clients to keep their resource in the foreground. Using the "molecular" metaphor, the client retrieves and keeps the atomic resource as part of the SoC to be maintained when reviewing the trauma.

Dissociation and Its Utilization

A primary defense mechanism utilized by trauma victims and others with PTSD is dissociation. In fact, intrusive symptoms are an attempt of the psyche to process the split-off or dissociated material (Horowitz, 1986; Epstein, 1989). Thus, the term *dissociation* usually refers to a splitting off of information or consciousness. This chapter suggests an alternative view. If a hypothetical world has only two states of mind, A and B and if a person is dissociated from state A, then that person must be associated to state B. Conversely, if a person is associated to A, then that person is dissociated from B. In this artificial world, it becomes clear that one is associated to one place or the other; "dissociation" becomes a relative condition.

A clear example of this view is found in the pathological condition of multiple personality disorder (MPD). A patient who is associated to one alter is dissociated from the others; the two are not integrated. The dissociation in MPD is pathological for several reasons. First, rules that govern the separate alter SoCs include separate memories and identities. Second, there are amnestic barriers between the alter SoCs.

Dissociation also comes in many more benign, if not helpful, forms. If a man had a bad day at the office and wants to be able to have a romantic evening, he might find it helpful to dissociate from the office and associate into a romantic mood. He would not think that he is dissociated in this circumstance. But, in fact, he is "dis-associated" from the office state of consciousness and associated into the romantic mood state of consciousness. In other words, dissociation is actually an illusion based on a point of reference. Therefore, the more germane questions are, from where is the person dis-associating, and to where is the person associating?[1] Of course, in the real world the actual state of consciousness that a person can be in can be very complex and essentially mixed. Frankl (1989) described how he minimized the effects of the Nazi concentration camps by dis-associating from his current time and associating to a resourceful future that included the potential for making meaning out of his Holocaust experiences, a classic example of associating into a resourceful state. The recognition of the dissociation/association mechanism as a dynamic process is crucial to understanding hypnotic treatment of PTSD.

HYPNOSIS AND HYPNOTIC TECHNIQUES

Informal Hypnotic Techniques (Using Hypnotic Language)

Dissociation and Distinctions

Dissociation is really a matter of making a distinction in regard to which SoC a person is associated. Purposeful use of language primes and reinforces distinctions that help a person stay associated to more resourceful SoCs. A variety of common distinctions are useful, including: then/now, there/here, them/you, and the you then/the you now.

It is important to distinguish clearly between what was happening then at the time of the trauma versus the resourcefulness of now. For instance, if the therapist is asking what the client is feeling when discussing the trauma, this inadvertently suggests to the client to associate into the trauma. To avoid this, one could say, "Keeping your current feelings present, what *did the you back then* feel?"

When dealing with situations of abuse, boundary violations, or secondary victimization, the distinction between "them" and "you" can be important. Sometimes clients have not made accurate distinctions about what they thought and felt and what others said they should think or feel. The therapist may need to question the client by asking, "Was that your idea, or was it something they said to you?"

It can often be useful to help clients dissociate their identity from the lack of resourcefulness that they experienced during the trauma by using language such as "the old you," "the twenty-year-old you," "that young child back there" (Erickson, 1992). This language-based use of dissociation helps clients consider the experience of what happened to them without identifying (in other words associating into the identity) with the person experiencing the trauma. This approach is actually used in many different "therapies." It is a fundamental aspect of "child within" work, transactional analysis, Gestalt work and even the "observing ego" of psychodynamic work (if one is observing something, one is dissociated from it). Even though there is an initial emphasis on dissociation, the final result is more on integration. The author refers to this phenomenon as "disowning in order to own."

Clients are linguistically associated into a resourceful aspect of the self in order to consider a less resourceful or more problematic aspect of themselves or their experiences. The therapist may need to spend considerable energy to keep the person in the resourceful identity while considering that person over there. For instance, the therapist may insist that the client talk in the third person (e.g., "He was feeling" or "She thought that"). From the position of strength the client can then understand and eventually integrate or own the material. While this approach may seem artificial, it actually protects the client from too much pain and too much shame. When clients do not feel debilitating shame or pain, they can obtain very good insight into themselves, with little resistance.[2]

Hinting at the Future

Another distinction is the then/now/will be distinctions of time. Therapists can be very specific when they talk about time. One good way to instill hope in people indirectly is to suggest that they will have a more positive future. It is important to use language that keeps the possibility of change open. Examples include "So you have not gotten over those nightmares, yet" and "When [not if] you have recovered."

Following the work of de Shazer (1988), Dolan (1991) derived a Solution-Oriented Recovery Scale for survivors of sexual abuse. She uses the scale to ask clients what they think will be signs of their recovering. The presupposition is that recovery will occur; the only question is what the signs will be. This type of future and solution orientation helps clients to begin to organize their attention toward healing.

Formal Hypnotic Techniques

Intrusive Aspects of PTSD

People continue to have intrusive experiences after trauma because they have not been able to assimilate and process the information from the traumatic experience (Horowitz, 1986; Epstein, 1989). Instead, because they used disso-ciative mechanisms to split off the material, it keeps coming back. When people describe being plagued by intrusive symptoms of PTSD, they are usually feeling, thinking, and/or acting as if they are still in the trauma. They are associated into the trauma state and dissociated from their current context as well as their resources. Therefore, the treatment method necessary to correct this measure is to help clients be able to be aware of the trauma, while remaining emotionally dissociated from the trauma and emotionally associated with their current context and their resources. All of these techniques should be used in the context of an overall treatment plan by clinicians who have sufficient training in hypnosis, imagery, cognitive restructuring, or other similar approaches.

The following technique utilizes the dissociative/associative processes to re-solve most of the intrusive symptoms of PTSD. The goal of the process—the main reason it works—is that it helps the person stay disassociated from the trauma state and associated to a resource state. However, as the reader will note, each of the four aspects that occur in survivors' solutions to trauma is present to some extent. (1) Survivors gain access to resources and can apply them to appropriate contexts; (2) they maintain appropriate boundaries (the boundaries of here and now to there and then); (3) they honor and value previously dissociated parts of the self (see step 6 in following section); (4) they can dissociate from the traumatized self and associate into a larger self (the part of them watching and then comforting the traumatized self).

Trauma Reassociative Conditioning[3]

The linear, cookbook format of this process allows for a clear and specific description of the sequence of steps in the process. It should be learned in the same manner in which a musician learns a specific scale. This does not preclude improvising or making adjustments, as is often necessary in real clinical situa-tions. It exemplifies the principles of accessing resources and the therapeutic utilization of dissociation.

1. Explain to clients the overall process, to let them know what will be happening, with appropriate rationale. Reassure them that the therapist will not let them fall back into the traumatic feelings/experiences (with the exception of the first time to know what it looks like). Formal trance induction is optional because, as persons follows the succeeding instructions, they will inevitably go into a trance.

2. Have clients briefly think of the traumatic experience. Watch them for the minimal cues (e.g., breathing rate, posture, skin color, muscle tonus) or earliest signs that they are associating into the trauma. Then re-orient them. Clients are not to be allowed to associate back into the trauma. During step 8, it is imperative that the therapist keep watching clients for these cues and not allow them to fall back into the traumatic feelings/experiences. If this does start to happen,

then the therapist brings clients back to the safety of here and now where they feel competent and safe.

3a. Ask clients to think of a strong and positive resource state that would have protected them and led to less traumatization had it been in the foreground of experience during the stressful event (e.g., self-confidence, feelings of competence, joy). This state does not have to have anything to do with the trauma; however, it does have to be a powerful enough resource to match the intensity of the trauma. If it is not sufficiently powerful, use additional resource states.

3b. Develop a signal or cue associated with the resource state. The cue could be the name the clients call the state or a touch. If the resource is strength, the therapist could firmly hold the clients' wrist. If the trauma was sexual abuse, touching clients by the therapist may not be the best course of action. An alternative could be making a fist.

3c. Have clients associate into the resourceful state and really be fully associated to the state. For instance, if the resource was joy at a time they were at the most beautiful place they had ever been, they should not be seeing themselves in that place (which is dissociated). They should be at the place, seeing what they saw, hearing what they heard, feeling what they felt, smelling the scents, and so on.

3d. While clients are associated to this resourceful SoC, associate the signal to this state. For instance, the therapist says, "joy" joyfully ("At this moment you are feeling joy. Just allow yourself to fully feel joy. With every fiber of your body feel the joy").

4. Have clients begin to establish a dissociated point of view. Have them imagine themselves to be in a movie theater sitting with the therapist watching a blank movie screen.

5. Ask clients to remember just before the traumatic incident. Instruct them to make a static picture of this moment. Ask them to see the younger self in detail in this first frame just before anything stressful happened and then put this frozen image on the screen.

6. Establish a double dissociation by suggesting that clients imagine floating either up to the control room or to the back or side of the theater so they can watch the therapist and themselves sitting and watching the movie screen. Clients are to experience themselves in the control room watching themselves with the therapist watch the movie. Associate a signal to this state (as in 3b and 3d) with touch or a sound. Then have clients return to the movie seat.

7a. Ask clients to get back the resource state and keep it constant. At the same time the therapist or clients apply the signal for this state. Once this aspect of the molecule is stabilized, then

7b. Ask clients to float out of their body into the projection booth, keeping the resourceful feelings present at all times (if a signal for this double dissociation has been established, it should now be used). At this point clients should be feeling the resource (e.g., joy) and be doubly dissociated up in the projection booth watching themselves and the therapist watching the screen with a frozen image of just before the trauma.

8. Instruct clients to let the movie of the past experience run. They are to watch to a point where the trauma was over and they knew they were no longer in danger. Reinforce dissociation with verbal suggestion (e.g., "As you continue to be in the projection booth, watching yourself sitting with me here and now in [this year] watching the younger you go through that experience then and feeling the joy, you can be learning about that experience, perhaps getting a new understanding, a new perspective"). The therapist must make sure there are no developing signs of traumatic feelings. If at any time clients start to develop the traumatic experience, reinforce the dissociation or resource state. If that does not work, bring them back to here and now. Reinforce the signals and/ or distance the movie by making it farther away or smaller or add more powerful resources. Sometimes it is enough to just remind clients not to associate into the movie.

9. When clients finish watching the old experience (they may need to watch it more than one time as a matter of clinical acumen and the clients' own desires), instruct them to float back to their body, still keeping the resourceful feelings. Have clients, from the here-and-now resourceful position, look at their younger self at the end of the experience. Suggest to them to go up to the movie screen or even to step into the picture, and instruct them to do whatever it takes to reassure and comfort the younger self. Suggest that they reassure the younger self that they made the best choice available to them at the time and that the present self appreciates and values the younger self and that they are who they are today partly because of what the younger self went through then. Reassure the younger self that the clients know they are going to be all right, since they are the younger person's future self. In this step, a variety of other restructuring and integrative work can be done as needed.

10a. Have clients bring the younger self off the screen and sit back down in the chair with the here-and-now self (re-integrate). Reorient clients to the here and now.

10b. [Optional.] Have clients think of a time in the future in a context where the old symptoms would likely come up. Tell the clients they now can watch themselves with their new learnings and resources. Then have them associate into the picture and experience themselves being more resourceful. This step stabilizes their resourceful SoC via rehearsal, expectation, and association.

10c. [Optional.] Suggest to clients that the therapist would like them to learn how much they have changed and think about the past trauma now with all that they have learned. This step, if clients do feel more resourceful, acts as further ratification that they are different. If clients still associate into the traumatic state, this step acts as feedback to the therapist that more work needs to be done. This process can be repeated, if necessary, for the same trauma or for similar traumas. An additional step suggests to clients that their unconscious mind is able to discover if there was some event prior to the trauma that primed them to have such a negative reaction. If such an event is discovered, it can be worked through.

The steps of this technique are guidelines for the clinician. The technique identifies the appropriate use of the dissociation/association distinction and the need to retrieve resources. Different variations of this approach exist from which the therapist can make adjustments and alterations in accordance with clients' idiosyncratic needs.

This approach is not a panacea for treating PTSD. However, as long as there is not a significant amount of secondary gain, it effectively alleviates intrusive symptoms and phobic avoidance. By itself, it is not as effective with long-term problematic character traits that existed prior to the trauma or solidified identities that resulted from poor adjustment to trauma. However, when dealing with beliefs and identity issues that result from trauma, this approach can be a good first step.

One variation that helps a client change decisions and beliefs that were made as a result of the trauma can be facilitated by a more involved interaction between the adult resourceful self and the child or adolescent self (when redecision work is needed, the trauma usually occurred at younger age). This process involves the following additional steps after the communication and nurturing between the adult and child self have been established (as in step 9).

1. Facilitate a recognition that any decisions made by the child of the past occurred due to limited resources.

2. Then suggest a trade of resources between parts for a more creative adjustment (Lankton, 1992). This often involves having the adult self-provide safety and love and having the child give back the resources that were dissociated off as a part of the decision, such as spontaneity or the ability to express anger. These resources are then linked to the future scenarios (Lankton, personal communication, 1992), as in step 11a.

Other Clinical Issues

A variety of issues relevant in this type of work need to be mentioned. First and foremost is the need for safety and protection (Dolan, 1991; Williams, Chapter 11). Several safety and protection issues relate especially to hypnosis. If memory retrieval is to be used with hypnosis, it must be done in a manner that is respectful of the client's defenses and resistance. Clients often ask the hypnotist to make them remember "no matter what." The hypnotist should never agree to this. Instead, the use of a comment such as the following is advised:

I understand that you really want to know what happened to you, and hypnosis can allow you to gain access to those experiences. But, we cannot go any faster than your unconscious mind will allow us. If your unconscious mind slows down the process or even stops the process, it is doing so in a desire to protect you in some way. So, we need to respect that important intention, and we will find ways together to make sure that your unconscious mind feels that you are safe and protected in whatever manner is relevant.

A second safety issue recognizes the need to access appropriate psychological resources before memory retrieval takes place. Some of the appropriate types of resources have already been mentioned. However, the need for sufficient dissociation cannot be overstated.

A third issue questions how much a person needs to recall in order to "get over" the trauma. It is important to recognize that similar to experimenters, therapists present certain demand characteristics to their clients (Orne, 1969). Clinicians should be careful not to suggest to clients that the only way to recover is to remember "everything" about the trauma. Dolan (1991) noted that the client needs to remember only what is necessary in order to heal. Clients can also use the desire to dig for the "truth" as a way to avoid dealing with current aspects of their life that are more relevant to solving their presenting problems. These matters need to be negotiated in the therapy process.

Ideomotor Signaling

Rossi and Cheek (1988) described the theory and use of ideomotor signaling to access traumatic memories. Ideomotor signaling differs from conscious and volitional movement. The movements are minimal and perseverative. An everyday example of this type of movement is the small, perseverative nodding people do when they are in agreement with a speaker. Ideomotor signaling involves asking the "unconscious mind" of the hypnotized person questions that can be answered "Yes," "No," and "Not ready to answer." These answers are usually assigned to a specific finger of one hand. Signaling does not necessarily need to be motoric. Signaling can be in the form of internal pictures (for instance, seeing a version of the self signal yes or no with head nods). Following the utilization principle, the hypnotist seeks to find some type of specific communication that will provide for client feedback.

How does this type of approach work? Traumatic memories become amnestic because they were encoded in a state-dependent form (i.e., a specific SoC). The SoC associated with the trauma is created and maintained at the biological level via neural modulation by neuropeptides. Ideomotor signaling can be helpful, according to Rossi and Cheek (1988), because "the relatively mild stress arousal that patients experience as they ideodynamically review their problems releases a pattern of information substances (peptides and stress hormones) similar to that which originally encoded their problem in a state bound form. . . . [This] accesses the state bound amnesia that have blocked the patient's previous efforts at self-understanding" (p. 77). Two possibilities derive from this hypothesis. First, actual, conscious, verbal recall is facilitated by taking this intermediate "ideomotor" approach. Second, actual conscious recall may not be necessary (or as necessary) to resolve the symptomatic problem.

The permissiveness of the approach has two therapeutic aspects. The goal of getting the memory becomes secondary to the process of activating these inner psychobiological processes of mind-body communication and healing in which the client must engage to answer the question (Rossi & Cheek, 1988). Any response from the client is utilized as feedback for the direction and pace of the therapy. As with any utilization, this approach minimizes the interpersonal problems and resistance that occur with direct or authoritarian methods.

Second, ideomotor signaling facilitates dissociation, which helps to deepen trance, and protects the client from a fully associated recall (a revivified memory) that the client is trying to avoid. Formal ideomotor signaling can be built into any approach, as can informal observation of the ideomotor signals or minimal cues communicated by the client. Rossi and Cheek (1988) described the retrospective approach and the progressive chronological approach. The *retrospective approach,* considered to be a safer technique, uses a "20 Questions" style of asking questions. The general pattern of questions (adapted from Rossi & Cheek, 1988, p. 29) is as follows:

1. Accessing the problem
   a. Is there a past trauma responsible for your symptoms? (If no, check for a group of events.)
   b. Did it occur before you were thirty years old? Twenty years old? [and so on].
   c. Did it occur at home? In Vietnam? [and so on].
   d. Allow your unconscious mind to review what is happening. When it knows what it is, your "yes" finger will lift. As it lifts, the memory will come up, and you will be able to talk about it. (If extra safety is desired, ask if it is OK for the conscious mind to know what it is.)
2. Therapeutic reframing
   a. Is it all right to tell me about it? [The patient tells what happens; therapeutic suggestions and reframing are used as needed. Aiding the client to bring the more mature or adult understanding to the situation is helpful.][4]
   b. Is there an earlier experience that might have set the stage or made you vulnerable to what you have just told me? (If yes, proceed as in step 1 above.)
3. Ratifying therapeutic gains
   a. Now that you know about this and have these new learnings (from the therapy in steps 2a and 2b), can you be well? (If the response is no, more work needs to be done.)
   b. Is there anything else we need to know before you can be free of this problem? (If the answer is yes, proceed to step c.)
   c. Let your unconscious mind give a "yes" signal when it is ready to give you a date of satisfactory resolution of the problem into your conscious mind. (If a satisfactory response does not occur, more therapeutic work needs to be done.) [An alternative approach is to ask the unconscious mind if it is willing to work on the problem over the week so more could be achieved in the following session.]

In the *progressive chronological approach,* considered a more advanced approach, the client is asked to go back to a time before the trauma occurred. He or she is taken forward in time to the point of the trauma and then through the various stages of, and reactions to, the trauma. Throughout the process, ideomotor signaling is used.

A benefit of the ideomotor approach is that it begins to access the SoC that contains the trauma without conscious awareness or recall. Lankton (personal communication, 1992) described a variation of this unconscious processing of the trauma, without conscious awareness, using multilevel dissociation if the client could not recall the trauma. After establishing a safe environment and retrieving the necessary resources, the therapist uses the following complex dissociation/association format (adapted from Lankton, 1992):

1. Ask the client to imagine a "grown or current self" (part I) in the middle of the room.
    a. This person is conscious and knows what the conscious mind knows.
    b. This conscious mind is to be the only "part" of the self that communicates with the client.
    c. The client then imagines communication taking place between this part and himself or herself.
    d. Ideomotor signaling is established for the therapist to continue with more intricacy.
2. Ask the client to ask the projected part to dissociate further.
    a. Projected part (part I) is asked to see another part.
    b. This second part (part II) is not seen by the client.
    c. Part II represents the unconscious and can communicate only via the ties with part I.
    d. Part I, therefore, becomes a buffer between the memory and the client.
    e. The client adds an additional part if needed, if the client becomes too anxious. (Usually, two parts plus the client are enough.)
3. Have the client ask part I to ask part II to review the trauma from a comfortable distance.
    a. Only by means of dialogue or signaling (such as seeing the "head nods") from the imaginary part I can the client know what is occurring.
    b. Conduct a careful elaboration of part II, reviewing the scenes and sharing with part I only what it is safe to share.
    c. Care should be taken to keep reinforcing the dissociation verbally by emphasizing the different levels of awareness of the self, part I and part II. (E.g., part I might know only that part II would have finished reviewing the trauma for the first time but not know what part II now knows.)
    d. The therapist should not be surprised or disconcerted if the client's conscious report is that he or she does not know what is going on.
4. Repeatedly review and communicate with the self from the past.
    a. Continually request and guide the client to instruct part I to ask part II (only) to review the trauma and to communicate with the self from the past.
    b. Help the client instruct part I to help part II help the self from the past (for instance, as in step 9 of the trauma process). In some instances the reassociation of learnings can take place at a completely unconscious level.

    If the client does not need to remember and is giving clear ideomotor signals that the problem has been resolved, the therapist can reinforce this with appropriate suggestions and safeguards (e.g., "If at some point you need to remember, it will be OK to do so''). The client can be instructed to take this resolution and apply it to his or her social context (as in steps 10a and 10b of the first technique described in this chapter). The therapist should not impose the idea that the trauma needs to be made conscious. After all, if the trauma can cause a problem from an SoC that is out of awareness, a therapeutic SoC that is out of awareness can be used to resolve the problem.

If memory retrieval is the goal, the following steps are taken, with the caveat that clients need to remember only what is necessary to heal (Dolan, 1991).

5. Remove the intermediate parts gradually.
   a. Have part II communicate to part I everything part I needs to know about the trauma.
   b. The client must repeat the above steps (D1–2) until part I has integrated the material, which is still out of the client's awareness. This eventually creates a one-level dissociation for the client.
6. Work to achieve the desired and agreed-upon goals in a one-level dissociation.

Reconnecting Clients with Their Social Environments

An aspect of the numbing and avoidance responses that occur in PTSD is the pulling away from loved ones, hobbies, and so on. Once the trauma itself has been processed, clients may spontaneously return to their social networks. This, too, is more likely to occur if the client is treated relatively soon after the trauma. If the PTSD has been chronic and the avoidance and disconnection have been occurring over periods of years, more active measures may be needed.

Appropriate resources need to be accessed. These may be new understandings that clients have of themselves due to the work done to process the trauma or specific SoCs that contain resources for involvement with others. For instance, clients can be age-regressed to a time before the trauma and allowed to re-associate into the more social self. They can then be asked to watch themselves with these feelings in a variety of current contexts that "were" (tense shift) problematic but now are more enjoyable. Next, they can be asked to associate into these experiences with their new resources. (This approach is modeled after Lankton & Lankton's (1983) self-image thinking.) During this process, a variety of suggestions can be given to clients to help them rediscover old resources in new ways and make adjustments to old learnings.

SUMMARY

This chapter described a state-of-consciousness model of trance and trauma as the foundation for hypnotic treatment of PTSD. The importance of providing clients with needed resources before dealing with traumatic memories was discussed. Emphasis was placed on the utilization of dissociative and associative processes to help survivors of trauma build states of consciousness that reassociate them to their resources, while dissociating them from the traumatic experience. Dissociative processes in the form of ideomotor signaling were also described.

NOTES

1. The author wishes to credit Robert Dilts and Todd Epstein from whom he first heard this idea.

2. This is actually a classic example of Erickson's utilization approach. It is the therapist who is suggesting the dissociation that clients usually do themselves. Since the therapist is suggesting that the person in the office is not the person back then, the client can actually consider the person back then and, quite spontaneously, have insight about him or herself.

3. This technique has been taught for a number of years in workshops and seminars. This process was first generalized by Bandler and Grinder for treating phobias, and was published by Lankton (1980).

4. Depending on what is remembered, the therapist might segue into the process for resolving intrusive symptoms at this point.

Part VIII

Special Group Interventions for Trauma Survivors

27

A Twelve-Theme Psychoeducational Program for Victims and Survivors

Joel Osler Brende

INTRODUCTION

The focus of this chapter is a psychoeducational program for patients who have suffered from stress and trauma. It is based on principles of group psychoeducational therapy first used by the author during the treatment of substance-abusing Vietnam veterans (Brende, 1984). It has been widely accepted that group therapy, including the rap group for recovering veterans (Brende, 1981), is a useful modality to help recovering trauma survivors. Psychoeducational approaches have been less widely publicized, although bibliotherapy has reportedly been used to help depressed psychiatric patients (Scogin, Jamison & Gochneaur 1989), survivors struggling with unresolved grief (Mahan, Schreiner & Green, 1983), and recovering substance abusers (Pardeck, 1991).

Traditional psychotherapy tends to use principles of (1) establishing a diagnosis and recommending the most suitable form of therapy; (2) establishing a therapeutic relationship; (3) appropriately managing the patient's regressive symptoms; (4) confronting and resolving the patient's unconscious resistances to recovery; (5) establishing therapeutic objectives; and (6) clarifying the ethical issues embedded in the therapeutic experience (Meissner & Nicholi, 1980). Psychoeducational groups, however, are less likely to consider these principles important.

This author's experience is that patients suffering from a variety of stressful or traumatic experiences can benefit from gaining a cognitive awareness of the key elements of trauma recovery. This is the primary focus of a psychoeducational program, a program that also integrates the following psychotherapeutic principles:

1. *Diagnosis*. Although it is widely recognized that no one form of therapy is appropriate for all patients, a psychoeducational program is appropriate for patients who share common experiences of stress and loss. In this author's experience, many of the participants benefiting from the program suffer from the diagnosis of post-traumatic stress disorder (PTSD), as well as depression, dissociative disorder, bipolar disorder, adjustment disorder, substance abuse, and borderline personality disorder. It is particularly helpful, however, when participants begin their participation in the program to take a PTSD assessment (Appendix I) to provide them with an idea of the nature and severity of their symptoms.

2. *Transference and Countertransference*. Transference and countertransference elements are often problematic during therapy, particularly if the therapist is a trauma survivor and has not fully resolved his or her symptoms (Brende, 1991a). At such times, the therapist's overprotective qualities might become aligned with the patient's victim identification (''victim-self''), resulting in the therapist's falling into enabling or rescuing behavior. This phenomenon can also cause splitting within a treatment team, a difficulty inherent in the treatment of trauma survivors with identity fragmentation syndromes (Parson, personal communication, 1992).

The advantage of the psychoeducational approach is a minimization of transference and countertransference problems. A trained group leader who primarily uses lecture and facilitation of discussion limits the potentially negative transference. Yet, a positive transference relationship between group leader and participants is also very important. A positive transference minimizes resistances to the learning process and weathers the negative feelings that could emerge in some patients who suffer from post-traumatic fragmentation symptoms. Furthermore, as the duration of the psychoeducational group extends over a longer period of time, the leader is often able to use techniques of confrontation and clarification during the discussions to increase a patient's self-awareness. These techniques have meaning only when the relationship is a trusting one.

3. *Regression*. Regression can be either destructive or constructive (Brende & McCann, 1984). One type of regression for a trauma survivor is a flashback, which, if it occurs during therapy, may lead to resolution of post-traumatic symptoms. On the other hand, when a survivor relives a trauma in the context of misunderstanding or rejection, a flashback becomes a retraumatizing experience, causing further shame and fragmentation. This psychoeducational program hopes to foster growth, not destructive regressions. While participants may recall traumatic experiences, they are encouraged not to ''open up'' until completing theme three, which focuses on resolving shame and building trust. Themes 5 through 8 also encourage traumatic recollections by helping participants understand how their destructive or painful emotions of anger, fear, guilt, and grief are linked to past traumatic experiences.

4. *Resistance*. Trauma survivors are unlikely to move forward without help. They have been in cycles of resistance for years, often repeating their traumatic experiences and self-destructive behaviors again and again. The psychoeduca-

tional format helps participants to understand their resistances and sometimes provides a supportive setting for confrontation.

5. *Therapeutic Objectives*. Trauma survivors often are not sure what help they need. The psychoeducational format helps them formulate their recovery objectives much more clearly. As group participants confront their issues and the twelve themes are more clearly defined, each can more easily grapple with important objectives. Furthermore, themes 2 and 5 are designed to specifically address issues of meaning and purpose.

6. *Ethical Issues*. This psychoeducational program includes themes with important ethical issues that revolve around the resolution of guilt (theme 7), control of self-destructive symptoms (theme 9), commitment to justice (theme 10), commitment to purpose (theme 11), and helping others (theme 12).

In 1984–86, the author developed a structured psychoeducational group approach in a specialized treatment program for Vietnam veterans in Bay Pines, Florida, VA Medical Center. During their average hospital stay of three months, veterans were helped to resolve chronic war-related post-traumatic symptoms, many of which were associated with unresolved issues of guilt and shame (Mahedy, 1986). The program also included a component of twelve spiritual steps (Brende & McDonald, 1989; Brende, 1990, 1991a, 1991c). It soon became apparent that there were a number of advantages in this treatment approach, including the following:

1. Participants gained new knowledge as a way of improving self-esteem.

2. Participants had specific information to read and reread after they left the program.

3. All participants were expected to gain the same basic knowledge about the acute and long-term affects of post-traumatic stress disorder and the principles of recovery.

4. Individuals could become part of a twelve-step trauma recovery group following completion of the program, called Combat Veterans Anonymous (Sorenson, 1985; Brende, 1990; 1991b).

The program was originally designed to fit the duration of a twelve-week hospitalization period. It encompassed twelve themes, one for each week, as follows:

1. Power versus victimization

2. Seeking meaning in survival

3. Trust versus shame and doubt

4. Self-inventory

5. Anger

6. Fear

7. Guilt

8. Grief

9. Life versus suicide

10. Justice versus revenge

11. Finding a purpose

12. Love and relationships

Four structured psychoeducational meetings were held each week. At the first meeting, the leader asked the members of the group to define the theme, wrote the various definitions on a blackboard, led a group discussion, and asked participants to complete theme-specific questionnaires and work sheets to be used for the next day's discussion. At the second meeting, the leader asked participants to discuss the completed work sheets, including a color-coded guide to measure progress. At the third meeting, participants discussed ways to improve their recovery process related to the specific theme, and at the fourth meeting, participants discussed the theme-specific spiritual step with the assistance of the hospital chaplain.

PROGRAM STRUCTURE AND APPLICATION FOR DIFFERENT TREATMENT SETTINGS

The author has used variations of this psychoeducational program in several other non-VA settings where each theme has required from one to seven hours a week to complete. The body of the chapter describes the structure of those sessions for each of the twelve themes, as they have been applied to the treatment of adults, both men and women, who suffered from a variety of traumatic experiences, including childhood sexual abuse, severe automobile accident, assault, industrial accident, and deaths of family members. The program has been used in various settings.

In a private day hospital in 1988–90, patients received treatment for three to fifteen months for emotional and behavioral symptoms with diagnoses including post-traumatic stress disorder, dysthymic disorder, Bipolar disorder, borderline personality disorder, and multiple personality disorder.

The psychoeducational group involved five hours of time each week in a total program consisting of thirty hours of treatment. One hour daily was used for group time. One theme was the focus of each week so that the entire twelve themes could be covered in three months.

In 1991–92, the author used the program in short-term hospital treatment for military dependents and retirees. The average length of stay was two to three weeks, and an average of twenty different patients with a full range of psychiatric diagnoses completed the program each month. In this program, all twelve themes were completed in a two-week period. Patients remaining longer than two weeks rotated through the two-week program as long as they remained in the hospital. At the time of admission, patients were given a workbook and asked to complete work sheets as assignments between meetings.

As a part of their aftercare program, patients were asked to return weekly for a group that included the twelve-theme format. A small group of six patients was involved in this aftercare group, spending a portion of each weekly therapy time to discuss a specific theme and spending from three to four weeks on each theme. All twelve themes were completed in four to six months.

An added component of this program was a twelve-step self-help group. Veterans started groups called Combat Veterans Anonymous (Sorenson, 1985; Brende & McDonald, 1989) or War Veterans Anonymous (Brende, 1991b). Survivors of other kinds of traumas formed a group called Trauma Survivors Anonymous (TSA), started by one of the graduates of a structured program led by the author (Brende, 1990, 1991b). The TSA group has met weekly in a local church since 1990 and spends approximately three weeks on each of the twelve different themes, with an additional emphasis on the spiritual step for each theme.

TWELVE-THEME PSYCHOEDUCATIONAL GROUP FORMAT

The format for the two-week short-term hospital program is as follows:

1. Administer a twelve-theme PTSD assessment at the beginning and completion of the program (Appendix I).
2. Use appropriate diagrams during the group (Appendix II).
3. Use twelve work sheets for homework (Appendix III).
4. Follow a format that is structured over a six-day week, preferably three hours a day (this can be condensed to a shorter time if necessary).
5. Structure meetings to include time for the leader to provide instruction and discussion of topic, often using a blackboard.
6. Include drawings and collages to add depth to the involvement.
7. Use theme-specific exercises or role playing if desired.
8. Include a spiritual step for each theme for those who are open to a twelve-step format.

Guidelines for Participants

1. Participants are expected to take the assessment at the beginning and after completing the program.
2. They are expected to complete the homework between meetings.
3. Rules applicable for all therapy groups pertaining to no violence or use of nonprescribed substances are in force in this program.
4. The primary purpose of this program is to learn. However, the best way to learn is to participate.
5. Participants do not have to reveal personal traumatic memories if they do not wish to do so and have the freedom to reveal as much as they would like when comfortable.

THEME 1: POWER VERSUS VICTIMIZATION

The goal of theme 1 is to present an overview of post-traumatic responses, victimization, destructive power, and positive power. In the first hour, the leader presents the figures in Appendix II in order to introduce the subject of post-traumatic stress disorder and involves the group in a discussion about their personal experiences as they apply to the diagrams. These diagrams are also discussed during future meetings. During the last ten minutes of this first meeting, the leader asks all participants to complete the PTSD assessment (Appendix I).

During the second hour, the therapist discusses the significance of the participants' total score and twelve theme-related scores on the PTSD assessment and their relationship to Figure A27.1. The color-coded system to determine severity of symptoms can also be discussed during this time: red means symptoms are destructive and potentially life-threatening; black means symptoms are significant enough to block recovery; yellow means symptoms are minimal, and there is motivation for recovery; green means there are no significant symptoms, and there is positive action toward recovery.

Next, the group leader discusses the definition of power. It is helpful to use the blackboard for this part of the hour. In two columns, the leader lists the participants' descriptions of positive power (the power of persuasion, the power of physical strength, the power of asking for help, the power of education) and destructive power (the use of brute force, the use of dictatorial methods, the destructive use of weapons, the use of manipulation and deception, the misuse of money).

Group members have an assignment to complete before the meeting—the work sheet for theme 1. In the third hour, participants can take turns reading the introductory paragraph on the work sheet and discuss the questions for colors red (destructive symptoms) and black (blocked symptoms). Participants can use the last half of the hour to discuss their plans to achieve positive power.

THEME 2: SEEKING MEANING

The goal of theme 2 is to present participants with the concept that traumatic experiences can open a door to positive events and can become opportunities for personal growth. In the first hour, the facilitator leads a discussion about the significance of surviving traumatic events. The blackboard is again a useful tool. Participants are encouraged to talk about the list of reasons they think they survived traumatic or frightening events, dissociative experiences, fight-flight-freeze responses to frightening events, emotional numbing and disbelief, and precognitive experiences.

In the second hour, members complete the theme 2 work sheet before the meeting. Participants can take turns reading parts of the work sheet and discussing the questions as well as their plans to seek meaning. Before the meeting, members read about (or view an appropriate videotape about) survivors who have discovered meaning from their traumatic experiences. One source is Victor Frankl's *Man's Search for Meaning* (1984). Discussion of these reading materials and their application to the participants takes place during the third hour.

THEME 3: TRUST VERSUS SHAME AND DOUBT

The goal of theme 3 is to help participants become aware of the relationship of shame to post-traumatic fragmentation as well as their difficulties with distrust, shame, and doubt; ways of resolving their difficulties; and ways to improve their trust level, particularly with other participants. In the first hour, the group discusses the definition of trust as well as definitions for shame and distrust. Figure A27.2 in Appendix II can be used to facilitate the discussion about the relationship of persistent shame to fragmentation symptoms. Participants are encouraged to talk about their own experiences of trust or distrust related to past traumatic experiences.

Members complete the work sheet for theme 3 before the meeting. During the second hour, participants can take turns reading parts of the work sheet and discussing the questions, as well as their plans to resolve shame and improve their trust level. They discuss ways to build trust within important relationships, with other group members, and with their higher power if they are participating in a 12-step program.

In the third hour, participants, with the help of a trained leader, do trust exercises. These can include the trust walk (individuals are blindfolded and safely led by another trustworthy person), falling backward into the supportive arms of group participants, and standing together and defining boundaries and needs for personal space. Following the exercises, the participants discuss their responses.

THEME 4: SELF-INVENTORY

The goal of theme 4 is self-inventory. In the first hour, the group discusses the topic truth versus secrets. Using a blackboard, the leader writes down the participants' various symptoms associated with either recalling or avoiding unpleasant or shameful memories: intrusive memories, nightmares, physiological memories, withdrawal, secrecy, distorting the truth, pathological lying, and exhibitionism. This is followed by a discussion about the pros and cons of self-revelation and the time and place when self-revelation and sharing of memories may become a healing experience instead of a retraumatization.

The assignment to be completed before the second hour is: "Draw the most significant traumatic experience that has happened to you. Then, on a separate sheet of paper, list every traumatic experience you have had, the date on which it happened, and the symptoms or other aftereffects since it occurred." During the group session, in the second hour, the leader uses Figure A27.3 (Appendix II) to talk about how victims may become "addicted" to traumatic experiences and repetitions of traumatic events in their lives. Participants can then discuss their drawings, experiences of victimization and addiction to trauma and stress, and the pros and cons of talking about their painful memories at this time. Before the meeting, members complete the work sheet for theme 4. In the third hour, participants can discuss their answers and then use the final portion of the hour to give feedback to one another, emphasizing at least one positive attribute.

THEME 5: ANGER

The goal of theme 5 is to help participants become aware of both positive and negative aspects of anger, their problems with destructive anger, and ways to express anger constructively. In the first hour, the leader directs a discussion about anger and both destructive and constructive aspects. Participants can see how problems with anger can be associated with symptoms of victimization: physical illness and passivity versus explosive outbursts. The facilitator leads a discussion about the relationship of anger to fear, guilt, and grief and discusses ways to recognize hidden anger in procrastination, habitual lateness, sadistic humor and sarcasm, overcontrolled speech, boredom and apathy, passivity, hyperirritability, clenched jaws, grinding the teeth, habitual fist clenching, depression, and physical illnesses.

Before the meeting, members complete the work sheet for theme 5. During the second hour, participants take turns reading questions on the work sheet and discussing the questions for destructive symptoms and blocked symptoms. Participants should also discuss how they can better express anger in positive ways.

The third hour focuses on assertiveness. The following assertiveness principles can be discussed:

1. You have the right to accept or reject criticism.
2. You have the right not to justify any of your behavior that does not hurt yourself or others.
3. You have the right to change your mind.
4. You have the right to decide if you are responsible for solving other people's problems.
5. You have the right to make mistakes and to take responsibility to correct them.
6. You have the right to say, "I don't know" and "I don't understand."

This time can also be used for assertiveness training exercises and role-playing exercises or to apply assertiveness principles.

THEME 6: FEAR

The goal of theme 6 is to help participants become aware of both the positive and negative aspects of fear and ways to cope more effectively with fear-related symptoms. In the first hour, the leader directs a discussion about the definition of fear and aspects of fear that are both constructive and destructive. The group can also discuss the relationship of persistent fear to victimization symptoms, including risk-taking behavior or panic, terrifying nightmares, compulsive symptoms, and phobias. Through the use of the blackboard, participants can list their definitions of both positive and destructive fear, using personal examples if they choose.

Before the meeting, members complete the work sheet for theme 6. In the second hour, participants can take turns reading parts of the work sheet, initially discussing the questions for destructive symptoms and blocked symptoms. During the last part of the hour participants can discuss their plans to resolve destructive fear, panic symptoms, frightening nightmares, and phobias.

Members are to draw their most frightening memories and their most common responses to fear, bring their drawings to the group, and discuss them and the ways they would like to resolve their fears during the third hour. As a group exercise, participants then choose an appropriate member of the group and draw on a large piece of paper how they will help this member resolve his or her problems with fear.

THEME 7: GUILT

The goal of theme 7 is to help participants become aware of both the positive and negative aspects of guilt and ways to cope more effectively with symptoms associated with unresolved guilt. In the first hour, the leader discusses the definition of conscience, the positive aspects of appropriate guilt feelings, and the destructive consequences of unresolved guilt. Figures can be used to facilitate a discussion about the relationship of unresolved guilt to victimization symptoms: antisocial or perverse acts versus excessive guilt feelings. Through the use of the blackboard, participants can list their definitions of both positive and destructive guilt, using personal examples if they choose.

Before the meeting, members draw a memory related to guilt. During the second hour, group members discuss each drawing with other members. They also do a group exercise: after choosing an appropriate member of the group, participants draw on a large piece of paper the ways they will help alleviate or resolve this member's guilt feelings.

In the third hour members complete the work sheet for theme 7 before the meeting. Participants can take turns reading parts of the work sheet, initially discussing the questions (destructive symptoms and blocked symptoms). During the last part of the hour participants can discuss their plans to resolve destructive guilt as listed in the yellow and green sections.

THEME 8: GRIEF

The goal of theme 8 is to help participants become aware of the normal phases of grief resolution and ways to cope more effectively with symptoms associated with unresolved grief. During the first hour, the leader directs a discussion about the definition of grief, the normal phases of grief resolution, and the destructive consequences of unresolved grief. There can also be a discussion about the relationship of persistent, unresolved grief to victimization symptoms of isolation, abandonment, and depression. Participants can discuss their understanding of the normal phases of grief resolution and symptoms caused by blocked grief phases, using personal examples if they choose.

Before the meeting, members draw a memory associated with unresolved grief. In the second hour, during the group meeting, they discuss the drawings with the group. Then, after choosing an appropriate member of the group, members complete a group exercise by drawing on a large piece of paper the ways they will help alleviate or resolve this member's persistent grief.

Before the next meeting, members complete the work sheet for theme 8. In the third hour, participants can take turns reading parts of the work sheet, initially discussing the questions (destructive symptoms and blocked symptoms). During the last part of the hour participants can discuss their plans to resolve destructive grief.

THEME 9: LIFE VERSUS DEATH

The goal of theme 9 is to help participants become aware of the ways they may be self-destructive or block their capacity to live life fully; a second goal is to then enable them to make a commitment to living. During the first hour, the leader involves the group in a discussion about the definition (both obvious and subtle) of self-destructive symptoms and the destructive consequences of retained suicide fantasies. He then leads a discussion about the relationship of unresolved suicide thoughts and feelings to victimization symptoms, including self-destructive habits and addictions of food, cigarettes, drugs, alcohol, sex, gambling, and so on. Participants are encouraged to share personal examples of self-destructive symptoms if they choose.

Before the next meeting, members draw their self-destructive thoughts or habits. In the second hour, they discuss the drawing with the group if they choose. Then they proceed with a group exercise: participants choose an appropriate member of the group and draw on a large piece of paper the ways they will help alleviate or resolve this member's self-destructive symptoms.

Before the meeting, members complete the work sheet for theme 9. During the third hour, participants can take turns reading parts of the work sheet, initially discussing the questions (destructive symptoms and blocked symptoms). During the last part of the hour participants can discuss their plans to resolve self-destructive symptoms.

THEME 10: JUSTICE VERSUS REVENGE

The goal of theme 10 is to help participants clarify the meaning of justice and to become aware of the relationship of long-standing bitterness to self-destructive symptoms, blocks to relinquishing long-standing bitterness, and the difference between justice and revenge. During the first hour, the leader directs a discussion about the definitions of justice and revenge, as well as the differences between the two. Participants' definitions of justice versus revenge are listed on the blackboard. It is also helpful to discuss the relationship of unresolved anger and bitterness to victimization symptoms, using personal examples if they choose.

During the second hour, participants can take turns reading questions on the work sheet. During the last part of the hour participants can discuss their plans to seek justice and resolve bitterness and anger. Before the next meeting, participants complete the work sheet for theme 10 and review the list of persons toward whom they feel anger or bitterness (as assigned on the work sheet). They also clarify with whom they would hope to pursue further justice and whom they would like to be able to forgive. These topics are discussed during the group session in the third hour.

THEME 11: FINDING A PURPOSE

The goal of theme 11 is to help participants clarify, individually, a sense of purpose pertaining to education, spirituality, relationships, and personal goals (both immediate and lifelong). During the first hour, the leader leads a discussion about the problems people may have because of a lack of purpose, followed by a discussion about victimization symptoms of purposelessness, fanaticism, and psychosis. Participants should also be encouraged to talk about the definition of having a purpose: being a part of something greater, making and completing personal goals, helping others, and so on.

Before the meeting, participants complete the theme 11 work sheet. During the second hour, participants can take turns reading parts of the work sheet and discussing the questions for colors red (destructive symptoms) and black (blocked symptoms). Participants can complete the hour by discussing their individual plans to find a purpose, as listed in the yellow and green sections.

The assignment to be completed before the third hour's meeting is to "draw yourself as you would like to be in one month, one year, and five years." During the group meeting, they discuss the drawings in the group. Members may also complete a group exercise of a group drawing or collage. On a large piece of paper, participants can make a group drawing or collage of a group project or common task that can improve their group, their program, or their community. If it is possible to do so, this project may then be planned for future completion.

THEME 12: LOVE AND RELATIONSHIPS

The goal of theme 12 is to help participants become aware of the ways they block meaningful and loving relationships, as well as ways to improve their capacity to love and to help others better. During the first hour, the leader directs a discussion about disturbed relationships, codependency, "addicted" relationships, and isolation. In addition the group discusses the definitions of friendship love, erotic love, unconditional love, and intimacy, using personal examples if they choose.

Before the meeting, members complete the work sheet for theme 12. During the second hour, participants discuss their answers and spend most of the remaining part of the hour discussing the attributes of a healthy family. In a healthy family:

1. the family members communicate and listen to one another;
2. they provide emotional support and protection for one another;
3. they trust each other;
4. there is mutual respect;
5. they can play and laugh together;
6. they are willing to share responsibility;
7. there is a healthy sense of right and wrong;
8. there are positive family traditions;
9. there is a good balance of interaction;
10. they share a common spiritual core;
11. there is a respect for one another's privacy;
12. they believe in providing service to others;
13. they sit down together and share meals and conversation;
14. they enjoy leisure activities together;
15. they are free to acknowledge their problems and seek help from one another.

Before the third hour meeting, participants review the list of persons with whom they would like to improve relationships and clarify whom they believe they have taken for granted, with whom they wish to improve capacity to give and receive love, and whom (particularly those with similar post-traumatic problems) they would like to help. The list is discussed during the third hour. The final part of the session is devoted to improving communication skills with a significant person, using role playing if they choose. Skills learned include:

1. Expressing what they are thinking, feeling, or wanting.
2. Expressing their feelings in positive terms. Saying what they are for, not what they are against.
3. Practicing listening without criticizing or giving advice.
4. Avoiding power struggles.
5. Understanding and clarifying their physical and emotional boundaries.

During the session, the leader uses the group to provide feedback to those members who have participated in this role-playing exercise.

CONCLUSIONS

This psychoeducational program can be extremely helpful as a part of the therapeutic regimen for victims and survivors suffering from post-traumatic symptoms, including those suffering from post-traumatic stress disorder, depression, dissociative disorder, bipolar disorder, adjustment disorder, substance abuse, and borderline personality disorder. The program can be used in short-term, long-term, day hospitalization, or outpatient treatment. Self-help programs have also been developed using the same themes and accompanied by spiritual steps or to complement individual or group psychotherapy. The advantage of this modality is that it provides a structure and cognitive approach to understanding post-traumatic symptoms and the main elements of recovery. This is particularly helpful when group leaders find that the traditional group process is inadequate as a treatment technique.

This psychoeducational program promotes the notion of growth and finding ways to break free from revictimization. Participants can begin by taking the PTSD assessment (Appendix I), which provides them with an idea of the severity of their symptoms.

Themes 1 through 4 are primarily meant to lay a groundwork of trust and self-inventory in order to proceed further. Group members may choose not to reveal painful memories within the format of the group, particularly prior to completing theme 3, which emphasizes trust building. Yet the full program provides a way to recall memories via the use of questionnaires, drawings, and discussions. Themes 5 through 8, in particular, encourage group members to remember, by learning how destructive or painful emotions of anger, fear, guilt, and grief are linked to past traumatic experiences. Themes 9 through 12 emphasize moving beyond the traumatic experience. Participants are encouraged to make a commitment to life (theme 9), justice (theme 10), purpose (theme 11), and loving relationships (theme 12).

Appendix I
Assessing Post-Traumatic Symptoms and the Twelve-Theme Program

The following assessment instrument can be used to determine the severity of PTSD symptoms as well as the severity of theme specific symptoms and problems. Participants in the program should answer each of the following questions by circling the number (0-4) which comes the closest to describing their symptoms.

0	1	2	3	4
Never	Occasionally	Some of the time	Quite Often	Nearly all the time

I. I can't stop the disturbing 'flashbacks' that seem to control my mind.
   0   1   2   3   4

2. The trauma was so upsetting that I wonder, "why did this have to happen to me?"
   0   1   2   3   4

3. My disturbing memories make me feel shameful and bad about myself.
   0   1   2   3   4

4. I have 'blackouts' or lapses of consciousness and do things without remembering what I did.
   0   1   2   3   4

5. I feel anger more than any other emotion when I think about what happened.
   0   1   2   3   4

6. I have rapid heart rate, chest tightness, upset stomach, and other symptoms that upset me.
   0   1   2   3   4

7. I have guilty memories and dreams about what I did or should have done.
   0   1   2   3   4

8. I stay numb and avoid people because I don't want to cry or have other feelings.
   0   1   2   3   4

9. I have urges to hurt myself.
   0   1   2   3   4

10. I have thoughts and dreams about hurting whoever was responsible.
   0   1   2   3   4

11. I have lost my purpose in life and wonder what will become of me.
   0   1   2   3   4

12. I often think that someone wanted this to happen to me.
   0   1   2   3   4

13. I feel like a victim and am afraid it's going to happen again and again to me.
   0   1   2   3   4

14. I often feel confused and have difficulty concentrating on anything.
   0   1   2   3   4

15. I may trust persons that can't be trusted or distrust those who want to help.
   0   1   2   3   4

16. It can seem like the traumatic event never happened.
   0   1   2   3   4

Appendix I (continued)

Never	Occasionally	Some of the time	Quite Often	Nearly all the time
0	1	2	3	4

17. I am easily provoked and can go into a rage.
    0   1   2   3   4

18. I am hypervigilant,'on guard' most of the time, and loud noises or sudden moves startle me.
    0   1   2   3   4

19. I feel guilty that I survived and think, "it should have been me instead of ..."
    0   1   2   3   4

20. Sometimes I feel numb and other times I can't keep from crying.
    0   1   2   3   4

21. I feel sad, fatigued, listless, depressed, and have thoughts I'd rather be dead.
    0   1   2   3   4

22. I am bitter and feel like hurting or killing those who were responsible.
    0   1   2   3   4

23. I feel alienated from God for what happened and detached from contact with God.
    0   1   2   3   4

24. I feel distant or cut off from other people and have trouble getting close to anyone.
    0   1   2   3   4

Answer the questions as honestly as possible in order to determine your score. In the event that you cannot answer all of the questions or have difficulty scoring, ask your therapist or group leader.

TOTAL SCORE:_____

To determine the severity of your symptoms, see where your score fits, as follows:

SEVERE	70 - 96
MODERATE	36 - 69
MILD	10 - 35
NOT SIGNIFICANT	0 - 9

To determine the severity of each of the theme specific scores, add up scores on the themes 1 + 13, 2 + 14, 3 + 15, etc.

___	___	___	___	___	___	___	___	___	___	___	___
___	___	___	___	___	___	___	___	___	___	___	___
Totals ___	___	___	___	___	___	___	___	___	___	___	___
1	2	3	4	5	6	7	8	9	10	11	12
Power	Meaning	Trust	Truth	Anger	Fear	Guilt	Grief	Life/Death	Revenge	Purpose	Love

Scores 6-8 on any theme indicate severe symptoms, 3-5, moderate symptoms, and 1-2 mild symptoms.

Source: All material in Appendix I is owned and copyrighted by Joel Brende.

Appendix II.A
Post-Traumatic Phases

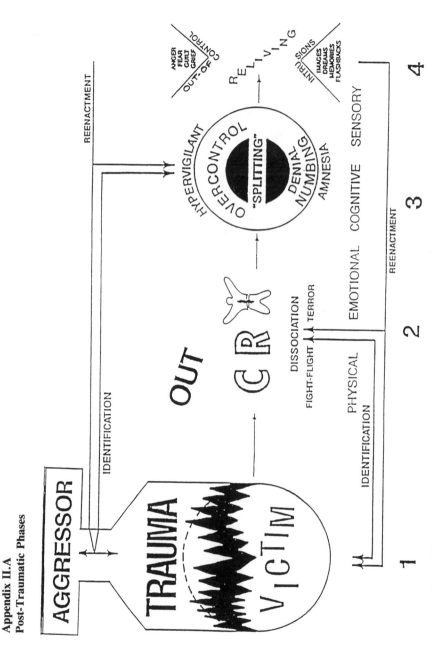

Source: All material in Appendix II.A is owned and copyrighted by Joel Brende.

Appendix II.B
Post-Traumatic Self-Fragmentation

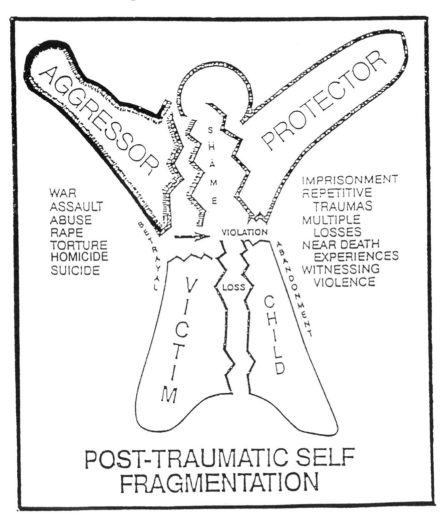

Source: All material in Appendix II.B is owned and copyrighted by Joel Brende.

437

Appendix II.C
Post-Traumatic Self-Fragmentation and "Addiction" Cycle

The "addiction" cycle of post-traumatic stress serves to temporarily shield the victim from hidden traumatic memories and emotions. But this is a precarious cycle which is easily destabilized. Victims often use substances as an attempt to maintain the shield of omnipotence and psychic numbing.

Victims may suffer traumatic re-enactments triggered by internal or external sources. When this happens, they may quickly regress into a state of fragmentation and identify with any of the four identity fragments - protector, child, victim, or aggressor.

Source: All material in Appendix II.C is owned and copyrighted by Joel Brende.

Appendix III
Sample Work Sheet

THEME ONE WORKSHEET: POWER vs. Victimization

This theme focuses on resolving problems related to power and victimization. What is the definition of victim? Do you feel like a victim? Have you been a victim of traumatic experiences? _____ If so, what post-traumatic symptoms do you have? Nightmares? _____ Angry Outbursts? _____ Panic Attacks? _____ Grief? _____ Flashbacks? _____ Guilt feelings? _____ Bad Memories? _____ Destructive Habits? _____ Destructive Behaviors? _____ Startle Reactions? _____ Hypervigilance? _____

How do you define power? _____
What is an example of positive power? _____
What is an example of destructive power? _____
Have you been a victim of someone in a position of power? _____

The answers to these and the following questions can become a basis for self-understanding and group discussion. If you answer any of the questions "Yes" in the Red or Black section on this or any of the other 12 worksheets which follow, professional consultation or treatment is recommended. Red symptoms are the most potentially destructive. Black symptoms mean that you have significant problems. If you discover you have problems you'd like to change, learn about how to use your own positive power to change them. If you realize you have problems you cannot change, learn how to seek help from sources of positive power outside of yourself to change them.

RED-DESTRUCTIVE:
Do you use your power to hurt others?	Yes _____	No _____
Do you frequently think of taking your own life?	Yes _____	No _____
Do you ever provoke others to the point that your life is at risk?	Yes _____	No _____

BLACK-BLOCKED:
Are you accident prone?	Yes _____	No _____
Do you repeat behaviors that cause you to be victimized again and again?	Yes _____	No _____
Are you often victimized by others in power?	Yes _____	No _____
Do others often worry that you might hurt them?	Yes _____	No _____

YELLOW-GOALS & PLANS:
Write a plan for each of the following on the back of this worksheet:
- How to enhance your positive power.
- How to improve your physical health.
- How to break your victimization patterns.
- How to recognize those times when it is okay to be helpless and ask others for help.
- How to seek help from your Higher Power.

GREEN-POSITIVE ACTION:
What are the sources of positive power in your life? _____
How are you making positive power work for you? _____
What are your methods for breaking patterns of victimization? _____
How are you using your Higher Power to help you? _____

ASSIGNMENT:
Keep a daily diary of the positive power methods that you use involving action, thoughts, and feelings: This can include meditation, exercise, helping others, seeking and accepting help, activities, hobbies, and readings.

COMMITMENT:
"I seek freedom from victimization and from using power destructively. I have taken steps and will continue to learn new ways of breaking victimization patterns and gaining positive power in my life."

_____
_____
_____
_____

Source: All material in Appendix III is owned and copyrighted by Joel Brende.

28

Group Therapy and Self-Help Groups for Adult Survivors of Childhood Incest

Jeremy Herman and Lana R. Lawrence

INTRODUCTION

When a child is sexually abused by an adult whom the child is supposed to be able to trust, the psychological stress is extreme, causes great psychological suffering, and influences personality development. Incest used to be considered rare. In the last decade or so, it has been revealed to be extensive. How extensive is not known, because of underreporting. What is known is that many survivors have not (until recently) received the assistance they need to heal and recover. One cannot recover from a trauma if one does not remember it or is afraid to reveal it and if one's family, society, and the professional community are unwilling or unable to acknowledge and deal with it.

In order for incest victims to be helped, the trauma they suffered must be recognized and its effects must be realistically addressed. This chapter explains two trauma-based approaches—leader-led group therapy program and the Twelve-Step Survivors of Incest Anonymous program.

GROUP THERAPY FOR ADULT SURVIVORS OF CHILDHOOD INCEST

There are many varieties of group therapy. This author (J.H.) has been working with adult survivors of childhood incest since 1985 and has developed a personal method and style. However, group therapy is a living, dynamic interaction of human beings, and every group has been significantly different.

The Basic Approach

No two humans and no two survivors are the same. However, most adults molested as children developed ways to cope with the abuse and exploitation that were adaptive when they were helpless children dealing with powerful adults but are now counterproductive and self-destructive. Psychological defenses, such as dissociation, fighting, fantasy, and dependency, prevent a person from engaging in a career or relating positively to others but can be psychologically lifesaving strategies to a youngster who is being threatened daily with sexual abuse by adults in a position of authority.

Conceptualizing survivors' symptoms and problems in this way—as earlier adaptive strategies—can be helpful in both individual and group therapy. In individual therapy, clients tend to be on their best behavior, relating to the therapist as positively and maturely as they can. The therapist primarily works on problems and relationships occurring outside the therapy room involving people not present—friends, lovers, coworkers, bosses, subordinates. When the therapist believes that a client is relating to him or her in a distorted way, pointing out and working with the distortion effectively can be very difficult. Even when the childhood connection is made, for example, that the client is seeing the therapist as the abusive or passive weak parent who did not protect him or her, and a childhood coping strategy, such as spacing out or fighting, is employed, it is very difficult to engage the adult ego sufficiently to confront the defense and overcome the threat felt by the client. In the group setting, as will be explained later, it is easier to demonstrate, clarify, and work effectively with interpersonal distortions.

Groups are small (six or seven people), are of mixed gender, meet once a week for two hours, and are open-ended. Prospective members who are not in individual therapy with the therapist meet with the therapist for a screening interview to determine if the kind of group therapy that is employed is the "right kind" for them. Groups have three phases. During phase 1 (the first few sessions), members share their childhoods and current lives. In phase 2 (several weeks), people continue to disclose themselves, and psychoeducation is added. In phase 3, analysis of members' interactions is added.

Screening Interview

The screening for this clinician's groups is not based upon diagnostic categories, for example, borderline or even schizophrenic. Most survivors who apply for individual or group therapy do have the borderline problems described in the *Diagnostic and Statistical Manual of Mental Disorders* (DSM III-R, APA, 1987): impulsivity, unstable and intense relationships, problems with anger, difficulties with identity, mood swings, self-destructive behavior, and depression (APA, 1987, pp. 346–47). The estimate of suitability for a group is based upon openness and interpersonal relatedness, as well as whether or not the client seems to have sufficient strength to tolerate and to benefit from the analysis of self and others based upon interactions in the group. For this clinician, the relevant questions to answer are: Does the person have a desire to change and help others to change that is strong enough to counter negative emotions and attitudes? Is there a core of decency and rationality? Are there a capacity and willingness to question and keep an open mind? Someone suffering from schizophrenia is, of course, not suitable for any kind of outpatient therapy as long as the psychosis is active, but if the severe symptoms are controlled by medication, the same criteria for admission to the group apply. Also, anyone who is suicidal or homicidal is not admitted, because concern for him or her will dominate group time. When someone seems inappropriate for this clinician's groups, I explain my opinion and rationale as directly and sensitively as I can and make a referral to other resources.

Deciding whether someone is appropriate for group therapy is difficult, and sometimes people who seriously interfere with group functioning will be admitted, people who are too hostile, self-centered, or fragile at this time in their lives to relate positively enough to other members. If efforts to help them are unsuccessful, they have to be referred to other resources. Removal of a member is painful and frightening for everyone, because it implies the felt threat that "bad behavior" means expulsion. However, it is necessary if the group is to accomplish anything (Yalom, 1985, pp. 323–25). The therapist must point out and stress that the member being asked to leave is intractable, reacting to the group as if it were his or her original family rather than people trying to correct that environment.

Phase 1

At the first meeting of the group the therapist reiterates, for everyone together, what has been told to each person individually during the screening interview or in individual sessions, namely, the basic rules, purpose, and method of the group. The three basic rules are (1) confidentiality, (2) regular attendance, and (3) no socializing outside the group, other than unavoidable contact before and after sessions. Since many group members attend, or have attended, self-help groups where attendance is voluntary and socialization outside meetings is permitted and usually encouraged, these two rules need to be explained.

Regular attendance is important. An individual therapy session can be made up. Missing a group meeting is a permanent loss of two hours of group content. This is detrimental to the absent member and to everyone else in the group. The regular attendance rule is usually accepted without too much objection.

The nonsocialization rule often encounters both overt and covert opposition. Many incest survivors are quite isolated and lonely. In the group, members share their lives with others, and some strong ties develop. The desire to spend more than session time together and to get involved as good friends or in a romance is only natural. Doing so, however, destroys a main purpose of the group—to explore and analyze early relationships and their repetitions in current relationships as they appear in direct, observable, face-to-face interaction. What would go on between group members outside the group would not be directly observable by the rest of the group.

After the rules are explained and discussed, the rest of the first session and the next several meetings are devoted to members' revelations concerning their childhoods and current lives. People ask each other questions, and there are back-and-forth sharing and accompanying emotional release. During these first few sessions, the therapist observes both positive and negative interpersonal attitudes but does not comment upon interactions unless they are disruptive, and, even then, comments do not contain interpretations. The idea behind this strategy is to keep the atmosphere congenial, accepting, and understanding.

Phase 2

As soon as members feel reasonably comfortable with each other, psycho-education is added. The approach used by this therapist is to clarify the symptoms and problems that members bring to the group, showing how they developed as a natural result of being sexually exploited and abused as children. Incest survivors feel extensive guilt and shame. They blame themselves for what happened and who they became as a result. The therapist must continually emphasize that they are not responsible for what happened, because they were helpless children dealing with powerful adults or older siblings. However, they can learn to be responsible now, as grown-ups, with potential adult strength.

Within this adult/child framework, several concepts are utilized to explain the psychological impact of incest. These explanatory ideas or theories are presented at whatever time seems appropriate as each group develops in its own way. Of obvious importance is education about the elements of "post-traumatic stress disorder" (PTSD) (APA, 1987, pp. 247–51). PTSD accurately and succinctly describes many of the symptoms and problems of trauma survivors, but in this therapist's view it is an incomplete explanation. It does not expressly include the problematic personality styles that people from dysfunctional, incestuous families develop—styles that cause personal suffering and also interfere with relationships. These styles are included in DSM-III-R but are, unfortunately, called "personality disorders" and are consequently rejected by many clinicians who view them as stigmatizing and blaming the victim (APA, 1987, pp. 35–58). This therapist believes that the various personality styles are quite accurately described and offer a very important dimension to understand and help people overcome the damaging psychological effects of chronic severe trauma inflicted upon them by other humans. Therefore, this therapist utilizes the phenomenological information and descriptions of the "personality disorders" section as an educational tool without citing the section as a reference or using the term.

Several concepts from psychoanalysis are utilized as well, especially transference, identification, splitting, and repetition compulsion (Miller, 1984). Victims of childhood incest have an understandable tendency to mistrust others and to be quick to display anger, fear, and other strong emotions. As a result of unconscious transference, a survivor sometimes completely misreads a friendly overture, viewing it as hostile. Other times, a small mistake or insignificant ambivalence is overblown, and the survivor splits someone who is mostly positive into someone who is essentially negative.

At early stages of recovery, when abuse memories are new and particularly upsetting and painful, survivors tend to split family members and view them as 100 percent evil or 100 percent weak; in other words, not as human beings. It is important to work on and to dissolve splitting so that survivors can see their family members realistically as people having mixtures of many characteristics, whose personalities and characters were also influenced by their childhoods. More importantly, survivors are thereby enabled to develop a more complete and accurate picture of their complex relationships with family members. Often, for example, even the relationship with the abuser contained some good elements of nurturing and closeness.

Human beings identify with people in their families. This identification is usually part conscious and part unconscious. Survivors, coming from families of which they are not proud, often have great difficulty seeing and acknowledging their "inherited" traits.

Another topic covered is the theory of repetition compulsion. It is explained as unconscious addiction to ways of thinking, feeling, and behaving learned in response to abuse and exploitation, as, for example, in learned helplessness.

Phase 3

At the point where group members have bonded strongly, have a fairly good beginning understanding of the psychological impact of childhood incest upon them as children, and have an understanding of how incest manifests itself in the symptoms and problems they face in their current lives, it is time to begin to analyze group members' interactions with one another. This analysis is stressful. Behavior patterns formed and developed over many years in dysfunctional families are difficult to recognize and modify. When human beings talk about relationships with bosses, friends, lovers, and spouses, they select information they remember and believe to be relevant. However, their emotions and defenses have unconsciously affected their experiences and have also affected what is remembered. Group interactions clearly demonstrate that members' perceptions of events are affected by their moods, concentration, and attitudes toward one another. As in their outside lives, people become afraid, angry, hurt, or ashamed and fight, appease, or dissociate.

In individual therapy, analysis of client distortions in the therapist-client relationship is difficult because clients very astutely focus on the therapist's distortions, rather than their own. In group therapy, several people in the room offer their viewpoints as to what is going on, so interpretations are more persuasive and more difficult to shrug off. It is also possible for analysis to be more subtle and complete.

In individual therapy, the therapist reveals only limited information about his or her personality and the part that it plays in interactions. Clients thereby have a realistic sense of the incompleteness of the transference/countertransference analysis, knowing quite well that they are often reacting, in varying degrees, to the therapist's unacknowledged difficulties. In group, analysis of members' interactions is not limited in this way, and can be complete. For example, at a session of one group that had been meeting for six months, member A described the childhood incest memories that caused her to panic or freeze during sex with her husband. Her chief attitude was distress for her husband and herself. Nevertheless, member B, a man with an acknowledged sadistic streak, attacked her for being seductive and then rejecting toward her husband, adding that her husband was a wimp to put up with her behavior. A became largely dissociative and was unable to respond effectively. C became frightened, remained alert, but withdrew. D felt upset and menaced by B's hostility, did not think it should be allowed by the therapist, and threatened to leave the group. The unconscious defenses of E, F, and G, which they had developed as children, were not triggered on this occasion, and they were able to help the therapist clarify and analyze the interactions of A, B, C, and D.

B had been sexually abused as a child by his mother. Her behavior toward him was highly inconsistent. Sometimes she would be affectionate and sexual and other times, rejecting and nasty. Her moods and behavior were volatile. Her mood and attitude toward him might last a few days, a few hours, or a few minutes and then change. On the other hand, she was more positive toward him than any other member of the family. His father and older sister disliked and avoided him. B's relationship with his mother, though complex, ambivalent, and dependent upon her moods, did contain positive elements. They did things together and talked, and she taught him a good deal and encouraged him to achieve.

A's mother was an alcoholic. When she and A's stepfather divorced, he got custody of A and had sex with her for several years. He trained her to be seductive and helpless—one of the ways she related to men after she was liberated. During sex with him, A would often feel overpowering shame, fear, and anger and would dissociate and imagine a rescuer. Sometimes, after initiating sex with her husband, she would perceive—literally see, hear, feel, smell—him as her stepfather and become filled with dread and sorrow. But, as with B, the traumatic and destructive relationship had positive qualities because, like all people, A's stepfather had positive qualities. He was successful, educated, and cultivated and was liberal and fair-minded in his social views. A benefited greatly from these aspects of her "home."

During the six months that the group had been meeting, A had flirted with most men in the group, and B had been cruel to most of the women. They had both also been honest, revealing, understanding, warm, and kind. They and other group members knew each other quite well. At this meeting, as A was describing her problem with her husband, her main attitude was pain for herself and her husband. Her body language was unconsciously slightly sexual, and she expressed a wish that her husband be stronger. B unconsciously reacted to these minor elements as if they were the only elements. He split A into a woman who was totally seductive, rejecting, and contemptuous toward men and, at the same time, weak and insecure. He reacted to her with strong transference, as if she were his mother. He felt angry, hurt, confused, and afraid. Simultaneously, he consciously saw that she was open and vulnerable and knew that his attack would wound her. In this respect, his aggression toward A was like his mother's aggression toward him. B's transference, splitting, and identification were so compulsive and powerful that he lost his affection for A and distorted her into his mother and himself.

Analytic and cognitive theorists disagree about the order of these reactions. Which one comes first—the emotional or the cognitive? If there is a first one, does it cause the other? This clinician takes no position on the issue and simply treats them both as equally worthy of attention and work.

A, as she spoke of her sexual problems with her husband, was essentially being open, vulnerable, and serious. She sincerely wanted the group's help to work on resolving her transference to her husband, perceiving him as her stepfather. She felt safe, and when A attacked her, she was overwhelmed and became dissociative. Unconsciously, she felt fear, anger, and powerlessness. In other words, mentally and emotionally, she was a child again in her stepfather's house. She split B into someone who was entirely the way he was at that moment. That he could be decent and understanding was not remembered. She also lost the knowledge that she was now an adult who could deal with B, and others, if they mistreated her.

C's father had a violent temper, and abused her mother physically and emotionally. During his rages, C would stay out of the way, trying to look unafraid and trying to mentally prepare herself for what always followed—being taken by him into the bedroom for sex. When B attacked A, C felt and behaved as she had as a child at home.

D's mother began having sex with her when she was eleven. D was an only child. Her mother was domineering, self-centered, and extremely critical of her husband and D. D's father was a successful professional, but he was afraid of his wife and let her run the house. When B attacked A, D was unconsciously back in that house as a helpless child with an ineffective weak father—the therapist.

A TWELVE-STEP RECOVERY MODEL

Twelve-step programs modify the Twelve Steps and Twelve Traditions of Alcoholics Anonymous (AA) to address a specific recovery issue, such as an addiction or being the victim of trauma. Groups utilizing the twelve-step model offer many child sexual abuse survivors the opportunity to examine the trauma of their childhoods in a mutually supportive environment. National offices of the two twelve-step recovery programs for adult survivors of childhood sexual abuse (Survivors of Incest Anonymous and Incest Survivors Anonymous) indicate that the number of individual group meetings has surged in recent years.

Because this author (L.R.L) is most familiar with Survivors of Incest Anonymous (SIA), discussion of the twelve-step model for survivors will be limited to this program. A revised version of the twelve steps is utilized for this discussion and can be found in the appendix to this chapter (SIA, 1990).

Although the structure of individual meetings within twelve-step programs for survivors may vary, meetings generally require participants to follow specific guidelines derived from the Twelve Traditions as adapted from Alcoholics Anonymous (SIA, 1990). The most beneficial meetings tend to have a clearly defined structure. Twelve-step groups are not facilitator-led; volunteers or persons designated by group conscience act as "leaders." These leaders read the opening literature and request that individuals initiate discussions. Other volunteers manage financial matters or "housekeeping" tasks.

Many groups adopt rules in order to protect individuals against unwanted touching or advice giving during the meeting. Depending on the preference of group members, meetings may be for women only, men only, or both men and women. Many groups clearly state that meetings are intended to provide mutual support but are not a replacement for a safe and therapeutic relationship where survivors can confront and process recovery issues with a trained professional. Meetings are free of charge, do not require a time commitment, and do not even require that the survivors identify themselves or share their abuse histories.

Twelve-step programs may provide survivors of all forms of child sexual abuse (not restricted to incest) with a more structured model for approaching recovery than conventional therapy or self-help groups might provide. The first step asks survivors to acknowledge powerlessness over the sexual abuse experience and its effects and the unmanageability of their lives. This step effectively asks survivors to examine the denial that has shielded them from the pain and rage of having been abused. Survivors may discover that this step must be repeatedly reexamined throughout the recovery process.

Steps 2 and 3 are, perhaps, the most difficult and/or controversial steps for many survivors, yet they are precisely the elements of the program that attract many survivors to this recovery model. These steps ask survivors to believe that a power greater than themselves can "restore hope, healing and sanity" and to make a decision to turn their "will and lives" over to the care of this higher power. Survivors are often encouraged to define the concept of a higher power in comfortable terms, such as the inner or true self, the part of themselves or others that is godlike (i.e., good, loving, and powerful), or a God of the survivors' understanding or religious choice. Many survivors consider the concept of the inner child to be the higher power that holds universal truth and that, when listened to, can lead to personal discovery and healing.

Many survivors have difficulty with these first three steps because they experienced a loss of control during the sexual abuse when the perpetrator, a person in a position of control or power, exploited their trust. The concept of giving control to someone or something outside themselves may, therefore, re-create those feelings of loss of control that originated during the abuse. These steps require that survivors trust their internal self-instincts or a spiritual figure. Equally as challenging for survivors is the constant struggle to move beyond the self-protective belief that they were somehow in control of, or responsible for, the abuse that occurred. When survivors remove the denial, they expose the pain and anger that have been, in many cases, long submerged. Recovery may then become more focused on trust and control issues. The steps attempt to restore a sense of control to the survivors by emphasizing that they are now choosing to give up control and to trust another being—control is not being taken from them again.

The spiritual component of the twelve-step model is one that many survivors believe is missing from more conventional group support systems or models. For example, if a survivor previously abandoned organized religion as a result of the effects of the abuse, twelve-step meetings can provide a sense of congregation or religious community. These meetings may enable survivors to reconcile previously held conflicts concerning their religious belief systems.

Step 4, which asks survivors to make a "searching and fearless moral inventory" of their abuse and the aftereffects, helps survivors to examine the destructive ways in which the abuse affected their lives. Survivors are asked only to examine the effects of the abuse; not until the fifth step are they encouraged to disclose the ways in which they destructively acted out their abuse. During the discussion of the fifth step, survivors are likely to hear others disclose painful accounts of self-defeating behaviors that consistently are linked with childhood sexual trauma. They include taking responsibility for the abuse aftereffects, such as inappropriately acting out anger, promiscuity, eating disorders, substance abuse/addiction, prostitution, self-mutilation, and reenactment of the abuse toward others (Gelinas, 1983). Discussion of survivor perpetration is allowed in some meetings but, usually, only if the survivor was a child while this reenactment of abuse occurred (SIA, 1990, Traditions). Steps 4 and 5 offer survivors an opportunity to break free from the shame, guilt, and isolation that they may have experienced as a result of hiding these behaviors from others. Survivors often experience tremendous relief when they reveal additional "secrets" that may have caused deep feelings of shame.

Steps 6 and 7 ask that survivors become ready to seek assistance from their higher power to remove "debilitating consequences of the abuse" or self-defeating aspects of the survivors' lives and personalities. Survivors are requested to examine the denial and/or excuses that have enabled them to continue such behaviors. A second portion of this step asks survivors to become "willing to treat ourselves with respect, compassion, and acceptance."

The eighth and ninth steps ask survivors to "make a list" and "make amends to all persons" they may have harmed as a result of the abuse. Survivors are encouraged, once again, to examine themselves and acknowledge ways in which the abuse may have influenced them to harm themselves and/or others. Examining, taking responsibility for, and apologizing to the self and others for emotional or physical harm are encouraged "except when to do so would injure" the survivors or others. These steps offer them the opportunity to accept the harmful actions and to repair the self or relationships. Survivors are discouraged from communicating with others who may attempt to emotionally or physically victimize them. For example, survivors are not encouraged to "make amends" to family members for angry verbal exchanges during confrontations if they believe that they will be emotionally or physically assaulted for having disclosed the sexual abuse.

The remainder of the steps ask survivors to "continue to take personal inventory," seek "through prayer and meditation to improve . . . conscious contact" with a higher power, and "carry" the message of recovery to others and "practice these [steps or] principles in all our endeavors."

Clearly, the twelve-step model offers survivors an opportunity to confront the reality of the sexual abuse in a structured manner. Survivors who have difficulty utilizing the steps may continue to attend meetings in order to benefit from the fellowship and community of other survivors. Gannon (1989) suggests that the groups can provide a sense of family that the survivors may not have experienced.

Among other benefits that meetings provide are the flexibility to attend on an as-needed basis and the freedom to approach issues at a comfortable pace. Survivors who are overwhelmed by abreactions may feel more in control of the experience if they know that they are free to leave the room and return when and if they are comfortable in so doing. In addition, survivors who frequently travel or move to new locations may benefit from the opportunity to attend an established meeting, with a structure that is familiar, in various geographical locations.

Although there are many benefits to twelve-step programs for adult survivors, there are also limitations that survivors may encounter. Some survivors may need a group setting with a trained facilitator to assist them in disclosing the painful memories and emotions stemming from sexual abuse. Theoretically, because of the nature of the group guidelines, a survivor could attend a twelve-step meeting indefinitely and never openly discuss the abuse and/or feelings.

Other difficulties may stem from what some survivors may perceive as benefits, such as the flexibility of the structure, which allows attendance only as often as is desired. For example, if a core group evolves and some members abruptly stop attending, survivors may feel abandoned and experience difficulty trusting new group members. Another benefit for all survivors—that the anonymity of the survivor will be respected—can suggest secrecy and shame if survivors wish to identify themselves in public as having been sexually abused.

Safety issues may arise for survivors who feel insecure when there is not a clearly defined leader to take responsibility for the meeting and facilitate conflict resolution as needed. Yet, survivors may also feel empowered by creatively resolving, through group conscience, conflicts and problems that may arise, including expelling abusive members or active perpetrators without the assistance of an authority figure.

Just as other supportive group environments can become unhealthy, twelve-step meetings may contain abusive elements. Any group that allows members to violate the emotional or physical boundaries of individuals who attend is clearly unsafe. Revictimization has been reported by members who received unwanted criticism and even sexual advances following a meeting. In order for support groups to assist survivors through the recovery process, the boundaries of others must be respected.

Additionally, meeting lengths vary from group to group; meetings that are lengthy (over an hour and a half to two hours) may leave survivors feeling revictimized by the volume and depth of the shared stories and emotions. Generally, most survivors find that they must approach painful feelings and memories gradually. Overexposure to abuse-related issues may accelerate the frequency of abreactions and emotionally overwhelm them.

Although survivors usually revisit many of the twelve steps over the course of several months or years as they accomplish many of the recovery tasks set forth by the program, twelve-step programs are not structured for in-depth processing of feelings and experiences (Toews and Palmer, 1991). Survivors in need of individual guidance in a group setting will more likely benefit from facilitator-led groups. Group interaction is limited to the sharing of individual stories and emotions. This format may provide survivors with an additional sense of safety because they know that they will not be subjected to unwanted interruption, advice, or criticism by other group members. This is typically described as the "no cross-talk rule."

As illustrated in this overview, the twelve-step recovery model has both benefits and limitations. It provides the opportunity for many survivors to break the secrecy and silence surrounding their abuse in a supportive environment with others who have had similar experiences. What follows is a case history of a survivor who had both positive and negative experiences while attending twelve-step meetings of adult survivors.

Rae had been sexually abused between the ages of three and seventeen by several perpetrators, including her father. She sporadically attended individual therapy for several years, seemingly approaching painful memories and emotions and then retreating from them when she felt out of control. Eventually, Rae began attending a therapy group for adult women survivors of childhood sexual abuse, and her progress, although gradual, assisted her in gaining consistent and ongoing individual therapy.

Although Rae benefited from the support, validation, and camaraderie that the group members provided, she felt somewhat revictimized because other members had the freedom to probe into her history of abuse without her requesting them to do so. She sensed that some survivors used the group to analyze each other—oftentimes as a defense against facing their own feelings. She began to refer to the structure of the group as the "sledgehammer approach" because she felt as though she was forced to confront memories and feelings that should have been examined in a gentle and nurturing manner.

As a coping strategy, Rae began to participate in this analytical approach with other group members. Soon, she discovered that she, too, was hiding behind the intellectualization that the group fostered. It was only after joining a twelve-step program, with a structure that did not allow others to comment on any aspect of her sharing or to probe deeper into her issues, that she began to feel safe enough, both in individual therapy and the support group, to experience and share more of the memories and emotions that she had repressed.

Rae learned that it was difficult, if not excruciating, at times, to sit through a meeting without being able to employ her previous defenses of analyzing or intellectualizing the issues of the other group members. As participants shared their stories, Rae had to sit with the emotions that she had been avoiding for most of her life. Eventually, she was able to restrict her sharing to her own experience and to disclose candidly many of the details of the abuse that she had endured.

The group felt safe to Rae because she was able to attend the meetings and share only if she chose to do so. On numerous occasions, she never talked and only listened to her fellow survivors share their experiences. This helped her truly hear the stories and emotions that others experienced, without minimizing her own trauma.

Rae continued in the group for four years. She has developed a support network of dozens of men and women upon whom she can rely in times of need. She has also developed a sense of family with many of the core group members who have lost their own families because of abuse. Rae and her fellow group members often share holidays with each other; they acknowledge her loss of family yet fulfill a need for fellowship with people who are supportive.

Rae now feels that she can eventually return to a therapy group, perhaps a group that uses experiential or expressive modalities. She continues to recognize that issues from her abusive childhood remain but believes that she will, one day, be free from the devastating effects.

CONCLUSION

This chapter presented two quite different group approaches designed specifically for adult survivors of childhood incest. In interactional groups, members react to each other with a full range of attitudes and feelings. Their interactions are clarified and analyzed in terms of childhood coping styles developed in reaction to original family members—styles that are counterproductive and ineffective now that they are adults. A combination of analytic, cognitive, and learning models is used.

Survivors of Incest Anonymous groups are explicitly noninteractional. To relieve the suffering of the survivor and produce change in attitudes, feelings, and behavior, SIA groups utilize spiritual and moral principles, along with role modeling. Group members do not analyze each other. Individuals are encouraged, by example, to heal and to change.

Both group approaches are useful and not as contradictory as they might seem. They both rely upon humans helping humans—people getting together in an attempt to correct the abuse and exploitation survivors experienced in their original families.

APPENDIX

Twelve Steps of Survivors of Incest Anonymous

1. We admitted we were powerless over the abuse, the effects of the abuse, and that our lives had become unmanageable.

2. Came to believe that a loving Higher Power, greater than ourselves, could restore hope, healing and sanity.

3. Made a decision to turn our will and our lives over to the care of a loving Higher Power, as we understood Her/Him.

4. Made a searching and fearless moral inventory of ourselves, the abuse, and its effects on our lives. We have no more secrets.

5. Admitted to a loving Higher Power, to ourselves, and to another human being our strengths and weaknesses.

6. Were entirely ready to have a loving Higher Power help us remove all the debilitating consequences of the abuse and became willing to treat ourselves with respect, compassion, and acceptance.

7. Humbly and honestly asked a loving Higher Power to remove the unhealthy and self-defeating consequences stemming from the abuse.

8. Made a list of all the people we had harmed (of our own free will), especially ourselves and our inner child, and became willing to make amends to them all.

9. Made amends to such people wherever possible, except when to do so would result in physical, mental, emotional or spiritual harm to ourselves or others.

10. Continued to take responsibility for our own recovery, and when we found ourselves behaving in patterns still dictated by the abuse, promptly admitted it. When we succeed, we promptly enjoy it.

11. Sought through prayer and meditation to improve our conscious contact with ourselves and a loving Higher Power as we understood Her/Him, asking only for knowledge of Her/His will for us and the power and courage to carry that out.

12. Having had a spiritual awakening as a result of these steps, we tried to carry this message to other survivors and practice these principles in all our endeavors.

NOTE

Material pertaining to Survivors of Incest Anonymous was reprinted from *The welcome, the closing, the twelve steps, the twelve traditions, and the adapted twelve steps.* © Revised 1991. Used by permission of Survivors of Incest Anonymous, Inc., Baltimore.

29

The Development of Groups for Partners of Survivors of Child Sexual Abuse

Wendi R. Kaplan

> The best way to take care of our [survivor] partners is to take care of ourselves first.
>
> —Steve (a partner)
>
> I'm not as alone as I was before this group started.
>
> —John (a partner)
>
> I feel like a bull in a china shop.
>
> —Earl (a partner)
>
> If I had been an astronaut, I wouldn't have faced more challenges than I have as a partner of a survivor and a multiple.
>
> —John (a partner)

INTRODUCTION

The vast societal epidemic of child sexual abuse has made its mark on millions of people all over the globe (Gelles & Cornell, 1985; Herman, 1981; Russell, 1984, 1986). It is estimated that one-third of all girls and one-fifth of all boys under the age of eighteen are victimized by this trauma. Therapists' offices are filled with women and men of all ages who have managed, each in her and his own unique way, to survive child sexual abuse traumas.

In the last fifteen years there has been an awakening to issues of family violence and abuse. Propelled by the feminist movement of the 1970s, therapists, mental health practitioners, medical practitioners, and members of society at large have become increasingly aware of the extent of child sexual abuse and its overwhelming impact on extensive numbers of victimized people (Courtois, 1988b; McCann & Pearlman, 1990b; Williams, 1991b).

In the last five years, in fact, an ever-increasing amount of information has become available (in books, journals, conferences, and workshops) to the mental health community to provide guidance to those who work with survivors and the aftereffects that they suffer. More and more women (primarily) and men (the numbers grow) have survived the trauma of child sexual abuse and are choosing therapy to courageously work through the issues that were created by the abuse trauma. Therapists, therefore, are continually seeking information and methods to help them assist survivors in that recovery process.

Initially, therapists worked primarily with adult survivors themselves. Occasionally, some therapists would see the "significant others" in survivors' lives in adjunctive treatment or consultation (Courtois, 1988b). The purpose of meeting with these significant others, primarily the partners of the survivors, was mostly to assist the survivor. Information was often provided about child sexual abuse to those partners in order to help them better understand the issues and provide additional support for those survivors.

As therapists met with partners on a case-by-case basis, they began to gain greater understanding about the survivors' current family systems in general and about the partners in particular. It became clear that partners needed more than just information. The partners, also often from dysfunctional families, needed skills and support as well (Davis, 1991; Gil, 1991b; Graber, 1991; Maltz, 1991).

WHO IS THE PARTNER?

Partners vary in many respects. Partners are men and women. They are heterosexual and homosexual. Partners are married to, living with, dating, or intimately involved in some way with other persons who were sexually abused as children. The partner can be known as an ally, lover, spouse, girlfriend, boyfriend, significant other, or special friend. They come from every race, religion, socioeconomic class, educational background, occupation, and neighborhood in this country. The partner, too, may be a survivor of childhood abuse.

PARTNER'S RESPONSE PATTERNS

While the survivor of child sexual abuse is directly affected by the trauma, the partner (as well as other family members and loved ones) also suffers. Courtois (1988b) defines this effect as "contact traumatization." Contact traumatization describes the wide variety and range of reactions experienced by partners and loved ones, including rescue, revenge, rejection, blame, ambivalence, avoidance, denial, hurt and empathy. McCann and Pearlman (1990b) and Figley (1983, 1986) have also written about the psychological distress that the survivors' significant others experience as they empathize with, and act strongly for, the survivor. This author has identified the pattern of emotional response that many partners exhibit as a form of grief reaction. The grief and loss a partner experiences have to do with the awareness of abuse, which frequently changes drastically the way in which he or she perceives the world. What he or she has known about the survivor and their relationship together is altered by the knowledge of child sexual abuse and its effect on their lives. The grieving reaction often begins with shock and is followed by a range of responses that may include denial, disbelief, fear, feelings of vulnerability, a sense of powerlessness, anxiety, hyperactive behavior, blunted emotions, disturbances in sleep and other physiological and behavioral functions, guilt, and anger. The intensity and sequence of the response vary according to the unique experience of each partner in each situation. Gradually, though, the partner regains equilibrium.

Initially many partners feel a sense of shock and disbelief or denial when they learn of the abuse. They may find it hard to believe that the survivor has had to suffer such victimization. They may doubt the survivor's story and may question the survivor's memory, wondering why previously dissociated abuse was not recalled before this time.

The partner may experience some degree of numbness (both behaviorally and emotionally). This numbness seems to be followed by anger (particularly for men, for whom anger is more socially acceptable and who are socialized to take action). Their anger is generally focused on the perpetrator but may be vented onto the survivor. It is not unusual, at this stage, for conflict to develop between the partner and the survivor, as each focuses on his or her own needs. While the partner experiences almost immediate anger, it often takes much longer for a survivor to muster up anger toward the abuser(s), whom the survivor often experienced as nurturing as well as frightening. In fact, the survivor may even defend the offender(s) to protect him or her from the partner's rage. Defensive reactions such as this are often very confusing to the partner.

In many cases, partners then find themselves flailing helplessly and impotently—not knowing what to do with the rage, while realizing they are in a place/situation with no familiarity. They begin to feel as if they were a victim as well, feeling a sense of helplessness and loss of control. If they are venting anger, it feels like an exercise of fighting shadows—no blow is effective, and increasingly the partners tire.

Partners may not immediately connect to their anger and rage. They often experience increased anxiety, followed by a need to act, fix, change or do something to alleviate that anxiety and to remedy the situation.

At this point, partners often begin to seek therapy themselves, or the survivor and her or his therapist will ask the partner to participate in conjoint sessions. Thus the survivor's story and knowledge of the abuse take on a new perspective: the experience and the situation become more real, concrete, and tangible. Partners begin to sense feelings of deep sadness for the survivor, for themselves, and for other affected family members and sadness about the tragedy of child sexual abuse and the damage it creates. Partners may experience feelings of guilt and sometimes self-recrimination because they were not aware of the abuse and the difficulties that the survivor faced. Partners think that if they had been more understanding or more sensitive, then they could have somehow made up for the abuse committed by the perpetrator(s). Fear may also emerge for partners as they gain awareness of the magnitude of the trauma of child sexual abuse and how it has affected, and continues to affect, the survivor and their relationship. Partners may also begin to be concerned about their children or other children who have had contact with the offender(s) and fear for their safety and well-being.

As partners' clarity about the abuse grows, they often begin to see how relationship issues are connected to the abuse experience. The survivors' childhood abuse and how that has directly impacted their current relationship become more evident to partners.

THE NEED FOR A PARTNERS GROUP

As therapists began to work with more and more partners, in both conjoint and individual therapy, the awareness of partners' emerging needs and feelings became increasingly evident. This author observed that partners were an isolated population and realized that group treatment would be most beneficial to them. A search for a group referral in 1989, however, revealed that no group was available in the entire Washington, D.C., metropolitan area.

The family service agency at which the author worked agreed to sponsor a group for partners as an "experiment" to see if anyone was interested. A flier was sent to mental health professionals in the area and was made available to clients in the waiting room. The response was overwhelming. Many calls were received from therapists who expressed excitement about this new resource. Calls from supportive and grateful survivors said they would try to talk their partners into coming. "Significant others," such as nonoffending parents, siblings, in-laws, and friends, asked if they could participate or requested a "significant others" group that would include them. Finally calls came from partners—not only from the immediate area but from the far corners of Virginia and Maryland and even Delaware and Pennsylvania. Many partners called just to talk and get information and validation via telephone. Although they were not ready to join a group, they were pleased to know a group was available. Thus the first group began with four partners.

Over the last few years the author has facilitated many partners groups (both short- and long-term) and workshops. The following information is derived from those facilitation experiences and, most importantly, from the partners themselves.

THE ROLE OF THE PARTNERS GROUP

The role of a group is invaluable to partners. They are able to attain immediate, as well as long-term, benefits from the group experience. As the partner benefits, the survivor and others close to the partner benefit.

The immediate results from participation in a group include:

- Safety and support. A group provides a safe place (sometimes the first experience of safety for a partner) for learning. Safety is created consciously by the facilitator by establishing guidelines that ensure confidentiality and respectful communication to allow partners to hear each other and understand the process. Receiving support is often a new experience for partners. They are frequently used to giving, but not receiving, support. Those who have difficulty giving often learn from others in the group.

- Reduced isolation. Partners frequently believe that they must avoid discussing the abuse and their personal feelings with others (including the survivor), in order to protect the survivor. They often shoulder the burden of the survivor's secrets alone. Being in a group gives them permission to open up and connect with others.

- Validation. By hearing others voice similar concerns and feelings, partners find that they are not alone and that others understand.

- Self-Care. The group provides the space and time for partners to focus on themselves and to get some of their own needs met. They learn options for taking care of themselves and find that in doing so they are then better able to hear and be supportive of the survivor.

Many long-term benefits derive from being in a partners group, as well:

- Empowerment. Group participation, by allowing the partners to be heard and to receive support and validation, is empowering. They learn to understand the issues of child sexual abuse in general and their own issues in particular. This awareness is empowering.

- Ego strength. Increased awareness of oneself, as well as connection with others, builds ego support. Each person's thoughts and feelings are allowed, respected, and given a chance to mature.

- Trust. Group membership allows partners to risk self-exposure and to deal with the trust issues that emerge from that risking. They learn to trust others to hear them and also hear the abuse stories entrusted to them by the survivor and by other partners.

- Communication skills. Many partners, as they learn to express themselves in group, develop better communication skills. They become better able to receive feedback and constructive criticism, as well as articulate their needs and have those needs heard. They learn how powerful and affirming it is to be heard.

- Boundary awareness. Partners need to understand boundaries for their own benefit and for the survivor's. The boundary issue becomes clearer with discussion and demonstration as partners learn to identify, set, and then respect the limits as established.

- Intimacy/relationship issues. As partners work on and discuss relationship and other intimacy issues in their lives, they build skills to carry outside the group. They learn to wait for other members to ask for assistance rather than just give advice, they explore the balance between overfunctioning and underfunctioning, and they discuss characteristics of healthy relationships.

HOW TO BEGIN A GROUP

Once a therapist decides to create a partners group, she or he will want to consider the following questions:

- What are the structure and format of the group?
- How is the group to be publicized?
- How are group members screened and selected?
- Is the group open to men, women, or both?
- What are the minimum and maximum numbers of participants?

Group Structure

Forming a group for partners offers many options. The therapist might consider creating a time-limited group (ten–twelve weeks seems to work well) or doing an ongoing group. This author has found that partners have been more responsive to groups with definable ends because they are often new to the therapy experience and also because, at least initially, they view the group as a tool to help the survivors rather than themselves.

One-day or half-day workshops for partners are also effective. The workshop not only provides information about child sexual abuse, survivors, and partners of survivors but also allows partners to experience a taste of what membership in a therapeutic group might entail. Most partners are willing to commit a few hours or a day to a workshop. However, during the workshop itself, they then find that the experience is beneficial. Participants often request that a group be formed to continue the work that they began in the workshop.

Long-term groups are also powerful and rewarding for partners. The longer commitment and the enhanced familiarity and stability of these groups allow for even deeper levels of intimacy and thus more involved and explicit exploration of issues. In a long-term group the specific group dynamics become more of an issue and allow each member to experience different styles and alternatives for dealing with issues among the members. Group members learn to problem-solve and deal with conflicts as well as to be sensitive and supportive as relationships evolve.

Publicizing the Group

Creating a flier or an announcement to publicize the group directly works well. A one-page flier can be mailed to mental health care providers, agencies, and hospitals. It can be made available at support groups for survivors and at meetings of twelve-step programs (such as Alcoholics Anonymous, Al-Anon, Adult Children of Alcoholics, and Survivors of Incest Anonymous).

Screening Group Members

The screening of group members is dependent on the format of the group. It is usually not necessary to screen for workshops because they are contained by the brevity of time allotted and usually by a more didactic format.

In both short- and long-term groups the facilitator may want to have a twenty- to thirty-minute screening session with each prospective group member. This provides the facilitator the opportunity to explain the group in more detail to prospective members and to go over the group guidelines and/or contract with them. It also allows the prospective group member and the facilitator to question each other in order to better determine the appropriateness of the group for that person at that time.

The Group

The group format can be educational, therapeutic, didactic, cognitive, experiential, or a combination of these. A partners group configuration that seems to be most helpful has the following parameters:

- Lasts ten to twelve weeks in 1 1/2-hour sessions
- Has a minimum of four and maximum of eight members
- Has as members both men and women, heterosexual and homosexual. Groups or workshops, in general, have been extremely accepting of all partners
- May have a cofacilitator or may be run effectively with one facilitator.

The primary goal of the first session of the partners group is to create a safe setting and to establish preliminary connections and a common purpose. Establishing rules of confidentiality in order to make the group safe is essential. Safety guidelines may also include establishing a tone of respect for each member's process and issues; giving members the right to speak and be heard, though all do not have to agree; encouraging natural emotional expression; and encouraging risk taking and asking for help and support.

The use of an introductory or warm-up exercise in this session is helpful. In addition, group members need to discuss their goals and expectations for the group in this session. The facilitator can help establish goals by providing information about child sexual abuse, sharing and developing coping strategies, identifying and expressing feelings, and building communication skills, as well as offering alternative options to help them meet those goals in future sessions.

The group then works on those established goals. A combination of methods works well in these groups. Sessions often begin by talking about a topic for a brief period of time. For instance, the group may have expressed an interest in understanding the behaviors of the offender. That interest might lead to a discussion of feelings toward the offender. Members may then express anger either verbally or through anger exercises. In another instance, one member of the group may be having difficulty communicating with the survivor. A psychodrama or role play is developed to help the partner understand the situation and create options. Each member of the group learns from, and has the opportunity to relate to, this situation and exercise in some way.

Useful Methods

The group, as simply a place to talk and hear and be heard, is invaluable to members. However, the group also provides partners with important skills and techniques to assist them in self-care. It is extremely useful to begin group sessions with an exercise that enables each member to experience relaxation and self-awareness. Because most groups are held at the end of the workday, this exercise provides group members the time and the vehicle to transition from the business mode to a more personal and reflective mode. It teaches members to focus exclusively on themselves safely and privately and to pay attention to their physical, emotional, and mental processes without judgment. Techniques such as guided imagery, self-hypnosis, progressive body relaxation, and ''centering'' exercises are effective tools that can be taught easily to the group. These techniques provide immediate results and are easily mastered.

Partners often express a need for a how-to manual or a list of partner dos and don'ts. Over the course of the twelve-week group cycle members are encouraged to write their wisdom and insights on newsprint posted around the room. At the end of the group cycle, the therapist makes copies of what has been written and distributes them to members. This list is a tangible ''manual'' that partners take with them and add to as they continue their own processes.

Partners groups should address topics such as grief and loss, anger, fear, shame, sexuality, self-care, communication, intimacy, family-of-origin issues, trust, boundaries and limit setting, dealing with conflict, guilt, and ''child within'' issues. The content of the groups can be formally structured by using a different topic as the focus of each session. In this structure the topics are facilitator-generated.

For example, one session may focus on the topic of sexuality. The facilitator(s) then has many options available to introduce this topic. The facilitator might give a brief talk about sexuality and how it relates to couples whose lives have been affected by child sexual abuse. Or the facilitator might ask a series of questions to stimulate discussion or even distribute a questionnaire about the subject. Often a simple writing exercise is an excellent tool for members to explore their thoughts and feelings privately before bringing them up (often for the first time) in a group. Then the members can discuss the issues of the topic that are prominent for them.

Partners groups can also be less structured and more open. Simply asking, ''How are you?'' or ''What's going on?'' will elicit current issues. The facilitator(s) can then use the issues that emerge in group to provide education, understanding, and support to the group-generated topic.

Expressive and experiential techniques are very useful in partners groups as ways to introduce topics as well as to understand and deal with issues. Experiential therapies such as Gestalt, psychodrama, art therapy, bioenergetics, and core energetics are invaluable to therapists who are well trained in these modalities. Techniques such as role play, storytelling, guided imagery, and use of drawing, writing, and music are extremely helpful as they assist group members to tap into deeper levels of feeling and into the creative aspects of themselves that are often latent and thus underused resources.

The facilitator can employ a variety of techniques to introduce topics; for example, a facilitator might play some music that evokes feelings of grief and loss and ask members to simply be aware of what happens as they listen or might read a therapeutic story with a loss theme. Other options might be to ask group members to write a list of losses they have experienced in their lives and how they dealt with those losses or identify the positive and negative models of dealing with loss that they have witnessed or experienced in their families, among friends, or in films and books. After talking about loss in general, the facilitator can help the group focus on the losses they have experienced within their current relationship that are a result of the abuse.

Experiential work is quite helpful as a means to deal with issues. The following case example illustrates this work.

In a discussion about intimacy, Bill brought up an example of "trying to communicate" with his wife at breakfast one morning. Bill's wife had expressed her unhappiness with her job. Bill and his wife then proceeded to have an argument, which left Bill confused and baffled.

Bill initially asked the group to help him identify options for his wife that he could present to her. He had assessed that the argument he and his wife had had that morning about her job was due to his inability to provide better alternatives to his wife. Bill explored this through psychodrama, reenacting the scene at the breakfast table with the help of the group. As the psychodrama progressed, "doubles" (psychodramatic technique) were added to portray Bill's feelings and his wife's feelings. Bill, a very rational and logical neurologist, was able to identify his feelings—prior to this, he did not have any awareness of them—and then was able to surmise his wife's feelings as well. Bill was astonished to realize that he was feeling frightened because he did not know what to do to "fix" this situation for his wife. He was also feeling sad because he realized, on some level, that they were not really communicating and the distance between them was growing. This led to a deepened awareness of his role in his family of origin, where he had felt inadequate, abandoned, and out of control after the death of his mother when he was eight years old.

Bill realized that he could support his wife simply by listening to her. The option of being supportive by not fixing was a new experience for Bill. By being attentive to his own process, Bill was able to allow his wife the space for her own process. Other members of the group were really able to identify with Bill's desire to "fix" things. They talked about wanting to make their partner's (the survivor's) life better and to "make up" for all of the pain the survivor had suffered. They also discussed how they had learned to be fixers and how that role was useful to them. The value of listening gained status in the group. Many were both surprised and relieved to learn how powerful "just listening" can be, including, most importantly, listening to one's own feelings.

This case example illustrates how one member's dilemma can be explored in a very concrete manner and how this exploration furthers insight for that member as well as for the other group members. Experiential work is particularly useful in dealing with issues of anger and shame, issues that are often difficult to understand and express in positive and helpful ways.

An important issue to address from the outset as well as throughout the group is the decision to stay in the relationship. It is important that partners know what brought them to that relationship and what keeps them there. They do have a choice.

Group Termination

The final session is a natural ending to each particular group. It is helpful to have members discuss what they have learned from the group, which goals were or were not met, and what issues continue to need attention and options for attending to those needs and issues. Partners often will choose to go through two or more twelve-week cycles of the group or come back to the group again after a period of time elapses.

Group members will frequently continue to see each other and support each other after the group ends. Some group members will continue rituals that began while in group such as meeting for dinner or calling each other on a regular basis to check in.

CONCLUSION

As the mental health community has become more knowledgeable about child sexual abuse and its aftermath, treatment has become more sophisticated and more comprehensive. Treatment of the survivor of child sexual abuse conducted in a vacuum only perpetuates the stigmatization and isolation of the trauma. Rather, it is important and necessary to include the survivor's significant others in the healing process. Partners, in particular, because of their intimate involvement with the survivor, are highly affected and often suffer secondary traumatization that necessitates therapeutic intervention.

Group therapy is a particularly effective method to address the unique issues of partners. It provides a sense of community and a forum by which to deal with subjects that, until very recently, have been taboo. In the group therapy process partners are given the opportunity to honestly explore their thoughts and feelings, to search for, and share, options for coping, and to generally understand how being a partner of a survivor of child sexual abuse has affected them.

As partners begin, in growing numbers, to embark on their own healing processes, they are experiencing surprising benefits. The journey begun in an effort to help the survivor often opens up deeper levels of self-awareness and therefore a greater capacity for intimacy and personal satisfaction in their lives. As Tim, a partner, said, "I came here [to the group] expecting to understand and ended up feeling."

30

Developing an Inpatient Dissociative Disorders Unit

Christine A. Courtois, Barry M. Cohen, and Joan A. Turkus

As increasing numbers of adult survivors of sexual child abuse and other child-hood traumas have sought mental health treatment, their needs and conditions have become known through clinical observation and research studies. They have been found to suffer from chronic post-traumatic conditions that often involve dissociative defenses and personality adaptation. Treatment technologies, generally for outpatient therapy, have been developed and become available only over the last five to ten years. Specialized inpatient treatment is now urgently needed to supplement outpatient services and to offer safety and containment for survivors needing such extra support. Currently, approximately twenty such specialized units are available to offer services to survivors with severe post-traumatic dissociative conditions.

This chapter describes the development of one such program, the empower-ment model. The first part of the chapter is devoted to a discussion of the prevalence of child abuse and dissociation, as well as the overlap found between severe childhood abuse and dissociative post-traumatic reactions. The initial and long-term effects are briefly discussed, as are the typical post-abuse diagnostic categories. These determine the treatment needs of the adult survivor. At present, individual and group outpatient treatment for adult survivors is relatively avail-able; however, specialized hospital treatment is only now being developed. This chapter describes the philosophy, admission circumstances, treatment planning and goals, treatment components, sequencing, staffing, and expected outcome of the inpatient program designed and implemented by the authors.

THE RELATION BETWEEN CHILDHOOD TRAUMA AND
THE DISSOCIATIVE DISORDERS

In the last decade, sexual child abuse has been identified as a major socio-political problem with far-reaching personal and social consequences. Whereas incest and other forms of sexual abuse were thought to occur so infrequently as to constitute aberrations that were taboo either to discuss or in which to engage, it is now recognized that they occur quite regularly in a substantial percentage of the population.

The recent discovery (or rediscovery) of the high prevalence of sexual child abuse is due to a confluence of social initiatives: the women's movement with its recognition of the high incidence of rape and other forms of sexual violence against women by strangers and by intimates; the fields of criminology and traumatic stress with their emphases on victimization and its aftermath; and sociological studies of the dynamics and aftereffects of child abuse and other forms of family violence. The aggregate findings of these studies refute the long-standing theory promulgated by Freud that sexual abuse was a fantasy or wish on the part of the child rather than a reality (Freud, 1896). These findings, instead, return attention to Freud's original discovery and theory—the seduction theory (or trauma theory)—which held that incest and other forms of sexual abuse are common occurrences for many children, with effects that are far-reaching, threatening both psychological development and mental health.

Subsequent to the identification of the high prevalence of sexual child abuse has been the recognition of the seriousness and extensiveness of the risk it poses to the victim. Sexual child abuse (especially incest) is now recognized as a traumatic stressor that is correlated with a host of potentially severe reactions occurring over the victim's life span. These qualify as post-traumatic stress reactions and frequently meet the criteria for the diagnosis of post-traumatic stress disorder (PTSD).

Over this same decade, a second area of study focused on the concept of dissociation and the dissociative disorders (DDs), especially multiple personality disorder (MPD). The study of dissociation was active from the 1800s up to approximately 1935; a hiatus in this research occurred between 1935 and 1965, due primarily to Freud's emphasis on the defensive process of repression rather than dissociation. Dissociation has received renewed interest since approximately 1965 (Counts, 1990). It has been identified as a normative process that can be induced under certain conditions (e.g., hypnosis) and, under conditions of extreme stress, is used as a spontaneous defense to protect the individual from the full psychological impact of a traumatic stressor. The hypothesized continuum of dissociation ranges from "a normal mental process that results in the erecting of barriers that exclude data from consciousness (or involves other types of interruption or the disconnecting of normally connected elements)" to dissociative disorders that "are instances involving gross or dramatic interruptions" (Counts, 1990, p. 474). Five dissociative disorders are listed in the *Diagnostic and Statistical Manual* III-R (DSM III-R, APA, 1987): (1) psychogenic amnesia, (2) psychogenic fugue, (3) depersonalization disorder, (4) multiple personality disorder, and (5) dissociative disorder, not otherwise specified.

The respective fields of child sexual abuse/family violence, dissociation/multiple personality disorder, and traumatology/traumatic stress studies have recently converged, recognizing that their populations of study substantially overlap and that traumatic stress response has similarities across stressors. The applicability of adult-onset post-traumatic stress disorder originated primarily with the study of veterans of Vietnam and other combat circumstances and has been extended to other traumatized populations such as refugees, political prisoners, victims of natural disasters, and crime victims. The most substantial extension of post-traumatic syndromes has derived from the study of child-onset trauma and trauma of a prolonged/chronic nature (which usually refers to abuse and neglect within the family).

Children are particularly prone to dissociation (some more than others) (Putnam, 1991). When faced with conditions of ongoing and escalating physical, sexual, and/or emotional abuse (particularly if abuse is severe and combines with inconsistency of nurturance, little or no hope of intervention, and therefore no escape), children resort to dissociative responses as coping strategies. Dissociation and post-traumatic stress responses have recently been found to be complementary; in fact, PTSD is now being described as a type of dissociative disorder that assists the victim to cope with ongoing abuse by alternately suppressing/numbing it and reexperiencing it in intrusive form. Over time, if the abuse persists in serious enough form within an otherwise interpersonally chaotic and inconsistent environment, post-traumatic reactions affect the developing child's personality and become embedded within it.

Severe trauma is defended against by encapsulation and dissociation, often for extended periods of time. A high percentage of adults lost direct memory of the abuse (and/or their entire childhoods); yet, they suffered from acute symptomatology sporadically and/or chronically across the life span. Their abuse was lost to them until its memory was triggered in some way. In today's culture, the almost constant barrage of media information about abuse serves as a triggering mechanism for the return of what was previously dissociated in the interest of survival. Dissociative disorders, including post-traumatic stress disorder, are increasingly recognized as affecting large numbers of adult survivors of sexual child abuse. The most serious and most rigidly encapsulated dissociative responses are found in those individuals suffering from multiple personality disorder.

PREVALENCE

Heretofore, dissociative disorders were not believed to be common either in the general population or in the clinical subpopulation. Recent research, as well as clinical findings, is suggesting just the opposite: they are common and have been overlooked due to psychiatry's emphasis on repression rather than dissociation (Counts, 1990). Ross (1991) conducted the first epidemiological study of dissociation, the dissociative disorders, and multiple personality disorder in the general population in Winnipeg, Manitoba, Canada, and found a prevalence of 5–10 percent of DDs in general and 1 percent of complex dysfunctional posttraumatic MPD in the general population. It was also noted that although these figures might seem exceedingly high, they are in line with epidemiological studies of the prevalence of other major mental illnesses, with recently available data concerning the high prevalence of childhood trauma (especially sexual child abuse) in North America, and with clinical findings reported later in this chapter. These research results, which remain to be replicated, indicated that the dissociative disorders are as common as the anxiety and affective disorders in the general population. As Ross noted, "The rationale for conducting a study of the prevalence of DDs in the general population is the realization that they occur commonly in clinical populations" (Ross, 1991, p. 507). Reports of diagnosed dissociative disorders, including multiple personality and of post-traumatic stress disorder in adult survivors of severe chronic child abuse, increased dramatically during the 1980s. With the diagnosis came the recognition within the professional mental health community of the dearth of treatment models to meet the needs of this exponentially growing clinical group.

THE TREATMENT NEEDS OF THE ADULT SURVIVOR

Adult survivors of child sexual, physical, and emotional abuse constitute a special at-risk population that has long been denied and neglected (Courtois, 1988b). The adult survivors of today grew up when abuse was unrecognized and held to be taboo. An atmosphere of denial and disbelief prevailed; very little assistance or intervention was available (except in the most egregious, undeniable cases, usually those brought to the attention of the authorities). Abused children coped as best they could under such circumstances. Because of the nonacknowledgment of abuse, its symptoms and aftereffects went unrecognized at the time of abuse and later. During the 1970s and 1980s, investigations yielded fairly consistent data on the prevalence and aftereffects of sexual abuse and other forms of childhood trauma. Current estimates, however, are that between one in three and one in four girls and one in four to one in seven boys in the United States were sexually abused in childhood (Courtois, 1988b). Abuse has been identified as a high-risk factor for serious symptoms and aftereffects both at the time of the abuse and throughout the life span. Carmen, Rieker, and Mills (1984) noted that a common aftermath of untreated victimization was the development of later mental health problems, a process they labeled as "victim-to-patient."

Browne and Finkelhor (1986) reviewed the available research on initial and long-term aftereffects of abuse and concluded that as a group, abused samples had more mental health and other disturbances than nonabused samples. Aftereffects are compounded over time, as suggested by Carmen, Rieker, and Mills

(1984), Courtois (1988b), and Gelinas (1983), and can be consolidated into seven major categories: (1) post-traumatic reactions (short- and long-term, chronic, and delayed); (2) emotional reactions (e.g., guilt, depression, anxiety, self-blame); (3) self-perceptions and belief systems or cognitive schemas (e.g., as bad, contaminated, shamed); (4) physical/somatic effects (e.g., chronic pain, headaches, hyperarousal); (5) sexual reactions (e.g., pain, aversion, compulsivity, desire disorder); (6) interpersonal relating (e.g., mistrust, fear, conflict, intimacy, and parenting difficulty); and (7) social effects (e.g., isolation and inability to function versus overfunctioning).

Many of these symptoms and aftereffects fit within the DSM III-R (APA, 1987) Axis I category (the symptoms and presenting concerns brought to treatment); however, both clinicians and researchers have identified a strong connection between a history of childhood trauma and Axis II diagnoses (long-standing, developmental, and applied to personality disturbances) (Briere & Runtz, 1985; Briere, 1989, 1991). In particular, a significant overlap, unacknowledged by previous researchers, has been found between the diagnosis of borderline personality disorder and a history of childhood trauma (Briere, 1989; Briere & Runtz, 1985; Herman & van der Kolk, 1987). Linkages have also been suggested among post-traumatic stress disorder, dissociative disorders (including multiple personality disorder), borderline personality disorder (Braun, 1980, 1986; Schultz, Braun & Kluft, 1987; Herman & van der Kolk, 1987; Ross, 1989), and other Axis II disorders (Fink, 1991). The diagnosis of "dissociative disorder, not otherwise specified: variants of multiple personality" has also been increasingly utilized.

Both Kluft (1991a) and Turkus (1991) have commented that the points on the dissociation continuum between post-traumatic stress disorder and "classic form" MPD provide pioneer territory for researchers and clinicians alike. It appears that multiplicity is clinically more common than previously estimated and is largely a complex set of post-traumatic symptoms arising from severe and chronic forms of childhood trauma. Multiplicity has gone unrecognized when its form does not fit the expectations or knowledge base of the clinician, when the clinician has no index of suspicion and/or does not screen for it. Furthermore, multiplicity is a condition of concealment with vacillating presentations. Similar to other traumatic stress reactions, it may be dormant for extended periods of time (Kluft, 1991a).

UNCHARTED TREATMENT TERRITORY: THE
DISSOCIATIVE POST-TRAUMATIC DISORDERS

The recognition of the prevalence of post-traumatic dissociative disorders led to a concomitant recognition of the lack of both adequate outpatient and adequate inpatient treatment technology for adult survivors of abuse. A concurrent set of research findings has suggested that survivors of childhood trauma (especially sexual abuse) make up a disproportionately large number of users of mental health services. Current estimates are that 50 percent of outpatients and 50 percent or more of inpatients have a history of childhood trauma (this percentage goes dramatically higher by diagnostic category: abuse survivors are estimated to comprise better than 60 percent of eating disorders, chemical dependency, borderline personality disorder, dissociative disorder, and multiple personality disorder (Briere, 1989; Courtois, 1988b; Herman & van der Kolk, 1987; Putnam, 1989). Survivors in treatment can be categorized according to their chronicity in the mental health system. One subgroup is highly symptomatic and may have been since childhood. Many members of this subgroup have become repeat and/ or chronic clients. They have received treatment for their presenting symptom(s) and their diagnosed psychopathology, but not for their childhood trauma(s), even when they disclosed occurrence. Until just recently, clinicians either denied or avoided reports of abuse and did not correlate abuse with their clients' symptom pictures. Societal taboo and denial concerning abuse and the often-extended intervening time period between the abuse and the development and elaboration of their symptoms have conspired to disconnect or decontextualize presenting problems from the abuse (Carmen, Rieker & Mills, 1984; Courtois, 1988b; Gelinas, 1983). Gelinas labeled this process "the disguised presentation," and, as noted previously, "the victim-to-patient" process was coined by Carmen, Rieker, and Mills (1984) to articulate this transformation over time.

Another subgroup of survivors who seek treatment consists of those who have no memory of the abuse, the "secret survivors" described by Blume (1990). The essential feature of a dissociative disorder is a disturbance or alteration in the normally integrative functions of identity, memory, or consciousness, according to the DSM III-R (APA, 1987, p. 269). Adult survivors who are amnestic for their abuse have usually dissociated or repressed memory in order to cope with the trauma. Thus, unless clinicians routinely ask about an abuse history, unless the presenting symptoms fit the postsexual abuse syndrome proposed by Briere (1989) and others, and unless clinicians recognize the possibility of a trauma history and ask about its occurrence, the history will likely continue to remain buried and unidentified. Similarly, symptoms of this subgroup will be treated and may, in fact, remit. But the untreated trauma remains as a "psychological time bomb" (Peters, 1976), ready to be cued unexpectedly throughout the life span in response to a large number of developmental and environmental trigger events (Courtois, 1988b).

To summarize, abuse survivors (whether their abuse is known and/or disclosed) compose a large number of mental health consumers (Briere, 1989; Courtois, 1988b). Many are repeatedly treated, and some become chronic clients with symptoms refractory to standard treatment based upon the existing medical model. A paradigm shift in mental health, as proposed by Ross (1989, 1991), is needed to gear treatment to the resolution of the trauma and its subsequent effects (Courtois, 1988b). A paradigm based on a trauma model of dysfunction or psychopathology provides an alternative model on which to develop treatment. Sequences and strategies of outpatient treatment, although still in need of refinement and expansion of alternative delivery models, have been described in the abuse literature. (See Briere, 1989, 1991; Courtois, 1988b, 1991b; Gil, 1988; Kluft, 1984b). Descriptions of two impatient models have thus far been published (Bloom, this volume; Kluft, 1991a).

INPATIENT TREATMENT OF DISSOCIATIVE DISORDERS EMPOWERMENT MODEL

Although patients with severe dissociative disorders frequently need inpatient treatment, few specialized programs are available as models. The empowerment model was developed and implemented by the authors to respond to the needs of these patients as well as to provide supportive, ego-enhancing, progressive treatment consistent with the shift in the American health care system from long-term to short-term inpatient care.

This model, which has been developed on an acute care specialty unit of a psychiatric hospital, encourages patients to reclaim their sense of self-worth and personal power and to function at the highest possible level during the course of their treatment. This approach is specifically designed to remove the patient from the passive victim role and to counteract contagious helplessness within the therapy. The model features mentoring, rather than reparenting, in guiding patients toward personal empowerment. Treatment is designed to be collaborative between the treatment team and the patient. Continuity of treatment with the outpatient caregiver, along with the patient's outside support network, is fostered. A cognitive framework for understanding the destructive impact of childhood trauma and child and adult defenses and aftereffects is presented. Expression and connection (rather than repression and disconnection) are encouraged by a multidisciplinary team, including therapists from various expressive therapy modalities, yet the pace is contained in order not to overwhelm the patient's capacities.

The therapeutic model is based on a solid theoretical foundation for outpatient care recently articulated in the child abuse, dissociative disorders/MPD and traumatic stress literature (Briere, 1989, 1991; Courtois, 1988b, 1991b; Herman, 1981; Kluft, 1989b). McCann & Pearlman, 1990b; Meiselman, 1990; Ochberg, 1988; Putnam, 1989. It is a "whole person" model that recognizes the mind/body impact of trauma (Ochberg, 1988; van der Kolk, 1987c) and is based upon current research and theory in the following areas: (1) feminism, by which gender and power-based relationships, the importance of individual experience in understanding the collective, and the normalcy of survival skills are legitimized; (2) traumatic stress, by which defenses and survivor skills are understood as normal, not pathological, responses to traumatic circumstances. These defenses and skills may cause later dysfunction, which, along with the original trauma and its effects, is in need of direct treatment for psychological mastery to occur; (3) developmental theory, by which the maturational impact of chronic trauma is understood and addressed, and undeveloped life and coping skills are taught;

(4) loss theory, by which the losses of victimization are understood and grieved; (5) interpersonal relations, by which the relational distortions and deficits caused by family dysfunction and abuse are addressed; (6) cognitive theory, by which the effects of emotional overload in response to the impacts of trauma on cognitive processes and personal schemas regarding self and relations with others are presented; and (7) dissociation theory, by which the individual's awareness, memory, and identity are altered (or split) to cope with trauma of an ongoing, overwhelming sort.

Criteria for Hospitalization

Most admissions occur during acute or crisis circumstances and/or stalemates in outpatient work that may benefit from an outside professional analysis and consultation. The most common reasons for admission include suicidal and/or homicidal ideation and behavior and/or serious self-mutilation; extreme disorganization related to a decline in functioning or an inability to function; danger during significant anniversaries or danger due to other events that trigger response; profound and incapacitating depression; heightened status of fear or physiological arousal; life-threatening addictions and compulsions, including unsafe sexualizing, eating disorders, or substance abuse; diagnostic crisis associated with the original diagnosis or its revision/upgrading (especially when MPD is diagnosed and greater degrees or intensity of trauma are discovered); and safety during intensive remembering, abreactive, and/or integrative work.

Treatment Planning and Sequencing

Treatment involves a multidisciplinary team led by a psychiatrist, psychologist, and art therapist/manager and includes nursing, social work, and expressive therapy staff, as well as adjunctive nutritional and chemical dependency staff as needed. As was mentioned, continuity of care is emphasized. Outpatient therapists are encouraged to continue to provide individual psychotherapy whenever feasible and are included in treatment planning. When the outpatient therapist is unable to treat the patient during the hospitalization, collaboration is sought in preadmission consultation, along with treatment and discharge planning.

A careful assessment regarding the need for stabilization versus uncovering, safety precautions, comorbidity, and social support systems contribute to appropriate goal setting for, and sequencing of, the treatment. Discharge planning is addressed from the outset of the hospitalization. The patient is stabilized before uncovering/remembering work is undertaken. Patients are actively taught pacing and containment strategies and are encouraged to slow or increase the pace on an individual basis. The entire milieu and the treatment team are involved in both the stimulation and the containment of the therapeutic material. The dissociated material is encouraged to return and is worked through within the newly taught cognitive framework and coping structure. Comorbid conditions are also assessed carefully. Often, differential diagnosis is difficult. Post-traumatic/dissociative conditions frequently encompass other symptoms that must be assessed and disentangled. Outside experts are consulted on an as-needed basis, and specialized procedures are utilized whenever required for diagnosis and comprehensive treatment planning.

The treatment program itself contains four major components: group therapy, expressive therapies, individual psychotherapy, and psychoeducation, backed up by nursing care, the therapeutic milieu, and adjunctive involvement and therapy of any significant others/family. Individual therapy is approached in a stage-appropriate means to focus and integrate the inpatient treatment. The treatment team actively teaches the patient about the etiology and symptomatology of post-abuse syndromes (including dissociation) while fostering a milieu of understanding coupled with expectations for personal accountability, responsibility, and self-nurturing. The atmosphere emphasizes healing and the expectation of recovery to counter the hopelessness/despair that is so often an aftermath of severe trauma.

The program is highly structured. The majority of the treatment is conducted in group formats. Patients have twice-weekly sexual trauma and psychodrama groups in addition to art therapy and a number of psychoeducation, special topic, and community groups per day. Individual therapy, including abreactive sessions when advisable, occurs at least three times per week. Couples and family meetings are also planned across the hospital stay.

Group therapy provides ongoing opportunities for sharing and connecting with others as both helper and helpee. Patients are encouraged in give-and-take, and groups enable the amelioration of shame and guilt, as well as the expression of other strong emotions such as rage and sadness. Groups provide a support network that extends the learning of the psychoeducational components as members hear their experiences reflected in the experiences of others. Members are actively encouraged to reassociate what has been previously split off, avoided, or denied and to assist others to do the same. Expressive therapy refers to the group of modalities based on visual, literary, and performing arts that includes art, dance/movement, music, poetry, and drama therapy/psychodrama. Expressive therapists are clinicians at the master's and doctoral levels who are specially trained and are registered in these modalities. Expressive therapies also allow for expression rather than repression/dissociation through symbolic productions and enactments. These productions are actively assessed and utilized in the interest of "putting the picture together" by staff. Expressive techniques provide the means by which patients can express that "for which there are no words" (Steele, 1989) and can circumvent verbalization that feels threatening and/or premature.

Nursing care is both continuous and crucial in this model. Nurses run the hospital milieu and have the most ongoing patient contact. They are called upon to monitor each patient and to reinforce and build upon the therapy in their interactions with patients. A major opportunity for nursing creativity and re-sourcefulness exists within this model. Nurses implement treatment plans and suggest specific tasks to patients.

Finally, intervention and adjunctive work with family and/or significant others is undertaken by social work staff who are active in assessment, education, and referral. Family and significant others can be a major source of support or distress to the patient. Supportive others have not received adequate inclusion in most survivor treatment and are only now being recognized in terms of their own needs and their potential for support (Davis, 1991; Panos, Panos & Allred, 1990; Williams, 1991a). On the other hand, partners and spouses may be part of the patient's problem when they are abusive and/or otherwise critical or unrespon-sive. Via family meetings, social workers attempt to assess strengths and weak-nesses and potential for support or distress and develop treatment strategies accordingly. These are then coordinated with the rest of the treatment team. Interventions range from psychoeducation, to active therapy, to referrals for individual, couples, or family therapy, to reports to child or adult protective services.

This brief review describes in general terms how the trauma work is paced and contained by the therapeutic milieu and connectedness between patients and staff. This model requires attention to staff communication and process, as well as the active maintenance of staff morale through teamwork and the processing of traumatic content. Staff expect to be vicariously traumatized (McCann & Pearlman, 1990b), and attempts are made to offer education, processing, and support to offset despair and professional burnout. The model's emphasis on collaboration, mentorship, and the empowerment of survivor patients also serves to support and maintain the staff. Staff members are selected for their personal and professional resonance to the treatment model and philosophy, their moti-vation, their ability to function both individually and as members of a team, and their potential as mentors. In this respect, they are knowledgeable in theory and practice, skilled in communication such as teaching and empathic listening, flexible and creative with good boundaries (neither too tight nor too loose), and dynamic and inspirational as "developers of people."

The healing process from childhood trauma and sexual abuse has been anal-ogized by Bass and Davis (1988) as similar to childbirth. This is a good analogy for staff as well as patients: the recovery process, like childbirth, is often ex-cruciating and close to intolerable. The reward, however, is nothing less than the rebirth of the individual, a most substantive and satisfying outcome.

SUMMARY

The empowerment model appears, from a clinical perspective, to be effective. Long-term outcome studies have, however, not yet substantiated these obser-vations. The authors have, thus far, treated approximately 300 survivors during the program's first year and a half of operation. They have also maintained an almost constant waiting list for admission, attesting to the need for specialized treatment for abuse aftermath and dissociative conditions. This chapter has not focused upon, but has alluded to, some of the difficulties in making an inpatient program work. These will be discussed in future publications as clinical research to measure the effectiveness of the model is conducted. The authors are quite aware of their responsibility to determine which treatment strategies and components are most therapeutic for this population and how some might be applied to general psychiatric units and the treatment offered to the abused/dissociated patient in that context.

In summary, the empowerment model is encompassing and heuristic. It builds upon recently available clinical knowledge regarding the trauma of childhood abuse and the serious initial and long-term consequences of that abuse. The significance of dissociation as a defense strategy and adaptational style utilized by abused children and into adulthood is emphasized. The treatment philosophy and strategy are based on relevant theory. A safe environment in which trauma work can progress and be contained is provided very deliberately. The trauma is reworked as new coping and relational skills are taught and reinforced. The treatment is progressive rather than regressive, encourages the highest level of functioning rather than traumatic reenactment and/or decline, and is geared to be short-term. The model provides the structure, varied therapeutic modalities, and therapeutic connectedness and containment for trauma resolution, personal development, and personal empowerment to occur.

The Sanctuary Model: Developing Generic Inpatient Programs for the Treatment of Psychological Trauma

Sandra L. Bloom

BACKGROUND

Most psychiatric unit directors today would state that their programs are based on the concept of the "therapeutic milieu" described by Gunderson (1978) as a methodology characterized by five functional variables: containment, support, structure, involvement, and validation. As is the case with many other areas of human endeavor, a wide gap between the real and ideal concept of the therapeutic milieu often exists (Abroms, 1969; Almond, 1974; Gabbard, 1988; Gutheil, 1985; Kirshner & Johnston, 1982; Leeman, 1986; Margo & Manring, 1989; Wilmer, 1981). Underlying assumptions upon which practice is constructed are confusing, contradictory, and divisive. The corollary of this lack of theoretical cohesion is a lack of agreement on treatment goals.

There is no longer any doubt about the strong connection among childhood trauma, disturbed development, and adult psychiatric illness (Beck & van der Kolk, 1987; Briere & Saidi, 1989; Bryer et al., 1987; Bulik, Sullivan & Rorty, 1989; Herman, 1986; Herman, Perry & van der Kolk, 1989; Jacobson & Herald, 1990; Jacobson, Koehler & Jones-Brown, 1987; Jacobson & Richardson, 1987; Morrison, 1989; Shearer et al., 1990; Sierles et al., 1983; Stone, 1981; Walker, Katon & Harrop-Griffiths, 1988).

A common human response to overwhelming life events is called the "post-traumatic stress response," upon which the trauma-based approach is based. This approach to treatment, foundation of the sanctuary model of inpatient treatment, makes certain fundamental assumptions about those patients who have survived significant traumatic experiences (Herman, 1981; van der Kolk, 1987c):

1. Patients begin life with normal potentials for growth and development, given certain constitutional and genetic predispositions, then become traumatized. "Post-traumatic stress reactions are essentially the reactions of normal people to abnormal stress" (Silver, 1986).

2. When people are traumatized in early life, the effects of trauma interfere with normal physical, psychological, intellectual, and moral development.

3. Trauma has psychological, biological, social, and moral effects that spread horizontally and vertically, across and through generations.

4. Many symptoms and syndromes are manifestations of adaptations, originally useful as coping skills, that have now become maladaptive or less adaptive than originally intended.

5. Many victims of trauma suffer chronic post-traumatic stress disorder (PTSD) and may manifest any combination of the symptoms of PTSD.

6. Victims of trauma become trapped in time, their ego fragmented. They are caught in the repetitive reexperiencing of the trauma, which has been dissociated and remains unintegrated into their overall functioning.

7. Dissociation and repression are core defenses against overwhelming affect and are present, to a varying extent, in all survivors of trauma.

8. Although the human capacity for fantasy elaboration and imaginative creation is well established, memories of traumatic experiences must be assumed to have at least a core of basis in reality.

9. Stressful events are more seriously traumatic when there are an accompanying helplessness and lack of control.

10. The more severe the stressor, the more prolonged the exposure to the stressor, the earlier the age, the more impaired the social support system, and the greater the degree of exposure to, or involvement in, previous trauma, the greater will be the resultant post-traumatic pathology.

11. Attachment is a basic human need. Enhanced attachment to abusing objects is seen in all studied species, including man.

12. Childhood abuse leads to disrupted attachment behavior, inability to modulate arousal and aggression toward self and others, impaired cognitive functioning, and impaired capacity to form stable relationships.

13. People who are repeatedly traumatized develop "learned helplessness," a condition that has serious biochemical implications.

14. Trauma survivors often discover that various addictive behaviors restore at least a temporary sense of control over intrusive phenomena.

15. Survivors may also become addicted to their own stress responses and, as a result, compulsively expose themselves to high levels of stress and further traumatization.

16. Many trauma survivors develop secondary psychiatric symptomatology and do not connect their symptoms with previous trauma. They become guilt-ridden and depressed and exhibit low self-esteem and feelings of hopelessness and helplessness.

17. Trauma victims have difficulty with the appropriate management of aggression. Many

survivors identify with the aggressor and become victimizers themselves. A vicious cycle of transgenerational victimization often ensues.

18. Although it may require lifelong processing, recovery from trauma experience is possible. Over the course of recovery, survivors may temporarily need safe retreats within which important therapeutic goals can be formulated and treatment can be organized.

These and other basic assumptions undergird the sanctuary model of inpatient treatment. They serve, as well, as working hypotheses for all patients. In this way, formerly incomprehensible symptoms become comprehensible, explicable, and often treatable.

SANCTUARY MODEL OF INPATIENT TREATMENT

Treatment Context

The sanctuary model is an elaboration of the therapeutic milieu concept. It uses the trauma-based approach as a philosophical structure for organizing treatment and a feminist-informed systems approach for organizing the milieu (Belenky et al., 1986; Engel, 1977; Gilligan, 1982; Marmor, 1983; Menninger, 1963; Miller, 1976; Ruddick, 1989; Wilkinson & O'Connor, 1982).

These concepts are applied to short-term hospital care. *Short-term* is defined as a length of stay of less than thirty days on an open, voluntary, 22-bed psychiatric unit.

Program Description

In 1980 a multidisciplinary group of mental health specialists created an open, voluntary, inpatient unit in a general hospital. Around 1985 as a result of some particularly instructive patients, staff began realizing that insufficient attention had been paid to the implications of severe childhood trauma in the histories of many of the patients. This led to a shift in emphasis in the evaluation phase of treatment toward a focus on underlying trauma. Staff stopped asking, in any number of ways, "What's wrong with you?" and began asking, "What happened to you?" When they began to ask different questions, they were astounded by the answers they received. The discovery that a majority of patients were victims of serious and significant childhood physical and sexual abuse led to a broadening of the treatment perspective and an ongoing search for more effective modalities of treatment.

In 1986, Silver described "sanctuary trauma" as a phenomenon that occurs when people who are expecting a protective environment find only more trauma. Psychiatric patients have been traumatized for centuries by institutions supposedly designed to provide asylum. This recognition led to an attempt to define and operationalize what has come to be called "the sanctuary at Northwestern."

At present, the program is comprised of twenty-two beds situated in a discrete unit within a private psychiatric hospital in the suburbs of Philadelphia, Pennsylvania. The target population is adults who have been—or are suspected of having been—abused as children. The staff is made up of a medical director and an assistant medical director, both of whom are psychiatrists; attending psychiatrists; a program director, who is a licensed social worker; a clinical nurse specialist; two psychologists; two clinical social workers; three creative therapists; and a complete nursing staff.

Patients receive daily individual psychotherapy sessions after having been given complete psychiatric, psychological, social service, and medical evaluations. Family therapy evaluations and the beginning of family therapy sessions are routinely provided. There are two community meetings a day, led by a community president.

In addition to individual sessions, the patients attend three to four groups per day. The unit provides about thirty-two to thirty-six group experiences per week. Psychoeducational groups are designed to provide didactic information about trauma and its effects on the individual and on the society. This cognitive information reframes the symptoms and places them into a more comprehensible intellectual structure that can assist the patient in learning how to use intellect to modulate affect.

Stress management groups help the patients learn new coping skills to replace compulsive, self-destructive habits. Traumatic reenactment groups focus on the ways in which patients reenact their own traumatic scenarios in the context of the community. Discharge planning groups prepare individuals to utilize the insights they have gained during their admission to anticipate and prepare for problems after discharge.

Psychodrama, art therapy, occupational therapy, and movement therapy all use the creative arts to help the patient express affect nonverbally, translate nonverbal into verbal expression that can be shared, and rehearse new behaviors. The creative therapy groups are often the most evocative of emotional, rather than cognitive, expression.

Each patient is assigned a "contact person" from every nursing shift so that individual problems can be addressed. The regular supervision and management of the nursing staff are coordinated by a nurse manager. Patients who have particularly destructive symptoms can be placed on special protocols to help manage problems of eating disorders, self-mutilation, dissociation, and traumatic reenactments. More individualized protocols are established as required.

The average length of stay is about three weeks. Patients will often be readmitted over the course of their overall treatment experience; these readmissions are not viewed as an aspect of "recidivism." Post-traumatic symptoms are so pervasive and affect so many aspects of a person's life that a sanctuary environment is frequently required at different stages in treatment or when there is relapse. Generally, however, there is a pattern of increasing function and productivity in between hospitalizations and decreasing disability during the rehospitalization.

The intensity of treatment requires a commensurate intensity of management. The entire treatment team meets twice weekly to review each case. However, each smaller treatment team that is assigned to the individual patient collaborates daily. Each patient is assigned a social worker, who coordinates family interventions and liaisons with the outpatient therapist and any other involved agencies. Family sessions are usually led conjointly by the social worker and primary therapist. Sessions involving the outpatient therapist frequently occur in preparation for discharge. In addition, the medical director, assistant medical director, program director, clinical nurse specialist, and nurse manager meet regularly to assess the overall treatment environment.

Patients must be sufficiently in control of their behavior to be maintained in an open and voluntary unit and must not be a danger to others. The most commonly admitted diagnostic categories from the Diagnostic and Statistical Manual (DSM III-R, APA, 1987) are major depressive disorder, borderline personality disorder, multiple personality disorder, and the other dissociative disorders. The unit is not gender-specific. The fundamental basis for admission is whether or not the physical, emotional, and social safety of the unit can be maintained and the person can be adequately treated using this specific therapeutic approach.

Most survivors enter psychiatric treatment because of self-destructive, self-abusive behaviors ranging from addictions of all kinds to self-mutilation, suicidal ideation, social withdrawal, self-sabotage, and impaired capacities for intimacy. They usually make no connections between present problems and earlier, often still completely repressed, traumatic experiences.

Some individuals may still be in abusive relationships, and their present needs for immediate safety outweigh concerns about the past. Many enter treatment manifesting the "negative symptoms" of PTSD: denial, numbness, depression, withdrawal, anhedonia. Others seek treatment only when they begin to experience the "positive" symptoms of hyperarousal, irritability, inability to control rage, flashbacks, behavioral reenactments, and pseudohallucinations.

Upon entering treatment, most patients feel defective, demoralized, and fearful of "going crazy" or losing control. Most have serious deficits in the capacity to trust. Hence, the ability to form stable and satisfying mutual relationships is often seriously impaired. Also, many suffer from a disturbance in the capacity to comprehend normal interpersonal boundaries.

Trauma, particularly trauma suffered at the hands of other humans, is, by definition, a boundary disorder. Thus, trauma survivors have difficulties establishing and maintaining normal, protective boundaries around the sense of self and frequently misinterpret the meaning of the more normal boundary operations of others. As a consequence, their quality of relating is often overly intense and unrealistic. They are also extremely sensitive to boundary incursions of all kinds, while attempting to reenact them compulsively.

As a part of this very complicated picture and as a direct result of PTSD, trauma survivors have difficulty modulating feelings of rage, fear, and grief and manifest extremes of emotional expression. They may also experience intrusive phenomena and flashbacks, manifestations easily mistaken for psychotic symptoms.

Stages of Treatment

Horowitz (1986) discussed a phase-oriented treatment of stress response syndromes. Lifton (1988) talked about confrontation, reordering, and renewal. Herman (1992) has simplified treatment into three stages: safety, reconstruction, and reconnection. No matter how these stages are defined, however, it is clear that interpenetration of all the stages occurs and that recovery proceeds along a continuum of treatment experience that includes outpatient individual, group, and often, inpatient treatment.

Safety

The essence of trauma is that a person's sense of safety in the world is seriously compromised. The provision of a safe environment is the most important aspect of the treatment of victims of trauma. The sense of safety must encompass physical, emotional, social, and moral levels of care.

Biological safety. Biological safety means providing for basic biological survival needs. Medical evaluation assesses the current physical status of the person. Medications assist in the treatment of stress-related physical illnesses, and psychopharmacological agents may be utilized if it is clear that they may do more good than harm. Antidepressants and antianxiety medications offer significant temporary benefit, as well.

Many psychiatric units mix voluntary with involuntary patients (Chiappa & Wilson, 1981; Leeman et al., 1981). Excluding involuntary admissions does not guarantee safety, but it does improve the odds. When voluntary patients are mixed with noncompliant, involuntarily committed patients, care usually sinks to what is required to keep the level of violence and disruption to a minimum. This is not adequate care for persons who have already been victims of violence. Screening out involuntary patients helps screen out violence.

Clear expectations must exist about the unacceptability of violent acting out as an intrinsic part of the therapeutic milieu. If violence does erupt, the behavior must be handled promptly, firmly, and decisively and may necessitate transfer of the offender to a more restrictive environment. Clear rules and effective response to sexual acting out applies to patients and staff alike. Sexual acting out must not be tolerated because, like violence, it is an act of boundary trespass.

An intensive therapeutic milieu is not appropriate for everyone. It can be too stimulating for acutely psychotic, manic, and chronically psychotic patients and can promote further deterioration (Kahn & White, 1989). These patients need special treatment programs designed to meet their needs and stabilize their illness as effectively as possible.

The achievement of biological safety also necessitates the substitution of healthier coping skills for compulsive, self-destructive behaviors. Issues of self-harm, including self-starvation, bulimia, self-mutilation, destructive dissociation, and addictions, must be addressed. In order to be admitted to the unit, patients must be willing to make a commitment to transforming their self-destructive habits into self-creative ones. Specific protocols are then constructed to achieve this goal.

If the patient is not yet willing to give up self-destructive behaviors, the decision and prerogative to pace treatment are respected. However, this person is not permitted to victimize the entire community with self-destructiveness and, if necessary, is returned to outpatient treatment or referred to a more restrictive and controlled setting, depending on the degree of potential lethality of the symptoms.

Self-destructive behaviors have been necessary coping skills to prevent even worse destruction for many survivors. If patients are to give up these behaviors, they must develop and substitute more creative and constructive strategies to cope with stress. In addition, the metacontext of the social milieu must substitute for the rewards of the harmful behavior, providing an opportunity for the patient to develop more meaningful and constructive attachments to other people and to the community. The comforting of other people must be substituted for the comfort of the knife.

Psychological safety. Psychological safety is a product of the therapeutic alliances formed with individual therapists and key staff members. Relationships that develop with other patients, often the roommates, also help to maintain a sense of psychological safety. A key to safety is the establishment of healthy boundaries. Trauma, by its very nature, is a boundary violation. For many patients, the experience of the treatment milieu is the first time that their own personal boundaries have been respected. Open discussion of boundary formation and function, as well as the continued negotiation and renegotiation about changes in boundaries, must occur.

Open discussion with patients helps to define what level of safety must be reached before they reveal memories to self and others or have any family confrontations. The first goal of treatment is the stabilization of initial unsafe practices. Achieving this goal may become the purpose of the entire hospitalization.

Social safety. Social safety, a by-product of the properly conducted therapeutic milieu, requires constant maintenance. Each patient must feel safe within the groups, with the other patients, and with the entire staff. This necessitates active and ongoing conflict resolution. Even more importantly, it necessitates a thorough understanding of the role of traumatic reenactment in the group setting. However, evolving concepts of "health" bear little relationship to concepts of "normality" and relate only minimally to the potential for true health that exists within human nature.

This criticism is even more true for social forms of treatment. A definition or methodology to formulate a "healthy" system is yet to be conceptualized completely. Therefore, attempts to create a healthy system are preliminary and still evolving. However, patients who are victims of trauma, particularly childhood abuse, come from such astonishingly dysfunctional systems that, in relative terms, attempts to achieve social safety are often significant improvements on previous experiences and provide corrective emotional experiences.

Patients must feel safe with other patients. The use of traditional therapeutic community techniques, including twice-daily community meetings with patient government, promotes this sense of safety. The staff also participates in meetings because of the short length of stay and rapid turnover of population. Responsibility to maintain confidentiality is reviewed repeatedly, and infractions of rules are dealt with promptly via community confrontation and special staffings. Continued infractions are considered grounds for discharge or transfer.

It is mandatory that all members of the therapeutic community, including the physicians, respect the integrity of the group process meetings. Community feeling is fostered, and the true therapeutic action of the community manifests itself within the context of the groups. Therefore, groups are not to be interrupted, and physicians must plan their visits around the functions of the groups, rather than the usual reverse situation in which physicians are permitted to disrupt boundaries and pull patients from group meetings at any time. This practice must be curbed.

Moral safety. Moral safety requires that the milieu in practice reflect the standards verbalized in theory. Staff must serve as models for personal empowerment. Patients must be able to observe staff share power with each other and with the patient community while modeling conflict resolution strategies and adult problem-solving behaviors. They must also be afforded the opportunity to assume increasing power over the course of their hospitalizations.

A morally safe environment must be a place where it is safe to freely and openly discuss issues of life's purpose and meaning, existential dilemmas, ethical quandaries, and spiritual impasses without fear of condemnation or censure. There must be room for hope, love, forgiveness, and atonement. It must also be a safe place to recognize the hypocrisy that is an implicit part of the lives of all patients and staff and of the society within which all are embedded. Thus, the most fundamental obligation of the therapeutic milieu is to provide an environment in which honesty mixed with compassion represents the overall therapeutic stance.

This creation of an atmosphere of relative moral safety leads directly to the sense of "survivor mission" (Herman, 1992). Perhaps a vital part of recovery is that the patient develops a recognition that suffering is part of a general pattern of traumatization, an outcome of human evolution that expresses itself through all of the problems of mankind. The patient comes to recognize that the possibility of healing on a social scale is the only key to prevention of further trauma; it transforms the victim into a socially active citizen and provides a useful model for larger social change.

Reconstruction

The second major stage of the recovery process involves the reconstruction of lost memories, including the physical, affective, and cognitive aspects of traumatic experiences. The onset of this stage is often characterized by the appearance or reappearance of positive symptoms of PTSD, including hyper-arousal, flashbacks, nightmares, increased dissociative experiences, sleep and concentration problems, and psychosomatic symptoms. In most cases of trauma, memory retrieval and abreaction are necessary.

The inpatient setting can provide the intensive level of care demanded through this acute phase. Emotional demands on the outpatient therapist during this period of overt emotional expression can be too much for one person to manage successfully. The inpatient unit provides enough staff to diffuse the emotional intensity, while continuing to allow the patient the opportunity to work through the trauma.

In addition, the inpatient structure provides the patient with some extremely reassuring external limits when enduring an abreactive experience. Regression can be planned, organized, and controlled to offer support and guidance as well as to maintain physical and emotional stability. The built-in cycles of work and relaxation, withdrawal and socialization are important to prevent physical and emotional collapse.

Reconstructive work is only a part of the overall treatment plan. Many levels of trauma may correspond to different ages of traumatic experiencing, different perpetrators, different ego states, and different developmental impasses; thus the reconstructive experience may occur in cycles with intervening periods of high functioning. When at all possible, reconstructive work should therefore be planned among the patient, the outpatient therapist, and the inpatient staff. Experienced survivors can set specific goals and time limits for themselves to help prevent further deterioration.

The goal of reconstructive work is to get beyond the need for the compulsive reexperiencing and reenactment of trauma. Catharsis, while important, is not an answer in and of itself. Ultimately the survivor must integrate the traumatic experience into a new definition of, and attitude toward, life that transcends that experience.

Reconstructive work is emotionally and morally draining to staff and patients. Treatment during this phase must be highly individualized. Survivors who feel shame and guilt as they retrieve memories may need time alone with supportive staff who monitor them for safety and comfort. Others require personal contact with a staff member or members during the reexperiencing but are overwhelmed by a group interaction. Still others feel most comfortable and safe within the confines of a group with whom they have already established meaningful relationships.

Group process. Most groups focus on specific issues or use specific modalities to achieve their ends. All group experiences foster changes away from trauma and toward a new relationship with self and others.

Early in treatment, group participation necessitates sharing of shame-laden memories and experiences. The subsequent validation by peers is profoundly supportive. As treatment continues, the group experience supports a cognitive restructuring of trauma-bound thought processes and enables the patient to evaluate the present situation in a new context, leading to deliberate attempts to change behavior and different affective experiences. As patients share their memories within the groups, they learn to tolerate and modulate affect within a comforting circle of people who understand through their own experience.

The group process allows the ongoing processing of reenactment behavior as it manifests in the group setting. When this behavior is understood, patients can begin to take more risks with each other (e.g., offering forgiveness) and experiment with new behaviors (e.g., atonement).

In the course of the stay, the junior members of the group become senior members, take increasing risks in trusting others, assume more responsibility for the community, and experience themselves as empowered persons who can make a difference in others' lives. These experiences produce a sense of social reconnection that has usually been missing from their experiences.

Anger work. One particular aspect of reconstructive work is "anger work." None of these patients have a comfortable working relationship with their own anger. No differentiation has been made between anger as self-protection and boundary-protector and rage as violence and boundary-trespasser. As a consequence, patients express anger either passively at the self, passive-aggressively toward others, or aggressively toward self or others. Various Gestalt and psychodramatic techniques teach patients ways of expressing physical rage without inflicting harm. When they discover that they can vent rage in a nonharmful way, without doing any damage to themselves or others, without "going crazy," they discover that they can still feel angry, without rage. Then their anger can serve a useful and constructive purpose.

Traumatic reenactment. The most lethal aspect of trauma is its profound tendency to be repeated throughout a lifetime. Traumatic reenactment is unconscious, often heavily disguised, and at the center of most individual and social pathology. It is to be expected, therefore, when twenty-two traumatized people are put together under one roof, they will unwittingly and symbolically re-create their individual traumatic scenarios with the inpatient unit as the stage, utilizing each other and the staff as players in their own personal drama. As the traumatic scenarios of the staff interact with the scripts of the patients, the result can be chaos. The job of the milieu is to wrest order from this chaos and engender constructive change through active management, constant vigilance, and an absolute commitment to true team treatment. The only counterforces to the tremendous push to repeat the past compulsively are knowledge, a sense of humor, compassion, a love of creative change, and a willingness to lean on one another.

Patients who have used hostility as a means to cope with the helplessness of previous trauma will unconsciously provoke rejection in the therapeutic environment. The intimacy of the milieu is so simultaneously threatening and enticing that as they get closer to the affect, they increase their rejectable behaviors. Patients who have been abused often provoke various forms of abuse as a form of traumatic reenactment, including a demand for physical and chemical restraint and demands for hypnotic interventions to "get the material out" of them.

It takes enormous forbearance on the part of the staff not to be coerced into the automatic repetition of rejection of the patient or into providing interventions that, under the guise of therapy, are in fact intrusive reenactments. When the patient's conduct becomes destructive, rejection of some sort is unavoidable. When this occurs, it is at least necessary to make this behavior conscious to enable the patient to pursue the opportunity to alter the outcome.

Patients who have used compliance and appeasement behavior to deflect the abuse of their perpetrator often unconsciously elicit boundary trespass from others. These are the patients who become "special" (Main, 1957), for whom rules are bent, special privileges assigned, special liaisons formed. However, the patient feels compelled to pay for this specialness by further shame and abuse.

At times, the entire community colludes to reenact a common scenario, often with one patient assuming the victim role (interestingly, often someone who has been a perpetrator as well) and other members of the community becoming quite vocally abusive, while the rest—often the healthier members of the community—stay quiet. This latter phenomenon, "the silence of the well," must be understood and confronted on a community level.

Many traumatic reenactment scenarios are routinely handled in the normal course of treatment by virtue of the treatment philosophy and practice. However, often the more profound the trauma that the person has experienced, the more difficult the reenactment scenario is to manage.

Special meetings of key staff members and the patient are used to help manage these difficult situations. The team meets together to discuss the situation. Conferring provides the staff an opportunity to vent feelings of frustration, fear, anger, and guilt in an atmosphere of safety and acceptance. The staff members then begin to construct the outlines of the patient's traumatic scenario and figure out how their countertransference feelings fit into the script. Once they have developed a working hypothesis, they set a time to meet with the patient. Specific actions are recommended to deal with the problem behavior. This redirection interrupts the compulsive cycle and usually produces the desired effect. It is designed to be a "corrective emotional experience."

Reconnection

Reconnection, the third stage, occurs when survivors begin to reconnect, in a real and symbolic way, with the outside world and begin to reconstitute their reality without trauma as the central core of identity. Memories begin to become actual memories and no longer carry the same power to control thought, action, and feelings.

This stage of recovery actually interpenetrates other stages and is promoted through the community milieu and group experiences. In addition, there is an implicit assumption in the philosophy of the unit that survivors are capable of transcending their pain. The unit offers no set formula for such a transformation— that is the mission of the survivor. However, perhaps the most essential function of the therapeutic community is to provide an atmosphere of hopefulness and multiple mastery experiences.

The Importance of Play

The saddest outcome of the loss of childhood is severe impairment in the capacity to enjoy or even participate in play. Patients who have been abused as children are made to feel ashamed or guilty about playfulness and the experience of joy. In many dysfunctional families, play is a punishable offense.

Curbing or erasing the natural and spontaneous joy in living becomes a significant part of the chronic depressive picture and numbing of emotions. For these patients, playfulness, humor, creative expression, and even laughter all require active permission and instruction. Constant work in itself can be a traumatic reenactment, a reenactment not at all unusual among the helping professionals who serve as role models for the patients.

A truly healing environment must have room for lightheartedness, spontaneity, laughter, joking, goofing-off, and general silliness. These qualities exist by virtue of not smothering them, rather than by any active intervention, and they are set by example of staff interactions, rather than by direct teaching or creation.

HOSPITALIZATION AS RITUAL PASSAGE

Van der Hart (1983) noted that rituals offer a behavioral framework in which changes surrounding a transition can occur. This ritualized passage makes movement to the next stage of development possible in a relatively stable way.

The act of coming into a hospital is itself the first stage of a ritual called the separation phase, a stage in which the interactions with the survivor's normative group are strongly reduced or cut off. In the second stage of ritual, called the threshold stage, the person is in a state of limbo; the old condition no longer exists, but the new one has not yet been reached. During this stage, the survivor undergoes whatever trials or experiences are necessary to make the transition. In this stage the rules of normal functioning are usually overturned, and ''all bets are off.'' The opportunity for change is present, but so is danger.

Most of the patient's hospital stay is spent in this threshold state, a state unlike ''normal'' functioning. Patients are expected to talk about the most personal and intimate details of their lives with virtual strangers. They are expected to allow and to support the expression of emotion and must subject themselves to restrictions that they would not tolerate at home.

The survivors participate in a level system in order to earn privileges. This system is based on successes through the symbolic ritual passage. Markers for an increase in privileges include participation and openness in individual and community group functions, expression of affective experience, cognitive restructuring, and behavioral change.

Patients enter and begin treatment by simply observing the progress of other patients. During this initial phase, multiple assessments occur, and the patients and staff get to know each other. The working phase occurs when the patients begin to serve as "auxiliaries" in other patients' psychodramas, actively work in individual and group psychotherapy, plan family sessions, and become actively involved in the overall life of the community.

A significant step occurs when patients decide to serve as protagonists for their own psychodramatic experience. This may be done in the general patient group or just with staff. Often at about the same time, the most difficult family sessions or confrontations are held. Quite noticeably, patients often denote this psychodramatic experience as the stepping over of a symbolic threshold, and, afterward, more rapid change occurs, behavior alters, affect lightens, and patients prepare more actively for discharge.

The final stage of ritual occurs when the participants step out of the threshold stage and commence a new life via the reunion with their social group. Often just prior to discharge, the other members of the group organize some kind of ritual good-bye that may include a special meal, flowers, cards, or other expressions of congratulations. Patients recognize the ritual nature of this passage back to "normal" life.

TREATMENT PITFALLS

Inadequate Leadership

The issue of milieu management has been given insufficient attention. The inpatient system must be viewed as an ecological system, an organic whole that is completely interdependent. An inpatient psychiatric system can be as dysfunctional as the most disturbed family system. Effective functioning of the system can be achieved only with a universal recognition that the whole is greater than the sum of the parts.

Effective functioning can be accomplished only if the unit is highly and visibly managed. Leadership of the unit must be provided by members of the various treatment disciplines, including, but not limited to, physician leadership. All managers must provide for the unit what the unit must provide for patients: protection, nurturance, and training (Ruddick, 1989).

All staff must feel physically and emotionally safe within the environment. This sense of safety can be achieved only if there are clear, although not rigid, boundaries between the unit and the outside world as represented by the medical staff and the hospital administration. Well-defined internal boundaries established through the ongoing process of policy development and implementation must also exist.

It is important that management nurture and support staff and each other. Conflicts must be resolved, hurt feelings attended to, chronic rage addressed. Staff will inevitably serve as role models for the patients; thus it is unrealistic to expect the patients to behave in a more mature manner than the staff.

An active in-service training program must be implemented by management. However, even more vital is an attitude that is conducive to learning and recognizes that learning usually occurs from mistakes. Therefore the unit leadership must have an attitude of respect, consideration, and basic benevolence toward the staff and each other.

In healthy inpatient units, as in healthy families, rules are clear but flexible, lines of authority and responsibility are well defined, conflicts are actively resolved, power is shared, and decisions are made as democratically as possible and are arrived at through a certain amount of compromise and negotiation with all parties.

Decentralized Admissions

The inpatient milieu, as a social system, must create adequate structure to ensure effective functioning while allowing for the flexibility to adjust to individual needs. On many units, a physician may admit anyone if a bed is available and insurance is adequate. In this case, decisions are made based on the needs of the individual—patient or physician—rather than the needs or requirement of the system.

No milieu can be totally flexible. If the milieu cannot define which people to treat and how to treat them, it is put in the untenable position of having responsibility without authority. When this situation is in effect, the milieu must devote more time to defending itself and responding to inappropriate admissions than it does to active treatment. When this occurs, the unit functions most of the time in a crisis mode and, as a result, often develops overly rigid and excessively primitive defenses.

Responsibility without authority can be avoided by centralizing admissions within one department—usually social service—and granting staff the final authority on admissions under the supervision of the medical director of the unit. It is then the responsibility of social service to evaluate the overall needs and responsibilities of the milieu and base admission decisions on what is in the best interest of the patient and the treatment environment.

Unidimensional Assessment

In many psychiatric settings only one assessment is heavily weighted. It may be the psychiatric opinion; at other times it may be the nursing assessment.

Whatever the case, a lack of integration of all points of view—including the patient's—defeats the purpose of a multidimensional milieu. The combined result of several independent evaluations gives clinicians the closest understanding of the truth and reality of the patient. Only then can treatment goals be made relevant to the whole person.

Incomplete Programming

Often, the psychiatric program revolves around the needs of the physicians, staff, hospital administration, or insurance companies rather than around the needs of the patient. Relegating patient needs to a secondary position replicates many dysfunctional families in which the children were used to satisfy the needs of the parents.

The sanctuary program makes attempts to address all the needs of the individual patient. Patients who are victims of trauma usually require the safety and security of an individual psychotherapy relationship. Yet they also need different kinds of group experiences, including psychoeducational groups, which facilitate the cognitive processing of traumatic experience, evocative groups, which provide the opportunity for catharsis and rehearsal of new behaviors, and focus groups, which can flexibly and spontaneously respond to specific issues (women's groups, men's groups, eating disorders groups).

No inpatient program is complete if it does not address the physical needs of the patient. Physicians must be available to prescribe appropriate medications and to interface effectively with other medical specialists, especially since the rate of somatic symptoms is so high in this population.

The family of the survivor cannot be ignored. Family evaluations and the initiation of family therapy should be an essential part of every treatment program. Family therapy may focus on the present family, or it may involve the family of origin, particularly in cases of childhood abuse (Courtois, 1988b).

Nonspecific, Overgeneralized Treatment Goals

A great deal of individual variation exists in what each patient can or will accomplish during a short-term hospitalization. While some patients surprise themselves and the staff and make major intrapsychic and behavioral changes, the common therapeutic mistake is that they try to do too much, too fast. The key word to emphasize is process. Inpatient goals must be specific, focused, and attainable within the short-term structure of the unit. Recovery from trauma is a long, multidimensional process, and inpatient hospitalization must be seen as simply an integral part of that recovery process.

Overemphasis on Catharsis

Abreaction appears to be a necessary, but not totally sufficient, aspect of treatment. A push for reconstructive work can be dangerous if the patient has not yet established an internalized sense of safety. The patient has developed symptoms as a defense against affect. If defenses are prematurely overwhelmed by affect, staff can anticipate an increase in self-destructive symptoms. This inevitable increase does not mean that reconstructive work should be avoided. However, it does mean that the burden must be on the patients to "prove" to the staff that they are ready to assume the responsibility for their feelings without becoming destructive to themselves or others. Several hospitalizations and extensive individual and group psychotherapy may be necessary before patients are ready to move from being "victims" to being "survivors."

Encouraging Dependency

The time spent on the inpatient unit is, for many patients, their first experience with a relatively caring and nurturing environment. It is understandable that there is frequently a great reluctance to leave such an environment and return to the often emotionally sparse homes in which these patients reside. By definition, however, continued residence in the inpatient milieu requires a willingness to sustain the patient role and therefore contradicts the goals of recovery.

Some patients appear to make progress until discharge becomes imminent. Their behavior may then deteriorate, and self-destructive behavior may again be threatened or acted out. These patients obviously are manifesting symptoms related to trauma, yet they may deny memories until just before a scheduled discharge and then begin to have threatening flashbacks. These patients can be considered "discharge-resistant" and often have suffered extreme and prolonged abuse in childhood. Significant countertransference problems (Main, 1957) may arise as the staff splits in disagreement. One half of the staff may empathize with the patient's distress over leaving the hospital and focus on the patient's apparent willingness to work on therapeutic issues in the face of the former resistance. The other half of the staff recognizes the need for the patient to move on, is often angry at the patient's dependency, and frequently uses words like "manipulative" to describe the patient's behavior.

Discharge resistance can be a crucial turning point for the patient, if handled properly. The hospital experience temporarily provides the ideal parenting experience from which the traumatized patient has been banned, often since early childhood. Understandably, the patient is reluctant to give up that kind of support. Unfortunately, because of the very nature of the hospital experience, continuing to receive that nurturing requires that the patient must remain in a sick, dependent, needy, and self-destructive role.

It is vital that staff members recognize their own internal splitting as early in the hospitalization as possible and use it as a way to predict which patients may have difficulties with discharge. In resisting discharge, the patient endeavors to avoid dealing with the extremely painful grieving process that accompanies finally giving up the hope of ever recovering the idealized parents. Ultimately, survivors must come to the recognition that the capacity for safety and security resides within themselves. Each must find a means to cease his or her compulsive, traumatic reenactments while transforming the pain of trauma into some form of personal transcendence.

It is important that the treatment staff be willing to share in the grief without participating in the regression. Refusal to grieve and ultimately give up the patient role must be sympathetically but firmly handled. Much of what has been called patient dependency is in fact iatrogenic.

The mental health field has been guilty of offering ambivalent messages to patients and to the public. Clinicians have not been fully convinced, and therefore have not been fully convincing, that patients can recover. Poor results in therapy have been blamed on "patient resistance" rather than therapeutic inadequacy. It has become dogma that therapy is always a very long and arduous process that may take many years. It is impossible to know how much this attitude has led to a self-fulfilling prophecy. If clinicians maintain the role of the expert, then the patient must always remain in the novice, childlike position, endlessly trying to recapture a childhood forever lost.

The benefits of the patient role must give way to the benefits of health. Therapists must be convinced that patients can get well; patients must be convinced that their therapists want them to get well. The patient has to grieve the loss of an idealized childhood. The therapist must grieve for the loss of the child-patient. Just when the patient becomes well enough to serve as an interesting and enjoyable companion, the therapist must send the patient out into the world, recovered and no longer in need of the therapist. As a result, the therapist suffers through the bad times but is deprived of the opportunity of sharing in the good times.

Burnout

When therapists allow themselves to share in the experience of survivors, their own assumptions about the nature of the world may also be damaged. The contagion of traumatic experience is a real and serious professional liability and has been called "vicarious traumatization" (McCann and Pearlman, 1990c). Probably the most effective coping method against burnout is regular consultation with other clinicians. Cotherapy, particularly with male-female cotherapy teams, also decreases the amount of stress and improves collaboration. The entire treatment team, including attending physicians, must meet several times weekly to review the progress of each patient, revise the treatment plan, and discuss countertransference and secondary traumatic stress issues.

CONCLUSION

Inpatient treatment is a powerful tool in the psychiatric armamentarium that can be used for good or ill. The recognition that trauma is a normative experience among the psychiatric population must influence the future course of inpatient care. Much is to be learned from the specialized care of trauma victims on an inpatient basis. Ultimately, the knowledge gained will have a positive influence on the entire field of inpatient treatment.

This chapter has reviewed the major tenets of an approach to inpatient treatment called the sanctuary model. The implicit assumption of this model is that the most severe effects of trauma relate to the social self. Therefore, only through social forms of treatment can those wounds be healed. Healing cannot occur until intrapsychic and interpersonal safety is achieved. Only then can the painful task of memory reconstruction and affective integration proceed, ultimately leading to a sense of restored intrapsychic and social reconnection.

The further development of the inpatient social milieu within which change can be fostered and sustained serves as a preliminary model for wider social change. The greater part of the twentieth century has been spent living out unimaginable trauma and imagining only more. It is the task of the new millennium to imagine healing that goes beyond repetition.

_____ Part IX

New Trends and Developments

32

Biological and Pharmacological Aspects of the Treatment of PTSD

Matthew J. Friedman

INTRODUCTION

From a biological psychiatric perspective, research on post-traumatic stress disorder (PTSD) has recently entered a new phase. The first phase, ushered in by Blanchard et al., (1982) established, beyond doubt, that PTSD is associated with psychophysiological and neurobiological abnormalities. Such findings led to a rediscovery of Abram Kardiner's prescient and seminal work with World War I veterans (1941); Kardiner and Spiegel (1947) stimulated further research and generated a number of provocative theoretical models (see reviews by Kolb, 1987, 1988; Kosten and Krystal, 1988; Bremner, Southwick, and Charney, 1991; van der Kolk, 1987a; Friedman, 1991). Of particular importance was the suggestion that well-studied experimental chronic stress animal models, such as learned helplessness/inescapable stress (Seligman and Beagley, 1975), kindling (van der Kolk, 1987a; Friedman, 1988), and potentiated startle (Davis, 1990), might be specifically applicable to an understanding of the PTSD syndrome.

Based on these theoretical perspectives, the new phase in PTSD research consists of hypothesis-driven studies in which clinical cohorts participate in elegant experimental paradigms derived from animal research. This approach improves efforts to explicate the specific neurobiological abnormalities associated with PTSD. With the aid of such biochemical and pharmacological strategies, researchers now have a much better understanding of the central adrenergic, hypothalamic-pituitary-adrenocortical (HPA) and endogenous opioid abnormalities associated with PTSD. Three other neurobiological systems, serotonergic, dopaminergic, and GABA-benzodiazepine, known to be disrupted in animals exposed to inescapable stress, kindling, or fear-potentiated startle paradigms

Table 32.1
Physiological Alterations Associated with PTSD

1. Heightened Sympathetic Arousal.
    a. Elevated resting heart rate and blood pressure
    b. Increased reactivity to neutral stimuli
    c. Increased reactivity to traumamimetic stimuli
2. Exaggerated Startle Response
    a. Lowered threshold
    b. Increased amplitude
    c. Loss of startle inhibition
3. Disturbed Sleep and Dreaming
    a. Poor quality of sleep 1) increased sleep latency, 2) decreased sleep time, 3) increased movement, 4) increased awakenings
    b. Possible abnormalities in sleep architecture (decreased slow wave sleep)
    c. Traumatic nightmares are unique
4. Abnormal Evoked Cortical Potentials
    a. Reducer pattern in response to neutral stimuli

(Charney, Southwick, and Krystal, in press), are just beginning to receive attention in clinical PTSD research. Obviously, the better the understanding of how specific neurotransmitter systems are dysregulated in PTSD, the better the chances of identifying specific drugs that might be expected to alleviate the symptoms of PTSD.

In addition to this hypothesis-driven search for effective pharmacotherapeutic agents, there is a growing body of empirical research in which a variety of drugs have been assessed for efficacy in PTSD. Most drugs tested so far have either been antidepressants or anxiolytics, with a few interesting exceptions such as clonidine, propranolol, carbamazepine, and valproate. Besides offering useful information on drug efficacy, these studies have provided data that contribute to theoretical efforts to conceptualize PTSD.

This chapter begins with a brief review of research findings on psychophysiological and neurobiological alterations associated with PTSD. It then reviews those results in the context of pathophysiological models pertinent to drug treatment of PTSD. Next, it reviews the current clinical psychopharmacological literature with regard to findings on drug efficacy, methodological concerns, and important unanswered questions and, finally, makes some recommendations for future research.

BIOLOGICAL ALTERATIONS ASSOCIATED WITH PTSD

Several symptoms diagnostic for PTSD, as delineated in the *Diagnostic and Statistical Manual* (DSM III-R; APA, 1987) and ICD-10 (World Health Organization, 1993) have been operationalized and reproduced in psychophysiological laboratories. As shown in Table 32.1, these include heightened sympathetic arousal, exaggerated startle response, disturbed sleep and dreaming, and abnormal evoked cortical potentials.

Among Vietnam combat veterans with PTSD, pulse rate and blood pressure appear to be consistently elevated in the resting state (as reviewed by Blanchard, 1990). Furthermore, PTSD patients exhibit greater cardiovascular arousal following exposure to either a neutral stimulus, a burst of white noise (Paige et al., 1990), or a meaningful traumamimetic stimulus such as the sounds or images of combat (Blanchard et al., 1982; Kolb, 1987; Malloy, Fairbank, and Keane, 1983; Pitman et al., 1987; McFall et al., 1990).

Vietnam war zone veterans with PTSD exhibited both a lowered threshold and increased amplitude of the acoustic startle eyeblink reflex in comparison to a control group of Vietnam war zone veterans without PTSD (Butler et al., 1990). With a related but more complex experimental protocol testing the eyeblink reflex, children with PTSD showed an age-related loss of startle inhibition in comparison to appropriate controls (Ornitz and Pynoos, 1989).

Disturbed sleep and dreaming have been considered a hallmark of PTSD (Kardiner and Spiegel, 1947; Archibald and Tuddenham, 1965; Horowitz, Wilner, and Alverez, 1979). Without doubt, PTSD patients exhibit difficulty initiating and maintaining sleep, show excessive movement during sleep, and demonstrate increased nocturnal awakenings (Friedman, 1988; Ross et al., 1989; ver Ellen and von Kammen, 1990; Rosen et al., 1991). Furthermore, there is considerable evidence that traumatic nightmares are unique phenomena that differ from classic nightmare/night terror, Stage 4 episodes, as well as from the dream anxiety attacks associated with rapid eye movement (REM) sleep (Friedman, 1981; Ross et al., 1989). It is controversial at this time, however, whether PTSD is associated with characteristic changes in sleep architecture. Inconsistent findings from sleep laboratory research in this regard may be due to a variety of methodological problems, such as small sample sizes, diagnostic imprecision, medication status, and diagnostic comorbidities (Friedman, 1991; ver Ellen and von Kammen, 1990). Preliminary sleep laboratory findings on forty Vietnam veterans with PTSD (Woodward, personal communication, 1992) suggested that PTSD may be associated with a marked reduction in slow-wave sleep.

The final psychophysiologic abnormality reported among PTSD patients is a single report by Paige and associates (1990) on the pattern of cortical evoked potentials elicited by auditory stimuli. In contrast to combat-exposed controls, Vietnam veterans with PTSD showed a reduced, rather than normal or augmented, pattern (Buchsbaum, 1976). The author suggested that these findings might indicate that PTSD patients are reducers in whom inhibitory feedback loops are activated to dampen a tonic state of hyperarousal.

Abnormal neurohumoral and neuroendocrinological abnormalities associated with PTSD are particularly pertinent to the search for effective pharmacotherapy. On one hand, they tie findings with PTSD patients more directly to neurobiological animal research with chronic stress paradigms. On the other hand, these results suggest specific categories of drugs to test in PTSD patients. As shown

Table 32.2
Neurohumoral/Neuroendocrinological Abnormalities Associated with PTSD

1. Adrenergic Hyperactivity
   a. Higher resting levels of urinary catecholamines
   b. Elevated catecholamine levels following traumamimetic stimuli
   c. Down regulation of alpha–2 and beta adrenergic receptors
   d. Yohimbine-induced panic and flashbacks
2. Hypothalamic-Pituitary-Adrenocortical Axis
   Abnormalities
   a. Decreased urinary free cortisol levels
   b. Increased glucocorticoid receptors
   c. Supersensitivity to dexamethasone
   d. Blunted ACTH response to CRH
3. Opioid System Dysregulation
   a. Lower pain threshold at rest
   b. Stress induced analgesia
   c. Lower beta-endorphin levels
   d. Abnormal met-enkephalin release and metabolism

in Table 32.2, current research suggests that PTSD is associated with adrenergic hyperactivity, HPA axis abnormalities, and opioid system dysregulation.

Many independent observations suggest that PTSD is associated with a hyperadrenergic state. Consistent with heightened sympathetic nervous system activity indicated in Table 32.1 is the finding that PTSD patients have higher resting, 24-hour urinary epinephrine and norepinephrine levels than normals and patients with most other psychiatric disorders (Mason et al., 1986; Kosten et al., 1987). Second, war zone Vietnam veterans with PTSD show significantly greater increases in plasma norepinephrine and epinephrine levels following exposure to traumamimetic stimuli reminiscent of combat sounds in contrast to combat veterans without PTSD (Blanchard et al., 1991; McFall et al., 1990).

If, as suggested by both of these observations, PTSD is associated with higher levels of circulating catecholamines, such increased adrenergic activity should subsensitize or down-regulate adrenergic receptors. This, indeed, appears to be the case since the number of both alpha–2 and beta adrenergic receptor sites is reduced in platelets and lymphocytes of combat veterans with PTSD (Perry et al., 1990; Lerer et al., 1990).

Finally, evidence that there is a central nervous system (CNS) component to the PTSD hyperadrenergic state comes from experiments with yohimbine, a centrally acting alpha–2 antagonist that can precipitate panic reactions, in panic-disordered patients (Charney et al., 1987). When Vietnam combat veterans with PTSD were given yohimbine in a double-blind experimental protocol, 60 percent of them exhibited hyperarousal, anxiety, panic, and intrusive recollections of traumatic combat experiences. In 40 percent of these patients, yohimbine elicited frank flashback (dissociative) episodes (Southwick, Krystal, et al., 1992). It should be noted that yohimbine has no such effects on normal controls free of panic disorder and/or PTSD.

Turning to the HPA axis, it appears that PTSD is associated with a specific abnormality that clearly distinguishes it from major depressive disorder and other DSM III-R diagnoses. Mason et al. (1986) reported that urinary free cortisol levels are lower in PTSD patients than in other psychiatric diagnostic groups. The major pathophysiological change appeared to be an excessive number of glucocorticoid receptors (Yehuda, Lowy, et al., 1991). Based on this finding, Yehuda and associates hypothesized that PTSD is associated with HPA glucocorticoid supersensitivity and predicted that PTSD patients would show excessive sensitivity to the glucocorticoid dexamethasone. Indeed, as predicted, Yehuda, Giller et al. (1991) elegantly demonstrated complete HPA suppression in PTSD patients with a 0.5-milligram (and in some cases a 0.25-milligram) dose of dexamethasone, a dose that is unable to suppress the HPA axis in normal controls. (It should be recalled that the HPA abnormality in depression is exactly the opposite. Depressed patients show glucocorticoid receptor subsensitivity as manifested by nonsuppression of the HPA system with 1.0 milligram dexamethasone). From a practical point of view, these results suggest that the dexamethasone suppression test (DST) may play an important diagnostic role in future PTSD research and treatment, if it continues to differentiate PTSD supersensitivity/suppression from depressive subsensitivity/non-suppression (Kudler, Davidson, and Meador, 1987; Halbreich et al., 1988; Olivera and Fero, 1990; Kosten et al., 1990; Yehuda, Lowy, et al., 1991). The final HPA abnormality in PTSD is a blunted ACTH (adrenocorticotropin hormone) response to CRH (corticotropin-releasing hormone) in contrast to normal controls (Smith et al., 1989).

The third dysregulated neurohumoral system listed in Table 32.2 is the endogenous opioid system. Clinical reports of lower pain threshold (Perry et al., 1987) and increased susceptibility to chronic pain (Benedikt and Kolb, 1986; Wolf, Alavi, and Mosnaim, 1988) suggested that PTSD is associated with lower resting levels of endogenous opioids. This is supported by the laboratory finding that PTSD patients have lower resting beta-endorphin levels (Hoffman et al., 1989). Additional evidence for opioid system dysregulation is data suggesting that PTSD patients have a lower rate of release of met-enkephalin into the circulation than normal controls (Wolf et al., 1990).

The most dramatic opioid system abnormality, however, is that stress-induced analgesia (SIA) could be produced in Vietnam veterans with PTSD after exposing them to videotaped Vietnam combat scenes from the movie *Platoon*. Such exposure produced a significant elevation in pain thresholds that could be prevented by pretreatment with the narcotic antagonist naloxone (Pitman et al., 1990). This experiment is valuable for two reasons. First of all, it shows that SIA, a well-known phenomenon in animal research on chronic stress, can be reproduced in

PTSD patients. Second, it provokes speculation that endogenous opioid fluctuations may serve as the biological vehicle for some of the avoidant/numbing symptoms associated with PTSD (van der Kolk et al., 1989).

Five other neurohumoral findings should be noted. Serum testosterone levels are significantly higher in PTSD patients than in other psychiatric disorders (Mason et al., 1990). Second, PTSD patients show marked elevation in most thyroid hormones (total and free thyroxine and total and free triiodothyronine), compared with non-PTSD psychiatric controls (Mason et al., 1990). Third, PTSD patients were distinguishable from depressed patients because they showed a normal response to the thyrotropin-releasing hormone (TRH) stimulation test, in contrast to depressed patients, who exhibited a blunted response (Kosten et al., 1990). Fourth, recent rape victims (who were not diagnosed with respect to PTSD) showed a dramatic increase in urinary conjugated dopamine in contrast to appropriate controls (Ende, Gertner, and Socha, 1990). Finally, among sexually abused boys, the growth hormone response to clonidine, but not to L-dopa, was abnormally sensitive, whereas among physically abused boys, the growth hormone response was abnormally sensitive to L-dopa but not to clonidine (Jensen et al., 1991). Although PTSD was not assessed in this last experiment, the findings suggest that biological strategies may play an important role in delineating different subtypes of PTSD. The last two experiments invite comparisons with animal studies that demonstrate dopaminergic abnormalities following exposure to inescapable stress and suggest that there may be an etiologic rationale for the use of neuroleptic agents in PTSD.

ANIMAL MODELS

As noted previously, three animal models have been proposed for PTSD: inescapable stress, fear-potentiated startle, and kindling. Although an exposition on each of these models is beyond the scope of this chapter, it is instructive to briefly review each model's implications for pharmacotherapy.

The inescapable stress model (Seligman and Beagley, 1975; van der Kolk et al., 1985; Kosten and Krystal, 1988) directs attention to limbic system and locus coeruleus abnormalities. It suggests that the neurotransmitter systems dysregulated in PTSD are likely to be noradrenergic (Anisman and Zacharko, 1986; Weiss et al., 1981), dopaminergic (Kalivas and Duffy, 1989), GABA-benzodiazepine (Weizman et al., 1989; Medina et al., 1983), and opioid (Stuckey et al., 1989).

The fear-potentiated startle model (Davis, 1990) suggests that the activity of the central nucleus of the amygdala and its projections to the brain stem are likely to be disrupted in PTSD. Drugs that affect this system include noradrenergic agents, benzodiazepines, and opiates.

Finally, the kindling/long-term potentiation model postulates sensitization of limbic nuclei involved with emotional arousal, memory, and other behaviors. Kindling is associated with increased benzodiazepine receptor binding along with sensitization of catecholaminergic neurons. Such a model suggests that anticonvulsants with antikindling potency might be effective in PTSD. It also suggests that clinical trials with benzodiazepines might be in order.

To bridge the chasm from theory to practice, basic research with PTSD patients and the animal models that have emerged from such research suggest that drugs affecting adrenergic, benzodiazepine, opioid, and, possibly, dopaminergic systems might be useful in PTSD. It also appears that the pathophysiology of PTSD may be exceedingly complex, with stable abnormalities in a number of interdependent systems. Such a possibility implies that successful pharmacotherapy for this disorder may require simultaneous administration of several drugs, each of which has a specific action on a specific neurobiological system.

There is also a growing interest in drugs that act primarily on serotonergic systems. It is apparent that among the growing family of serotonin receptors, several (5-HT1A, 5-HT2, 5-HT3) appear to mediate anxiety (Gonzalez-Heydrich and Peroutka, 1990). It is less apparent whether serotonergic activity has been altered in PTSD, as it has been in other anxiety disorders (such as obsessive-compulsive disorder). Perhaps the best evidence to date comes from preliminary experiments in which Vietnam veterans with PTSD experienced panic attacks and flashbacks after receiving the serotonergic agonist mCPP (m-chlorophyl-piperazine) (Southwick, Yehuda et al., in press). Such findings, if replicated, would suggest that there might be an etiological basis for prescribing serotonergic agents in the treatment of PTSD.

DRUG TRIALS

Despite numerous published articles on open trials of different drugs in the treatment of PTSD, there have been very few controlled pharmacological trials. These consist of three controlled trials with tricyclic antidepressants (TCAs) (Frank et al., 1988; Davidson et al., 1990; Reist et al., 1989), two with monoamine oxidase inhibitors (MAOIs) (Frank et al., 1988; Shestatzky, Greenberg, and Lerer, 1988), one with the beta-adrenergic antagonist propranolol (Famularo, Kinscherff, and Fenton, 1988), and one with the triazolo-benzodiazepine, alprazolam (Braun et al., 1990). Several reviews catalog case reports and open trials with TCAs, MAOIs, sympatholytic agents (propranolol and clonidine), anxiolytics, carbamazepine, lithium, and neuroleptics (van der Kolk, 1987a; Friedman, 1988, 1991; Silver, Sandberg, and Hales, 1990). The comprehensive review by ver Ellen and van Kammen (1990) presented details on most open and closed drug trials through 1990. Since that time there have been reports on open trials with buspirone, fluoxetine, cyproheptidine, alprazolam, valproate, and TCA/clonidine combination therapy that have not been reviewed elsewhere. In general, the aforementioned reviews of published case reports and open trials indicated significant anti-PTSD efficacy for a variety of drugs. On the other hand, these same reviews concluded that results from controlled trials have been mixed. A common finding in almost all published reports, however, is that successful pharmacotherapy for PTSD generally results in attenuation of DSM III-R intrusive recollections (especially nightmares) and arousal (especially insomnia, startle, and irritability) symptoms. Avoidant/numbing symptoms usually do not respond to medication. An exciting preliminary result in this regard, however, is that fluoxetine may reduce the severity of avoidant/numbing as well as the other PTSD symptoms (discussed later) (Davidson, Roth and Newman, 1991; McDougle et al., 1990).

Tricyclic Antidepressants and MAO Inhibitors

Based on the previous discussion, it would appear that any drug that can dampen physiologic hyperactivity, ameliorate the disturbed sleep/dream cycle, attenuate sympathetic hyperarousal, or reduce anxiety should be helpful in the treatment of PTSD. For these reasons, antidepressants, both TCAs and MAOIs, would appear to be good choices since they are effective anxiolytic and antipanic agents that can dampen sympathetic arousal through a variety of mechanisms (Kahn et al., 1986; Sheehan, Ballenger, and Jacobsen, 1980; Charney, Menkes, and Heninger, 1981).

A quantitative review of treatment outcomes from TCA pharmacotherapy—including open, as well as double-blind, trials—suggests that they effectively reduced specific PTSD symptoms such as hyperarousal, intrusive recollections, traumatic nightmares, and flashbacks (Southwick, Yehuda, et al., 1994). Furthermore, when depressive symptoms are monitored concurrently with PTSD symptoms, TCAs appear to have much greater efficacy against the former, suggesting that clinical success may have more to do with an antidepressant than an anti-PTSD effect (for references, see ver Ellen and von Kammen, 1990; Friedman, 1991).

The three published double-blind trials of TCAs reported mixed results and are somewhat difficult to interpret. Frank et al. (1988) in an eight-week double-blind comparison of imipramine (a TCA), phenelzine (a MAOI), and placebo in thirty-four Vietnam combat veterans with PTSD found significant reduction in intrusion but not avoidant symptoms as measured by the Impact of Events Scale (IES) (Horowitz, Wilner, and Alverez, 1979). Davidson et al. (1990), using the IES in an eight-week double-blind comparison of amitriptyline versus placebo in forty-six Vietnam veterans with PTSD, reported modest reductions in PTSD symptoms. It is noteworthy that the data also show a small reduction in avoidant symptoms for PTSD patients. Davidson and associates also observed that depressed PTSD patients appeared to show greater remission than non-depressed patients. They suggested that improvement was most likely attributable to amitriptyline's antidepressant and anxiolytic potency rather than to a specific anti-PTSD effect. Finally, Reist et al. (1989) reported no difference between the TCA desipramine and placebo in a four-week double-blind comparison.

The two MAOI studies, both with phenelzine, also have contradictory results. In the imipramine, phenelzine, placebo eight-week double-blind trial by Frank et al. (1988), mentioned earlier, phenelzine was superior to imipramine (and both were significantly more effective than placebo) in reducing intrusive symptoms such as nightmares, intrusive recollections, and flashbacks, as measured by the IES. (It should be noted that since the IES does not monitor hyperarousal symptoms, we have no information on this important component of the PTSD syndrome in any of these double-blind trials with TCAs and MAOIs.) Finally, a four-week double-blind crossover comparison between phenelzine and placebo showed no difference between the two treatments with regard to PTSD symptom reduction (Shestatzky, Greenberg, and Lerer, 1988).

Kudler et al. (1989) criticized the two negative studies (Reist et al., 1989; Shestatzky, Greenberg, and Lerer, 1988) on several methodological grounds. Based on their criticism, it is recommended that any drug trial in PTSD be carried out for a minimum of eight to ten weeks; that a better instrument than the IES be used in future drug trials; and that future research designs include adequate controls for disorders frequently comorbid with PTSD such as major depressive disorder (MDD) (Reaves, Hansen, and Whisenand, 1989) and alcoholism/substance abuse (Kofoed, Friedman and Peck, 1993). With regard to MDD, it is possible that recent findings by Yehuda, Giller, et al., 1991 and Yehuda, Lowy, et al., 1991 on different HPA axis abnormalities in PTSD and MDD may enable future researchers to identify and separate patients with PTSD-alone from patients with PTSD + MDD. Such a separation will make it possible to determine whether TCAs and MAOIs have a specific anti-PTSD action or whether their efficacy is due to their antidepressant and anxiolytic properties.

Clonidine and Propranolol

There are theoretical and practical reasons that drugs that antagonize adrenergic activity might prove to be effective agents in PTSD treatment. Research cited previously indicates that sympathetic hyperarousal and adrenergic dysregulation occurs in PTSD patients (Tables 32.1 and 32.2). Second, adrenergic abnormalities are detectable in all three of the animal models (inescapable shock, fear-potentiated startle, limbic kindling) proposed for PTSD. Finally, since MAOIs and TCAs are very potent antipanic agents and since panic disorder is an adrenergic dysregulation syndrome (Charney et al., 1987), the effectiveness of TCAs and MAOIs in PTSD may be attributable to their antiadrenergic antipanic/anxiolytic properties.

Clonidine is an adrenergic alpha–2 agonist, and propranolol is a postsynaptic adrenergic beta-blocking agent. Both drugs reduce sympathetic arousal and anxiety through different mechanisms of action (Tanna, Penningroth, and Woolson, 1977; Charney et al., 1986; Ravaris et al., 1991). There has been surprisingly little interest in either clonidine or propranolol despite the fact that Kolb, Burris, and Griffiths (1984) reported several years ago that in open trials on Vietnam veterans with PTSD, both drugs effectively reduced PTSD symptoms such as nightmares, intrusive recollections, hypervigilance, insomnia, startle reactions, and angry outbursts. Kinzie and Leung (1989) conducted an open trial of clonidine in combination with the TCA imipramine in Cambodian refugee patients suffering from both PTSD and depression. They reported that PTSD symptoms such as insomnia, nightmares, and startle reactions (as well as depressive symptoms) improved in most patients. There are also other reports that the clonidine/imipramine combination was effective in treating Southeast Asian refugees with PTSD (Friedman and Jaranson, in press).

Although propranolol was ineffective in an open trial with Cambodian refugees with PTSD (Kinzie, 1989), it had marked efficacy in American children with acute PTSD who had been physically and/or sexually abused (Famularo, Kinscherff, and Fenton, 1988). In an A-B-A design (off-on-off medication), eight out of eleven children receiving 2.5 milligrams/kilogram/day exhibited significant reductions in PTSD intrusion and arousal symptoms during the active drug phase of this clinical trial. Furthermore, when placebo was substituted for propranolol, all symptoms returned with the same intensity as before.

Benzodiazepines

Use of benzodiazepines in PTSD is controversial, despite their proven efficacy as anxiolytics. In some settings up to 71 percent of PTSD patients have received benzodiazepines (Ciccone et al., 1988) while in other settings clinicians are very reluctant to prescribe these drugs because of the risk of addiction/dependency among patients who already have very high rates of alcoholism and chemical abuse/dependency (Kofoed, Friedman, and Peck, 1993). In the case of alprazolam, these concerns are augmented by the additional risk of rebound anxiety and severe withdrawal symptoms (Higgitt, Lader, and Fonagy, 1985; Noyes et al., 1985). In fact, Risse et al., (1990) reported on eight Vietnam veterans who experienced severe exacerbation of their PTSD symptoms during alprazolam withdrawal. The patients exhibited anxiety, sleep disturbance, rage reactions, hyperalertness, increased nightmares, intrusive thoughts, and homicidal ideation.

Despite these reservations, benzodiazepines in general are excellent anxiolytics, and alprazolam, in particular, has potent anxiolytic/antipanic actions. Furthermore, the kindling model of PTSD offers a theoretical reason to consider these drugs since limbic kindling is associated with increased benzodiazepine receptor binding (McNamara et al., 1985; Morita et al., 1985; Tietz, Gomaz, and Berman, 1985). There are two published reports on alprazolam in PTSD treatment. Feldman (1987) conducted an open trial and found that sixteen out of twenty veterans with PTSD treated with alprazolam showed reduced insomnia, anxiety, irritability, and hyperarousal. Evidence for benzodiazepine-induced emotional disinhibition is indicated, however, by Feldman's report that four of these patients showed an increase in outbursts of anger. Braun et al. (1990) carried out a randomized double-blind five-week crossover trial of alprazolam versus placebo on Israeli patients with PTSD. Although there was a general reduction in anxiety level during alprazolam treatment, the drug had no effect on specific PTSD symptoms.

Antikindling Agents

Carbamazepine and valproate are two antikindling agents with reported efficacy in treatment of PTSD. Kindling is a relatively stable neurobiological alteration that has been hypothesized to develop after exposure to traumatic stress (van der Kolk, 1987a; Friedman, 1988). It is a process by which neuroanatomic structures, especially those in the limbic system, become increasingly sensitized following exposure to electrical stimulation or stimulant (cocainelike) drugs. Once established, kindling can lead to profound CNS disruption as manifested by neurophysiological abnormalities, grand mal seizures, and aberrant behavior. Post and Kopanda (1976) invoked kindling as a model for lithium-refractory bipolar affective disorder. Van der Kolk (1987a) and Friedman (1988) independently suggested that the chronic CNS sympathetic arousal associated with PTSD produced an endogenous state that optimized conditions that promote limbic kindling.

Two positive reports on successful open trials with carbamazepine are consistent with the kindling hypothesis. Lipper et al., (1988) observed marked reductions in intensity and frequency of traumatic nightmares, flashbacks, and intrusive recollections among Vietnam combat veterans treated with carbamazepine. Wolf, Alavi, and Mosnaim (1988), also treating Vietnam veterans in an open trial, observed reductions in impulsivity, irritability, and violent behavior. In order to rule out complex partial seizures, which have been postulated to cause PTSD symptoms (Greenstein, Kitchner, and Olsen, 1986; Stewart and Bartucci, 1986), Wolf, Alavi, and Mosnaim (1988) monitored electroencephalograms (EEGs) in conjunction with their carbamazepine protocol; they found that all patients had normal EEGs and none had evidence for complex partial seizures.

Valproate is an antikindling agent that was tested by Fesler (1991) because patients could not tolerate the side effects of carbamazepine (and lithium). Of sixteen Vietnam veterans with PTSD who participated in this open trial of valproate, ten exhibited significant improvement on both hyperarousal and avoidant/ numbing symptoms. The other report on valproate is a case report on a single patient whose flashbacks were controlled by valproate (Brodsky et al., 1990).

Lithium

There are uncontrolled reports about lithium's efficacy in PTSD (van der Kolk, 1983; Kitchner and Greenstein, 1985). In an open trial, fourteen out of twenty-two PTSD patients treated with lithium exhibited markedly diminished autonomic hyperarousal, greater capacity to cope with stress, and reduced alcohol consumption. Reporting on these findings, van der Kolk (1987a) stated that this response was clinically indistinguishable from the response to carbamazepine.

It is noteworthy in this regard that among its many complex pharmacological actions, lithium is also an effective antikindling agent. Another pharmacological property of lithium, however, is its enhancement of 5-HT release from nerve terminals, especially in the hippocampus (Treiser et al., 1981).

Serotonergic Agents

Open trials have been reported on three different types of drugs that affect the serotonergic system: fluoxetine, a potent antidepressant serotonin reuptake inhibitor; buspirone, an anxiolytic 5-HT1A partial agonist; and cyproheptadine, a 5-HT receptor antagonist. In addition to theoretical reasons, mentioned earlier, for consideration of 5-HT mechanisms in PTSD, there are also clinical reasons for focusing on serotonergic drugs. A number of symptoms and comorbid disorders seen frequently in PTSD patients may result from serotonergic disruption. These include impulsivity, disinhibition, hostility, depression, obsessive-compulsive behavior, and alcohol and substance abuse/dependency (Yager, 1976; Penk et al., 1981; Branchey, Davis, and Lieber, 1984; Yager, Laufer, and Gallops, 1984; Jelinek and Williams, 1984; Carol et al., 1985; Cloninger, 1987; Hyer et al., 1986; Keane et al., 1988; Kofoed, Friedman, and Peck, 1993).

Fluoxetine is a 5-HT reuptake inhibitor that is a potent antidepressant. Drugs of this type have also been found effective in treating obsessive-compulsive disorder and alcoholism. Davidson, Roth, and Newman (1991) reported successful treatment of five male and female adults with PTSD who had been exposed to industrial/motor vehicle accidents or sexual assault. Treatment was continued for 8–32 weeks, and dosage ranged from twenty to eighty milligrams. In contrast to reports on other drugs, fluoxetine treatment reversed both intrusive and avoidant symptoms. Similar findings were reported by McDougle et al. (1990), who observed marked improvement in avoidant and intrusive symptoms in thirteen of twenty Vietnam combat veterans with chronic PTSD. In a third open trial, Shay (1992a) reported that following fluoxetine treatment, thirteen out of eighteen depressed Vietnam veterans with PTSD exhibited reduced explosiveness and elevated mood.

Buspirone is a 5-HT1A partial agonist with proven efficacy as an anxiolytic. Wells et al. (1991) administered buspirone, thirty-five to sixty milligrams daily, to three combat veterans who fought in World War II, Korea, and Vietnam, respectively. In all cases, anxiety, insomnia, flashbacks, and depressed mood improved following treatment. Unlike trials with fluoxetine, however, buspirone produced no improvement in avoidant symptoms.

Harsch (1986) and Brophy (1991) contributed interesting case reports on two and four PTSD patients, respectively, who received cyproheptadine for traumatic nightmares. In five out of six cases, this 5-HT antagonist successfully suppressed traumatic nightmares within a few days on bedtime doses between four and twenty-eight milligrams. There are additional reports that over eighty patients have now been treated successfully with cyproheptadine for traumatic nightmares

(Michael Brophy, personal communication, 1992). Furthermore, methyergide, a serotonergic antagonist similar to cyproheptadine, has also alleviated sleep and nightmare problems in a small sample of Vietnam veterans with PTSD (Andrew Morgan, personal communication, 1992).

Obviously, more research is needed, especially double-blind clinical trials. These preliminary results are certainly promising and suggest that serotonergic drugs may have an important place in the treatment of PTSD.

Neuroleptics

The pendulum has swung dramatically during the past twenty-five years regarding use of neuroleptics in the treatment of post-traumatic syndromes. During the pre–DSM III (1980) era, before PTSD was classified as a recognized psychiatric syndrome and before it was conceivable that there might be treatable biological alterations in PTSD, clinicians had little conceptual or empirical information to guide them. This was especially true at Veterans Administration (VA) hospitals where Vietnam veterans with (unrecognized) PTSD sometimes appeared to have a bizarre and explosive psychiatric disorder marked by agitation, paranoid thoughts, loss of control, potential for violence, and brief psychotic episodes now called PTSD flashbacks. Symptom relief became the primary goal of treatment. Consequently, neuroleptics were frequently prescribed.

The material reviewed in this chapter indicates that certain biological systems are disrupted in PTSD patients, provides conceptual models suggesting that PTSD has a unique pathophysiology, and suggests through empirical findings that certain drugs may be effective in this disorder. In fact, the pendulum has swung so far in the other direction that there have been no systematic evaluations of neuroleptic treatment for PTSD patients, and none appear to be under serious consideration. After two decades of overuse and misuse, it appears that neuroleptics have no place in the routine treatment of PTSD.

This does not mean that neuroleptics have no place at all in PTSD treatment. Animal research has shown that inescapable stress increases dopamine metabolism in specific mesocortical neurons, especially in the prefrontal cortex (Kalivas and Duffy, 1989). Reports on sexually abused boys (Jensen et al., 1991) and women who had been raped recently (Ende, Gertner, and Socha, 1990) suggest that dopaminergic abnormalities can be detected following traumatization. Finally, clinical reports suggest that neuroleptics may have a specific role in the treatment of refractory PTSD in which patients exhibit paranoid behavior, aggressive psychotic symptoms, overwhelming anger, fragmented ego boundaries, self-destructive behavior, and frequent flashback experiences marked by frank auditory and visual hallucinations of traumatic episodes (Walker, 1982; Atri and Gilliam, 1989; Friedman, 1988). In fact, Mueser and Butler (1987) recommended that neuroleptics be prescribed when PTSD patients present with auditory hallucinations.

In short, the best approach to treatment is to anticipate that TCAs, MAOIs, and other first-line drugs will attenuate PTSD target symptoms such as hyper-arousal and intrusive recollections. Such symptom reduction usually results in amelioration of more dramatic manifestations of this syndrome, such as flash-backs, hypervigilance/paranoia, loss of control, and rage. If these symptoms persist, however, it is time to consider neuroleptic treatment.

CONCLUSIONS

Biological theory and research on PTSD is a dynamic and expanding field. It appears that PTSD is a clinical syndrome that lends itself to a variety of fun-damental experimental paradigms, such as inescapable stress, fear potentiated startle, and kindling. In that regard it potentially opens up a wealth of animal research findings for extrapolation to clinical situations.

Biological research with PTSD patients has raised many exciting questions on the pathophysiology of this disorder and on possible pharmacological inter-ventions that may ultimately provide relief of some PTSD symptoms. Although the actual number of publications on neurobiological aspects of PTSD is small, there is an elegant consistency in results from one laboratory to another.

Controlled drug trials, to date, in addition to being few in number, are dis-appointing in outcome. Not only are the results themselves sometimes incon-sistent but effect sizes have often been disappointing in magnitude. It is one thing to demonstrate that drug A is significantly better than drug B from a statistical perspective. It is quite another to say that this statistical difference is important from a clinical perspective.

Future PTSD research will have to address a number of concerns with regard to neurobiological alterations and clinical psychopharmacology. These include lack of standard protocols, lack of standard assessment tools, and failure to control for different comorbid diagnoses (such as depression, alcoholism, sub-stance abuse, and panic disorder) that are frequently found in PTSD patients. Most biological and psychopharmacological research to date has been performed with male veterans exposed to war zone trauma. Future studies must apply the same protocols to women and to individuals exposed to a variety of traumatic situations.

Finally, there is a serious shortage of double-blind drug trials. It is encouraging that the pace of systematic drug evaluation has picked up in recent years and that there are a number of promising results that need further exploration. Given the neurobiological complexity found in animals exposed to inescapable stress and given the evidence from clinical cohorts that is consistent with such animal research findings, it appears likely that a number of interdependent biological systems are disrupted in PTSD. Furthermore, it is also possible that several drugs, each with a different specific action, may need to be prescribed simul-taneously to achieve optimal pharmacotherapeutic results in PTSD (e.g., optimal treatment of congestive heart disease often consists of simultaneous prescribing of complementary drugs such as digitalis, a diuretic, a vasodilator, and a calcium channel blocker). In PTSD, the first suggestion that this may be the case comes from Kinzie and Leung (1989), who found that Cambodian refugees with PTSD had much greater symptom relief from combination treatment with imipramine and clonidine than from either drug alone.

It is apparent from these concluding remarks that researchers have not yet discovered a penicillin or even a lithium for PTSD. Although that remains an experimental and therapeutic goal, other possibilities must be considered. Fortunately, it is abundantly clear that drugs have an important role to play in the current treatment of PTSD, even if they cannot eradicate all of its symptoms. When successful, pharmacotherapy results in attenuation of intrusive recollections and arousal symptoms. Preliminary findings suggest that avoidant/numbing symptoms may also respond to certain drugs. Drug-mediated reduction in intensity of certain target symptoms facilitates psychotherapeutic work on other PTSD symptoms such as impacted grief, guilt, avoidance of emotional expression, problems with intimacy, and moral pain.

In short, medication, at the very least, can be extremely useful as an adjunct to ongoing intrapsychic or behavioral treatment of PTSD. Hopefully, future research will discover single or combination drug treatments that will produce profound improvement in symptom severity and functional capacity for patients who suffer from PTSD.

33

Traumatology: Implications for Training, Education, and Development Programs

David P. Niles

INTRODUCTION

Successful legal defenses of violent crimes using the ''post-traumatic stress disorder defense'' have greatly increased the general public's awareness of this often long delayed stress syndrome. Concurrently, increasing numbers of researchers are focusing on the psychophysiological reactions of human beings to violent, traumatic life experiences.

As traumatology emerges as a recognized field of study, many professionals, paraprofessionals, and victims are seeking programs to enhance their understanding of trauma through training, education, and development programs. These programs, focusing on the predictive-preventive-intervention-recovery trauma continuum, are being developed worldwide to fill these existing needs.

However, there appears to be little evidence that a clear, conceptual framework regarding the content of training, education, and development programs exists. Numerous workshops and seminars present various aspects or parochial views of traumatology. Lack of expert consensus on traumatic reaction symptomatology relating to the more severe post-traumatic stress disorder (PTSD) adds to the confusion. The lack of credentialing, licensing, and ethical standards regarding practitioners in the field of traumatology is of even greater concern. The fundamental basis of this concern is untrained individuals attempting to help victims of violence, inadvertently retraumatizing the victim through inappropriate intervention techniques.

The purpose of this chapter is to provide a conceptual framework for traumatology in order to design meaningful traumatological training, education, development, and credentialing programs. This framework is expanded by including definitions relating to traumatology, levels of traumatic reaction, and traumatologist expertise associated with the various levels of traumatic reactions. Finally, ethical and moral considerations are examined relating to the credentialing and licensing of professional and paraprofessional traumatologists.

TRAUMATOLOGICAL TERMS AND CONCEPTS DEFINED

Traumatological Terms

The rapidly expanding field of traumatology uses terms often associated with other fields of study without reframing definitions meaningful to the unique field of traumatology. For example, the term *traumatology* traditionally refers to a branch of surgery dealing with wounds and disability from injury. However, the usage of traumatology relating to a truly emerging, unique field of study is of very recent origin (Donovan, 1991). Donovan's definition is limited to three worlds of the human condition and does not include the spiritual dimension. Yet, consideration of spirituality is often crucial for those diagnostic-prognostic-interventive strategies used to help victims of trauma (Brende & McDonald, 1989). The following reframed definitions of traumatology and other trauma concepts are offered as a means to help develop needs assessments relating to traumatological training, education, and development programs.

Traumatology: the study of natural (e.g., earthquakes, disasters) and man-made (e.g., sexual, war, crime) trauma affecting the psychological, biological, sociological, and spiritual domains of healthy human personality development with associated predictive-preventive-intervention-recovery strategies evolving from that study of trauma.

Personality: the dynamic developmental structuring within a person of interacting psychological, biological, sociological, and spiritual domains determining one's unique self-image and interaction with the universe, or external world of existence.

Traumatic personality reaction: a normal, not necessarily healthy, human reaction to abnormal, violent life events disrupting and/or disintegrating the healthy, dynamic developmental personality structuring within an individual. This traumatic personality fracturing reaction may occur immediately after exposure to trauma or may be delayed for years.

Traumatologist: a professional or paraprofessional working in the field of traumatology providing expertise commensurate with the levels of traumatic reaction for which the practitioner is trained, educated, and credentialed in helping victims of trauma.

Traumatology Training, Education, and Development Programs: Terms and Concepts

Before programs for traumatologists are developed, terms relating to needs and expectations of professionals and paraprofessionals must be defined. For example, the terms *training* and *education* are often used in conjunction with each other. Yet, these two types of programs and their implications for practitioners and victims are clearly different. Seminars conducted for persons with various levels of training, expertise, and expectations often lead to confusion and disappointment by many attendees. The field of human resource development (HRD) and Nadler's (1984) critical events model (CEM) provide a framework by which to develop the three distinct traumatology training, education, and development programs.

Traumatology training, education, and development programs: organized learning experiences integrating traumatological definitional concepts. These different types of learning experiences are designed to increase individual understanding of traumatology at various levels of expertise.

Traumatology training programs: designed to provide learning experiences for individuals to immediately use in their current capacities as traumatologists in helping victims of trauma. An example is traumatic stress reaction (TSR) interventions associated with critical incident debriefings and disaster relief programs.

Traumatology education programs: designed to provide an individual with expertise in the field of traumatology or prepare the individual to become a professional or paraprofessional working within the field of traumatology. As with any professional field, credentialing, certification, and ethical standards are part of the educational process. For example, higher-level education programs prepare the individual for the field of psychotherapeutic trauma counseling and/ or a clinical focus in the field of traumatology.

Traumatology developmental programs: designed to develop individual and/ or group awareness of concepts related to traumatology. These programs are related not to a specific present or future job by the individual but to self-awareness and expanded knowledge about trauma and traumatic personality reactions. This type of program is often presented to victims, significant others, and/or families of victims to help them understand the effects of violent trauma. These programs are also presented to professional and business organizations to illustrate the impact of trauma on organizational efficiency and productivity. Organizations can then develop meaningful programs to help their members deal with traumatic events.

LEVELS OF TRAUMATIC REACTION

A layered conceptual framework of traumatology leads to a multidimensional trauma reaction modality (Figure 33.1). This multimodal framework provides the foundation for the needs assessment relating to traumatology training, education, and development programs.

Level 1: Traumatic reaction (TR) suggests a healthy, positive reaction by the individual. Healthy personality development requires constant integration and balancing of often conflicting components of existence. Unhealthy, stagnant,

Figure 33.1
Levels of Traumatic Reactions

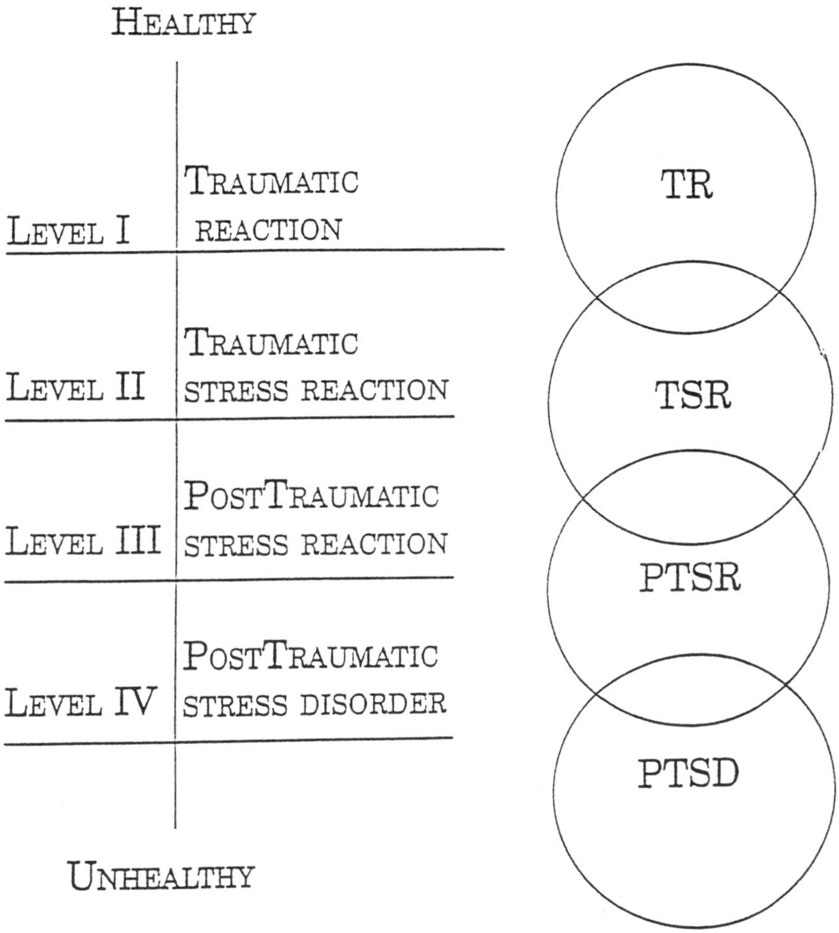

HEALTHY

LEVEL I	TRAUMATIC REACTION	TR
LEVEL II	TRAUMATIC STRESS REACTION	TSR
LEVEL III	POSTTRAUMATIC STRESS REACTION	PTSR
LEVEL IV	POSTTRAUMATIC STRESS DISORDER	PTSD

UNHEALTHY

confused, inhibited existence emerges when the integration of meaningful, divergent perspectives breaks down, or traumatic disintegration occurs. Traumatic reaction suggests the individual possesses and implements healthy coping mechanisms in dealing with traumatic life experiences, allowing for healthy personality development. The fundamental example of healthy, positive traumatic reaction is the ''spanking at birth,'' causing a traumatic reaction resulting in autonomous functioning and a true transformation of the fetus into the essence of human existence.

Level 2: Traumatic stress reaction (TSR) relates to the immediate reaction by victims of overwhelming, often life-threatening traumatic experience(s), which may have delayed stress reactions. Although the victims continue to work through the experience themselves, often professionals and paraprofessionals are called in to assist in the cathartic and elucidating expression of the experience. These TSR professionals and paraprofessionals are providing not psychotherapy, but support and understanding during the immediate post-trauma stage. The provision of a sense of safety to allow victims to ventilate and validate, as well as predict post-trauma possibilities, is the primary objective. A form of brief TSR therapy may be seen in employee assistance programs (EAPs). The EAP often conducts short crisis interventions relating to traumatic, work-related stress reactions, such as referrals to alcohol treatment programs. The brief interactive therapy provided by EAPs is an example of a more active therapeutic role.

Level 3: Post-traumatic stress reaction (PTSR) is manifested by large numbers of individuals who are not aware of the impact traumatic events have had upon their current life situations. Manifesting symptoms are often depression, anxiety, and substance abuse. The less severe PTSR symptoms are manifested as mistrust, guilt, shame, doubts, existential anxieties, angry outbursts, avoidance of feelings, sleep disturbances, and a pervading sense that one's quality of life is somewhat diminished (problematic relationships and so on). Although these are normal reactions to abnormal life events, the coping mechanisms of the victims are less than healthy or mature. Victims are often quite professionally competent and successful using obsessive-compulsive behavior, attempting to maintain control of emerging PTSR/PTSD symptomatology. However, the quality of life diminishes, and the inability to become intimate with others increases as the delayed PTSR symptoms become more severe. The practitioner now becomes actively involved in the psychotherapeutic process, providing mental health expertise to help the victim integrate the traumatic event(s) into her or his unique life experience.

Level 4: Post-traumatic stress disorder (PTSD) is the clinical manifestation of delayed reactions to severe chronic/acute traumatic violence. Severe symptomatology emerges and is associated with clinical manifestations of PTSD (flashbacks, psychogenic amnesia, physiologic reactivity, psychic/emotional numbing, and intrusive/fixated thoughts on the violent experience[s]). Overlapping *Diagnostic and Statistical Manual* (DSM III-R, APA, 1987) Axis I and Axis II symptomatology, leading to differential diagnoses of substance dependency and personality disorders, must be considered in the diagnosis (borderline, multiple, narcissistic, dissociative personality disorders). Possible inpatient intervention to ensure the safety of the victim and others may result. The practitioner plays an expanded role in the decision-making process in helping the victim deal with the overwhelming reaction to severe, violent trauma.

INTEGRATING LEVELS OF TRAUMATIC REACTIONS, TRAUMATOLOGICAL EXPERTISE, AND THE CRITICAL EVENTS MODEL (CEM)

At Level 1, traumatic reaction (TR), the victim is in total control, dealing with the traumatic reaction in a healthy, dynamic, developmental process. At Level 2, traumatic stress reaction (TSR), the victim(s) is in control. However, shock, anger, and denial may be manifested shortly after the traumatic event. Professional and paraprofessional traumatologists offer supportive facilitating expertise and assistance. The EAP practitioner is often the conduit to the next level of reaction. At Level 3, post-traumatic stress reaction (PTSR), the victim is coequal with the traumatologist who is providing professional intervention techniques. At Level 4, post-traumatic stress disorder (PTSD), the traumatologist may, in fact, take control if the victim is harmful to self and others and PTSD symptomatology is too overwhelming for the victim's personality coping mechanisms.

Intervention Training and Education Expertise

When developing traumatology programs, the level of traumatic stress reaction and implications regarding its intervention strategies and skills of the traumatologist must be considered. At each level of traumatic reaction, specific intervention modalities must be employed. Roles, expectations, and skill levels change for both the victim and traumatologist in the various modalities at each level of traumatic reaction and must be clearly defined and understood. The commensurate intervention strategies and skills of the traumatologist run on a continuum from the nonclinical to clinical. The fundamental intervention focus at all levels is to avoid revictimizing the victim, respect the victim's wisdom in dealing with his or her traumatic experience(s), and help reestablish trust in self with an internalized sense of control. Without professional training and education, it is possible for the unskilled professional and paraprofessional to revictimize the victim with inappropriate intervention strategies and techniques.

Designing Traumatology Programs and the Critical Events Model (CEM)

The primary focus in designing traumatology programs is determining the needs and expectations of the learner. Nadler's (1984) CEM provides a framework to help design programs to meet learning needs and goals (see Figure 33.2.).

The major critical events relate to (1) assessing the needs and objectives of the target audience related to the levels of traumatic reactions; (2) identifying the level of expertise needed by the instructor and the expected intervention expertise by the learner resulting from these programs; (3) identifying the specific needs of the traumatologist; (4) determining the objectives of the specified pro-

Figure 33.2
The Critical Events Model

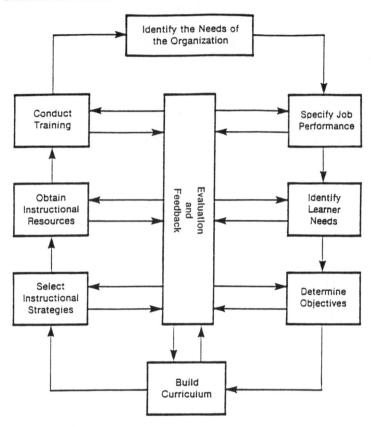

gram related to the needs of the traumatologist; (5) building a curriculum to meets these assessed traumatological needs and expectations; (6) selecting methods of presentation, instruction, and materials; (7) obtaining all needed materials to conduct the traumatology program; and (8) conducting the specified traumatological training, education, or development program. Throughout the entire process constant evaluation and feedback are conducted to keep the needs assessment updated. This relates to constantly analyzing, redesigning, developing, implementing, and controlling the emerging programs throughout the process (Wiggs, 1984).

Training programs. An organization may need professionals and/or paraprofessionals to provide TSR expertise, such as critical incident debriefings and disaster relief training. The expectations are that the learners are, in fact, going to use this training to work with victims of trauma using nonclinical intervention techniques. Based on this needs assessment and evaluation, objectives are developed and a curriculum is built to provide the skills commensurate with the traumatological intervention strategies. Instructional strategies are developed, and instructional resources are gathered. The training is conducted with levels of expertise measured to ensure the learners meet the standards associated with the training program. Constant evaluation and feedback provide for constant improvement of the program. Clinical programs are designed to enable professionals to improve their skills related to the clinical manifestations of traumatic reactions. Constant feedback related to research, emerging clinical techniques, medication, differential diagnostic problems, and so on must be made. Case studies, dynamic group processes, and so on can help develop these skills. The fundamental similarity of nonclinical and clinical training programs is that traumatology training received is commensurate with the level of manifesting trauma symptomatology. The immediate application of this training expertise is in working with victims of trauma.

Education programs. The focus of traumatology education programs is to produce professional traumatologists holding advanced degrees in the field of traumatology counseling and psychology that relate to post-traumatic stress reaction and post-traumatic stress disorder. The CEM once again provides a step-by-step process in developing education programs. Nonclinical and clinical factors must be part of the needs assessment related to education and training provided by the education program. These needs assessments can involve EAPs, master's degree practicums in counseling, or doctoral clinical internships. The types of education programs and training expertise required become part of the needs assessment in conjunction with the other steps in the CEM. For example, the EAP might need further education relating to substance abuse, post-traumatic stress disorder, and brief intervention therapy to gain understanding of trauma in the workplace and subsequent referral policies. Counseling programs may be developed around a core curriculum related to counseling with specific courses focusing on PTSD (substance abuse, family violence, PTSD and diagnostic implications, and so on) and practicum experience working with victims of trauma (rape, incest, molestation, victims of crime, and so on). Advanced degrees associated with clinical internships include differential diagnostic and prognostic problems, diagnostic testing and PTSD, psychopharmacology, neuropsychology, and PTSD research. Internship experience involves inpatient clinical work with patients suffering from chronic and complex post-trauma problems (multiple personality disorder and PTSD). In developing advanced degree programs, the definitional concepts provide a framework. For example, programs must include philosophical/religious components in order to prepare the counselor to deal with these complex issues when they arise during the therapeutic process. Sadly, this aspect of the human condition is ignored by the majority of advanced degree programs or subsumed under bioethics courses. For trauma victims, spirituality is often a primary focus and an extremely important aspect of the diagnostic process.

It is also extremely important to develop programs focusing on paradoxical side effects of intervention techniques further traumatizing the victims (relaxation techniques resulting in traumatic flashbacks with which the student is not prepared to intervene clinically and so on). Advanced degree programs should focus on a balanced curriculum related to the developmental aspects of the biopsychosocio-spiritual domains of the human condition with clear understanding of how traumatic violence inhibits healthy development of the unique personality.

Development programs. These programs are designed to help develop awareness by victims, families, organizations, and society regarding the impact violent trauma has upon human beings. Once again, the CEM provides a framework. The primary focus of development programs is to provide information for increased awareness of traumatic violence and its impact on individuals, families, and organizations. From this emerging awareness, steps can be taken by individuals, families, and organizations in dealing with levels of post-trauma reactions. For example, organizations can gain awareness of how substance abuse and PTSR/PTSD are often a synergistic problem interfering with organizational efficiency. EAPs can provide intervention strategies, if properly trained and educated to deal effectively with these major organizational problems. Individuals and families who develop an awareness of post-trauma problems related to chronic and/or acute events in their lives can make better personal choices in selecting trained and educated therapists in the field traumatology. Furthermore, traumatologists can use the CEM as a framework to design programs to help develop expanded awareness of their unique training and education qualifications in the field of traumatology.

Ethical and Licensing Considerations

Since traumatology is a relatively new field, a code of ethics with clear credentialing and licensing procedures is lacking at this time. This can lead to misdiagnosis, inappropriate intervention techniques, and misuse of medication, exacerbating underlying, undiagnosed PTSD through paradoxical side effects that lead to severe, if not fatal, consequences. Retraumatization of trauma victims by untrained and uneducated professionals leading to suicide by victims is a major concern of professional traumatologists. There is no current limitation as to who may claim to be skilled in the field of traumatology. Advanced degrees do not mean one is skilled in dealing with PTSD and the paradoxical side effects of interventions normally used by one's profession or skilled in intervening immediately concerning the abreactive, flashback episodes associated with PTSD and traumatology interventions.

Establishing a code of ethics for those providing professional or paraprofessional interventions to trauma victims is essential. Ethical behavior by traumatologists must be guided by their level of expertise commensurate with the level of traumatic reactions. Professionals and paraprofessionals must be held accountable for the severe consequences of inappropriate interventions that can lead to victim retraumatization and severe, if not fatal, reactions.

The CEM may be useful in designing developmental programs to expand awareness of the specialized field of traumatology and establishing licensing procedures. Credentialing and licensing programs based upon a respected code of ethical behavior help ensure professional control over those entering into, and claiming expertise in, the field of traumatology. This leads to the societal development of awareness of trauma and of those experts who can help alleviate suffering from post-trauma reactions.

SUMMARY

Since the field of traumatology is a new, rapidly expanding field of study with an emerging research-based foundation, there is increased need to consolidate efforts to develop meaningful needs assessments related to the future direction of the profession, which is only slightly more than a decade old.

Only highly trained, educated, and skilled professionals and paraprofessionals should practice in the field of traumatology. Currently, without a traumatology code of ethics and/or a credentialing, licensing organization, the revictimization of trauma victims by unskilled practitioners is an extremely serious problem. The critical events model and the human resource development (HRD) field provide a resource framework to develop programs to help rectify this severe problem in the field.

34

Ethical Considerations in Trauma Treatment, Research, Publication, and Training

Mary Beth Williams, John F. Sommer, Jr., B. Hudnall Stamm, and C. J. Harris

INTRODUCTION

Ethical standards are guidelines for practice and theory as well as standards of conduct or action, the "oughts" of what a professional is or is not to do in given situations. According to Reiser et al. (1987), ethics, as a discipline, is "concerned with . . . the right-making and wrong-making characteristic of actions" (p. 1). It provides both the philosophy and decision rules (*APA Monitor*, 1991) to establish at least minimally acceptable levels of behaviors (Van Hoose & Kottler, 1985).

Ethical statements of professional organizations are based upon a consensus of beliefs of the members of those organizations as well as cultural mores, traditions, legal decisions, and historical conventions (Reiser et al., 1987). Members of the International Society for Traumatic Stress Studies (ISTSS) form a community of multidisciplinary professionals with common beliefs concerning the impact of stressful events upon the lives of individuals, as well as upon communities and cultures.

The persons, communities, and cultures studied, treated, and investigated by trauma researchers and therapists frequently are overwhelmed and in states of crisis. When the research effort occurs years after the traumatic event, that research may reawaken the earlier crisis state and thereby retraumatize the participant. Trauma survivors are often vulnerable as they seek to find meaning in what has occurred to them and their lives. Ethical principles help to protect this vulnerability.

The end goals of ethical practice in the trauma field are to improve the quality of service given to traumatized populations (Van Hoose & Kottler, 1985), in a culturally nonbiased manner, to educate the public, and to serve public interest. A statement of ethical principles provides a sense of value-driven identity and includes statements of responsibilities to the profession and professional development, to clients, to research participants, and to society (Gellerman, Frankel & Ladenson, 1990). While this chapter focuses on that responsibility within the area of research and the client-patient relationship, ethical issues in training, publication, and presentation are also discussed (Reiser et al., 1987).

ETHICS IN RESEARCH

The Focus of Post-Traumatic Research

The researcher who investigates vulnerable, traumatized populations cannot avoid making decisions that have ethical implications when conceptualizing, conducting, and/or reporting research. This decision making often involves consideration of competing, if not contradictory, values within a reality-based setting (Reiser et al., 1987). Ethically oriented decisions provide the framework to decide which research goals, obligations, and responsibilities are most important. Decisions may involve whether or not to try to create an ideal practice or best-world scenario in research or to be content to use generally agreed upon standards shared by the post-traumatic stress research community.

Consideration of the ethical implications of a research proposal frequently helps resolve dilemmas. Dilemmas might include, for example, bettering the many versus exploiting the few to obtain data; advancing the understanding of traumatic reactions versus impinging on the rights of participants; studying profound traumatic effects superficially to get a general understanding or studying them in depth, even though it might mean retraumatizing the individual participant; and providing informed consent versus deceiving.

Research with victims of trauma has human, social, political, and economic consequences. For example, if research dealing with the need for treatment of sexual abuse traumatizes many of the participants and there is no suitable, available facility for them to obtain treatment or if they cannot afford appropriate treatment, then that research may be too costly to conduct because of the individual (personal) and social consequences. One survivor who participated in a recent doctoral research study (Williams, 1990) wrote the following:

It seemed irresponsible (and still does) to put a questionnaire of this intensity (and subject matter) into the hands of some already very troubled (at least I am) women, with no supervision or safe environment, in some cases, to be protected or supported in the event a crisis might arise, over a question designed to project one back to a time of horror and revulsion.

Ethical problems may be unforeseen, or they may be inadequately anticipated by the researcher. Other ethical problems may be foreseen but unavoidable; for example, administering a questionnaire that asks respondents to reimage their trauma is frequently intrusive and stimulates further memories, as the previous quote noted. However, that reexperiencing ultimately may be positive if it moves the person toward healing or seeking help. In some cases, if the respondent does not provide detailed information, research knowledge gained will not be as extensive. Ethical problems also may be unclear, necessitating the opinions and inputs of others, including human subjects committees.

The type of research undertaken also impacts ethical decision making. Ethical decisions may be involved in attempting to draw a valid sample while protecting subjects' privacy. How private matters in the lives of subjects can be studied—for example, persons who participated in war atrocities or who were abusers themselves—may involve ethical controversies. Data are not immune from subpoena, and, if the researcher identifies criminal activities, then the ethical question is whether or not that researcher reports the violation to authorities.

Social experimentation and random assignment also incorporate ethical dilemmas. Do all clients have the right to adequate treatment without the use of a placebo? Are subjects informed of the real purposes of a study and the actual existence of a control group? Does the control group, who is also "hurting," not have the right to new treatments as well? When does a researcher let subjects know, if at all, that they were withheld treatment, particularly when the treatment resources are scarce or costly?

Values guide research. No research, by virtue of a choice of a specific theoretical paradigm as a framework, is value-free. The value systems of the researchers themselves help decide what measures to use, what samples to utilize, and what theory bases to espouse. Ideally, researchers studying traumatic symptoms value and respect the autonomy and well-being of subjects, desire to avoid unnecessary harm to, and suffering by, those subjects, and value the equitable distribution of research benefits. As the research problem is operationalized, though, intrusive aspects of design and instrumentation must be minimized, while making instruments as value-free as possible.

Areas of Ethical Decision Making for Research

Three major areas of research involve ethical decision making. These include treatment of participants; design of research protocols and analysis of data, particularly when the project has been poorly conceived and data collection and/or analysis has been poorly done; and reporting and dissemination of research results.

Benefits of Participation for Society

The major goal of post-traumatic stress research and work is to benefit others: this statement is value-laden. To the extent that researchers/practitioners acknowledge this goal, rather than a goal of self-aggrandizement without concern for the benefit to others, they also acknowledge the basic rights of those who participate in that research or seek treatment. However, is inflicting harm on individuals ever justified and, if so, to what extent? Who has the right to determine if anything negative has occurred during or after participation to any aspect of the individual—researchers, therapists, participants or clients themselves, family members of the persons, or any others who must pick up the pieces at the conclusion of the research or unethical treatment?

The respondent who wrote the following recognizes this potential harm: ''This is dangerous business. . . . Many of us are on very shaky grounds anyway. This form [the research questionnaire] should have very strict regulations that a therapist should adhere to when handing these out to clients: #1. Supervision. #2. Therapist on call (and available).''

If trauma-victim respondents or clients are vulnerable and in crisis, as is the case with many research participants whose symptoms are being measured or clients who are being offered treatment, then the need to protect them from harm and negative outcomes is even greater. Completing a research protocol or intake form that requires reimaging an event can restimulate a reenactment, reactivating the trauma in all its behavioral, affective, sensate, and knowledge (BASK) aspects (Braun, 1988). The previously quoted respondent addressed this retraumatizing potential by stating: ''Just don't be surprised [*sic*] if this document results in suicide attempts, and return to drug abuse in some individuals—I don't think I'm being melodramatic in suggesting these possibilities and worse! I'm doing a disservice if I don't send this letter.''

It is essential that researchers recognize that all survivors must be empowered to maintain as much control as possible and that researchers balance individual costs against societal benefits to minimize or reduce potential negative impacts. The belief of ''above all, do no harm'' ultimately guides this choice. This balancing may occur through the use of the following techniques when designing a research study:

1. developing pilot studies or pretest/posttest designs using instruments and assessments;
2. screening and subsequent elimination of potentially emotionally fragile participants to minimize retraumatization;
3. incorporating procedures to assess harm from the research in the protocol;
4. identifying benefits to participants for participation, including the possible means to work out unresolved issues, to receive counseling if needed, and to help others who have or will experience similar traumas by contributing to the development of a theoretical framework or computer model by which to view their reactions;
5. allowing respondents to end participation at any time without incurring feelings of guilt or fearing negative consequences for withdrawal (this is a difficult endeavor and may eventuate in psychological discontinuity for the participant, who then attributes a ''badness'' to self for failure to complete or handle the study);
6. having the protocol reviewed by others;
7. establishing a backup for referrals to competent therapists for those seriously impacted; and

8. offering a debriefing at the conclusion of the study, which may include education
   about post-traumatic stress disorder (PTSD) reactions as normative occurrences following traumas.

Research must be perceived by participants as nonmalicious in intent while
guaranteeing the basic legal, cultural, and moral rights of participating individuals.

Informed Consent

Informed consent assures the subjects that they are not being coerced into
participation in research, treatment, or public revelation and gives subjects the
right to self-determination and control over the extent of that participation.

Western culture and legal concerns are the basis for the principle of informed
consent. Further, he suggested the priority that Western society gives to freedom
makes it all but imperative that informed consent exists. This principle therefore
presupposes that participants are competent and rationally able to determine what
is in their own best interests (Elliott & Gunderman, 1990). It also reduces
concomitant legal liabilities.

Incorporation of a consent principle into a research protocol or treatment
contract is particularly relevant if respondents or clients have been previously
traumatized by unpredictable, abnormal events. This trauma has probably shattered their expectations of control and challenged their previously accepted beliefs
of safety, trust, power, esteem, and intimacy (Williams, 1990). Giving them
the choice to participate or stop participating, to continue or terminate treatment,
while weighing individual risks or benefits, helps reestablish their beliefs of
safety, trust (in researchers and therapists), and control (over their own actions).

However, informed consent for research participation is not possible if participants are not aware they are being studied or if they are being manipulated
in a disguised field experiment. Informed consent is also not possible if research
involves participant observation in a private setting or an "add-on" project to
institutional or action research or if informed consent is obtained from third
parties (e.g., the principal of a school without the students' or parents' knowledge). Additional questions to consider include the following. Do parents have
the right to give permission for potentially retraumatizing participation for their
children, particularly if children are twelve years old or younger? Is the age of
consent for participation in research or therapy the age of majority, or are teens
able to decide for themselves if they choose to participate?

Harris (1986) proposed that informed consent protects the individual by (1)
increasing the freedom to choose based on information given about possible risks
and benefits (thereby weighing the extent of personal victimization against possible future victimization); (2) screening out those who feel that participation
may be harmful; (3) helping potential participants who feel they may be harmed
to reveal the sources of the harm, thereby helping research staff or therapists to
generate better safeguards for other potential participants or clients; (4) increasing

the trust in science and therapy by potentially distrustful participants; and (5) suggesting cooperation between staff or therapists and participants or clients.

A valid question is, How much information needs to be provided in an informed consent form? Enough information must be given for the potential client or participant to make an informed decision without compromising the parameters of research or therapy. Informed consent reduces the negative impact of the investigation or process, thereby reducing the degree of harm that individuals may experience. The possibility of deception is also reduced since most of the research parameters and many of the treatment parameters are open for review and, within limits, question. Privacy is maintained; anonymity is assured. Some mild deception by omission of information about the project or in answers to questions about treatment may occur. However, the participant retains the right to ''drop out/terminate'' altogether. Participants and clients alike are debriefed at the end of the study or throughout the treatment process.

Sieber (1982) and Diener and Crandall (1978) suggest the following guidelines. It is possible to use whichever guidelines seem more appropriate to the researcher's, trainer's, or therapist's work. Each and every guideline is not applicable in all cases.

1. Include the overall purpose of the research or treatment.
2. Describe the role of the research participant and why he or she was chosen, thereby reducing confusion and minimizing fear of participation (Hartman & Burgess, 1985). Describe why post-traumatic therapy is appropriate to the client.
3. Explain any procedures, treatment strategies, or techniques to be used, without compromising the results or process.
4. Discuss any risks and discomforts that may be incurred both in the short term and in the long term.
5. List the benefits to the respondent for participation. Make sure that this listing does not increase participant's or client's guilt, should they choose not to participate in research or initiate treatment.
6. Offer to answer questions about the research and/or treatment and give suggestions as to whom to contact to help the individual make a reasonably informed decision to become involved or refuse involvement.
7. Acknowledge the right to withdraw and terminate participation at any time, even after beginning the study or treatment (or in the middle of completion of a traumatizing questionnaire or therapy process), making this as guiltless a choice as possible.
8. Identify the sponsorship of the research.
9. Identify likely gains in knowledge or the purposes of the research (e.g., to improve principles of post-traumatic treatment for survivors of sexual abuse).
10. Discuss how the data will be used and how they will be disseminated or how information gained through therapy concerning techniques, methods, and strategies will be shared with other clients or professionals.
11. Offer to give any additionally needed information to the participants at the conclusion of the research or during the therapy process.

12. Offer to send results and then incorporate a mechanism for doing so into the research protocol. Be sure to follow up on that offer.

13. Keep any promises made to participants prior to their participation or promises made to clients during therapy.

14. Clarify and honor all obligations and responsibilities of both researcher and participants, as well as therapist and clients, for example, a commitment to pay for research participation or the commitment to read clients' journals.

15. Ask participants to help formulate research questions and measures or successful techniques and methods of treatment. After all, they are the experts and are most knowledgeable about potential impact.

16. Write the informed consent letter or form in clear, understandable language, without excessive detail.

17. Identify time, effort, and resource expenditures necessary for participation, as well as the costs, rules, and boundaries of therapy.

18. Avoid placing duress or pressure on subjects to participate in research, by directly or subtly appealing to their sense of altruism. Avoid creating motives to participate or "catastrophizing" effects of failure to obtain treatment as signs of instability or a character flaw. Use of this method in research could result in false positive responses.

19. Provide information about services and therapy available, should retraumatization occur from research participation or should potential clients seek to "shop around."

Ethical principles for informed consent must take into consideration all these concerns. Survivors' abilities to cognitively process the positives and negatives of research participation or treatment vary, as did their original abilities to process what happened during the traumatic events (Lazarus & Folkman, 1984).

As Harris (1986, p. 18) noted, appraisal depends upon the significance of the process for the well-being of the participant, the coping resources of the participant, and the reapplication of new information gained after participation. The eventuality that the participant or client may view the process as traumatic and anxiety-producing must be taken into account.

Privacy Issues

At times, information that is sensitive or personally threatening or has the potential to bring harm is gathered by researchers or therapists. Harris (1986) noted that many trauma survivors distrust nonsurvivors and place great value on privacy of their personal settings and personal histories (Diener & Crandall, 1978).

Anonymity in publication of results must be ensured to participants. Confidentiality measures make sure that identifying data are not accessible to others. Coding of data must avoid inclusion of identifying information that could be traced back to specific subjects. If the data must be included as part of the protocol, then they must be deleted prior to being made accessible to others. If this is not possible, then the researcher must make sure that those others will become liable if confidentiality is bridged.

One ethical question to be resolved is whether or not data can be donated or sold to data banks at the conclusion of a study. Another is whether or not other researchers should have the right and ability to use those data for further studies. A third asks how long researchers must keep raw data and how or where that data should be stored. Decisions as to when it is possible, if ever, to destroy raw data need to be made. Inappropriate, illegal sharing of raw data or private information about traumatic events and traumatized individuals is a form of revictimization.

Confidentiality is also of utmost importance in areas of training and clinical practice. For a detailed discussion of this area of practice, consult Williams (Chapter 11) in this text.

Deception

Deception in research may occur by commission during the investigation (e.g., telling direct lies to the participant) or by omission (misleading respondents by withholding or failing to provide relevant information). The American Psychological Association, in its revised Code of Ethics (APA, 1991), professes that a researcher must never deceive persons about potential negative aspects of research that would lessen willingness to participate, for example, physical risks, discomfort, and resultant unpleasant emotional experiences.

Why does deception in research need to occur? At times, deception is necessary to ensure methodological control and create a setting for research, for example, field research that introduces scenarios that the subject believes are real but, in actuality, are staged. As Harris (1987) noted, the efficacy and appropriateness of disguised participant observation with victims must be questioned. Traumatized individuals seek empowerment and control (Green, Wilson & Lindy, 1985). However, disguised participant observation as deception undermines an internal locus of control of participants. When revealed, it, too, may lead to retraumatization. In other cases, deception may be based on pragmatic reasons of limited time and money.

When and if respondents or participants learn that they have been deceived, they may then warn other subjects, will quite possibly feel used, and may come to distrust "science" and the scientific community. A statement concerning the potential use of deception, as well as the purposes, magnitude, and specificity of the deception used, therefore needs to be included in ethical guidelines for traumatic research. One component of the statement would include guidelines as to when deception as an integral part of a research design would be revealed (i.e., as early as feasible and no later than at the conclusion of the research) (*APA Monitor*, 1991).

Deception must also be avoided in treatment and training. The therapist must never profess to have abilities or expertise that does not exist. Techniques and strategies, such as hypnosis or trance induction, must be explained prior to their use. Training brochures must accurately and honestly describe what will be presented and the methods that will be used.

The Ethics of Quantitative Research

Although medical, psychological, and educational research traditionally has been used in decision-making processes, decisions that affect lives broadly in areas of public policy and even marketing are being influenced by quantitative methods. It seems incumbent upon researchers, therefore, to consider the ethical implications of the quality of their research, which may be the basis of decision making that affects people's public and/or private lives directly. This may be particularly true in an area as sensitive as traumatology.

By representing themselves as professionals and by engaging in research, professionals bring upon themselves certain responsibilities as to the quality of the research process. Presumably a professional who chooses to initiate a research project does so because there is an identifiable question of interest and an appropriate population of which to ask this question. The researcher has responsibility to the following four major areas: the quality and appropriateness of the variables selected; the quality and adequacy of the sampling method employed; the quality and completeness of the research design; and the appropriateness, both in choice and in execution, of the analysis. Taken together, in the context of the question of interest, these four areas determine the manner in which the research will be interpreted and its ultimate usefulness to the scientific community and, by extension, the general population.

This chapter is broad in scope; therefore this section cannot attempt to cover all of the issues that might arise in the arena of quantitative ethics. However, a brief review of the four areas delineated above follows as a means to assist the reader in his or her thinking about ethics and research methodology.

The variables. The most common area of concern when considering the quality of variables (which may or may not be found in the form of an instrument) is the reliability and validity of those variables. In short, can the subject's response be replicated, and do the variables measure what they are supposed to measure? (Campbell & Stanley, 1966; Lord & Novick, 1967).

Less commonly considered is the level of measurement. Are the variables continuous or discrete? More important, is it even realistic to assign numbers to the qualitative variables? A simple example of quantifying qualitative information and the difficulties encountered therein is the coding of "sex." Commonly, researchers code sex as a variable, with $1 = $ male and $2 = $ female. Numerically, a computer then considers "female" as having two times as much sex as "male"; this presents rather interesting problems with interpretation. On the other hand, if femaleness ($0 = $ no, $1 = $ yes) is considered as the variable, being male is representative of the absence of femaleness (0), while femaleness is represented as the presence of that characteristic (1). The second coding scheme is quantitatively more meaningful. Although this example is quite fundamental, it exemplifies the fact that the manner by which a researcher chooses to code qualitative variables can lead to differences in interpretation.

Subjects. At the heart of subject selection is the issue of the generalizability of the interpretation of the results. Specifically, has the researcher selected a sample that permits the answer to the question being asked to be related to the population of interest?

Beyond this most basic consideration, which is assumed to be met, how the sample is gathered from that larger population must be considered. Although random sampling is appealing from the viewpoint of statistical theory, it does not guarantee that the population is represented adequately. Knowing some of the characteristics of the population can assist in determining the application of appropriate sampling techniques, for example, stratified random sampling or sampling from specific, predetermined populations.

Inevitably, the question of how many subjects to include arises. The key to answering this question lies in the desired quality of the estimates of the standard errors of the parameters, which is reflected in the degree of accuracy of the result. Viewed from an interpretability perspective, how much confidence does the researcher have in the final result? The reader will recognize this as the issue of power.

Although larger sample sizes generally produce results in which researchers have more confidence, and certainly they must have a sample of sufficient size to be able to observe the presence of an effect, there is a point at which increasing the size may become detrimental. Specifically, if the sample is sufficiently large, it becomes possible to find trivial differences that are statistically significant. Interpretability, grounded in astute judgment, continues as the central heuristic in that "it is necessary to guard against the human tendency to find patterns whether or not they exist" (Kruskal & Wish, 1978, p. 36).

Design. As with variables, validity is a crucial component to the quality of the research design itself. Did the observed effect actually arise due to the treatment (internal validity), and is this observed effect generalizable beyond the confines of the subjects in the research (external validity)? Together these are the two key facets of the design, which form a base from which the interpretation is derived.

Many other issues can arise in design, but, in some way, almost all of them can be related to validity (Campbell & Stanley, 1966). For instance, one of the most common problems encountered in design is whether or not the instrument or treatment creates a systematic bias in the manner in which the subjects are responding. Another common problem is whether or not all of the subjects experience the same set of events during the research process. Likely, they did not. Problems such as these strongly affect the validity of the research and ultimately its interpretability.

Analysis. The analysis technique can literally drive the interpretation. Results and, subsequently, the interpretation may appear to be completely different depending on how researchers choose to conceptualize the level of measurement present in the variables and the options they choose as they proceed through an analysis technique.

The proliferation of high-powered desktop computers and menu-driven statistical packages has increased the risk of confusion in the analysis process. Often, in a sincere effort to create a friendly environment in which the computer and researcher can work, applying a technique has been made so simple that it is possible to apply it without ever knowing what process has occurred in the analysis. Although difficulties can arise with univariate techniques, this potential for difficulty is amplified with multivariate analysis techniques.

Multivariate techniques can be beneficial in that they attempt to reduce the sheer number of measured variables by creating a smaller number of new theoretical variables. On the positive side, the creation of theoretical variables enhances global interpretations and reduces the probability of obtaining seemingly conflicting univariate results. On the negative side, the processes by which these theoretical variables are created are complex and may, in themselves, cause confusion. Moreover, in most cases of multivariate analysis, a computer will generate results while remaining blind to the intrinsic quality of the very results it is producing.

The interpretability—making meaning—of research is the ultimate goal. Statistical significance in and of itself does not convey meaning (Bieber, 1986). In judging the quality of the result, it is not just the significance that must be considered. Because most tools for analysis will produce a result, without regard to the quality of that result, the researcher must look beyond significance tests to the interpretability of the results in order to assess their quality.

Section Summary

Researchers are focused upon the interpretation of research. Making meaning of quantitative information is one of the goals of research. This meaning making is interpretation. Beyond the usual standards, for example, avoiding overgeneralization, interpretations should be guided and, in some sense, restrained by knowledge of the field, knowledge of the data as well as the design, and, finally, knowledge of the analysis procedure and application with which the researcher is working.

FALSIFICATION AND PUBLICATION

Another major area of research-oriented ethical concern concerns the falsification of research findings and the publication of those results. Gellerman, Frankel, and Ladenson (1990) noted that inaccurate, falsified reporting contaminates scientific knowledge, especially if those data are then used as a rationale for further studies. Researchers are ultimately responsible for making sure that their statements do not deceive. For example, if they hear their findings are being deceptively presented, then they must try to correct the deception. It is of the utmost importance that researchers do not make fraudulent claims to the public in either research or practice arenas.

A Case of Flawed Government Studies Relating to Special Problems of Vietnam Veterans

The following case is an example of a study influenced by political considerations not supported by science. The right to search for truth implies also a duty; one must not conceal any part of what one has recognized to be true (Albert Einstein).

Until the past decade, scientists, research institutions, and government agencies relied solely on a system of self-regulation based on shared ethical principles and generally accepted research practices to ensure integrity in the research process (David, 1992).

The U.S. government, more specifically its Centers for Disease Control—an agency within the Department of Health and Human Services—has been charged with using flawed science in concluding that a valid scientific study of the long-term health effects of Agent Orange, a defoliant used extensively in Southeast Asia during the Vietnam War, cannot be conducted (Conyers et al., 1990).

Agent Orange, so named because of the orange stripe painted on the 55-gallon barrels in which it was stored, was a mixture of two chemicals, 2,4,D and 2.4.5-T, the latter of which contained 2,3,7,8-tetrachlorodibenzo-dioxin. Better known as dioxin, it has been recognized to be one of the most toxic chemicals created by man, and studies have proven that it is carcinogenic in animals. Over 11 million gallons of Agent Orange were sprayed in part of Southeast Asia during the period 1962 to 1971.

In the late 1970s, veterans who served in Vietnam and the survivors of deceased Vietnam veterans began filing claims for disability compensation and dependency and indemnity compensation for diseases and deaths based on the allegation that they were caused by the veterans' exposure to Agent Orange.

In 1979, Congress passed and the president signed into law PL 96–151, which, among other things, required the then administrator of veterans affairs to design a protocol and conduct an epidemiological study of any long-term adverse health effects resulting from exposure to phenoxy herbicides (including Agent Orange) and the class of chemicals known as dioxins. The study was to be conducted in accordance with a protocol approved by the director of the Office of Technology Assessment.

The agency that was then the Veterans Administration (VA), after three years of no progress and a great deal of foot-dragging, relinquished the responsibility for the epidemiological study in January 1983 to the Centers for Disease Control (CDC), after a CDC official testified during a House Veterans Affairs Committee hearing that the agency could design and carry out the study better and faster than VA.

The study seemed to get off the ground finally when CDC developed a protocol that was approved by the Office of Technology Assessment. Officials from CDC visited many Agent Orange–involved individuals and agencies, including the American Legion and other veterans service organizations, to elicit input and concerns regarding the conduct of the study. On the surface things appeared to be going well.

However, it became apparent that the progress was slowly deteriorating, and by mid–1985 it became mired in major administrative and methodological problems that forced the study to a complete standstill. The position of study director changed several times. CDC began working outside the originally approved study protocol. Thus the Office of Technology Assessment, the agency charged by Congress to monitor the study, recommended that it be delayed until a revised protocol, including an acceptable exposure assessment method (Sommer, 1990), was developed and approved.

The study population for this research was severely limited by changing criteria. Among the veterans eliminated from consideration were those who served more than one tour in Vietnam, those who served in one of the selected units for fewer than 180 days, individuals who were above the rank of E–5, those transferred from one unit to another during their tour, and any veteran who served any number of days before or after the proposed study window (January 1967–December 1968). Only army personnel who served in III Corps were included, to the exclusion of veterans of all other branches of services and army veterans who served in any of the three other corps tactical zones in South Vietnam. These constraints eliminated thousands of veterans, many of whom were, no doubt, heavily exposed to Agent Orange. It has been reported that 83 percent of the possible study subjects were disqualified based on these criteria established by CDC (Sommer, 1990).

Following the premature abortion of the Agent Orange ground troop study, CDC introduced the notion that examining the blood of veterans by measuring the amount of dioxin therein would be the validating factor to determine who was exposed to Agent Orange. In the pilot study, CDC measured the current level of dioxin in the blood of a subset of the veterans whom the agency had selected as the exposed cohort for the Agent Orange study that had been mandated by PL 96–151 and compared it with the current level of dioxin in the blood of a group of veterans who had served somewhere other than Vietnam. CDC concluded, in part, that the current level of dioxin in an individual's blood was a suitable measure of exposure fifteen to twenty years ago. They found that the current levels of dioxin in the blood of the selected exposed cohort were no higher than the current levels in the blood of those who did not serve in Vietnam. Therefore, it was not possible scientifically to conduct the mandated Agent Orange exposure study.

In its November 1987 final report entitled "Comparison of Serum Levels of 2,3,7,8-TCDD with Indirect Estimates of Agent Orange Exposure in Vietnam Veterans," CDC concluded that the findings of this study and the conclusions from the White House Agent Orange Working Group Science Panel report on exposure assessment did not identify any method for utilizing military records or self-reported exposure to distinguish between U.S. Army ground combat troops who were and were not exposed to Agent Orange in Vietnam, as would be needed for a cohort study of possible health effects.

This conclusion has been used by CDC and the federal government to cancel the mandated study, end all government attempts to study the health effects of Agent Orange exposure, and discredit any nongovernment studies on this subject.

One of the studies CDC attempted to discredit was the American Legion and Columbia University Vietnam Veterans Study, which found, through the use of an Agent Orange exposure index using military herbicide spray records, that there are diseases related directly to Agent Orange exposure. The findings include increased incidence of benign fatty tumors, skin rash with blisters, change in skin color, and increased sensitivity of the eyes to light. Additionally, the miscarriage rate among spouses of Vietnam veterans who were exposed to Agent Orange was significantly higher than in spouses of those not exposed. Cancers or birth defects were not analyzed (Stellman, Stellman & Sommer, 1988).

The Centers for Disease Control, on March 29, 1990, released a report on the purported findings of its "Selected Cancers Study," which was an add-on to the aborted study mandated by PL 96–151. CDC officials admitted that the study of selected cancers among Vietnam veterans was in no way related to Agent Orange but then led the public to believe that the cancers were not related to Vietnam service.

CDC studied only 166 Vietnam veterans with cancers. An exposure index was not used to determine whether or not there was any actual exposure to Agent Orange and, if so, to what extent the individual was exposed. Instead, CDC used the very technique it has routinely condemned when used by others, self-reporting of exposure.

Of major importance was the extent to which CDC did or did not heed the advice of a National Academy of Sciences, Institute of Medicine Advisory committee. The committee warned CDC to avoid data-dredging subgroup analysis beyond its initial hypotheses. This advice was not taken, and an unexpected, unexplained significant association of service in the navy with non-Hodgkin's lymphoma was reported (Stellman & Stellman, 1992).

When CDC abandoned the Agent Orange exposure study, it should also have abandoned the Selected Cancers Study or clearly and openly stated that the Selected Cancers Study was not an Agent Orange study. Instead, it allowed Congress and the American people to continue to believe that it was studying Agent Orange and cancer.

It is impossible to illustrate in this chapter all of the scientific manipulation that has been perpetrated by the Centers for Disease Control and others in the federal government in attempts to cover up the fact that there is growing evidence Agent Orange is causing health problems in many veterans who were exposed to it during the Vietnam War. However, in a recent report by the House Government Operations Committee entitled "The Agent Orange Cover-Up: A Case of Flawed Science and Political Manipulation," prepared following a lengthy investigation by its Subcommittee on Human Resources and Intergovernmental Relations, the following findings are set forth:

A. The CDC Agent Orange Exposure Study should not have been canceled because it did not document that exposure of veterans to the herbicide could not be assessed, nor did CDC explore alternative methods of determining exposure.

B. The original protocol for the CDC Agent Orange study was changed to the point that it was unlikely for the heaviest exposed soldiers to be identified.

C. The blood serum analysis, which was used as proof by CDC that an Agent Orange exposure study could not be conducted, was based on erroneous assumptions and a flawed analysis.

D. The White House compromised the independence of the CDC and undermined the study by controlling crucial decisions and guiding the course of research at the same time it had secretly taken a legal position to resist demands to compensate victims of Agent Orange exposure and industrial accidents.

There is no doubt that the American scientific establishment is the best in the world, and it should be made aware of the distortions and misrepresentations of the past. What is needed is an ethical scientific program to answer the questions about the health of Vietnam veterans and the effects of herbicides on them. What is further needed is a political program to rectify the wrongs that have already been done in the name of science and medicine (Sommer, 1990).

THE ETHICS OF CLINICAL PRACTICE WITH TRAUMATIZED CLIENTS

Many similar issues and ethical dilemmas face practitioners and researchers alike. The motivating force of clinical practice in the trauma field also is "above all, do not harm." Clients and practitioners develop good-faith relationships based on the intent of clinicians to act primarily for the benefit and in the best interests of the clients. Ethical clinicians inform the client of the extent and limitations of their services, expertise, and treatment style, as well as limits to maintenance of confidentiality (e.g., suicide threat or gesture, child abuse perpetration, and/or intent to harm others).

The framework of post-traumatic therapy rests upon a model of empowerment and collaboration, recognizing the client's expertise in the healing process. The power held by the therapist, by virtue of degree or position, is to be used to empower, not to control, that client. The client makes the ultimate choice whether or not to remember or abreact a trauma, share a memory, or even feel safe in the therapy setting. For a detailed discussion of pacing and timing issues, see Williams (Chapter 11) in this book.

As a means to deal with a tightening of mental health service provision, practitioners are also developing short-term methods to lessen intrusive aspects of traumatic reenactments and the post-traumatic cycle (Muss, 1991). Short-term methods are often not acceptable; then therapy must fit the needs of the severely abused or severely otherwise traumatized client. There is no one "way" to heal, no one road map of healing. The decision ultimately rests with clients as to which technique, strategy, or approach to utilize based on their needs, preferences, and style. Interactions between practitioner and client, however, help influence those decisions. If the client is a child, the level of self-autonomy may be limited, or different issues may come into play. Still, the aim is empowerment (James, Chapter 4 in this book).

The traumatologist therapist is loyal to, and respects, each client without being judgmental. If countertransference issues or vicarious traumatizations become overwhelming, then that therapist has the ethical obligation to deal with, and confront, those issues. Therapists who bring their own unresolved issues to sessions may retraumatize clients. If the issues are not resolvable, then another therapist must be found and the client must be informed in an honest, open manner about reasons for transfer.

Rules of therapy must promote safety and attempt to build beginning levels of trust. The therapist may be viewed by the client as a potential violator of sacred boundaries, as a threatening force, or as a betrayer. Traumatologists therefore generally take a more active stance. They frequently must deal with clients' intense, angry feelings, which need to be expressed within safe limits. Physical violence toward the therapist is never allowed, tolerated, or excused and may result in immediate termination of the therapeutic relationship.

Therapy promotes healing in the client; it does not exist to fulfill the needs of the therapist. To be sure, as a client heals, the therapist may feel that he or she is "needed," has value as a practitioner, and is effective. However, the therapist's needs for affection, connection, and self-worth are not to be met through that therapeutic relationship.

Exploitation of the client is also to be avoided. Dual relationships are unethical. Clients should never be asked or permitted to provide services to the therapist. They are not to clean house, baby-sit, house-sit, do office work, or perform other similar tasks. Therapists need to make individual, ethically based decisions as to the limits of extra-session personal interaction with clients. Does the clinician attend a Christmas open house at a client's home or a "going away" party for a terminating client who, after four years of therapy, is moving across the country? The answers may be yes if that clinician maintains a professional stance at these events or no if the clinician recognizes that attendance would violate relationship boundaries and harm the course of therapy.

If the therapist is participating in a research project or has been asked by other researchers to assist them to obtain a research sample, it is essential for that clinician to put no pressure on a client to participate. Clients may feel obligated, through transference reactions, to "do what the therapist asks," much as the good little child did what the powerful perpetrator wanted. Requests must not resemble prior traumatic experiences and must respect the autonomy of the client.

Similar issues center around the use of client art productions (collages, drawings) or poetry, as well as client histories and stories. The ultimate ethical question guiding the use of client materials, stories, or first-person interviews is, If clients tell their story, will that telling do them harm (malficience) in any way? If they give an interview to a newspaper or on a television talk show, will their identity be hidden and will the facts be presented correctly without the writer's or host's modifying or changing those facts to sensationalize the information? If clients offer to tell their story as part of a presentation at a professional conference or workshop, will that telling retraumatize them in any way? How will the use of the client as part of the presentation impact the future of the therapeutic relationship? Have benefits and risks of telling been discussed in depth, prior to the presentation? Has the presentation been rehearsed, and have the motivations (to please the therapist, to ventilate anger in an unhealthy or inappropriate manner, to educate the audience) of all client-participants been clarified?

How can the therapist help to protect the client during the telling and after the telling (e.g., after the interview appears in print, particularly if the interview has been misquoted or modified without client permission)? What control does the client have over what happens, and how can control be assured? How is the client to be debriefed after the interview, media appearance, or conference presentation is completed? If the client begins to "fall apart," have a flashback or dissociation, or switch personalities (alters), in the case of multiple personality disorder, how will the therapist handle that situation? Has this possibility been addressed prior to participation? Should the client give an interview, presentation, or testimony without the immediate physical presence of the therapist? All of these questions must be answered, assuring that ethical boundaries of practice are maintained.

If the client has an intense emotional reaction during the telling of the story, audience members may feel uncomfortable or angry and may themselves be vicariously traumatized. Any telling must respect and ensure safety for the client. First and foremost, benefits to the client for participation in this process must exist; in addition, those benefits must outweigh the potential benefits to be gained by the audience. Violation of ethics concerning the publication or preservation of these testimonies (e.g., a videotape or audiotape of a presentation in which the client gives a personal account of abuse and, during that accounting, falls apart) may do great harm and undermine that client's healing. The client may need to request that the "story" be excluded from the tape before it is made available for distribution.

Issues in Ethical Forensic Practice

Ethical issues also surround forensic aspects of the work of a traumatologist/ therapist or diagnostician. In what way does the issue of who hires practitioners as witnesses impact testimony? If they are hired by the defense of a perpetrator and if they fear governmental reprisals should evidence of governmental incompetence or even governmentally instituted trauma be revealed, to what extent will these practitioner-witnesses withhold evidence that points to guilt or to traumatization? What if a client reveals information that implicates local officials and those officials, knowing that the information has been disclosed, begin to harass the practitioner? What if a practitioner needs, wants, or could utilize consultation or supervision about a case, yet revealing information about the case might bring harm to both client and therapist? This scenario might be evident particularly if the client has been involved in cult-related activities.

On the other hand, what if a witness/therapist is hired by the defense and the person accused of a crime, in spite of a history of negative experiences and traumas, does not exhibit clear symptoms of post-traumatic stress or dissociation that may have impacted the commission of that crime? To what extent does the practitioner, as employee, "stretch" or manipulate the existent symptoms in such a manner to "prove" the existence of a traumatic reaction? Testimony needs to be backed by "harder" evidence than just the expert's presumptions and beliefs, if at all possible. It is important to utilize instruments that have been validated over time to corroborate conclusions and to document the existence of traumatic stress and dissociative reactions. Furthermore, what if the witness is hired by the prosecution and is requested to demonstrate the long-term impact of traumatic experiences on that individual? Again, conclusions need to be "backed up" with paper-and-pencil evidence (including drawings, journals, test results) indicating the extent of trauma-related impairment. It is very difficult to establish causation between traumatic events and subsequent impairments in cognitive, affective, somatic, interpersonal, and relational areas of functioning. Yet connections can be made, and the client's own assessment of attribution can be assessed by a competent professional. Ethical implications of each of these scenarios must be considered prior to agreeing to serve as an expert witness.

ETHICS OF TRAINING

Ethical issues must also be considered when designing and implementing training programs. The traumatologist as trainer must operate within a competency-based model. In other words, only persons who have theoretical knowledge of trauma and clinical expertise with traumatized persons should be trainers in this field. These individuals have both specific and general theoretical knowledge, as well as knowledge of practical strategies, diagnostic methods, and treatment techniques. The competent trainer must also have up-to-date knowledge of trauma-specific research, theoretical models, and treatment principles and skills. The competent trainer, furthermore, designs the training event to fit the audience and acknowledges the audience's needs, interests, and level(s) of experience when developing the program. But what if the design of the training program is unethical or, once implemented, traumatizes the participants unnecessarily? What if the sponsoring agency sets up a training program dealing with secondary traumatization that includes exposure to gruesome material? It is up to the trainer to recognize the possible negative consequences of this approach, weigh them, and either decline to do the training, revise the format, or give ample warning to participants before the material is presented to them. Applying ethical principles before a training can save trainers emotional and mental anguish when they realize or are confronted with the extent of potential harm that could occur.

The ethical trainer (and clinician) must always take into account cultural issues and values, including communication style, use of language, belief systems, proxemics, and others. The trainer views trainees as collaborative equals who are to be involved in the training process. If those trainees hold cultural beliefs and values that vary from those of the trainer, it is the responsibility of the trainer to become aware of the cultural milieu in which he or she is working.

The trainer must be knowledgeable, responsive, attentive, and credible. Training formats should be mutually planned, taking into account the learning needs of the participants while focusing on specific, jointly created objectives. The trainer's primary task is to create a learning environment that involves the audience, involves continuity and a planned focus, and presents the appropriate information in a multimodel fashion. Materials that may be used include handouts and appropriately designed audiovisuals. Participants need to be given opportunities to process what they have learned via a small group format as the trainer directs and monitors their learning.

VALUE-ORIENTED ISSUES

An additional area to consider in establishing ethical principles involves the relationship among science, values, various cultures, and society. How do societal interests and concerns dictate types of research to be done and the types of questions to be investigated and types of treatment offered? If the societal "push" is for short-term, brief therapy that limits sessions and if clients cannot resolve their serious trauma issues within those limits, what are the ethical role and position of the therapist? How can these clients be helped when insurance coverage is limited or does not exist? Cultural concerns also impact the type of treatment utilized or the research projects in which persons participate. Rules of confidentiality vary among cultures (Pedersen, 1988), and culturally relevant values also impact research, training protocols, and practice.

In the research arena, cultural and societal concerns frequently impact which hypotheses are tested, which populations or samples are selected, which instruments are or can be used, and which statistical analyses are undertaken. Consideration of cultural issues is especially important when an organization has an international focus or membership. This is true for the International Society for Traumatic Stress Studies, in particular.

CONCLUSIONS

Ethical principles for traumatic research and the practice of traumatic therapy need to be developed and standardized. Diener and Crandall (1978, p. 215) have explained the rationale for this need for general research principles:

1. Ethical decisions have value implications.
2. Concern for the well-being of participants and future uses of knowledge gained must be taken into account in research.
3. Participants must be protected from harm.

Establishing ethical standards helps to protect the rights of victims without penalty or insinuation of blame or gender bias. These guidelines provide a way for traumatologists who are unsure of ethical implications to find direction and assistance. Researchers need to be encouraged to develop studies that look at specific treatment techniques as well as diagnostic and assessment instruments that are consistent with the theoretical framework of PTSD, within a social context.

Many needs in the field of traumatic research and trauma-oriented therapy and training exist (Baum, Solomon & Ursano, 1987). However, without the establishment of ethical guidelines, those needs cannot satisfactorily be addressed and met. Therapy and/or research with trauma survivors is difficult yet challenging. The development of internationally recognized ethical principles for post-traumatic research, practice, publication, forensic representation, and training will help minimize potential revictimization or retraumatization of respondents. Any work with traumatized persons has as its goal the betterment of life for those individuals. If a traumatologist keeps that goal in mind and adheres to a consensually established statement of ethical principles, ethical decision making will be easier.

35

Countertransference and Trauma: Self-Healing and Training Issues

Yael Danieli

Reflecting upon a previous chapter on treatment (Danieli, 1988b), I realized that what I proposed there was what has been described as good therapy throughout the history of the discipline, and in that chapter I wondered whether the "need to reiterate these factors as the goals and principles of working with survivors of the Nazi Holocaust and their offspring [as well as with other populations of victim/survivors] perhaps attests to the crippling effects of countertransference, which often renders the therapist unable to listen, a necessary condition for fulfilling his/her therapeutic contract" (p. 291). Indeed, the phrase *conspiracy of silence* has been used to describe the typical interaction of Holocaust survivors and their children with psychotherapists when Holocaust experiences were mentioned or recounted (e.g., see Barocas & Barocas, 1979; Krystal & Niederland, 1968; Tanay, 1968), as it had been used to describe the pervasive interaction of survivors with society in general. Elsewhere, I reviewed in detail the literature on the conspiracy of silence (Danieli, 1982b), and described its harmful, long-term impact on the survivors (Danieli, 1981c, 1989), their families (Danieli, 1981a, 1981b, 1985), and their psychotherapies (Danieli, 1984, 1988a, 1993).

As one therapist put it: "I think the biggest problem is not having any guide-lines to deal with the Holocaust. The fear is of going into uncharted territory where your only guide is your patient, and yet you are in the role of expert." Another stated, "I dread being drawn into a vortex of such blackness that I may never find clarity and may never recover my own stability so that I may be helpful to this patient." Although these statements were reported by two of the participants in my original research, titled "Therapists' Difficulties in Treating Survivors of the Nazi Holocaust and Their Children" (Danieli, 1982b), they seem to articulate obstacles hindering therapists treating victim/survivors of many other traumatic events, such as intrafamilial violence against women and children, sexual abuse, crime, war, political repression and torture, refugee and hostage experiences, technological, environmental, and natural disasters, and high-risk occupational experiences.

These statements reflect, in part, the only recently acknowledged fact that traditional training generally has not prepared professionals to deal with massive real (adult) trauma and its long-term effects. The International Society for Traumatic Stress Studies has begun to ameliorate this lack of training, among other activities, through its Initial Report from the Presidential Task Force on Curriculum, Education, and Training (see Danieli & Krystal, 1989). This report contains model curricula formulated by leading international specialists in the field and is composed of subcommittees representing different technical specialties or interests, including psychiatry, psychology, social work, nursing, creative arts therapy, clergy, and media; organizations, institutions, and public health; paraprofessionals and other professionals; and undergraduate education. The need to cope with, and work through, countertransference difficulties was recognized as imperative and necessary to optimize training in this field by all expert groups.

Whereas society has a moral obligation to share its members' pain, psychotherapists and researchers have, in addition, a professional contractual obligation. When they fail to listen, explore, understand, and help, they too inflict the "trauma after the trauma" (Rappaport, 1968), or "the second injury to victims" (Symonds, 1980) by maintaining and perpetuating the conspiracy of silence.

BACKGROUND

The major countertransference themes that have appeared in the literature related to the Holocaust are based almost entirely on anecdotal comments, confessional self-reports, and impressionistic statements and observations. The most striking phenomenon encountered in reviewing this professional literature is that most of the writers seem to feel compelled to share their emotional and/or moral reactions to their subject matter.

This chapter first briefly reports some of the major findings of a study that systematically examined the nature of the emotional responses and other problems experienced by psychotherapists in working with Nazi Holocaust survivors and their offspring. It then discusses ways of using these findings preventively and therapeutically.

Participants in this study were sixty-one psychotherapists, forty women and twenty-one men, with four to forty years of experience. Within this group, twenty-eight were social workers, twenty-three were psychologists, and ten were psychiatrists. Fifty had completed postgraduate training, and all but one had undergone psychoanalysis or psychoanalytic psychotherapy. A survivor in this study is defined as one who was in Nazi-occupied Europe and subjected to Nazi persecution sometime after 1938 until 1945. Of the fifty-six Jewish (eight Israeli) participants, ten were themselves Holocaust survivors, and eight were postwar children of survivors.

They were recruited for interviewing by announcements at professional conferences, through contact with colleagues known to be working with survivors and their family members, and through contact with the Group Project for Holocaust Survivors and their Children (see Danieli, 1982a, 1988c). They responded with great eagerness and astonishing candor. The open-ended interviews ranged from one to three meetings, of an hour to six hours each, and were sometimes completed via telephone conversations or mail. The atmosphere of the interviews tended to be intense and serious. Many of the participants were deeply involved in the process and expressed themselves with much emotion. All participants stated that their reported reactions in working with survivors or children of survivors of the Nazi Holocaust were unique to this population.

COUNTERTRANSFERENCE THEMES

Bystander's Guilt

The most common of the affective reactions therapists reported in their work with survivors and their children is bystander's guilt: "I feel an immense sense of guilt because I led a happy and protected childhood while these people have suffered so much."

Merely asking a question, they feared, would hurt the patient "who has suffered so much already," and they stopped asking and exploring when they saw tears in the survivors' eyes, despite the fact that tears are a perfectly appropriate reaction. Afraid that survivors were so fragile that they would fall apart, some therapists overlooked the fact that these people had not only survived but also rebuilt families and lives—often literally based on ashes—despite their immense losses and traumatic experiences. Similarly, therapists tended to attribute fragility to survivors' offspring.

Guilt often resulted in the therapist's inability to set reasonable limits, to the point of patronizing survivors and their children and not respecting their strengths. The survivors or their offspring were allowed to do anything, for example, call the therapist at any time of day or night. This resulted in the therapist's not wanting to listen and adopting a masochistic position in relation to the survivor and in additional guilt over the therapist's resulting rage.

Therapists also felt guilty in reaction to their own rage at these individuals. Researchers reported feeling guilty for using survivors as subjects and then trying to put such human suffering into a "cold," objective, scientific design. Some therapists feared that demonstrating the long-term negative effects of the Holocaust was tantamount to giving Hitler a posthumous victory. In contrast, others feared that demonstrating these individuals' strengths was equivalent to saying that because people could adapt, "it couldn't have been such a terrible experience, and it is almost synonymous with forgiving the Nazis."

Rage

Rage is the most intense and one of the most difficult affective reactions experienced by therapists in working with survivors and their children. Therapists often reported that they became enraged listening to Holocaust stories and were overwhelmed by the intensity of their reactions.

Survivors remind therapists of their own anger and destructiveness. Some therapists accused victims of bringing the Holocaust upon themselves, which appears to be a rationalization of their displacement.

Therapists resorted to counterrage in three major instances: (1) in response to transferentially being viewed by survivors or their offspring as Nazis; (2) when survivors did not live up to expectations to rise above hate and prejudice (e.g., "I hate all Germans"); or (3) when they became terrified of the extent of rage they anticipated in survivors.

Therapists' inability to cope effectively with the rage they experienced toward survivors and their children led some to reject them or to shorten their therapy. They often justified their actions with reference to "patient's resistance," which again appears to be a rationalization. Some therapists sought further psychotherapy primarily to work through issues surrounding rage and related imagery.

Dread and Horror

Another reaction that occurs frequently among psychotherapists is dread and horror. Therapists felt traumatized, as if attacked by their own emotions and fantasies, and dreaded "being drawn into a vortex of such blackness." They also reported horror in reaction to cathartic experiences that survivors tend to relive with much vividness and intensity. A few found themselves sharing the nightmares of the survivors they were treating. Those therapists who attempted to control their own reactions often experienced the sessions and the treatment as draining.

Shame and Related Emotions

One aspect of shame is derived from therapists' fantasies of what the survivor must have done in order to survive. Disgust and loathing in response to instances of humiliation and degradation frequently impelled the therapist to silence survivors and their offspring. Therapists who accepted the myth of the Jews during the Holocaust as going like sheep to the slaughter tended to feel contemptuous toward, and condemn, survivors for having been passive, weak, vulnerable, and abused.

In addition to Freud's depiction of the three blows to humanity's naive self-love or narcissism, perhaps the deepest aspect of shame is what I have called the fourth narcissistic blow. Nazi Germany gave humanity the fourth (ethical) blow by shattering our innocent belief that the world we live in is a just place in which human life is of value, to be protected and respected. Not only therapists, but all of us, in various degrees of awareness, share this sense of shame. Indeed, this fourth narcissistic blow may have caused many in society to avoid confronting the Holocaust by refusing to listen to survivors and their offspring, who bear witness to the experience and its consequences.

Grief and Mourning

Therapists also reported experiencing deep sorrow and grief during and after sessions with survivors and their offspring, especially when losses and suffering were recounted. Some found themselves tearful or actually cried at those times. Others spoke of "sinking into despair" and fearing to be "engulfed by anguish."

The anguish is related to the impossibility of adequately mourning so massive a catastrophe as the Holocaust. Therapists who work with members of survivors' families encounter individuals whom the Holocaust deprived of the normal cycle of the generations and ages and of natural, individual death (Danieli, 1981c) and normal mourning.

Therapists who were unable to contain these feelings in themselves and in their patients became intolerant or immobilized. Some therapists attempted to avoid listening to pain and suffering by asking such questions as, "How did you survive?" instead of "What happened to you?" or "What did you go through during the war?"

Victim/Liberator

Therapists may view survivors as either victims or heroes. When they view survivors as victims, they are seen as fragile, helpless martyrs. This image generates bystander's guilt, rage, and shame in them, reactions sometimes generalized to the survivors' offspring. Some therapists, however, viewed the offspring as victimized by their parents and attempted to rescue the children from their survivor parents, compete with their survivor parents, and/or compensate for parental deprivation.

Viewing the Survivor as Hero

When therapists view survivors as heroes, awed by the courage, hope, and determination in their Holocaust accounts, they glorify them as superhumanly strong and capable figures. The therapists thus render themselves insensitive to the pain and suffering that brought the survivor to therapy.

The idealization of both victims and heroes can lead therapists to view their own lives as trivial and may result in envious and competitive feelings toward survivors, feeling excluded or like an outsider. Most therapists preferred working with heroes to working with victims.

"Me Too"

The "me too" reaction, also stated as "We are all survivors," may stem from a sincere attempt on the therapist's part to empathize with his or her patient. It poses a danger of blurring distinctions among various kinds of survival experiences, under various conditions and degrees of trauma.

Many therapists who are survivors and/or children of survivors used similarity of experience in the service of empathy and understanding, which they reported to be helpful to their patients. However, it was sometimes used in the service of defense or was otherwise problematic, as in using foreclosing remarks like, "I know what you mean; I am a survivor [or, a child of survivors], too."

Sense of Bond

Therapists who are survivors and/or children of survivors were uniformly convinced that they were better able to understand and help survivors and their offspring because of their shared experiences, culture, language(s), and customs. Some acknowledged that they wanted to help themselves. This sense of kinship and "connectedness" was often related to these therapists' need to reestablish their own sense of family and community. Some expressed conflict over maintaining professional roles and authority in working with "their people."

Privileged Voyeurism

Privileged voyeurism, in contrast to the "countertransference reactions" described previously, tends to lead therapists to dwell excessively on the Holocaust/ trauma. These therapists tended to ask numerous questions, many of which may not have been relevant to the particular survivor's experiences. Sometimes they totally ignored their patient's pre- and post-trauma and present life situation, thereby perpetuating the traumatic rupture, discontinuity, and loss.

Defense

The various modes of defense against listening to victimization experiences and against therapists' inability to contain their intense emotional reactions comprised the most frequent "countertransference phenomena" repeatedly reported by psychotherapists and researchers in working with survivors and their children. Unable to contain their intense emotional reactions, some therapists numbed themselves. Others accused their patients of exaggerating. Therapists reported "forgetting," "turning off," "tuning out," and "getting bored with the same story repeated over and over again." Many used distancing. They listened to the stories as though they were "science fiction stories" or "as if it happened 5,000 years ago." Some used the word *death* to describe the fate of the survivor's relatives, friends, and communities, which appears to be a defense against acknowledging murder as possibly the most crucial reality of the Holocaust. Others became very abstract, "professional," and intellectual, frequently lecturing the patient and clinging to available methods, theories, theoretical jargon, and prescribed roles.

IMPLICATIONS FOR TRAINING AND SELF-CARE

As early as 1980 (Danieli, 1980), when I published the preliminary thematic overview of this study, I stated:

While this cluster [of countertransference reactions] was reported by professionals working with Jewish Holocaust survivors and their offspring, I believe that other victim/survivors populations may be responded to similarly and may suffer . . . similar [consequences]. . . . It will be of interest and importance to investigate what components of this cluster may be shared by different victim/survivors populations, and what other components may [constitute] clusters specific to other populations. Defining the[se] reaction-clusters . . . will lead therapists and investigators to be better able to [recognize them so that they can monitor,] contain and use them preventively and therapeutically (p. 366).

In 1981 (Danieli, 1981c) I noted that these reactions "seem very similar to alexithymia, anhedonia, and their concomitants and components which, according to Krystal, characterize survivors" (p. 201). In 1989, in the context of training (Danieli, 1989b) I referred to these phenomena as the "vicarious victimization of the care-giver."

Indeed, the ensuing literature reflected a growing realization among professionals working with other victims/survivors of the need to describe, understand, and organize different elements and aspects of the conspiracy of silence. Haley (1974) and Parson (1988b) reported, and Lindy (1988) has adapted and revised, the countertransference categories previously mentioned to compare and contrast them with responses from therapists of Vietnam veterans with post-traumatic stress disorder (PTSD). Comas-Diaz and Padilla (1990) and Fischman (1991) discussed countertransference themes related to torture; Mollica (1988) and Kinzie (1989), to refugees; Chu (1988) and Kluft (1989a), to multiple personality disorders (MPD); McCann and Pearlman (1990c), who similarly named these phenomena "vicarious traumatization," to adult survivors; and Herman (1992), to adult survivors of childhood sexual abuse.

Countertransference reactions are integral to our work, ubiquitous and expected. Our work calls on us to confront, with our patients and within ourselves, extraordinary human experiences. This confrontation is profoundly humbling in that at all times these experiences try our view of the world we live in and challenge the limits of our humanity.

Indeed, countertransference reactions are the building blocks of the societal, as well as professional, conspiracy of silence. They inhibit professionals from studying, correctly diagnosing, and treating the effects of trauma. They also perpetuate the traditional lack of training necessary for professionals to cope with massive, real, adult trauma and its long-term effects.

Although information cannot undo unconscious reactions, knowledge about traumas in their historic context does provide the therapist with a factual and, for example, gender, ethnic, racial, religious, cultural, and political perspectives that help him or her know what to look for, what may be missing in survivors' accounts of their experience, and what types of questions to ask.

Familiarity with the growing body of literature on the long-term psychological sequelae of trauma on its survivors and their offspring also helps prepare mental health professionals. Nonetheless, they should guard against the simple grouping of individuals as "survivors," who are expected to exhibit the same "survivor syndrome" (Krystal & Niederland, 1968), or PTSD, and the expectation that children of survivors will manifest a single, transmitted "child-of-survivor syndrome" (e.g., Phillips, 1978).

The reader may note that many of the aforementioned examples are reactions to patients' Holocaust stories rather than to their behavior. The unusual uniformity of psychotherapists' reactions suggests that they are in response to the Holocaust—the one fact that all the otherwise different patients have in common. Because the Holocaust seems to be the source of these reactions, I suggest that it is appropriate to name them countertransference reactions to the Holocaust, rather than to the patients themselves. I also believe that therapists' difficulties in treating other victim/survivors populations may similarly have their roots in the nature of their victimization (event countertransference).

PROCESSING EVENT COUNTERTRANSFERENCE

Regarding event countertransferences as dimensions of one's inner, or intrapsychic, conspiracy of silence about the trauma allows us the possibility to explore and confront these reactions to the trauma events prior to, and independent of, the therapeutic encounter with the victim/survivor patient, in a variety of training and supervisory settings and by ourselves. I now present an exercise process that has proven helpful in numerous seminars, workshops, training institutes, and supervisory and consultative relationships around the world, to work through event countertransference. While it originally evolved, and is still done optimally, as a part of a group experience, it can also be done alone and assist the clinician working privately. As one veteran traumatologist who does it regularly stated, "It is like taking an inner shower when I am stuck with this patient and things are a mess." The following is the version adapted for individual use.

The first phase of the process will be private, totally between you and yourself. Take a large piece of paper, a pen or a pencil. Create space for yourself. [If in group setting.] Please, don't talk with each other during this first phase.

Choose the victimization/trauma experience most meaningful to you. Please, let yourself focus in to it.

1. Draw everything and anything, any image that comes to mind when you think _____ [the experience you chose]. Take your time. We have a lot of time. Take all the time you need.

2. When you have completed this task, turn the page, and please, write down every word that comes to mind when you focus on this experience.

3. When you finish this, draw a line underneath the words. Please, look through/reflect on the words you wrote. Is there is any affect or feeling word that you may not have included? Please, add them now. Roam freely around your mind, and add any other word that comes to mind now.

4. When was the very first time you ever heard of _____, the very first time? How did you hear? What was it like for you? Who did you hear it from? Or what did you hear it from? Go back and explore that situation in your mind with as much detail as you can: What was it like? How old were you? Where are you in the memory? Are you in the kitchen, in the bedroom, living room, in class, in the movies, in the park? Are you watching TV? Are you alone or with other people? With your parents, family, friends? What are you feeling? Do you remember any particular physical sensations? What are you thinking?

5. Are you making any choices about life, about people, about yourself at the time? Decisions like "Because this happened, therefore . . . " or "This means that life is . . . that people are . . . that the world is . . . " What are you telling yourself? Are you coming to any conclusions? This is very important. Stay with that.

6. Think of yourself today; look at that situation. Are you still holding those choices? Do you still believe what you concluded then? Would you say, "This is still me" or "This is not me anymore? What is the difference? What changed and why?

7. Have you talked with other people about it? Who did you talk to [both in the past and now]? Who did you talk to if you did? What was their reaction? What was your reaction to their reaction?

8. Is there anything about this that you haven't told anyone, that you decided is not to be talked about, that is "unspeakable"? Is there any area in it that you feel is totally your secret, that you dealt with all alone and kept to yourself? If there is, please put it into words such as, "I haven't shared it because . . . " or "I am very hesitant to share it because . . . " Would you please mention the particular people with whom you won't share it, and why.

9. Moving to another aspect of the interpersonal realm, do you personally know survivors of _____ or their family members—as friends, neighbors, or colleagues?

10. There are secrets we keep from others to protect either ourselves or them, and there are self secrets. Take your time. This is very important. Imagine the situation of the very first time you ever heard anything about it. Roam inside your mind. Is there anything about it that you have never talked to yourself

about, a secret you have kept from yourself? An area that you have sort of pushed away or kept at arm's length from yourself? Or about which you say to yourself, "I can't handle that"? Why is it the one thing that was too much for you? What haven't you put into words yet, that is still lurking in that corner of your mind you have not looked into yet?

11. What is your personal relationship to the trauma? Please, do write the answers, because even the way you write makes a difference. Did your place of birth figure in your relationship to the trauma? Does your age figure in your relationship to the trauma?

12. What is your religious, ethnic, cultural, political, racial, gender identity? Do these parts of your identity figure in the choices you made, influence your relationship to the experience? How? You can answer these one by one.

13. Let us move to your professional self. What is your professional discipline? How long have you been working in it? What is your professional relationship to the _____? Within your professional practice, have you seen survivors or their children of _____? How many?

14. What therapeutic modality did you employ? Emergency/crisis intervention, short- or long-term, individual, family, and/or group therapy? Was it in an inpatient or outpatient basis? What modality have you found (or would you find) most useful, and why?

15. Was it the only victim/survivor population you have worked with professionally?

16. Have you ever been trained to work with victim/survivors of trauma? In school, on the job? If you were, what have you found to be the crucial elements of your training without which you won't feel prepared to do the job?

The sequence of the first phase of the processing of event countertransference is from the immediate visual imagery, through free associations, to the more verbal-cognitive material. It then moves to articulate how the trauma fits within the therapist's experience, personal and interpersonal development, and the gender, racial, ethnic, religious, cultural, and political realms of her or his life. It begins with one's private world of trauma and proceeds through the context of one's interpersonal life to one's professional work. While the material can be analyzed privately, the second phase of the process works best by sharing and analyzing it in a group setting, as is often the case in treating survivors and children of survivors of the Nazi Holocaust (Danieli, 1982b; 1988c; 1989) and other victim/survivors.

This training process assumes that the most meaningful way to tap into event countertransferences is to let them emerge, in a systematic way, from the particularity of the therapist's experience. Therapists can thus be better able to recognize and become familiar with their reactions so that they can monitor them, learn to understand and contain them, and use them preventively and therapeutically. The exercise process also helps built awareness of caregivers' vulnerability to being vicariously victimized by repeated exposure to trauma and trauma stories and awareness of the extent of the toll countertransference reactions take on their intrapsychic, interpersonal, and family lives. It makes poignantly clear the paramount necessity of carefully nurturing, regulating, and ensuring the development of a self-protective, self-healing, and self-soothing way of being a professional and a full human being.

The importance of self-care and self-soothing is acknowledged in the exercise in building into the process instructional elements such as: "Take your time. . . . Take all the time you need" and a caring, respectful attention to every element explored.

SOME PRINCIPLES OF SELF-HEALING

The following principles are designed to help professionals recognize, contain, and heal event countertransference.

A. To Recognize One's Reactions
   1. Develop awareness of somatic signals of distress—chart warning signs of potential countertransference reactions, for example, sleeplessness, headaches, perspiration.
   2. Try to find words to name accurately and to articulate inner experiences and feelings. As Bettelheim (1984) commented, "What cannot be talked about can also not be put to rest; and if it is not, the wounds continue to fester from generation to generation" (p. 166).
B. To Contain One's Reactions
   1. Identify one's personal level of comfort in order to build openness, tolerance, and readiness to hear anything.
   2. Knowing that every emotion has a beginning, a middle, and an end, learn to attenuate your fear of being overwhelmed by its intensity and try to feel its full life cycle without resorting to defensive countertransference reactions.
C. To Heal and Grow
   1. Accept that nothing will ever be the same.
   2. When feeling wounded, take time, accurately diagnose, soothe, and heal before continuing to work.
   3. Any one of the affective reactions (grief, mourning, rage) may interact with old, unworked-through experiences of the therapists.
   4. Seek consultation or further therapy for previously unexplored areas triggered by patients' stories. This utilizes professional work purposefully for personal growth.
   5. Establish a network of people to create a holding environment (Winnicott, 1965) within which one can share one's trauma-related work.
   6. Therapists should provide themselves with avocational avenues for creative and relaxing self-expression in order to regenerate energies.

Being kind to oneself and feeling free to have fun are not a frivolity in this field but a necessity without which one cannot fulfill one's professional obligations or professional contract.

NOTE

The event countertransference exercise described in this chapter is owned and copyrighted by Yael Danieli.

36

Toward the Development of a Generic Model of PTSD Treatment

Mary Beth Williams and
John F. Sommer, Jr.

As Everstine and Everstine (1993) noted, the first step in the treatment of a traumatic reaction is for "the therapist to enter the shattered reality of the victim and see it through the victim's eyes, while maintaining a clinical perspective" (pp. 49, 50). The more traditional approaches to treatment, based on the medical model of disease and pathology, as the authors of the present volume have illustrated, are often not appropriate for post-traumatic healing. The goal of this final chapter is to integrate the techniques, methods, and strategies of those authors into a comprehensive, active treatment model.

Although not all aspects of the model are applicable to all individuals, the four-stage, nonlinear framework can serve as a beginning point for the development of a treatment plan and a guide for ongoing clinical work. The model may be applied to children as well, taking into consideration developmental stage and age (see Williams, in press, for further explication). In the following sections of the chapter, chapters in this book that illustrate the various stages are included in parentheses or in the text.

Treatment of post-traumatic stress disorder (PTSD) must be flexible; it varies with client needs and level of development and helps integrate traumatic material into the past while building a new framework by which to view the present and the future. Treatment utilizes a phenomenological approach that places ultimate responsibility for recovery on the client as he or she attempts to master the events to a reasonable degree, reduce body chemistry arousal, reduce "undue emergence mobilization reactions and avoid any unnecessary kindling phenomena that can lead to hypervigilance, sleep disturbance," reduce the "endorphin opiate-like withdrawal'' (Flannery, 1992, p. 143), find meaning in, and make sense of, the traumatic events, and reattach to the world and others.

STAGE 1. ENCOUNTER/EDUCATION

Establish Safety and the Safety Milieu

Boundaries and rules of therapy are introduced immediately to help create a safety milieu for the traumatized individual (Chapter 11) in the biological, psychological, social, and moral arenas (Chapter 31). The framework of therapy includes setting fee schedules, time frames, and procedures and establishing rights, responsibilities, and contracts. Through this process the client begins to develop a collaborative relationship with the therapist. This relationship is constantly renegotiated in order to establish some level(s) of trust. Areas of conflict are faced openly and dealt with directly.

Assess Immediate Safety Levels and Set Up Emergency Responses

Traumatized individuals cannot begin to heal in an unsafe external-to-therapy environment, for example, a battered woman who returns from therapy to a potentially lethal situation. Therefore it is important to assess the safety level of the client. Child clients also must be safe from harm and must not be harming others (Chapter 4). At times, the therapist must take the role of advocate should the individual need assistance to find safety (Chapter 9). This function may include providing information about available services or assuming some of the rights of self-determination for a client who is unable to provide safety for self (Chapter 10).

Emergency response plans also need to be created for anniversary dates and holidays (e.g., if ritual abuse occurred) and for other potentially dangerous situations. Hospital programs designed to treat dissociative disorders and PTSD can offer a safe place during these times, if insurance permits the hospitalization (Chapters 30 and 31).

Begin with Crisis Intervention If Necessary; Set the Cultural Framework

Initial treatment of a traumatic reaction frequently takes the form of crisis intervention. Presently occurring traumatic events are crises that require immediate triage, defusing, and debriefing (Chapter 17). Crisis intervention may occur via a call to a radio show or hot line (Chapter 16) or through team intervention in a school (Chapter 5), community, or organization (Chapter 18). The timing of crisis intervention is critical and should occur as near in time to the event's occurrence as possible. Quick speed of response is essential for early healing (Chapter 18). When workplace trauma occurs, debriefing should happen as soon as possible after the event (Chapter 20). However, survivors of secret, hidden traumas that are not remembered fully or even partially until later in life do not benefit from early crisis interventions. Their crises generally focus on present-day events rather than the past traumas.

All aspects of treatment must incorporate a cultural awareness of beliefs, values, norms, customs, and attitudes (Chapters 9, 14, and 16). This is particularly true when crisis intervention occurs following a death. The role of culture in the processing of death is "particularistically" significant. Thus the therapist must utilize both universal and culturally specific crisis intervention techniques (Chapter 14).

Build an Empathic Connection and Begin to Establish the Relationship

The therapist must approach the traumatized individual as a helper, an empathic "other" who believes in, and thus is willing to collaborate in, the recovery process. According to the Committee for Children (1992), the "first component of empathy is the ability to identify how another person feels through physical cues of facial expressions and body language, verbal cues of language and tone, and situational cues of what is happening." The second component of empathy is the ability "to understand another person's point of view," that is, another's experiences, feelings, values, motivations, and needs. The third component of empathy is the ability to respond emotionally to them, hopefully in an enhancing manner.

The dynamic relationship is established only if the therapist respects the client/patient's capacities, values, customs, ethnocultural background, and present belief systems. The therapist tries to understand and focus on the motivations, strengths, and expectations of the individual and uses flexible, strategically chosen techniques. Establishing this relationship frequently takes a long time and involves repeated testing of the therapist. Belief in the client by the therapist is essential.

The post-traumatic therapist must be secure in his or her personal identity, have control of personal trauma history, and be confident as to personal competence (Chapter 14). The therapist also must be able to tolerate the intense, painful imagery the client presents (Chapter 3). The therapist models self-soothing abilities in this process and is sensitive to the reactions of clients. Issues of transference and countertransference that inevitably develop must be acknowledged and dealt with by both client and therapist (Chapter 35).

Assessment and Initial Diagnosis

Assessment occurs throughout the intake process as well as throughout ongoing therapy. Assessment is a dynamic process that examines the needs of the client as well as resources and coping skills, present level of functioning (Chapter 19), self capacities, approach/avoidance escape strategies, level of external and internal connection, prior trauma history (Chapter 3), need for medications, referrals (Chapter 9), traumatogenic states, and available resources (Chapter 4).

Assessment is multidimensional if possible and uses psychophysiological, behavioral, and cognitive components. A variety of structured instruments are being developed to assess trauma history (Chapter 3) and present level of functioning (Chapter 2). Early assessment leads to early intervention and may also involve observation (e.g., of play) and the use of drawings or other paper-and-pencil tasks. If chronic PTSD exists, ongoing assessment can monitor alterations in ego defenses as well as improvement or decline (Chapter 21). Assessment of secondary and personality disorders also occurs at this step.

The intake process during this initial step varies in level of structure and flexibility. The use of extensive testing, questionnaires, or inventories needs to be timed appropriately and should not occur too early. Survivors need to have as much control of the initial telling of their stories as possible.

Setting the Trauma Paradigm

The therapist has the responsibility to set the frame of treatment for the client. This frame provides a trauma-based view of post-event reactions. It assumes a measure of health and states that a post-traumatic stress reaction is a normal reaction to abnormal events. The trauma paradigm serves as a structure for organization through a variety of models ranging from information processing to psychosocial, to psychodynamic, to behavioral, to cognitive appraisal, to object relations, to psychophysiological, to interactive (Chapters 1 and 11). The paradigm recognizes that some individuals have dissociated their traumatic experiences and do not recognize the impact of those events on their lives or may not view what is remembered as traumatic.

Education

An extremely important component of the initial stage of treatment is education. Clients may need to be taught that they are not crazy, even though they feel out of control and disconnected to self and others and experience a loss of meaning (Chapter 12). Clients need to know that PTSD is not a pathological reaction (Chapter 6) and that exposure to trauma changes the psychobiological state, cognitive-processing abilities, memory capacity, beliefs, self-structure, object relations, and orientation to society (Chapter 1).

The therapist teaches that the impact of trauma varies greatly and is more acute if it involves certain event and survivor characteristics:

Bereavement or loss (Chapters 1 and 12)
Life threat (Chapters 1, 10, 12, and 20)

Violation of self-boundaries (Chapters 9 and 12)

Exposure to death and dying (Chapter 12)

Witnessing, observing directly (Chapters 9 and 12)

Greater degree of feelings of responsibility for the occurrence (Chapter 12)

Longer duration (Chapter 1)

History of past trauma (Chapters 9 and 20)

Greater degree of moral conflict (Chapter 1)

Absence of a support system (Chapters 9 and 20)

Human design (Chapter 9)

Relationship with the perpetrator (Williams, 1990)

Betrayal (Chapter 20).

Each individual has a threshold of tolerance for traumatic stressors that is dependent upon personality variables (traits, coping style, beliefs, abilities), stressor dimensions, and the post-trauma milieu (Chapter 1).

Education may be indirect or didactic; at times, the therapist gives the client written material, shows videos, or verbally presents the information (Chapter 9). Several sessions may be needed to frame client reactions as post-traumatic stress response (PTSR) or PTSD and discuss the nature of trauma (Chapter 6) as well as the process of memory retrieval (Chapter 3) and the nature of dissociation. It is crucial that individuals of all levels of education and training who work with trauma be trained to provide accurate information to their clients (Chapters 10, 16, 18, and 20).

Since many traumatic events occur to children, education of school system officials is an essential component of regular education as well as post-crisis intervention (Chapter 5). Teaching children directly about trauma helps them gain physical and behavioral mastery (Chapter 4). Psychoeducation is also important at the inpatient level of treatment (Chapters 30 and 31).

Establishing Beginning Control over Retraumatizing Behaviors

Retraumatizing behaviors must be brought under control as soon as possible in this initial stage of therapy. Many trauma survivors are self-destructive through avoidance (substance usage and other addictions) and approach (thrill seeking, behavioral reenactment) behaviors (Chapters 6, 12, and 13). Clients must learn to identify what triggers these behaviors (Chapter 6). It is also essential that clients maintain as normal a functioning as possible during this stage of treatment, even if superficial. Clients need to be encouraged to follow daily routines, keep their jobs, and engage in social activities.

Children can learn to manage self-disturbing, trauma-reactive behaviors (Chapter 4) through the use of self-soothing statements and supportive images (Chapter 3). The creation of a physically or mentally safe place that can serve as a refuge can help diffuse symptoms (Chapter 11). If symptoms are so intense that control is not possible, short-term or longer hospitalizations can help clients develop coping skills. This is particularly true if the client is suicidal, destructively dissociative, at risk for the physical consequences of bulimia or anorexia, or extremely self-mutilatory (Chapter 31). Chemical and nonchemical habituating behaviors also must be addressed and their treatment integrated into therapy. Trauma survivors frequently self-medicate (Chapters 10 and 21), and PTSD frequently coexists with substance abuse (Chapter 6). Dual disorder treatment is helpful when addiction becomes the means by which clients deny, minimize, avoid, or survive trauma (Chapter 13). Nonchemical habituating behaviors can also become addictive and/or destructive. These may include gambling, over-exertion, thrill seeking, workaholism, and religion (Chapter 13).

Symptom Management

The initial stage of treatment must include the introduction and use of behavioral and cognitive techniques to promote self-control and symptom management (Chapters 9 and 12). A variety of arousal management strategies for anger control, relaxation, thought stopping, sleep disturbance modification, and trigger awareness can be presented (Chapter 9). The development of stress management skills is an ongoing part of therapy and uses biofeedback, stress inoculation training, contracting, naming of responses, and so on (Chapters 10 and 19).

STAGE 2. EXPLORE THE TRAUMA AND ITS IMPACT: DOING THE WORK

Working with Memories

Telling the story prior to this stage of treatment should be more cognitive and utilize dosing, pacing, and appropriate timing. Clients initially may want to flood themselves with their stories; however, moderation and titration are essential until safety and behavioral control have been established. Also, therapists may want to "get into" and explore the traumatic material at too early a point in the therapeutic process (Chapter 3). The use of flooding and implosion is risky before the second stage of treatment, if not outright dangerous (Chapter 12).

During this step in the treatment process, clients can be taught to listen to, recognize, and honor their memories. Deliberate facilitation of memories through the use of drawings, photos, and imagery occurs only with preparation and pacing (Chapter 10). Although the seeds of recovery lie within these trauma stories, telling must proceed slowly and carefully and only if there are an atmosphere of safety and some degree of trust (Chapter 15).

Detailed, chronological accounting of trauma stories must be combined with relaxation and other self-soothing exercises (Chapter 21). Telling often is repetitive in order for both adults and children to make sense of what happened

(Chapter 11). Thus, the traumatologist must be willing and able to hear these horrific stories over and over again. This stage of treatment is major in impact and scope. Identification of critical incidents and accompanying triggers in all their behavioral, affective, sensate, and knowledge (BASK; Braun, 1988) components is necessary. Flashbacks and planned and unplanned abreactions often occur. Not all traumas must be fully remembered and reexperienced. However, the client must accept the reality of the existence of trauma and its impact. Past and present must be connected if healing is to occur. It is possible that the trauma story may be underrepresented, overrepresented, minimized, distorted, or remembered partially rather than in full. Identification of triggers that lead to remembering may help to facilitate building a more complete picture. Triggers include words, body sensations, fantasies, sounds, and smells, among others.

Chu (1992) noted that abreactive work is very difficult and may lead to partial regression or temporarily full regression. Abreactive work should not occur without adequate preparation, education about the process, and therapeutic and familial support. The work is likely to occur in spurts, over an extended period of time when intrusions are more intense. Abreaction involves constantly processing to put the relived traumas into the past without accompanying feelings of guilt, shame, or self-blame. Chu (1992) wrote that "abreaction of past trauma frees abuse survivors from fear of their own repressed memories" (p. 359). However, rules for the pacing and timing must be established to give clients a feeling of at least minimal control.

Inevitability of Secondary Traumatization

Consequences of trauma exist intergenerationally as well as concurrently in both families of survivors and in therapists themselves (Chapters 8 and 35). The impact of trauma on other family members necessitates their inclusion in the treatment process if at all possible (Chapters 11 and 12). Family members can function as sources of either support or distress (Chapter 30). It is important, for example, that the caretakers of traumatized children be involved in their treatment (Chapter 4). Partners groups can teach boundaries, self-care, and empowerment as well as help in the development of communication and relationship skills (Chapter 29). Partners and children of trauma survivors are at risk for long-term secondary effects. They may exhibit symptoms of depression and anxiety or show symptoms of guilt, aggression, confusion, and hopelessness. The effects of trauma on relationships impact areas of safety, trust, power, esteem, and intimacy (Chapters 3 and 11).

When secondary reactions are identified and treated, traumatized family members can become helping, supportive assistants (Flannery, 1992). The victim's family is "the first potential major resource" (p. 165) and can help the victim restore a sense of mastery through its emotional support, as well as psychological and physical assistance. If the family is not supportive or if it perpetrates additional trauma, friends and significant others can serve as resources.

Examining and Integrating the Emotional Impact of Trauma

As clients work through traumas in a more detailed fashion, they need to learn healing rituals appropriate to their individual circumstances. These rituals may focus on safety, abreactive work, or examining and feeling the emotional impact of the traumatic events, including work with anger, grief, or leave-taking (Chapters 11, 15, and 21). It is necessary to grieve the specific temporary and permanent losses that trauma has caused. Mourning these losses is essential. For example, persons traumatized through moving need to grieve the lost home, attachments, and accompanying disruptions (Chapter 19). Victimization also brings many losses (e.g., innocence, childhood) that must be grieved (Chapter 30).

An additional emotion that frequently accompanies trauma and must be resolved is rage/intense anger toward self and others. Self-anger is often operationalized through self-blame and guilt. Anger toward others may range from aggressive acting out to vague dissatisfaction.

Remembering must incorporate processing of affect as well as cognitive knowledge, behaviors, and sensations (Braun, 1990). It is essential to experience associated emotions fully in addition to labeling them in a cognitive manner (Chapter 10). Clients must learn to feel, as well as name, their feelings (Chapter 6). The initial approach to emotions is more cognitive, often through the use of metaphors, bibliotherapy, and stories so that clients (particularly children) are not overwhelmed (Chapter 4). Abreactions of traumatic events that incorporate emotional release have been shown "to be effective in alleviating acute symptomatology" (Chu, 1992, p. 352).

Use of Action Strategies

Action activities can be utilized in a therapeutic manner to assist the work of therapy (Chapters 12 and 25). These activities stimulate reexperiencing in a symbolic and metaphoric way as well as in a physical manner. They are alternatives to talking therapy and use the power of context while promoting fun and laughter (Chapter 25).

Linking Mind and Body

The role and use of medications also have to be considered in cases where intrusions become too intense to prohibit normal daily functioning (Chapter 6) or if depression and anxiety become too overwhelming. The biological perspective cannot be ignored. A variety of drugs is now being utilized and studied as adjuncts to therapy (Chapter 32). Medications can provide significant temporary benefits (Chapter 31) and help relieve emotional flooding, making clients more amenable to intervention (Chapter 21).

The use of medication recognizes the connection between mind and body and promotes a whole-person model (Chapter 30). Body memories also indicate the link between mind and body and, when addressed directly, may pave the way for further remembering. Activities that encourage relaxation and promote joy and fun also recognize and utilize the mind-body connection (Chapter 7). Hypnosis and the states of consciousness model help individuals to reassociate and recognize inner experiences. During trance, the survivor can be helped to gain mastery over trauma and can learn specific techniques to resolve intrusive symptoms and neutralize fear (Chapter 26).

The Use of Other Adjunctive Therapies

A variety of adjunctive, experiential, and reflective techniques can assist in the recall and processing of traumatic material. These include the following:

1. Play therapy (Chapter 4) to help the child or inner child begin to develop a core self.
2. Music therapy (Chapter 23) through specific songs and the creation of personal music.
3. Dance/movement therapy (Chapter 23), which facilitates spontaneous movement, uses stretch and extended movement, gives a means to express thoughts and feelings, and helps build body awareness.
4. Psychodrama (Chapter 23) as a group method to enact relevant events and core experiences, allowing for emotional discharge and exploration with group members as auxiliary egos.
5. Logotherapy/bibliotherapy (Chapters 4, 7, and 11), using metaphors, a focus on meaning, stories, written materials about trauma, workbooks, first-person accounts, symbols within, and the development of a personal language.
6. Writing (Chapters 21 and 24) to preserve memory, conduct private dialogue, bear witness, and integrate experience from a distance.
7. Art therapy (Chapters 22, 23, and 30) as a visual dialogue and form of phenomenological expression to create an individual drama on a visual surface. Art captures the historical narrative and associated affect and serves as a modality for safer personal testimony and a way to tell secrets without the threat of consequences that accompanies verbal telling (Chapter 22).
8. Groups (Chapters 5, 16, 19, 27, 28, 29, and 30) are excellent arenas for processing trauma through mutual interaction and support. Groups may be open or closed in membership, structured or unstructured, time-limited or ongoing. Support groups provide additional resources to survivors and/or their families. Groups help normalize and validate reactions while allowing for sharing and providing connection in a therapeutic environment. No one form of therapy is appropriate for all trauma survivors. Psychoeducational twelve-step groups can be used in a variety of settings, as can leader-led groups and twelve-step groups modeled on Alcoholics Anonymous (AA).

Vicarious Traumatization of Therapists

It is inevitable that the traumas of survivors vicariously impact trauma workers (Chapter 35). Traumatologists must learn to recognize the symptoms of helper stress and take proactive steps to counter its inevitable impact (Chapter 20). Self-care for the therapist is essential and ethically necessary; it involves the processing and evaluation of the therapist's own trauma history and issues (Chapter 9), seeking support of peers through networking, and obtaining supervision and training (Chapter 10). Vicarious traumatization impacts therapists' cognitive schemas, relationships, psychophysiological functioning, emotional state, spiritual orientation, and meaning. Vicarious traumatization may cause therapists to require assistance to assess and establish personal limits and boundaries both within the client-therapist relationship and in other relationships. Therapists need to play, express creativity, rest, and care for themselves and their bodies, among other nurturing activities, to counteract countertransference and secondary traumatization.

STAGE 3. SKILL BUILDING AND CLIENT EMPOWERMENT

Belief System Change

Clients have a variety of mind-sets about themselves and the world that impact their functioning (Matsakis, 1992; Glover, 1984). They may blame themselves for their victimization and may develop perfectionistic shoulds, which are generally unrealistic. Some survivors deny that their traumatic experiences have had any negative impact and devalue mental health services. Others display all-or-nothing, black-or-white thinking that leads to absolutist self-perceptions or perceptions about others.

During traumatic experiences, survivors employ a variety of defenses and behavioral strategies that help them survive. However, these defenses may become maladaptive over time and may lead to impaired beliefs about safety, trust, power, esteem, and intimacy (Chapters 3 and 11). Helping clients develop a personal bill of rights assists in the repairing of damaged self-esteem (Chapter 11). The social support system can also serve as a buffer between the client's belief system about self and the world and resulting actions (Chapter 20). The use of cognitive techniques to identify and describe beliefs, for example, belief inventories (McCann & Pearlman, 1990b; Williams, 1990), can prove helpful. Restructuring of beliefs occurs generally after clients have identified and processed memories. Identification of, and work with, coping styles also occur at this step in the process.

Social Skills Development

As clients continue to heal, they are ready to focus on building social skills that will help them survive in the everyday world. Therapists should incorporate a variety of communication skills exercises, assertiveness skills, and conflict management and anger management skills into this stage of therapy (Chapters

6 and 11). It is also important to develop stress management skills that do not rely on substances or other addictions (Chapter 10).

Establishing/Reestablishing Emotional Intimacy

Clients need to learn to develop or reestablish emotional intimacy with self and others. Individuals who are not in relationships learn to make choices as to whether or not they want new relationships. They also learn to monitor any indicators that safety is at risk and trust may be violated (Chapter 10). Fear helps to interfere with the formation of intimate relationships and generally involves fear of merger, exposure, abandonment, attack, and personal destructive impulses. The use of indirect or metaphorical techniques (sharing meditation, healing metaphors) effectively help to build intimacy (Chapter 7). Clients can also be encouraged to self-nurture through play and leisure, as well as the building of positive rituals.

Empowerment

Empowerment of the self beyond survivorship is the ultimate goal of therapy. All interventions are designed to empower the client to build options, develop positive coping strategies, and engender resilience (Chapter 10). Tasks also aim to help clients learn new coping skills involving positive power. The resilient, empowered client knows how to deal with manipulation and deception. Clients may be encouraged to develop physical strength through exercise, tae kwon do, or bodybuilding. The empowerment model also guides inpatient treatment (Chapter 30).

STAGE 4. EVALUATION, INTEGRATION, TERMINATION

Finding Meaning

A cognitive reframing of meaning is essential for healing (Chapter 12). This includes restructuring of self-blaming messages or inaccurate beliefs, thoughts, and feelings (Chapter 9). Clients need to come to terms with their shattered assumptions while reestablishing a conceptual system that makes sense of the world (Chapters 3, 10, and 30). This is one of the most difficult tasks of therapy. However, trauma often has positive aspects that can lead to personal growth (Chapter 27). Recognizing these positive aspects of trauma can lead to healing and transformation (Chapter 10). Reframing traumas in more positive terms can help the client accept what has happened and make plans for the future (Chapters 6 and 19).

Finding a Mission

Part of the positive change brought by trauma includes finding a cause or mission (Chapter 12). For example, the NAIM Foundation during the Gulf War became an advocate for the Arab community (Chapter 16). Educating others about victims' issues, becoming an advocate for victims, developing prosocial action plans, and initiating prosocial activities help facilitate recovery (Chapter 10).

Reconnecting Spiritually

The role of spirituality cannot be ignored in the healing process. Clients who are involved in twelve-step-modeled programs learn to seek help from a higher power and accept personal spirituality (Chapter 28). Traumatized children also need to address spiritual beliefs directly (Chapter 4). Therapy with survivors of trauma ultimately must explore, address, and process issues of dying, pain, suffering, death, justice, and injustice (Chapter 9).

Spiritual healing may be necessary before the client can resolve survival guilt. Forgiveness of self is often a process of nurturing and dialogue. This is particularly true if the survivor wronged others and needs to confess those actions and do restitution for them.

Prevention of Further Distress

Preventive interventions with survivors and others help lessen instances of relapse or treatment failure. Therapists as well need to undertake preventive measures to keep themselves in balance, including training and consultation (Chapters 17, 18, 20, 35). Therapists may collect or develop handouts that review or explain what they know, for example, about crisis intervention. They may also help develop clear, competency-based training models that are culturally sensitive (Chapters 11 and 33).

Termination

Ideally, termination occurs when client and therapist agree that the utility of therapy has been exceeded and that the client has reinvested energy beyond the trauma and has a sense of future. Clients who are "ready" for termination have reconnected with self and others and recognize that their trauma history will always be a part of their past. If possible, clients should be given an "open door" to be allowed to check in periodically when they deem it necessary.

CONCLUSIONS

Recovery from trauma is often a long, arduous process. However, recovery is possible. While these stages and steps of therapy serve merely as a guideline, they may also help client and therapist alike to focus on the process of therapy and ''what needs to be done next.''

The diverse treatment models presented in this book are also designed to stimulate thought and serve as references. It is the hope of the editors and authors that these will be useful for clinicians and clients as they proceed on their journeys to healing.

References

Abroms, G. M. (1969). Defining milieu therapy. *Archives of General Psychiatry*, 21, 553–560.

Abueg, F., and Fairbank, J. (1991). Behavioral treatment of the PTSD substance abuser. In P. A. Saigh (ed.), *Post-traumatic stress disorder: A behavioral approach to assessment and treatment*. New York: Pergamon Press, 111–146.

Abueg, F. R., J. A. Kriegler, H. Falcone & F. Gusman. (1989). Relapse prevention training with alcoholic Vietnam veterans with PTSD: A treatment outcome study with one-year follow-up. In (F. Abueg, Chair), Comorbidity in traumatic stress disorders with attention to substance use/dependence. Paper presented at the Annual Meeting for the Association for Advancement of Behavior Therapy (AABT), Washington, DC.

Agger, I. (1989). Sexual torture of political prisoners. *Journal of Traumatic Stress*, 2(3), 305–318.

Agosta, C. & M. Loring. (1991). Ending Violence Effectively Inc. program description pamphlet. Boulder, CO.

Ahmed, I. & N. Adadow-Gray (eds.). (1988). The Arab-American family: A resource manual for human service providers. Detroit: Access Publishing.

Albeck, J. (1989a). Learning from survivor's videotaped testimonies. *One Generation After Newsletter*, 11(2), 6.

———. (1989b). *Songs for the last survivor*. Boston: One Generation After.

Alexander, D. W. (1990). Secondary victims of violent crime: Examining the effects on child siblings through play therapy. Ph.D. diss., University for Humanistic Studies, Del Mar, CA.

Algier, R. (1991). Effects of trauma on children. *Trauma and Recovery*, 4(1), 9.

Allodi, F. & A. Rojas. (1985). The health and adaptation of victims of political violence in Latin America. In P. Pichot et al. (eds.). *Psychiatry: The state of the art*. Vol. 6. New York and London, Plenum Press.

ALMACAN. (1986). AFA EAP: An exemplary program. August.

Almagor, M. & G. Leon. (1989). Transgenerational effects of the concentration camp experience. In P. Marcus & A. Rosenberg (eds.), *Healing their wounds: Psychotherapy with Holocaust survivors and their families*. New York: Praeger, 189–196.

Almond, R. (1974). *The healing community*. New York: Jason Aronson.

American Psychiatric Association (APA) (1980). *Diagnostic and statistical manual, edition III*. Washington, DC: American Psychiatric Association.

———. (1987). *Diagnostic and statistical manual, edition III-R*. Washington, DC: American Psychiatric Association.

American Psychological Association (APA) (1991, June). Draft of APA ethics code published. *APA Monitor*, 22, 30–35.

Amick-McMullan, A., D. G. Kilpatrick, L. J. Veronen & S. Smith. (1989). Family survivors of homicide victims: Theoretical perspectives and an exploratory study. *Journal of Traumatic Stress*, 2, 21–35.

Amnesty International. (1988). *Amnesty International report 1988*. London: Author.

———. (1984). *Torture in the eighties*. London: Author.

———. (1975). *Report on torture*. London: Duckworth.

Angell, M. & A. Relman. (1989). Redundant publication. *New England Journal of Medicine*, 320, 1212–1213.

Anisman, H. & R. M. Zacharko. (1986). Behavioral and neurochemical consequences associated with stressors. *Annual New York Academy of Sciences*, 467, 205–229.

Anthony, E. J. & B. Cohler (eds.). (1987). *The invulnerable child*. New York: Guilford Press.

APA Task Force. (1991). *DSM-IV option book*. Washington, DC: American Psychiatric Press.

Archibald, H. C. & R. D. Tuddenham. (1965). Persistent stress reaction after combat: A 20-year follow-up. *Archives of General Psychiatry*, 12, 475–481.

Argueta, M. (1987). *Where the southern sea beats*. New York: Vintage Books.

Armstrong, K., W. O. O'Callahan & C. R. Marmar. (1991). Debriefing Red Cross disaster personnel: The multiple stressor debriefing model. *Journal of Traumatic Stress*, 4(4), 581–593.

Armsworth, M. & M. Holaday. (1993). The effects of psychological trauma of children and adolescents. *Journal of Counseling and Development*, 72(1), 49–56.

Aronoff, J. & J. P. Wilson. (1985). *Personality in the social process*. Hillsdale, NJ: Lawrence Erlbaum.

Atkinson, D., M. Maruyama & S. Matsui. (1978). The effects of counselor race and counseling approach on Asian Americans' perceptions of counselor credibility and utility. *Journal of Counseling Psychology*, 25, 76–83.

Atri, P. B. & J. H. Gilliam. (1989). Comments on post-traumatic stress disorder. [Letter], *American Journal of Psychiatry*, 146, 128.

Auerhahn, N. C. & E. Prelinger. (1983). Repetition in the concentration camp survivor and her child. *International Review of Psycho-Analysis*, 10, 31–46.

Baker, A. M. (1989a, December). The impact of the Intifada on the mental health of Palestinian children living in the Occupied Territories. Paper presented at the

Sixty-Seventh Annual Meeting of the American Orthopsychiatric Association, Miami, FL.

———. (1989b, October). Psychological reactions of Palestinian children to environmental stress. Paper presented at the Fifth Annual Meeting of the Society for Traumatic Stress Studies, San Francisco, CA.

Baker, G. R. (1992, February). Sleep disturbance. In G. R. Baker & M. D. Salston (Chair), Management of PTSD-related intrusion and arousal symptoms. Workshop conducted at the meeting for the International Association of Trauma Counselors, San Diego, CA.

Baker, G. R. & M. D. Salston. (1989). Survivors of homicide victims: Power regained. Presented at the meeting of the National Organization for Victim Assistance, Chicago, IL, August.

Baker, R. (1984). Alcohol, drugs and Vietnam: "Triple threat" for veterans. *Vet Center Voice*, 9, 11–12.

Bard, M. & H. Connolly. (1982). *A retrospective study of homicide adaptation.* Rockville, MD: National Institute of Mental Health.

Bard, M. & D. Sangrey. (1986). *The crime victim's book.* 2d ed. Secaucus, NJ: Citadel Press.

Barker, P. (1985). *Using metaphors in psychotherapy.* New York: Brunner/Mazel.

Barnett-Queen, T. & L. H. Bergmann. (1988). Critical Incident Training I, ISFSI *Instructo-Gram: Training Keys for the Fire Officer.* 9, 4.

Barocas, H. A. & C. B. Barocas. (1979). Wounds of the fathers: The next generation of Holocaust victims. *International Review of Psycho-Analysis*, 6, 1–10.

Barse, H. (1984). Post-traumatic stress disorder and the American Indian Vietnam vet. *Stars and Stripes*, April 19.

Basoglu, M., I. M. Marks & S. Segün. (1992). Amitriptyline for PTSD in a torture survivor: A case study. *Journal of Traumatic Stress*, 5(1), 77–83.

Bass, E. & L. Davis. (1988). *The courage to heal.* New York: Harper & Row.

Baum, A. & L. Davidson. (1985). A suggested framework for studying factors that contribute to trauma in disaster. In B. Sowder (ed.), *Disasters and mental health: Selected contemporary perspectives.* Rockville, MD: National Institute of Mental Health, 29–40.

Baum, A., R. Fleming & J. E. Singer. (1983). Coping with victimization by technology disaster. *Journal of Social Issues*, 39(2), 117–138.

Baum, A., S. D. Solomon, & R. Ursano. (1987, September). *Emergency/disaster research issues: A guide to the preparation and evaluation of grant applications dealing with traumatic stress.* Bethesda, MD: Uniformed Services University of the Health Sciences.

Baum, C., M. Hyman & S. Michel. (1983). *The Jewish-American woman in America.* New York: New American Library.

Bean-Bayog, M. (1988a). Alcoholism as a cause of psychopathology. *Hospital and Community Psychiatry*, 39(4), 352–354.

———. (1988b). The Hispanic Vietnam veterans: Mental health issues and therapeutic approaches. In R. M. Becerra & K. M. Escobar (eds.), *Mental health and Hispanic Americans.* New York: Grune & Stratton.

Beattie, M. (1987). Codependent no more. New York: Hazelden Foundation, Harper & Row.

Becerra, R. M. (1982). The Hispanic Vietnam veteran: Mental health issues and therapeutic approaches. In R. N. Becerra & K. M. Escobar (eds.), *Mental health and Hispanic Americans*. New York: Grune & Stratton.

Beck, J. C. & B. A. Van der Kolk. (1987). Reports of childhood incest and current behavior of chronically hospitalized psychotic women. *American Journal of Psychiatry*, 144, 1474–1476.

Becker, E. (1971). *The birth and death of meaning*. (2nd ed.). New York: The Free Press.

Beebe, G. W. (1975). Follow-up studies of World War II and Korean War prisoners; II: Morbidity, disability and maladjustments. *American Journal of Epidemiology*, 101, 400–422.

Beere, D. (1990). The experience of shame and traumatization. Paper presented at the annual meeting of the American Psychological Association, Atlanta, GA, August.

Begmann, M. S. & M. E. Jucovy (eds.). (1982). *Generations of the Holocaust*. New York: Basic Books.

Beiser, M. (1985). A study of depression among traditional Africans, urban North Americans, and Southeast Asian refugees. In A. Kleinman & B. Good (eds.), Culture and depression: Studies in the anthropology and cross-cultural psychiatry of affects and disorder. Berkeley, CA: University of California Press.

Belenky, M. F., B. M. Clinchy, N. R. Goldberger & J. M. Tarule. (1986). *Women's ways of knowing: The development of self, voice and mind*. New York: Basic Books.

Benedikt, R. A. & L. C. Kolb. (1986). Preliminary findings on chronic pain and post-traumatic stress disorder. *American Journal of Psychiatry*, 143, 908–910.

Benner, A. (1982). Concerns cops have about shrinks, Presentation to a Symposium on Psychology Therapy and Law Enforcement, San Francisco.

Berg, K. & K. E. Trarioy. (1983). *Research ethics*. New York: Alan R. Liss.

Berger, A. (1988). Working through grief by poetry writing. *Journal of Poetry Therapy*, 2, 11–19.

Berger, A. & M. Giovan. (1990). Poetic interventions with forensic patients. *Journal of Poetry Therapy*, 4, 83–92.

Berger, P. (1980). Documentation of physical sequelae. *Danish Medical Bulletin*, 27, 215–216.

Berk, J. (1992). PTSD and type III environment. Ph.D. diss., Union Institute of Graduate Studies, Cincinnati, OH.

Berry, J. (1969). On cross-cultural comparability. *International Journal of Psychology*, 4, 119–128.

Bettelheim, B. (1984). Afterword to C. Vegh, *I didn't say goodbye* (R. Schwartz, trans.). New York: E. P. Dutton.

———. (1979). *Surviving and other essays*. New York: Alfred A. Knopf.

Bieber, S. L. (1986). Multiple regression and its alternatives. *Social Science Journal*, 25(1), 1–19.

Birnbaum, S. (1989). Veterans' tours to Europe more numerous than ever. [Tacoma WA] *Sunday News Tribune*, April 9, F–5.

Black, C. (1981). *It will never happen to me*. New York: Ballantine Books.

Black, D. & T. Kaplan. (1988). Father kills mother: Issues and problems encountered by a child psychiatric team. *British Journal of Psychiatry*, 153, 624–630.

Blackman, J. (1989). *Intimate violence: A study of injustice*. New York: Columbia University Press.

Blake, D. D., B. T. Litz, T. M. Keane & R. De Young. (1990). Using the SCL–90 to assess combat-related post-traumatic stress disorder. Paper presented at the meeting of the Society for Traumatic Stress Studies, New Orleans, LA, October.

Blake, D. D., F. W. Weathers, L. M. Nagy, D. G. Kaloupek, G. Klauminzer, D. Charney & T. M. Keane. (1990). A clinician rating scale for assessing current and lifetime PTSD: The CAPS–1. *Behavior Therapist*, 18, 187–188.

Blanchard, E. B. (1990). Elevated basal levels of cardiovascular response in Vietnam veterans with PTSD: A health problem in the making? *Journal of Anxiety Disorders*, 4(3), 233–237.

Blanchard, E. B., L. C. Kolb, R. J. Gerardi, P. Ryan & T. P. Pallmeyer. (1986). Cardiac response to relevant stimuli as an adjunctive tool for diagnosing post-traumatic stress disorder in Vietnam veterans. *Behavior Therapy*, 17, 592–606.

Blanchard, E. B., L. C. Kolb, T. P. Pallmeyer & R. J. Gerardi. (1982). The development of a psychophysiological assessment procedure for post-traumatic stress disorder in Vietnam veterans. *Psychiatric Quarterly*, 54, 220–229.

Blanchard, E. B., L. C. Kolb & A. Prins. (1991). Psychophysiological responses in the diagnosis of post-traumatic stress disorder in Vietnam veterans. *Journal of Nervous and Mental Disease*, 179, 99–103.

Blanchard, E. B., L. C. Kolb, A. Prins, S. Gates & G.C. McCoy. (1991). Changes in plasma norepinephrine to combat-related stimuli among Vietnam veterans with post-traumatic stress disorder. *Journal of Nervous and Mental Disease*, 179, (6), 371–373.

Blank, A. S. (1987). Irrational reactions to post-traumatic stress disorder and Vietnam veterans. In S. M. Sonnenberg (ed.), *The trauma of war: Stress and recovery in Vietnam veterans*. Washington, DC: American Psychiatric Association Press.

Blatner, A., and A. Blatner. (1988). *Foundations of psychodrama, history, theory, and practice*. New York: Springer.

Bleich, A., R. Garb & M. Kottler. (1986). Treatment of prolonged combat reaction. *British Journal of Psychiatry*, 148, 493–496.

Bloom, B. L. (1979). Prevention of mental disorders: Recent advances in theory and practice. *Community Mental Health Journal*, 15, 179–181.

Bloom, S. (1993). The sanctuary model. In M. B. Williams & J. Sommer. *Handbook of post-traumatic therapy*. Westport, CT: Greenwood Publishing Group.

Blume, E. S. (1990). *Secret survivors: Uncovering incest and its aftereffects in women*. New York: Wiley.

Boehnlein, J. K., J. D. Kinzie, R. Ben et al. (1983). One year follow-up study of post-traumatic stress disorder among survivors of Cambodian concentration camps. *American Journal of Psychiatry*, 142, 956–960.

Bograd, M. (1986). Holding the line: Confronting an abusive partner. *Networker*, 10(4), 44–47.

———. (1984). Family systems approaches to wife battering: A feminist critique. *American Journal of the Orthopsychiatric Association*, 54(4), 558–568.

Bolin, R. (1985). Disaster characteristics and psychological impacts. In B. Sowder (ed.), *Disasters and mental health: selected contemporary perspectives*. Rockville, MD: National Institute of Mental Health, 3–28.

Bolin, R. & P. Trainer. (1978). Modes of family recovery following disaster: A cross-national study. In E. L. Quarantelli (ed.), *Disaster theory and research*. Beverly Hills, CA: Sage.

Borkman, T. J. (1990). Experiential, professional, and lay frame of reference. In T. J.

Powell (ed.), *Working with self-help groups*. Silver Spring, MD: NASW Press, 3–30.

Boscarino, J. (1979). Current excessive drinking among Vietnam veterans: A comparison with other veterans and non-veterans. *International Journal of Social Psychiatry*, 27, 204–212.

Boudewyns, P. (1991). Chronic combat-related PTSD and concurrent substance abuse: Implications for treatment of this frequent "dual diagnosis." *Journal of Traumatic Stress*, 4(4), 549–560.

Boudewyns, P. A., L. Hyer, M. G. Woods, W. R. Harrison & E. McCranie. (1990). PTSD among Vietnam veterans: An early look at treatment outcome using direct therapeutic exposure. *Journal of Traumatic Stress*, 3(3), 359–368.

Bowen, G. R. & J. A. Lambert. (1986). Systematic desensitization therapy with post-traumatic stress disorder cases. In C. R. Figley (ed.), *Trauma and its wake, vol. 2: Traumatic stress theory, research, and intervention*. New York: Brunner/Mazel, 280–291.

Bowen, M. (1978). *Family therapy in clinical practice*. New York: Jason Aronson.

Bowman, D. (1991). A veteran's recovery and the use of poetry therapy. *Journal of Poetry Therapy*, 5, 21–30.

Branchey, L., W. Davis & C. S. Lieber. (1984). Alcoholism in Vietnam and Korea veterans: A long-term follow-up. *Clinical and Experimental Research*, 8, 572–575.

Brand, A. (1980). *Therapy in writing*. Lexington, MA: Lexington Books.

Braun, B. G. (1989). Iatrophilia and iatrophobia in the diagnosis and treatment of MPD. *Dissociation: Progress in the Dissociative Disorders*, 2(2), 66–69.

———. (1988). PTSD and dissociative disorders in children: Similarities and differences. Presidential Annual Lecture, Fourth Annual Meeting of Society for Traumatic Stress Studies, Dallas, TX, October.

———. (1986). *Treatment of multiple personality disorder*. Washington, DC: American Psychiatric Press.

———. (1984). Symposium on multiple personality. *Psychiatric Clinics of North America*, 7, 1.

———. (1980). Hypnosis for multiple personalities. In H. J. Wain (ed.), *Clinical hypnosis in medicine*. Chicago: Year Book Medical Publishers.

Braun, P., D. Greenberg, H. Dasberg & B. Lerer. (1990). Core symptoms of post-traumatic stress disorder unimproved by alprazolam treatment. *Journal of Clinical Psychiatry*, 51, 236–238.

Bremner, D., S. M. Southwick & D. S. Charney. (1991). Animal models for the neurobiology of trauma. *PTSD Research Quarterly*, 2(4), 1–7.

Brende, J. O. (1991a). *Acute trauma debriefing. Special focus—Law enforcement & police chaplains: Twelve-step workbook for leaders and participants*. Columbus, GA: Trauma Recovery Publications.

———. (1991b). *A workbook for survivors of war: A twelve-step recovery program workbook supplement for group leaders and participants*. Columbus, GA: Trauma Recovery Publications.

———. (1991c). When PTSD rubs off. In S. Sabon (ed.), *Voices*, 27(1–2), 139–143.

———. (1990). *Trauma recovery for victims and survivors: Twelve-step workbook for leaders and participants*. Columbus, GA: Trauma Recovery Publications.

———. (1985). The use of hypnosis in post-traumatic conditions. In W. E. Kelly (ed.),

Post-traumatic stress disorder and the war veteran patient. New York: Brunner/Mazel, 193–210.

———. (1984). An educational-therapeutic group for drug and alcohol abusing combat veterans. *Journal of Contemporary Psychotherapy*, 14(1), 122–136.

———. (1981). Combined individual and group therapy for Vietnam veterans. *International Journal of Group Psychotherapy*, 31(3), 367–378.

Brende, J. O. & B. D. Benedict. (1980). The Vietnam combat delayed stress syndrome: Hypnotherapy of "dissociative symptoms." *American Journal of Clinical Hypnosis*, 23, 34–40.

Brende, J. O. & I. L. McCann. (1984). Regressive experiences in Vietnam veterans: Their relationship to war, post-traumatic symptoms and recovery. *Journal of Contemporary Psychotherapy*, 13, 57–73.

Brende, J. O. & E. McDonald. (1989). Post-traumatic spiritual alienation and recovery in Vietnam combat veterans. *Spirituality Today*, 41(4), 319–340.

Brende, J. O. & E. R. Parson. (1985). *Vietnam veterans: The road to recovery*. New York: Plenum.

Breslau, N. & G. C. Davis. (1987). Posttraumatic stress disorder: The etiologic specificity of wartime stressors. *American Journal of Psychiatry*, 144, 578–583.

Brett, E. A. & R. Ostroff. (1985). Imagery and post-traumatic stress disorder: An overview. *American Journal of Psychiatry*, 142, 417–424.

Briere, J. (1991). *Treating victims of child sexual abuse*. San Francisco: Jossey-Bass.

———. (1989). *Therapy for adults molested as children: Beyond survival*. New York: Springer.

———. (1984). The effects of childhood sexual abuse on later psychological functioning: Defining a post-sexual abuse syndrome. Paper presented at Third National Conference on Sexual Victimization of Children, Washington, DC, April.

Briere, J. & M. Runtz. (1985). Symptomatology associated with prior sexual abuse in a non-clinical sample. Paper presented at the annual meeting of the American Psychological Association, Los Angeles, CA.

Briere, J. & L. Y. Saidi. (1989). Sexual abuse histories and sequelae in female psychiatric emergency room patients. *American Journal of Psychiatry*, 146, 1602–1606.

Brinson, T. & V. Treanor. (1988). Alcoholism and post-traumatic stress disorder among combat Vietnam veterans. *Alcoholism Treatment Quarterly*, 5(3/4), 65–82.

Brodsky, L., A. L. Doerman, L. S. Palmer, G. F. Slade & F. A. Munasifi. (1990). Post-traumatic stress disorder: An eclectic approach. *International Journal of Psychosomatics*, 37, 89–95.

Brody, V. (1992). The dialogue of touch: Developmental play therapy. *International Journal of Play Therapy*, 1, 21–30.

Bromet, E., H. C. Schulberg & L. Dunn. (1982). Reactions of psychiatric patients to the Three Mile Island nuclear accident. *Archives of General Psychiatry*, 39, 725–730.

Brophy, M. H. (1991). Cyproheptadine for combat nightmares in post-traumatic stress disorder and dream anxiety disorder. *Military Medicine*, 156(2), 100–101.

Brown, L. S. & M. P. Root (1990). *Diversity and complexity in feminist therapy*. New York: Harrington Park.

Brown, P. (1984). Legacies of war: Treatment considerations with Vietnam veterans and their families. *Social Work* 29 (August): 372–379.

Browne, A. & D. Finkelhor. (1986). Impact of child sexual abuse: A review of the literature. *Psychological Bulletin*, 99, 66–77.

Browne, A. & K. R. Williams. (1989). Exploring the effects of resource availability and the likelihood of female-perpetrated homicides. *Law and Society Review*, 23(1), 75–94.

Brownmiller, S. (1975). *Against our will: Men, women and rape*. New York: Bantam Books.

Bryce, J. & H. Armenian. (1986). In wartime: The state of children in Lebanon. In J. Bryce and H. Armenian (eds.), *In wartime: The state of children in Lebanon*. New York: Syracuse University Press, 155–159.

Bryer, J. B., B. A. Nelson, J. B. Miller & P. A. Krol. (1987). Childhood sexual and physical abuse as factors in adult psychiatric illness. *American Journal of Psychiatry*, 144, 1426–1430.

Buchsbaum, M. S. (1976). Self-regulation of stimulus intensity. In G. E. Schwartz & D. Shapiro (eds.), *Consciousness and self-regulation*. New York: Plenum Press.

Bulik, C. M., P. F. Sullivan, & M. Rorty. (1989). Childhood sexual abuse in women with bulimia. *Journal of Clinical Psychiatry*, 50, 460–464.

Burge, S. K. (1983). Rape: Individual and family reactions. In C. R. Figley & H. I. McCubbin (eds.), *Stress and the family: Vol. 2, Coping with catastrophe*. New York: Brunner/Mazel.

Burgess, A. W. & L. Holmstrom. (1976). Rape and its effects on task performance at varying stages in the life cycle. In J. J. Walker & S. L. Brodsky (eds.), *Sexual assault*. Lexington, MA: Health, 23–24.

Burnstein, A., P. E. Ciccone, R. A. Greenstein, N. Daniels, K. Olsen, A. Mazarek, R. Decatur & N. Johnson. (1988). Chronic Vietnam PTSD and acute civilian PTSD: A comparison of treatment experiences. *General Hospital Psychiatry*, 10, 245–249.

Butcher, J. N., W. G. Dahlstrom, J. R. Graham, A. Tellegen & B. Kaemmer. (1989). *Minnesota Multiphasic Personality Inventory (MMPI–2): Manual for administration and scoring*. Minneapolis: University of Minnesota Press.

Butcher, J. N., E. A. Egli, N. K. Shiota & Y. S. Ben-Proath. (1988). Psychological interventions with refugees. Prepared for the Refugee Assistance Program: Technical Assistance Center, University of Minnesota. Sponsored by the National Institute of Mental Health. Contract #278–85–0024 "CH".

Butcher, J. N. & C. Hatcher. (1988). The neglected entity in air disaster planning: Psychological services. *American Psychologist*, 43(9), 724–729.

Butler, R. W., D. L. Braff, J. L. Rausch, M. A. Jenkins, J. Sprock & M. A. Geyer. (1990). Physiological evidence of exaggerated startle response in a subgroup of Vietnam veterans with combat-related PTSD. *American Journal of Psychiatry*, 147(10), 1308–1312.

Calia, V. (1966). The culturally deprived client: A reformulation of the counselor's role. *Journal of Counseling Psychology*, 13, 100–105.

Callahan, S. (1969). *Exiled to Eden*. New York: Sheed & Ward.

Calof, D. (1991). Adult survivors of incest and child abuse. Paper presented at the Eastern Regional Conference on Abuse and Multiple Personality, Alexandria, VA, June.

Campbell, D. T. & J. C. Stanley. (1966). *Experimental and quasi-experimental designs for research*. Skokie, IL: Rand McNally.

Campbell, J. (1986). Nursing assessment for risk of homicide with battered women. *Advances in Nursing Science*, 8(4), 36–51.

Cannon, D. S., W. E. Bell, R. H. Andrews & A. S. Finkelstein. (1987). Correspondence between MMPI PTSD measures and clinical diagnosis. *Journal of Personality Assessment*, 51, 517–521.

Caplan, G. (1964). *Principles of preventive psychiatry*. New York: Basic Books.

Capps, W. (1982). *The unfinished war: Vietnam and the American conscience*. Boston: Beacon.

Card, J. (1983). *Lives after Vietnam: The personal impact of military service*. Lexington, MA: Lexington Books.

Carmen, E. H. & P. P. Rieker. (1989). A psychosocial model of the victim-to-patient process: Implications for treatment. *Psychiatric Clinics of North America* 12(2), 431–443.

Carmen, E. H., P. P. Rieker & T. Mills. (1984). Victims of violence and psychiatric illness. *American Journal of Psychiatry*, 14, 37–38.

Carol, E. M., D. B. Rueger, D. W. Foy & C. P. Donahoe. (1985). Vietnam combat veterans with post-traumatic stress disorder: Analysis of marital and cohabiting adjustment. *Journal of Abnormal Psychology*, 94, 329–337.

Carrington, F. (1991, April). Editorial: Habeas Corpus reform. *Networks*, 6, 2, 4. (Available from National Victim Center, 307 W. 7th St., Suite 1001, Ft. Worth, TX 76102).

Cathcart, L. M., P. Berger & B. Knazan. (1979). Medical examination of torture victims applying for refugee status. *Canadian Medical Association Journal*, 121, 179–184.

Charney, D. S., A. Brier, P. I. Jathow & G. R. Heninger. (1986). Behavioral, biochemical and blood pressure responses to alprazolam in healthy subjects: Interactions with yohimbine. *Psychopharmacology*, 88, 133–140.

Charney, D. S., D. B. Menkes & G. R. Heninger. (1981). Receptor sensitivity and the mechanism of action of antidepressant treatment: Implications for the etiology and therapy of depression. *Archives of General Psychiatry*, 38, 1160–1180.

Charney, D. S., S. M. Southwick & J. H. Krystal. (in press). The psychobiology of PTSD. In G. Adelman & B. Smith (eds.), *Neuroscience year: The yearbook encyclopedia of neuroscience*. Boston: Birkhauser Boston Publishing.

Charney, D. S., S. W. Woods, W. K. Goodman & G. R. Heninger. (1987). Neurobiological mechanisms of panic anxiety: Biochemical and behavioral correlates of yohimbine-induced panic attacks. *American Journal of Psychiatry*, 144, 1030–1036.

Cheng, L. & H. Lo. (1991). On advantages of cross-cultural psychotherapy: The minority therapist/mainstream patient dyad. *Psychiatry*, 54, 386–396.

Chernick, N. & B. Chernick. (1979). *In touch*. Scarborough, Ontario: Signet.

Chester, B. (1990). Because mercy has a human heart: Centers for victims of torture. In P. Suedfeld (ed.), *Psychology and torture*. Washington, DC: Hemisphere Publishing Corporation, 165–185.

———. (1989). Issues involved in providing treatment for torture victims in the context of a center. Paper presented to the Fifth Annual Society for Traumatic Stress Studies, San Francisco.

———. (1987). Center for victims of torture: Salvaging lives. *Northwest Report*, 24–26.

Chester, B. & K. Dhillon. (1991). Torture in India: A feasibility study. Unpublished manuscript.

Chiappa, F. W. & S. J. Wilson. (1981). The effect of a locked door on a psychiatric inpatient unit. *Hospital and Community Psychiatry*, 32, 801–802.

Chu, J. (1992) The therapeutic roller coaster: Dilemmas in the treatment of childhood abuse survivors. *Journal of Psychotherapy Practice and Research*, 1(4), 351–370.

———. (1988). Ten traps for therapists in the treatment of trauma survivors. *Dissociation*, 1, 24–32.

Chutis, L. (1987). Flashbacks. Unpublished article.

Ciccone, P. E., A. Mazarek, M. Weisbrot, R. A. Greenstein, K. Olsen & J. Zimmerman. (1988). [Letter], *American Journal of Psychiatry*, 145, 1484–1485.

Cienfuegos, A. J. & C. Monelli. (1983). The testimony of political repression as a therapeutic instrument. *American Journal of Orthopsychiatry*, 53, 43–51.

Cloninger, C. R. (1987). Neurogenetic adaptive mechanisms in alcoholism. *Science*, 236, 410–416.

Coates, D. & T. Winston. (1983). Counteracting the deviance of depression: Peer support groups for victims. *Journal of Social Issues*, 39(2), 169–194.

Cohen, A. A. (1981). *The tremendum: A theological interpretation of the Holocaust.* New York: Crossroad.

Cohen, J. (1960). A coefficient of agreement for nominal scales. *Educational and Psychological Measurement*, 20, 37–46.

Cohen, S. & T. A. Wills. (1985). Stress, social support and the buffering hypothesis. *Psychological Bulletin*, 98, 310–357.

Cole, C. H. & E. E. Barney. (1987). Safeguards and the therapeutic window: A group treatment strategy for adult incest survivors. Paper presented at Sixty-Fourth Annual Meeting of the American Orthopsychiatric Association, Washington, DC.

Coles, R. (1967). *Children of crisis: A study of courage and fear.* Boston: Atlantic Monthly Press.

Coles, R. & T. F. Dugan. (1989). *The child in our times.* New York: Brunner/Mazel.

Colodzin, B. (1989). *Trauma and survival: A self-help learning guide.* Laramie, WY: Ghost Rocks Press.

Comas-Diaz, L. & A. Padilla. (1990). Countertransference in working with victims of political repression. *American Journal of Orthopsychiatry*, 60, 125–34.

Comas-Diaz, L. & F. Jacobsen. (1991). Ethnocultural transference and countertransference in the therapeutic dyad. *American Journal of Orthopsychiatry*, 61, 392–402.

Combs, A. W. (1989). A theory of therapy: Guidelines for counseling practice. Newbury Park, CA: Sage.

Committee for Children. (1992). What is empathy? Paper presentation. Los Angeles, CA: ISTSS.

Conyers, J. (1990, August 9). *The Agent Orange coverup: A case of flawed science and political manipulation.* Twelfth Report by the Committee on Governmental Operations. Washington, DC: U.S. Government Printing Office.

Cooper, N. A. & G. A. Clum. (1989). Imaginal floodings as a supplementary treatment for PTSD in combat veterans: A controlled study. *Behavioral Therapy*, 13, 499–510.

Coughlan, K. & C. Parkin. (1987). Women partners of Vietnam vets. *Journal of Psychosocial Nursing*, 25, 25–27.

Counts, R. M. (1990). The concept of dissociation. *Journal of the American Academy of Psychoanalysis*, 18(3), 460–479.

Courtois, C. A. (1991a). Countertransference and vicarious traumatization. Paper presented to the Northern Virginia Sexual Abuse Network, Falls Church, VA.

———. (1991b). Theory, sequencing, and strategy in treating adult survivors. In J. Briere (ed.), *Treating victims of child sexual abuse*. San Francisco: Jossey-Bass.

———. (1988a). Adult survivors of incest. *NOVA Newsletter*, 3–4.

———. (1988b). *Healing the incest wound: Adult survivors in therapy*. New York: Norton.

Crnich, K. & J. Crnich. (1991). *Shifting the burden of truth*. Lake Oswego, NY: Recollex.

Crocker, L. & J. Algina. (1986). *Introduction to classical and modern test theory*. New York: Holt, Rinehart & Winston.

Cronbach, L. J. (1990). *Essentials of psychological testing*. 5th ed. New York: Harper Collins.

Cruden, J. (ed.). (1985). Post-treatment group assessing dependency problems; client history reveals abusive chemical usage pattern; caseloads dictate types of dependency therapy offered. *Vet Center Voice*, 6(10), 8–11.

Curran, C. (1972). Sexuality and sin. In M. Taylor (ed.), *Thoughts for contemporary Christians*. New York: Doubleday.

Cutler, B. (1989). Meet Jane Doe. *American Demographics*, 11(6), 25–27.

Danieli, Y. (1993). The diagnostic and therapeutic use of the multi-generational family tree in working with survivors and children of survivors of the Nazi Holocaust. In J. P. Wilson & B. Raphael (eds.), *The international handbook of traumatic stress syndromes*. New York: Plenum, 2889–898.

———. (1989a). Mourning in survivors and children of the Nazi Holocaust: The role of group and community modalities. In D. R. Dietrich & P. C. Shabad (eds.), *The problem of loss and mourning: Psychoanalytic perspectives*. Madison, WI: International Universities Press, 427–460.

———. (1989b, August). Countertransference and trauma: Vicarious victimization of the care giver. Workshop presented at the Critical Incident Conference, Federal Bureau of Investigation, Behavioral Science Instruction and Research Unit, Federal Bureau of Investigation Academy, Quantico, VA.

———. (1988a). Confronting the unimaginable: Psychotherapists' reactions to victims of the Nazi Holocaust. In J. P. Wilson, Z. Harel & B. Kahana (eds.), *Human adaptation to extreme stress from the Holocaust to Vietnam*. New York: Plenum, 219–237.

———. (1988b). Treating survivors and children of survivors of the Nazi Holocaust. In F. M. Ochberg (ed.), *Post-traumatic therapy and victims of violence*. New York: Brunner/Mazel, 278–294.

———. (1988c). The use of mutual support approaches in the treatment of victims. In E. Chigier (ed.), *Grief and bereavement in contemporary society: Vol. 3. Support systems*. London: Freund Publishing House, 116–123.

———. (1985). The treatment and prevention of long-term effects and intergenerational transmission of victimization: A lesson from Holocaust survivors and their children. In C. R. Figley (ed.), *Trauma and its wake*. New York: Brunner/Mazel, 295–313.

———. (1984). Psychotherapists' participation in the conspiracy of silence about the Holocaust. *Psychoanalytic Psychology*, 1(1), 23–42.

————. (1982a). *Group project for Holocaust survivors and their children.* Washington, DC: National Institute of Mental Health, Mental Health Services Branch.

————. (1982b). Therapists' difficulties in treating survivors of the Nazi Holocaust and their children. Ph.D. diss., New York University, 1981. (University Microfilms International, #949–904.)

————. (1981a). Differing adaptational styles in families of survivors of the Nazi Holocaust: Some implications for treatment. *Children Today,* 10(5), 6–10, 34–35.

————. (1981b). Families of survivors of the Nazi Holocaust: Some short- and long-term effects. In C. D. Speilberger, I. G. Sarason & N. Milgram (eds.), *Stress and anxiety,* vol 8. New York: McGraw-Hill/Hemisphere, 405–421.

————. (1981c). On the achievement of integration in aging survivors of the Nazi Holocaust. *Journal of Geriatric Psychiatry,* 14(2), 191–210.

————. (1980). Countertransference in the treatment and study of Nazi Holocaust survivors and their children. *Victimology: An International Journal,* 5(2–4), 355–367.

Danieli, Y. & J. H. Krystal. (1989). *The initial report of the Presidential Task Force on Curriculum, Education and Training of the Society for Traumatic Stress Studies.* Chicago: Society for Traumatic Stress Studies.

Daniels, L. & R. M. Scurfield. (submitted). War-related post-traumatic stress disorder, chemical addictions and non-chemical habituating behaviors.

David, E. E., Jr. (1992). *Responsible science: Ensuring the integrity of the research process,* vol. 1. New York: National Academy Press.

Davidowicz, L. (1976). *The war against the Jews 1933–1945.* New York: Baytown.

Davidson, J., H. Kudler, R. Smith, S. L. Mahorney, S. Lipper, E. Hammett, W. B. Saunders & J. O. Cavenar. (1990). Treatment of post-traumatic stress disorder with amitriptyline and placebo. *Archives of General Psychiatry,* 47, 259–266.

Davidson, J.R.T. & E. B. Foa. (1991). Diagnostic issues in post-traumatic stress disorder: Considerations for the DSM-IV. *Journal of Abnormal Psychology,* 100, 346–355.

Davidson, J.R.T., S. Roth & E. Newman. (1991). Fluoxetine in post-traumatic stress disorder. *Journal of Traumatic Stress,* 4(3), 419–423.

Davidson, J.R.T., R. D. Smith & H. S. Kudler. (1989). Validity and reliability of the DSM-III criteria for post-traumatic stress disorder: Experience with a structured interview. *Journal of Nervous and Mental Disorders,* 177, 336–341.

Davis, L. (1991). *Allies in healing.* New York: HarperCollins.

Davis, M. (1990). Animal models of anxiety based on classical conditioning: The conditioned emotional response (CER) and the fear-potentiated startle effect. *Pharmacology and Therapeutics,* 47(2), 147–165.

Davis, N. (1990). *Once upon a time . . . : Therapeutic stories to heal abused children.* Rev. ed. Oxon Hill, MD: Psychological Associates of Oxon Hill.

DeFazio, V. J. (1978). Dynamic perspectives on the nature and effects of combat stress. In C. R. Figley (ed.), *Stress disorders among Vietnam veterans: Theory, research and treatment.* New York: Brunner/Mazel, 23–42.

Derogatis, L. R. (1977a). Confirmation of the dimensional structure of the SCL–90: A study in construct validation. *Journal of Clinical Psychology,* 33(4), 981–989.

————. (1977b). *SCL–90: Administration, scoring, and procedure manual-I for the R (revised) version.* Baltimore: Johns Hopkins University School of Medicine.

————. (1973). SCL–90: An outpatient psychiatric rating scale: Preliminary report. *Psychopharmacology Bulletin*, 9, 13–28.

de Shazer, S. (1988). *Clues: Investigating solutions in brief therapy*. New York: Norton.

Dewayne, C. J. (1984). Posttraumatic stress disorder in medical personnel in Vietnam. *Hospital and Community Psychiatry*, 35(12), 1232–1234.

Diener, E. & R. Crandall. (1978). *Ethics in social and behavioral research*. Chicago: University of Chicago Press.

Disabled American Veterans. (1980). Forgotten warriors: America's Vietnam era veterans. *Disabled American Veterans Magazine*, Jan., 8–13.

Dohrenwend, B. P. & P. E. Shrout. (1984). "Hassles" in the conceptualization and measurement of life-stress variables. *American Psychologist*, 40, 780–786.

Dolan, Y. M. (1991). *Resolving sexual abuse: Solution-focused therapy and Ericksonian hypnosis for adult survivors*. New York: Norton.

Donaldson, M. A. & R. Gardner, Jr. (1987). Diagnosis and treatment of traumatic stress among women after childhood incest. In C. R. Figley (ed.), *Trauma and its wake: The study and treatment of post-traumatic stress disorder*. New York: Brunner/ Mazel, 356–377.

Donovan, D. (1991). Traumatology: A field whose time has come. *Journal of Traumatic Stress*, 4(3), 433–435.

Drabek, T. E. & W. H. Key. (1976). The impact of disaster on primary group linkages. *Mass Emergencies*, 1(2), 89–105.

Draguns, J. (1981). Cross-cultural counseling and psychotherapy: History, issues, current status. In A. J. Marsella & P. B. Pederson (eds.), *Cross-cultural counseling and psychotherapy*. New York: Pergamon Press, 3–27.

————. (1975). Resocialization into culture: The complexities of taking a worldwide view of psychotherapy. In R. W. Brislin, S. Bochner & W. J. Lonner (eds.), *Cross-cultural perspectives on learning*. New York: Sage, 8–44.

Drug Action Forum. (1990). Post torture state of mental health: Report of the medical study on the delayed effects of torture on Nagas in Manipur. West Bengal S/3/5, Sector 111. Salt Lake, Calcutta: Author.

Dunning, C. (1990). Mitigating the impact of work trauma: Administrative issues concerning intervention. In J. T. Reese, J. M. Horn & C. Dunnings (eds.), *Critical incidents in policing*. Washington, DC: U.S. Government Printing Office, 73–82.

————. (1988). Intervention strategies for emergency workers. In M. Lystad (ed.), *Mental health response to mass emergencies: Theory and practice*. New York: Brunner/Mazel, 284–307.

Durkheim, E. (1973). *On morality and society: Selected writings*. Chicago: University of Chicago Press.

Dutton, M. A. (1992a). *Women's response to battering: Assessment and intervention*. New York: Springer.

Dutton, M. A. (1992b). Assessment and treatment of PTSD among battered women. In D. Foy (ed.), *Treating PTSD: Procedure for combat veterans, battered women, adult and child sexual assaults*. New York: Guilford Press.

Dutton, M. A. & S. Painter. (1981). Traumatic bonding: The development of emotional attachments in battered women and other relationships of intermittent abuse. *Victimology: An International Journal*, 6, 139–155.

Dutton, M. A., S. Perrin, K. Chrestman & P. Halle. (1990). MMPI trauma profiles for battered women. Paper presented at the Annual Convention of the American Psychological Association, Boston, MA.

Dutton, M. A. & F. L. Rubinstein. (In press). Trauma workers. In C. F. Figley (ed.), *Trauma and its wake.* Vol. 3. New York: Brunner/Mazel.

Dutton-Douglas, M. A. & L.E.A. Walker (eds.). (1988). *Feminist psychotherapies: Integration of therapeutic and feminist systems.* Norwood, NJ: Ablex Publishing Co.

Dwortzsky, J. P. (1982). *Psychology.* (2nd ed.). St. Paul, MN: West Publishing Company.

Ebert, B. W. (1988). Hypnosis and rape victims. *American Journal of Clinical Hypnosis,* 31(1), 50–56.

Effects of PTSD on incest survivors. (1991). Presentation to the Northern Virginia Sexual Abuse Network, Falls Church, VA.

Egendorf, A. (1985). *Healing from the war: Trauma and transformation after Vietnam.* Boston: Houghton Mifflin.

———. (1982). The postwar healing of Vietnam veterans: Recent research. *Hospital and Community Psychiatry,* 33, 901–908.

———. (1975). A Vietnam veteran rap group and themes of post-war life. *Journal of Social Issues,* 31(4), 111–124.

Egendorf, A., C. Kadushin, R. Laufer, G. Rothbart, & L. Sloan. (1981). *Legacies of Vietnam: Comparative adjustment of veterans and their peers.* A study prepared by the Center for Policy Research for the Veterans Administration, Superintendent of Documents. Washington, DC: U.S. Government Printing Office.

Einstein, A. Statue inscription located on A. Einstein statue on the grounds of the National Academy of Sciences, Washington, DC.

Eisenhart, R. (1975). You can't hack it, little girl: A discussion of the covert psychological agenda of modern combat training. *Journal of Social Issues* 31(4), 13–23.

Ellenson, G. S. (1985). Detecting a history of incest: A predictive syndrome. *Social Casework: Journal of Contemporary Social Work,* 66, 525–532.

Elliott, C. & R. Gunderman. (1990). Ethics in psychiatric research. *Current Opinion in Psychiatry,* 3, 664–667.

Ende, N., S. B. Gertner & B. Socha. (1990). Unexpected changes in urinary catecholamines and vanillylmandelic acid following rape assault. *Hormones and Behavior,* 24(1), 62–70.

Engel, G. L. (1977). The need for a new medical model: A challenge for biomedicine. *Science,* 196, 129–136.

Epstein, H. (1977). Heirs of the Holocaust. *New York Times Magazine,* 14, June 19.

Epstein, S. (1991). The self concept, the traumatic neuroses, and the structure of personality. In D. Ozer, J. M. Healy, Jr., and A. J. Stewart (eds.), *Perspectives on personality,* vol. 3. Greenwich, CT: JAI Press.

———. (1989). Beliefs and symptoms in maladaptive resolutions of the traumatic neurosis. In D. Ozer, J. M. Healy & A. J. Stewart (eds.), *Perspectives on personality,* vol. 3. Greenwich, CT: JAI Press.

Erickson, M. H. (1992). Creative choice in hypnosis. In E. L. Rossi & M. O. Ryan (eds)., *The seminars, workshops and lectures of Milton H. Erickson,* vol. 4. New York: Irvington.

———. (1980a). Deep hypnosis and its induction. In E. L. Rossi (ed.), *The collected papers of Milton H. Erickson on hypnosis,* vol. 1. New York: Irvington, 139–167.

————. (1980b). Further clinical techniques of hypnosis: Utilization techniques. In E. L. Rossi (ed.), *The collected papers of Milton H. Erickson on hypnosis*, vol. 1. New York: Irvington, 177–205 (original work published 1959).

Erikson, E. H. (1968). *Identity: Youth and crisis*. New York: Norton.

Erikson, K. (1976). *Everything in its path: Destruction of community in the Buffalo Creek Flood*. New York: Simon & Schuster.

Erschak, G. M. (1984). The escalation and maintenance of spouse abuse: A cybernetic model. *Victimology*, 9, 247–253.

Everson, M. & B. James. Traumagenic impact of maltreatment rating summary. Unpublished.

Everstine, D. S. & L. Everstine. (1993). *The trauma response: Treatment for emotional injury*. New York: W. W. Norton.

Fagan, J. & P. McMahon. (1984). Incipient multiple personality in children: Four cases. *Journal of Nervous and Mental Disease* 172, 26–36.

Fairbank, J. A. & R. A. Nicholson. (1987). Theoretical and empirical issues in the treatment of post-traumatic stress disorder in Vietnam veterans. *Journal of Clinical Psychology* 43(1), 44–66.

Falcon, S., C. Ryan, K. Chamberlain & G. Curtis. (1985). Tricyclics: Possible treatment for post-traumatic stress disorder. *Journal of Clinical Psychiatry*, 46, 385–389.

Famularo, R., R. Kinscherff & T. Fenton. (1988). Propranolol treatment for childhood post-traumatic stress disorder, acute type: A pilot study. *American Journal of Diseases of Children*, 142, 1244–1247.

Farberow, N. L. & N. S. Gordon. (1979). *Training manual for human service workers in natural disasters*. Rockville, MD: National Institute of Mental Health.

Feldman, L. B. (1979). Marital conflict and marital intimacy: An integrated psychodynamic-behavioral-systemic model. *Family Process*, 18, 69–78.

Feldman, T. B. (1987). Alprazolam in the treatment of post-traumatic stress disorder. [Letter], *Journal of Clinical Psychiatry*, 48, 216–217.

Fesler, F. A. (1991). Valproate in combat-related post-traumatic stress disorder. *Journal of Clinical Psychiatry*, 52(9), 361–364.

Feuer, B. (1988). One union EAP's response to posttraumatic stress. *EAP Digest*, September/October.

————. (1987). Innovations in employee assistance programs: A case study at the association of flight attendants. In A. Riley & S. Zaccaro (eds.), *Occupational health and organizational effectiveness*. New York: Praeger Press, 217–227.

Figley, C. R. (1994). Compassion fatigue. In *Trauma counselors: Assessment, treatment, and prevention*. Charleston, SC: The Wolf at Your Doorstep, International Association of Trauma Counselors Annual Meeting.

————. (1988). Post-traumatic family therapy. In F. M. Ochberg (ed.), *Post-traumatic therapy and victims of violence*. New York: Brunner/Mazel, 83–110.

————. (1986). Traumatic stress: The role of the family and social support system. In C. R. Figley (ed.), *Trauma and its wake*, vol. 2: *Traumatic stress theory, research, and intervention*. New York: Brunner/Mazel, 39–54.

————. (1983). Catastrophe: An overview of family reactions. In C. R. Figley & H. I. McCubbin (eds.), *Stress and the family*, vol. 2: *Coping with catastrophe*. New York: Brunner/Mazel, 3–20.

————. (ed.). (1985). *Trauma and its wake: The study and treatment of post-traumatic stress disorder*. New York: Brunner/Mazel.

Figley, C.R. & Leventman, S. (eds.). (1980). *Strangers at home: Vietnam Veterans since the war*. New York: Praeger.

Figley, C. R. & D. H. Sprenkle. (1978). Delayed stress response syndrome: Family therapy implications. *Journal of Marriage and Family Counseling*, 4, 195–184.

Fine, C. (1990). Cognitive therapy with MPD. Paper presented at Eastern Regional Conference on Abuse and Multiple Personality. Training in Treatment, Alexandria, VA.

Fink, D. (1991). The comorbidity of multiple personality disorder and DSM-III-R Axis II disorders. *Psychiatric Clinics of North America*, 14(3), 547–566.

Finkelhor, D. & K. Yllo. (1983). *License to rape: Sexual violence against wives*. New York: Holt & Rinehart.

Firestone, R. W. (1989). *The fantasy bond*. New York: Human Sciences Press.

Fischman, Y. (1991). Interacting with trauma: Clinician's responses to treating psychological aftereffects of political repression. *American Journal of Orthopsychiatry*, 61, 179–185.

Fisher, C. S. (1987). *Networks and places: Social relations in the urban setting*. New York: Free Press.

Fisher, M. & G. Stricher. (eds.). (1982). *Intimacy*. New York: Plenum Press.

Flannery, R. B. (1992). *PTSD: A victim's guide to healing and recovery*. New York: Crossroad.

Foa, E., G. Steketee & B. O. Rothbaum. (1989). Behavioral/cognitive conceptualizations of post-traumatic stress disorder. *Behavior Therapy*, 20, 155–176.

Foa, E. B., B. Olasov-Rothbaum, D. S. Riggs & T. B. Murdock. (1991). Treatment of post-traumatic stress disorder in rape victims: A comparison between cognitive-behavioral procedures and counseling. *Journal of Consulting and Clinical Psychology*, 59, 715–723.

Foa, E. B., G. Steketee & B. Olasov-Rothbaum. (1989). Behavioral/cognitive conceptualization of posttraumatic stress disorder. *Behavior Therapy*, 20, 155–176.

Fogelman, E. & B. Savran. (1980). Brief group therapy with offspring of Holocaust survivors: Leader's reaction. *American Journal of Orthopsychiatry* 50, 96–108.

Foreman, C. (1990). Police stress response to a civilian aircraft disaster. In J. Reese, J. Horn, & C. Dunning (eds.), *Critical Incidents in Policing*. Washington, DC: Government Printing Office, 131–147.

Forhoud, L. & H. Zurayk. (1990). Impact of the war on the mental health of the family. Paper presented at Naim Foundation Conference on Children and Trauma, October, Washington, DC.

Foster, D. & D. Sandler. (1985). A study of detention and torture in South Africa: Preliminary report. Institute of Criminology, University of Cape Town, South Africa.

Fox, R. (1982). Enriching clinical practice. *Social Work Journal*, 10, 94–102.

Foy, D. W., S. S. Osato, B. M. Houskamp & D. A. Neumann. (1993). PTSD etiology. In P. A. Saigh (ed.), *PTSD: A behavioral approach to assessment and treatment*. New York: Pergamon Press, 28–49.

Frank, E. & B. P. Anderson. (1987). Psychiatric disorders in rape victims: Past history and current symptomatology. *Comprehensive Psychiatry*, 28, 77–82.

Frank, J. B., T. R. Kosten, E. L. Giller & E. Dan. (1988). A randomized clinical trial of phenelzine and imipramine for post-traumatic stress disorder. *American Journal of Psychiatry*, 145, 1289–1291.

Frankl, V. E. (1989). *Man's search for meaning: An introduction to logotherapy.* Boston: Beacon Press.

———. (1984). *Man's search for meaning.* Boston: Beacon Press.

———. (1969). *The will to meaning.* Cleveland: New American Library.

Frankle, H. (1978). The survivor as a parent. *Journal of Jewish Communal Services,* 54(3), 241–246.

Freud, S. (1896). The aetiology of hysteria. (J. Strachey, trans.). In J. Strachey (ed.), *The complete psychological works of Sigmund Freud,* vol. 3. London: Hogarth Press, 1962, 179–221.

Freud, S. (1957). *Introductory lectures on psychoanalysis.* New York: Liveright, 1966.

Frey-Wouters, E. & R. S. Laufer. (1986). *Legacy of a war: The American soldier in Vietnam.* Armonk, NY: M. E. Sharpe.

Frick, R. & L. Bogart. (1982). Transference and countertransference in group therapy with Vietnam veterans. *Bulletin of the Menninger Clinic,* 46, 429–444.

Friedman, J. (1990). Bringing kids home from abroad. *Washington Post,* September 18, B3.

Friedman, M. J. (1993). Psychobiology and pharmacological approaches to treatment. In J. P. Wilson & B. Raphael (eds.), *The international handbook of traumatic stress syndromes.* New York: Plenum Press, 785–794.

———. (1991). Biological approaches to the diagnosis and treatment of post-traumatic stress disorder. *Journal of Traumatic Stress,* 4(1), 67–91.

———. (1988). Towards rational pharmacotherapy for posttraumatic stress disorder. *American Journal of Psychiatry,* 145, 281–285.

———. (1981). Post-Vietnam syndrome: Recognition and management. *Psychosomatics,* 22, 931–943.

Friedman, M. J. & J. M. Jaranson. (1994). The applicability of the PTSD concept to refugees. In A. J. Marsella, T. H. Borneman & J. Orley (eds.), *In peril and pain: The mental health and well-being of the world's refugees.* Washington, DC: American Psychological Press, 207–228.

Friedman, M. J., C. K. Schneiderman, A. N. West & J. A. Corson. (1986). Measurement of combat exposure, post-traumatic stress disorder, and life stress among Vietnam combat veterans. *American Journal of Psychiatry,* 143, 537–539.

Fromuth, M. E. & B. R. Burkhart. (In press). The nature of childhood sexual abuse and its relationship with family background. *Victimology.*

Furey, J. A. (1991). Women Vietnam veterans: A comparison of studies. *Journal of Psychosocial Nursing,* 29(3), 11–13.

Gabbard, G. O. (1988). A contemporary perspective on psychoanalytically informed hospital treatment. *Hospital and Community Psychiatry,* 39, 1291–1295.

Ganley, A. (1989). Integrating feminist and social learning analyses of aggression: Creating multiple models for intervention with men who battered. In P. Caesar & L. Hamberger (eds.). Treating men who batter. New York: Springer, 196–235.

Ganley, A. (1981). *Court mandated treatment for men who batter.* Washington, DC: Center for Women Policy Studies.

Gannon, J. Patrick. (1989). *Soul survivors: A new beginning for adults abused as children.* New York: Prentice-Hall.

Garmezy, N. & M. Rutter. (eds.). (1983). *Stress, coping and development in children.* New York: McGraw-Hill.

Garrett, C. & M. Ireland. (1979). A therapeutic art session with rape victims. *American Journal of Art Therapy*, 18, 103–106.

Gass, M. A. (1991). Enhancing metaphor development in adventure therapy programs. *Journal of Experiential Education*, 14(2), 6–13.

Gelinas, D. J. (1983). The persisting negative effects of incest. *Psychiatry*, 46, 313–332.

Gellerman, W., M. S. Frankel & R. F. Ladenson. (1990). *Values and ethics in organization and human systems development: Responding to dilemmas in professional life.* San Francisco: Jossey-Bass.

Gelles, R. J. & C. P. Cornell. (1985). *Intimate violence in families.* Beverly Hills, CA: Sage.

Gerardi, R., T. M. Keane & W. Penk. (1989). Utility: Sensitivity and specificity in developing diagnostic tests of combat-related post-traumatic stress disorder. *Journal of Clinical Psychology*, 45, 691–703.

Gerlock, A. A. (1991). Vietnam: Returning to the scene of the trauma. *Journal of Psychosocial Nursing*, 29(2), 4–8.

Gersons, B.P.R. (1989). Patterns of post-traumatic stress disorder among police officers following shooting incidents; the two-dimensional model and some treatment implications. *Journal of Traumatic Stress*, 2(3), 247–257.

———. (1988). Adaptive defence mechanisms in post-traumatic stress disorders and leave-taking rituals. In O. van der Hart. *Coping with loss.* New York: Irvington Publishing, 135–149.

Getzel, G. S. & R. Masters. (1984). Serving families who survive homicide victims. *Social Casework Journal for Contemporary Social Work*, Fall, 138–144.

Gil, E. (1991a). *The healing power of play.* New York: Guilford Press.

———. (1991b). *Outgrowing the pain together: A book for partners and spouses of adults abused as children.* New York: Dell Bantam Doubleday.

———. (1988). *Treatment of adult survivors of childhood abuse.* Walnut Creek, CA: Launch Press.

Gilbert, M. (1987). *The Holocaust.* London: Collins/Fontana.

Gilligan, C. (1982). *In a different voice: Psychological theory and women's development.* Cambridge: Harvard University Press.

Gilligan, S. G. & C. E. Kennedy. (1989). Solutions and resolutions: Ericksonian hypnotherapy with incest survivor groups. *Journal of Strategic and Systemic Therapy*, 8(4), 9–17.

Gist, R. (1990). Debriefing and related activities. In G. A. Jacobs (Chair), *Flight 232: Case study of psychology's response to air disasters.* Symposium conducted at the Ninety-Eighth Annual Convention of the American Psychological Association, Boston.

Gist, R. & B. Lubin. (eds.). (1989). *Psychological aspects of disasters.* New York: Wiley.

Glover, H. (1984). Survival guilt and the Vietnam veterans. *Journal of Nervous and Mental Disease*, 172, 393–397.

Gold, E. R. (1986). Long-term effects of sexual victimization in childhood: An attributional approach. *Journal of Consulting and Clinical Psychology*, 54, 471–475.

Goldberg, J., W. R. True, S. A. Eisen & W. G. Henderson. (1991). A twin study of the effects of the Vietnam war on post-traumatic stress disorder. *Journal of the American Medical Association* 263(9), 1227–1231.

Goldfeld, A., R. F. Mollica, B. H. Pesavento & S. V. Faraone. (1988). The physical and psychological sequelae of torture. *Journal of the American Medical Association*, 259(18), 2725–2729.

Goldston, W. E. (1977). Defining primary prevention. In G. W. Albee & J. M. Joffee (eds.), *Primary prevention of psychopathology*, Vol. 1: *The issues*. Hanover, NH: University Press of New England.

Goleman, D. (1990). PTSD: Crisis can alter brain chemistry. *MADDVOCATE*, Fall, 21.

Gonzalez-Heydrich, J. & S. J. Peroutka. (1990). Serotonin receptor and reuptake sites: Pharmacologic significance. *Journal of Clinical Psychiatry*, 51, 4 (suppl.), 5–12.

Good, B. & M. Good. (1985). The cultural context of diagnosis and therapy: A view from medical anthropology. In M. Miranda & H. Kitano (eds.), *Mental health research in minority communities—development of culturally sensitive training programs*. Rockville, MD: NIMH, 8–44.

Gordon, S. (1984). PTSD and chemical dependency: Concurrent treatment. *Vet Center Voice*, 9, 9–10.

Gorelick, K. (1989). Poetry as the final common pathway of the psychotherapies: Private self, social self, self-in-the-world. *Journal of Poetry Therapy*, 3, 5–18.

Gorski, T. (1989). Relapse prevention and warning signs. Paper presented to the University of Utah School on alcoholism and other chemical dependencies, Salt Lake City, UT, June 1989.

Graber, K. (1991). *Ghosts in the bedroom: A guide for partners of incest survivors*. Deerfield Beach, FL: Health Communications.

Graham, J. R. (1990). *MMPI–2: Assessing personality and psychopathology*. New York: Oxford University Press.

Graham, D., E. Rawlings & N. Rimini. (1988). *Battered women as survivors: An alternative to treating learned helplessness*. Lexington, MA: Lexington Books.

Greeley, A. M. (1969). *Why can't they be like us?* New York: Institute of Human Relations Press.

Green, B. L. (1991). Evaluating the effects of disasters. *Psychological Assessment: A Journal of Consulting and Clinical Psychology*, 3, 538–546.

———. (1990). Defining trauma: Terminology and generic stressor dimensions. *Journal of Applied Social Psychology*, 20, 1632–1642.

Green, B. L., M. C. Grace & G. G. Gleser. (1985). Identifying survivors at risk: Long-term impairment following the Beverly Hills Supper Club fire. *Journal of Consulting and Clinical Psychology*, 53, 672–678.

Green, B., M. Grace, J. Lindy & A. Leonard. (1990). Race differences in response to combat stress. *Journal of Traumatic Stress*, 3, 379–406.

Green, B. L., J. P. Wilson & J. D. Lindy. (1985). Conceptualizing post-traumatic disorder: A psychosocial framework. In C. R. Figley (ed.), *Trauma and its wake: The study and treatment of post-traumatic stress disorder*. New York: Brunner/Mazel, 53–69.

Greenstein, R. A., I. Kitchner & K. Olsen. (1986). Post-traumatic stress disorder, partial complex seizures, and alcoholism. *American Journal of Psychiatry*, 142, 1203.

Greenwood Mortuary. (1988). *Survey of the support of the clergy at the time of the death of a loved one*. San Diego, CA: Author.

Griffin, C. (1987). Community disasters and PTSD: A debriefing model for response. In T. Williams (ed.), *Post-traumatic stress disorder: A handbook for clinicians*. Cincinnati, OH: Disabled American Veterans, 267–293.

Groves, D. & B. I. Panzer. (1989). *Resolving traumatic memories: Metaphors and symbols in psychotherapy*. New York: Irvington.

Gunderson, J. G. (1978). Defining the therapeutic processes in psychiatric milieus. *Psychiatry*, 41, 327–335.

Gutheil, T. G. (1985). The therapeutic milieu: Changing themes and theories. *Hospital and Community Psychiatry*, 36, 1279–1285.

Halbreich, U., J. Olympia, J. Glogowski, S. Carson, S. Axelrod & C. M. Yeh. (1988). The importance of past psychological trauma and pathophysiologic process as determinants of current biologic abnormalities. *Archives of General Psychiatry*, 45, 293–294.

Haley, S. A. (1985). Some of my best friends are dead. In W. E. Kelly (ed.), *Post-traumatic stress disorder and the war veteran patient*. New York: Brunner/Mazel, 54–71.

———. (1984). The Vietnam veteran and his preschool child: Child rearing as a delayed stress in combat veterans. *Journal of Contemporary Psychotherapy*, 14, 114–121.

———. (1974). When the patient reports atrocities: Specific treatment considerations in the Vietnam veteran. *Archives of General Psychiatry*, 30, 191–196.

Hamada, R. S., C. C. Chemtob, B. Sautner & R. Sato. (1988). Ethnic identity and Vietnam: A Japanese-American Vietnam veteran with PTSD. *Hawaii Medical Journal* 47, 100–109.

Hammond, K. W., R. M. Scurfield & S. C. Risse. (1993). Post-traumatic stress disorder. In D. L. Dunner (ed.), *Current psychiatric therapy*. W. B. Saunders.

Harkness, L. (1992): Transgenerational transmission of war-related trauma. In J. P. Wilson & B. Raphael (eds.), *The international handbook of traumatic stress syndromes*. New York: Plenum Press, 635–644.

Harris, C. J. (1991). A family crisis-intervention model for the treatment of post-traumatic stress reaction. *Journal of Traumatic Stress*, 4, 195–207.

———. (1986). The use and abuse of research participants: Trauma victims with post-traumatic stress disorder. Paper presented at Second Annual Meeting of the Society for Traumatic Stress Studies, Denver, CO.

Harsch, H. H. (1986). Cyproheptadine for recurrent nightmares. *American Journal of Psychiatry*, 143, 1491–1492.

Hart, B. J. (1988). Research on family violence: Identifying and answering the public policy questions. Paper presented at Harry F. Guggenheim Foundation Seminar Presentation, American Enterprise Institute for Public Policy Research, New York.

———. (1987). Ethical principles for woman abuse research. Paper presented at the Third National Family Violence Research Conference, Durham, NH.

Hartman, C. R. & A. W. Burgess. (1985). Illness and related PTSD: A cognitive-behavioral model of intervention with heart attack victims. In C. R. Figley (ed.), *Trauma and its wake*, vol. I. New York: Brunner/Mazel, 338–355.

Hartsough, D. & D. A. Myers. (1985). *Disaster work and mental health: Prevention and control of stress among workers*. Rockville, MD: National Institute of Mental Health.

Hathaway, S. R. & J. C. McKinley. (1983). *Minnesota Multiphasic Personality Inventory: Manual for administration and scoring*. New York: Psychological Corporation.

Havens, L. (1979). Explorations in the uses of language in psychotherapy: Complex empathic statements. *Psychiatry*, 42, 40–48.

Heath, C. P. (1982). *Children's reactions to death: Coping with disaster: A reference* guide for teachers: Preschool and elementary school. Santa Cruz, CA: Project Cope.

Helzer, J. E. (1984). The impact of combat and later alcohol use by Vietnam veterans. *Journal of Psychoactive Drugs*, 16, 183–191.

Helzer, J. E., L. Robins & L. McEvoy. (1987). Post-traumatic stress disorder in the general population: Findings of the Epidemiologic Catchment Area Survey. *New England Journal of Medicine*, 317, 1630–1634.

Hendin, H. & A. P. Haas. (1984). Combat adaptations of Vietnam veterans without post-traumatic stress disorders. *American Journal of Psychiatry*, 141(8), 956–960.

Herman, J. D. (1989). Sudden death and the police officer. *Issues in Comprehensive Pediatric Nursing*, 12, 327–332.

Herman, J. L. (1992). *Trauma and recovery*. New York: Basic Books.

———. (1988). Father-daughter incest. In F. M. Ochberg (ed.), *Post-traumatic therapy and victims of violence*. New York: Brunner/Mazel, 175–195.

———. (1986). Histories of violence in an outpatient population: An exploratory study. *American Journal of Orthopsychiatry*, 56, 137–141.

———. (1981). *Father-daughter incest*. Cambridge: Harvard University Press.

Herman, J. L., J. C. Perry & B. A. van der Kolk. (1989). Childhood trauma in borderline personality disorder. *American Journal of Psychiatry*, 146, 490–495.

Herman, J., D. Russell & K. Trocki. (1986). Long-term effects of incestuous abuse in childhood. *American Journal of Psychiatry*, 143(10), 1293–1296.

Herman, J. & B. van der Kolk. (1987). Traumatic antecedents of borderline personality disorder. In B. van der Kolk (ed.), *Psychological trauma*. Washington, DC: American Psychiatric Press, 111–126.

Herndon, A. D. & J. G. Law. (1986). Post-traumatic stress and the family: A multimethod approach to counseling. In C. Figley (ed.), *Trauma and its wake*, vol. 2. New York: Brunner/Mazel, 264–279.

Hierholzer, R., J. Munson, C. Peabody, and J. Rosenberg. (1992). Clinical presentation of PTSD in World War II combat veterans. *Hospital and Community Psychiatry*, 42(8), 816–820.

Higginbotham, H. N. (1979). Cultural issues in providing psychological services for foreign students in the United States. *International Journal of Intercultural Relations*, 3, 49–85.

———. (1977). Culture and the role of client expectancy in psychotherapy. In R. W. Brislin & M. Hammet (eds.), *Topics in culture learning*. Honolulu, HI: East-West Center, 107–124.

Higgitt, A. C., M. H. Lader & P. Fonagy. (1985). Clinical management of benzodiazepine dependence. *British Medical Journal*, 291, 688–690.

Hodgkinson, P. E. & M. Stewart. (1991). *Coping with catastrophe: A handbook of disaster management*. London, England: Routledge.

Hoehn-Saric, R., J. J. Frank, S. Imber, E. Nash, A. Stone & C. Battle. (1964). Systematic preparation of patients for psychotherapy. I: Effects on therapy behavior and outcome. *Journal of Psychiatric Research*, 2, 267–281.

Hoff, L. A. (1984). *People in crisis: Understanding and helping*. (2d ed.) Menlo Park, CA: Addison-Wesley.

Hoffman, L., P. D. Watson, G. Wilson & J. Montgomery. (1989). Low plasma beta-endorphin in post-traumatic stress disorder. *Australian and New Zealand Journal of Psychiatry*, 23, 269–273.

Holm, T. (1984). Intergenerational rapprochement among American Indians: A study of thirty-five veterans of the Vietnam War. *Journal of Political Military Sociology*, 12, 161–170.

Holman, F. (1989). Women veterans sail toward new awareness. *Vet Center Voice*, 10(5), 4, 10.

Holmes, T. H. & R. H. Rahe. (1967). The Social Readjustment Scale. *Journal of Psychosomatic Research*, 11, 213–218.

Horowitz, M. J. (1986). *Stress response syndromes*. (2d ed.) Northvale, NJ: Jason Aronson.

———. (1976). *Stress response syndrome*. New York: Jason Aronson.

Horowitz, M. J. & G. F. Solomon. (1978). Delayed stress syndromes in Vietnam veterans. In C. R. Figley (ed.), *Stress disorders among Vietnam veterans*. New York: Brunner/Mazel, 268–280.

Horowitz, M. J., N. Wilner & W. Alvarez. (1979). Impact of events scale: A measure of subjective stress. *Psychosomatic Medicine*, 41, 209–218.

Howard, S. (1976). The Vietnam warrior: His experience and implications for psychotherapy. *American Journal of Psychotherapy*, 30, 121–135.

Hunter, E. J. (1978). The Vietnam POW veteran: Immediate and long-term effects of captivity. In C. R. Figley (ed.), *Stress disorders among Vietnam veterans*. New York: Brunner/Mazel, 188–206.

Hyer, L., W. C. Olary, R. T. Saucer, J. Blount, W. R. Harrison & P. A. Boudewyns. (1986). Inpatient diagnosis of post-traumatic stress disorder. *Journal of Consulting and Clinical Psychology*, 54, 698–702.

Hyer, L., R. H. Scurfield, D. Smith, J. Burke, and S. Boyd (submitted). Effects of Outward Bound experiences as an adjunct to inpatient PTSD treatment of war veterans.

Hynes, A. & M. Hynes-Berry. (1986). *Bibliotherapy—The interactive process*. Boulder, CO: Westview Press.

Jacob, M. R. (1987). A pastoral response to the troubled Vietnam veteran. In T. Williams (ed.), *Post traumatic stress disorders: A handbook for clinicians*. Cincinnati, OH: Disabled American Veterans, 51–74.

Jacobson, A. & C. Herald. (1990). The relevance of child sexual abuse to adult psychiatric inpatient care. *Hospital and Community Psychiatry*, 41, 154–156.

Jacobson, A., J. E. Koehler & C. Jones-Brown. (1987). The failure of routine assessment to detect histories of assault experienced by psychiatric patients. *Hospital and Community Psychiatry*, 38, 386–389.

Jacobson, A. & B. Richardson. (1987). Assault experiences of 100 psychiatric inpatients: Evidence of the need for routine inquiry. *American Journal of Psychiatry*, 144, 908–913.

Jaffee, P., D. A. Wolfe, S. Wilson & L. Zak. (1986). Emotional and physical health problems of battered women. Canadian Journal of Psychiatry, 31(7), 625–629.

Jamal, R., M. Shaya & H. Armenian. (1986). The emergency health survey. In J. Bryce & H. Armenian (eds.), *In wartime: The state of children in Lebanon*. New York: Syracuse University Press, 11–26.

James, B. (1989). *Treating traumatized children*. New York: Macmillan.

Jampolsky, G. (1979). *Love is letting go of fear*. New York: Bantam Books.

Janoff-Bulman, R. (1992). *Shattered assumptions towards a new psychology of trauma*. New York: Free Press.

———. (1989). Assumptive worlds and the stress of traumatic events: Applications of the schema construct. *Social Cognition*, 7(2), 113–136.

Janoff-Bulman, R. (1985). Criminal vs. non-criminal victimization: Victim's reactions. *Victimology: An International Journal*, 10, 498–511.

Janoff-Bulman, R. & I. H. Frieze. (1983). A theoretical perspective for understanding reaction to victimizations. *Journal of Social Issues*, 39(2), 1–17.

Jehu, D., M. Gazan & C. Klassen. (1988). *Beyond sexual abuse: Therapy with women who were childhood victims*. Chichester, England: Wiley.

Jelinek, J. & T. Williams. (1987). Post-traumatic stress disorder and substance abuse: Treatment problems, strategies and recommendations. In T. Williams (ed.), *Post-traumatic stress disorders: A handbook for clinicians*. Cincinnati, OH: Disabled American Veterans, 103–117.

————. (1984). Post-traumatic stress disorder and substance abuse in Vietnam combat veterans: Treatment problems, strategies and recommendations. *Journal of Substance Abuse Treatment*, 1, 87–97.

Jensen, J. B., J. J. Pease, R. ten Bensel & B. D. Garfinkel. (1991). Growth hormone response patterns in sexually or physically abused boys. *Journal of the American Academy of Child and Adolescent Psychiatry*, 30(5), 784–790.

Johnson, D. (1987). The role of the creative arts therapies in the diagnosis and treatment of psychological trauma. *Arts in Psychotherapy*, 14, 7–14.

Johnson, D. & R. A. LaDue. (1990). The function of traditional healing: A cultural and community process. Paper presented at the Annual Conference of the International Society for Traumatic Stress. New Orleans, October.

Johnson, D. & J. Miller. (1990). Expressive art therapies in work with PTSD combat veterans. Paper presented at Fifth International Conference of Traumatic Stress Society, New Orleans.

Kahana, B., Z. Harel, E. Kahana & T. Rosner. (1988). Coping with extreme trauma. In J. P. Wilson, Z. Harel & B. Kahana (eds.), *Human adaptation to extreme stress: From the Holocaust to Vietnam*. New York: Plenum Press, 55–79.

Kahn, E. M. & E. M. White. (1989). Adapting milieu approaches to acute inpatient care for schizophrenic patients. *Hospital and Community Psychiatry*, 40, 609–614.

Kahn, R. J., D. M. McNair, R. S. Lipman, L. Covi, K. Rickels, R. Downing, S. Fisher & L. M. Frankenthaler. (1986). Imipramine and chlordiazepoxide in depression and anxiety disorders. *Archives of General Psychiatry*, 43, 79–85.

Kalivas, P. W. & P. Duffy. (1989). Similar effects of daily cocaine and stress on mesocortiolimbic dopamine neurotransmission in the rat. *Biological Psychiatry*, 25, 913–928.

Kardiner, A. (1941). *The traumatic neurosis of war*. Psychomatic Medicine Monograph (I–II). Washington, DC: National Research Council.

Kardiner, A. & H. Spiegel. (1947). *The traumatic neuroses of war*. New York: Paul Hoeber.

Katz, P. (1984). The psychiatrist and the minority group adolescent. *Clinical Update in Adolescent Psychiatry*, 1(22), 1–10.

Keane, P. (1977). *Sexual morality: A Catholic perspective*. New York: Doubleday.

Keane, T. M., J. M. Caddell & K. L. Taylor. (1988). Mississippi Scale for Combat-Related PTSD: Three studies in reliability and validity. *Journal of Consulting and Clinical Psychology*, 56, 85–90.

Keane, T. M., J. A. Fairbank, J. M. Caddell & R. T. Zimmering. (1989). Implosive (flooding) therapy reduces symptoms of PTSD in Vietnam combat veterans. *Behavior Therapy*, 20, 245–260.

Keane, T. M., J. A. Fairbank, J. M. Caddell, R. T. Zimmering & M. E. Bender. (1985). A behavioral approach to assessing and treating PTSD in Vietnam veterans. In C. R. Figley (ed.), *Trauma and its wake*. New York: Brunner/Mazel, 257–294.

Keane, T. M., J. A. Fairbank, J. M. Caddell, R. T. Zimmering, K. L. Taylor & C. A. Mora. (1989). Clinical evaluation of a measure to assess combat exposure. *Psychological Assessment: A Journal of Consulting and Clinical Psychology*, 1, 53–55.

Keane, T. M., R. J. Gerardi, J. A. Lyons & J. Wolfe. (1988). The interrelationship of substance abuse and post-traumatic stress disorder: Epidemiological and clinical considerations. *Recent Developments in Alcoholism*, 6, 27–48.

Keane, T. M., R. J. Gerardi, S. J. Quinn & B. T. Litz. (1992). Behavioral treatment of post-traumatic stress disorder. In S. M. Turner, K. S. Calhoun & H. E. Adams (eds.), *Handbook of clinical behavior therapy*. (2d ed.) New York: Wiley.

Keane, T. M., P. F. Malloy & J. A. Fairbank. (1984). Empirical development of an MMPI subscale for the assessment of combat-related posttraumatic stress disorder. *Journal of Consulting and Clinical Psychology*, 52, 888–891.

Keane, T. M., W. O. Scott, G. A. Chavoya, D. M. Lamparski & J. A. Fairbank. (1985). Social support in Vietnam veterans with post-traumatic stress disorder: A comparative analysis. *Journal of Consulting and Clinical Psychology*, 53, 95–102.

Keane, T. M. & J. Wolfe. (1990). Comorbidity in post-traumatic stress disorder: An analysis of community and clinical studies. *Journal of Applied Social Psychology*, 20, 1776–1788.

Keane, T. M., J. Wolfe & K. L. Taylor. (1987). Post-traumatic stress disorder: Evidence for diagnostic validity and methods of psychological assessment. *Journal of Clinical Psychology*, 43, 32–43.

Kemp, A., E. Rawlings & B. Greene. (1991). Post-traumatic stress disorder (PTSD) in battered women: A shelter sample. *Journal of Traumatic Stress*, 4(1), 137–148.

Kepner, E. (1990). *Principles of Gestalt psychology*. Research Triangle Park, NC: Fielding Institute Summer Session Psychology Workshop.

Kestenberg, J. (1989). Transposition revisited: Clinical, therapeutic, and developmental considerations. In P. Marcus & A. Rosenberg (eds.), *Healing their wounds: Psychotherapy with Holocaust survivors and their families*. New York: Praeger, 67–82.

Khamis, V. (1990). Handicaps and adjustments: Victims of the Intifada. Paper presented at the Naim Foundation Conference on Children and Trauma, Washington, DC, October.

Kiev, A. (1972). *Transcultural psychiatry*. New York: Free Press.

Kilpatrick, D. G., A. Amick & H. S. Resnick. (1990, Fall). Post traumatic stress disorder following murders and drunk driving crashes. *MADDVOCATE*, 20.

Kilpatrick, D. G., C. L. Best, L. J. Veronen, A. E. Amick & L. A. Vileponteaux. (1985). Mental health correlates of criminal victimization: A random community survey. *Journal of Consulting and Clinical Psychology*, 53, 866–873.

Kilpatrick, D. G. & H. S. Resnick. (1991). Empirical findings of criterion A: Methods for assessment of multiple stressor events leading to PTSD diagnosis. Paper presented at the meeting of the International Society for Traumatic Stress Studies, Washington, DC, October.

Kilpatrick, D. G., B. E. Saunders, A. Amick-McMullan, C. L. Best, L. J. Veronen & H. S. Resnick. (1989). Victims and crime factors associated with the development of crime-related post-traumatic stress disorder. *Behavior Therapy*, 20, 199–214.

Kilpatrick, D. G., L. J. Veronen, B. E. Saunders, C. L. Best, A. Amick-McMullan & J. Paduhovich. (1987). *The psychological impact of crime: A study of randomly surveyed crime victims.* Washington, DC: National Institute of Justice.

Kingsbury, S. J. (1988). Hypnosis in the treatment of post-traumatic stress disorder: An isomorphic intervention. *American Journal of Clinical Hypnosis*, 31(2), 81–90.

Kinzie, J. D. (1989). Therapeutic approaches to traumatized Cambodian refugees. *Journal of Traumatic Stress*, 2(1), 75–91.

Kinzie, J. D. & J. K. Boehnlein. (1989). Post-traumatic psychosis among Cambodian refugees. *Journal of Traumatic Stress*, 2, 185–198.

Kinzie, J. D., R. H. Fredrickson, B. Rath, J. Fleck & W. Karls. (1984). Post-traumatic stress disorder among survivors of Cambodian concentration camps. *American Journal of Psychiatry*, 141, 645–650.

Kinzie, J. D. & P. Leung. (1989). Clonidine in Cambodian patients with posttraumatic stress disorder. *Journal of Nervous and Mental Disease*, 177, 546–550.

Kirshner, L. A. & L. Johnston. (1982). Current status of milieu psychiatry. *General Hospital Psychiatry*, 4, 75–80.

Kitchner, I. & R. Greenstein. (1985). Low dose lithium carbonate in the treatment of post-traumatic stress disorder: Brief communication. *Military Medicine*, 150, 378–381.

Kivens, L. (1980). *Evaluation and change: Services for survivors.* Minneapolis, MN: Minneapolis Medical Research Foundation.

Kluckhohn, C. & H. Murray. (1953). Personality formation: The detriments. In C. Kluckhohn, H. Murray & D. Schneider (eds.), *Personality in nature, society, and culture.* New York: Knopf, 30–65.

Kluft, R. P. (1991a). Hospital treatment of multiple personality disorder: An overview. *Psychiatric Clinics of North America*, 14(3), 695–720.

———. (1991b). Hypnotic techniques in the treatment of MPD. Paper presented at Post-conference Course, Eastern Regional Conference on Abuse and Multiple Personality: Training in Treatment, Alexandria, VA.

———. (1989a). The rehabilitation of therapists overwhelmed by their work with MPD patients. *Dissociation*, 2(4), 243–249.

———. (ed.) (1989b). Treatment of victims of sexual abuse. *Psychiatric Clinics of North America*, 12, 2.

———. (1984a). Multiple personality in childhood. *Psychiatric Clinics of North America*, 7, 9–29.

———. (1984b). Treatment of multiple personality disorder. *Psychiatric Clinics of North America*, 7, 1, 9–30.

Kobasa, S. C. (1979). Stressful life events, personality, and health: An inquiry into hardiness. *Personality and Social Psychology* 37, 1–11.

Kofoed, L., M. Friedman & R. Peck. (1993). Alcoholism and drug abuse in patients with PTSD. *Psychiatric Quarterly*, 151–171.

Kolb, L. C. (1988). A critical survey of hypotheses regarding post-traumatic stress disorders in light of recent findings. *Journal of Traumatic Stress*, 1, 291–304.

————. (1987). A neuropsychological hypothesis explaining post-traumatic stress disorders. *American Journal of Psychiatry*, 144, 989–995.

Kolb, L. C., B. C. Burris & S. Griffiths. (1984). Propranolol and clonidine in the treatment of the chronic post-traumatic stress disorders of war. In B. A. van der Kolk (ed.), *Post-traumatic stress disorder: Psychological and biological sequelae*. Washington, DC: American Psychiatric Press, 97–105.

Kolb, L. C. & L. R. Mutalipassi. (1982). The conditioned emotional response: A subclass of the chronic and delayed post-traumatic stress disorder. *Psychiatric Annals*, 12, 979–987.

Korb, M. P., J. Gorrell & V. Van De Riet. (1989). *Gestalt therapy: Practice and theory* (2nd ed.). New York: Pergamon Press.

Kordon, D. R., L. I. Edelman, D. M. Lagos, E. Nicoletti & R. C. Bozzolo. (1988). *Psychological effects of political repression*. Buenos Aires, Argentina: Planeta Publishing Company.

Koretzky, M. B. & A. H. Peck. (1990). Validation and cross-validation of the PTSD subscale of the MMPI with civilian trauma victims. *Journal of Clinical Psychology*, 46, 296–300.

Koss, M. P. & C. A. Gidycz. (1985). Sexual experiences survey: Reliability and validity. *Journal of Consulting and Clinical Psychology*, 53, 422–423.

Kosten, T. R. & J. Krystal. (1988). Biological mechanisms in post-traumatic stress disorder: Relevance for substance abuse. *Recent Developments in Alcoholism*, 6, 49–68.

Kosten, T. R., J. W. Mason, E. L. Giller, R. B. Ostroff & L. Harkness. (1987). Sustained urinary norepinephrine and epinephrine elevation in post-traumatic stress disorder. *Psychoneuroendocrinology*, 12, 13–20.

Kosten, T. R., V. Wahby, E. L. Giller & J. Manson. (1990). The dexamethasone suppression test and thyrotropin-releasing hormone stimulation test in post-traumatic stress disorder. *Biological Psychiatry*, 28, 657–664.

Kovach, J. (1983). The relationship between treatment failures of alcoholic women and incestuous histories with possible implications for post-traumatic stress disorder symptomatology. *Dissertation Abstracts International*, 44, 710A.

Kraemer, H. C. (1987). The methodological and statistical evaluation of medical tests: The dexamethasone suppression test in psychiatry. *Psychoneuroendocrinology*, 12, 411–427.

Krause, N. (1987). Exploring the impact of a natural disaster on the health and psychological well-being of older adults. *Journal of Human Stress*, 13, 61–69.

Krell, R. (1982). Family therapy with children of concentration camp survivors. *American Journal of Psychotherapy*, 139, 513–522.

Kriegler, J. A. (1991). Chronic PTSD and polysubstance abuse: A relapse prevention model. Paper presented at International Society of Traumatic Stress, Washington, DC, ISTSS.

Krupnick, J. & M. J. Horowitz. (1981, April). Stress response syndromes. *Archives of General Psychiatry* 38, 428–435.

Kruskal, J. B. & M. Wish. (1978). Multidimensional scaling. Newbury Park, CA: Sage.

Krystal, H. (1988). *Integration and self-healing*. Hillsdale, NJ: The Analytic Press.

————. (ed.). (1968). *Massive psychic trauma*. New York: International Universities Press.

Krystal H. & W. G. Niederland. (1968). Clinical observations on the survivor syndrome.

In H. Krystal (ed.), *Massive psychic trauma*. New York: International Universities Press, 327–348.

Kubey, C., D. Addlestone, R. O'Dell, K. Snyder, B. Stichman & Vietnam Veterans of America. (eds.). (1985). *The Viet vet survival guide. How to cut through the bureaucracy and get what you need—and are entitled to*. New York: Ballantine Books.

Kuch, K. & B. J. Cox. (1992). Symptoms of PTSD in 124 survivors of the Holocaust. *American Journal of Psychiatry*, 149(3), 337–340.

Kudler, H., J. Davidson & K. Meador. (1987). The DST and post-traumatic stress disorder. *American Journal of Psychiatry*, 144, 1068–1071.

Kudler, H. S., J.R.T. Davidson, R. Stein & L. Erickson. (1989). Measuring results of treatment of PTSD. [Letter] *American Journal of Psychiatry*, 146, 1645–1646.

Kulka, R. A., W. E. Schlenger, J. A. Fairbank, R. L. Hough, B. K. Jordan, C. R. Marmar & D. S. Weiss. (1990). *Trauma and the Vietnam war generation: Report of findings from the National Vietnam Veterans Readjustment Study*. New York: Brunner/Mazel.

———. (1988). *National Vietnam veterans readjustment study (NVVRS): Description, current status, and initial PTSD prevalence estimates*. Washington, DC: Veterans Administration.

Kulka, R. A., W. E. Schlenger, J. A. Fairbank, B. K. Jordan, R. L. Hough, C. R. Marmar & D. S. Weiss. (1991). Assessment of post-traumatic stress disorder in the community: Prospects and pitfalls from recent studies of Vietnam veterans. *Psychological Assessment: A Journal of Consulting and Clinical Psychology*, 3, 547–560.

Kushner, M. G., K. J. Sher & B. D. Beitman. (1990). The relationship between alcohol problems and the anxiety disorders. *American Journal of Psychiatry*, 147(6), 147.

Kuznik, F. (1991, April). Fraud busters. *Washington Post Magazine*, 22–26, 31–33.

Lacoursiere, R. B., K. E. Godfrey & L. M. Ruby. (1980). Traumatic neuroses in the etiology of alcoholism: Vietnam combat and other trauma. *American Journal of Psychiatry*, 137, 966–968.

Lagomarisino, B. (1991, July). Congressional newsletter. 19th Congressional District, CA.

Laidlaw, T. A., C. Malmo & Associates (eds.). (1990). *Healing voices: Feminist approaches to therapy with women*. San Francisco: Jossey-Bass Publishers.

Lamartine, C. (1985). *Suicide prevention in educational settings. After a suicide death*. Pamphlet. Dayton, OH: Suicide Prevention Center.

Lang, P. J. (1985). The cognitive psychophysiology of emotion: Fear and anxiety. In A. H. Tuma & J. D. Maser (eds.), *Anxiety and the anxiety disorders*. Hillsdale, NJ: Lawrence Erlbaum.

Langer, L. (1991). *Holocaust testimonies, the ruins of memory*. New Haven, CT: Yale University Press.

Lankton, S. R. (1985). A state of consciousness model of Ericksonian hypnosis in S. R. Lankton (ed.), *Ericksonian monographs*, vol. 1, *Elements and dimensions of an Ericksonian approach*. New York: Brunner/Mazel, 26–41.

———. (1980). *Practical magic*. Cupertino, CA: Meta Publications.

Lankton, C. & S. Lankton. (1986). *Enchantment and intervention in family therapy: Training in Ericksonian approaches*. New York: Brunner/Mazel.

Lankton, S. R. & C. Lankton. (1983). *The answer within: A clinical framework of Ericksonian hypnotherapy.* New York: Brunner/Mazel.

Laufer, R. S. (1988). The serial self: War trauma, identity and adult development. In J. P. Wilson, Z. Harel & B. Kahana (eds.), *Human adaptation to extreme stress: From the Holocaust to Vietnam.* New York: Plenum Press, 33–53.

Laufer, R. S., E. Frey-Wouters & M. S. Gallops. (1985). Traumatic stressors in the Vietnam War and post-traumatic stress disorder. In C. R. Figley (ed.), *Trauma and its wake: The study and treatment of post-traumatic stress disorder.* New York: Brunner/Mazel, 73–90.

Laufer, R. S., M. Gallops & E. Frey-Wouters. (1984). War and stress trauma: The Vietnam veteran experience. *Journal of health and Social Behavior,* 25, 65–85.

Lawson, B. Z. (1989). The trauma of helping: Management responses to traumatic reactions in human service workers. Paper presented at the meeting of the NASW Conference, San Francisco.

————. (1987). Work-related post-traumatic stress reactions: The hidden dimension. *Health and Social Work,* 12(4), 250–258.

Lazarus, R. S. & S. Folkman. (1984). *Stress, appraisal, and coping.* New York: Springer.

Lee, E. & F. Lu. (1989). Assessment and treatment of Asian-American survivors of mass violence. *Journal of Traumatic Stress Studies,* 2(1), 93–120.

Leedy, J. (1969). *Poetry therapy.* Philadelphia: Lippincott.

Leeman, C. P. (1986). The therapeutic milieu and its role in clinical management. In L. I. Sederer (ed.), *Inpatient psychiatry.* Baltimore: Williams & Wilkins.

Leeman, C. P., L. I. Sederer, J. Rogogg, H. S. Berger & J. Merrifield. (1981). Should general hospitals accept involuntary psychiatric patients? *General Hospital Psychiatry,* 3, 245–253.

Lehman, D. R., C. B. Wortman & A. F. Williams. (1990, Fall). Long-term effects of losing a spouse or child in a motor vehicle crash. *MADDVOCATE,* 13.

Lerer, B., A. Bleich, E. R. Bennett, R. P. Ebstein & J. Balkin. (1990). Platelet adenylate cyclase and phospholipase C activity in post-traumatic stress disorder. In M. E. Wolf & A. D. Mosnaim (eds.), *Post-traumatic stress disorder: Etiology, phenomenology, and treatment.* Washington, DC: American Psychiatric Press.

Lerer, B., A. Bleich, M. Kotler, R. Garb, M. Herzberg & B. Levin. (1987). Post-traumatic stress disorder in Israeli combat veterans. *Archives of General Psychiatry,* 44, 976–981.

Lerner, A. (1978). *Poetry in the therapeutic experience.* New York: Pergamon Press.

Levi, P. (1965). *The reawakening.* New York: Macmillan.

Levy, L. (1982). Mutual support groups in Great Britain. *Social Science Medicine,* 16, 1265–1275.

Lifton, R. J. (1988). Understanding the traumatized self: Imagery, symbolization, and transformation. In J. P. Wilson, Z. Harel & B. Kahana (eds.), *Human adaptation to extreme stress: From the Holocaust to Vietnam.* New York: Plenum Press, 7–31.

————. (1979). *The broken connection: On death and the continuity of life.* New York: Simon & Schuster.

————. (1978). Advocacy and corruption in the healing professions. In C. R. Figley (ed.), *Stress disorders among Vietnam veterans.* New York: Brunner/Mazel, 209–230.

————. (1973). *Home from the war: Vietnam veterans: Neither victims nor executioners*. New York: Simon & Schuster.

————. (1967). *Death in life: Survivors of Hiroshima*. New York: Simon & Schuster.

Lindberg, F. H. & L. J. Distad. (1985). PTSD in women who experienced childhood incest. *Child Abuse and Neglect*, 9(3), 329–334.

Lindemann, E. (1944). Symptomatology and management of acute grief. *American Journal of Psychiatry*, 101, 141–148.

Lindy, J. (1988). *Vietnam: A casebook*. New York: Brunner/Mazel.

————. (1986). An outline for the psychoanalytic psychotherapy of post-traumatic stress disorder. In C. R. Figley (ed.), *Trauma and its wake*, vol. 2. New York: Brunner/Mazel, 195–212.

Lindy, J. & M. Grace. (1985). The recovery environment: Continuing stressor versus a healing psychosocial space. In B. J. Sowder (ed.), *Disasters and mental health: Selected contemporary perspectives*. Rockville, MD: National Institutes of Mental Health, 137–149.

Lindy, J. D., B. L. Green, M. Grace, J. McLeon & L. Spitz. (1987). *Vietnam: A casebook*. New York: Brunner/Mazel.

Lindy, J. D. & J. L. Titchener. (1983). Acts of God and man: Long-term character change in survivors of disasters and the law. *Behavioral Sciences Law*, 1, 85–96.

Lipper, S., J.R.T. Davidson, T. A. Grady, J. D. Edingar, E. B. Hammett, S. L. Mahorney & J. O. Cavenar. (1988). Preliminary study of carbamazepine in post-traumatic stress disorder. *Psychosomatics*, 27, 849–854.

Lira, E., D. Becker & M. I. Castillo. (1988). Psychotherapy with victims of political repression in Chile: A therapeutic and political challenge. Paper presented at the meeting of the Latin American Institute of Mental Health and Human Rights, Santiago, Chile.

Little, M. (1957). The analyst's total response to the patient's needs. *International Journal of Psycho-Analysis*, 38, 240–254.

Litz, B. T., D. D. Blake, R. G. Gerardi & T. M. Keane. (1990). Decision-making guidelines for the use of direct therapeutic exposure in the treatment of post-traumatic stress disorder. *Behavior Therapy*, 13(4), 91–93.

Litz, B. T., T. M. Keane, L. Fisher, B. Marx & V. Monaco. (1992). Physical health complaints in combat-related post-traumatic stress disorder: A preliminary report. *Journal of Traumatic Stress*, 5, 131–141.

Litz, B. T., W. E. Penk, R. Gerardi & T. M. Keane. (In press). Behavioral assessment of PTSD. In P. Saigh (ed.), *Post-traumatic stress disorder: A behavioral approach to assessment and treatment*. New York: Pergamon Press, 50–84.

Litz, B. T., W. E. Penk, S. Walsh, L. Hyer, D. D. Blake, B. Marx, T. M. Keane & D. Bitman. (1991). Similarities and differences between Minnesota Multiphasic Personality Inventory (MMPI) and MMPI–2 applications to the assessment of post-traumatic stress disorder. *Journal of Personality Assessments* 57, 238–253.

Loeb, V. (1990). Making peace with the war. *Inquirer*, May 27, 10–17, 31.

Long, R. P., P. Wine, W. Penk, T. Keane, D. Chew, C. Gerstein, J. O'Neill & T. Nadelson. (1989). Chronicity: Adjustment differences of Vietnam combat veterans differing in rates of psychiatric hospitalization. *Journal of Clinical Psychology*, 45(5), 745–753.

Lord, F. & M. Novick. (1967). *Statistical theories of mental test scores.* Reading, MA: Addison Wesley.

Lyons, J. A. (1991). Strategies for assessing the potential for positive adjustment following trauma. *Journal of Traumatic Stress Studies,* 4(1), 93–112.

Lyons, J. A. & T. M. Keane. (1992). Keane PTSD scale: MMPI and MMPI–2 update. *Journal of Traumatic Stress,* 5, 111–117.

Lystad, M. (ed.). (1988). *Mental health response to mass emergencies, theory and practice.* New York: Brunner/Mazel.

Mac Ian, P. S. & L. A. Pearlman. (1992). Development and use of the TSI Life Event Questionnaire. *Treating abuse today: The International Newsjournal of Abuse, Survivorship and Therapy,* 2(1), 9–11.

Macksoud, M. S. (1989). The war traumas of Lebanese children. Paper presented at the Naim Foundation Conference on Children's Trauma, Washington, DC, October.

Mahan, C. K., R. L. Schreiner & M. Green. (1983). Bibliotherapy: a tool to help parents mourn their infant's death. *Health Social Work,* 8(2), 126–32.

Mahedy, W. (1986). *Out of the night: The spiritual journey of Vietnam vets.* New York: Ballantine.

Mahjoub, A. (1990). Approche psycholosociale des traumatismes de guerre des enfants et adolescents Palestines. Louvain-la-Neuve: Université Catholique de Louvain.

Main, T. F. (1957). The ailment. *British Journal of Medical Psychology,* 30, 129–145.

Major, E. F. (May 1991). The effects of the Holocaust on the second generation: A Norwegian study. *WISMIC Newsletter,* Oslo, Norway.

Malan, D. H. (1979). *Individual psychotherapy and the science of psychodynamics.* London: Butterworth.

Malchiodi, C. (1990). *Breaking the silence: Art therapy with children from violent homes.* New York: Brunner/Mazel.

Malloy, P. F., J. A. Fairbank & T. M. Keane. (1983). Validation of a multimethod assessment of post-traumatic stress disorders in Vietnam veterans. *Journal of Consulting and Clinical Psychology,* 51, 488–494.

Maltz, W. (1991). *The sexual healing journey: A guide for survivors of sexual abuse.* New York: HarperCollins.

Manson, E. C. (1989). *Critical incident stress debriefing team training manual.* Culpeper, VA: Virginia CISD Team Training.

Marcus, R. & J. Katz. (1990). Inpatient care of the substance-abusing patient with a concomitant eating disorder. *Hospital and Community Psychiatry,* 41, 59–62.

Margo, G. M. & J. M. Manring. (1989). The current literature on inpatient psychotherapy. *Hospital and Community Psychiatry,* 40, 909–915.

Marin, P. (1981). Living in moral pain. *Psychology Today,* 6, 68–80.

Marmar, C. R. & M. Freeman. (1988). Brief dynamic psychotherapy of post-traumatic stress disorders: Management of narcissistic regression. *Journal of Traumatic Stress,* 1(3), 323–337.

Marmor, J. (1983). Systems thinking in psychiatry: Some theoretical and clinical implications. *American Journal of Psychiatry,* 140, 833–838.

Marsella, A. & P. Pederson. (1981). *Cross-cultural counseling and psychotherapy.* New York: Pergamon Press.

Marsella, A. J., C. M. Chemtob & R. Hamada. (1990). Ethnocultural aspects of PTSD in Vietnam War veterans. *NCP,* a clinical newsletter of the National Center for Post-Traumatic Stress Disorder, U.S. Department of Veterans Affairs, 1(2), 1, 3, 4.

Maslow, A. H. (1970). *Motivation and personality*. New York: Harper & Row.

———. (1954). *Motivation and personality*. New York: Harper & Row.

Mason, J. W., E. L. Giller, T. R. Kosten, R. Ostroff & L. Harkness. (1986). Urinary free-cortisol in post-traumatic stress disorder. *Journal of Nervous and Mental Diseases*, 174, 145–149.

Mason, J. W., E. L. Giller, T. R. Kosten & V. S. Wahby. (1990). Serum testosterone levels in post-traumatic stress disorder inpatients. *Journal of Traumatic Stress*, 3, 449–457.

Mason, J. W., T. R. Kosten, S. M. Southwick & E. L. Giller. (1990). The use of psychoendocrine strategies in post-traumatic stress disorder. *Journal of Applied Social Psychology*, 20 (21 [pt 1]), 1822–1846.

Mason, P. (1990). *Recovering from the war: A woman's guide to helping your Vietnam vet, your family and yourself*. New York: Penguin Books.

Matsakis, A. (1992). *I can't get overt: A handbook for trauma survivors*. Oakland, CA: New Harbinger.

Matsakis, A. (1990). *When the bough breaks: A helping guide for parents of sexually abused children*. Oakland, CA: New Harbinger.

———. (1989a). Dual trauma couples. *Vet Center Voice*, 10(6), 3–5.

———. (1989b). Triple and quadruple trauma couples. *Vet Center Voice*, 10(7), 11–13.

———. (1988). *Vietnam wives*. Kensington, MD: Woodbine House.

Matsuoka, J., B. Coalson, D. Duenas, K. Bealer, I. Orloff, B. Brown, B. Kilauano, R. Hamada and R. Torigoe. (1991). Asian-Pacific American Vietnam veterans: A study of war-time experiences and post-war adjustment. Unpublished manuscript. Available from the first author, School of Social Work, University of Hawaii. Honolulu, HI.

Mazza, N., C. Magaz & J. Scaturo. (1987). Poetry therapy with abused children. *Arts in Psychotherapy*, 14, 85–92.

McCann, L. & L. A. Pearlman. (1990a). Constructivist self-development theory as a framework for assessing and treating victims of family violence. In S. Stith, M. B. Williams & K. Rosen (eds.), *Violence hits home: Sourcebook for the treatment of family violence*. New York: Springer, 305–329.

———. (1990b). *Psychological trauma and the adult survivor: Theory, therapy and transformation*. New York: Brunner/Mazel.

———. (1990c). Vicarious traumatization: A framework for understanding the psychological effects of working with victims. *Journal of Traumatic Stress*, 3(1), 131–149.

McCann, I. L., D. K. Sakheim & D. J. Abrahamson. (1988). Trauma and victimization: A model of psychological adaptation. *The Counseling Psychologist*, 16(4), 531–594.

McCollum, A. (1990). *The trauma of moving*. Newbury Park, CA: Sage.

McCormack, N. A. (1988). Substance abuse among Vietnam veterans: A view from the CAP control perspective. *International Journal of the Habituations*, 23(12), 1311–1316.

McCubbin, H. I. & J. M. Patterson. (1983). Family transitions: Adaptations to stress. In H. I. McCubbin & C. R. Figley (eds.), *Stress and the family*, vol. 1, *Coping with normative transitions*. New York: Brunner/Mazel, 5–25.

McDougle, C., S. Southwick, R. St. James & D. Charney. (1990). An open trial of fluoxetine. *PTSD Research Quarterly*, 1(2), 7.

McFall, M. E., M. Murburg, D. K. Roszell & R. C. Veith. (1989). Psychophysiologic and neuroendocrine findings in post-traumatic stress disorder: A review of theory and research. *Journal of Anxiety Disorders*, 3, 243–257.

McFall, M. E., M. M. Murburg, G. N. Ko & R. C. Veith. (1990). Autonomic responses to stress in Vietnam combat veterans with post-traumatic stress disorder. *Biological Psychiatry*, 27(10), 1165–1175.

McFall, M. E., D. E. Smith, D. K. Roszell, D. J. Tarver & K. L. Malas. (1990). Convergent validity of measures of PTSD in Vietnam combat veterans. *American Journal of Psychiatry*, 147, 645–648.

McFarlane, A. (1992). Avoidance and intrusion in post-traumatic stress disorder. *Journal of Nervous and Mental Disease*, 180(7), 439–445.

———. (1989). The treatment of post-traumatic stress disorder. *British Journal of Medical Psychology*, 62, 81–90.

———. (1988). The aetiology of post-traumatic stress disorders following a natural disaster. *British Journal of Psychiatry*, 152, 116–121.

———. (1984). The Ash Wednesday bushfires in South Australia: Implications for planning for future post-disaster services. *Medical Journal of Australia*, September, 286–291.

McGoldrick, M. & R. Gerson. (1985). *Genograms in family assessment*. New York: W. W. Norton.

McKay, M., P. Rogers & J. McKay. (1989). *When anger hurts: Quieting the storm within*. Oakland, CA: New Harbinger.

McMahon, E. (1986). Creative self-mothering. In B. Zilbergeld, M. G. Edelstein & D. L. Araoz (eds.), *Hypnosis questions and answers*. New York: Norton, 150–154.

McNamara, J. O., D. W. Bonhaus, C. Shin, B. J. Crain, R. L. Gellman & J. L. Giacchino. (1985). The kindling model of epilepsy: A critical review. *Critical Reviews of Clinical Neurobiology*, 1, 341–391.

McNiff, S. (1981). *The arts and psychotherapy*. Springfield, IL: Charles Thomas.

Meadow, A. (1982). Psychopathology, psychotherapy, and the Mexican-American patient. In E. E. Jones & S. J. Korchin (eds.), *Minority mental health*. New York: Praeger, 351–361.

Mechanic, D. (1986). The concept of illness behavior: Culture, situation and personal predisposition. *Psychological Medicine*, 16, 1–7.

Medina, J. H., M. L. Novas, C.N.V. Wolfman, M. Levi De Stein & E. DeRobertis. (1983). Benzodiazepine receptors in rat cerebral cortex and hippocampus undergo rapid and reversible changes after acute stress. *Neuroscience*, 9, 331–335.

Meichenbaum, D. (1977). *Cognitive behavior modification*. New York: Plenum.

Meiselman, K. C. (1990). *Resolving the trauma of incest: Reintegration therapy with survivors*. San Francisco: Jossey-Bass.

Meissner, W. W. & A. M. Nicholi. (1980). The psychotherapies: Individual, family, and group. In A. M. Nicholi (ed.), *The Harvard guide to modern psychiatry*. Cambridge, MA: Belknap Press.

Meleis, A. (1981). The Arab-American in the health care system. *American Journal of Nursing*, 81, 1180–1183.

Meleis, A. & A. Jonsen. (1983). Ethical crises and cultural differences. *Western Journal of Medicine*, 138, 889–893.

Meleis, A. & C. LeFever. (1984). The Arab-American. *Perspectives in Psychiatric Care*, 22, 72–86.

Meleis, A. & L. Sorrell. (1981). Arab-American women and their birth experiences. *American Journal of Maternal Child Nursing*, 6, 171–176.

Menninger, K. (1963). *The vital balance*. New York: Viking Press.

Meyer, C. (1987). Stress: There's no place like a first home. *Family Relations*, 36, 198–203.

Milgram, N., Y. Toubiana, A. Klingmqan, A. Raviv & I. Goldstein. (1988). Situational exposure and personal loss in children's acute and chronic stress reactions to a school bus disaster. *Journal of Traumatic Stress*, 1, 339–352.

Miller, A. (1984). *Thou shalt not be aware*. New York: Farrar, Straus, Giroux.

Miller, J. B. (1976). *Toward a new psychology of women*. Boston: Beacon Press.

Miller, S., D. Wackman, E. Nunnally & P. Miller. (1989). *Connecting: Instructor's manual*. Littleton, CO: Interpersonal Communication Programs.

Miller, W. R. & M. DePilato. (1983). Treatment of nightmares via relaxation and desensitization: A controlled evaluation. *Journal of Consulting and Clinical Psychology*, 51, 870–877.

Minuchin, S. (1974). *Families and family therapy*. Cambridge: Harvard University Press.

Mitchell, J. T. (1988). The history, status and future of critical incident stress debriefings. *Journal of Emergency Medical Services*, 13(11), 49–52.

———. (1983). When disaster strikes: The critical incident. Stress debriefing process. *Journal of Emergency Medical Services*, 8(1), 36–39.

Mitchell, R. E. & E. J. Trickett. (1980). Task force report: Social networks as mediators of social support: An analysis of the effects and determinants of social networks. *Community Mental Health Journal*, 16, 27–44.

Mize, E. (1975). A mother mourns and grows. In E. Kübler-Ross (ed.), *Death: The final stage of growth*. Englewood Cliffs, NJ: Prentice-Hall, 97–104.

Model mugging. (1990). Descriptive pamphlet.

Mollica, R. F. (1988). The trauma story: The psychiatric care of refugee survivors of violence and torture. In F. M. Ochberg (ed.), *Post-traumatic therapy and victims of violence*. New York: Brunner/Mazel, 295–314.

Moreno, Joseph, J. (1991). Musical psychodrama in Naples. *The Arts in Psychotherapy*, 18, 331–339.

Morita, K., M. Okamoto, K. Seki & J. A. Wada. (1985). Suppression of amygdala-kindled seizures in cats by enhanced GABAergic transmission in the substantial innominata. *Experimental Neurology*, 89, 225–236.

Morrison, J. (1989). Childhood sexual histories of women with somatization disorder. *American Journal of Psychiatry*, 146, 239–241.

Moss, R. (1981). *The I that is we*. Millbrae, CA: Celestial Arts.

Mothers Against Drunk Driving. (1991). *A 1991 summary of statistics: The impaired driving problem*. Dallas, TX: Author.

Mowbray, C. (1988). Post-traumatic therapy for children who are victims of violence. In F. M. Ochberg (ed.), *Post-traumatic therapy and victims of violence*. New York: Brunner/Mazel, 196–212.

Mueser, K. T. & R. W. Butler. (1987). Auditory hallucinations in combat-related chronic post-traumatic stress disorder. *American Journal of Psychiatry*, 144, 299–302.

Munro, R. H. (1989). A therapeutic return: Former U.S. soldiers go back to Vietnam to help build a clinic. *Time*, April 24, 43.

Muss, D. (1991). *The trauma trap*. London: Doubleday.

Mutter, C. B. (1986). Posttraumatic stress disorder: Hypnotherapeutic approach in a most unusual case. *American Journal of Clinical Hypnosis*, 30(2), 81–86.

Nadler, L. (1984). *The handbook of human resource development*. New York: John Wiley & Sons.

National Mental Health Association. (1991). *Helping children in grief: A fact sheet*. Washington, DC: Author.

National Organization for Victim Assistance. Network Information Bulletin. (1985). *Survivors of homicide victims*. Washington, DC: Author.

Neff, A. (1988). *The Arab-Americans*. New York: Chelsea House.

Ness, R. (1985). The Old Hag phenomenon as sleep paralysis: A biocultural interpretation. In R. C. Simmons & C. Hughes (eds.), *The culture-bound syndromes*. Dordrecht: Reidl, 60–82.

Newberry, T. B. (1985). Levels of countertransference toward Vietnam veterans with posttraumatic stress disorder. *Bulletin of the Menninger Clinic*, 49, 151–160.

NiCarthy, G., K. Merriam & S. Coffman. (1984). Talking it out: A guide to groups for abused women. Seattle: Seal Press.

Niles, D. (1989). Relationships between combat experiences, post-traumatic stress disorder symptoms and alcohol abuse among active duty Vietnam veterans, George Washington University, 1988, 203 pp., *Dissertation Abstracts International*, 9(7).

Nolan, Paul. (1989). Music therapy, improvisation techniques with bulimic patients. In Lynn M. Hornyak & Ellen K. Baker (eds.), *Experiential therapies for eating disorders*. New York: Guilford Press, 167–187.

Norman, E. M. (1988). Post-traumatic stress disorder in military nurses who served in Vietnam during the war years: 1965–1973. *Military Medicine*, 153, 238–242.

Noyes, R., J. Clancy, W. H. Coryell, R. R. Crowe, D. R. Chaudhry & D. V. Domingo. (1985). A withdrawal syndrome after abrupt discontinuation of alprazolam. *American Journal of Psychiatry*, 142, 114–116.

Oboler, S. (1987). American prisoners of war—An overview. In T. Williams (ed.), *Post-traumatic stress disorders: A handbook for clinicians*. Cincinnati: Disabled American Veterans, 131–144.

Ochberg, F. (1988). *Post-traumatic therapy and victims of violence*. New York: Brunner/ Mazel.

Olivera, A. A. & D. Fero. (1990). Affective disorders, DST, and treatment in PTSD patients: Clinical observations. *Journal of Traumatic Stress*, 3(3), 407–414.

Orne, M. T. (1969). Demand characteristics and the concept of quasi controls. In R. Rosenthal & R. L. Rosnow (eds.), *Artifacts in behavioral research*. New York: Academic Press.

Ornitz, E. M. & R. S. Pynoos. (1989). Startle modulation in children with post-traumatic stress disorder. *American Journal of Psychiatry*, 146, 866–870.

Ostrov, E.J.D. (1986). Police/law enforcement and psychology. *Behavioral Sciences & the Law*, 4(4), 353–370.

Ott, J. (1985). Women Viet Nam veterans. In S. Sonnenberg, A. S. Blank & J. Talbott (eds.), *The trauma of war: Stress and recovery in Viet Nam veterans*. Washington, DC: American Psychiatric Press, 309–320.

Paige, S., G. Reid, M. Allen & J. Newton. (1990). Psychophysiological correlates of PTSD. *Biological Psychiatry*, 27(4), 419–430.

Paivio, A. (1986). *Mental representations: A dual coding approach*. New York: Oxford University Press.

Pallmeyer, T. P., E. B. Blanchard & L. C. Kolb. (1985). The psychophysiology of combat-induced post-traumatic stress disorder in Vietnam veterans. *Behavioral Research and Therapy*, 24, 645–652.

Palmer, S. & M. Harris. (1983). Supportive therapy for women partners of Vietnam veterans. *Family therapist*, (4)2, 3–11.

Panos, P. T., A. Panos & G. H. Allred. (1990). The need for marriage therapy in the treatment of multiple personality disorder. Dissociation, III, 10–14.

Pardeck, J. T. (1991). Using books to prevent and treat adolescent chemical dependency. *Journal of Adolescence*, 26(101), 201–208.

Pardeck, J. & J. Pardeck. (1984). Treating abused children through bibliotherapy. *Early Child Development and Care*, 16, 195–204.

Parente, Alice Ball. (1989). Music as a therapeutic tool in treating anorexia nervosa. In Lynn M. Hornyak & Ellen K. Baker (eds.), *Experiential therapies for eating disorders*. New York: Guilford Press, 305–328.

Parkes, C. M. (1988). Bereavement as a psychosocial transition: Processes of adaptation to change. *Journal of Social Issues*, 44, 53–65.

Parson, E. R. (In press). Intercultural communication: Black veterans in war stress therapy: Part II. Culture, symptoms, and phases of war stress therapy. *The Black American*.

———. (1991). Post-traumatic psychocultural therapy (PTpsyCT): Integration of trauma and the social shattering labels of the self. *Journal of Contemporary Psychotherapy*, 20, 237–258.

———. (1990). Agent Orange stress response syndrome: Recognition and management. In P. Atwood (ed.), *Agent Orange: Medical, scientific, legal, political, and psychological aspects*. Boston: William Joiner Center, University of Massachusetts, 72–82.

———. (1989). Healing in the refugee community: Lessons learned from the Vietnam veteran experience. Paper presented at a Symposium of the William Joiner Center for the Study of War and Social Consequences, University of Massachusetts, Boston.

———. (1988a). Post-traumatic self disorders: Theoretical and practical considerations in psychotherapy of Vietnam war veterans. In J. P. Wilson, Z. Harel & B. Kahana (eds.), *Human adaptation to extreme stress: From the Holocaust to Vietnam*. New York: Plenum Press, 245–284.

———. (1988b). The unconscious history of Vietnam in the group: An innovative multiphasic model for working through authority transferences in guilt-driven veterans. *International Journal of Group Psychotherapy*, 38, 275–301.

———. (1985a). *The black Vietnam veteran: His representational world in post-traumatic stress disorder and the war veteran patient*. New York: Brunner/Mazel, 314–337.

———. (1985b). Ethnicity and traumatic stress: The intersecting point in psychotherapy. In C. R. Figley (ed.), *Trauma and its wake: The study and treatment of post-traumatic stress disorder*. New York: Brunner/Mazel.

———. (1985c). The intercultural setting: Encountering black Vietnam veterans. In S. Sonnenberg, A. S. Blank & T. Talbott (eds.), *The trauma of war: Stress and recovery in Vietnam veterans*. Washington, DC: American Psychiatric Press, 361–387.

————. (1985d). *Vietnam veterans: The road to recovery.* New York: Plenum.

————. (1984). The role of psychodynamic group therapy in the treatment of the combat veteran. In H. J. Schwartz (ed.), *Psychotherapy of the combat veteran.* New York: SP Medical and Scientific Books, 153–220.

Paul, E. A. (1985). Wounded healers: A summary of the Vietnam Nurse Veteran Project. *Military Medicine,* 150, 571–576.

Payton, J. B. & M. Krocker-Tuskan. (1988). Children's reactions to loss of parent through violence. *Journal of American Academy of Child and Adolescent Psychiatry,* 27, 563–566.

Pearlman, L. A. & Mac Ian, P. S. (In preparation). *Vicarious traumatization among trauma therapists: Empirical findings.*

Pearlman, L. A., P. S. Mac Ian, G. Johnson, & K. Mas. (1992). Understanding cognitive schemas across groups: Empirical findings and their implications. Presentation at the Eighth Annual Meeting of the International Society for Traumatic Stress Studies, Los Angeles, CA.

Pearlman, L. A. & K. W. Saakvitne. (In preparation). *Trauma and the therapist: Countertransference and vicarious traumatization in psychotherapy with adult incest survivors.* New York: W. W. Norton.

Pedersen, P. (1988). *A handbook for developing multi-cultural awareness.* Alexandria, VA: American Association for Counseling and Development.

Pena, G. (1985). Diagnosis and treatment of post-traumatic stress disorder in Hispanic Vietnam veterans. In S. Sonnenberg, A. Blank & J. Talbott (eds.), *The trauma of war: Stress and recovery from Vietnam.* Washington, DC: American Psychiatric Press, 389–402.

Pence, E. & M. Paymar. (1986). *Power and control: Tactics of men who batter: An educational curriculum.* Duluth: Minnesota Program Development, Inc.

Penk, W. (1986). Researcher investigates trauma and substance abuse. *Vet Center Voice,* 7(9), 5.

Penk, W. & I. Allen. (1991). Clinical assessment of post-traumatic stress disorder (PTSD) among American minorities who served in Vietnam. *Journal of Traumatic Stress,* 4, 41–66.

Penk, W. E., T. M. Keane, R. Rabinowitz, D. R. Fowler, W. E. Bell & A. Finkelstein. (1988). Post-traumatic stress disorder. In R. Greene (ed.), *The MMPI: Use with specific populations.* New York: Grune & Stratton, 193–213.

Penk, W., R. Rabinowitz, J. Black, M. Dolan, W. E. Bell, W. Roberts & J. Skinner. (1989). Co-morbidity: Lessons learned about post-traumatic stress disorder (PTSD) from developing PTSD scales for the MMPI. *Journal of Clinical Psychology,* 45, 709–717.

Penk, W. E., R. Robinowitz, W. R. Roberts, E. T. Paterson, M. P. Dolan & H. G. Atkins. (1981). Adjustment differences among male substance abusers varying in degree of combat experience in Vietnam. *Journal of Consulting and Clinical Psychology,* 49, 426–437.

Perls, F. S. (1973). *The Gestalt approach.* Palo Alto, CA: Science and Behavior Books.

Perry, B. D., S. M. Southwick, R. Yehuda & E. L. Giller. (1990). Adrenergic receptor regulation in posttraumatic stress disorder. In E. Giller (ed.), *Biological assessment and treatment of post-traumatic stress disorder.* Washington, DC: American Psychiatric Press, 87–114.

Perry, S. W., D. F. Cella, J. Falkenberg, G. Heidrich & C. Goodwin. (1987). Pain perception in burn patients with stress disorders. *Journal of Pain and Symptom Management*, 2, 29–33.

Peters, J. J. (1976). Children who are victims of sexual assault and the psychology of offenders. *American Journal of Psychotherapy*, 30, 398–421.

Peterson, C., M. Prout & R. Schwarz. (1991). *Post-traumatic stress disorder: A clinician's guidebook*. New York: Plenum Press.

Phillips, R. D. (1978). Impact of Nazi Holocaust on children of survivors. *American Journal of Psychotherapy*, 32, 370–378.

Piaget, J. (1970). *Structuralism*. New York: Basic Books.

———. (1969). *The theory of stages in cognitive development: An introduction*. Englewood Cliffs, NJ: Prentice-Hall.

Pichot, J. (1991). Preventive mental health in disaster situations: Terror on the autobahn. *Military Medicine*, 156(10), 540–543.

Pina, G. (1985). Hispanic Vietnam veterans. In S. Sonnenberg, A. S. Blank & J. Talbott. (eds.), *The trauma of war: Stress and recovery in Vietnam veterans*. Washington, DC: American Psychiatric Press, 389–402.

Piper, O. (1960). *The biblical view of sex and marriage*. New York: Scribner.

Pitman, R. K., S. P. Orr, D. F. Forgue, J. B. de Jong & J. M. Clairborn. (1987). Psychophysiologic assessment of post-traumatic stress disorder imagery in Vietnam combat veterans. *Archives of General Psychiatry*, 44, 970–975.

Pitman, R. K., B. A. van der Kolk, S. P. Orr & M. S. Greenberg. (1990). Naloxone-reversible analgesic response to combat-related stimuli in posttraumatic stress disorder. A pilot study. *Archives of General Psychiatry*, 47(6), 541–544.

Post, R. M. & R. T. Kopanda. (1976). Cocaine, kindling and psychosis. *American Journal of Psychiatry*, 133, 627–634.

Progoff, I. (1981). Journal workshop, Dialogue House Library, New York.

Punamaki, R. (1987). Psychological stress responses of Palestinian mothers and their children in conditions of military occupation and political violence. *Quarterly Newsletter of the Laboratory of Comparative Human Cognition*, 9, 76–84.

———. (1986). Stress among women under military occupation: Women's appraisal of stressors, their coping modes, and their mental health. *International Journal of Psychology*, 21, 445–462.

Putnam, F. W. (1991). Dissociative disorders in children and adolescents: A developmental perspective. *Psychiatric Clinics of North America*, 14(3), 519–532.

———. (1989). *Diagnosis and treatment of multiple personality disorder*. New York: Guilford Press.

Pynoos, R. S. & S. Eth. (1984). The child as a witness to homicide. *Journal of Social Issues*, 40, 87–107.

Pynoos, R. & K. Nader. (1990). Children's exposure to violence and traumatic death. *Psychiatric Annals*, 20(6), 334–344.

Rakoff, V., J. J. Sigal & N. B. Epstein. (1967). Children and families of concentration camp survivors. *Canada's Mental Health*, 14, 24–26.

Ram Doss, B. (1970). *The only dance there is*. New York: Jason Aronson.

Rand, A. (1943). *The fountainhead*. New York: Bobbs-Merrill.

Rando, T. A. (1984). *Grief, dying, and death: Clinical interventions for caregivers*. Champaign, IL: Research Press.

Range, L. M. & N. Niss. (1990). Long-term bereavement from suicide, homicide, accidents, and natural deaths. *Death Studies*, 14, 423–433.

Range, L. M. & K. E. Thompson. (1987). Community responses following suicide, homicide, and other deaths: The perspective of potential comforters. *Journal of Psychology*, 12, 193–198.

Rapaport, M. H. (1987). Chronic pain and post-traumatic stress disorder. *American Journal of Psychiatry*, 144, 120.

Raphael, B. (1977). The Granville train disaster: Psychological needs and their management. *The Medical Journal of Australia*, 1(9), 303–305.

Raphael, B., T. Lundin & L. Weisaeth. (1989). A research method for the study of psychological and psychiatric aspects of disaster. *Acta Psychiatrica Scandiavica Supplementum*, 80.

Rappaport, E. A. (1968). Beyond traumatic neurosis: A psychoanalytic study of late reactions to the concentration camp trauma. *International Journal of Psycho-Analysis*, 49, 719–731.

Rappaport, L. (1965). The state of crisis: Some theoretical considerations. In H. J. Parad (ed.), Crisis intervention: Selected readings. New York: Family Services of America.

Rasmussen, O. V. (1990). *Danish Medical Bulletin*, Supplement No. 1. Copenhagen, Denmark, 1–48.

Rasmussen, O. V. & Lunde. (1980). Evaluation of investigation of 200 torture victims. *Danish Medical Bulletin*, 27, 421–423.

Ravaris, C. L., M. J. Friedman, P. J. Hauri & G. J. McHugo. (1991). A controlled study of alprazolam and propranolol in panic-disordered and agoraphobic outpatients. *Journal of Clinical Psychopharmacology*, 11, 344–350.

Reaves, M. E., T. E. Hansen & J. M. Whisenand. (1989, May). The psychopharmacology of PTSD. *VA Practitioner*, 65–72.

Regier, D., M. Farmer & D. Rae. (1990). Comorbidity of mental disorders with alcohol and other drug abuse: Results from the epidemiologic catchment area (ECA) study. *Journal of the American Medical Association*, 19, 2511–2518.

Reid, J. & T. Strong. (1987). Torture and trauma: The health care needs of refugee victims in New South Wales. *A Report to the Western Metropolitan Health Region of the New South Wales Department of Health*. Sydney, Australia: Cumberland College of Health Sciences.

Reinberg, L. (1986). The combat survivor in the family context: Treating traumatized families. Paper presented at the Second Annual Meeting of the International Society for Traumatic Stress Studies, Denver, CO.

Reiser, S. J., H. J. Bursztajn, P. S. Appelbaum & T. G. Gutheil. (1987). *Divided staffs, divided selves: A case approach to mental health ethics*. New York: Cambridge University Press.

Reist, C., C. D. Kauffmann, R. J. Haier, C. Sangdahl, E. M. Demet, A. Chicz-Demet & J. N. Nelson. (1989). A controlled trial of desipramine in 18 men with post-traumatic stress disorder. *American Journal of Psychiatry*, 146, 513–516.

Resnick, H. S., D. G. Kilpatrick & J. A. Lipovsky. (1991). Assessment of rape-related post-traumatic stress disorder: Stressor and symptom dimensions. *Psychological Assessment: A Journal of Consulting and Clinical Psychology*, 3, 561–572.

Rheault, B. (1988). Outward Bound builds self-esteem through hard work. *Vet Center Voice*, 9(6), 7.

———. (1987). Outward Bound as an adjunct to therapy in the treatment of Vietnam veterans. In T. Williams (ed.), *Post-traumatic stress disorders: A handbook for clinicians.* Cincinnati, OH: Disabled American Veterans, 233–237.

Risse, S. C., A. Whitter, J. Burke, S. Chen, R. M. Scurfield & M. A. Raskand. (1990). Severe withdrawal symptoms after discontinuation of aprazolam in eight patients with combat-induced post-traumatic stress disorder (PTSD). *Journal of Clinical Psychiatry,* 51, 206–209.

Robbins, A. (1989). *The psychoaesthetic experience.* New York: Human Sciences Press.

Rogers, C. R. (1961). *On becoming a person.* Boston: Houghton Mifflin.

———. (1951). *Client-centered therapy.* Boston: Houghton Mifflin.

Rogler, L. (1989). The meaning of culturally sensitive research in mental health. *American Journal of Psychiatry,* 146, 296–303.

Rosal, M., M. A. Dutton-Douglas & S. Perrin. (1990). Anxiety in battered women. Paper presented at the 98th Annual Convention of the American Psychological Association, Boston.

Rose, S. L. & J. Garske. (1987). Family environment, adjustment, and coping among children of Holocaust survivors: A comparative investigation. *American Journal of Orthopsychiatry,* 57(3), 332–344.

Rosen, J., C. F. Reynold, A. L. Yeager, P. R. Houck & L. F. Hurwitz. (1991). Sleep disturbances in survivors of the Nazi holocaust. *American Journal of Psychiatry,* 148, 62–66.

Rosenheck, R. (1985). Malignant post-Vietnam stress syndrome. *American Journal of Orthopsychiatry,* 55(2), 166–176.

Rosewater, L. & L. Walker. (eds.). (1985). *Handbook of feminist therapy: Women's issues in psychotherapy.* New York: Springer.

Ross, C. (1991). Epidemiology of multiple personality disorder and dissociation. *Psychiatric Clinics of North America,* 14, 503–518.

———. (1989). *Multiple personality disorder: Diagnosis, clinical features, and treatment.* New York: Wiley.

Ross, R. J., W. A. Ball, K. A. Sullivan & S. N. Caroff. (1989). Sleep disturbance as the hallmark of post-traumatic stress disorder. *American Journal of Psychiatry,* 146, 697–707.

Rossi, E. L. & D. B. Cheek. (1988). *Mind-body therapy: Methods of ideodynamic healing in hypnosis.* New York: Brunner/Mazel.

Rossi, P. (1980). *Why families move.* Beverly Hills, CA: Sage.

Roth, S. & L. J. Cohen. (1986). Approach, avoidance, and coping with stress. *American Psychologist,* 41, 813–819.

Roth, S. & E. Newman. (1991). The process of coping with sexual trauma. *Journal of Traumatic Stress,* 4(2), 279–297.

Rothenberg, A. (1988). *The creative process of psychotherapy.* New York: Norton.

Roy, R. E. (1983). Alcohol misuse and posttraumatic stress disorder (delayed). An alternative interpretation of the data. *Journal of Studies of Alcohol,* 44, 198–202.

Rozynko, V. & H. Dondershine. (1991). Trauma focus group therapy for Vietnam veterans with PTSD. *Psychotherapy,* 28(1), 157–161.

Ruch, L. O., J. W. Gartrell, A. Ramelli & B. J. Coyne. (1991). The clinical trauma assessment: Evaluating sexual assault victims in the emergency room. *Psychological Assessment: A Journal of Consulting and Clinical Psychology,* 3, 405–411.

Ruddick, S. (1989). *Maternal thinking: Towards a politics of peace.* Boston: Beacon Press.

Russell, A. (1982). Family/marital therapy with second generation Holocaust survivor families, questions and answers. *The Practice of Family Therapy,* 2, 233–237.

Russell, D.E.H. (1986). *The secret trauma: Incest in the lives of girls and women.* New York: Basic Books.

———. (1984). *Sexual exploitation: Rape, child sexual abuse, and workplace harassment.* Beverly Hills, CA: Sage.

Saakvitne, K. W. (1990). Psychoanalytic psychotherapy with incest survivors: Transference and countertransference paradigms. Paper presented at the annual convention of the American Psychological Association, Boston, August.

Sa'ar, K. & H. Armenian. (1986). Child health in a city at war. In J. Bryce & H. Armenian (eds.), *In wartime: The state of children in Lebanon.* Syracuse, New York: Syracuse University Press, 27–44.

Saigh, P. (1986). Three measures of childhood psychopathology in Lebanon. In J. Bryce & H. Armenian (eds.), *In wartime: The state of children in Lebanon.* Syracuse, New York: Syracuse University Press, 117–121.

Salston, M. D. (1992). Victims of violent crime: Assessment and treatment. Workshop conducted at the meeting for the International Association of Trauma Counselors, San Diego, CA, February.

Sandecki, R. (1987). Women veterans. In T. Williams (ed.), *Post-traumatic stress disorders: A handbook for clinicians.* Cincinnati, OH: Disabled American Veterans, 159–168.

Sanders, C. M. (1989). *Grief: The mourning after.* New York: John Wiley & Sons.

Sandoval, J. (1985). Crisis counseling: Conceptualizations and general principles. *School Psychology Review,* 14(3), 257–265.

Sanner, P. (1983). Stress reactions among participants in mass casualty simulations. *Annals of Emergency Medicine,* 12(7), 426–428.

Sartore, R. (1990). Poetry and childhood trauma. *Journal of Poetry Therapy,* 3, 229–234.

Sartre, J. (1967). *What is literature?* London: Methuen.

Saunders, B. E., K. A. Mandoki & D. G. Kilpatrick. (1990). Development of a crime-related post-traumatic stress disorder scale within the Symptom Checklist–90 Revised. *Journal of Traumatic Stress,* 3, 439–448.

Savin, D. L. (1987). The expression of mourning in an eight-year-old girl. *Clinical Social Work Journal,* 15, 121–135.

Savina, L. (1987). *Help for the battered woman.* South Plainfield, NJ: Bridge.

Scarano, T. (1982). Family therapy: A viable approach for treating women partners of Vietnam veterans. *Family Therapist,* 3(3), 9–16.

Scarry, E. (1985). *The body in pain.* Oxford, England: The Oxford University Press.

Schechter, S. (1987). *Guidelines of mental health practitioners in domestic violence cases.* Washington, DC: National Coalition Against Domestic Violence.

Schlenger, W. E., R. A. Kulka, J. A. Fairbank, R. L. Hough, B. K. Jordan, C. R. Marmar & D. S. Weiss. (1988). *Contractual report of the findings from the national Vietnam veterans readjustment study.* Research Triangle Park, NC: Research Triangle Institute.

Schnair, J. A. (1986). Women veterans and their mental health adjustment. In C. R. Figley (ed.), *Trauma and its wake,* vol. 2. New York: Brunner/Mazel, 97–132.

Schultz, R., B. G. Braun & R. P. Kluft. (1987). The most significant findings of the interface between multiple personality disorder (MPD) and borderline personality disorder (BPD). Unpublished raw data.

Schwartz, H. J. (1984). *Psychotherapy of the combat veteran*. New York: SP Medical and Scientific Books.

Schwarz, R. A. (1984). Ph.D. diss. Clinical methodologies of hypnotic pain control. Hahnemann University, Philadelphia, PA.

Schwarz, R. A. & M. F. Prout. (1991). Integrative approaches in the treatment of post-traumatic stress disorder. *Psychotherapy*, 28, 364–372.

Schwarzwald, J., Z. Solomon, M. Weisenberg & M. Mikulincer. (1987). Validation of the Impact of Event Scale for psychological sequelae of combat. *Journal of Consulting and Clinical Psychology*, 55, 251–256.

Sclapobersky, J. (1989). Torture as the perversion of a healing relationship. In Janet Gruschow and Kari Hannibal (eds.), *Health services for the treatment of torture and trauma survivors*. Washington, DC: American Association for the Advancement of Science, 51–72.

Scogin, F., C. Jamison & K. Gochneaur. (1989). Comparative efficacy of cognitive and behavioral bibliotherapy for mildly and moderately depressed older adults. *Journal of Consulting & Clinical Psychology*, 57(3), 403–407.

Scrignar, C. B. (1988). *Post-traumatic stress disorder: Diagnosis, treatment and legal issues*. New York: Praeger.

Scurfield, R. M. (Submitted). Healing the warrior: Admission of two Native American war-veteran cohort groups to a specialized inpatient PTSD unit.

———. (1993a). Treatment of PTSD in Vietnam veterans. In J. P. Wilson & B. Raphael (eds.), *The international handbook of traumatic stress syndromes*. New York: Plenum, 879–888.

———. (1993b). Post-traumatic stress disorder in Vietnam veterans. In J. P. Wilson & B. Raphael (eds.), *The international handbook of traumatic stress syndromes*. New York: Plenum, 285–295.

———. (1992). The collusion of sanitization and silence about war: One aftermath of operation Desert Storm. *Journal of Traumatic Stress*, 5(3), 505–512.

———. (1991a). Needs of returning Gulf War veterans and their families. Presentation on the U.S. Department of Veterans Affairs national satellite teleconference, "The VA/DOD continuing response to our returning veterans," VA Regional Learning Resources Center, Salt Lake VA Medical Center, UT.

———. (1991b, September). Where do we go from here? Presentation on the U.S. Department of Veterans Affairs national satellite teleconference, "The VA/DOD continuing response to our returning veterans," VA Regional Learning Resources Center, Salt Lake VA Medical Center, UT.

———. (1989). Vietnam revisited: A journey of healing. *Western Express*, 1(2), 4, 5, 8.

———. (1988). A critique of the rationale to delete "survival guilt" from the DSM-III-R criteria for PTSD. *PTSD Quarterly Newsletter*, 5(2).

———. (1985). Post-traumatic stress assessment and treatment: Overview and formulations. In C. R. Figley (ed.), *Trauma and its wake*, vol. 1. New York: Brunner/Mazel, 219–256.

———. (1980). An integrated approach to case services and social reform. *Social Casework*, 61(10), 610–618.

Scurfield, R. M. & A. S. Blank. (1985). A guide to the Vietnam veteran military history. In S. Sonnenberg, A. S. Blank & J. Talbott (eds.), *The trauma of war: Stress and recovery in Vietnam veterans*. Washington, DC: American Psychiatric Press, 263–292.

Scurfield, R. M., T. Johnson, P. Gongla & R. Hough. (1984). Three post-Vietnam rap/therapy groups: An analysis. *Group*, 8(4), 3–21.

Scurfield, R. M., S. K. Kenderdine & R. J. Pollard. (1990). Inpatient treatment for war-related PTSD: Initial findings on a longer-term outcome study. *Journal of Traumatic Stress*, 3(2), 115–202.

Scurfield, R. M. & S. Tice. (1992). Interventions with psychiatric and medical casualties from Vietnam to the Gulf War and their families. *Military Medicine*, 157(2), 88–97.

Scurfield, R. M., L. E. Wong & E. B. Zeerocah. (1992). An evaluation of the impact of "helicopter ride therapy" for in-patient Vietnam veterans with war-related PTSD. *Military Medicine*, 157(2), 67–73.

Seidenberg, R. (1973). *Corporate wives—corporate casualties?* New York: American Management Association.

Seligman, M. (1975). *Helplessness on depression, development and death*. San Francisco: Freeman.

Seligman, M.E.P. & G. Beagley. (1975). Learned helplessness in the rat. *Journal of Comprehensive Physiological Psychology*, 88, 534–541.

Selye, H. (1946). The general adaptation syndrome and the diseases of adaptation. *Journal of Clinical Endocrinology*, 6, 117–130.

Sexton, R. E. & V. S. Sexton. (1982). Intimacy: A historical perspective. In M. Fischer & G. Stricher (eds.), *Intimacy*. New York: Plenum Press, 1–20.

Shalit, B. (1988). *The psychology of conflict and combat*. New York: Praeger.

Shapiro, F. (1989a). Efficacy of the eye movement desensitization procedures in the treatment of traumatic memories. *Journal of Traumatic Stress*, 2, 199–223.

———. (1989b). Eye movement desensitization: A new treatment for post-traumatic stress disorder. *Journal of Behavior Therapy and Experimental Psychiatry*, 20, 211–217.

Shapiro, R. (1984). Transference, countertransference and the Vietnam veteran. In H. J. Schwartz (ed.), *Psychotherapy of the combat veteran*. New York: SP Medical and Scientific Books, 85–102.

Shatan, C. F. (1978). Stress disorders among Vietnam veterans: The emotional content of combat continues. In C. R. Figley (ed.), *Stress disorders among Vietnam veterans: Theory, research, and treatment*. New York: Brunner/Mazel, 43–52.

———. (1974). Through the membrane of reality: "Impacted grief" and perceptual dissonance in Vietnam combat veterans. *Psychiatric Opinion*, 11, 5–14.

———. (1973). The grief of soldiers: Vietnam combat veterans' self-help movement. *American Journal of Orthopsychiatry*, 43, 640–653.

Shawcross, W. (1989). A tourist in the refugee world. In Carol Kismaric (ed.), *Forced out: The agony of the refugee in our time*. New York: Random House.

Shay, J. (1992a). Fluoxetine reduces explosiveness and elevates mood of Vietnam combat veterans with PTSD. *Journal of Traumatic Stress*, 5, 97–101.

———. (1992b). Reclaiming Homer's gods. Unpublished manuscript.

———. (1991). Learning about combat stress from Homer's *Iliad*. *Journal of Traumatic Stress*, 4(4), 561–580.

Shearer, S. L., C. P. Peters, M. S. Quaytman & R. L. Ogden. (1990). Frequency and correlates of childhood sexual and physical abuse histories in adult female borderline inpatients. *American Journal of Psychiatry*, 147, 214–216.

Sheehan, D. V., J. Ballenger & G. Jacobsen. (1980). Treatment of endogenous anxiety with phobic, hysterical and hypochondriacal symptoms. *Archives of General Psychiatry*, 37, 51–59.

Sheehan, P. L. (1991). Critical incident trauma and intimacy. In J. T. Reese, J. M. Horn & C. Dunning (eds.), *Critical incidents in policing*. Washington, DC: Federal Bureau of Investigation, U.S. Department of Justice, 331–333.

————. (1989). Ph.D. diss. Relationships among combat trauma, fear of close personal relationships, and intimacy. Indiana University, Bloomington.

————. (1985). Treating intimacy issues of Vet Center couples. Unpublished paper. Indianapolis, IN: Psychiatric/Mental Health Nursing, Indiana University School of Nursing.

Shestatzky, M., D. Greenberg & B. Lerer. (1988). A controlled trial of phenelzine in post-traumatic stress disorder. *Psychiatry Research*, 24, 149–155.

Shields, N. M., P. A. Resick & C. R. Hanneke. (1990). Victims of marital rape. In R. T. Ammerman & M. Hersen (eds.), *Treatment of family violence: A sourcebook*. New York: John Wiley & Sons, 155–182.

Shor, R. E. (1959). Hypnosis and the concept of the generalized reality orientation. *American Journal of Psychotherapy*, 13, 582–602.

Shortridge, J. L. (1980). The utilization of the FIRO-B for the comparison of selected differences among disabled Vietnam combat and non-combat veterans. *Dissertation Abstracts International*, 41(8), 3381 SECA. (University Microfilms No. ADG81–03421).

Sieber, J. E. (1982). *The ethics of social research: Surveys and experiments*. New York: Springer-Verlag.

Sierles, F. S., J. J. Chen, R. E. McFarland & M. A. Taylor. (1983). Post-traumatic stress disorder and concurrent psychiatric illness: A preliminary report. *American Journal of Psychiatry*, 140, 1177–1179.

Sierles, F. S., J. Chen, M. L. Messing, J. K. Besyner & M. A. Taylor. (1986). Concurrent psychiatric illness in non-Hispanic outpatients diagnosed as having post-traumatic stress disorder. *Journal of Nervous and Mental Disease*, 174, 171–173.

Sigal, J. J. (1989). Reconciliation of contradictions between clinical and empirical findings in studies of children of Holocaust survivors. Paper presented at Society for Traumatic Stress Studies, San Francisco, October.

Sigal, J. J. & M. Weinfeld. (1989). *Trauma and rebirth*. New York: Praeger.

Silver, J. M., D. P. Sandberg & R. E. Hales. (1990). New approaches in the pharmacotherapy of post-traumatic stress disorder. *Journal of Clinical Psychiatry*, 51 (Supplement 10), 33–38, 44–46.

Silver, S. M. (1986). An inpatient program for post-traumatic stress disorder: Context as treatment. In C. R. Figley (ed.), *Trauma and its wake*, vol. 2. New York: Brunner/Mazel, 213–231.

Silver, S. M. (ed.). (1984). *Worth of the Warrior Project: The national working group on American Indian Vietnam era veterans*. Washington, DC: Readjustment Counseling Service, Department of Veterans Affairs Central Office.

Silver, S. M. & W. E. Kelly. (1985). Hypnotherapy of post-traumatic stress disorder in combat veterans from WWII and Vietnam. In W. E. Kelly (ed.), *Post-traumatic stress disorder and the war veteran patient.* New York: Brunner/Mazel, 43–53.

Silver, S. M. & J. P. Wilson. (1988). Native American healing and purification rituals for war stress. In J. P. Wilson, Z. Harel & B. Kahana (eds.), *Human adaptation to extreme stress: From the Holocaust to Vietnam.* New York: Plenum Press, 337–355.

Silverstein, S. (1981). *The missing piece meets the big o.* New York: Harper & Row.

Simon, R. & C. Hughes. (1985). *The culture-bound syndromes.* Dordrecht: Reidl.

Simpson, M. (1992). Traumatic stress and the bruising of the soul: The effects of torture and coercive interrogation. In J. P. Wilson & B. Raphael (eds.), *The international handbook of traumatic stress syndromes.* New York: Plenum, 601–622.

Siporin, M. (1975). *Introduction to social work practice.* New York: Macmillan.

Smead, V. S. (1991). *Best practices in crisis intervention. Resources in crisis intervention—school, family, and community applications.* Silver Spring, MD: National Association of School Psychologists.

Smith, J. R. (1985). Rap groups and group therapy for Viet Nam veterans. In S. Sonnenberg, A. S. Blank & J. Talbott (eds.), *The trauma of war: Stress and Recovery in Vietnam veterans.* Washington, DC: American Psychiatric Press, 165–193.

———. (1982). Personal responsibility in traumatic stress reactions. *Psychiatric Annals*, 12, 1021–1030.

———. (1980). The roles, stages and structure of rap groups in the treatment of post-traumatic stress disorders. Paper presented at Dartmouth Medical School, November.

Smith, M. A., J. Davidson, J. C. Ritchie, H. Kudler, S. Lipper, P. Chapell & C. B. Nemeroff. (1989). The corticotrophin-releasing hormone test in patients with post-traumatic stress disorder. *Biological Psychiatry*, 26, 349–355.

Smith, S. (1990). Two decades and a wake-up. Documentary broadcast by Public Broadcasting Service (PBS) nationwide, November 1.

Smith, S. M. (1983). Disaster: Family disruption in the wake of disaster. In C. R. Figley & H. McCubbin (eds.), *Stress and the family*, vol. 2, *Coping with catastrophe.* New York: Brunner/Mazel, 120–147.

Solkoff, N. (1992). Children of survivors of the Nazi Holocaust: A critical review of the literature. *American Journal of Orthopsychiatry*, 62(3), 342–358.

Solomon, R. (1987). Coping with vulnerability. Unpublished.

Solomon, S. (1989). Research issues in assessing disaster's effects. In R. Gist & B. Lubin (eds.), *Psychosocial aspects of disaster.* New York: John Wiley, 308–340.

———. (1985). Enhancing social support for disaster victims. In B. J. Sowder (ed.), *Disasters and mental health: Selected contemporary perspectives.* Rockville, MD: National Institute of Mental Health, 107–121.

Solomon, S., E. Gerrity & A. Muff. (1992). Efficacy of treatments for posttraumatic stress disorder, *Journal of the American Medical Association*, 268, 5, 633–638.

Solomon, Z. & R. Bengenishty. (1986). The role of proximity, immediacy, and expectancy in front line treatment of combat stress reaction among Israelis in the Lebanon war. *American Journal of Psychiatry*, 143, 613–617.

Solomon, Z., R. Bengenishty & M. Mikulincer. (1991). The contribution of wartime, pre-war, and post-war factors to self-efficacy: A longitudinal study of combat stress reaction. *Journal of Traumatic Stress*, 4, 345–362.

Solomon, Z. & M. Mikulincer. (1987). Combat stress reactions, post-traumatic stress disorder, and social adjustment: A study of Israeli veterans. *Journal of Nervous and Mental Disease*, 175, 277–285.

Solomon, Z., M. Mikulincer & E. Avitzur. (1988). Coping, locus of control, social support, and combat-related post-traumatic stress disorder: A prospective study. *Journal of Personality and Social Psychology*, 55, 270–285.

Solomon, Z., M. Mikulincer & S. Hobfoll. (1987). Objective versus subjective measurement of stress and social support: Combat-related reactions. *Journal of Consulting and Clinical Psychology*, 55(4), 577–583.

Solursh, L. (1988). Combat addiction—Post traumatic stress disorder re-explored. *Psychiatric Journal of the University of Ottawa*, 13(1), 17–20.

Sommer, J. F., Jr. (1990). Testimony before the Subcommittee on Compensation, Pension and Insurance, Committee on Veterans' Affairs. Washington, DC: U.S. House of Representatives.

Somnier, F. & I. Block. (1987). Remarks on record of a round table discussion held on June 2, St. Paul, Minnesota.

Somnier, F. & I. Genefke. (1986). Psychotherapy for victims of torture. *British Journal of Psychiatry*, 149, 323–329.

Sonkin, D. J. & M. Durphy. (1982). *Learning to live without violence. A handbook for men*. San Francisco: Volcano Press.

Sonnenberg, S., A. Blank & J. Talbott. (1985). *The trauma of war: Stress and recovery in Vietnam veterans*. Washington, DC: American Psychiatric Press.

Sorenson, G. (1990a). Earthquake (Entire Issue Devoted to the Topic). *Vet Center Voice*, 11(7), 2–24.

———. (1990b). Tracking natural disaster. *Vet Center Voice*, 11(6), 3–7.

———. (1988). Survey measures symptoms among successful veterans. *Vet Center Voice* 11(7): 2–24.

———. (1985). Twelve steps to PTSD treatment prove successful. *Vet Center Voice*, December.

Southwick, S. M., J. H. Krystal, D. R. Johnson & D. S. Charney. (1992). Neurobiology of post-traumatic stress disorder. *Annual Review of Psychiatry*, 12, 347–370.

Southwick, S., R. Yehuda, E. L. Giller & D. S. Charney. (1994). The use of tricyclics and monoamine oxidase inhibitors in the treatment of post-traumatic stress disorder: A quantitative review. In M. M. Murburg (ed.), Catecholamine function in PTSD: Emerging concepts. Washington, DC: American Psychiatric Press, 293–305.

Spiegel, D. (1988). Dissociation and hypnosis in post-traumatic stress. *Journal of Traumatic Stress*, 1(1), 17–34.

———. (1981). Vietnam grief work using hypnosis. *American Journal of Clinical Hypnosis*, 24(1), 33–40.

Spiegel, D. & E. Cardena. (1990). New uses of hypnosis in the treatment of post-traumatic stress disorder. *Journal of Clinical Psychiatry*, 51(10, supp.), 39–43.

Spiegel, D., T. Hunt & H. E. Dondershine. (1988). Dissociation and hypnotizability in posttraumatic stress disorder. *American Journal of Psychiatry*, 139, 431–437.

Spitzer, R. L., J.B.W. Williams, M. Gibbon & M. B. First. (1990). *Structured clinical interview for DSM-III-R patient edition (SCID-P, Version 1.0)*. Washington, DC: American Psychiatric Press.

Spodick, P. (1983). The case of Joan Sommers: A six-year-old amnesia victim of rape.

In J. Shorr, G. Sobel-Wittington, P. Robin & J. Connella (eds.), *Imagery: Theoretical and clinical applications*, vol. 3. New York: Plenum Press.

Sprang, M. V., J. S. McNeil & R. Wright, Jr. (1989). Psychological changes after the murder of a significant other. *Social Casework*, 70, 159–164.

Spring, D. (In press). Red drawings: Ben and others. In Evelyn Virshup (ed.), *California art therapy trends*. Chicago: Magnolia Street Press.

———. (1993). *Shattered images: Phenomenological language of sexual trauma*. Chicago: Magnolia Street Press.

———. (1992a). Artistic symbolic language and treatment of multiple personality disorder. In Estelle Kluft (ed.), *Expressive and functional therapies in the treatment of multiple personality disorder*. Springfield, IL: Charles C. Thomas, 85–98.

———. (1990). Color scripts and victim myths. Unpublished manuscript.

———. (1989). Victim meets victim. Paper presented at the American Art Therapy Association Conference, San Francisco.

———. (1988a). Lifelong effects of sexual abuse. Paper presented at the Annual Conference of the American Art Therapy Association, Chicago, November.

———. (1988b). Sexual abuse and post-traumatic stress reflected in artistic symbolic language. *Dissertation Abstracts International* (University Microfilms) Pub. No. 90–02893.

———. (1985). Symbolic language of sexually abused, chemically dependent females in a recovery home. *American Art Therapy Journal*, 24(1), 13–21.

———. (1984). *A perspective: Art therapy treatment model for the effects of sexual abuse*. Ventura, CA: Earthwood Center.

———. (1983). Art therapy: An integrator for victimology. In Joseph Shorr, G. Sobel-Whittington, P. Robin & J. Connella (eds.), *Imagery, theoretical and clinical applications*, vol. 3. New York: Plenum Press, 355–375.

———. (1981). Bridging through imagery: An integration of the selves through art therapy, a visual dialogue. In Eric Klinger (ed.), *Imagery, concepts, results and applications*. New York: Plenum Press, 357–369.

———. (1980). Jane, a case study of a rape victim rehabilitated by art therapy. In J. E. Shorr (ed.), *Imagery: Its many dimensions and applications*. New York: Plenum Press, 375–390.

———. (1978). Change in maladaptive growth of abused girl through art therapy. *Art Psychotherapy*, 5, 99–109.

———. (1976). A treatment modality for rape victims. *American Art Therapy Association Archives*.

St. Just, A. (1991). The still point. There the dance is: Wilderness experience as a therapeutic tool in the healing of post-traumatic stress responses. Unpublished manuscript, Olympia Institute, Bolinas, CA.

Stamm, B. H., S. L. Bieber & L. A. Pearlman. (1991). A preliminary report on scale construction and generalizability of the TSI Belief Scale. Paper presented at the International Society for Traumatic Stress Studies Meeting, Washington, DC, October.

Stanton, M. D. (1980). The hooked serviceman: Drug use in and after Vietnam. In C. R. Figley & S. Leventman (eds.), *Strangers at home: Vietnam veterans since the war*. New York: Praeger, 279–292.

Stark, A., S. Arlwynne & T. McGeehan. (1989). Dance/movement therapy with bulimic patients. In Lynn M. Hornyak & Ellen K. Baker (eds.), *Experiential therapies for eating disorders*. New York: Guilford Press, 121–143.

Stark, E., A. Flitcraft, D. Zuckerman, A. Grey, J. Robison & W. Frazier. (1981). Wife abuse in the medical setting: An introduction for health personnel. *Domestic Violence*, 7, 1–54.

Staudacher, C. (1987). *Beyond grief: A guide for recovering from the death of a loved one*. Oakland, CA: New Harbinger.

Steele, K. (1989). Sitting with the shattered soul. *Pilgrimage: Journal of Psychotherapy and Personal Exploration*, 15, 6.

Steele, K. & J. Colrain. (1991). Abreactive work with sexual abuse survivors: Concepts and techniques. In M. Hunter (ed.), *The sexually abused male: Application of treatment strategies*, 1–55.

Steinberg, A. (1989). Holocaust survivors and their children: A review of the clinical literature. In P. Marcus & A. Rosenberg (eds.), *Healing their wounds: Psychotherapy with Holocaust survivors and their families*. New York: Praeger, 23–48.

Steketee, G. & E. B. Foa. (1987). Rape victims: Post-traumatic stress responses and their treatment: A review of the literature. *Journal of Anxiety Disorders*, 1, 69–86.

Stellman, S. D. & J. M. Stellman. (1992). Review of the health effects in Vietnam veterans of exposure to herbicides. Paper presented at the Institute of Medicine's Committee, Washington, DC.

Stellman, S. D., J. M. Stellman & J. F. Sommer, Jr. (1988). Combat and herbicide exposures in Vietnam among a sample of American Legionnaires. *Environmental Research*, 47, 112–128.

———. (1985). *The American Legion-Columbia University Vietnam veterans study*. Washington, DC: American Legion.

Stember, C. J. (1977). Printing with abused children: A first step in art therapy. *American Journal of Art Therapy*, 16(3), 104–109.

Stenger, C. A. (1985). *American POWs in WWI, WWII, Korea and Vietnam: Statistical data concerning numbers captured, repatriated and still alive as of January 1, 1985*. Washington, DC: Veterans Administration.

Stern, E. (1982). *Elie Wiesel: Witness for life*. New York: KTAV Publishing House.

Stewart, J. R. & R. J. Bartucci. (1986). Post-traumatic stress disorder and partial complex seizures. *American Journal of Psychiatry*, 143, 113–114.

Stiver, I. (1990). *Dysfunctional families and wounded relationships, part I*. Wellesley, MA: Stone Center.

Stone, M. H. (1981). Borderline syndromes: A consideration of subtypes and an overview, directions for research. *Psychiatric Clinics of North America*, 4, 3–13.

Stover, E. & E. O. Nightingale. (1985). *The breaking of bodies and minds: Torture, psychiatric abuse and the health professions*. New York: W. H. Freeman.

Stratton, J. G., D. A. Parker & J. R. Snibbe. (1984). Post-traumatic stress. Study of police officers involved in shooting. *Psychological Reports*, 55, 127–131.

Straus, M. A. & R. J. Gelles. (eds.). (1990). *Physical violence in American families*. New Brunswick, NJ: Transatlantic Publishers.

Straus, M. A., R. Gelles & S. Steinmetz. (1980). *Behind closed doors: Violence in the American family*. New York: Doubleday.

Stuckey, J., S. Marra, T. Minor & T. Insel. (1989). Changes in mu opiate receptors following inescapable shock. *Brain Research*, 476, 167–169.

Stutman, R. K. & E. L. Bliss. (1985). Post-traumatic stress disorder, hypnotizability and imagery. *American Journal of Psychiatry*, 142, 741–743.

Styron, W. (1979). *Sophie's choice*. New York: Bantam Books.

Sudhaker, M. & K. O'Brien. (1987). Acute post-traumatic stress disorder in victims of a natural disaster. *Journal of Nervous and Mental Disease*, 175, 286–292.

Sue, S. & N. Zane. (1987). The role of culture and cultural techniques in psychotherapy: A critique and reformulation. *American Psychologist*, 40, 37–45.

Suedfeld, P. (1990). Torture: A brief overview. In P. Suedfeld (ed.), *Psychology and torture*. Washington, DC: Hemisphere Press, 1–12.

Sullivan, H. S. (1953). *The interpersonal theory of psychiatry*. New York: Norton.

Summit, R. (1989). The centrality of victimization. *Psychiatric Clinics of North America*, 12(2), 413–429.

———. (1983). The child sexual abuse accommodation syndrome. *Child Abuse and Neglect*, 7, 177–193.

Survivors of Incest Anonymous (SIA). (1991). *The Welcome, the closing, the twelve steps, the twelve traditions, the adapted twelve steps*. Baltimore: SIA World Service.

———. (1990). *Twelve and twelve*. Baltimore: SIA World Service.

Sutker, P. B., M. Uddo-Crane & A. N. Allain. (1991). Clinical and research assessment of post-traumatic stress disorder: A conceptual overview. *Psychological Assessment: A Journal of Consulting and Clinical Psychology*, 3, 520–530.

Symonds, M. (1980). The "second injury" to victims. *Evaluation and Change*, Special Issue, 36–38.

Taini, R. (1991). Thoughts regarding the use of (ropes) activities with post-traumatic stress disorder Vietnam veterans. Unpublished notes. Colma, CA: Proaction Associates.

Talbot, A., M. Manton & P. J. Dunn. (1992). Debriefing the debriefers: An intervention strategy to assist psychologists after a crisis. *Journal of Traumatic Stress*, 5, 45–62.

Tanay, E. (1968). Initiation of psychotherapy with survivors of Nazi persecution. In H. Krystal (ed.), *Massive psychic trauma*. New York: International Universities Press, 219–232.

Tanna, V. T., R. P. Penningroth & R. F. Woolson. (1977). Propranolol in the treatment of anxiety neurosis. *Comprehensive Psychiatry*, 18, 319–326.

Terr, L. C. (1991). Childhood traumas: An outline and overview. *American Journal of Psychiatry*, 148(1), 10–20.

———. (1990). *Too scared to cry*. New York: Harper & Row.

———. (1985). Children traumatized in small groups. In S. Eth & R. S. Pynoos (eds.), *Post-traumatic stress disorder in children*. Washington, DC: American Psychiatric Press.

Terry, W. (1984). *Bloods: An oral history of the Vietnam War by black veterans*. New York: Ballantine.

Theileke, H. (1964). *The ethics of sex*. New York: Harper & Row.

Thomas, T. (1989). *Men surviving incest*. Walnut Creek, CA: Launch Press.

Thompson, C. L. & P. Kennedy. (1987). Healing the betrayed: Issues in psychotherapy with child victims of trauma. *Journal of Contemporary Psychotherapy*, 17, 195–202.

Thompson, J., R. Sandecki, L. Barajas-Gallagos, E. Alvarez, C. Garcia & M. Solganick.

(1982). *Report of a working group on women Vietnam veterans and the operation outreach Vietnam Vet Center Program.* Washington, DC: Readjustment Counseling Service, Veterans Administration Central Office.

Thornton, L. (1988). *Imagining Argentina.* New York: Bantam Books.

Tice, S., R. Hinds, E. Bialobok, H. Carter, J. Cecil, D. Koverman, N. Makowski, R. Pierson & A. R. Batres. (1988). Report of the working group on physically disabled Vietnam veterans. Washington, DC: Readjustment Counseling Service, Department of Veterans Affairs.

Tietz, E. I., F. Gomaz & R. F. Berman. (1985). Amygdala kindled seizure stage is related to altered benzodiazepine binding site density. *Life Sciences,* 36, 183–190.

Titchener, J. L. (1982). Post-traumatic decline: A consequence of unresolved destructive drives. In C. R. Figley (ed.), *Trauma and its wake, traumatic stress theory, research and intervention,* vol. 2. New York: Brunner/Mazel, 5–19.

Titchener, J. L. & F. T. Kapp. (1976). Family and character change at Buffalo Creek. *American Journal of Psychiatry,* 133(3), 295–299.

Toews, M. & L. Palmer. (1991). Finding a healthy support or therapy group. *Moving Forward,* November/December, 15.

Tolman, R. (1989). The development of a measure of psychological maltreatment of women by their male partners. *Violence and Victims,* 4(3), 159–177.

Torem, M. (1990). Healing self-affirmations. *Many Voices,* 2(6), 14.

Torrey, E. F. (1986). Witchdoctors and psychiatrists. New York: Harper & Row.

———. (1969). The case for the indigenous therapist. *Archives of General Psychiatry,* 20, 365–373.

Treiser, S. L., C. S. Cascio, T. L. O'Donohue, N. B. Thoa, D. M. Jacobowitz & K. J. Kellar. (1981). Lithium increases serotonin release and decreases serotonin receptors in the hippocampus. *Science,* 213, 1529–1531.

Trimble, M. R. (1985). Post-traumatic stress disorder: History of a concept. In C. R. Figley (ed.), *Trauma and its wake: The study and treatment of post-traumatic stress disorder.* New York: Brunner/Mazel, 5–14.

———. (1981). *Post-traumatic neurosis.* Chichester, England: Wiley.

Trimpey, M. L. (1989). Self-esteem and anxiety: Key issues in an abused women's support group. Special Issues: Family violence. *Issues in Mental Health Nursing,* 10(3–4), 297–308.

Tsai, M., S. Feldman-Summers & M. Edgar. (1979). Childhood molestation: Variables related to differential impacts on psychosexual functioning in adult women. *Journal of Abnormal Psychology,* 88, 407–417.

Tseng, W. & R. Hsu. (1980). Minor psychological disturbances of everyday life. In H. Triandis & J. Draguns (eds.), *Handbook of cultural psychology: Psychopathology,* vol. 6. Boston: Allyn Bacon.

Turkus, J. (1991). Psychotherapy and case management for multiple personality disorder: Synthesis for continuity of care. *Psychiatric Clinics of North America,* 14, 3, 649–660.

Turner, S. & C. Gorst-Unsworth. (1990). Psychological sequelae of torture: A descriptive model. *British Journal of Psychiatry,* 157, 475–480.

Tyler, F., D. Brome & J. Williams. (1991). Ethnic validity, ecology, and psychotherapy: A psychosocial competence model. New York: Plenum.

Tymchuk, A. J. (1980). Ethical decision-making and psychological treatment. *Journal of Psychiatric Treatment and Evaluation*, 3, 507–513.

U.S. Department of Veterans Affairs. (1991). *War-zone stress among returning Persian Gulf troops: A preliminary report*. West Haven, CT: Northeast Program Evaluation Center, Evaluation Division of the National Center for PTSD, Veterans Affairs Medical Center.

U.S. Department of Veterans Affairs. (1980). *POW: Study of former prisoners of war*. Washington, DC: VA Office of Planning and Program Evaluation.

U.S. Government, General Accounting Office (GAO). (1982). *Actions needed to insure that female veterans have equal access to VA benefits*. Washington, DC: Government Printing Office.

U.S. Senate, Committee on Foreign Relations, Republican Staff. (1991). An examination of U.S. policy toward POW/MIAs. Congressional Record, May 23.

Ursano, R. J. (1985). Vietnam era prisoners of war: Studies of U.S. Air Force prisoners of war. In S. Sonnenberg, A. S. Blank & J. Talbott (eds.), *The trauma of war: Stress and recovery in Viet Nam veterans*. Washington, DC: American Psychiatric Press, 339–358.

———. (1981). The Viet Nam era prisoner of war: Precaptivity personality and the development of psychiatric illness. *American Journal of Psychiatry*, 138(3), 315–318.

Ursano, R. J., J. A. Boydstun & R. D. Wheatley. (1981). Psychiatric illness in U.S. Air Force Viet Nam prisoners of war: A five-year follow-up. *American Journal of Psychiatry*, 138(3), 310–314.

van der Hart, O. (1988). *Coping with loss*. New York: Irvington.

———. (1983). *Rituals in psychotherapy: Transition and continuity*. New York: Irvington.

van der Hart, O. & S. Boon. (1988). Schrijfopdrachten en hypnose voor de verwerking van traumatische herinneringen. *Directieve Therapie*, 8, 4–44.

van der Kolk, B. (1992). Biological basis of trauma. In J. P. Wilson & B. Raphael (eds.), *The international handbook of traumatic stress syndromes*. New York: Plenum Press, 25–34.

———. (1989). The compulsion to repeat the trauma: Reenactment, revictimization and masochism. Treatment of victims of sexual abuse. *Psychiatric Clinics of North America*, 12(2), 389–412.

———. (1988). The trauma spectrum: The interaction of biological and social events in the genesis of trauma response. *Journal of Traumatic Stress*, 1(3), 273–290.

———. (1987a). The drug treatment of post-traumatic stress disorder. *Journal of Affective Disorders*, 13, 203–213.

———. (1987b). The psychological consequences of overwhelming life experiences. In B. van der Kolk, *Psychological trauma*. Washington, DC: American Psychiatric Press.

———. (1986). *Psychological trauma*. Washington, DC: American Psychiatric Press.

———. (1983). Psychopharmacological issues in post-traumatic stress disorder. *Hospital and Community Psychiatry*, 34, 683–691.

van der Kolk, B. A., M. Greenberg, H. Boyd & J. Krystal. (1985). Inescapable shock, neurotransmitters, and addiction to trauma: Toward a psychobiology of post-traumatic stress. *Biological Psychiatry*, 20, 314–325.

van der Kolk, B., D. Pelcovitz, J. Herman, S. Roth, S. J. Kaplan & R. L. Spitzer. (1991). Structured interview for SCID-DESNOS, conceptual discussion.

van der Kolk, B. A., R. K. Pitman, S. P. Orr & M. S. Greenberg. (1989). Endogenous opioids, stress induced analgesia, and post-traumatic stress disorder. *Psychopharmacology Bulletin*, 25, 108–112.

van der Kolk, B. A. & O. van der Hart. (1991). The intrusive past: The flexibility of memory and the engraving of trauma. *American Imago*, 48(4), 425–454.

van der Ploeg, H. & W. Kleijn. (1989). Being held hostage in the Netherlands: A study of long-term effects. *Journal of Traumatic Stress*, 2, 153–169.

Van Devanter, L. (1983). *Home before morning: The story of an army nurse in Vietnam*. New York: Beaufort.

van Hoose, W. H. & J. A. Kottler. (1985). *Ethical and legal issues in counseling and psychotherapy: A comprehensive guide*. 2d ed. San Francisco: Jossey-Bass.

Venn, J. (1988). Hypnotic intervention with accident victims during the acute phase of posttraumatic adjustment. *American Journal of Clinical Hypnosis*, 31(2), 114–117.

Ver Ellen, P. & D. P. van Kammen. (1990). The biological findings in post-traumatic stress disorder: A review. *Journal of Applied Social Psychology*, 20, (21, pt. 1), 1789–1821.

Vietnam Veterans Video Production Company. (1985). *Wall of tears*. Berkeley, CA: Author.

Volpe, J. (1982). *The flight attendant subculture: An ethnography*. An unpublished research study. Washington, DC: Association of Flight Attendants.

Waigandt, A. & L. Phelps. (1990). The effects of homicides and suicides on the population longevity of the United States. *Journal of Traumatic Stress*, 3, 297–304.

Wakefield, K. & J. M. Hyland. (1988). The importance of a female therapist in a male Vietnam veterans' psychotherapy group. *Bulletin of the Menninger Clinic*, 52(1), 16–29.

Walker, E., W. Katon & J. Harrop-Griffiths. (1988). Relationships of chronic pelvic pain to psychiatric diagnoses and childhood sexual abuse. *American Journal of Psychiatry*, 145, 75–80.

Walker, J. (1983). Comparison of "rap" groups with traditional group therapy in the treatment of Vietnam combat veterans. *Group*, 2, 48–57.

Walker, J. & J. Nash. (1981). Group therapy in the treatment of Vietnam combat veterans. *International Journal of Group Psychotherapy*, 31, 376–78.

Walker, J. I. (1982). Chemotherapy of traumatic war stress. *Military Medicine*, 147, 1029–1033.

Walker, K. (1985). *A piece of my heart. The stories of twenty-six American women who served in Vietnam*. New York: Ballantine Books.

Walker, L.E.A. (1984). Battered women, psychology, and public policy. *American Psychologist*, 39(10), 1178–1182.

———. (1979). *The battered woman*. New York: Harper & Row.

Wallas, L. (1990). *Stories that heal*. New York: Norton.

Warheit, G. (1985). A propositional paradigm for estimating the impact of disasters on mental health. In B. Sowder (ed.), *Disasters and mental health: Selected contemporary perspectives*. Rockville, MD: National Institute of Mental Health, 196–214.

Waring, E. M. & J. R. Reddon. (1981). The measurement of intimacy in marriage: The Waring Intimacy Questionnaire. *Journal of Clinical Psychology*, 39(1), 53–59.

Watkins, J. (1949). *Hypnotherapy of war neurosis*. New York: Ronald Press.

Watson, C. G., M. P. Juba, V. Manifold, T. Kucala & P.E.D. Anderson. (1991). The PTSD Interview: Rationale, description, reliability, and concurrent validity of a DSM-III-based technique. *Journal of Clinical Psychology*, 47, 179–188.

Watson, C. G., T. Kucala & V. Manifold. (1986). A cross-validation of the Keane and Penk MMPI scales as measures of post-traumatic stress disorder. *Journal of Clinical Psychology*, 42, 727–732.

Watson, J. (1980). Bibliotherapy for abused children. *School Counselor*, 27, 204–208.

Watts, A. (1958). *Nature, man and woman*. New York: Vintage Books.

Weathers, F. W., D. D. Blake, K. E. Krinsley, W. Haddad, J. M. Huska & T. M. Keane. (1992). The clinician-administered PTSD scale: Reliability and validity. Paper presented at the Twenty-Sixth Annual Conference for the Association for Advancement of Behavior Therapy, Boston, MA.

Wegscheider, S. (1983). *The family trap: No one escapes from a chemically dependent family*. St. Paul, MN: Nurturing Networks.

Weinberg, R. B. (1990). Serving large numbers of adolescent victims-survivors: Group interventions following trauma at school. *Professional Psychology: Research and Practice*, 21(4), 271–278.

Weinfeld, M. & J. J. Sigal. (1986). Knowledge of the Holocaust among adult children of survivors. *Canadian Ethnic Studies*, 18(1), 66–78.

Weisaeth, L. & L. Eitinger. (1991a). Research on PTSD and other post-traumatic reactions: European literature—Part I. *PTSD Research Quarterly*, 2(2), 1–8.

———. (1991b). Research on PTSD and other post-traumatic reactions: European literature—Part II. *PTSD Research Quarterly*, 2(3), 1–7.

Weiss, J. M., P. A. Goodman, B. G. Losito, S. Corrigan, J. M. Charry & W. H. Bailey. (1981). Behavioral depression produced by an uncontrollable stressor: Relationship to norepinephrine, dopamine, and serotonin levels in various regions of rat brain. *Brain Research Reviews*, 3, 167–205.

Weizman, R., A. Weizman, K. A. Kook, F. Vocci, S. I. Deutsch & S. M. Paul. (1989). Repeated swim stress alters brain benzodiazepine receptors measured in vivo. *Journal of Pharmacology and Experimental Therapeutics*, 249, 701–707.

Wells, B. G., C. Chu, R. Johnson, C. Nasdahl, M. A. Ayubi, E. Sewell & P. Statham. (1991). Buspirone in the treatment of post-traumatic stress disorder. *Pharmacotherapy*, 11(4), 340–343.

Werner, E. E. (1984). Resilient children. *Young Children*, November, 68–72.

Wertsch, M. E. (1991). *Military brats*. New York: Harmony Books.

Westen, D. (1991). Social cognition and object relations. *Psychological Bulletin*, 109, 429–455.

———. (1990). *Social cognition and object relations*. Unpublished manuscript.

Westermeyer, J. (1989). Cross-cultural care for PTSD: Research, training & service needs for the future. *Journal of Traumatic Stress*, 2(4), 515–536.

Westley, D. (1981). *Redemptive intimacy*. Mystic, CT: Twenty-Third Publications.

White, G. (1982). The ethnographic study of cultural knowledge of "mental disorder." In A. Marsella & G. White (eds.), *Culture and therapy*. Dordrecht: D. Reidl, 80–93.

White, S. G. & C. Hatcher. (1988). Violence and the trauma response. *Occupational Medicine*, 3(4), 677–693.

Wiggs, G. (1984). Designing learning programs. *The handbook of human resource development*, 7.1–7.35.

Wilkinson, C. B. & W. A. O'Connor. (1982). Human ecology and mental illness. *American Journal of Psychiatry*, 139, 985–990.

Williams, C. M. (1987). Peacetime combat. In T. Williams (ed.), *Post-traumatic stress disorder: A handbook for clinicians*. Cincinnati, OH: Disabled American Veterans National Headquarters, 221–231.

Williams, C. M. & T. Williams. (1987). Family therapy for Vietnam veterans. In T. Williams (ed.), *Post-traumatic stress disorder: A handbook for clinicians*. Cincinnati, OH: Disabled American Veterans National Headquarters, 221–231.

―――. (1985). Family therapy for Viet Nam veterans. In S. Sonnenberg, A. S. Blank & J. Talbott (eds.), *The trauma of war: Stress and recovery in Viet Nam veterans*. Washington, DC: American Psychiatric Press, 193–210.

Williams, M. (1969). *The velveteen rabbit*. New York: Doubleday.

Williams, M. B. (In press). Secondary trauma in children. In C. R. Figley (ed.), *Trauma and its wake III*. New York: Brunner/Mazel.

Williams, M. B. (1991a). Clinical work with families of multiple personality disorder patients: Assessment and issues for practice. *Dissociation*, 4, 92–98.

―――. (1991b). Effects of PTSD on incest survivors. Paper presented to the Northern Virginia Sexual Abuse Network, Falls Church, VA.

―――. (1991c). Verbalizing silent screams: The use of poetry to identify the belief systems of adult survivors of childhood sexual abuse. *Journal of Poetry Therapy*, 5, 5–20.

―――. (1990). Post-traumatic stress disorder and child sexual abuse: The enduring effects. Ph.D. diss., The Fielding Institute, Santa Barbara, CA.

Williams, T. (1987a). Diagnosis and treatment of survivor guilt-the bad penny. In T. Williams (ed.), *Post-traumatic stress disorder: A handbook for clinicians*. Cincinnati, OH: Disabled American Veterans National Headquarters, 75–92.

―――. (ed.). (1987b). *Post-traumatic stress disorders: A handbook for clinicians*. Cincinnati, OH: Disabled American Veterans.

Wilmer, H. A. (1981). Defining and understanding the therapeutic community. *Hospital and Community Psychiatry*, 32, 95–99.

Wilson, J. P. (1989a). Culture and trauma: The sacred pipe revisited. In J. P. Wilson (ed.), *Trauma, transformation and healing: An integrative approach to theory, research, and post-traumatic therapy*. New York: Brunner/Mazel, 38–74.

―――. (1989b). The psychobiology of trauma. In J. P. Wilson (ed.), *Trauma, transformation and healing: An integrative approach to theory, research, and post-traumatic therapy*. New York: Brunner/Mazel, 21–37.

―――. (1989c). Reconnecting: Stress recovery in the wilderness. In J. P. Wilson (ed.), *Trauma, transformation and healing: An integrative approach to theory, research, and post-traumatic therapy*. New York: Brunner/Mazel, 159–195.

―――. (1989d). *Trauma, transformation and healing*. New York: Brunner/Mazel.

―――. (1980). Towards an understanding of post-traumatic stress disorders among Vietnam veterans. Testimony before the U.S. Senate, May 21.

―――. (1978). Conflict, stress and growth: The effects of the Vietnam War on psychosocial development among Vietnam veterans. In C. R. Figley & S. Levantman (eds.), *Strangers at home: Vietnam veterans since the war*. New York: Praeger, 123–166.

Wilson, J. P. & G. E. Krauss. (1985). Predicting post-traumatic stress syndromes among Vietnam veterans. In W. Kelly (ed.), *Post-traumatic stress disorder and the war veteran patient*. New York: Brunner/Mazel, 102–147.

Wilson, J. P. & J. Lindy. (1994). *Countertransference in the treatment of post-traumatic stress disorders*. New York: Guilford Press.

Wilson, J. P., W. K. Smith & S. K. Johnson. (1985). A comparative analysis of PTSD among survivor groups. In C. R. Figley (ed.), *Trauma and its wake: The study and treatment of post-traumatic stress disorder*. New York: Brunner/Mazel, 142–172.

Winkelman, M. (1986). Trance states. *Ethos*, 13(2), 174–203.

Winnicott, D. W. (1965). *The maturational processes and the facilitating environment*. London: Hogarth Press.

Wirtz, P. & A. Harrell. (1987). Effects of post-assault exposure to attack-similar stimuli on long-term recovery of victims. *Journal of Consulting and Clinical Psychology*, 55, 10–16.

Woeber, M. (1969). Distinguishing centri-culture from cross-cultural tests and research. *Perceptual and Motor Skills*, 28, 488.

Wohl, Agnes & Bobbie Kaufman. (1985). Silent screams and hidden cries. New York: Brunner/Mazel.

Wolf, M. E., A. Alavi & A. D. Mosnaim. (1988). Post-traumatic stress disorder in Vietnam veterans: Clinical and EEG findings; possible therapeutic effects of carbamazepine. *Biological Psychiatry*, 23, 642–644.

Wolf, M. E., A. D. Mosnaim, J. Puente & R. Ignacio. (1990). Methionine-enkephalin in post-traumatic stress disorder: Plasma levels and degradation. *Research Communications in Psychology, Psychiatry, and Behavior*, 15(1–2), 73–78.

Wolfe, V. V., C. Gentile & D. A. Wolfe. (1989). Impact of sexual abuse on children: A PTSD formulation. *Behavior Therapy*, 20, 215–228.

Wolpe, J. (1969). *The practice of behavior therapy*. New York: Pergamon Press.

World Health Organization. (1993). *Manual of the International Statistical Classification of Disease*. (10th ed.). Geneva: Author.

———. (1990, May). Mental and behavioral disorders, diagnostic criteria for research. ICD–10. Geneva: Author.

———. (1978). ICD: Mental Disorders: Glossary and guide to their classification in accordance with the Ninth Revision of the International Classification of Diseases. Geneva: Author.

———. (1975). *Schizophrenia: A multidimensional study*. Geneva: Author.

World Medical Association. (1975). Declaration of Tokyo.

Yablonsky, Lewis. (1981). *Psychodrama*. New York: Gardner Press.

Yager, J. (1976). Post-combat violent behavior in psychiatrically maladjusting soldiers. *Archives of General Psychiatry*, 33, 1332–1335.

Yager, T., R. Laufer & M. Gallops. (1984). Some problems associated with war experience in men of the Vietnam generation. *Archives of General Psychiatry*, 41, 327–333.

Yalom, Irvin D. (1985). *The theory and practice of group psychotherapy*. 3d ed. New York: Basic Books.

———. (1980). *Existential psychotherapy*. New York: Basic Books.

Yandrick, R. (1990). Critical incidents. *EAPA Exchange*, Fall, 18–23.

Yates, Marsha & Kim Pawley. (1987). Utilizing imagery and the unconscious to explore and resolve the trauma of sexual abuse. *Art Therapy Journal*, 4(1), 36–41.

Yehuda, R., E. L. Giller, D. Boisoneau, M. T. Lowy, S. M. Southwick & S. W. Mason. (1991). The low dose DST in PTSD, NR 324, New Research Program. Paper presented at 144th Meeting, American Psychiatric Association. New Orleans, May 11–16.

Yehuda, R., M. T. Lowy, S. M. Southwick, D. Shaffer & E. L. Giller. (1991). Lymphocyte glucocorticoid receptor number in posttraumatic stress disorder. *American Journal of Psychiatry*, 148, 499–504.

Young, M. A. (1988). The crime victims' movement. In F. M. Ochberg (ed.), *Posttraumatic therapy and victims of violence*. New York: Brunner/Mazel, 319–329.

Zilberg, N. J., D. S. Weiss & M. J. Horowitz. (1982). Impact of Event Scale: A cross-validation study and some empirical evidence supporting a conceptual model of stress response syndromes. *Journal of Consulting and Clinical Psychology*, 50, 407–414.

Zogby, J. (1990). *Arab America today: A demographic profile of Arab-Americans*. Washington, DC: Arab-American Institute.

Index

About the Contributors

NUHA ABUDABBEH is a clinical psychologist practicing in Washington, DC. She was born in Jaffa, Palestine, and has lived in Turkey, Palestine, Lebanon, and Libya. She trained in her field at several community mental health centers in the Washington, DC, area and at Johns Hopkins University in Baltimore. She recently retired after twenty-two years as a staff forensic psychologist at St. Elizabeth's Hospital. In 1987 she established the Naim Foundation, in memory of her father, to meet Arabic-speaking people's health and social needs. She is a recipient of several awards and the author of several publications in her field. Presently she hosts a weekly call-in radio program in Arabic on mental health issues.

JOSEPH H. ALBECK is an instructor in psychiatry at Harvard Medical School and associate psychiatrist at McLean Hospital. He is past president of One Generation After and a member of the New England Holocaust Memorial Committee. He is currently chairperson of the Transgenerational Interest Area Group of the International Society for Traumatic Stress Studies. His book *Songs for the Last Survivor* describes his personal journey in coming to terms with the Holocaust.

SANDRA L. BLOOM is a board-certified psychiatrist who has been running an inpatient psychiatric unit for over twelve years. She is currently president of the Alliance for Creative Development, an outpatient practice and psychiatric management company. She is Medical Director of the "Sanctuary at Northwestern," an inpatient unit at Northwestern Institute, Washington, Pennsylvania, that specializes in the treatment of adults abused as children. She serves as the Chairperson of the Inpatient and Partial Hospitalization Special Interest Group for the International Society for Traumatic Stress Studies, and is a nationally and internationally known lecturer.

JOEL OSLER BRENDE is director of Psychiatric Inpatient Services for Military Dependents and Retirees, Ft. Benning, Georgia; consultant at the Pastoral Institute and the Trauma and Crisis Response Team at the Bradley Center, Inc., Columbus, Georgia; and Clinical Professor of Psychiatry, Mercer School of Medicine, Macon, Georgia. He worked with the VA for eighteen years, specializing in research and treatment for Vietnam veterans with PTSD. He has authored many scientific publications and is a presenter and trainer in the field of trauma and stress.

INGRID V. E. CARLIER is senior researcher at the Critical Incidents in Policework research project at the Department of Psychiatry, Academic Medical Center in Amsterdam, the Netherlands.

BARBARA CHESTER is an associate of the Hopi Foundation in Flagstaff, Arizona, where she works primarily with Native American groups, including Havasupai, Hopi, Navajo, and Pima people. She has taught at the university level and provided professional consultation in both the United States and abroad. She has helped to establish a number of private, nonprofit agencies that work with severe emotional trauma, including the Center for Victims of Torture, where she was clinical director.

BARRY M. COHEN is the program director for the Center for Abuse Recovery and Empowerment, Psychiatric Institute of Washington, Washington, DC. A registered art therapist, he has lectured and published in the United States and abroad about his research on drawing and psychiatric diagnosis. He founded the Eastern Regional Conference on Abuse and Multiple Personality in 1989 and has chaired it each year since that time.

CHRISTINE A. COURTOIS is a psychologist in private practice in Washington, DC, and is clinical director, Center for Abuse Recovery and Empowerment, Psychiatric Institute of Washington, Washington, DC. She is a consultant to community mental health centers in Virginia. She conducts workshops nationwide on the treatment of incest and other forms of sexual assault. She has coedited an issue of *The Counseling Psychologist* on the topic of victimization and its aftermath and is the author of *Healing the Incest Wound: Adult Survivors in Therapy*.

YAEL DANIELI is a clinical psychologist in private practice in New York City. She is cofounder and Director of the Group Project for Holocaust Survivors and Their Children; director of Psychological Services, Center for Rehabilitation of Torture Victims; and cofounder and past president of the International Society for Traumatic Stress Studies. She has served in many representative and consultative roles to the United Nations as well as to the Federal Bureau of Investigation.

LORI R. DANIELS worked at the American Lake VAMC in Tacoma, Washington, from 1988 to 1992 in the Inpatient Alcohol/Drug Abuse Program, in the Inpatient Post-Traumatic Stress Treatment Program, and in one of nine newly developed Substance Use/Post-Traumatic Stress outpatient treatment programs (SUPTs) in the country. She has given training to mental health providers and local universities throughout the state of Washington and Oregon regarding PTSD and the dual diagnoses of PTSD and chemical dependency. Since late 1992, she has been the director of the Post-Traumatic Stress Disorder Clinical Team at the Honolulu VA in Hawaii.

MARY ANN DUTTON is a professor of clinical psychology and director of the Family Violence Program at Nova University. She has published in the field of family violence and serves as an expert witness in criminal and civil court cases.

SUSAN C. FELDMAN is coordinator of Common Ground, Grant Street Partnership, New Haven, Connecticut. She is the former director of family therapy at the National Center for PTSD, VA Medical Center, West Haven, Connecticut.

BARBARA FEUER is the director of the Association of Flight Attendants Employee Assistance Program (AFA EAP). She supervises the activities of 150 peer counselors from nineteen airlines throughout the United States. Dr. Feuer trains and consults on team building, communications skills, conflict resolution, stress management/burnout prevention, and workplace trauma intervention.

CLAY FOREMAN, a counselor, trainer, and researcher in traumatic stress, is chief consultant for Traumatic Stress Recovery, Inc., Napa, California. He is a member of the International Society for Traumatic Stress Studies and a board member of the International Association of Trauma Counselors. He has presented both nationally and internationally on critical incident stress debriefing in disasters and has been a member of various teams responding to natural and man-made disasters.

MATTHEW J. FRIEDMAN is executive director of the Veterans Administration's National Center for PTSD, a four-part consortium with divisions at White River Junction, Vermont, Boston, Massachusetts, West Haven, Connecticut, and Menlo Park, California. Dr. Friedman is a Professor of Psychiatry and Pharmacology at Dartmouth Medical School. He has published numerous articles and chapters in the area of the psychopharmacology of PTSD.

BERTHOLD P. R. GERSONS is professor of psychiatry in the Department of Psychiatry, Academic Medical Center in Amsterdam, the Netherlands. He is a well-known researcher, author, and presenter in the field of police-related trauma.

JUDITH HALPERN is a clinical social worker in private practice in Falls Church, Virginia. She also has specialized training in the treatment of children.

C. J. HARRIS is presently a clinical associate with Linder, Waddell and Harris, in Greenville, South Carolina. He provides general marriage and family therapy while specializing in the prevention, assessment, and treatment of PTSD in individuals and their families. Dr. Harris serves on the editorial board of the *Journal of Traumatic Stress*. He is listed nationally in the Technical Advisory Service for Attorneys as an expert on PTSD. He is a clinical member of the American Association for Marriage and Family Therapy and a Charter Member of the International Society for Traumatic Stress Studies.

JEREMY HERMAN is an interpersonal psychoanalyst practicing individual and group psychotherapy in New York City. He specializes in PTSD, adults from dysfunctional families, self-help groups, and critical incident stress debriefing. He serves on the Mayor's New York City Task Force Against Sexual Assault and is cochair of the Interest Group of the International Society for Traumatic Stress Studies, which builds bridges between professionals and self-help groups.

BEVERLY JAMES is a psychotherapist and professional educator who specializes in issues related to childhood trauma. She utilizes a multidimensional, trauma-focused approach in her clinical practice in Hawaii. She provides professional training nationally and internationally. Her publications include *Treating Traumatized Children* (1989) and *Treating Sexually Abused Children and Their Families* (1983).

DAVID READ JOHNSON is an associate professor in the Department of Psychiatry, Yale University School of Medicine, and Chief, Specialized Inpatient PTSD Unit, National Center for PTSD, VA Medical Center, West Haven, Connecticut. He is the former chairperson of the National Coalition of Arts Therapy Associations. He is coauthor of *Waiting at the Gate: Creativity and Hope in the Nursing Home*.

WENDI R. KAPLAN is an experiential therapist in private practice in Alexandria, Virginia. She works with survivors of child sexual abuse and other traumas and their significant others. She is also an adjunct Professor at the American University and has been an editorial adviser to *Moving Forward: A Newsletter for Survivors of Sexual Child Abuse and Those Who Care for Them*. She is a certified Gestalt therapist and has training in bioenergetics, hypnotherapy, feminist therapy, couples therapy, and play therapy.

LANA R. LAWRENCE is a licensed funeral director and editor of *Moving Forward: A Newsletter for Survivors of Sexual Child Abuse and Those Who Care for Them*. She frequently speaks about child sexual abuse and appears regularly in the national media. She has also published several articles on sexual abuse and bereavement-related topics in a variety of publications.

BRETT T. LITZ is the deputy director for Education and Training at the National Center for Post-Traumatic Stress Disorder, Behavioral Science Division, Boston Department of Veterans Affairs Medical Center. He is an Assistant Professor in

Psychiatry at Tufts University School of Medicine. He has published in the areas of information processing in PTSD and the assessment of PTSD.

I. LISA MCCANN is currently in practice in Kansas City, Missouri, where she specializes in the treatment of women who have experienced psychological trauma, including sexual assault, childhood sexual or physical abuse, and domestic violence. She is clinical consultant to the Masters and Johnson Sexual Trauma Unit at Two Rivers Hospital in Kansas City. She is widely published in the area of traumatic stress and is on the editorial boards of the *Journal of Traumatic Stress* and *Treating Abuse Today*. She is also on the Board of Directors of the International Society for Traumatic Stress Studies.

APHRODITE MATSAKIS has worked with combat veterans, family abuse victims, and other trauma survivors for over seventeen years as a clinical psychologist at the Veterans Administration Medical Center in Washington, DC and at the Vietnam Veterans Outreach Center in Silver Spring, Maryland. She is the author of numerous books and articles.

DAVID P. NILES is a board-certified medical psychotherapist and board-certified trauma counselor. He has clinical neuroscience inpatient experience and is in private practice in the vicinity of Washington, DC, specializing in individual, group, and family therapy with victims of trauma. He is director of the Trauma Recovery and Counseling Center. He is internationally known for his work with Russian Afghanistan war veterans and is chair of the Trauma Recovery Special Interest Network of the American Mental Health Counselors Association. He is an adjunct professor at George Washington University.

MARILYN OLLAYOS is assistant head nurse, Specialized Inpatient PTSD Unit, National Center for PTSD, VA Medical Center, West Haven, Connecticut.

ERWIN RANDOLPH PARSON is a clinical psychologist and psychoanalyst and consultant to the PTSD Clinical Team and the Trauma Recovery Center at the DVA, Perry Point, Maryland. He is chief investigator of the U.S.-Vietnam Full Circle Project and a former professor of war and social consequences, University of Massachusetts at Boston. He is editor-in-chief of the *Journal of Contemporary Psychotherapy*, and an international expert in the clinical assessment and treatment of PTSD and intercultural psychotherapy.

LAURIE ANNE PEARLMAN is a clinical psychologist and research director of the Traumatic Stress Institute. Her research focuses on understanding the unique psychological experience of adult trauma survivors and on measurement of psychological needs. She does psychotherapy and clinical supervision at the Institute's Center for Adult and Adolescent Psychotherapy. Her clinical interests include treatment of adult survivors of child sexual abuse, couples experiencing relationship difficulties, women's issues, and women's personal psychological development.

MARYDALE SALSTON is in private practice in San Diego, California. She previously worked as a counselor at San Diego State University and was director of clinical services at a private, nonprofit agency serving victims of violent crime. She has provided training at the national level to professionals at numerous conferences, as well as at the state and local level. She is the coauthor of the *Social Work Curriculum for the ISTSS Presidential Task Force on Curricula for PTSD*.

ROBERT A. SCHWARZ is director of the Institute for Advanced Clinical Training in Villanova, Pennsylvania. He organized the 1992, 1993, and 1994 Advances in Treating Survivors of Sexual Abuse conferences on the east and west coasts, as well as the three eastern Eriksonian Hypnosis conferences. He is coauthor of *Post-Traumatic Stress Disorder: A Clinician's Guide*, as well as the author of several articles on hypnosis, PTSD, and pain. He is currently working on a new book, *Tools for Transforming Trauma*. In addition, he is involved with a research project investigating advanced stages of recovery from sexual abuse. A licensed psychologist, he is also an assistant clinical professor at Widener University as well as an adjunct clinical member of the Department of Psychiatry at the University of Pennsylvania.

RAYMOND MONSOUR SCURFIELD served as a psychiatric social work officer in the U. S. Army in Vietnam and has held several leadership positions with the U.S. Department of Veterans Affairs. He has been a featured speaker at over 180 trainings throughout the United States and has published articles and contributed chapters to a variety of journals and books. He is director of the Pacific Center for PTSD and War-Related Disorders, Department of Veterans Affairs, Honolulu, Hawaii.

PATRICIA L. SHEEHAN is presently employed by the VA Medical Center in Indianapolis, Indiana, and also is in private practice. She is a registered nurse in Indiana and is certified as a clinical specialist in adult psychiatric and mental health nursing. She serves as Adjunct Assistant Professor to the Department of Psychiatric/Mental Health Nursing of the Indiana University School of Nursing and serves as a consultant to Vietnam Veterans Outreach Centers. She is a member of the editorial board of the *Journal of Traumatic Stress*.

JOHN F. SOMMER, Jr., is executive director of the Washington, D.C. office of the American Legion. He has coauthored articles and facilitated research projects dealing with Agent Orange effects on Vietnam veterans. He has been involved in ongoing POW/MIA investigations, has testified before congressional committees, and has made two recent trips to Vietnam and other areas in Southeast Asia. He is a charter member of the International Society for Traumatic Stress Studies and is cochair of the Ethics Task Force/Committee of ISTSS. He has presented nationally on a variety of trauma-related topics. He currently chairs the Department of Veterans Affairs Advisory Committee on the Readjustment of Vietnam and Other War Veterans.

DEE SPRING has specialized in the treatment of sexual trauma and dissociative disorders for the past twenty years. Currently, she is executive director of Earthwood Center in Ventura, California, and teaches for the University of California at Santa Barbara and Maryhurst College. She is the chief instructor for the Sexual Trauma and Multiple Personality Symposia sponsored by the American Art Therapy Association.

B. HUDNALL STAMM, as a traumatologist and statistical consultant, has contributed to numerous U.S. and international research projects. She is a member of the Ethics Task Force and Committee of the International Society for Traumatic Stress Studies, working with ethics and issues related to trauma victims, particularly in the area of the ethical use of research methods and quantitative techniques. She has presented in research methodology and ethical issues at a variety of national and international conferences.

JOHN H. STEIN is deputy director of the National Organization for Victim Assistance. He has trained experimental teams of community service police officers, worked with prosecutors to develop victim/witness advocates, and was deputy director of a program for elderly crime victims. He was elected to the NOVA Board in 1978 and received its Founders Award in 1980. He serves as NOVA's liaison to the U.S. Congress, law enforcement agencies, and the judiciary. He is the senior editor of the NOVA *Newsletter* and is coauthor of many of NOVA's major publications.

CYNTHIA M. STUHLMILLER is affiliated with the University of San Francisco, Department of Veterans Affairs, Palo Alto, California, and the American Red Cross, Palo Alto Disaster Action Team. She is a private consultant and lecturer and has worked as a clinical nurse specialist with Vietnam veterans with PTSD at the National Center for PTSD Clinical Laboratory and Education Division. She conducts ongoing research with rescue and emergency works, which has led her to propose incorporation of action-based techniques to augment or replace the traditional critical incident debriefing model.

JOAN A. TURKUS practices general and forensic psychiatry in Virginia. She is medical director for the Center for Abuse Recovery and Empowerment, Psychiatric Institute of Washington, Washington, DC, and was previously affiliated with St. Elizabeth's Hospital in Washington, DC. She has extensive clinical experience in the diagnosis and treatment of MPD and is frequently called upon by therapists in the metropolitan Washington, DC, area for supervision, consultation, and teaching.

JEAN VOGEL is a licensed social worker. She has an outpatient practice with the Alliance for Creative Development and is the psychodramatist for the Sanctuary Unit at Northwestern Institute of Psychiatry in Fort Washington, Pennsylvania. She has had extensive psychodramatic training. She has participated in the evolution of the sanctuary model of inpatient care.

FRANK W. WEATHERS is a clinical research psychologist at the National Center for Post-Traumatic Stress Disorder, Behavioral Science Division, Boston

Department of Veterans Affairs Medical Center. He is a Clinical Instructor in Psychiatry at Tufts University School of Medicine. He has published in the area of assessment of PTSD and is active in training mental health professionals in the assessment and treatment of trauma.

MARY BETH WILLIAMS is currently in private practice in Warrenton, Virginia, where she specializes in the treatment of trauma and dissociative disorders. She has also been a school social worker in Falls Church, Virginia, for twenty-one years. She is book editor of the *Journal of Traumatic Stress*, a member of the board of directors of the International Society of Traumatic Stress Studies, president of the Washington, DC, chapter of ISTSS, and editorial adviser to Moving Forward. She has authored a variety of articles and book chapters, including coauthoring the *Social Work Curriculum for the ISTSS Task Force*.

JOHN P. WILSON is a professor of psychology at Cleveland State University, Director of the Center for Stress and Trauma, and Chairman of Emergency Services for the American Red Cross in Cleveland, Ohio. He is past president and cofounder of the International Society for Traumatic Stress Studies. His most recent book, coedited with Beverley Raphael, is the *International Handbook of Traumatic Stress Syndromes* (1993).

MARLENE A. YOUNG has been the executive director of NOVA since 1981 and is vice-president of the World Society of Victimology. She has been a board member and officer of the ISTSS. She has developed victim-oriented curricula used in the training of law enforcement officers and curricula for use in crisis intervention in community disasters. Dr. Young is widely published, and trains in the area of victims rights throughout the world.

ISBN 0-313-28143-2

9 780313 281433

HARDCOVER BAR CODE

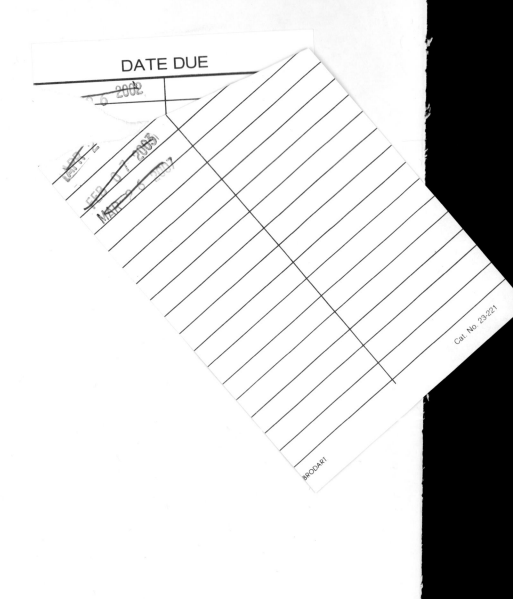